PEOPLE AND POLITICS

AN INTRODUCTION TO POLITICAL SCIENCE

PEOPLE AND POLITICS
AN INTRODUCTION TO POLITICAL SCIENCE

HERBERT R. WINTER
Rhode Island College

THOMAS J. BELLOWS
University of Arkansas

in collaboration with

CONRAD WALIGORSKI
University of Arkansas
and
STANLEY R. ERICKSON, Professor Emeritus
Augustana College, Rock Island, Illinois

JOHN WILEY & SONS
New York • Santa Barbara • London • Sydney • Toronto

Cover design: Eileen Thaxton
Cover photos: NASA
Library of Congress
Riboud/Magnum
Wide World Photos

Library of Congress Cataloging in Publication Data:

Winter, Herbert R, 1928–
People and politics.

Includes bibliographies and indexes.
1. Political science. 2. Political sociology.
3. Pluralism (Social sciences) I. Bellows, Thomas J.,
1935– II. Title.
JA71.W47 320 76-26629
ISBN 0-471-95485-3

Printed in the United States of America

10 9 8 7 6 5 4 3 2 1

To Our Children:

John and Nadia Winter
Roderick, Adrienne, Jeannine,
Derek, and Marshall Bellows

Preface

For a number of years we have been engaged in teaching the introductory political science course to first-year students. In writing this book we have been guided by our classroom experiences. Our purpose is to relate the subject matter clearly and instructively to you, the political practitioners of tomorrow.

This is a book for beginning students of political science—for those who will be majoring in the field as well as for those who are majoring in other areas but wish to understand the subject matter of political science. The book surveys the major areas and aspects of the political process, relating the parts of the political system to each other. The topics follow in logical order, progressing from the basics of political analysis through analysis of the political processes to international politics.

Part One describes the foundation of political science, namely the scope of the discipline, its approaches and concepts, as well as the fundamentals of political theory. Part Two examines the input activities, those forces that form the major popular participatory part of the political process. Included in this section are the formation of political attitudes, political participation as reflected in elections and representation, and the roles of political parties and interest groups. Part Three is devoted to an examination of the output agencies, which make, administer, and enforce policy. This includes the legislative system, the executive branch with the bureaucracy, as well as the judiciary.

Part Four deals with political change, emphasizing the process of modernization and its variations. Although societal change can be brought about by peaceful or violent means, violence has always played an important role. For this reason we have included a chapter on political violence. The peaceful aspect of change is previously discussed in Chapter 5 ("Representation and Elections"). Finally, Part Five focuses on international relations—politics among the nation-states. This section includes a discussion of international politics, of international organization, and of regional integration.

Pluralism and systems analysis provide the core of this book. Pluralism refers to the assumption that numerous, competing groups are involved in the political process. Although societies differ in terms of the number of groups and amount of competition, no society is so dominated by one person or one group that there is no competition. One important question always is how this competition takes place.

The entire framework of analysis, especially Chapters 4 through 9 and, to a lesser extent, Chapters 10 and 11, is based on the systems approach (which is explained in detail in Chapter 2). By systems approach we mean that politics can be viewed as an assembly or combination of mutually interacting units that affect each other and form a complex whole, such as the nation-state. By emphasizing how the different parts of the political system interact and affect each other, we can make some sense out of the seeming confusion of modern politics. This approach stresses that the political systems of the 150-odd nation-states of our time share similar characteristics.

All countries are influenced by their particular cultures, which may range from the long evolutionary growth of democracy in Britain to the authoritarian tradition of Russian society. All countries contain processes for the political socialization of young and old—though again these processes differ from society to society and range from a ninth-grade civics class to totalitarian brainwashing.

Political societies adhere to an ideology of one kind or another, be it capitalist democracy, social democracy, communism, fascism, or Third World socialism. Countries have systems for selecting their legislative, executive, and judicial officials. In the Western democracies this selection procedure is constitutionalized: officials are elected or appointed according to established law. In contrast, in many other countries change still occurs by violence, and gross nepotism is exercised in the appointment of government officials.

The Western democracies have viable input agencies for articulation and aggregation, in the form of interest groups and political parties. They serve as instruments for popular participation, for expression of public opinion, and for the selection of candidates for public office. The input process is different in Communist countries; they have basically one-party systems, and interest groups follow the course set by the reigning party. The developing countries still have little in terms of established interest groups or viable political parties. As the economic systems of these countries become more developed, however, we anticipate that these societies will become more pluralistic, which usually induces the formation of interest groups and political parties.

All countries have institutions for rule making, rule application, and rule adjudication in the forms of a legislature, an executive, and a judiciary. These agencies are more viable in certain countries than in others. For example, the United States has a fairly viable tripartite national government. In contrast, the executive branch dominates the governmental process in most of the developing countries. In these, legislatures and judiciaries have not yet developed to a state of coequality with the executive. In the Communist countries the politburo of the Communist Party is the basic rule-making body, and the legislature, the executive, and the judiciary play secondary roles.

All political systems are subject to change. Political change can take one of two forms: it can be evolutionary and relatively peaceful through such means as using the ballot, or change can be brought about by revolutionary means, using the gun to alter the political system. The latter is usually more drastic and far-reaching (for example, the Russian Revolution of 1917) than evolutionary change.

The systems approach permits us to use political features common to all societies as convenient *starting points* for our analysis and discussion. It provides an orderly framework for the comparative examination of political phenomena and is, perhaps, the most logical way to scrutinize a variety of political systems.

The examples used for illustrative purposes are drawn from many countries. However, we have made it a point to include in almost all of the chapters representative examples from Western democracies, Communist countries, and non-Communist developing societies.

Some of our examples are drawn from the realm of micropolitics and others from macropolitics. Micropolitics focuses on the individual rather than political groups or institutions. The area of micropolitics has received increasing attention since World War II because of the growing number of studies in voting behavior. These studies have looked at individual political behavior: Did he or she vote? How did he vote? Did she work in a campaign? Was money donated to political candidates and why? These studies have also looked at preference attitudes—whether, for example, a person identifies himself with a particular party or how she feels about particular issues.

But individual actions or preferences do not alone explain collective decisions, institutional behavior, or political processes. Desires and opinions are often organized by group action. Macropolitics focuses on groups and institutions. Micropolitics and macropolitics complement each other. The behavior of any group or institution manifests, in part, the attitudes and beliefs of the individuals involved.

This book discusses the various ways in which people organize to make political decisions or to influence the decision makers. Thus we examine political organizations as well as individual attitudes and behavior.

We believe our approach contains a healthy mix of traditionalism and behavioralism. No introductory text can include detailed discussion of all aspects of a discipline. We emphasize those subjects we consider important in teaching.

We hope that this book will give you a better understanding of politics and the institutions and processes it entails. We also hope that it kindles in you a deeper interest in politics and political analysis and provides a helpful basis for more specialized studies in political science. Our principal objective is to make it possible for you to participate more effectively in the political process.

Herbert R. Winter
Thomas J. Bellows

Acknowledgements

This book has emerged with the assistance of a number of people. A sincere note of thanks goes to our families who, for more years than we intended, accepted the numerous inconveniences that result from the work and distracted minds of authors in labor.

We are grateful to those undergraduate and graduate students who have shared parts of the manuscript with us at various times. Our faith in students continues to be bolstered by their pertinent questions and insightful suggestions. One student, Dale Plaxco, deserves to be mentioned in particular, because of his steady optimism and the many hours that he contributed to this project. Our cheerful and competent secretaries also deserve to be thanked publicly. We are grateful for a timely travel grant from the Faculty Research Committee of Rhode Island College.

The political science profession continues to have dedicated colleagues willing to review drafts and re-drafts. Their suggestions stimulated our thinking and gave us an opportunity to see the forest when sometimes we were too concerned with the trees. John Perrotta, Carey Rickabaugh, and Milburn Stone of Rhode Island College provided important help by reviewing the initial drafts of several chapters and offering constructive suggestions. Alfred Diamant of Indiana University reviewed the political development chapter and demonstrated again his gentle but incisive intellect. We have been assisted by the advice of Samuel Huntington of Harvard University, who saw us off to a good start. We have been aided by the constructive criticism of Afak Haydar of Arkansas State University, and we are especially grateful to Norma Noonan of Augsburg College and Norman Thomas of the University of Cincinnati, who helped us considerably in seeing the work through to completion.

We thank our Wiley editors. They are Gerald Papke, who encouraged us to commence the project, Carl Beers who guided it through the initial stage and, especially, Wayne Anderson, whose patience and quiet conviction uplifted our flagging spirits at crucial times and motivated us to complete the project.

A brief comment should be made about our division of labor. Winter wrote Chapters 1, 8, 12, and 13. Bellows produced Chapters 2, 5, 7, and 10. Waligorski composed Chapters 4 and 11. Erikson wrote Chapters 3 and 9. Chapter 6 was written jointly by the authors. Winter carried the senior responsibility for coordinating the work and for pre-editing the entire manuscript before it was sent to the publisher.

We have accepted many suggestions and made many changes. Each of you who has assisted us has made this a better book. We take the responsibility for the remaining omissions and commissions.

H. R. W.
T. J. B.

Contents

PART ONE
Foundation and Fundamentals

PART TWO
The Input Agencies

PART THREE
The Output Agencies

PART FOUR
Dynamics of Political Change

PART FIVE
The International System

Part One

Foundation and Fundamentals

Chapter 1

The Nature and Scope of Political Science

War, peace, inflation, unemployment, busing, civil rights, corruption, conflicts in the Middle East and Africa are a few of the many issues confronting today's citizen. These are problems in the public realm, problems we expect to deal with through political action. The public realm includes the activities and effects of all input and output agencies. Input agencies include political parties, interest groups, public opinion, and even violence. Outputs include the activities, decisions, and regulations of governmental agencies at the local, state, national, and international levels. These interact in a system of politics to produce the complex, often interdependent, problems that scream for our attention from the daily headlines. We are challenged to understand and deal with the world. Failure to do so may spell disaster for our country and ourselves.

Past generations have also had their share of crises and problems, but people often tend to feel that present-day public problems are more severe than those of the past. Modern politics is on a larger scale, involving more people and more questions than ever before. The public sector, that is, the sum total of all decisions made by public authorities in a society, has expanded considerably in most countries.[1] This expansion has brought the government closer to the people, while making it more complex and difficult to understand. More public services are available, but concurrently,

[1] For information on the growth of the public sector, see Bruce M. Russet et al., *World Handbook of Political and Social Indicators* (New Haven: Yale University Press, 1964), pp. 56–68.

1950

1960

1970

1974

The effect of inflation!

governments encroach increasingly on the day-to-day affairs of their citizens.

Contemporary people are politically better informed and more attentive than their forefathers; however, one may ask whether the increase in available information and the growth of governmental activities have made man a more active political participant. One standard indicator used to examine political participation is that of voter turn-out on election day. By and large, voter turnout has remained fairly constant in the developed countries or has even slightly declined during the last two decades. It is still too early to ascertain trends of this type in the developing countries.

Rather than a general increase in the standard types of political participation, the past decade has shown a pattern of "flash" activities and movements centering around specific issues. The many domestic demonstrations against United States' military involvement in Southeast Asia illustrate this. Currently, we are witnessing a rising concern about pollution, natural resource depletion, and conservation. The composite picture of political behavior in the 1960s and 1970s seems to show an additional phenomenon. Rising interest in the public issues of the day has been accompanied by a specific concern about priorities set by governments and the corresponding allocation of resources.

Many of the demonstrations staged by students, members of minority groups, and others in this country have had to do with governmental priorities, because these priorities are associated with individual and group welfare. Governmental decisions made in Washington may have a bearing on whether an American will have to fight in Asia or some other part of the world, whether his taxes will be increased, and whether a larger amount of

("The Small Society" by Brickman © Washington Star Syndicate, permission granted by King Features Syndicate 1973.)

his tax money will be used for furthering the arms race—or for improving medical services, public transportation, and conservation efforts.

Demonstrations protesting governmental policies are common outside the industrialized countries of the West. In many of the developing countries demonstrations are a common occurrence, as people who do not have a voice in public office attempt to make their wants known. The same applies to demonstrations in Communist countries. Thousands of workers and students rioted in Poland's port cities in December, 1970, protesting the government's economic policies. Dissent in the Soviet Union has been expressed in the form of small demonstrations or clandestine publications, as when some Soviet citizens demonstrated in public in 1968 against the Warsaw Pact intervention in Czechoslovakia. One of those protesting was the renowned nuclear physicist Andrei Sakharov, who become known in the West for his essay *Progress, Coexistence and Intellectual Freedom.*[2]

These criticisms indicate a growing civic awareness in segments of the population here and abroad. Among students in North America and Western Europe rising civil and social consciousness has led, during the 1960s, to a burgeoning enrollment in social science courses, in subjects that focus on the economic, political, and social behavior of man.

This book addresses itself to these interests and concerns by placing them into an analytic framework, that of political science.

What Is Political Science?

Political science is a discipline within the social sciences. It deals with politics, the political behavior of individuals, groups, societies, and the factors and conditions affecting politicians, political events, and institutions. It is akin to the other social science disciplines (anthropology, economics, geography, history, sociology, social psychology) in that all of them examine related aspects of human behavior and of society. All social behavior occurs through the interaction of individuals and groups of people, and therefore, all social science study is concerned with the nature of human interaction, group behavior, decision making, leadership, and so forth. An examination of the political behavior of men lends itself readily to the application of anthropological, economic, psychological, and sociological analyses. Almond and Verba, in their famous comparative analysis, *The Civic Culture,* applied a broad range of modern social science research techniques to study the political aspirations, beliefs, emotions, and partici-

[2] Andrei D. Sakharov, *Progress, Coexistence and Intellectual Freedom* (New York: W. W. Norton, 1968).

pation in Italy, Mexico, the United Kingdom, United States, and West Germany.[3]

In the past political scientists relied more on history and jurisprudence, but today they look to economics, sociology, social psychology, and statistics for research methods, tools, and analysis.[4]

THE FOCUS OF POLITICAL SCIENCE

Political science, we have said, deals with the political behavior of men. In short, it deals with politics. What is politics? What are its features and ingredients? The word "politics" stems from *polis,* the Greek city-state, such as Athens at the time of Plato and Aristotle. Aristotle, in his discussion of human associations, stated that the "most sovereign and inclusive association is the *polis,* as it is called, or the political association."[5] The complexity of the term "politics" is illustrated by the variety of the following responses, which were given by students in an introduction to political science class in an urban college in New England when they were asked to register their associations to the word:

authority	decision	political bosses
bargaining	dirty politics	political machines
bribery	dishonest	political parties
campaign	elections	politicians
candidates	elite	power
coercion	equal opportunity	president
committee	favoritism	propaganda
competition	government	public issues
complexity	influence	public office
compromise	law	secrecy
Congress	leadership	struggle
conservative	manipulation	summit meetings
corruption	money	voting
debate	mudslinging	war
deception	party loyalty	Watergate

A search through political science textbooks confounds the student with a number of definitions, stating that politics is the process of making

[3] Gabriel A. Almond and Sidney Verba, *The Civic Culture* (Boston: Little Brown, 1965).

[4] For a perceptive discussion of the relationship between political science and the other social sciences, see Seymour Lipset, ed., *Politics and the Social Sciences* (New York: Oxford University Press, 1969).

[5] Ernest Barker, ed. and trans., *The Politics of Aristotle* (New York: Oxford University Press, 1962), p. 1.

governmental policies, the making of decisions by public means, the authoritative allocation of values, the quest for power, and so forth. The ethical scope of political activities has been candidly expressed by Peter Merkl in the following words: "At its best, politics is a noble quest for a good order and justice; at its worst, a selfish grab for power, glory and riches."[6]

To most political scientists the word "politics" denotes all the activities and processes that take place in the public realm, some overt and others of a more covert nature. Our discussion in the following chapters will be limited to the public scope of politics.

The following are some of the more pertinent attempts to define politics. Quincy Wright, in his classic study of international relations, defines international politics as "the art of influencing, manipulating, or controlling major groups in the world so as to advance the purposes of some against the opposition of others."[7] This definition could readily be applied to domestic as well as international politics.

According to Vernon Van Dyke, "Politics can be defined as a struggle among actors pursuing conflicting desires on public issues."[8] A sizable number of American political scientists adhere to a definition attributed to David Easton, "Politics is the authoritative allocation of values."[9]
While Van Dyke's definition lacks reference to the outcome of the struggle between the actors and limits politics to the public realm, the definition attributed to Easton lacks reference to the competition and struggle that occur before an allocation of values can set in. But the two definitions complement each other. We suggest a comprehensive definition that contains elements of the thoughts of Van Dyke and Easton, namely that *politics can*

[6] Peter H. Merkl, *Political Continuity and Change* (New York: Harper and Row, 1967), p. 13.

[7] Quincy Wright, *The Study of International Relations* (New York: Appleton-Century-Croft, 1955), p. 130.

[8] Van Dyke's complete definition reads as follows: "Politics can be defined as (1) activity occurring within and among groups, (2) which operate on the basis of desires that are to some extent shared, (3) an essential feature of the activity being a struggle among actors, (4) to achieve their desires, (5) on questions of group policy, group organization, group leadership, or the regulation of intergroup relationships, (6) against the opposition of others with conflicting desires." See Vernon Van Dyke, *Political Science: A Philosophical Analysis* (Stanford, Cal.: Stanford University Press, 1960), p. 134.

A closely related definition comes from Meyerson and Banfield, who speak of politics as "the activity by which an issue is agitated and settled." Martin Meyerson and Edward C. Banfield, *Politics, Planning, and the Public Interest* (Glencoe, Ill.: Free Press, 1955), p. 304.

[9] This definition is a loose paraphrase of statements made by David Easton. At no place does he give the above definition verbatim. See David Easton, "An Approach to the Analysis of Political Systems," *World Politics* IX (1957), pp. 383–400; *A Framework for Political Analysis* (Englewood Cliffs, N.J.: Prentice-Hall, 1965) p. 47 ff., and *The Political System: An Inquiry into the State of Political Science,* 2nd ed. (New York: Alfred A. Knopf, 1971) p. 129 ff.

be defined as a struggle between actors pursuing conflicting desires on issues that may result in an authoritative allocation of values. Political science involves the systematic analyses and study of politics in the public realm.

THE RANGE OF POLITICS

Political activities may be considered legitimate or nonlegitimate. Legitimate activities are sanctioned by law and custom. Examples of legimitate political functions would be the act of voting on election day, the passage of a statute by a legislative body, a demonstration permitted by the authorities. But politics goes beyond the legitimate area: a demonstration held despite the authorities' refusal to grant permission is a political act, though this type of politics might lead to turmoil and fights in the streets. A coup d'etat is a political act, though it might involve military force. A revolution has clearly political overtones. The Prussian General Karl von Clausewitz went even further by saying that:

> *War is not merely a political act, but also a political instrument, a continuation of political relations, a carrying out of the same by other means.*[10]

While political scientists deal primarily with politics within the public realm, politics is *not* limited to the public realm. As stated by Robert Dahl, the political arena transcends the public realm. In his words, "A political system is any persistent pattern of human relationships that involves, to a significant extent, power, rule, or authority."[11]

His definition implies that politics is not limited to the public realm, but includes conflict of interest situations, struggles for power, as well as policy-making activities in business firms, civic groups, religious organizations, crime syndicates, college organizations, families, and other groups.

College students demonstrating against an undesirable policy set by their institution's administration are engaged in politics. Members of a minority group rioting in order to protest their miserable living conditions pursue politics. The phenomenon of politics can be found in the armed forces, be it in cases of promotion to high-level rank or the interservice rivalries having to do with areas of jurisdiction or budget allocations. Politics is found in business where promotion to a high-ranking executive position may involve a great deal of maneuvering behind the scenes. Those who have been active in an established church are probably aware that the hiring or

[10] Quoted in Frederick A. Hartmann, *The Relations of Nations,* 3rd ed. (New York: The Macmillan Company, 1967), p. 171.

[11] Robert A. Dahl, *Modern Political Analysis,* 2nd ed. (Englewood Cliffs, N.J.: Prentice-Hall, 1970), p. 6.

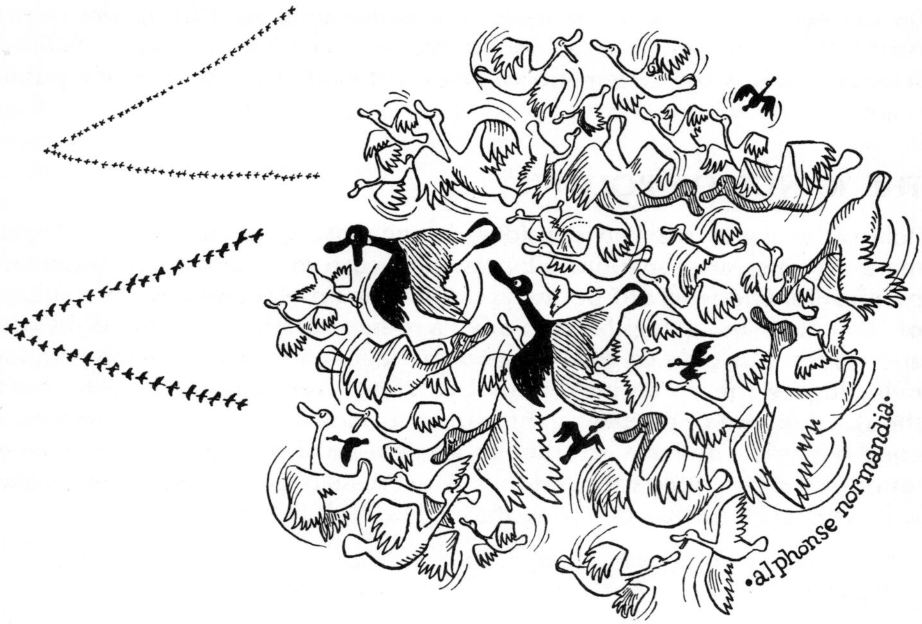

"There are times when I wish we had a somewhat stronger organization."

firing of a minister involves, at times, a fair amount of politics. The world of academe involves, at some institutions, considerable politics.

There is also an enormous amount of politics in organized crime: politics that has to do with the maintenance of hierarchical order, promotions within the syndicate, discussions about the ends to be pursued and the methods to be employed, and debate about the division of territory among the families. There is also politics in the sense that in some communities the activities of crime syndicates are tightly interlocked with those of the established authorities.

The smallest group subject to politics is the family. The pursuit of desires and issues in the family will often have political overtones in that father and mother will pursue differing, or at times contradictory, aims and will compete for the children's support for their stand. The playing of favorites will serve as enticement or as payoff. Children, at times, will try to play the parents against each other. These examples, we hope, will serve to illustrate that the phenomenon labelled "politics" is an unavoidable fact of human life and that everybody is involved in it in one fashion or another.

MAN AND HIS POLITICAL ENVIRONMENT

Politics surrounds everyone. Modern man is unlikely to play, either by choice or by fate, the isolated role of Robinson Crusoe. Man is by necessity an actor or a subject in the web of politics. His role will be that of a given type in the societal authority structure; for example, he might be a leader, an active participant, a passive subject, or he will play a role somewhere in between. What importance does a certain role or position have for man? Politics, if used wisely, can enhance the freedom and the well-being of man. While no man can achieve all his desires, he can, through political pursuit, exercise more choice and achieve some of his aspirations to render his life more secure and master a greater degree of his own fate.

The political role that an individual can play in a society depends upon the authority structure of a given society. A person living in a strongly regimented (totalitarian) society enjoys less freedom than his counterpart in an authoritarian society, who in turn has less leeway than the person in a Western-type democracy. Freedom of action, in the above context, involves such matters as freedom of speech, assembly, press, religion, travel mobility (both within and beyond one's country), and social and economic advancement and opportunity. All these freedoms are relative in the sense that there is no country where there prevails complete freedom and none where there exists no degree of freedom at all. However, a society's authority structure has a considerable bearing on the degree of freedom that prevails.

We have said above that everybody is enmeshed in the web of politics, but that not everybody is equally involved in political life. Robert Dahl, in *Modern Political Analysis,* identifies four different participatory groups: (1) the powerful, (2) the power seekers, (3) the political stratum, and (4) the apolitical stratum.[12]

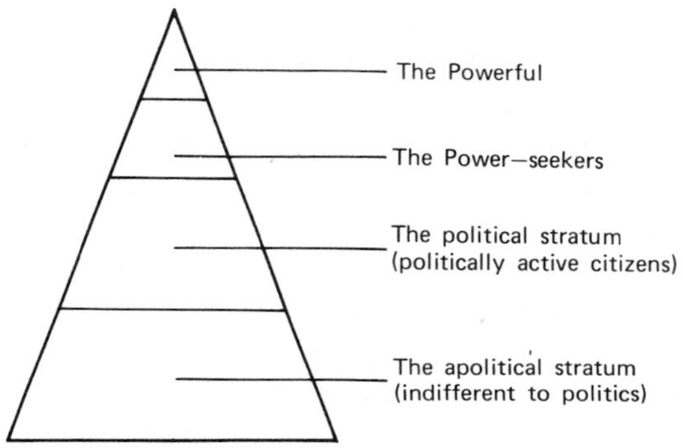

[12] Dahl, op. cit., pp. 77–92.

The powerful are the ruling elites, those who form the inner core of the *political system*. They are those who gain, because of their resources (such as economic wealth, time, influence, skill, and motivation), more power than others in the society. The power seekers are similar to the powerful in terms of skill and motivation but have fewer resources available and therefore will not reach the position held by the powerful. The above two categories form the two inner layers of the political system and are surrounded by other people who are active in political life, but less active and/or less successful than the strata of the power seekers and the powerful.

The apolitical category is made up of those who show an apathetic attitude toward politics and remain relatively inactive in political affairs. There are no clearly defined boundaries between these layers—each shades over into the next. The size of each category is influenced by the society's authority structure, that is, the totalitarian, autocratic, or democratic nature of a society. The stratum of the powerful is relatively small in all societies, but will involve a slightly larger percentage of people in the advanced industrialized countries, such as the United States, than in underdeveloped countries, as Afghanistan or Haiti. For similar reasons, the category of the power seekers and the lower-level political stratum may be larger in one country than in another and, therefore, produce a smaller apolitical stratum. The significance of Dahl's theory of authority structure will be discussed in some detail in subsequent chapters, especially as it pertains to political participation and the selection of decision makers in the executive and legislative realms.

THE IMPORTANCE OF POLITICS

Politics is concerned, among other factors, with the allocation of scarce resources by government. This presumes that the resources people regard as important are never sufficient, whether we are talking about clean air, clean water, or money. This does not mean that government determines or influences all aspects of our lives. If it did, we would be living in a completely totalitarian state as depicted in George Orwell's *1984*. But where government is involved, it is usually making a decision (a choice between alternatives) about how a resource shall be allocated. One situation that occurs regularly concerns appropriations for education. We may have to raise taxes or spend less on defense, highways, welfare measures, etc., if we are going to allocate more for schools.

Once man has gone beyond an idyllic "state of nature" where populations are small, people are assumed always to be rational and there are few, if any, conflicts; people are either forcibly organized or organize themselves into a society with rules and obligations. At this point some members of the society believe that certain objectives (for example, defense, security, transportation network) or values (such as respect for human life) can be achieved only by rules or laws that bind everyone. If many are legally allowed to participate in deciding procedures, objectives, policies, and values, we have some form of what is commonly called democracy. If few have the right to participate, we have some type of authoritarian or totalitarian system. The institution to promulgate and enforce such laws is government, and government in one aspect or another is a subject in which all political scientists are interested. Disagreements, competing points of views, or conflicts that are appealed to government for response, we call political conflicts. The age we live in is much more politicized than those of previous generations because many more conflicts involve government and therefore are political. There are several reasons for this:

(1) Today there are more than 150 sovereign countries in the world. When the United States declared its independent in 1776, there were approximately 40 sovereign countries; there were 70 sovereign countries in 1945. Thus, the number of independent countries has more than doubled during the last thirty years. The main reason for this increase in sovereign nation-states is the dissolution of the colonial empires. Most of the people who have achieved independence from colonial rule since 1945 live in Africa, Asia, and the Middle East. These people are no longer the generally docile colonial subjects of an imperial foreign power. With independence they progressively come to acquire a sense of common political identity and recognize they are now governed by individuals from their own country, although not necessarily from the same tribe or region. The effort, sometimes involving armed struggle, to achieve independence, made the majority of the world's population more politically aware. The world is more politicized because more people are self-consciously organized into sovereign states.

(2) Related to the first point is the fact that on occasion more people are participating in the political system. Now, after several years of independence, many of the developing world's peoples have become involved in influencing government policy or political leaders. Over the last several years one can point to such countries as Ghana, India, Indonesia, Jordan, Nigeria, and Syria, where substantial elements of the population have been active in the political process since independence. In much of the developing world and even in most Communist countries there are more or less regularly scheduled elections; however, in a majority of these political systems few if any opposition candidates are permitted. One purpose of single-party elections in these countries is to manipulate political awareness and create support for the government. In contrast, the United States

serves as an example where enfranchising segments of the population has led to a meaningful increase in political participation due to the passage of the Nineteenth, Twenty-Third, and Twenty-Sixth Amendments to the United States Constitution. The Nineteenth Amendment, ratified in 1920, granted suffrage to women. The Twenty-Third Amendment, ratified in 1961, gave voters in the District of Columbia the right to vote for president and vice-president. The Twenty-Sixth Amendment, ratified in 1971, gave citizens 18 years and older the vote in federal, state, and local elections. More people are participating in the political process in the contemporary world, whether mobilized by authoritarian governments or voluntarily, as in the United States.

(3) We also have become more politicized in the last hundred years as citizens have increasingly turned to government to solve problems previously considered outside the jurisdiction of government. Formerly, most governments throughout the world were responsible principally for defense, internal security, and maintaining some form of transportation–communication network. Today governments are often held responsible not only for inflation and deflation, but also for the price of gasoline and sugar, for encouraging industrialization to provide jobs, for establishing minimum wages and working conditions, for implementing retirement systems such as social security, etc. The list could go on for several pages. The notion of what government responsibilities are has expanded severalfold within the last hundred years. As groups support certain issues, such as gun registration or increasing the minimum wage, other groups oppose them. It is inevitable that political competition and disagreement expand as more issues are being pursued by various groups or individuals. The cumulative impact leads to increased politicization.

The more complex, specialized, and interdependent economic and social systems become within a country and the more economic, political, and national security policies are influenced by international forces outside the country, the more governments must respond on behalf of the political community. Governments are expected to deal with multiplying problems, national and international. The balancing and accommodating of numerous demands and pressures and the choice among alternatives often are decisions only governments can make and enforce. Even in this age of specialization and division of labor, governments should not, however, be expected "to do everything" and solve all problems. However, the role of political institutions is critical. The linchpin status of government today results in increased politicization.

(4) Another reason for increased politicization is that we have experienced a communications revolution in this century. Radio increased political participation and awareness in the United States and abroad. Tele-

vision has brought a new dimension to observing events and has replaced radio as the prime source of political information in the more advanced countries, though participation did not itself increase. Television is the principal source of news for approximately 70 percent of the population in the United States. Greater in-depth understanding does not necessarily occur, but awareness of the politically newsworthy and dramatic events of the moment is increased. Riots, wars, the impeachment proceedings are filmed live or shown within hours of the event. This is superficial politicization of the dramatic. It may actually draw attention away from a reasoned and studied understanding of major political problems, but superficial politicization is a phenomenon that occurs in many countries that have developed mass communications systems (newspapers, radio, television).

In sum, the world of today is more politicized than ever before, and politics is an important element of our life.

THE LANGUAGE OF POLITICS

One other item merits discussion before we turn to the discipline of political science per se. The metallurgist speaking on iron or lead, the ornithologist speaking on bluebirds or goldfinches, the artist discussing the techniques of Rubens or Van Dyck can speak more objectively about his subject than the political scientist discussing democracy or communism because these two labeles refer to something of an amorphous quality, in contrast to the known entities of iron, lead, bluebirds, goldfinches, or the paintings of Rubens and Van Dyck. Many of the terms used to describe political phenomena have, at best, ambiguous meanings. This language complexity is obviously not unique to political science vocabulary, but presents a problem in other social science disciplines too.

While the social scientist attempts to define his terminology with some precision, society at large often uses political labels very loosely. What do we mean by "democracy," by "communism," by "fascism," by "socialism"? What is a "liberal," what are the characteristics of a "conservative"? Which societies are "democratic," which "authoritarian," and which "totalitarian"? During the past three decades it has been in vogue in this country to speak of "the free countries," leaving the assumption that all countries not included in the above category are the opposite—enslaved countries. In discussions on matters of international politics basic terms such as "state" and "nation" have been used quite loosely too.

We shall discuss the ideological terms in some detail in our chapter on political theory and ideology. For our present purposes we would like to point out that even within a society such as the United States, people's concepts as to what constitutes democracy, socialism, communism, or fascism differ considerably. While the social scientist may attach basic models to each of these "isms," only to find that these models have little applicability to contemporary societies, the layman will use these terms in a still less thoughful way. One's own political perspective will have a bearing on how one applies the labels. The language used during the demonstrations in the United States in the late 1960s serves as an interesting illustration. People strongly opposed to the demonstrations were quite likely to label the demonstrators "communists," while in turn some of the demonstrators who were taken into custody by the police would accuse the police (and other officials) of being "fascists" or "fascist pigs." Obviously, the labels, in their true meanings, do not apply to either of the groups.

Still more confusion arises about the proper use of such terms as "liberal" and "conservative." People sharing the political philosophy of former Governor Reagan or Senator Towers (two leaders who are generally considered to be conservative) will view those who are less conservative as being "liberal." In turn, many supporters of such "liberals" as Senators Bayh or McGovern will look upon those who are less liberal than they are as being "conservative." The point is that the terms "liberal" and "conservative" are used not so much in reference to ideologies, but in a relative way, describing a person's political philosphy relative to one's own.

In a related way, this thesis could be partially applied to the use of such terms as democracy, socialism, fascism, and communism. There has been a tendency among many Americans, including high-ranking governmental officials, to label as "Communists" those at home and abroad who have opposed one or several of our foreign policies, while some of the domestic and foreign adversaries to United States foreign policies have accused the government of this country of being "fascist."

At the Yalta Conferece in 1945 Churchill, Roosevelt, and Stalin agreed that a "democratic" government would be established in Poland after World War II. It is obvious that Stalin's concept of what this government was to be like differed considerably from that of his Western conference partners. The point is that the use of political words is often purely verbal, that it is based on linguistic habits and conventions but tells us little or nothing about the matter of fact.[13]

Political vocabulary has more meaning if the user clarifies how he uses a term and what he means by it. One important service political scientists render is to help to define political vocabulary more clearly.

THE DISCIPLINE OF POLITICAL SCIENCE

After having examined the scope of political science, we would like to discuss the discipline per se. Political science is a relatively young academic

[13] For a more detailed discussion of the complexities of political labels, see T. D. Weldon, *The Vocabulary of Politics* (London: Penguin Books, 1953), pp. 9 ff.

field in the United States. The first political science courses were taught at Columbia University in the 1850s and 1860s. During the following decades the political science program at Columbia served as a model for similar programs being established at a number of American universities.[14]
The discipline has grown rather speedily, and today political science departments exist independently at many colleges and universities in this country. In other colleges political science is still part of a conglomerate social science department or forms a department jointly with history or economics. Among the approximately 2000 colleges and universities in the United States, 747 had independent political science departments in 1970, and of these 108 offered a Ph.D. program in the field.[15]

The United States has more trained political scientists than the rest of the world together. According to Gabriel Almond, "Nine out of every ten political scientists in the world today are American, and probably two out of every three political scientists who ever lived are alive and practicing today.[16]

What do political scientists do? How successful are they in pursuing their aims? Most political scientists are teaching about politics at colleges and universities. Their teaching and research have largely to do with politics in the public realm. Political science as a teaching field has traditionally been subdivided into the areas of American politics, comparative politics, international relations, political theory, public administration, and public law. Very little has yet been written by political scientists about politics in the world of business, social organizations, religious organizations, or organized crime.[17] The importance of one of these categories to political scientists was stated some time ago by Hans Morgenthau:

> *The curriculum of political science must take theoretical notice of the actual development of private governments in the form of giant corporations and labor unions. These organizations exercise power within their organizational limits, in their relations to each other, and in their relations to the state. The*

[14] The following are informative sources on the growth of political science in the United States: Albert Somit and Joseph Tannenhaus, *The Development of American Political Science: From Burgess to Behavioralism* (Boston: Allyn and Bacon, 1967); Bernard Crick, *The American Science of Politics: Its Origins and Conditions* (Berkeley: University of California Press, 1964); Francis J. Sorauf, *Political Science: An Informal Overview* (Columbus, Ohio: Charles E. Merrill Books, 1965), and Harold D. Laswell, *The Future of Political Science* (New York: Atherton Press, 1963), ch. 2.

[15] From data compiled by the personnel office of the American Political Science Association.

[16] Gabriel A. Almond, "Political Theory and Political Science," in Ithiel Pool, ed., *Contemporary Political Science: Toward Empirical Theory* (New York: McGraw-Hill, 1967), p. 3.

[17] Perhaps the most informative book on organized crime in the United States has been written by a former police officer and a journalist. See Ralph Salerno and John S. Tompkins, *The Crime Confederation* (Garden City: Doubleday, 1969).

state in turn exercises power in regard to them. These power relations constitute a new field for theoretical understanding.[18]

A similar reasoning could be applied to the political importance of the other categories too. The fact is, however, that most political scientists have assumed, and perhaps still assume, that political science should deal with legitimate politics in the public realm. Only in recent years have such areas of inquiry as domestic turmoil and revolutionary change become panel topics at political science conventions and have scholarly publications bearing such titles as *Political Violence, The Dynamics of Aggression,* and *Revolutionary Change* begun to appear.

What are the legitimate tasks of those who teach political science? What are the values of studying political science? Most of us would presumably agree with Dwight Waldo who speaks of teaching citizenship as the first pursuit of the political science teacher. We are talking about citizenship in the sense of providing data, facts, and methods of analysis pertaining to political processes and systems so that students hopefully become interested in politics and become more intelligent observers of, and participants in, the political arena. While political scientists do not have ready-made answers to all political issues and problems, they can—and should—educate students in citizenship.

A second task of those who teach political science is to provide pre-professional and professional training, such as preparing young people for public service. Each year thousands of college graduates take jobs with the federal, state, and local governments. Many of these are political science majors whose academic training has given them a suitable academic and pre-professional background for their future careers. A third task, according to Waldo, is to train students for political science research.[19] The last function is more applicable to graduate instruction than to undergraduate.

THE SCIENTIFIC CONTENT OF POLITICAL INQUIRY

How scientific a science can political science be? No single school or mood in political science provides the exclusive answer to the question. For, as Gaetano Salvemini has stated so succinctly:

Scientific research is a series of successive approaches to the truth, comparable to an exploration in an unknown land. Each explorer checks and adds to the findings of his predecessors, and facilitates for his successors the attainment of the goal they all have in common. This is why history and the social sciences,

[18] Hans J. Morgenthau, "Power as a Political Concept," in Roland Young, ed., *Approaches to the Study of Politics* (Evanston: Northwestern University Press, 1958), p. 77.

[19] Dwight Waldo, "Values in the Political Science Curriculum," in Roland Young, ed., *Approaches to the Study of Politics* (Evanston: Northwestern University Press, 1958), p. 110.

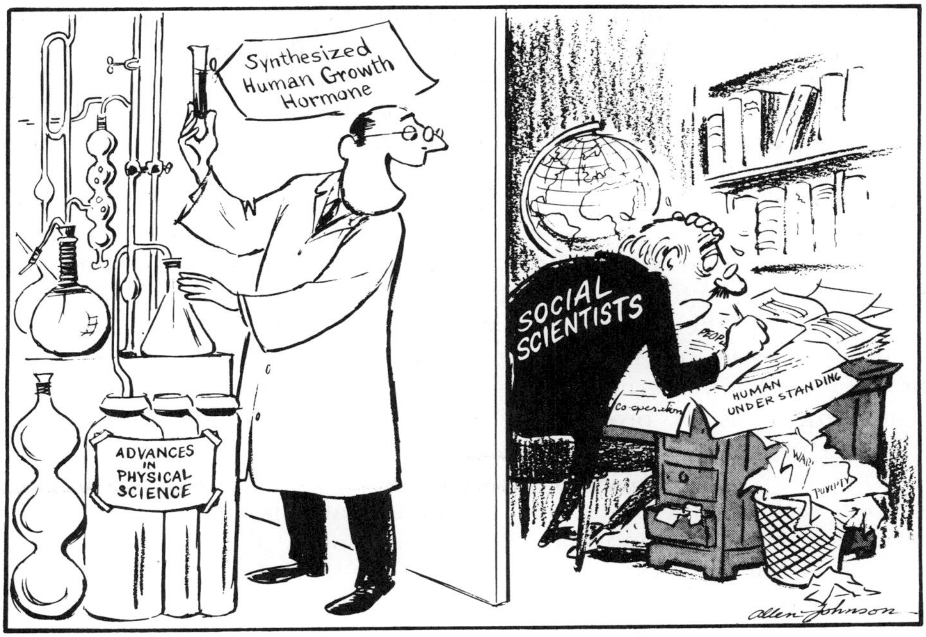

"How're you doing, Professor?"
(Allen Johnson, Providence Journal.)

more than any of the physical sciences, need an atmosphere of free competition between different schools of thought, in which all hypotheses and all proconceptions [sic] can be pitted one against the other. If liberty is suppressed in favor of a single school, it is the death warrant of our studies. . . . If they do not demand free competition not only for themselves but for their rivals as well, the historian and the social scientist, more than any scholars, accept both moral and intellectual degradation.[20]

Political science, as a social science, it not a science in the sense of the so-called hard sciences, such as biology, chemistry, or physics. These "hard" sciences deal with phenomena that can be examined in controlled experiments in a laboratory setting, while in political science inquiry it is just not possible to examine a voter, a political candiate, or an office holder in the same fashion. Furthermore, the natural scientist can pursue his research with a neutral or value-free attitude toward the object of his experiments.

In contrast, the researcher of political phenomena has a certain amount

[20] Gaetano Salvemini, *Historians and Scientists* (Cambridge. Mass.: Harvard University Press, 1939), pp. 112–113.

of personal psychological involvement in the subject of his inquiry, be it an urban problem, an aspect of national government policy, or a particular issue of United States' involvement abroad. A political scientist's findings are by nature more subjective than those of the natural scientist. The complexity of political phenomena and the influence of values make it impossible for the political scientist to be as objective as his colleague in the natural sciences. This does not mean, however, that political science inquiry is not scientific. For science starts with empiricism, the observation and verification of facts, and the formulation of generalizations and propositions. Scientific inquiry calls for adding new knowledge to what is known already. The perennial debate over the scientific nature of any or all of the social sciences has all too often been influenced by the commonly held notion that the term "science" should be reserved to those disciplines that show constant progress in obvious ways and use standard-type research techniques to achieve this progress.

However, we should take note of Abraham Kaplan: "Each science—and indeed, each inquiry—finds some techniques appropriate and others inappropriate and even impossible. The microscope is of very limited use to astronomy (for the present, at least), while the biologist cannot learn much about terrestrial life with the telescope. But to note this difference is not to say that these two sciences have different methods."[21]

In his essay *The Structure of Scientific Revolutions,* Thomas S. Kuhn defines science as "research firmly based upon one or more past scientific achievements that some particular scientific community acknowledges for a time as supplying the foundation for its further practice."[22]

Political science is self-conscious about the need to be as "scientific" as possible. It strives to be scientific in its methods, in the ways facts are collected, examined, and organized. The rigorous survey research that occurs in the United States is an example and outgrowth of this scientific research. Nationwide surveys by the Gallup and Harris polls or the Michigan Survey Research Center interview 1200 to 1600 adults. These surveys describe American political opinion or vote intention of more than 100 million adults within a maximum of 2 or 3 percent margin of error.[23]

[21] Abraham Kaplan; *The Conduct of Inquiry: Methodology for Behavioral Science* (San Francisco: Chandler Publishing, 1964), p. 31.

[22] Thomas S. Kuhn, *The Structure of Scientific Revolutions* (Chicago: The University of Chicago Press, 1962), p. 10.

[23] For further discussion of the scientific nature of political science, see Andrew Hacker, *The Study of Politics: The Western Tradition and American Origins* (New York: McGraw-Hill, 1963), pp. 5–8; Charles S. Hyneman, *The Study of Politics* (Urbana, Ill.: University of Illinois Press, 1959), pp. 75–80; Alan C. Isaak, *Scope and Methods of Political Science: An Introduction to the Methodology of Political Inquiry* (Homewood, Ill.: The Dorsey Press, 1969), pp. 22–30 and 45–57; Austin Ranney, ed., *Political Science and Public Policy* (Chicago: Markham Publishing Company, 1968), and Vernon Van Dyke, *Political Science: A Philosophical Analysis* (Stanford, Cal.: Stanford University Press, 1960), pp. 191–205.

As the student will see in the following chapters, political science is making progress in identifying and explaining political relationships. Moreover, new theories have been developed and older ones have been re-examined in new settings. New horizons have been opened for research. Political science has grown to become a more exact and more scientific discipline of scholarly pursuit. One other sign of its growth importance can be seen in the fact that in the past two decades the presidents of this country, as well as state executives, have increasingly sought the advice of selected political scientists.

Having examined the nature and scope of political science, we now turn our attention to the approaches or methods used by political scientists to study political phenomena and the key concepts involved.

Selected Readings

An excellent collection of essays on the relationship between political science and the other social sciences is *Politics and the Social Sciences** (New York: Oxford University Press, 1969), edited by Seymour Martin Lipset. For a treatment of the relationship between political science and mathematics, see Hayword R. Alker, *Mathematics and Politics** (New York: Macmillan, 1965).

Among the more useful of the numerous studies that focus on the scope and methods of political science are Charles E. Hyneman, *The Study of Politics: The Present State of American Political Science** (Urbana, Ill.: University of Illinois Press, 1959); Vernon Van Dyke, *Political Science: A Philosophical Analysis** (Stanford, Cal.: Stanford University Press, 1960) and, by the same author, "The Optimum Scope of Political Science," in James C. Charlesworth, ed., *A Design for Political Science: Scope, Objectives, and Methods** (Philadelphia: The American Academy of Political and Social Sciences, 1966); Harold D. Laswell, *The Future of Political Science** (New York: Atherton, 1963); David Easton, *A Framework for Political Analysis* (Englewood Cliffs, N.J.: Prentice-Hall, 1965) and, by the same author, *The Political System: An Inquiry into the State of Political Science,** 2nd ed. (New York: Alfred A. Knopf, 1971); William A. Welsh, *Studying Politics** (New York: Praeger, 1973), and Alan C. Isaak, *Scope and Methods of Political Science: An Introduction to the Methodology of Political Inquiry*, rev. ed. (Homewood, Ill.: The Dorsey Press, 1975). A good collection of recent essays on political science and the functions of political scientists is George J. Graham, Jr., and George W. Carey, eds., *The Post-Behavioral Era: Perspectives on Political Science** (New York: David McKay, 1972).

* Available in paperback.

A superb analysis of the political environment of society is Robert A. Dahl, *Modern Political Analysis,** 3rd ed. (Englewood Cliffs, N.J.: Prentice-Hall, 1976). Two other studies that focus on the same general topic are Harold D. Laswell, *Politics: Who Gets What, When, How** (Cleveland: The World Publishing Company, 1958), and David R. Segal, *Society and Politics: Uniformity and Diversity in Modern Democracy** (Glenview, Ill.: Scott, Foresman, 1974).

Very little has been written on "the language of politics." The best treatment is chapter 3 in T. D. Weldon, *THe Vocabulary of Politics** (London: Penguin Books, 1953).

Two informative books on the development of political science in the United States are Bernard Crick, *The American Science of Politics: Its Origins and Conditions* (Berkeley: University of California Press, 1964) and Albert Somit and Joseph Tannenhaus, *The Development of Political Science: From Burgess to Behavioralism* (Boston: Allyn and Bacon, 1967). For a discussion of its present status, see Heinz Eulau and James G. March, eds., *Political Science** (Englewood Cliffs, N.J.: Prentice-Hall, 1969). A though-provoking study with emphasis on futurism is Albert Somit, *Political Science and the Study of the Future** (Hinsdale, Ill.: Dryden, 1974).

Two good treatments of the subfields in political science are Marian D. Irish, ed., *Political Science: Advance of the Discipline** (Englewood Cliffs, N.J.: Prentice-Hall, 1968) and Michael Haas and Henry S. Kariel, eds., *Approaches to the Study of Political Science* (Scranton, Pa.: Chandler, 1970).

* Available in paperback.

Chapter 2

Political Science: Approaches and Concepts

Approaches to the Study of Politics

Political scientists use various methods to conduct their inquiries. Modern political science has been shaped by different methodological approaches and considerable debate over the appropriateness of each. The period during the late nineteenth century was heavily legalistic and philosophically oriented, as illustrated by the title of one of the major works of that era, John Burgess, *Political Science and Comparative Constitutional Law* (1890). Many American political scientists of that time had received at least some of their graduate training at European universities and were influenced by the legalistic training in these schools. But already during Burgess' years, some political scientists in this country had begun to shift away from constitutionalism and legal inquiry, moving toward a comparative historical and structural study of governmental institutions and organizations. This can be seen, for example, in Woodrow Wilson, *Congressional Government: A Study in American Politics* (1885).

A new mood or spirit entered political science in the 1920s, when some political scientists began to supplement their library research with interview and survey fieldwork, thereby adding a new vista to the historical, legalistic, and constitutional approaches employed by the traditionalists. The new movement, soon to become known as behavioralism, aimed at making political science a more scientific discipline, which analyzed politics as it operated in the contemporary, real world.

Behavioralism, which should not be confused with the behaviorist school in psychology, initially focused on man as the political actor. The emphasis on individual and group behavior led the behavioralist to study the leadership role of a president, the performance roles of congressmen and judges and how they carry out their responsibilities, instead of focusing on the Constitution, the executive, the Congress, or the judiciary per se. In other words, while the traditionalist's concern was largely with formal institutions, the behavioralist has focused principally on individuals rather than large political units.

The behavioralists have acquired some of the research tools used in anthropology, economics, mathematics, psychology, and sociology. They have advocated a more rigorous empiricism, extensive use of statistical methods for quantifying the data and the recording of these on charts, graphs, scales, and tables. A major effort of the behavioralists was survey research undertaken to assess attitudes and beliefs. Table I, for example, taken from one of the major "voting studies," shows the results of a survey research questionnaire that was interested in measuring the influence of primary groups (face-to-face groups one regularly associates with, such as family, friends, and fellow workers) on voters' behavior. The table shows only that there is a fairly close correspondence between the individual's political vote and the group with which he associates. In part, this may result from primary group pressure to conform, or at least to discourage

Table I Party Preferences of Individuals and Primary Groups with Which the Individuals Affiliate[a]

Respondent Voted	Spouse Voted		Family Voted[b]		Friends Voted		Work Associates Voted	
	Dem.	Rep.	Dem.	Rep.	Dem.	Rep.	Dem.	Rep.
Democratic	89%	7%	80%	8%	83%	15%	79%	24%
Republican	11	93	20	92	85	85	21	76
Total	100%	100%	100%	100%	100%	100%	100%	100%
n[c] =	337	496	75	108	355	574	271	290

Source: Angus Campbell et al., *The American Voter* (New York: John Wiley, 1960), p. 77. Reprinted by permission of the publisher.

[a] This tabulation is limited to persons who reported voting for a major party candidate for president and who could attribute to the primary group in question a clear partisan preference

[b] Asked only of unmarried respondents

[c] Includes a small number of persons who voted for a minor party candidate

substantial levels of political disagreement and tension within the group. Political similarity in primary groups also results from the fact that most members share the same experiences and characteristics, which generally results in similar attitudes.

The behavioral approach seeks to achieve a greater accuracy in explaining political phenomena and to make generalizations applicable to a variety of political systems. The most successful areas of inquiry for the behavioralist have been studies of voting behavior and investigations of beliefs and attitudes held by individuals.

During the past decade behavioralism has become an integral part of the political science discipline and many members of the profession rely now on a combination of methods of inquiry derived from the traditional and behavioral schools. In a very real sense almost all political scientists are behavioralists if we summarize the behavioral movement as an effort to make political science more empirical and scientific. This new post-behavioral synthesis is not concerned exclusively with individuals, but is also concerned with the functioning and impact of political institutions and the influence of relevant geographic, economic, historical, legal, and cultural factors. This synthesis has been increasingly influenced by the political and social crises of our time. One important credo of post-behavioralism is *relevance,* that is, the effort to make political science teachers and research as relevant as possible to current domestic and international problems and, if possible, to contribute to resolving these problems. A major subfield that has emerged in the last few years is called public policy, committed to improvement of government policy making. Two relatively new journals representative of this trend are *Policy Sciences* and *Public Policy.*

This text is designed to use the most appropriate approaches for the beginning student in his or her study of politics. We believe that a basic familiarity with political science principles will enable the student to better understand contemporary political issues and to analyze and contribute toward the making of public policy.

We believe that the most appropriate approach to political science for the beginning student is a combination of systems analysis and pluralism. Both of these orientations are concerned with the interaction, cooperation, and conflict of diverse parts. The underlying organization of this book presumes that such a focus provides the most useful means for understanding the political world.

THE POLITICAL SYSTEM AND SYSTEMS THEORY

We do not consider all the complexities and nuances of systems theory. We will focus on the concept of political system as a means to recognizing and understanding patterns or regularities when confronted with what is often an unorganized mass of political information. Herbert Spiro has summarized this need:

> *Anyone who attempts to study politics scientifically must at least implicitly think of politics as though it were functioning as some sort of system. That is, he must assume that more or less regular relationships can be discerned among various aspects of politics and between phenomena he describes as political and certain other phenomena not so described.*[1]

We have used the term "political system" several times. At this point a definition and more thorough explanation are in order. Most political scientists agree that we study political systems and not just government. Government is the focal point or center of the political system, but many other parts are involved. The political systems approach does two things: it enables us to perceive selectively and to organize what is significant politically when we look at the whole political process; and it also alerts us to the interrelationships between obviously political phenomena—for example, political parties, the chief executive, civil service commission—and other phenomena in society that are sometimes politically important—such as the family and educational or economic systems.

Any system, whether we are discussing the political system, the heating system in a house, or the individual's physiological system, has certain characteristics:

1. The system is made up of many parts.
2. The parts interact.
3. To varying degrees the parts are interdependent.
4. The system has boundaries.

A major difference between an example such as the heating system of a house and the political system is that in the former the boundaries are tangible and readily observable. The components of the heating system (thermostat, furnace, wiring, ducts) are apparent to the eye, and it is obvious where the physical boundaries are. This is not true with the political system; its boundaries are abstract and must be discerned and explained by the political scientist. You are not participating in the political system if you take a date to a movie or a football game. You are in the political system if you attend a political rally, write a letter to a political official, vote, or study and discuss politics.

In any system some parts are more important than others, and some parts interact more than others. Changes in one part may or may not affect other parts or processes in the system. If you have your appendix removed, there

[1] Herbert J. Spiro, "An Evaluation of Systems Theory," in James C. Charlesworth, ed. *Contemporary Political Analysis* (New York: Free Press, 1967), p. 164.

is little apparent change in your physiological system. If you lose a kidney the consequences are serious, and without a heart the body will not function. There are similar variations in the critical nature and frequency of variation in the political system. Political parties and elections are very important in the American political system. The military and/or bureaucracy may be the most important institutions to study in some other political system. In fact, the latter situation is true for many political systems in Africa, Asia, Latin America, and the Middle East. An understanding of what we mean by political system will assist you in studying political science and particular countries or processes (for example, elections, revolutions, rule making, political socialization), but the concept of political system will not itself explain particular events. The first step, however, is to organize data within a general framework, in this case, the political system. Figure 1 will help you visualize what we are discussing.

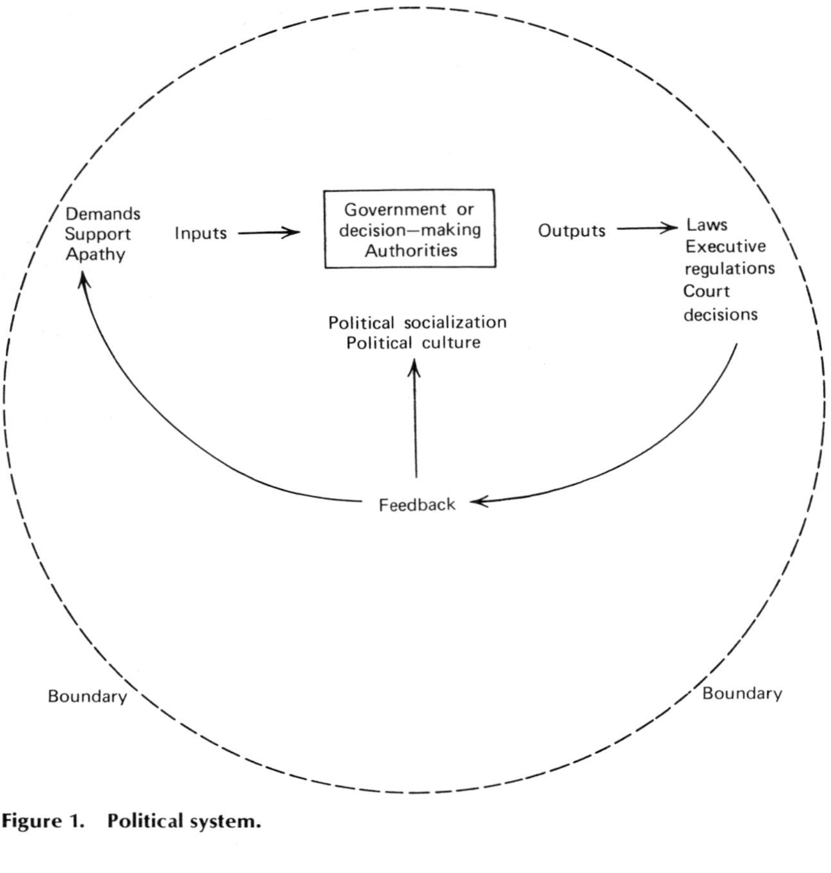

Figure 1. Political system.

Government Defined

Government is the focal point or center of any political system. A government is viable when it successfully upholds a claim to the exclusive regulation of the legal use of physical force in enforcing its rules within a given territorial (geopolitical) area. It is the most inclusive institution in society. No other organization (fraternity, sorority, trade union, church) in society includes everyone within its jurisdiction or membership.

Government sometimes allows other groups to use physical force, but only in a restricted manner. A parent may physically discipline a child, but this must be limited; too much physical force becomes child abuse. Child abuse is against the law. Generally, when physical force is used by other than government officials it is done illegally. Much violence that actually occurs in society is outside the law, or what is generally described as crime. If crime and violence become too widespread, government effectiveness rapidly diminishes and the existence of a particular government may actually be threatened. When individuals organize and declare a government illegal, initiate political violence in an effort to establish a different government, or change drastically the existing political system, then there is an insurgency or a revolution and political instability.

The use of force is the ultimate government sanction. Generally the less force required, the more effective government is and the more it is accepted by the population. The arbitrary and unpredictable use of force characterizes totalitarian governments, which seek to terrorize and thus more easily control their subjects. A government such as the American, uses force relatively infrequently, but it is used. So that a government does not have to allocate extensive resources to internal security, 90 to 95 percent of the population should—out of commitment, understanding, self-interest, or habit—obey the law. If a police officer had to be on duty 24 hours a day to enforce stoplights, an unacceptable share of government resources (taxes, appropriations, personnel) would have to be committed to this area of government responsibility. Fortunately, most drivers obey traffic signals.

One example of the role of government and the uncommon but ultimate use of physical coercion by democratic governments is eminent domain. In the United States, eminent domain, or the acquiring of private property for public use after the payment of fair compensation, is usually accomplished without a court trial or resort to force. There are exceptions, such as the hypothetical individual who is required to sell his property for an interstate highway interchange. The person may believe the price the government offers for the property is too low. Therefore, a jury trial becomes necessary to determine the price. On a few tragic occasions, government force is used. The following example also involves the question of whether or not "justice" was actually served:

Consider the 1964 case of a Los Angeles resident named Steven Anthony who refused to vacate his home which had been condemned by Los Angeles County under the laws of eminent domain. The land was to be turned over to a private group for the construction of the Hollywood Motion Picture and Television Museum. For ten weeks Anthony barricaded himself in his home, holding off with a shotgun the deputies who sought to evict him. Finally, two plainclothes policemen gained access by posing as sympathizers. Anthony was arrested and jailed. The next day the house was demolished by court order. The judge labeled this previously unknown man "an anarchist, a rabble rouser, and a publicity seeker" and sentenced him to a year in jail for battery and resisting arrest. . . .

All plans for building the museum have been abandoned due to dissension among the ranks of the Hollywood promoters. The property is currently being used as a parking lot.[2]

Inputs

Government, because of its unique characteristics, is at the center of the political system, but many other activities and institutions are included as part of the system.

The input side of Figure 1 includes: claims or demands; supports; and

Voters in Wisconsin line up to cast their ballots in a primary election.

[2] Susan Love Brown et al., *The Incredible Bread Machine* (San Diego: World Research, 1974), pp. 2–3. The original story appeared in the *Los Angeles Times,* April 4, 1965.

apathy. *Demands* refer to actions people want government to undertake or reject. The method by which to involve peacefully the largest number of people is that of competitive elections where most of the adult population is eligible to vote. Voters make few specific policy choices, but they do select candidates who have committed themselves on specific issues. Demonstrations, petitions and individual letters to newspapers or government officials are also means of making input.

Interest groups and political parties, discussed in more detail in chapter 5, are also means of making claims. For example, the National Rifle Association actively and successfully opposes gun control legislation. In a pluralistic or more open political system, the opportunities are greater for groups to organize without the supervision or control of government. A variety of competing claims are made in this type of political system. Ultimately, some part of government makes a decision (or refuses to take action), whether it be a law, a court decision, or an executive order prohibiting the importation of beef from Canada. Individuals can also make claims or present demands by writing letters, meeting a government official, running for office, and, of course, through the electoral ballot.

Supports are given to the political system as a whole and to that part of the system referred to as the regime. Regime refers to the overall constitutional process or political rules of the game, to "those arrangements that regulate the way in which the demands put into the system are settled and the way in which decisions are put into effect."[3] Supports evolve over decades or even centuries and are basically loyalty to the system and regime, without necessarily being in agreement with the individuals or political party in office. You may have voted against the president or the congressman representing you, but still are loyal to the existing political arrangements, which in the case of the United States is a constitutional representative government.

Supports can be divided into two basic types: manifest or observable; and affective. Manifest supports are usually actions that show or promote loyalty and identity with the political system. Examples include voting as an act of citizenship or paying taxes because of a feeling of commitment and identity. Affective supports are states of mind that are predispositions and attitudes of loyalty, patriotism, and commitment. These attitudes sometimes become manifest supports; at other times they remain simply a psychological orientation that creates what may be described as diffuse, indirect support.

Supports evolve because governments and regimes have responded over several decades and generations (see political integration in chapter 10).

[3] David Easton, "An Approach to the Analysis of Political Systems," *World Politics,* IX, No. 1 (April, 1957), p. 392.

Supports hold a political community together, even though there are sharp differences over particular policies or individuals in office. When the widely shared supports are few, the political system is endangered and radically different political arrangements may be introduced. During the closing days of Weimar Germany (1918–1933), shortly before Adolf Hitler assumed full power in 1933, the Communists and Nazis together were winning 50 percent of the votes. (In the November, 1932, Reichstag elections, the Nazi Party won 33 percent of the vote and the Communists 17 percent.) This lack of support for constitutional democracy made it easier for the Nazis to achieve power and transform the German government from a representative to a totalitarian political system.

Apathy or indifference can be either a support or a potential reservoir from which revolutionaries can mobilize support. For example, in the United States approximately 20 percent of the eligible electorate is apolitical or apathetic. Some people are apathetic because the electoral process involves so many people that they feel one vote makes no difference; others are uninterested because "things will not get better," or they lack the mental ability to understand and organize political information. In some political systems fear and coercion encourage apathy. For others, apathy reflects general satisfaction with the political system and therefore there is no need to become concerned with political rhetoric. People may be very intelligent and have many interests, but simply not be interested in political issues. If politics becomes so intense that it turns into a war of one side against the other, orderly procedures, such as secret ballot and the defeated candidate acknowledging the winner's right to assume office, will soon be ineffective. Apathy, positively viewed, reflects the genuine right of a person to be apolitical. This bloc of people, by their presence, reduces the intensity of competition among the politically concerned.

Political apathy can also reflect a sense of hopelessness and withdrawal from the political system. Apathy in an authoritarian state is commonly a defense mechanism. It does not overtly challenge the regime, but it seeks to preserve in one of the few ways possible a degree of individual privacy and autonomy. It prevents the complete politicization of the individual in the name of the state. Given the proper circumstances, such apathy may be interrupted by spontaneous antiregime demonstrations, as happened in East Germany in 1953, in Hungary in 1956, in Czechoslovakia in 1968, and in Thailand in 1973. Apathy based on a sense of hopelessness or a controlled, dormant hostility is not a support, and it becomes an input when triggered.

In the case of the Thai "student revolution," which occurred in Bangkok in October, 1973, troops fired on students and at least 69 students died. High-ranking military officers then refused to order the troops against the students again. Three days of demonstrations forced the most unpopular

Thai students scatter to avoid fire from troops during clashes that led to the collapse of the military government, 1973.

government–military leaders to flee the country. The generally politically uninterested Bangkok population was mobilized by the students' actions and discontent. In Thailand apathy had been a form of support for many years. As this apathy moved from a form of support to latent hostility, the student demonstration drew on and organized popular feelings. The result was input that had crucial political implications. A civilian prime minister was appointed by the king, and one year later, in October, 1974, a new, more liberal constitution was promulgated.

Apathy, as we have seen, can provide support for the political system or it can be a potential source for mass agitation against the system. If a government is struggling against an insurgency, the apathy of the population in its effort to physically survive generally is a disadvantage for the government.

Outputs

Outputs are government decisions. They may be laws, court decisions, executive–administrative orders, or conscious refusals to make a decision. The work and even intentions of the government are measured by its outputs. Public administration is the subfield of political science that studies how decisions are implemented and if implementation is effective, often with more concern for procedures (such as budgeting and personnel policies) than substance of decisions. Non-decisions, the refusal of government to intervene or take an action concerning a problem or dispute in society, is also a form of output. For example, during a labor strike, either management or the union may go to court and request an injunction. The burden for settling the dispute rests then almost entirely on the two parties involved—management and labor—with limited outside intervention.

Laws as output are apparent: eighteen-year-olds are enfranchised by Constitutional amendment, social security benefits are raised, or the speed limit is set at 55 miles per hour by act of Congress. One of the most famous judicial outputs in the United States was the Supreme Court decision in *Brown* v. *Board of Education* (1954), in which racial segregation in public schools was declared unconstitutional. The implementation of that decision since 1954, though slow, has had a tremendous impact on society.

An example of an executive or administrative output was the action taken by President Ford in 1974 imposing a quota on the importation of Canadian beef and pork. President Nixon had suspended import quotas on foreign beef in 1972 to reduce inflationary pressures. President Ford's reimposition of quotas on Canada resulted from the American government's belief that Canada had established "unjustifiable import restrictions" on American Products. A White House spokesman explained that the President's proclamation was intended "to bring an end to the Canadian quotas."[4]

Unfortunately, most political science writing is not concerned with the output side of the political system. Relatively little research is done on the impact that output decisions have or on the question of whether they actually accomplish their purpose. Laws, rules, appropriations, and good administrative procedures do not guarantee that the result will be the one anticipated. Most political science literature focuses either on inputs or the government decision-making.

Conversion and Political Culture

Government in all of its parts (executive, legislative, and judicial branches) can be described as the decision-making authority that has conversion as a principal function:

> *The conversion processes, or functions, are the ways systems transform inputs into outputs. In the political system this involves the ways in which demands and support are transformed into authoritative decisions and are implemented.*[5]

The more people participate freely in making demands, as in a pluralistic system, the more effort required by government to balance, modify, approve, or reject some claims, and convert the inputs into policy or outputs. Much of what political scientists study is concerned with govern-

[4] *Washington Post,* November 17, 1974.

[5] Gabriel Almond and G. Bingham Powell, Jr., *Comparative Politics: A Developmental Approach* (Boston: Little, Brown 1966), p. 29.

ment institutions: history, organization, and functioning. Government is crucial to political science because of its ultimate sanction—the legal use of physical force, and also because of its decision-making and conversion roles.

As government decisions are made and policies carried out, they pass through a feedback process that affects the political culture, as well as the more immediate input side. Political culture (discussed in detail in chapter 4) is shaped in part by outputs, but it also affects the input process. Political culture refers to those aspects of our social heritage concerned with dispositions, attitudes, values, and behavior pattern affecting the way people perceive and behave in the political system. Political culture grew out of the concept of national character, which presumes the presence of modal national traits having political significance, for example, general acceptance of a ruling elite not subject to competitive elections. Modal behavior, or the mode, refers to the characteristic that occurs most often in the group. The characteristic is not present in everyone, and sometimes is not even present in a majority of the universe measured, but it is the most common trait or set of traits.

Political culture is important in the conversion process. It influences the thinking and actions of those actually making government decisions. It also influences the range of claims and the style (voting, letters, demonstrations, riots, or apathetic obedience) with which the conversion process must deal. For example, during the Tokugawa period (1603–1857) in Japan, the emperor was a figurehead, and military lords, or *daimyo,* controlled the government. Rule was often arbitrary. The political culture fostered uniformity and self-conscious apolitical behavior. There were few, if any, popular demands and political claims were nil. An in-depth study of the period by a cultural anthropoligist shows how the samurai warriors enforced detailed government rules by instantly decapitating anyone whose actions were "other than expected." Those Japanese who survived in the Tokugawa political system "learned in early chilhood to keep their own counsel, trust no one, and conform fanatically to whatever might be ordered."[6]

Feedback

Feedback is a movement of perceptions resulting from output. It increases or decreases support for the system. It may affect the types of inputs or claims that are made (from lower taxes to creating a totally new type of government), as well as how the claims are presented (voting to revolu-

[6] Douglas G. Haring, "The Formation of National Character in Tokugawa and Meiji, Japan," reprinted in Thomas J. Bellows, Stanley Erikson, and Herbert Winter, eds., *Political Science: Introductory Essays and Readings* (Belmont, Calif.: Duxbury Press, 1971), p. 166.

tion). Feedback in an authoritarian political system, as in the case of Tokugawa Japan, may be controlled by the government so as to compel obedience, with the result that popular input is nonexistent.

Feedback is filtered through the political culture. It influences the political culture, as well as the nature and method of inputs. Relative satisfaction with output leads one to support the political system or even particular candidates and political parties. In a direct and clear-cut feedback loop (see Figure 1) legislators may raise social security benefits or welfare payments shortly before an election.

Feedback also can affect general political orientation as in the case of postwar Japan, which underwent one of the most successful land reform programs in this century. The American occupation required the Japanese Diet (legislature) to enact far-reaching land reform legislation in October, 1946. The number of farmers owning all their land increased from 36 percent to 62 percent within three years, and the number of farmers owning less than half their land dropped from 17 to 7 percent. The agrarian objectives and feedback related to these reforms were accomplished. The land reform campaign was to restructure village relationships so that the mass of peasants were not dominated by a few village landlords. Radical agrarian movements found little support among the new peasant-owners. Political attitudes and the input were greatly influenced by the government's agrarian policies. The peasants were mainly interested in conserving their new gains. The new peasant-owners "became the chief support of the conservative political parties."[7]

Communications and information are part of the feedback loop. The presumption is that with more information governments are more effective. David Easton, the political scientist who has written the most extensively on political systems, believes that information is important for two principal reasons: public officials need as much information as is feasible about the political system so they can act to meet any possible loss of support; and public officials also should be aware of the effects of future decisions as well as "be able to evaluate the consequences of whatever behavior they have already undertaken or are in the process of undertaking."[8]

Feedback through elections, the party organization, newspapers, interest groups, etc., provides information about the impact of outputs. Nevertheless, in this information explosion era we live in, we often do not have sufficient information, nor are we able to utilize fully what we potentially have access to. Even in a pluralistic system with a wide range of competing

[7] Franz H. Michael and George E. Taylor, *The Far East in the Modern World* (New York: Henry Holt, 1956), p. 546.

[8] David Easton, *A Systems Analysis of Political Life* (New York: John Wiley, 1965), pp. 364–65.

inputs, the amount of information moving through the feedback loop is inadequate or cannot be feasibly retrieved at the moment it is required. It almost appears at times that there is a dichotomy between the world of action and the world of thought. A man who has achieved success in both worlds, as a government decision maker and as an eminent political scientist at Harvard University, Secretary of State Henry Kissinger, spoke on the inevitable information gap confronting political leaders as they make what are often difficult choices and judgments: "Facts are not clear and this is difficult in the best of circumstances."[9]

We are suggesting that even when all parts of the political system appear to be functioning at a high level, the system will always be less than "perfect." Even in a competitive, pluralistic environment with considerable subsystem (interest group, parties, individual freedom) autonomy, resulting in a great flow of claims and information feedback, policies and choices are subject to the "human factor." Anthony Downs has pointed this out in his analysis of the civil servant as a decision maker. Downs discusses several inevitable, if not innate, limitations to decision making:

1. Each decision maker can devote only a limited amount of time to decision making.
2. Each decision maker can mentally weigh and consider only a limited amount of information at one time.
3. The functions of most officials require them to become involved in more activities than they can consider simultaneously; hence, they must normally focus their attention on only part of their major concerns.
4. The amount of information initially available to every decision maker about each problem is only a small fraction of all the information potentially available on the subject.
5. Additional information bearing on any particular problem can usually be procured, but the costs of procurement and utilization may rise rapidly as the amount of data increases.
6. Important aspects of many problems involve information that cannot be procured at all, especially concerning future events; hence, many decisions must be made in the face of some ineradicable uncertainty.[10]

The world we live in is fallible. We can never achieve a mechanical functioning of the political system that will provide a perfectly harmonious and rational interaction. During any given period of time political conflict and

[9] Henry Kissinger, *Speech before the Annual Dinner of Alfred E. Smith Memorial Foundation* (Department of State, Bureau of Public Affairs, PR 427, October 16, 1974), p. 75.

[10] Anthony Downs, *Inside Bureaucracy* (Boston: Little, Brown, 1967), p. 75.

disagreements are inevitable, with regard to both the substance and administration of policy. We believe, though, that systems analysis provides an effective orientation to analyze political events.

Systems analysis has alerted us to what now appears obvious but was not always recognized, namely, that while everything may relate to everything ultimately, some things relate more than others. For example, government-supported agricultural research can lead to the migration of farm populations, which then has consequences for cities. A knowledge of what we mean by political system should assist us in identifying those components that have significant influence. Beyond this, there are limitations.

Criticisms of the Systems Approach

It is difficult to test the whole systems model, in fact, it has never been operationalized (hypotheses developed and empirically tested) in its entirety. It is easier to study parts or subsystems that are performing important functions, such as political parties, interest groups, or the bureaucracy. The components of a political system are distinct and different from one another. All of the parts do not mutually depend on one another. Some parts are vital, some are intermediary, some are incidental. In one political system autonomous interest groups are important in maintaining competition and freedom of expression, while in a totalitarian system, interest groups are just another instrument of control and provide no input. We must study a specific political system in detail to determine which parts are essential and how they influence and are influenced by other parts. Change or destruction of one component will not necessarily have much impact on the system. Parts and processes may function in relative isolation from one another. Adjustments between parts and/or processes may be delayed. It often is difficult to predict response or determine with any degree of accuracy what a change in one component (literacy, birthrate, lowered voting age) may have on another (increased political support, weakened extremist parties).

Finally, we might note the frequent criticism that systems analysis is biased toward the status quo and is sympathetic toward only limited change. Although regularly denied, this is sometimes true. There is more than a suspicion in systems theory that the continuous interaction and interdependence of parts implies self-regulation and self-maintenance because the principal goal is survival. We cannot assume all parts are working for survival (for example, a revolutionary party), nor have any measures been constructed to determine when a system is being adequately maintained. What is the threshold, determined by measuring such crucial variables as caloric intake, literacy, employment, education, and political assassinations, that when taken as an interrelated group will reveal to us that a political system is about to disintegrate or, having faced challenges, is surviving and relatively stable?

Summary
Despite its problems, systems analysis provides the political scientist with a useful framework for analysis. It is the beginning point for a study of one or more individual political systems or for a study of international politics. It provides a general orientation and reminds us that there are certain basic processes, such as inputs, decision making, outputs, and feedback that are performed in all systems. Which parts are important, how they interact, and what functions each performs can only be determined by analyzing specific cases.

PLURALISM

We now turn to another approach to the study of politics—pluralism. Pluralism and the systems approach are not mutually exclusive concepts, but in fact complement one another. We believe some form of pluralism is necessary if a political system is to facilitate the optimum level of human progress and freedom. Pluralism is defined as extensive participation in the political process through competing and autonomous groups and hence competing viewpoints. Citizens, though, continue to participate as individuals, as discussed below. Pluralism recognizes that many, though not all, important political decisions are influenced most effectively by organized groups (interest groups) concerned with the political question at hand. Pluralism requires that there be various competing groups not government sponsored or manipulated. In addition to a multiplicity of associations, there should be some multiplicity of affiliations: "Individuals belong to several groups, no one group is inclusive of its members' lives."[11]

In a pluralist system, many groups have members with a variety of social characteristics (class, education, age, religion, ethnic, or racial identifications, etc.) and a majority of individuals will belong to more than one organization. The various organizations will serve different needs and will be independent of each other. No group will dominate a person's thinking. Multiple memberships will give the individual a variety of perspectives and sometimes even conflicting signals. Hopefully, the impact of various memberships will not be cumulative in a monolithic, doctrinaire way, which will give the individual a rigid and closed view of the political world, for example, the Communist who belongs to the Communist trade union, reads a Communist newspaper, and belongs to a social group whose members are all Communists.

[11] William Kornhauser, *The Politics of Mass Society* (New York: The Free Press, 1959). p. 80.

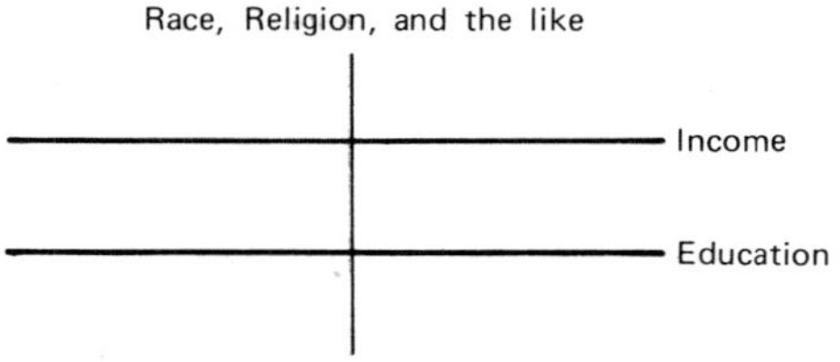

Figure 2.

One of the pioneer studies of pluralism and the importance of groups to a community was undertaken in the late 1930s in Newburyport, Massachusetts. One-third of the 357 associations studied in this city had members from 3 of the 6 social classes the authors had previously identified. Another third of the groups had members from 4 classes. Approximately 13,000 members were surveyed in conjunction with the study of the 357 associations. Almost two-thirds of these individuals belonged to associations in which 4 or more of the 6 classes were represented. More than 50 percent belonged to associations in which 2 or more of the 4 major religious faiths were represented. Pluralism, as in Newburyport, is based on a large number of organized groups.[12] This type of pluralism moderates political conflict. Associations composed of people with different religious, ethnic, and class characteristics prevent one line of social cleavage from becoming dominant and cumulative in the organization. The actions of the group are usually moderated because the organization must respect the various identities of its members, lest it alienate any segment of its membership. This mixing of memberships and identifications is characteristic of a society where individuals have cross-cutting and often competing identifications. (See Figure 2.)

We have used cross-cutting here in the sense of a grid. Vertical divisions in society, represented as |, are principally inherited genetically or socially and include male–female, young–old, religion, language, and race. Vertical divisions generally do not involve a quantity or characteristics that may vary in the degree to which they are present. One is either Catholic or Methodist, a native Mali speaker or a native Chinese speaker. Horizontal divisions, represented ———, generally measure the degree of presence or absence of something such as income (high or low) or education (grade school or university). An example of a person with cross-cutting identifications would be a high school educated, wealthy businessman, who follows a particular religion.

[12] See W. Lloyd Warner and P. Lunt, *The Social Life of a Modern Community* (New Haven: Yale University Press, 1941), pp. 341, 346, and 349.

A cumulative set of traits not cross-cutting might typify a society where all Malays are Muslims; almost all have a grade school education or less; and are living at the poverty level or below. Here each characteristic reinforces the other in such a way as to set apart the group from the rest of society. No identifications are shared with other groups. Interaction and tolerance among groups frequently breaks down. Barriers are erected that prevent accommodation of different needs and concerns of individuals and groups.

Pluralism presumes that the largest possible number of people will participate in the political input process through universal adult suffrage or interest group activity. It also assumes that the widest range of alternative proposals will compete. Competition is subject to restriction only to those who call for deliberate violence, propose to drastically reduce participation, or substantially restrict the types of alternatives that can be proposed legally. One such example was the Nazi Party of Germany. The Nazis participated extensively and effectively in the competitive electoral system of Weimar Germany before forming the government in 1933. Yet the Nazis were dedicated to eliminating all political freedoms and all opposition parties once they seized power. There is no absolute answer, but a realistic approach suggests that a pluralistic system must by some means constrain those who would participate in order to destroy the system.

Nazi rally in Nuremberg, 1936.

Pluralism encourages individual action, such as voting, and collective action through group membership. These two types of participation are not necessarily contradictory or mutually exclusive. Classical democratic theory stressed individual responsibility and individual choice based on rational evaluation of all factors involved. This type of individual participation is still common in a pluralist system as manifested in the private act of voting, writing a letter to a government department or a public official, or meeting with an elected official. The individual also may participate collectively through membership in and support of one or more interest groups. Commonly, this act of association with a group is a matter of individual choice. Nevertheless, in a pluralist system groups with an organized membership, monetary resources, administrative skills and contacts, and offices in the state or national capitals, are often the most successful in influencing policy. We live in a specialized, complex, and interdependent world. The most effective means by which an individual gains access to and influences decisions in the political system is frequently through the groups with which he is affiliated.

A recent and insightful study that addressed the concept of pluralism occurred in New Haven, Connecticut, in the late 1950s. This study was undertaken by political scientists at Yale University.[13] One of the conclusions of the study was that no single group dominates politics. Pluralism as it existed in New Haven, and was hypothesized as existing in the United States, identifies power with issues. Issues generally are transitory or semipermanent. Each issue provokes coalitions among different individuals and groups. Pluralism means limited participation in many situations because of specializations of interest or competence. When issues affecting a large number of people are involved, however, wider participation is required. Nelson Polsby, who participated in the study, concluded that political decision makers were relatively free to deal with issues that were routine or minor. "Other kinds of decision-making—of a nonroutine, unbureaucratized, or innovative variety—seem to require special consent by citizens who fall outside the small decision-making group."[14]

Pluralism allows restricted participation, depending on the nature of the issue and the possibility of its becoming controversial. At times a broad popular mandate is required, as occurs at general elections or when questions, such as a city income tax or an amendment to the state consititution, are decided as a referendum item on the ballot. Different groups and various numbers of people participate according to the issue, and no single

[13] The first of several books to appear based on this study was Robert A. Dahl, *Who Governs? Democracy and Power in an American City* (New Haven: Yale University Press, 1961).

[14] Nelson W. Polsby, *Community Power and Political Theory* (New Haven: Yale University Press, 1963), p. 128.

group dominates most decisions. On critical issues, a broad consensus usually is sought from the general public. Specialization and limited participation in input is controlled by the need to maintain popular support.

Pluralists also usually support a division of power and a series of checks and balances so that no group, not even a popular majority, can exercise unrestrained power. Robert Dahl has summarized the basic principle of political pluralism:

> *Since even legal and constitutional arrangements will be subverted if some citizens or groups of citizens gain disproportionate opportunities for power in comparison with other citizens, the potential power of one citizen or group must be balanced by the potential power of other citizens.*[15]

At the national level, this balance and division of power was achieved by the Constitution. Some examples are: certain powers are denied to Congress (Article I); Congress is bicameral and legislation must be approved by both houses (Article I); the president can veto laws passed by Congress (Article II); and the federal judiciary is largely independent of the president and Congress (Article III); the national government is prohibited from undertaking certain acts, or rights are guaranteed to the citizens (Amendments 1–9).

Pluralism regards concentrations of power as dangerous, whether in government, large corporations, powerful trade unions, or landed estates. Pluralism sees countervailing centers of power as allowing broad inputs and checking the consolidation of private or public power. Competition and regulated conflict are accepted as inevitable. An important function of government is the maintenance of rules of the game to prevent undue accumulation of power in the private sector and to maintain individual freedoms. Interest groups not only should organize and express opinion and thus continually bear witness to the right of freedom of association, providing information to the public and government officials, but also act as a check on excessive amassing of power in the hands of government officials or in other interest groups.

Pluralism means negotiation and compromise. Decisions are reached more slowly and may not always be as logically consistent because of the need to accommodate diverse inputs. Multiple centers of power mean various groups may have the power to dilute, delay, or veto. Pluralistic politics is often consensual politics. Ideally, no affected group should be ignored in the solution, even if no group entirely realizes its objectives. Coalition building around specific issues, bargaining, negotiating, and accommodating diverse viewpoints are key aspects of pluralism. This process has been described at the national level of American politics.

[15] Robert A. Dahl, *Pluralist Democracy in the United States: Conflict and Consent* (Chicago: Rand McNally, 1967), p. 40.

> *The most conspicuous problem that American political parties face is to achieve a record of advocacy and accomplishment in public policy while harmonizing the interest of Presidential and Congressional wings. Legislative policy is approved or rejected by building a majority coalition through a process of bargaining and the proposal of objectives appealing to a wide variety of interests. With no central authority to dictate decisions, administrative politics requires the formation of coalitions among the many dispersed centers of power.*[16]

The need to coalition-build, whether between branches of government, within a multiparty legislature, or at election time characterizes most pluralistic political systems.

Criticisms of Pluralism

Pluralism has its critics, and objections have been raised to this type of political system.

A. Classical democratic theory emphasized the rational, informed, and thoughtful political participation of the individual. Pluralism, with its emphasis on political competition among groups, policy alternatives as advanced by various coalitions of group interests, and the resulting competition among leadership elites, implicitly rejects classical individual participation. It is charged that pluralists more generally consider the typical voter uninformed and only occasionally interested. Some contend that pluralists are overly concerned about "the role of demagogic leadership, mass psychology, group coercion, and the influence of those who control concentrated economic power," and as a result the individual's participatory capability is neglected.[17] Meaningful political competition–participation is among elites. The masses exercise some power because of the right to vote among alternatives at regularly held elections. However, individual input at the mass level is limited.

B. Moreover, pluralism assumes that individuals identify with and belong to associations that advance individual as well as group interests. It anticipates that many individuals will belong to more than one interest group. Multiple memberships expose a person to various opinions and thus increase political information and political tolerance. But in actual practice it is said that group memberships may not be as extensive as often assumed.

A recent cross-national survey by a Canadian sociologist asked the following question: "Are you a member of any organization now—trade or labor union, business organization, social group, professional or farm organization, cooperative, fraternal or veteran's group, athletic club, political,

[16] Nelson W. Polsby and Aaron B. Wildavsky, *Presidential Elections,* 3rd ed. (New York: Charles Scribners Sons, 1971), pp. 294–96.

[17] Jack L. Walker "A Critique of the Elitist Theory of Democracy," *The American Political Science Review,* LX, No. 2 (June, 1966), p. 285.

charitable, civic, or religious organization, or any other organized group?"[18] In the case of the United States, 57 percent belong to an organization and 32 percent belong to more than one association. Excluding union membership, 50 percent belong to one organization and 29 percent have multiple memberships. The figures for Canada were almost as high.

Critics of pluralism point to the fact that more than 40 percent of the adult population has no organizational membership. Furthermore, those who do voluntarily belong are the better educated, wealthier, and predominantly from the middle and upper classes. A significant strata of the population is thus on the periphery of a functioning pluralism.

We might observe that if there is such a thing as a "perfect" pluralist political system, it comes closest to being realized in the United States and Canada. And while memberships as percentage of adult population seem low, they are higher than in most countries. The sociologist who directed the cross-national membership survey described the United States and Canada as "nations of joiners."[19] Where memberships are voluntary in a political system, one cannot expect anything approximating 100 percent of the population belonging to one or more organizations.

One point of comparison might be the level of participation in American presidential elections. Statistics for 1972 reveal that only 63 percent of the eligible adult population voted in the presidential race. Twenty-five percent of the 18-year-olds and over had not registered.[20] One of the keystones of pluralism and also classical democratic theory is voluntary participation. A political system that does not require participation must expect a measure of political uninterest or even apathy. Whether participation in groups and voting is high or low in the United States (and in Canada in the case of association memberships), and if this is caused by political pluralism or is independent of pluralism are questions still being studied. A person can, of course, still vote, write letters, go to see an elected official, or march in a demonstration, even if he or she does not hold any group membership.

C. Critics of pluralism also argue that interest group competition dominates the political system and thereby restricts the input of individual citizens. Moreover, since many groups are oligarchically organized, the average association member has little influence on the organization's policies. Robert Michels was the first modern scholar to conclude that the "iron law of oligarchy" was an inherent trait of organizations. In his analysis

[18] The results of the survey are analyzed in James Curtis, "Voluntary Association Joining: A Cross-National Comparative Note," *American Sociological Review,* Vol. 36 (October, 1971), pp. 872–80.

[19] *Ibid.,* p. 875.

[20] "Voters and Registration in the Election of November 1972," *Current Population Reports, Population Characteristics and Registration in the Election of November, 1972,* pp. 1 and 17.

of the German Social Democratic Party during the period before 1915, Robert Michels concluded that even in groups committed to an open political system, whoever "says organization says oligarchy." Michels claimed that monopoly of organizations by the full-time professional staff was inevitable. Consequently, leaders' perspectives are no longer those of the members. Seymour Martin Lipset has summarized Michels's position concerning organization leadership.

1. Superior knowledge, for example, they are privy to much information that can be used to secure assent for their program.
2. Control over the formal means of communication with the membership, for example, they dominate the organization press; as full-time salaried officials, they may travel from place to place presenting their case at the organization's expense; and their position enables them to command an audience.
3. Skill in the art of politics, for example, they are far more adept than nonprofessionals in making speeches, writing articles, and organizing group activities.
4. Those who become full-time officials of unions, political parties, or who serve as parliamentary representatives, "whilst belonging by social position to the class of the ruled, have in fact come to form part of the ruling oligarchy." That is to say, the leaders of the masses are themselves part of the "power elite," and develop perspectives and interests derived from their position among the more privileged elements.[21]

After summarizing Michels, Lipset then points out that the pessimistic, oligarchical, and unrepresentative structures described by Michels frequently have not come into being. More recent research reveals that many political parties and interest groups in the United States and Western Europe vary significantly from the organizational structure described by Michels. Michels's forecast was "overdeterministic." Lipset then continues with additional examples to show that "the iron law of oligarchy" is not a universal phenomenon.[22]

A case study by Samuel Eldersveld of party organization in Wayne County, Michigan, reveals a fluid structure, where the leadership is heavily dependent on support from the membership. This is summarized as a "reciprocal deference system," quite the opposite of the "iron law of oligarchy." Undoubtedly, some organizations are oligarchical; others are

[21] Seymour Martin Lipset, "Introduction" in Robert Michels, *Political Parties,* Edan and Cedar Paul, trans. (New York: The Free Press, 1962), pp. 16–18.

[22] *Ibid.,* pp. 27–33. See also Samuel Eldersveld, chapter 1 in *Political Parties* (Chicago: Rand McNally, 1967).

not. Additional data must be collected and analyzed before we can conclude that organizations have an inherent oligarchical nature, which fundamentally undermines pluralism.

D. Pluralism assumes checks and balances resulting from group conflict, with no group or coalition emerging permanently victorious. Critics claim that too often there is inequality of bargaining power among groups. Many times well-led groups representing narrow interests have acquired much political expertise in achieving their goals. Their goals, such as higher milk prices, may be achieved at the expense of most other segments of the population. Related to this is the observation that producer groups, especially those producing essential products, even when the number of individuals involved is not large, achieve inordinate success under a pluralistic system. Consumer groups tend to be more amorphous, poorly organized, and less successful in the political system. The evidence is mixed, as described below. The student who investigates this topic further will discover carefully analyzed examples on the several sides of the question.

E. The final argument advanced is more logical and deductive than replete with specific examples. It was advanced more than two decades ago, and has occasionally appeared in writing since that time. Simply stated, it is the "no government leadership" hypothesis, which maintains that the public interest, representing the essential concerns and needs of the whole political society, is neither articulated nor promoted in a pluralist system. Government does not advance specific national interest policies. Rather, it plays an umpire role. As groups compete, government maintains the rules of the game in the political arena. The bargaining, negotiation, and compromises that ensue produce some benefits for the groups involved, but no group completely achieves its objectives. Equilibrium is a principal objective and government plays a key role in maintaining the dialog, monitoring the competition, and finally through laws and regulations, implementing the eventual compromises. Government is a responsive institution, which plays a regulative-balancing role. Government does not initiate policy or promote policies that will respond to a broad public interest beyond the narrower concerns of competing group interests.

Pluralism: An Overview

We have summarized the major criticisms of pluralism. They do not include all of the criticisms, nor does each critic include every major argument in his analysis of pluralism. We recognize that no series of political arrangements is beyond improvement. Pluralism is a form of democracy that has evolved; it was not constructed or deliberately planned. In no small measure it has emerged in the last two centuries as social and economic life became more specialized, complex, and interdependent. Undoubtedly, pluralism will continue to change. These changes may or may not be improvements. In the imperfect world we live in, however, we believe pluralism is a political form that facilitates organizational and individual autonomy in the political system. It can be improved, but it has many virtues as it actually functions. It seems to be one means by which authoritarian politics can move toward more personal freedom and citizen input. A distinguished political scientist and proponent of pluralism, Robert A. Dahl, has observed how we must deal with the empirical political world we live in, not an ideal model that can never be realized.

Dahl first concludes that there are no students of modern politics who deny the proposition "that leaders do, as a matter of fact, have great weight in large, modern representative systems."[23] Dahl goes on to state:

> *At the empirical level, experience with and systematic study of political life in cities and countries with democratic governments has turned up evidence that, if valid, raises interesting and important empirical questions. . . . This evidence seems to demonstrate rather conclusively, I think, that rates of participation vary widely, that a rather large fraction of adults participate in political life barely at all, and that a small proportion of adults participate a very great deal. Confronted by this evidence, political scientists have had either to reject it as factually false, which it is increasingly difficult to do, or to accept it provisionally as correct.*

Pluralism is not a utopian blueprint. It has evolved as societies became more specialized and interdependent. It exists today in fewer than forty political systems. Pluralistic systems are concentrated in North America and Western Europe and scattered haphazardly in the rest of the world, for example, in Japan, Costa Rica, Sri Lanka, Singapore, Malaysia, Venezuela, and a few others. Part of the evolution of pluralism has also been in response to the rates of political participation described in the above quote. Pluralism is an input process that potentially includes large numbers of people despite the fact that many people in a democracy are only marginally interested in politics. Finally, like it or not, it is characteristic of most modern political systems commonly labeled "democratic."

We believe systems analysis and pluralism are two important and helpful approaches for the student studying political science. Political scientists mav disagree on the effectiveness of general approaches or specific methodologies. Most, though, agree on the range of phenomena we study. In the remainder of this chapter we consider certain terms with which the student should be familiar. The terms we discuss are political analysis, insti-

[23] Robert A. Dahl, "Further Reflections on 'The Elitist Theory of Democracy,'" *The American Political Science Review,* LX, No. 2 (June, 1966), pp. 298–99) Professor Dahl's article was in reply to Professor Jack Walker's article, which maintained that pluralists were in effect promoting an elitist theory of democracy. Under such a system of democracy, the mass citizens had only a peripheral political role.

tution, role, power and influence, authority and legitimacy, and conflict and adjustment.

POLITICAL ANALYSIS

The business of political scientists is political analysis. Most adults are aware of and discuss some political happenings. The political scientist, however, brings systematic training to bear on the study of politics. At its simplest, analysis is work undertaken by a trained person, which requires studying a problem, issue, decision, policy, or situation by organizing the data into categories or elements and then relating these to one another. Basic to the analytical process is selective perception—choosing the elements or variables that are of primary significance as opposed to those of secondary importance or even irrelevant to the study. Analysis should lead to generalization, explanation, and the offering of hypotheses for further study. Scientific analysis seeks to relate two or more political phenomena (type of political leadership, for example, and effectiveness of government decisions) with one another.

Negating a generalization is also part of analysis. For example, for many years after World War II it was argued that democracy is unstable if religion is politicized and religious parties are active, as in Lebanon, Northern Ireland, and the French Fourth Republic (1946–58). As this generalization has been tested in other political systems, such as postwar Germany, Austria, and the Netherlands, it was found that the relationships between religious political parties and instability did not always hold. Therefore, religious political parties do not inevitably lead to instability. Other factors or variables, still being determined, must be present.

Analysis requires training and a basic knowledge of the subject matter. The determination of crucial variables and identification of nonobvious patterns, such as channels of recruitment to political leadership, the policy role of the bureaucracy, and cultural fragmentation, are most effectively analyzed by individuals who have spent a good deal of time studying these problems. Certain a priori assumptions about which are the key institutions and processes serve to determine the appropriate focus of the investigation and guide the selection and ordering of one's observations. A priori expectations and insights based on prior study and research are fundamental to sophisticated political analysis. The deductive establishment of testable propositions precedes the inductive, empirical research. One objective of this book is to help the student acquire basic political science principles and data for effective political analysis.

Robert Merton has described and analyzed American political machines in the late nineteenth and early twentieth centuries in a study widely quoted as an excellent example of political analysis. Merton pointed out the "human" side of the political machine. The political machine saw its roots in the local neighborhood, where residents were principally concerned with personal problems and needs. The machine won its elections in the precincts through elaborate networks of personal ties and obligations.

> *The precinct captain is forever a friend in need. In our prevailingly impersonal society, the machine, through its local agents, fulfills the important social func*tion of humanizing and personalizing all manner of assistance *to those in need. Foodbaskets and jobs, legal and extra-legal advice, setting to rights minor scrapes with the law, helping the bright poor boy to a political scholarship in a local college, looking after the bereaved—the whole range of crises when a feller needs a friend, and above all, a friend who knows the score and who can do something about it—all these find the ever-helpful precinct captain available in the pinch.*[24]

Political machines were corrupt. They often used public moneys to benefit the leader and their friends. But they also helped new migrants to the big cities to adjust to the problems of urbanization and industrialization. The machines helped these immigrants, some of whom could not speak English, to survive in an alien environment. Professor Merton's analysis shows how political machines helped to integrate people into society through welfare services and similar programs aimed at individual adjustment. These were latent functions, or functions not originally intended by political machines, which were created to win elections. The extended analysis goes on to suggest that in our study of organizations we should be alert to the importance of latent functions in a social or political system. Merton's analysis explained, generalized, and hypothesized.

The organization of components, their interrelationships, and how they function vary in many ways among the 150-plus sovereign states in today's world. Analysis and understanding of political system *A* will not necessarily enable you to use the same approach or methods of analysis and arrive at a quick understanding of political system *B*. An expert on Ford automobiles will have little difficulty in working on a Plymouth motor. The same does not hold true for political systems. The importance of certain components or institutions in one system does not mean they are important in another political system. If the relative importance of parts varies, the pattern of interaction obviously varies even more. For example, knowledge of the organization and functioning of American political parties will not lead to an immediate understanding of French parties. It will, though, make you better able to analyze the French party system. One reason for a large number of diverse examples in the text is to enable you to understand better when studying new material and new situations.

[24] Robert Merton, *Social Theory and Social Structure,* 3rd ed. (Glencoe, Ill.: The Free Press, 1968), pp. 127–29, *passim.*

INSTITUTION

Institutions are more than tangible objects made out of steel and brick, although many people think first of the physical structures when discussing institutions. Institutions are patterns of human relationships. They are regularized patterns of interaction, usually evolving over time, which are then formalized by custom or written form through rules of procedure or laws. Institutions may develop rather quickly if rules are promulgated and behavior must conform to such rules. For example, one of the inheritances common to former British colonies is the Public Service Commission (PSC). The PSCs were introduced in the British colonies to handle recruitment, promotion, and often job assignments in the colonial civil services. Most such PSCs are less than fifty years old. Yet these personnel procedures and the PSCs through which they are implemented have rapidly become

Democratic National Convention, 1976.

important institutions in many of the now independent developing countries formerly under British rule. In some developing countries the PSC may be one of the most important institutions in the political system because of its control over the bureaucracy.

Political parties are also institutions. No mention is made of them in the American Constitution. Their crucial role today tells us much about the evolution of the American political system. American political parties and the party conventions that nominate the presidential and vice-presidential candidates have become important political institutions in our nation. As parties and conventions evolved, states passed laws dealing with such matters as non-discriminatory practices in primary elections and regulations affecting the choice or voting commitments of convention delegates (as, for example, a delegate must support the individual who won the party's presidential primary in the state on the first convention ballot). Over the nineteenth century, we can observe the institutionalization of party and convention processes.

The "action" in stable political systems occurs in the principal institutions. (By political stability we mean change without noticeable violence.) Institutionalization should not mean rigidity or ossification. To remain effective, institutions must be flexible in organization and adaptable in terms of performing new and discarding old functions. Institutions should allow for and structure change, but not prevent it. Russian civil administration under the czar prior to World War I represents an institution that collapsed when it could not adapt to fundamental challenges—World War I and the fight against the Austro-Hungarian and German Empires, along with the desperate domestic economic crises resulting from the war.

When we study institutions, an important aspect is the individual and the role he occupies and how he is limited by or expands the role.

ROLE

It is essential to appreciate the significance of role if one is to study institutions. Role refers to the relationship between individual and institution.[25] In all societies people develop standard expectations about how they and others should behave in specific situations or within particular institutional contexts. When many people share generally similar expectations, we refer to this as a role.

A role guides behavior in a socially defined position. It establishes the broad parameters but not every detail. Students have rather clear ideas about the role of the student and the teacher in a college or university.

[25] This discussion of role draws heavily from Robert A. Dahl, *Modern Political Analysis* (Englewood Cliffs, N.J.: Prentice-Hall, 1966), p. 11.

However, within the general role expectations there is wide latitude for individual behavior.

Each American president must fulfill certain role obligations while he is in office. Individuals are expected to perform certain actions and to function in certain ways. The individual in the role, considered to be the actor, also has the opportunity to modify or expand the role. Role suggests incremental but not radical change. Radical change would so alter the parameters of the role that the new role would resemble only in name the previous role. The presidential role in the United States has undergone substantial incremental changes, but generally within restrictive yet adaptive guidelines. In an excellent analysis of the role of the American chief executive, Louis W. Koenig has pointed out that it is individual presidents responding to great crises who have had the major impact on shaping the presidency:

> *Crisis is a crucible in which a President and his administration are tested as nowhere else. No other condition tries so vigorously the capacity of the President for decision, perceptiveness, physical endurance, self-confidence and prudence.*[26]

An example of role adaptation is the regular holding and use of press conferences, which have become an important part of the presidential role. This was first mastered and developed by Franklin Delano Roosevelt (1933–45) as part of his response to the Depression crisis:

> *Roosevelt's approach to the crisis was a massive venture in public relations. Like Hoover, interestingly, Roosevelt considered the root cause of the depression to be psychological. . . . "The only thing we have to fear is fear itself," he said memorably in his inaugural. He perfected two techniques to bathe the country regularly in the ointments of hope and optimism—the press conference and the fireside chat. He transformed the press conference. . . . into a vehicle of lively and informative interchange between the President and the press.*[27]

While reading the rest of the book, the student should be training himself to pick out the key institutions and roles in whatever political system he or she is studying. An understanding of role, institutions, and power are essential if one is to analyze politics.

POWER AND INFLUENCE

We can say that power is the ubiquitous phenomenon of politics. Robert Dahl has defined politics or a political relationship as involving to a signifi-

[26] Louis W. Koenig, *The Chief Executive* (New York: Harcourt, Brace, & World, 1964), p. 362.
[27] *Ibid*, p. 373.

cant extent "power, rule, or authority."[28] We are more restrictive because we limit our focus to power that is part of the political system in the public realm. We are not so much concerned with power, rule, and authority as they may affect family relationships, the election of a union representative, a business reorganization, or the selection of a college president, except if some of the activities of the preceding occasionally overlap into the public political system. We restrict politics in this text to the political system. We do not use it in the more popular sense, which refers to any situation (such as the election of a student body or club president or a new chairman of the board in Corporation X), which involves influence, power, authority, rules or regulations, and the person(s) exercising these.

Power is innate to the study of politics, because in many ways this is what politics is all about. Harold Laswell's oft quoted analysis of politics is entitled *Politics—Who Gets What, When, How.*[29] The "who" in the title refers to who has power or who has access to those holding power. Those with power are most able to control the allocation of scarce resources in society for which there is competition.

We define power in the following way: one person or group exercises power over another when it is intentional and done in such a way as to affect in a predictable way the action(s) of another or others. Three aspects are involved: relationship; intention; and predictability. Power usually involves sanctions or rewards, but the instruments of power can also be rational persuasion or appeals to the emotions.

The difference between influence and power is predictability. Power suggests that the intended outcome will more likely occur. Thus, the sanctions and rewards are considerably more severe or greater in the hands of the person or group exercising power. A teacher can influence a student to study. Frequently, the sanction or reward, as the case may be, is the grade. For some students the grade is an important influence; for a few it is relatively insignificant because it is regarded as having only short-run consequences. In terms of grading, teachers generally have influence, not power.

The power base is composed of a few or many assets. The power base requires some but not all of the following: wealth, social status, control of force (military/police), office, skills (legal, managerial, technical, etc.), personal magnetism, friendships and other forms of extended personal relationships, such as family, ethnic group, religion, etc. A person exercising power has one and usually more of the preceding. A public official not only has his office (legislator, judge, mayor) but he also has several other

[28] Robert A. Dahl, *Modern Political Analysis,* 2nd ed. (Englewood Cliffs, N.J.: Prentice-Hall, 1970), pp. 4–6.

[29] Harold Lasswell, *Politics—Who Gets What, When, How* (New York: McGraw-Hill, 1936).

assets that enable him to achieve office. In the case of the United States, a typically successful candidate will possess wealth, social status, education (legal training, for example), as well as some measure of personal magnetism. The following description of President Franklin Roosevelt indicates the importance of personality.

> *His flashing smile, his cigarette holder set at a jaunty angle, his ready humor and booming laugh were the trademarks of his self-possession against the pressures of crisis. A brief exposure to Roosevelt was enough to repair the panicky, quiet the agitated, and inspirit the downhearted.*[30]

Power is relational and reciprocal. It is affected both by the exerciser and the recipient. A nation with adequate energy reserves is not nearly as dependent on the goodwill of the petroleum-producing countries as a nation that must import 90 percent of the energy resources it consumes. A poor man may be more susceptible to the demands of a rich man than another rich man. A person may be willing to endure severe penalties for a cause to which he or she is committed. Joan of Arc was not swayed by violence, even when she was under sentence of death and eventually executed.

The concept of nonautonomous change (NAC) is closely associated with the "relational" aspect of power. NAC refers to the effort or amount of change that the exerciser must expend if power is to be exercised. NAC is the adoption of a decision or policy need to exert influence. When President Lyndon Johnson sent troops to the Dominican Republic in 1965 to prevent what was believed to be a possible Communist takeover, relatively little effort had to be expended by the United States. Compare the Dominican case with American involvement in Vietnam. The American objective was to prevent insurgents, supported by North Vietnam, from winning control of South Vietnam. Beyond that, one can only debate the extent to which the United States desired to influence the policies and choice of political leaders of the Republic of Vietnam. American offers to exercise power or influence in Vietnam extend back to President Truman's second administration (1948–52).

Many nonautonomous changes occurred in the United States. The NACs that occurred would not have taken place if we were not attempting to exercise power or influence in this ravaged Southeast Asian nation. Examples of NACs in the Vietnam case are higher taxes, an expanded military draft, larger defense budgets, accelerated military and civilian aid to the Republic of Vietnam, and troop dispositions—at one point more than 500,000 American military personnel were assigned to Vietnam. Eventually, these NACs became so burdensome and unpopular that the American

[30] Koenig, *op. cit.*, p. 373.

government reduced its efforts to exercise power or influence and agreed to a truce agreement in Vietnam in January, 1973. The ultimate result was a Communist takeover in South Vietnam during the spring of 1975.

American involvement in Vietnam will be debated for many years, but it does illustrate a situation where the NACs necessary to exercise power became unacceptable and policy was modified accordingly. Frequently, the objective desired is not considered as important as the scarce resources that must be allocated to achieve the objective. Another example is a recent analysis that explores the growth of opposition political parties in the West. This book identifies several reasons for their emergence. Many of these have their origin in the unique historical circumstances of the political systems studied.[31] The common denominator is the fact that governments, which probably had the power to restrain opposition, ultimately decided that the NACs necessary to exercise this restraining power did not justify the objective:

> *Opposition is likely to be permitted in a political system if (1) the government believes that an attempt to coerce the opposition is likely to fail, or (2) even if the attempt were to succeed, the costs of coercion would exceed the gains.*[32]

Nonautonomous change is a key but often overlooked factor in analyzing power. Another facet of power and influence is authority, which in turn is related to legitimacy.

AUTHORITY AND LEGITIMACY

Authority is one type of power. Authority is power that is regarded by citizens as generally rightful or legitimate. This does not mean that one agrees in each instance with the decision by the person in authority. There is, though, a general belief in the rightfulness or appropriateness of the authority. There should also be an inverse relationship between authority and force. The greater the authority of the person or group exercising power, the less need there will be to use force.

Legitimacy is the principle upon which authority rests in a political system. Legitimacy has three dimensions:

1. Procedural norms should be used in acquiring power. In the Western democracies such procedures most commonly are competitive elections in which all enfranchised persons may vote. Legitimacy is a relative term. What is legitimate in one political system may not be regarded as legitimate

[31] In his preface to this study, the editor, Robert Dahl, observes that in 1964 there were "only about 30 . . . political systems in which full legal opposition among organized political parties had existed throughout the preceding decade." *Political Oppositions in Western Democracies* (New Haven: Yale University Press, 1966), p. *xiii.*

[32] *Ibid.*, p. *xiv.*

in another. In some societies rule by a council of elders (gerontocracy) has been considered appropriate. Age, experience, and wisdom are interdependent traits, and age is the criteria for membership on the council. For many centuries blood descent (as in a king or emperor) was regarded as the procedure to qualify for office and power. Political systems with a monarch as the head of state actually exercising power (as opposed to a constitutional monarchy today in which the king or queen is a figurehead) were based not on election or age but on the fortuitous circumstances of birth. The latter two procedures for acquiring power are not, obviously, regarded as legitimate in the American political system, but they were legitimate in other political systems.

2. Procedural norms (generally accepted procedures) should generally be followed in exercising power. In constitutional systems, where a constitution and laws restrain government officials, even those at the highest level of power and discretion must follow the legal procedures expected of the office. This is contrary to some political systems where there are relatively few procedural limitations on a ruler who has acquired office. For most of recorded history, it was regarded as an act of treason to remove even the most rapacious and incompetent ruler. Few people made an effort to justify rebellion. One famous political philosopher who did allude to the problem of tyranny and procedural standards in exercising power was Thomas Aquinas (1225–74). Saint Thomas distinguished between a person who usurps power—a tyrant or *titulo*—and a ruler, who is the legitimate sovereign but who abuses his power.

> *He [Saint Thomas] argues that a tyrant* a titulo *can legitimize his power if he governs with justice; that is, in the interest of his subjects. He admits that in extreme cases when tyranny becomes unbearable and inflicts sinful actions on his subjects, rebellion is justified.*[33]

Only during the last few centuries have we made progress toward a commitment to limited or constitutional government. This means that in some political systems the rulers and other government officials will lose legitimacy as happened to President Nixon as a result of Watergate if they flagrantly violate the minimal procedural norms in exercising their political office. In some cases this may only involve replacing (sometimes violently) one ruler or group of rulers for another, but not changing the fundamental rules of the game in the system. In other situations the political system itself has been drastically altered.

China represents both cases. During its 4000-year history, Imperial China experienced numerous rebellions and civil wars. Often the usurper was vic-

[33] Gaetano Mosca, *A Short History of Political Philosophy* (New York: Thomas Y. Crowell Company, 1972), p. 60. Translated by Sondra Z. Koff. Originally published in 1937.

torious, and a new dynasty was established. The imperial political system as such, with the emperor as head of state, was not changed. The Chinese revolution of 1911 was a sharp break with the past. Not only did new rulers seize office, but the political system was fundamentally changed. A republic replaced the empire, which had been based on blood descent. The Republic of China, led by Chiang Kai-shek, was eventually replaced by a Communist state after fighting that lasted intermittently from 1927 to 1949.

3. Legitimacy involves the notion that government and the political system should function in such a way that government generally performs the tasks citizens expect of it. Popular expectations of the functions, if not obligations, of government have changed measurably during the last two hundred years. During the nineteenth century the most common political system was the "night watchman state." Governments were expected to maintain domestic security, protect the borders, and construct, maintain and protect communication and transportation networks. For example, immediately after the American colonies won their independence, two of the most important cabinet departments were the State Department and the Post Office Department. Expectations about government responsibilities have evolved worldwide over the ensuing decades. People now turn to government to solve inflation, unemployment, land reform, energy shortages, retirement benefits, protection of the environment, zoning, water and sewers, free public education, and so on. The obligations of government, or expected government outputs, vary among political systems. Thus, political systems in the developing world, where governments have fewer monetary and technical resources, are not expected to provide extensive retirement programs or unemployment benefits.

We might only note that where governments do not provide the minimal outputs the prevailing values deem necessary, the government and the rules of the game may be completely changed. One of the most difficult situations any system confronts is an insurrection or internal war, often aided and abetted by outside powers. In such circumstances the preponderant allocation of resources goes to combat the insurgents. This almost inevitably erodes legitimacy because governments are unable to deliver other outputs believed necessary in the contemporary world. The "revolution of rising expectations" refers in part to the services citizens expect from their governments.

Legitimacy in all of its aspects is relative rather than absolute and varies among countries. It is a long and evolving process and is an objective for all political systems. In our discussion of the developing world, chapter 10, we shall see that it is a difficult goal to reach in the short run.

Conclusion

CONFLICT AND ADJUSTMENT

In concluding this chapter, we note that in the first two chapters of this text we have provided the student with a basic overview of the underlying concerns of politics and the academic discipline that studies it—political science. We also have discussed certain basic approaches such as systems analysis and pluralism, which are the underlying organizational principles in the following eleven chapters. These concepts are necessarily selective of many available in the political science literature. They represent what we believe are the more feasible ways of organizing a great bulk of material for students being introduced to political science. Although we focus on systems analysis and pluralism, we do not believe there is one approach or a single key to understanding politics. There are many writers who adopt an exclusive theme. One example is Hans Morgenthau, a distinguished author in the international politics field since the 1950s. Morgenthau believes all men share drives to live, reproduce, and dominate. He expands this assertion by declaring that all political life is a struggle for power.

> *Both domestic and international politics are a struggle for power, modified only by different conditions under which this struggle takes place in the domestic and international spheres.*[34]

We do not believe there is a single, underlying principle such as a struggle for power that is the basis for understanding politics. We believe that a broader approach will enable a student to understand better the ever changing phenomena we study.

Our final point is implicit in much of what you have read so far. Change, transition, and competition are integral to what we are studying. The history of politics is the history of men striving to have their way with their fellowmen. Politics is development, adjustment, or regression. Seldom, if ever, is there a period that can be described as a time of status quo equilibrium.

Change, power, and competition are the ever present phenomena of modern politics. Karl Mannheim has correctly observed that when we study the political we inevitably deal with "tendencies and strivings in a constant state of flux." There are many changes consistent with the existing political and social institutions: one president is elected and another leaves office; one party replaces another as the majority party in parliament; the social security deduction or the income tax is raised or lowered. Formal structures and processes are not altered by these changes.

[34] Hans J. Morgenthau, *Politics Among Nations,* 5th ed. (New York: Alfred A. Knopf, 1973), pp. 34–5.

A second type of change is more substantial and may fundamentally affect the functioning and organization of the political system: a presidential type of government replaces a parliament-dominated political system, as occurred in 1958 when the French Fifth Republic replaced the Fourth Republic; an hereditary monarch has his powers removed and in his place a junta of young, reform-minded, military officers makes government decisions. This happened in Ethiopia in 1974. Change may be peaceful or violent, but it is always pervasive. A never-ending task of political science is to attempt to explain the nature and types of change that are occurring.

Our analysis of change means that political systems that appear stable are actually in a condition of homeostatic equilibrium. By this we mean a relatively stable functioning of the political system with regard to ongoing competition among contending individuals, groups, and ideas. Homeostatic equilibrium is present when institutions and procedures have evolved for peaceful rather than violent competition and facilitate the peaceful adjustment of conflict.

Throughout the remainder of this text students should carefully analyze what they perceive to be those institutions that encourage the peaceful adjustment of disagreement in the most reasonable and fair manner. By fair we mean equity, responding to the maximum degree possible to the various viewpoints in resolving a conflict. We offer no solutions, except to note that political conflict will probably always exist, even with the best of intentions. John Stuart Mill stated it ably:

> *As soon as any part of a person's conduct affects prejudicially the interests of others, society has jurisdiction over it, and the question whether the general welfare will or will not be promoted by interfering with it, becomes open to discussion.*[35]

We believe political science should make it possible for the student to understand better the political process. The student is being trained to: perceive selectively and to focus on the key factors in the political system; organize data; retrieve previously learned and relevant concepts and data as he or she interprets contemporary political events; and analyze the functioning of different political systems or components of a system (for example, your city or state, the United States, one or more foreign governments, the international system, or specific institutions and processes such as political parties, legislatures, political violence, and political socialization, all discussed subsequently). Perception, organization, retrieval, and explanation as they relate to the political process are the capabilities you are beginning to acquire as you read this book.

[35] John Stuart Mill, *On Liberty,* from Marshall Cohen, ed., *The Philosophy of John Stuart Mill* (New York: The Modern Library, 1961), p. 272.

Selected Readings

There are several brief introductions to the major questions in the discipline. These are read to better advantage by students who have had one or two basic courses. Three of the more useful works are Robert A. Dahl, *Modern Political Analysis,* 3rd ed.* (Englewood Cliffs, N.J.: Prentice-Hall, 1976); Francis J. Sorauf, *Political Science: An Informal Overview** (Columbus, Ohio: Charles E. Merrill Publishing Co., 1965); and Victor Wiseman, *Politics: The Master Science** (New York: Pegasus, 1969).

A more comprehensive review of most of the fields in political science, with an extensive bibliography, more appropriate for seniors or beginning graduate students is Stephen L. Wasby, *Political Science: The Discipline and Its Dimensions* (New York: Charles Scribner's Sons, 1970). Also useful is Heinz Eulau and James G. March, eds., *Political Science** (Englewood Cliffs, N.J.: Prentice-Hall, 1969). Albert Somit and Joseph Tanenhaus have traced major trends in the discipline from the "prehistory" (before 1880) period through the mid-1960s in *The Development of American Political Science* (Boston: Allyn and Bacon, 1967).

Two works that provide useful evaluations of the various approaches and methodologies in the discipline are James A. Bill and Robert L. Hardgrave, Jr., *Comparative Politics: The Quest for Theory** (Columbus, Ohio: Charles E. Merrill Publishing Co., 1973) and James C. Charlesworth, ed., *Contemporary Political Analysis** (New York: The Free Press, 1967). A basic overview and evaluation of the behavioral movement in political science is Robert Dahl's "The Behavioral Approach in Political Science: Epitaph for a Monument to a Successful Protest," *The American Political Science Review,* LX, No. 4 (December, 1961), pp. 763–72. A readable critique by a statistician of some of the quantitative methods used by political scientists is Edward R. Tufte, "Improving Data Analysis in Political Science," *World Politics,* XXI, No. 4 (July, 1961), pp. 641–54.

The initiator and leading exponent of the systems approach in political science is David Easton. The most efficient introduction to his writings is "An Approach to the Analysis of Political Systems," *World Politics,* IX, No. 3 (April, 1957), pp. 383–400. A more recent and expanded interpretation of his theories is his *A Systems Analysis of Political Life* (New York: John Wiley, 1965). Evaluations and criticisms of the systems approach are found in the Bill and Hardgrave and Charlesworth works cited above. A difficult but a "must" evaluation of recent political research, including a section on the systems approach, is Joseph LaPalombara, "Macrotheories and Microap-

* Also available in paperback.

plication in Comparative Politics: A Widening Chasm," *Comparative Politics,* I, No. 1 (October, 1968), pp. 52–78.

A short but superior summary of pluralism, pro and con, is in Thomas R. Dye, Lee S. Greene, and George S. Parthemos, *American Government: Theory, Structure and Process* (Belmont, Calif.: Wadsworth Publishing Co. 1969), pp. 174–76. Pluralism as an approach or treated as a particular form of democracy has evolved rather than being formally presented as a theory. Two authors who present a sympathetic and reasoned defense are Robert Dahl, "Further Reflections on the Elitist Theory of Democracy," *American Political Science Review,* LX, No. 2 (June, 1966), pp. 296–305; and William Kornhauser, *The Politics of Mass Society* (Glencoe: Ill.: The Free Press, 1954).

The critics of pluralism are, if anything, more numerous than its proponents. Two representative critical presentations are William E. Connolly, ed., *The Bias of Pluralism** (New York: Atherton Press, 1969); and Jack L. Walker, "A Critique of the Elitist Theory of Democracy," *American Political Science Review,* LX, No. 2 (June, 1966), pp. 285–95.

The most helpful introduction to power and its relationship to influence and authority is chapter 3 in Robert Dahl, *Modern Political Analysis,** cited above. A more difficult and comprehensive work is Harold D. Lasswell and Abraham Kaplan, *Power and Society* (New Haven: Yale University Press, 1950). Nelson Polsby, *Community Power and Political Theory** (New Haven: Yale University Press, 1963) is a well-written effort to organize the theoretical implications of local power studies. The volume edited by John R. Champlin, *Power** (New York: Atherton Press, 1971) includes various viewpoints on the definitions and applications of power.

Robert E. Lane, *Political Life** (Glencoe, Ill.: The Free Press, 1959); and Seymour Martin Lipset, *Political Man** (Garden City, N.Y.: Doubleday and Company, 1960) discuss some of the major generalizations about how man behaves politically. Students will find these two books provide valuable background as they follow and participate in political events after leaving college.

Finally, we might note that essays and bibliographies on most of the terms and concepts used in this chapter are available in the useful volume *International Encyclopedia of the Social Sciences* (New York: Macmillan and Free Press, 1968).

* Also available in paperback.

Chapter 3

Political Theory and Ideology

Introduction

The study of political theory and ideology are integral parts of political science. Both are analytic methods, or ways of looking at political phenomena, which is an important part of politics. As noted in chapter 1, values and value arguments are part of politics and are among the most important things studied by political theorists. Moreover, in reviewing the development of political theory, we are looking at the origin of both political science and many of our basic institutions and values. For this reason we now turn to political theory and ideology, to help provide the foundation for understanding the political value conflicts that make up the heart of subsequent chapters.

Political philosophy generally deals with man and the state. From early times men have speculated about their relationship to the state, the various kinds of state, and the best way to attain a just state. The Western political tradition is still the source of much wisdom, and many basic concepts of modern political life had their origin in the Greco-Roman world and the Middle Ages.

In developing their theories, many great political thinkers have attempted to find an answer to some political problem or crisis of their day, such as Saint Augustine and the capture of Rome by the barbarian tribes or Karl Marx and the evils of the industrial evolution in the middle of the nineteenth century. In this sense philosophers are dated but all the great thinkers, in developing answers, have raised issues and answers that transcend the problems of their day. It is this feature that gives their works a timeless quality.

That political thought influences actual political institutions is unquestionable. The relationship between Karl Marx and the political and economic developments in the Soviet Union is obvious. This is not to suggest that present-day Russia is a blueprint of Marx's ideas, for it obviously is not. There are many developments that Marx did not anticipate and many of his ideas have perhaps worked out differently from what he expected. Yet it would be hard to think of the Russian Revolution without Karl Marx.

There is also a close relationship between the ideals of John Locke, the English philosopher of the late seventeenth century, and American political principles and practices. Not only is the American Declaration of Independence a restatement of Locke's philosophy, but such concepts and practices as limited government, a written constitution, and a bill of rights are derived from Locke as well as similar theorists.

In this brief survey of leading Western political philosophers the student should ask himself not which man is "right," for none has provided a complete answer to the perennial problems of politics, although some developed a metaphysical system they believed was final. Rather, the question should be what insights do these men offer in helping to understand the great issues of politics.

In answering the above question, it does not necessarily follow that a recent philosopher in time, say John Dewey, is necessarily more relevant than Plato. Although John Dewey still has his followers, many believe his rather facile optimism is superficial because it reflects an exaggerated and unjustified confidence in the ability of the scientific method to solve our political problems. Furthermore, men whose philosophical systems we may reject as erroneous may still offer many insights. We may reject the "dialectical materialism" of Marx, but few can deny the truth of his analysis of the evils of mid-nineteenth-century capitalism.

GREEK POLITICAL THOUGHT

Plato and Aristotle are leading, seminal political philosophers of all time. Plato (427–347 B.C.) was an Athenian aristocrat. He was greatly influenced by his friend and teacher, Socrates, whose death decreed by the Athenian state led Plato to distrust Athenian democracy, which was at its height in the fourth century B.C. In Athens citizens were entitled to participate directly in the government of the city by voting in the assembly of all citizens or serving on a jury. Selection for office was very democratic. The procedures employed were lot and rotation in office. Although the

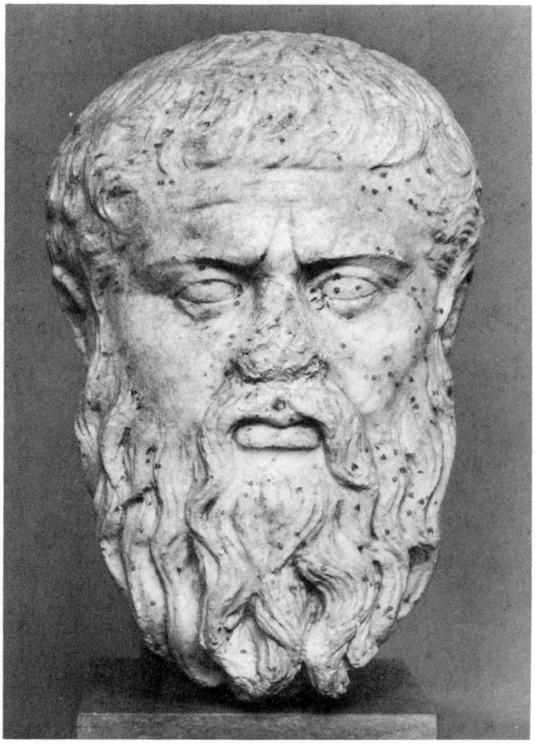

Plato.

Athenians prized their democracy and citizenship highly, there was also a dark side to their political system. Only a minority of the inhabitants of Athens were citizens and slavery was accepted as natural. Demagogues as well as statesmen were elected to office and, as has already been mentioned, Athenian democracy put Socrates to death.

Plato's greatest political work is *The Republic* in which he describes the ideal state. *The Republic* was not a utopia in the modern sense, for Plato regarded the ideal state to be the most real state and the standard by which actual states were to be judged. Plato believed that behind the world of appearances there was an inner reality. To him objects perceived through the senses are particular manifestations of universal ideas. To understand these universal categories was the task of philosophy. For Plato the idea of the triangle was more real than a particular triangle. To understand the ideal state was more important than studying actual historical states. These principles were the exact opposite of the school of philosophers known as

Sophists who argued that there is no truth or absolute moral principles, only opinion and social convensions. To Plato the Sophists' philosophy was not only erroneous but dangerous.

Justice was the cornerstone on which *The Republic* was to be based. By this term Plato meant a society in which each person performed a function in society for which he was best suited. The structure of society was aristocratic, with an artisan class of workers, farmers, and merchants at the bottom who performed economic functions. Above them were the auxiliaries, consisting of men and women whose role was that of defense. At the top were the ruling class of philosopher or "philosopher-king" if one was available. The philosopher class was to undergo a long period of training and education as preparation for the task of governing, which Plato regarded as an exacting science.

More important than the details of *The Republic* are the political ideals it reflects. Plato firmly believed that man by nature is a moral being and that the good man is also the good citizen. Despite his distrust of Greek democracy as exemplified in Athens, Plato was not a believer in arbitrary government. To him tyranny was the worst form of government.

Plato's concept of the philosopher-king as the ideal ruler is a magnificent idea and consistent with his basically aristocratic philosophy, that those of superior wisdom and virtue should rule. Perhaps the closest approximation of a philosopher-king in Western history is the Roman Emperor Marcus Aurelius who ruled from A.D. 160 to 180. He was famous for his statesmanship, love of philosophy, and moral character. In the eighteenth century Age of Enlightenment the ideal of "enlightened despots" had great appeal even to men of liberal persuasion, such as Voltaire, the famous French philosopher. Today the idea of the expert in government is a practical variation of Plato's ideal. And the United States Supreme Court, especially in recent years, has at times been said to perform a function similar that of the Platonic guardians. Interestingly enough, this comment has been made by critics as well as supporters of the Court. Critics have suggested that in interpreting the Constitution, the Court, a body of men appointed for life, has in recent years ignored past precedents and read their own views of what is wise into the Constitution. The implication, of course, is that no group of men is wise or expert enough to perform this function. Apart from the question of whether this criticism of the Court is fair, the argument does suggest dangers in Plato's thought. Is any man or group of men, however learned, to be trusted with vast power? Furthermore, is government more than a matter of knowledge? Perhaps it is also an art.

Like Plato, Aristotle (384–322 B.C.), a former student of Plato's, believed that man is a rational, moral being who could attain the good life only through the state, which Aristotle considered the highest form of organization. Aristotle believed that by nature man is a "political animal" and that the state is the result of man's social instinct. He believed the state grew out of the household and was the ultimate human organization.

Unlike Plato, Aristotle was less concerned with the ideal state and more with the best practical state, which he called "polity" or a mixture of aristocracy and democracy. Aristotle laid great stress on economic conditions as the basis of a good state. Extremes of wealth and poverty worked for political instability. Polity would be possible in a political society with a strong middle class. The idea of a government under law was important in Aristotle's philosophy. Plato, in his ideal state ruled by philosophers, dispensed with the need for law. But *The Statesman,* a product of Plato's old age when he realized the ideal state was unattainable, stressed the need for law as a "second best," to compensate for the inability to find all-wise philosophers.

There are obvious shortcomings in Greek political thought. Both Plato and Aristotle were unable to go beyond the Greek city-state, which was already becoming obsolete. Aristotle, for example, served as tutor to Alexander, son of Philip, king of Macedonia. Within a short time Macedonia was to conquer the Greek city-states and under Alexander the Great establish an empire for the Hellenistic world. Yet Aristotle's experience at the Macedonian Court as tutor to the young Alexander apparently made no impression on his political thought. Both Plato and Aristotle had a conception of citizenship limited to a leisure class that would be free of economic concerns. Aristotle in particular defended slavery and assumed the natural superiority of Greeks to the "barbarians."

Yet both Plato and Aristotle laid the basis for a science of politics. Both men accepted the civic ideal of a state based on reason and aiming for the good life. Aristotle in particular established a logical method of political inquiry. And Plato accepted the complete equality of the sexes.

STOIC AND MEDIEVAL CONTRIBUTIONS

Following the death of Aristotle in 322 B.C. and with the advent of world empires in the Western world—for a brief time Alexander's empire and subsequently the Roman Empire—political thought showed a marked change as the independent city-state became politically obsolete. The dominant school of thought was that of Greek and Roman Stoics. Stoicism was a school of thought rather than a philosophy identified with a particular individual. The Stoics equated God with universal reason, which they believed to be immanent in nature and in man. Politically, the Stoics emphasized the basic equality of all men, regardless of differences in wealth or social position. Gone was any distinction between Greeks and barbarians. Even a slave was a "laborer hired for life." The individual was a citizen not only of the secular state into which he was born but of the community of all men as well.

The Stoics also introduced the concept of natural law, which was to dominate Western political thought through the eighteenth century. Natural law, in the words of the Roman philosopher and politician Cicero, a great popularizer of Stoicism, was "right reason in agreement with nature; it is of universal application, unchanging and everlasting; it summons to duty by its commands, and averts from wrongdoing by its prohibitions."[1] This law is the foundation of the state as it existed from eternity. And the state or commonwealth exists to promote ethical purposes or it is nothing.

Although no attempt was made to implement Stoicism in a political sense, it is unlikely that political democracy in the modern sense could develop unless the idea of the basic equality of all men won general acceptance. The Stoic idea of the role of natural law has probably contributed to the later concept of natural rights and the present-day practice of judicial review.

Christianity as a body of thought was consistent with Stoicism in stressing the basic equality of all men. It also believed government to be of divine origin and stressed the duty of obedience. But it introduced a dualism unknown to the ancient world. Man is not only a citizen of an earthly kingdom but also, potentially at least, a member of the kingdom of God. Thus, there is a potential divided loyalty as illustrated in the Gospels—a loyalty to Caesar and to God. Perhaps as George Sabine has suggested, civil liberties would not have played the role they have in the modern world were it not for the concept of divided loyalty.[2]

The idea of divided loyalty or rights against the state was unknown to the Greeks. To Plato and Aristotle the state served a moral purpose and men could achieve their complete development only through the state. But the state was considered prior to the individual and the idea of the individual asserting rights against the state was unknown to them.

The great political work of the early Middle Ages was the *City of God* by Saint Augustine (354–430). The immediate purpose of this work was to defend Christianity against the charge that the abandonment of the Pagan gods was responsible for the capture of Rome by the barbarian tribes and the decay of the Roman Empire. He asserted Christians did not need the corrupt Roman Empire.

To Saint Augustine, history was a record of conflict between the City of

[1] Michael B. Foster, ed., *Plato to Machiavelli,* Vol. 1 in *Masters of Political Thought* (Cambridge: The Riverside Press, 1964), p. 188.

[2] George H. Sabine and Thomas Landon Thorson, *A History of Political Theory,* 4th ed. (Hinsdale, Ill.: Dryden Press, 1973) pp. 180–81.

God and the City of Man. Only to a limited degree did these two cities correspond to Church and State. Man, according to Saint Augustine, was a fallen creature corrupted by sin, especially pride. The state based on law and coercion is necessary because of sin. Private property and slavery were also explained as consequences of sin. No earthly state could provide more than an approximation of a just society. All earthly states like the Roman Empire were tainted with sin.

To many secular-minded students of the present day this philosophy may seem irrelevant. However, a distinguished contemporary political philosopher and theologian, the late Reinhold Niebuhr, considered Saint Augustine to be the first political realist in that he recognized that states are not the product of pure reason and that frequently they claim to be far more just than they actually are. In minimizing the contribution of Rome, Augustine probably did not do complete justice to its many achievements, but he was more realistic than Cicero who presented an idealized version of the Roman Republic.[3]

The climax of medieval political philosophy is found in Saint Thomas Aquinas (1225–1274), the great medieval philosopher and theologian. Aquinas sought to incorporate the complete works of Aristotle into Christian thought. These were not known to the Western world until the twelfth and thirteenth centuries. Aquinas accepted as true most of Aristotle's idea about the origin, nature, and functions of the state. The state was necessary for the good life in this world, but he pointed out that Aristotle, not being a Christian, did not realize that man's ultimate destiny lay in the life after death. But in accepting Aristotle's idea of the state growing out of man's social nature, he disagreed with Saint Augustine who explained the origins of the state in terms of man's sinfulness.

Law also played a great role in the philosophy of Thomas Aquinas, who accepted the Stoic conception of natural law. To this he added divine and eternal law. The highest law is the eternal law of God, which is the source of all law. Divine law is God's plan for man's salvation found in the Christian revelation. Natural law is based on man's participation in the eternal law as a rational creature. Human law grows out of man's need to apply natural law to changing human conditions. But human law is binding only insofar as it is based on principles of natural law.

Probably the greatest contribution of the Middle Ages was its emphasis on law and kingship. A king presumably derived his authority from God, by inheritance as the oldest son, and in a vague sense from the people. A just king was one who ruled according to the law of God, reason, and the customs of the realm. A tyrant was no king. Unfortunately, no method was dis-

[3] Reinhold Niebuhr, *Man's Nature and His Communities* (New York: Charles Scribner's Sons, 1965), p. 44.

covered for dealing with tyranny or requiring a king to observe principles of justice except the dubious remedy of tyrannicide. But the importance of medieval thought is that it contributed to the theoretical foundations of modern constitutionalism and limited government. But the machinery to implement these principles were not developed until modern times, with the rise of representative assemblies and constitutions.

THE RISE OF INDIVIDUALISM

One of the characteristics of the modern age, which began in about 1500, is the rise of individualism, which was manifested in all walks of life. In religion individualism is identified with the Protestant Reformation, which stressed individual salvation made possible by God's grace without the intervention of the Catholic Church. The modern age was associated with the rise of capitalism, which emphasized individual endeavor and financial rewards for those who were successful. Another influence was the Renaissance, which was characterized by a revival of interest in the Greek and Roman classics. The result was a new humanism centering on man as the "measure of all things." Fundamentally, the new individualism was a rebellion against the existing restraints of the traditional social order and a movement toward personal autonomy.

In political philosophy the new individualism gave rise to the social contract theory of government, which unlike previous political philosophy began with the autonomous individual rather than the state. The individual according to the new approach created the state through the social contract. The leading advocates of the new school were Thomas Hobbes (1588–1679) and John Locke (1632–1704), both Englishmen. Although the social contract philosophy frequently stresses limited government and the right of revolution, this type of thinking is not always present. Certainly in the thought of Hobbes it was absent. Instead, Hobbes's philosophy led to emphasis on the dangers of anarchy and the need for a strong government to make life tolerable. Hobbes's philosophy reflected the social and political turmoil of his age characterized by the struggle between Charles I and the Puritan majority in Parliament, the subsequent civil war between the king and his supporters and the Puritans, the execution of Charles I, the rule of Oliver Cromwell, and the royalist restoration.

Yet Hobbes was an individualist in the sense that the starting point of his philosophy was the state of nature, a presocial state, characterized as a condition in which life was "solitary, poor, nasty, brutish, and short." To make life tolerable men created an "artificial" community, the state, to which men turned over all power. As the state was the beneficiary of the contract and not a party to it, there was no possibility of asserting rights against the state.

Hobbes was also a materialist who ridiculed the traditional natural law philosophy and revealed religion. To him the only law was that made by the sovereign of a state. It was the sovereign who would determine the religion of the state.

In every state, according to Hobbes, there was a sovereign in which ultimate power rested. In a democracy this might be a parliament, in a monarchy the king. Whoever the sovereign might be he was all powerful except for the rather ineffective right of the individual to resist the infliction of death or injury on himself. What liberty there might be in a state existed only at the sufference of the sovereign, whether the latter was a king or a democratic parliament. The only difference between the all-powerful state and a democracy was the way in which sovereign power was exercised.

To Hobbes monarchy was the best government. Despite his preference for a strong monarchy, Hobbes should not be considered an advocate of modern dictatorship as exemplified in twentieth-century Fascist or Communist states. Hobbes's monarch would preserve order and suppress any movements leading to possible anarchy, but he did not expect the monarch to engage in thought control and purges as contemporary dictators do. The ideal monarch would provide security and presumably a limited area of intellectual freedom for enlightened men like Hobbes.

Hobbes's overemphasis on the dangers of anarchy is in part a product of the age in which he lived. Without doubt Hobbes was overly pessimistic about the possibilities of limited government and he overstressed the role of force in maintaining order. Yet today we may find some insights in Hobbes in a period characterized by revolutions, riots, and social unrest. Even in a democratic state, force is the ultimate weapon in maintaining order when the community is threatened by disorders.

The idea of sovereignty that Hobbes developed was destined to be of great importance in nineteenth-century thinking, especially in England. In every state, as previously mentioned, there is an ultimate authority to make laws subject to no limitation. This may be the people or a legislative body like parliament. Such English legal philosophers as John Austin took Hobbes's theory of sovereignty to develop the idea of parliamentary supremacy.

Of greater significance for Americans was John Locke, the defender of the "glorious revolution" of 1688, which deposed James II, the last of the Stuart kings and the last English monarch claiming to rule by divine right. In his place the English Parliament, as spokesman for the nation, called William and Mary, rulers of the Netherlands, to the throne.

In his *Second Treatise on Government* Locke, like Hobbes, assumed that man originally lived in a state of nature. But Locke's primitive state was prepolitical rather than presocial like Hobbes's. Locke accepted the tradi-

John Locke.

tional philosophy of natural law. To this he added natural rights, the rights to liberty and property that men enjoyed in the state of nature. To better secure these rights men entered into a social contract, thus creating a political society.

The next step is the formation of a government by majority decision, as contrasted with the unanimity necessary for the social contract. To Locke the government was trustee of society's rights. A government that failed to protect the individual's rights to liberty and property violated the trust and could no longer claim the obedience of its citizens. For a flagrant abuse of power the people could resort to revolution.

Locke's philosophy not only justified the English Revolution of 1688 but the American Revolution as well. In the Declaration of Independence Thomas Jefferson restated the essentials of Locke:

> *That, to secure these Rights, Governments are instituted among Men, deriving their just Powers from the Consent of the Governed; that, whenever any Form of Government becomes destructive of these Ends, it is the right of the People to alter or abolish it, and institute new Government, laying its Foundation on*

such Principles, and organizing its Powers in such Forms, as to them shall seem most likely to effect their Safety and Happiness.

The American Constitution, with its emphasis on the powers of government being limited to those delegated and implied, reflects Locke's influence. And the Bill of Rights is a practical application of the idea of natural rights.

Today the philosophy of natural law and natural rights is not as strongly held as formerly. Few if any now believe in the social contract as a historical fact. Nevertheless, Locke's philosophy is still of great significance. It is a way of explaining the importance of the individual and his priority to the state and the state as a constitutional relationship based on consent.

THE POLITICAL COMMUNITY

Political thought in the eighteenth century was greatly influenced by the French "Enlightenment." The political philosophy of the Enlightenment undermined the intellectual foundations of the absolute monarchy in France. The basic assumptions of the Enlightenment were:

1. Confidence in the ability of human reason and science to cure the social ills of man.
2. The belief that social evils are the result of bad institutions but that human nature is essentially good.
3. Belief in the idea of progress.
4. Opposition to revealed religion.
5. Glorification of nature and worship of the God of nature.

Jean-Jacques Rousseau (1712–1778), one of the great political philosophers of the eighteenth century, shared many of the tenets of the Enlightenment, but he was atypical in stressing the primacy of feelings and emotion over reason. Rousseau was a romanticist who disliked the abstract, deductive reasoning characteristic of the Enlightenment.

"Man was born free and everywhere he is in chains," states Rousseau in his famous book, *The Social Contract*. But paradoxically the freedom of the state of nature can be regained through the establishment of a legitimate civil society to which men give up their natural freedom in return for which they participate in the general will of the community. As each individual agrees to be ruled as well as to rule, all men are free. This is the social contract.

One of Rousseau's basic contributions is popular sovereignty. The political community created by the social contract alone possesses supreme power or sovereignty. All legitimate governments, according to Rousseau, are basically democratic. In a democracy the people rule directly. Even a monarch rules only as long as the sovereign people permit. Rousseau did not approve of representative institutions, for they violated his idea of direct rule by the people. He also believed the only state that could be based on his philosophy was a small one comparable to the Greek city-state.

The concept of the general will is another important contribution of Rousseau. The general will is an expression of what the common good requires. It is more than an expression of the majority viewpoint.

The weakness in the idea of the general will is that Rousseau failed to safeguard minority rights. Only in the creation of the political community is unanimity required. Otherwise the will of the majority prevails. The people are never wrong according to Rousseau, but he acknowledged that they might be misled. In all democracies there will always be dissent. But Rousseau believed that dissenters, if they are not in agreement with the general will, must acknowledge their error. They may be "forced to be free" if necessary—that is, coerced. This is clearly not democratic and suggests the confusion inherent in the concept of the general will.

Although Rousseau was a democrat, his philosophy with slight modification can lead to totalitarianism. The general will need not be the will of the majority. It is conceivable that a small group or even one man might speak for the community. Hitler claimed to express the will of the German nation and Stalin spoke not only for the Russian Communist Party but for the entire nation.

Rousseau's influence has been tremendous. The Declaration of the Rights of Man of the French Revolution stresses popular sovereignty. American democratic thought in the nineteenth century also reflects Rousseau's philosophy that all power is derived from the people.

Yet Rousseau presents a utopian conception of democracy. Today for many it is hard to believe that the people are never wrong and that man is naturally good. Instead it has been argued that it is the weakness of human nature that makes democracy a necessity, not man's innate goodness. And as has been stated, Rousseau's rather mystical idea of the general will can also support totalitarianism.

EDMUND BURKE AND CONSERVATISM

Edmund Burke (1729–1797) was without question the outstanding critic of the philosophy of the Enlightenment, especially the philosophy of Rousseau. Burke did not write any systematic work on political science. Instead, his ideas are scattered through speeches, letters, pamphlets, and books. Burke was a member of the House of Commons from 1765 to 1794, a period covering both the American and French revolutions.

Burke was particularly critical of metaphysical and abstract political theory. It was such theorizing, rather than practical reason, that he attacked. To him morality is not comparable to mathematics and the most important qualification for a statesman was practical wisdom rather than the abstract, deductive reasoning of the leaders of the French Revolution, who believed it possible to create a new civilization by drawing up a new constitution based on theoretical "rights of man."

According to Burke man is a complex animal of both reason and passion. Reason is influenced by passions, loves, fears, and habit. Although Burke accepted the idea of natural law, he regarded the social contract theory of government as an oversimplified fiction. A political society was not an invention of men but a living organism with roots deep in the past that evolved slowly over the years and reflected the political experience of a particular nation. He considered the British settlement of 1688, with its limited monarchy and division of power between the king and Parliament, to be the best possible reconciliation of liberty and authority. No wonder Burke has often been called the philosopher of "common sense."

Burke defended the American Revolution while bitterly criticizing the French. The Americans in his opinion were fighting to retain the ancient liberties of Englishmen which were threatened by the policies of the king and Parliament. The French Revolution, on the other hand, was seeking to overturn the entire political order and create a new order based on abstract rights without concern for history or tradition.

Burke was not opposed to all change or reform, as his attitude toward the American Revolution indicates. No doubt he idealized the British House of Commons and overlooked its unrepresentative character. Also in criticizing the excesses of the French Revolution, he minimized the evils of the old regime in France. Nevertheless, Burke performed a great service in showing the weaknesses of a philosophy that assumed the perfectibility of human nature and the belief that all social evils result from a bad environment and can be eradicated overnight by a revolution based on abstract theories.

Burke's *Reflections On the Revolution in France* (1790) is usually considered the beginning of conservatism as a philosophical movement. There have been far fewer conservative than liberal writings and conservatism has been far more influential in Europe than in the United States. Much of what passes for conservatism in the United States is actually either a continuation of early liberalism or a revival of the philosophy that stressed laissez-faire economics, an important part of American "conservatism."

Although European conservatism began as a reaction against the French Revolution and its philosophy, it is not inherently a reactionary movement opposed to all social change. The French philosopher Joseph De Maistre (1753–1821), who sought a restoration of absolute monarchy in France and of a traditional class system, is not typical of conservative philosophy.

Conservatism originated among the aristocracy of Europe but it was accepted by considerable sections of the working class. Conservatism is characterized by basic attitudes rather than specific beliefs.[4] Support of established churches, whether Protestant or Catholic, and a belief that traditional institutions such as the family are important is part of the conservative creed. Traditionally, conservatives supported monarchy and generally still do where constitutional monarchies continue to exist. Conservatives also believe in an organic conception of society similar to Burke and accept the traditional class structure of society.

Although conservatives support private property as necessary for political and economic stability, they have not been committed to a belief in economic laissez-faire, as were many liberals in the early nineteenth century. Nineteenth-century English conservatives such as Benjamin Disraeli favored not only enfranchisement of the working class but paternalistic legislation to protect them against the evils of industrialism.[5]

LIBERALISM

Liberalism, as George Sabine and Thomas Thorson have suggested, is used in two different senses. In a narrower sense it designates a position that is midway between conservatism and socialism. It is thus favorable to reform but opposed to radicalism. In a broader sense it is belief in a democracy in a popular sense as opposed to dictatorship, whether Fascist or Communist. In this sense liberalism is identified with the defense of a democratic suffrage, representative, and responsible government and constitutionalism.[6]

Earlier liberalism is often identified with individualism and the philosophy of John Locke who, as has been explained, put the individual prior to the state in his social contract theory of government. Early English liberalism was a middle-class movement, which advocated traditional civil liberties, representative government, and constitutional monarchy. In economics early liberals advocated laissez-faire, the doctrine that the state should as a matter of principle not regulate the economy. The latter policy would abolish traditional mercantilist restrictions on trade and industry. As the rising middle class was identified with trade and industry, removal of these restrictions served middle class interests. Its political policy served to check the power of monarchy and the landed aristocracy. Although the liberal movement was primarily middle class, its program transcended purely middle class interests. And its philosophical roots, as set forth by Locke with emphasis on natural law, were definitely Christian.

[4] Compare the section on liberalism.

[5] See F. J. C. Henshaw, *Conservatism in England* (London: MacMillan, Ltd., 1933) pp. 22–3.

[6] George H. Sabine and Thomas Landon Thorson, *op. cit.*, pp. 668–69.

In the nineteenth century as a result of the industrial revolution the liberal movement faced a crisis. A liberal movement that opposed state intervention in the economy as a matter of principle meant that the working class would find no relief from sweat shops, subsistence wages, child labor, and a host of other such evils of early capitalism.

Some liberals, such as the English sociologist Herbert Spencer (1820–1903), who was a follower of Darwin, developed a philosophy of rugged individualism that assumed that society was based on a ruthless struggle for existence. To him it was futile for the state to try to interfere through welfare legislation, since it was natural that some should be poor and others rich as a result of the struggle for existence. The unsuccessful were the weak and incompetent. Their lot was regrettable, but nothing could be done about it. Spencer's concept of the role of the state was distinctly negative and limited to preserving order. Spencer's American counterpart was the famous Yale sociologist William Graham Sumner (1840–1910).

In the closing decades of the nineteenth century and early part of the present century Spencer's extreme individualism was perhaps the dominant political philosophy of the United States. Even the United States Supreme Court read Spencer's doctrine "freedom of contract" into the Constitution. The Court ruled that many labor laws setting maximum hours and all minimum wage laws violated "freedom of contract," which in the Court's opinion were part of the concept of "due process of law" included in the Fourteenth Amendment.[7]

Today some American "conservatives," like Senator Barry Goldwater of Arizona, are really adherents of the older liberal tradition of Spencer and Sumner in their strong opposition to state intervention in the economy.

But in the late nineteenth century the main body of the liberal movement broke with laissez-faire philosophically. John Stuart Mill (1806–1873), the famous English philosopher and economist, had been an adherent of the individualistic utilitarian school of philosophy. In later life Mill adopted an economic philosophy close to democratic socialism.

Perhaps more important was another English philosopher, Thomas Hill Green (1836–1882), who rejected laissez-faire by adopting Aristotle's conception of the state as a means of developing the moral life of man. To Green, victims of poverty in modern industrial society had no share in the civilization of England. Genuine freedom must be an actual as well as a legal possibility. The state may pass legislation to remove obstacles to the achievement of the good life, such as gross inequalities in bargaining power between employer and employee. Green also favored laws abolishing child labor and setting maximum hours of work when necessary.

[7] See the opinion of Justice Peckham in *Lochner versus New York* (1905) and Justice Holmes's dissent in the same case for a criticism of the majority for reading Herbert Spencer's social philosophy into the Constitution.

Green also believed that there is a social impulse in human nature and that there should be a mutual relationship between the individual and the community. A liberal society, according to Green, recognizes the social impulse and should create conditions that will make its realization possible.

The new liberalism in England, which Green helped to fashion, gave rise to the liberal legislation of the period 1906 to 1914, when the Liberal government of that country laid the basis for the present welfare state by enacting laws that removed barriers against trade unions and provided for unemployment insurance, old age pensions, and other welfare legislation.

In the United States the flowering of liberalism was in the Progressive movement of the early part of the century and the New Deal legislation of the 1930s. The former stressed making democracy more effective by such reforms as the direct primary, the strengthening and better enforcement of antitrust laws, effective regulation of monopolies such as the railroads, and reform of the banking system. The New Deal was a response to the Depression and led to a modified capitalism in which the role of government regulation of the economy was vastly extended and extensive welfare legislation was passed to protect the disadvantaged in society.

The philosophical basis of American liberalism grew out of Dewey's pragmatism more than Green's idealism. John Dewey (1859–1952) regarded the search for truth as a process of inquiry. In solving governmental problems, Dewey favored a process of trial and error under the guidance of the scientific method, which had been so successful in our natural sciences. Dewey had a great dislike of traditional metaphysics and was totally uninterested in such issues as the state, sovereignty, natural rights, and similar "abstractions" that had intrigued earlier philosophers. Despite his dislike of metaphysics, Dewey assumed certain axioms. Among these was confidence in human nature and the ability of man to disinterestedly apply the scientific method to social problems if freed from certain mistakes of the past, including belief in ideas such as first causes and ultimate goals. This approach disavowed Marxism with its belief in the class struggle and the inevitability of revolution, as well as traditional liberalism and conservatism. There is an affinity between Dewey's thinking and the experimental nature of Roosevelt's New Deal. Dewey also reflected the traditional American optimism in his belief that all problems are capable of solution. His thinking also has much in common with certain types of democratic socialism, especially Fabian socialism.[8]

SOCIALISM

Today when the term "socialism" is used, the doctrines of Karl Marx are often thought of. In fact, some individuals would tend to identify socialism

[8] See section on revisionist socialism.

primarily with Marx or with the interpretations of Marx by Soviet and Chinese revolutionary leaders, such as Lenin and Mao Tse-tung. Marx, of course, is perhaps the leading and most influential socialist philosopher. But there are many variations of socialism, and it is not at all necessary that one be a Marxist to be a socialist.

Socialism is a response to the industrial revolution and to the conditions it created. The early socialists of the first part of the nineteenth century were known as utopian socialists. Their socialism was based on a humanitarian outlook and belief in the perfectibility of human nature. They hoped to bring about an ideal socialist society as a result of the soundness of their arguments and were opposed to force and revolution.

An early French socialist was Count Henri de Saint-Simon (1780–1825), who proposed a new social order based on the leadership of the producing class. Society would be a productive association similar to an ideal factory. More important was Robert Owen (1771–1858), an English factory owner, who sought to create utopian communities organized along socialist lines. He set up such communities for brief periods in New Lanark in Scotland and New Harmony, Indiana.

Socialists believe that human progress and justice are hindered by private ownership of the means of production. The problem, as they see it, is to limit or abolish private property. The answer for the socialist is the common ownership of the means of production and exchange to varying degrees. In this way the inevitable unequal distribution of wealth under capitalism will be corrected. The difference between communism and socialism is in the means used to transform capitalism into socialism. Socialists believe the transformation can and should be attained through peaceful and democratic means. Communists, on the other hand, believe that the change must be accomplished by revolutionary means and that dictatorial government is necessary at least for a transitional period. The term "communist" is usually applied to the revolutionary regimes of the Soviet Union and the People's Republic of China.

Marxian Socialism

Karl Marx (1818–1883) was born in the Rhineland, Germany, but spent most of his life as an exile in England because his radical views brought him into conflict with the Prussian authorities. In his political activity and writing, he worked closely with his lifelong associate, Friedrich Engels.

As a young man Marx had studied the dialectical philosophy of Georg Wilhelm Friedrich Hegel at German universities. Marx took Hegel's philosophy and transformed it. According to Hegel, the dialectic is the way the human mind learns the truth about anything. A doctrine is advanced about some subject but such a doctrine is necessarily partial and one-sided because of human fallibility and is limited by the historical perspective of the period. Critics develop an opposite doctrine to correct the errors in the initial thesis. As this second doctrine, or antithesis, will also be one-sided and only partial in its truth, it will lead to a third doctrine, or synthesis, of the true elements in the original thesis and its opposite antithesis. However, the synthesis is not the complete truth and the dialectical process will start again with another antithesis. To Hegel this dialectical process was more than a way of acquiring knowledge; it was the essence of reality itself and its unfolding was the will of God or the Absolute.

Marx took Hegel's dialectic and transformed it into "dialectical materialism," which assumed that the ultimate reality is matter in motion. Reality is in a constant state of change and truth is no more than what the general laws of motion bring about. The Marxian dialectic works itself out in history. For example, the practical methods of industrial production, such as tools and machines, and the physical and cultural conditions of production, such as topography and climate, create various relationships such as landlord and tenant or factory owner and laborer. These economic forces and relationships determine the character of the state and its institutions, and the cultural and religious ideas of any given period. What is produced in society and how it is distributed are the ultimate causes of social change. The minds of men and ideas about truth and justice reflect changes in the methods of production and exchange.

Marx regarded religion as the opium of the masses and an illusion, since it is not God who creates man but man who creates God. To him religious ideas merely reflect alterations of economic relations.

Marx believed that the history of all human societies is a record of class struggles. Capitalism grew out of feudalism. With the discovery of America and the opening of new markets throughout the world as the result of progress in navigation, commerce, and industry, the old feudal order disintegrated. The development of capitalism led to the industrial revolution, which brought about the modern industrial working class, or proletariat. Under capitalism, labor becomes a commodity to be bought or sold and the wage earner becomes a wage slave as the average wage tends to become a subsistence wage.

Capitalism tends to destroy itself. The accumulation and centralization of capital leads to overproduction of both capital and commodities as the purchasing power of the masses or workers is inadequate to purchase the output of industry. Economic depressions become more frequent and severe. The middle class is destroyed and sinks into the proletariat. Eventually, there will be a final collapse of capitalism as there remain only the factory owners and proletariat whose economic lot becomes one of increasing misery. As the working class increases in size, its poverty becomes more pronounced. As its members become more class conscious, a communist movement develops among the proletariat. To Marx, the

Karl Marx.

communist movement is an instrument of history and a mechanism for the creation of a new social order.

To Marx the state or the government was always the tool of the dominant class. As the state was essentially an instrument of suppression under capitalism, the ruling bourgeoisie would use force against the proletariat if the latter sought to better itself. The idea of the state as an entity based on law, which sought to treat all groups and classes equally, was rejected by Marx.

Marx was not always consistent in his views as to how the transition to a socialist society would take place. In general he believed a violent revolution to be necessary. However, late in life he suggested that in England, America, and perhaps Holland there was hope of a peaceful change.[9]

The revolution according to Marx will be followed by the "dictatorship of the proletariat," by which he apparently meant the rule of the working class. But he was not clear as to the meaning of this phrase except that the

[9] J. H. Hallowell, *Main Currents in Modern Political Thought* (New York: Henry Holt and Company, 1950) p. 428.

proletariat would use political power against the bourgeoisie. Just how the proletariat was to be represented in the governing group was never explained.

The dictatorship of the proletariat would continue during the transition from capitalism to communism. There would still be differences in pay as labor would be compensated on the basis of skill. However, there would be no exploitation because the means of production would be owned by the state.

At some point, according to Marx, the dictatorship of the proletariat will destroy the last vestiges of capitalism. When this occurs there will be a classless society and no further correction will be necessary. Under the dictatorship of the proletariat, the political power of the state is used to destroy the remnants of the bourgeoisie. With the advent of the classless society, the state as an administrative machinery for managing the instruments of production remains even though it no longer employs force.

With the new society, religion, the family, and marriage will all disappear according to Marx. Marriage, in the traditional sense, will be replaced by alliances between the sexes based on mutual affection. With the abolition of private property, the family will be superfluous.

Revisionist Socialism

Following the death of Karl Marx many of his followers became revisionists. They realized that Marx was not an infallible guide and criticized him in a number of respects. Many revisionists believed individuals and nations develop an increasing freedom in shaping their progress, contrary to Marx and the materialist interpretation of history. The revisionists also contended that the lot of the proletariat was improving and that a violent revolution was not necessary in democratic states.

The revisionists, like Edward Bernstein (1850–1932) in Germany, accepted Marx as a great thinker who proved that capitalism does exploit the great majority of workers and does tend to undermine itself. But to Bernstein and others, Marx's philosophy would have to be revised in the light of experience, as he had been proved wrong on a number of points. The growing socialist parties in France and Germany tended to become increasingly revisionist in practice even though in theory they might remain orthodox Marxist parties.

In England Marx had relatively little influence. The Fabians, a group of intellectuals including such distinguished men of letters as H. G. Wells and George Bernard Shaw, took their name from the Roman general, Fabius, who through delaying tactics ultimately defeated the Carthaginians even though he lost many battles. The "Fabian Essays" presented the case for a democratic and evolutionary socialism in plain language that everybody could understand. Sidney and Beatrice Webb (1859–1947) and (1858–1943) were the leading theorists of the society.

Fabian socialism regarded socialism as a logical next step in the progress of society. To them socialism was a scheme under which the means of production and exchange would be under the administration of the civil service. They had no doubt that trained civil servants would fairly administer the economic system. The injustices of the industrial system that Marx denounced were in the eyes of the Fabians the result of inept social arrangements. They also assumed that their version of socialism was completely compatible with political democracy.

Fabian doctrine had great influence upon the British Labour Party, which was organized in 1906 and is now one of the two leading British parties. Fabian leaders, such as Sidney Webb, also served in Labour cabinets when that party was in power.

In the United States socialism has never been a factor of great significance in public life because it has never had any real working class support. What little strength the party had in the early part of the century probably derived from first-generation immigrants of socialist persuassion and a segment of American middle class radicalism, which was not really socialist in outlook.

Socialism, however, has been a powerful force in Europe. In Britain and the Scandinavian countries in particular, socialistic parties have been in power for considerable periods of time. Socialism also promises to be of importance in the new nations of Africa and Asia. But the socialist program has frequently been modified by socialist governments.

Socialism in office has often been the program of the "middle way" of reformed capitalism, with emphasis on the welfare state rather than nationalization of industry. Today many socialist leaders themselves disavow nationalization. In Britain it is primarily "sick" industries—the railroads, coal, and electricity, which were experiencing economic difficulties under capitalism—that were taken over by the government.

Democratic socialist parties still continue and some are in office, as in Britain, West Germany and the Scandinavian countries. But the traditional socialist philosophy is in a state of decay. On the continent Marxist influence is slight and the faith in politics and economics as a way of salvation is pretty well gone. In Britain the Labour party is hardly the "way of life" it once was. In Sweden anti-Americanism seems to be a tenet of the Social Democrats. In short, democratic socialism today is in some respects indistinguishable from liberalism.[10]

[10] For a popular and interesting review of socialism, see Will Herberg, "Appraisal of Socialism," *Commonweal* (October 12, 1956), pp. 42–44.

Soviet Communism

As a result of the Russian Revolution of November, 1917, there was for the first time in history a government established on the principles of Marxian Socialism. The man who headed the new regime, Vladimir Lenin (1870–1924), was an unusual combination of active revolutionary and political and economic theorist. Lenin's philosophy was based on Marx, but a Marxism modified in the light of developments in Russia. Lenin differed from Marx in a number of respects. First, since Russia was not a well-developed capitalist country, it was not a likely candidate for the type of revolution Marx predicted. Lenin explained the Communist victory in Russia as a result of the country having experienced capitalism "vicariously." Second, he believed that capitalism had entered the imperialist phase because the European powers were engaged in a worldwide imperialistic war in a struggle for world markets. Consequently, revolutionary activity was possible anywhere and Russia, as a result of World War I, had an unusually unstable government.

Lenin also differed from Marx in his interpretation of the role of the proletariat in bringing about revolutionary activity. Unlike Marx, Lenin believed the working class by itself was not capable of developing a revolutionary consciousness. A revolution according to Lenin could come about only through a vanguard of dedicated revolutionaries who would supplant the old regime as rulers. Thus the dictatorship of the proletariat became the dictatorship of the Communist Party in Russia. The party ruled in the name of the proletariat.

Lenin was more explicit than Marx about the period of transition following the revolution. He believed that an extended period of time was necessary before the attainment of communism was possible. Following the revolution there would be a period of revolutionary transformation during which time suppression of the minority of exploiters still remaining would be necessary. The state would continue but would rule in the name of the proletariat. During the period of transition inequalities of wealth would still exist but exploitation of the many would no longer be possible, for the means of production would cease to be in private hands. Only when society is capable of attaining the formula of "from each according to his ability—to each according to his needs" will the state disappear. When this stage would occur was not clear.

On the question of revolution Lenin believed that a violent overthrow of the old regime was necessary. He also had only contempt for institutions of parliamentary democracy that were common in Western Europe.

Lenin's emphasis on the need for a revolutionary vanguard to instigate the revolution and rule in the interim period before the state withers away prepared the way for the Soviet dictatorship, which began under Lenin and has continued to the present. While Lenin lived, dictatorial power was vested in the Communist Party leadership. Under his successor Joseph Stalin (1879–1953) power gravitated into the hands of Stalin alone, who acquired nearly absolute power through purges of party members. Since Stalin's death in 1953, the dictatorship has been relaxed in some respects but the Soviet Union is still far from the democratic republic it is supposed to be according to the Constitution of 1936, which on paper provides for a bicameral legislature with a cabinet responsible to the legislative branch. Actual power still does and always has been lodged in the party Central Committee and Politburo. There is no sign of the withering away of the state.

In economic terms the Soviet Union has achieved a high degree of socialization and is now a leading industrial power. But this accomplishment has been at a very high cost in human terms. Industrialization was achieved through a series of five-year plans, which imposed the cost of industrial progress on the masses through the maintenance of a low standard of living. Thus, drastic limitations on the production of consumer goods was the necessary price for rapid industrialization. And collectivization of agriculture led to liquidation of millions of peasants who resisted the abolition of private property in agriculture.

Chinese Communism

Chinese Communism is of importance for several reasons. First, it marks the second major nation to accept the creed of Marx. Second, the Chinese interpretation of Marxism has some ideological characteristics of its own that differ from the Soviet version. Lastly, the People's Republic of China, instead of strengthening the worldwide Communist movement by becoming a partner of the Soviet Union, as first seemed likely, has accentuated polycentrist tendencies in the Communist world by following policies of its own and attacking the Soviets as bitterly as any capitalist power. The principal charge against the Soviets was that of deviating from the principles of Marxist Leninism.

The Chinese Communists through their leader, Mao Tse-tung, emphasize the revolutionary doctrines of Marx rather than the philosophical and economic aspects of his philosophy. Since China is a developing nation, Mao has based his revolutionary techniques on the peasants rather than the proletariat which was virtually nonexistent in China. Since 1949 great efforts have been made to develop a proletariat through industrialization.

Probably the most important contribution of Mao to Communist ideology is the theory of guerrilla warfare as both a military and political principle. The military principles emphasize attacking isolated enemy forces, winning rural areas and small cities first and big cities later, mobile warfare, and making use of the periods between campaigns to consolidate the revolutionary forces. To retain the revolutionary army a strong territorial base is necessary. This requires control of an area where there is a revolutionary peasant government that has redistibuted land. By following the above tactics, the Chinese Communists were able to defeat the forces of the Chinese nationalist government headed by Chiang Kai-shek between the end of World War II in 1945 and 1949.

The tactics of the Chinese Communists following their victory in the mainland in 1949 were to apply the principles of Mao's pamphlet *On the People's Democratic Dictatorship*. A coalition government was formed, which originally included non-Communist elements. Agrarian reforms were introduced. To carry out these changes landlords were publicly executed as well as other "counterrevolutionary" individuals. In 1953 the first five-year plan to nationalize most of the economic structure was introduced. By 1956 most Chinese farmers were organized into cooperative farms.

In 1966 China launched the Great Proletarian Cultural Revolution. Young students, organized into Red Guards, were used to bring about an extensive cultural revolution and political purge of party members guilty of "bourgeois" thinking. For a while the revolutionary movement got out of control and Chinese society approached a condition of anarchy until the army restored order. According to Thomas L. Thorson the apparent purpose of the Cultural Revolution was to preserve Chinese society from the threat of destruction by industrialization and excessive bureaucratization of life.[11]

The Importance of Marx and Marxism

Marx is important not so much for his economic doctrines and ideology, but for his realistic analysis of the evils of capitalism in mid-nineteenth-century England. His doctrines became the basis of a secular religion. Perhaps as Christopher Dawson and others have suggested, Marx was of the "seed of the prophets" and offered a secularized version of the ancient doctrine of the Jewish prophets concerning the coming of the Messianic kingdom.[12] Despite Marx's antireligious point of view, the Marxian dialectic possessed religious values, for it was to serve as an instrument of universal salvation that would usher in a new and pure social order on earth. The God of tradition was rejected, but he returned in a modified form in the dialectic that provided a new source of meaning to life. For Marx private property is the source of evil that will eventually be purged from life.

These "spiritual" promises of Marxism, rather than the basic economic doctrines which were frequently obscure and sometimes mistaken, were the basis of the appeal of the new creed to the working classes of Europe. This appeal compensated for the inadequacies of his purely economic doc-

[11] George H. Sabine and Thomas Landon Thorson, *op. cit.*, p. 788.
[12] J. H. Hallowell, *op. cit.*, p. 436.

trines and led to the formation of socialist parties throughout much of Western Europe.

Marx's mistake was in assuming that his diagnosis of capitalism was of universal application and unchanging. He did not foresee that the lot of the proletariat would generally improve rather than grow worse as he predicted. Also many of his specific economic doctrines have not stood the test of time.

As has been seen in the discussion of revisionist socialism, the socialist movement as an outgrowth of Marxism never made much headway in the United States. However, Soviet Communism appealed to a limited number of American intellectuals and a small group of labor leaders. This tendency was manifested particularly in the 1930s and 1940s, not so much in the growth of the American Communist Party but in the phenomenon of the "fellow traveler." The latter is a person who consistently follows the policies of the Communist Party but is not a party member. Fellow travelers did not join the party because they felt their influence would be diminished if they were identified with the party.

Activities of fellow travelers were generally limited to justifying the foreign policies of the Soviet Union and stressing the great achievements of the Soviet Union in industrializing its economy, while at the same time "explaining away" or ignoring the more obnoxious features of the Soviet dictatorship. For a brief time during World War II and a few years after its end, Communists infiltrated a few labor unions.

The appeal of the Soviet Union was the result of the Great Depression of the 1930s and the rise of Hitler. In the early stages of the Depression the United States seemed to be drifting, with economic conditions growing worse, while the Soviets were engaged in economic planning. The gallant fight of the Russians against the Nazi military machine during World War II also encouraged fellow travelers to view the Soviets favorably.

What weakened the movement ultimately was first the Nazi–Soviet nonaggression treaty of 1939, which gave Hitler the green light to start World War II. This traumatic event made it increasingly difficult to believe in the antifascism of the Soviets. Second, the tyranny of Stalin was a fact even "true believers" found hard to ignore. Lastly, the development of the Cold War and the Korean War dealt a fatal blow to fellow travelers. Today relatively few look at the Soviet Union through rose-colored glasses. On the other hand, there is evidence of a growing tendency among some individuals to idealize the Chinese Communists.[13]

The basis attraction of Marxism—of whatever variety—is its quasi-religious appeal as a solution to the world's political and economic problems.

[13] Sheila K. Johnson, "To China with Love," *Commentary*, Vol. LV, No. 6, (June, 1973), pp. 37–45.

FASCISM AND NATIONAL SOCIALISM

Even though the two leading Fascist powers—Germany and Italy—were defeated in World War II and their regimes overthrown, it would be a mistake to assume that the conditions that led to the creation of these regimes could not recur in some country. There were considerable differences between the two Fascist countries but the similarities were greater. It is therefore appropriate to call both regimes Fascist even though the German system was called National Socialism. Primary consideration will be given to Hitler's dictatorship, as it was the most powerful militarily and more extreme in its ideology.

Fascist writers do not contribute a great deal to an explanation of the ideology of the movement. Mussolini stressed the "will to power" and the supremacy of the state over the individual. German writers like Alfred Rosenberg stressed the myth of Aryan racial superiority. But the basic elements of Fascist ideology would seem to be the glorification of the irrational, a social Darwinism employed to justify national and racial superiority, a totalitarian one-party state, and the leadership principle.

The Nazis stressed Aryan supremacy and justified the extermination of "inferior" races, such as the Jews, whom the Nazis blamed for the ills of Germany. The nationalism of both the Italian and German versions of fascism glorified war as the climax of human achievement.

But perhaps most important was the leadership principle. Hitler as *Fuhrer* presumably embodied within himself the ability to speak for the entire German nation. Only Hitler could express the will of the German people. This might be considered a perversion of Rousseau's concept of the general will. Hitler as leader provided religious as well as political values to the regime. Hermann Göring, a Nazi leader, claimed Hitler was infallible.

Thus Fascism, like Marxism, has served as a secular religion which supplies meaning to life.

There is no agreement among scholars as to the exact nature of fascism except that Fascist systems are dictatorships. There are, however, a number of theories of importance that have been advanced.[14]

One interpretation, the Marxist, holds that fascism is the final stage of capitalism in which capitalists conspire to save themselves by establishing a dictatorship. In support of this view it is pointed out that a number of German capitalists subsidized Hitler financially since he promised to save the country from communism. Although many of these financial angels regarded Hitler as a demagogue, they believed that he could be managed so that their economic interests would be protected. Hitler was strongly anti-Communist and appealed to the fear of communism not only among the industrialists but the middle class as well. Supporters of this view point

[14] This discussion follows to a considerable degree the analysis of John H. Hallowell, *op. cit.*, pp. 591–617. Hallowell considers the fourth interpretation to be the most satisfactory.

out that Germany was in a state of severe economic crisis when Hitler came to power and that a probable alternative regime was a Communist one.

This interpretation has elements of truth but ignores the fact that Hitler's dictatorship encroached upon property rights to such an extent that many industrialists were reduced to the status of paid managers of their own enterprises. Some businessmen had their property seized by the Nazi government. The Marxist interpretation also ignored the strong popular support for Hitler among the masses and the broad appeal of the Nazi movement as a new form of socialism.

Fascism has also been described as essentially a personal dictatorship comparable to the rule of Napoleon. This view ignores the mass support of the Nazis and obscures the totalitarian character of the dictatorship, which goes beyond the realm of the political and includes all aspects of individual life.

Another interpretation stresses the fact that Hitler's movement grew out of the strong military tradition that had roots deep in Germany history. According to this theory, the Nazi dictatorship was basically a new and extreme version of German militarism. This explanation overlooks the fact that Hitler differed in kind as well as degree from older militarists such as the German Emperor William II of World War I or Bismarck or Frederick the Great. These men were militaristic and authoritarian but they did not repudiate the basis values of Western civilization as Hitler did. They did not believe in the Nazi racial theories or seek military domination to the same extent as the Nazis.

A fourth view of fascism interprets it as a political manifestation of a crisis of Western civilization that occurred in Germany and Italy because of special circumstances in those countries. But these conditions could develop anywhere. The basis of fascism, according to this view, is despair caused by the loss of faith on the part of the German and Italian people in the ability of their political and economic institutions to solve their social problems. As a result, they accepted a tyranny that promised to restore some degree of order and provide a meaning to life. But the new order was the embodiment of naked power and repudiated reason and all Western values. The last court of appeal in a Fascist system is the will of the leader but his will is not influenced by reason or justice.

The preceding explanation contains elements of truth the other three ignore. But this approach is perhaps too philosophical and intellectual.

Conclusion

In looking back on the various schools of political thought that have developed since the birth of democracy at Athens, several diverse trends are apparent. The basic approach of Plato and Aristotle was to look upon the state as an agency for moral improvement and to see the individual as part of the state. This approach was revived by Rousseau in the eighteenth century with his emphasis on the importance of the community. T. H. Green, in justifying state intervention in the economic life of the community as a way of removing obstacles to the full development of the individual, stood in this tradition. The great insight of this approach is the recognition of man as a social being. The great weakness is that too often the rights of the individual are not adequately protected, as in Rousseau.

Stoicism, the second great school of thought discussed, differed from Plato and Aristotle in developing the concepts of natural law and the basic equality of all men.

Individualism for the first time starts with the individual for whose benefit the state is created in the social contract philosophy of Locke. It is important to remember that present-day liberalism had its origins in Locke's social contract, with his emphasis on limited government and natural rights, which were reinforced by his doctrine of natural law. The weakness of Locke is his concept of the state as a "passive policeman," which if unmodified in an industrial age can lead to the extreme and unrealistic ideas of Herbert Spencer. Perhaps one of Locke's great insights was his idea of the political community and its values that were brought into existence from the social contract. Today Americans can appreciate the buffeting the political community has received as a result of the stresses and strains induced by the Vietnam War, the Watergate scandals, and the civil rights revolution.

Another important philosophy is socialism. That Marxian doctrine had led to totalitarianism in the Soviet Union and the People's Republic of China is perhaps as much the result of the absence of a strong democratic tradition in those countries as it is of Marx's ideas. It would not have surprised Edmund Burke to learn that the new order in these countries includes much of the undemocratic past. Socialism, where it has been democratic, as in Western Europe, has served liberal values. But socialism in terms of pure economic policy can be as unliberal or inhumane as the worst capitalistic state, as evidenced by the Soviet Union. On the other hand, democratic socialism seems to differ from modern liberalism in degree rather than in kind. The dominant philosophical trend in the Western democracies is either liberalism or democratic socialism.

Lastly, more recent liberal political philosophy, which is dominant in the United States, has been "realistic" and pragmatic in the tradition of Dewey. Whether modern liberalism can continue to promote traditional liberal values when divorced from its philosophical roots, which assumed a world of transcendental values as set forth by Locke and Green, remains to be seen. Nevertheless, the current trends of liberal thought is away from such abstractions as the nature of the state, natural law, and natural rights and toward emphasis on political theory that is useful and factual.

The survey of political theory in this chapter points the way to our major focus—discussion and analysis of major political institutions and processes. We will begin to use and apply the insights developed in the first three chapters. As you progress in your reading keep in mind the ideas previously developed: that politics is part of a wider system of interactions and processes, that we are studying interactions.

Selected Readings

George H. Sabine and Thomas L. Thorson, *History of Political Theory,* 4th ed. (Hinsdale, Ill.: Dryden Press, 1973) is an excellent survey of Western political theory from the Greeks to the twentieth century. Thorson updates this classic work of the late George Sabine. For an interpretation of political thought from Locke to the twentieth century from a Christian and natural law point of view, see John H. Hallowell, *Main Currents in Modern Political Thought* (New York: Henry Holt, 1950).

A recent challenging study of political thought is John Rawls, *A Theory of Justice** (Cambridge, Mass.: Belknap Press of Harvard University Press, 1971). Rawls presents a theory of justice that rejects utilitarianism and reinterprets the traditional theory of the social contract as represented by Locke and his successors as its philosophical justification. For a work that surveys in detail the scientific foundation of twentieth century political thought, see Arnold Brecht, *Political Theory* (Princeton: Princeton University Press, 1959).

Hannah Arendt is the author of two excellent studies on certain aspects of political thought. *The Origins of Totalitarianism,** 2nd ed. (Cleveland, and New York: A Meridian Book, The World Publishing Co., 1967) analyzes the historical roots of totalitarianism. *Between Past and Future* (New York: The Viking Press, 1968) consists of eight essays in political thought. Chapter 3, "What is Authority?" in particular is outstanding.

For a modern study of the state as an instrument for satisfying human needs under changing conditions, see R. M. MacIver, *The Modern State,* rev. ed. (London: Oxford University Press, 1964). Another book about the state is Sir Ernest Barker's *Principles of Social and Political Theory** (London: Oxford University Press, 1961). Barker discusses the state and society historically and the development of justice and law.

* Available in paperback.

Of the many books on the political philosophy of Plato and Aristotle, mention will be made of only one. Sir Ernest Barker, *The Political Thought of Plato and Aristotle** (New York: Dover Publications, 1959) analyzes the philosophy of these classic Greek thinkers within the framework of T. H. Green's political thinking.

There are several good studies of ideologies. Kenneth M. and Patricia Dolbeare in *American Ideologies** (Chicago: Markham Publishing Co., 1971) present an introduction to current competing American political beliefs, such as various schools of liberalism, conservatism, capitalism, Black Liberation, the New Left, and American Marxism. C. Wright Mills, *The Marxists* (New York: Dell Publishing Co., 1962) is a primer on Marx and various schools of thought developed by his followers.

There are a number of philosophical books dealing with democratic theory. *Plato: Totalitarian or Democrat?* edited by Thomas L. Thorson (Englewood Cliffs, N.J.: Prentice-Hall, 1963) is a collection of essays on the question of whether Plato's philosophy was totalitarian or democratic in its implications. R. H. S. Crossman and Karl Popper view Plato as the ancestor of totalitarianism, while John Wild and John H. Hallowell see him as the ancestor of democracy. Henry B. Mayo, *An Introduction to Democratic Theory** (New York: Oxford University Press, 1960) develops a few basic principles necessary to the operation of a political system. They are popular control, elections, the franchise, political freedoms, and majority rule and its limits.

An unconventional vindication of democracy and criticism of its traditional defense is made in Reinhold Niebuhr, *The Children of Light and the Children of Darkness* (New York: Charles Scribner's Sons, 1944). The "children of light" are those who believe that self-interest should be brought under the control of a higher law, whereas the "children of darkness" are the moral cynics who recognize no law above their self-interest. A dilemma known to professional students of politics is that of choosing between justifying political systems or being scientific. Thomas L. Thorson, *The Logic of Democracy** (New York: Holt, Rinehart and Winston, 1962) explores this problem and proposes a solution. Walter Lippmann, *The Public Philosophy* (Boston: Little, Brown, 1955) is an eloquent plea for a restoration of belief in the "public philosophy," an objective order based on natural law.

For a classic study of the optimism of the eighteenth century Enlightenment, which had great influence on political theory, see Carl L. Becker, *The*

* Available in paperback.

Heavenly City of the Eighteenth Century Philosophers (New Haven: Yale University Press, 1932). Louis Hartz, *The Liberal Tradition in America* (New York: Harcourt, Brace and World, 1955) is an excellent interpretation of American Political thought since the Revolution, with emphasis on the liberal tradition.

Part Two

The Input Agencies

Chapter 4

Formation of Political Attitudes

Political life involves a constant interaction between institutions, individuals, values, and group activities. It includes attitudes, attitude formation, and many aspects of a country's culture. These help shape how institutions and processes operate. In this chapter, the opening chapter to our discussion of input processes, we will look at the formation of political understanding and attitudes. Attitude formation is an important input in terms of helping to regulate how people view their political system and what they will expect from it. It is also an important output of the political processes because people everywhere attempt to regulate and control the content and direction of political learning.

Each of us has probably asked where a particular person acquired his or her political ideas. Quite often we ask where they may have gotten their "*crazy*" ideas. In this chapter we will look at one answer to this question. Political culture—the political–social–economic–cultural–value milieu within which individuals and institutions operate—and political socialization—the process by which individuals learn to participate in or oppose their society—help explain the origin of many political values and behaviors. They illustrate the mechanism through which common values and orientations necessary to maintaining political–social cohesion operate, as well as offering clues as to why people in other nations or in previous eras have acted in ways we may consider incomprehensible or self-destructive. Fundamentally, we are what we consciously and unconsciously learn to be. Transferring a newborn infant from one cultural–political environment to another means he or she will learn a different language, religion, set of values, and expectations about politics. That is obvious. Less obvious is an explanation of why this is so. In the process of asking "why," we will rely less on the institutional orientation of other chapters in order to examine factors influencing formation of political attitudes, values, and norms.

Political Culture[1]

Culture refers to the widely shared rules, values, norms, cognitions, and ways of life of the members of a particular social group. This includes cognitive orientations, "basic premises and sets of assumptions."[2] Political culture is a specialized part or aspect of a whole culture, referring to the totality of attitudes, values, and beliefs that are relevant to politics in any society. These include empirical beliefs about what is actually happening in a society, generalized beliefs about the goals and values of that society, and beliefs and values that may be relevant to politics, even though they are not specifically political.

This attitudinal environment in which every political system operates affects and sets limits to that system as much as actual political institutions. As noted by Sidney Verba, political culture affects and helps to determine people's interaction with other people: who talks to whom; what roles and attitudes of superiority or deference they may have; the nature of political processes; how formal institutions operate; how ideologies are interpreted in daily activities; and what the orientation of members of a political system is to the functioning and structure of that particular system.[3] Political culture provides clues to proper collective and individual behavior, as well as defining the content of specific roles and the relationship between roles. It can be a dynamic and changing concept if we emphasize mutual interaction and interdependence of values, factual knowledge, and everyday experience.

[1] This discussion of political culture draws heavily from Gabriel A. Almond and Sidney Verba, *The Civic Culture* (Princeton: Princeton University Press, 1963), *passim;* George M. Foster, *Traditional Cultures and the Impact of Technological Change* (New York: Harper and Row, 1962), *passim;* Lucian W. Pye and Sidney Verba, eds., *Political Culture and Political Development* (Princeton: Princeton University Press, 1965), *passim;* James C. Scott, *Political Ideology in Malaysia: Reality and the Beliefs of an Elite* (New Haven: Yale University Press, 1968), *passim;* and Donald J. Devine, *The Political Culture of the United States* (Boston: Little, Brown, 1972), pp. 1–32.

[2] Foster, *op. cit.*, p. 11; George M. Foster, "Peasant Society and the Image of Limited Good," in Jack M. Potter, May N. Diaz, and George M. Foster, eds., *Peasant Society: A Reader* (Boston: Little, Brown, 1967), pp. 300–23.

[3] Pye and Verba, *op. cit.*, pp. 517–18.

Since it refers to a set of understandings, values, and assumptions, political culture is not uniform either between or within political systems. Diversity and even inconsistency are common. Political culture is the result or "product" of the history of any system, as well as the individual socialization of its members. Common values and socialization are the keys to political culture. Collective history and individual socialization may interact to produce a set of political attitudes very different from those that are dominant or at least those most commonly voiced. While we may speak of a common political culture in any society, its interpretation and meaning will vary greatly, depending on the roles, socialization, and experiences of different groups. We must consider the development of subcultures and countercultures, groups who have or develop substantially different social and political values from those that are dominant within their nation. Differences of opinion and orientations are very common. Different political cultures distinguish the United States from Germany, and to a more limited extent, eastern, white, elite values from southern, black, agricultural values.

Political culture is important because it gives people clues to proper political behavior and helps them to understand what kinds of behavior will be required of them. In a traditional political system, dominant values may indicate that the majority of people are unable or incompetent to participate in politics. Government may be treated as a mystery, understandable only by the high born, the highly educated, or by initiates into an arcane philosophy or ideology. Society may be pyramidically or hierarchically organized—the major injunction is obey the law and be loyal; do not question, do not participate.

In a democratic system, dominant values may emphasize participation—the idea that common people are rational and intelligent enough to participate, that governors gain their privilege of governing and decision making only from the consent of the governed. Whether or not these values actually operate, they set limits to government and spell out relations between governed and governors that could not exist in traditional political cultures.

Obviously, attitudes affect politics. Where they are supported by political and economic institutions they can be conducive to stability. Where they clash with new or changing institutions, or where older values, such as the primacy of self-help, clash with new realities, such as an urbanized, industrialized, highly interdependent economy, psychic dislocation and civil strife will result.

People socialized to an older political culture, one that emphasized authority, obedience, and deference, as in pre-World War II Germany, or local ties, limited opportunities, and stability of expectations, as in many developing states, may find it difficult or impossible to cope with their new situation. Their familiar political culture may be gone or disappearing, and the new world confusing and alien. Orientation becomes difficult because the old behavior clues no longer refer to reality.

Political culture and political socialization are related to each other. Political culture may be viewed as the "macro" level, the sum total of values, attitudes, and orientations that affect politics and political behavior. Political socialization may be viewed as the "micro," or individual, level "as the acquisition by an individual of the political culture which surrounds him."[4] Political culture and political socialization interact, with dominant political values largely determining the content of political socialization, while the process of successful socialization helps maintain and transmit the political culture. When culture and socialization are similar, political stability usually results. Where they diverge and disagree, the likely result will be political instability unless there is widespread agreement on the desirability of changing dominant values.

Political Socialization[5]

In the same way that political culture is a specialized part of culture, political socialization is a specialized part of socialization. Socialization refers to the total process of learning how to interact with other people and of developing our individual personalities. There is fairly widespread agreement on the components of a definition of political socialization, even though political scientists disagree about whether we should study only child learning, the content of what is learned, and/or adult learning about politics.

"Political socialization is the gradual learning of the norms, attitudes, and behavior accepted and practiced by the ongoing political system." Its goal "is to so train or develop individuals that they become well-functioning members of the political society," that is, a person "who accepts (internalizes) society's political norms and who will then transmit them to future generations."[6]

Or "socialization refers to the process by which persons acquire the knowledge, skills, and dispositions that make them more or less able members of their society."[7]

[4] Edward S. Greenberg, *Political Socialization* (New York: Atherton, 1970), p. 7.

[5] The first major work on political socialization was Herbert H. Hyman, *Political Socialization: A Study in the Psychology of Political Behavior* (New York: Free Press, 1959). Hyman summarized most previous work in the new field, and popularized the term "political socialization."

[6] Roberta Sigel, "Assumptions About the Learning of Political Values," *Annals of the American Academy of Political and Social Science,* 361 (September, 1965), pp. 1–9.

[7] Orville G. Brim and Stanton Wheeler, *Socialization After Childhood* (New York: John Wiley, 1966), p. 3.

Political socialization is a process of learning about politics. People are taught to participate or not to participate. They are taught what is proper behavior, how to interact with other people and with government. In modern developing systems people may be taught to focus their energies on national development. In democratic states people may be taught they have a right, perhaps even a duty, to participate. In most political systems people may be taught to disapprove of dissent. The essence of political socialization, therefore, involves learning and teaching, acceptance and transmission of group values and norms.

As a working definition we may consider political socialization as the continuing process by which people acquire motivations, information, norms, attitudes, and values about their society, economy, political system, and their role or place in these. People become members of their political system through political socialization. They learn what is expected of them and how to live and interact with society and the political system. The content of this learning is different from system to system, and even within the same political system because of different experiences and milieus. Regardless of the content, however, political socialization refers to political learning, and that is where its importance lies. Throughout the rest of this chapter we will be concerned largely with the process of political socialization, which shows less variations within and across systems than does the content of political socialization.[8]

THE IMPORTANCE OF POLITICAL SOCIALIZATION

Today, as in the past, people fervently hold an almost infinite variety of political-social-economic beliefs. Politically, men have supported every system from emperor worship to anarchism. Economically, they have supported every system from total state control to complete laissez-faire. Socially, people have condoned systems based on slavery and those promising equality. Human beings have practiced cannibalism and vegetarianism; cooperation and constant civil war; secularism and millenarianism. These illustrate the way in which human beings may be shaped and molded, particularly when we emphasize fairly general characteristics and societal averages rather than individual attributes. This does not mean that an individual's personality can be shaped in any direction. It does mean that the institutional-value milieu within which people develop has an important input into their political-social-economic behavior, and largely determines the nature of the values that are passed from generation to generation or, as the case often is, modified in the process of transmission.

[8] For a discussion of some of the different ways political scientists view political socialization, see Fred Greenstein, "A Note on the Ambiguity of 'Political Socialization:' Definitions, Criticisms, and Strategies of Inquiry," *Journal of Politics,* 32 (November, 1970), pp. 969–78.

Political socialization is important because it permits us to carry on an organized social–political life. Without political socialization there could be no continuation of political life. The very concepts of government, the state, and society would cease to exist. Clearly this is both inconceivable and impossible. Some political learning will always go on, simply because political learning is necessary to maintain any political system. It occurs in every political system, no matter how simple or complex. By creating common values, assumptions, and loyalties, it enables us to develop stable expectations about the behavior of others and integrates us into whatever common enterprises society is engaged in by supplying us with understanding of our position and roles. The choice is simple. Either people agree on some common values and ways of running their political system, or the system will be based on force and coercion. Yet even force and coercion are ultimately based on agreement to use them, that is, on some value agreement.

Therefore, while we are not certain of the *exact* relation between learning and particular features and characteristics of political systems, it is clear that how people learn to perceive politics, and what content they put into politics, ultimately affects community and regime characteristics. This fact has held out to many people the possibility that manipulation of the learning process may create a more desirable political system.

POLITICAL SOCIALIZATION IN POLITICAL THEORY

Political socialization is one of the oldest issues in political literature. The Greek philosopher Plato (427–347 B.C.), in his *Republic* and *Laws,* considered citizen training and education to be society's most important function. He proposed that everyone would have access to basic physical and mental training. This would be the first step in sorting people out to their different roles and activities. People who did not have the necessary intellectual equipment to master advanced education would be trained to accept unquestioningly the duties of citizenship. Internalization of citizen duties, loyalty, and acceptance of their social role as absolutely unchangeable and just, as well as physical remoteness from other sources of influence, guaranteed for Plato widespread acceptance of the values and ideas that produced a stable political system.

In addition to basic education, the most talented would be selected for further training and education. Their education, directed toward discovering and creating the guardians and philosopher-king, revolved around training the gifted few to understand and carry out what was necessary to achieve stability, justice, and congruence between society and what Plato considered to be the fundamental reality of the universe. Ultimately, good government depended upon this elite's understanding of the ideas or forms, which Plato considered to be the basic reality behind the transitory nature of physical existence. This understanding, in the *Republic,* would give the philosopher an absolutely perfect claim to rule. Through the proper system of education, society could literally be made perfect. No other theorist has claimed more for either philosophy or education.

Other theorists emphasized education. Aristotle discussed the necessity of legislation that would insure that young men received the education necessary to fulfill their role as citizens, to be able to rule and be ruled in turn. The Italian Renaissance theorist Niccolò Machiavelli (1469–1527) argued that civic loyalty and civic virtue made Republican Rome great, and that a resurrection of civic loyalty, or devotion to the affairs of the state, could unite Italy, freeing it from foreign invasions. In *The Prince* he indicated that the prince should attempt to create the kind of loyalty and sense of duty that would accomplish this. In his *Discourses* he presented models of civic devotion that he felt exemplified dedication to the state.

In the eighteenth century Jean-Jacques Rousseau, in his *Consideration on the Government of Poland,* emphasized the need for training, which would make people willing to dedicate their lives to a strong united Poland. In his *Social Contract* the only possible way the "general will" could operate would be through citizens trained to accept and articulate the same values. Throughout the eighteenth, nineteenth, and twentieth centuries theorists as diverse as Thomas Jefferson, Alexis de Tocqueville, Karl Marx, and John Dewey emphasized some form of education and civic training as prerequisites to citizen participation in their ideal political systems. Today B. F. Skinner's *Walden Two* represents an extreme belief in socialization and the effects of psychological conditioning to produce a cooperative, well-adjusted person. Based more on faith than empirical analysis, Skinner's model culminates more than 2300 years of efforts to argue for an ideal political system through manipulation of the educational system or, in some cases, the entire learning process.

POLITICAL SOCIALIZATION AND POLITICAL LIFE

If philosophers have dreamed of manipulating education, political power holders and social–political factions have continuously attempted to use education as the means to their ends or simply to perpetuate the values and institutions they upheld. Every political system that has existed anywhere, at any point in time, has been concerned with what kind of values and attitudes people were learning and, more importantly, how these affected behavior. In ancient Greece and Rome, although there was no formal educational system for the masses of people, the various governments were deeply concerned with controlling the population. Civic religions, games, and family training all contributed to maintaining political continuity. In the

Middle Ages the Church helped teach peasants proper political deference through emphasis on religious sanctions. Thomas Jefferson proposed a system of universal primary education to insure a population sufficiently educated to participate in public affairs and create an American republic of liberty. Throughout the nineteenth century in Europe and North America political reformers and civic leaders emphasized the need for widespread popular education to improve the position of the newly created industrial working class, but they fought bitterly over who would control the content of education.

Socialization is a political concern throughout the world, particularly during crisis periods or when old values and institutions appear to be weakened or in danger. Since World War II vocal and angry public debates have occurred in the United States, France, West Germany, Canada, the

Young Pioneers are assembled on the Red Square in Moscow to celebrate the 50th anniversary of the All-Union Young Pioneer League (May 19, 1972).

United Kingdom, and elsewhere over whether the educational system and mass media were inculcating necessary values for national survival. In the twentieth century, particularly in totalitarian states, or in response to their challenge, mass education has been consciously and systematically politicized. This is particularly true where the leadership attempts to control all social and cultural institutions, such as schools, clubs, and youth organizations. This enables the state to insure that children will receive the same message of dedication and loyalty to the regime, while countering the possibility that families will teach or inculcate antiregime values. Such education emphasizes the child's usefulness and duty to the country, rather than development of individual talents and potential as ends in themselves.

In the Soviet Union Lenin and Stalin emphasized the absolute necessity of teachers' conforming to the regime's values. Starting with virtually no school facilities and a largely passive and illiterate population, Soviet leaders created an educational system designed both to train effective workers and develop loyal citizens. In the process of creating an advanced educational system, they have employed formal methods, such as teaching history and economics from their ideological perspective, and informal methods, such as emphasizing cooperation and the individual's duty to society, to instill loyalty and pride in the Soviet Union. In addition, Young Pioneer and Komsomal organizations provide out-of-school reinforcement.

Nazi Germany reveals a slightly different pattern.[9] When Hitler came to power in 1933 he did not need to create an efficient educational system, but to take an advanced and sophisticated system and convert it into an active instrument of Nazi politics. To insure creation of a loyal population, the new Nazi government forbade Jews to teach, and subjected teachers to vigorous indoctrination and observation to insure that they were politically reliable. Teacher training emphasized race and physical prowess. German education was centralized in a Ministry of Education, thereby ending state educational independence and a tradition of university autonomy. The entire educational curriculum was changed to reflect Nazi teaching. Exceptions were forbidden. Most teachers and students rapidly cooperated. Based on prior socialization patterns, which emphasized obedience to authority, Hitler demanded that German education be concerned with creating healthy, racially "pure" bodies, development of obedience to authority, and teaching of useful tasks. This was supplemented by strong doses of historical studies, which were to teach patriotism, love of country, and willingness to sacrifice for Germany. History was taught as a struggle, out of which a racially "pure" Germany was emerging.

[9] See George Frederick Kneller, *The Educational Philosophy of National Socialism* (New Haven: Yale University Press, 1941); William L. Shirer, *The Rise and Fall of the Third Reich* (New York: Simon and Schuster, 1960), pp. 248–256.

In the process German education suffered a catastrophic decline. Between 1933 and 1939 the number of university students declined from 127,920 to 58,325.[10] The quality of education also suffered. Even before the war scientists had begun to complain that new graduates were unfit for creative work. To Hitler, that did not matter, as long as they had the proper political attitudes.

Nonschool activities were also organized and centrally controlled. Organization of children started at age six in Hitler Youth. Modeled on traditional youth clubs and organizations, it was organized in 1925 to provide an auxiliary service to the Nazi Party. After 1933 efforts were made to induce all youth to join, although it never achieved universal membership. At 18, young men went into the *Arbeitsdienst*, or Labor Service, for six months where their political education was continued while they engaged in labor. All these organizations sought to socialize German youth to Nazi ideology

Young members of the Hitler Youth at a Party rally in Nuremberg.

[10] Shirer, *op. cit..*, p. 252.

and break down class barriers that could have prevented total dedication to Germany.

Following World War II the victorious Allies engaged in systematic "de-Nazification" programs, passing on teacher certification, issuing new textbooks, and creating new youth groups, all aimed at resocializing German youth.

Without going to Nazi extremes, many leaders in developing countries emphasize education and new socialization patterns as keys to economic and social development. Given the strength of family, cultural, religious, ethnic, linguistic, and local groups in many developing states, common or nationwide patterns of loyalties, values, and expectations have not developed. This makes economic and social modernization impossible because people do not have the common images, trust, and patterns of interaction necessary to cooperate with each other. Instead, they often focus on the things that divide them. For the developing states education has a doubly difficult task: it must provide the skills and motivations necessary to modernize economically and it must overcome the certrifugal forces of localism by providing value orientations that can produce national consciousness, common identity, and integration. In the absence of cohesion and widespread agreement on goals, leaders of developing states seek control of socialization to achieve modernization.

POLITICAL SOCIALIZATION AND POLITICAL INDOCTRINATION

Students constantly ask how can we distinguish socialization from indoctrination. Indoctrination is a heavily value-laden word, which immediately conjures up images of manipulation, control, and perhaps questionable purposes. Nevertheless, indoctrination occurs, and this question must be faced.[11]

Facetiously, political socialization and civic education go on in systems we approve of, and indoctrination occurs in systems we disapprove of. Seriously, we may distinguish transmission of values, a neutral concept, from the content of values, which may have a heavy moral–normative content. Learning goes on in every system. Within Western, liberal democratic values, however, political socialization involves more than learning

[11] Our question cannot be answered in a completely value-free way. Some elements of subjectivism must enter, though we are not dealing with complete value relativism. Moreover, this question may be impossible to answer adequately, because most, if not all, that people prefer doing is a result of a learning process. No one ever has a completely free choice. Most of our preferences reflect past learning. There is always and perhaps inevitably restraint on alternatives. Therefore, any answer must acknowledge that every person is in large part a product of his or her experiences.

values. Ideally, it should also emphasize individual development, flexibility, ability to respond to new and changing conditions, development of critical judgment, including analysis of accepted values and institutions, and the right to question values learned during socialization.

Conversely, indoctrination can be understood as teaching that makes impossible acquisition of alternative values. It forbids seeking of political–social–economic alternatives, emphasizes the absolute truth of one set of values to the exclusion of all others, demands uncritical acceptance of, and dedication to, a set of values prescribed by the group or state, and includes injunctions that only one way of life is legitimate.

Given these criteria, no system is completely free of some elements of indoctrination. As with so many other questions involving values or behavior, political socialization versus political indoctrination is not an either/or, yes/no question. Rather, it is a "more or less" question (see figure 1). Societies may be ranked on a simple (more or less) ordinal scale, depending on their relative openness and receptivity to criticism of accepted values. The difference between socialization and indoctrination is a matter of degree. We may argue that the more conformity to a single strandard is demanded, and as alternatives are forbidden, the more we are in a situation of indoctrination. The more critical awareness is emphasized and the tools and ideas necessary for critical analysis are developed, the more we are dealing with a situation of socialization. Still, some elements of indoctrination will be present in every system. Children do not have any choice as to what language they will speak, what religion they will initially follow, or what values their parents will support. No one can learn to think

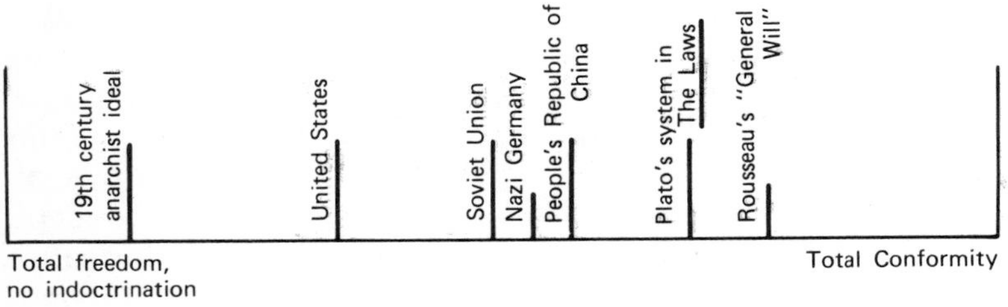

Figure 1. At the pole of total freedom there would be the danger that some values and information absolutely necessary to modern organized life would not be conveyed, such as, language, basic curbs on ego, ability to interact with other people, as well as simple conventions such as driving on the right side, rather than on the left side of the road, or stopping at a red traffic light rather than a green one. At the total conformity pole, children would be carbon copies of their parents, and there would be little or no intergenerational change. Neither pole is possible. (Note that distances are for illustrative purposes only and represent relative, not absolute, degrees of difference.)

critically until he or she has learned to think, has developed analytic tools, and has some minimum facts. Even participation and awareness are learned. Therefore, in seeking our own answer to this perennial question, we must try to look at the purposes, tendencies, content, and orientation of the entire learning process.[12]

POLITICAL SOCIALIZATION: REFINING OUR DEFINITION

By now it is apparent that we favor a definition of political socialization that is wide enough to include all politically relevant learning. Political socialization may be divided into "specifically political learning" and nonpolitical, but "politically relevant leaning."[13] *Specifically political learning* refers to the acquisition of information, attitudes, and evaluations about politics. Whether formal, as in school, or informal, through group discussion and the mass media, people learn a great deal about how their political system works, to whom it responds, what its basic institutions and values are, what their role is or should be, what kinds of values are dominant, and so forth.

Nonpolitical learning is also important, perhaps more important than specifically political learning. Through the political culture and formation of their personalities, people acquire attitudes and values which, while not specifically political in content, have an impact on how the political system functions and on their roles in the political system. In the family and at school children learn attitudes and habitual responses to authority, order, and obedience which *may* have an impact on their political attitudes and the broader political system. In pre-World War II China and Japan children were constantly taught obedience to their parents and superiors, and this habit of obedience to authority figures may have transferred to military and political affairs. Adults from families where, as children, they were encouraged to participate in family decisions tend to have a greater sense of personal efficacy and tend to participate more in politics than adults from families that emphasized obedience to parental decisions and exclusion from family decision making. Attitudes toward sex, race, and class, while not usually political in intent or content, do condition people's involvement in politics. Feelings that "politics is man's business" or attitudes of racial superiority are learned during childhood, usually from parents and close associates, but condition people's attitudes toward sex and race for the rest of their lives. Generalized exclusion of women and

[12] For a discussion of indoctrination intended to develop unquestioning political loyalty, see Hoang Van Chi, "Political Indoctrination in North Vietnam" in Thomas J. Bellows, Stanley Erickson, and Herbert R. Winter, *Political Science: Introductory Essays and Readings* (Belmont, Calif.: Duxbury Press, 1971), pp. 150–159.

[13] Fred J. Greenstein, *Children and Politics* (New Haven: Yale University Press, 1965), p. 12.

racial minorities from the professions and positions of power, as well as racial animosity, are partly traceable to casual remarks, parental attitudes, and parental models of behavior that children learn and imitate before they are able to make independent judgments. If you add to this the high probability that personality—openness, adaptability, ability to cooperate, willingness to tolerate ambiguity, need for order, inflexibility, assumptions about progress, etc.—affects politics, and that basic personality patterns develop through our interaction with institutions and other people as we grow up, it is easy to see the potential impact of nonpolitical learning on politics.

We may also distinguish formal and informal political socialization. Everyone is familiar with *formal* political socialization—that is, deliberate efforts by parents, groups, or government to teach information, values, and attitudes they feel may affect the political system. A structured teacher–student situation is the most typical forum for such instruction. Reading patriotic literature and classroom history or civics instruction are the most common forms of formal political learning. Governmental educational programs and propaganda may also be included. While political scientists are uncertain of the exact impact of formal instruction, parents and governments constantly emphasize its importance to the continued existence of preferred values and institutions.

Children and adults acquire a vast amount of political information and shape values and attitudes through *informal* learning situations as well. Much of our politically relevant learning goes on incidental to other activities. Much of it is at the subconscious level, where information and attitudes are acquired in an unstructured forum. Children absorb attitudes and values from their parents without being aware of this. Casual remarks about other races or honesty in government; formal parental statements about honesty versus efforts to bribe a policeman instead of paying a fine; simple explanations about why a car cannot be parked in a particular area—all these help form a child's attitude toward government and his or her place in government. A black child does not need formal classroom instruction to discover discrimination. A white child does not need a lesson in history to discover the story of slavery. Any child growing up in the 1950s did not need to attend school to discover that the Russians were the "bad guys." All of us are imbedded in an institutional-value milieu that constantly "teaches" us to accept or reject certain groups, ideas, or values. Even though political scientists have no precise way to measure this information learning or its impact, it seems to have a profound impact on politics and attitudes toward political life.

A further distinction follows from what we have said—the difference between cognitive socialization, affective socialization, and evaluation of the political system.[14] *Cognitive socialization* refers to "transmitting political knowledge and information."[15] This includes information about the formal structure of government, its officers, their roles and function, official values, the nature of political inputs and outputs, and information about accepted political behavior. Information may be acquired either formally or informally, but is specifically political in content. Acquisition of information about the political system is of obvious importance because citizens could not know how to function without it. This knowledge, however, is often minimal. In the United States half of the 17-year-olds in a recent study did not know that presidential candidates are nominated at national party conventions, and 29 percent did not know the Supreme Court has the power to declare acts of Congress unconstitutional.[16]

Cognitive socialization alone is insufficient to explain political stability. While knowledge of how the system works is necessary, *affective socialization* helps explain feelings of loyalty, support, and affection for the system. Affective socialization refers to acceptance of commonly held values, feelings, and beliefs about the political system. In terms of support and stability it is more important than cognitive socialization. Even before children acquire any understanding of their country's political system, they learn to have highly positive feelings toward it. In the United States:

> *The child's early relationship to the country is highly positive although his conceptualization of it is vague. . . . This attachment develops despite a fragmentary and incomplete view of the nation and its government.*[17]

Without feelings of support and affection, no system could survive for any extended period of time. This support and affection—or the lack of support—are taught in much the same way as factual information. As we will see below, families and schools are major agents teaching loyalty, affection, and support.

Evaluation judgments combine both factual information and values. They express judgments and opinions about the political system. Evaluation, or appraisal of political phenomena based on some moral criteria (good or bad) or empirical criteria (something is or is not working the way we agree it should work), is the essence of political judgment. Everyone constantly makes such judgments. Whether it is a question of agreement or

[14] Dean Jaros, *Socialization to Politics* (New York: Praeger, 1973), p. 9; Almond and Verba, *op. cit.*, p. 15. See also Lewis A. Froman, Jr., "Learning Political Attitudes," *Western Political Quarterly*, 15 (1962), pp. 304–13.

[15] Jaros, *op. cit.*, p. 9.

[16] Review of a National Assessment of Educational Progress Report in *DEA News*, No. 2, Spring-Summer, 1974, p. 6.

[17] Robert D. Hess and Judith V. Torney, *The Development of Political Attitudes in Children* (Chicago: Aldine, 1967), p. 26.

disagreement over personal conduct, such as extramarital sex, or political morality, such as calling a particular politician honest or crooked, we are expressing value judgments. These value judgments do not materialize out of thin air. Rather, they are based on a set of acquired and developed assumptions about what is or is not proper conduct. People may be taught to respond in predetermined ways—all capitalists (or communists) are bad—or they may be taught to develop the tools and criteria from which they can make reasonably independent political judgments.

Regardless of the source of our value judgments, statements about proper political conduct condition people's responses to political events. They help to determine what people will consider legitimate or illegitimate. For a person who accepts the tenets of a free enterprise system, governmental control of major parts of the economy will be considered illegitimate. He or she would probably oppose a proposal that the federal government in the United States acquire control over steel mills. Differing value judgments and efforts to implement them provide much of the content of political conflict. They arise because people have been socialized to expect different conduct and actions from government. One of the purposes of indoctrination is to insure that people will make the same value judgments, and will uniformly approve of the conduct of their governments.

Finally, political socialization is not directed toward a simple undifferentiated "thing," the political system. As stated in chapter 2, political scientists distinguish among "community," "regime," and "government" or authorities.[18] The same distinction applies to differentiation in political socialization. Children first acquire affection for the country, with affection and understanding of the regime coming later. Government or authority orientation is most easily changed. More importantly, a distinction among community, regime, and authority helps us to understand political stability in the midst of political disagreement. By being able to distinguish loyalty and affection toward the idea of maintaining a common community, values, and institutions from disagreements on specific issues or personalities, people are able to interact and disagree with each other without undermining the state or government. For example, during the Watergate crisis, politicians as different as Senator Barry Goldwater and Senator George McGovern could agree on the desirability of Richard Nixon's resignation (the individual) from the office of president (the regime) as a way of preserving that office and saving the nation (community) from a potentially divisive conflict. They were able to agree because of a common dedication to the regime and community, even though they disagree on most policy issues.

In short, socialization to community and/or regime provides the com-

[18] See especially, Jaros, *op. cit.*, pp. 33–50.

mon stock of ideas and values which enable people in the same country to disagree over particular political issues without resort to violence or civil war. Agreement on fundamental rules and institutions helps to account for the long-term stability of the United States and Great Britain. Where agreement is lacking, as in the question of the role of ethnic minorities, violence often results. In states where fundamental splits occur over whether there should be a single political community, as in Northern Ireland or Lebanon, socialization to different ethnic, religious, or national identities insures conflict and perpetuation of separate nationalisms. In the rare cases where several different groups and colonies joined together, as in the United States or Canada, it has been necessary to create a common community identification and to socialize people into accepting this identity. This identity provides the foundation upon which other, more specific, patterns of behavior are built.

CHILD SOCIALIZATION

By the time children enter high school they have acquired a vast amount of political and politically relevant information, ideas and attitudes. Informal politically relevant learning may begin as early as age two or three when children are forming their personalities and acquiring basic attitudes toward authority and rules. Ideas about law, justice, rules, government, and public roles develop long before children have any possibility of having an impact on politics. Childhood political learning is important because values and attitudes acquired at a tender age may last through a person's life. They may help condition a person's acceptance or rejection of institutions and values met in later life.

Logically there ought to be a link between childhood learning and adult attitudes and behavior. However, "the existing body of basic knowledge linking childhood experience and adult behavior is quite rudimentary."[19] We simply do not know the mechanism by which child socialization affects development of later policy orientations. At best we can say that child socialization does have some as yet unspecified impact on later issue orientations, and probably has a basic, but not controlling, influence on adult attitudes and values. It appears that the earliest values we acquire, especially loyalty and attachment, are the most deeply rooted and long lasting. Children learn political and social values uncritically. They do not usually have the necessary experience to see alternatives. Much childhood politically relevant learning is at the unconscious level, and people tend to

[19] Greenstein, *op. cit.,* p. 43. See also, Donald D. Searing, et al., "The Structuring Principle: Political Socialization and Belief Systems," *American Political Science Review,* 67 (June, 1973), pp. 415–32.

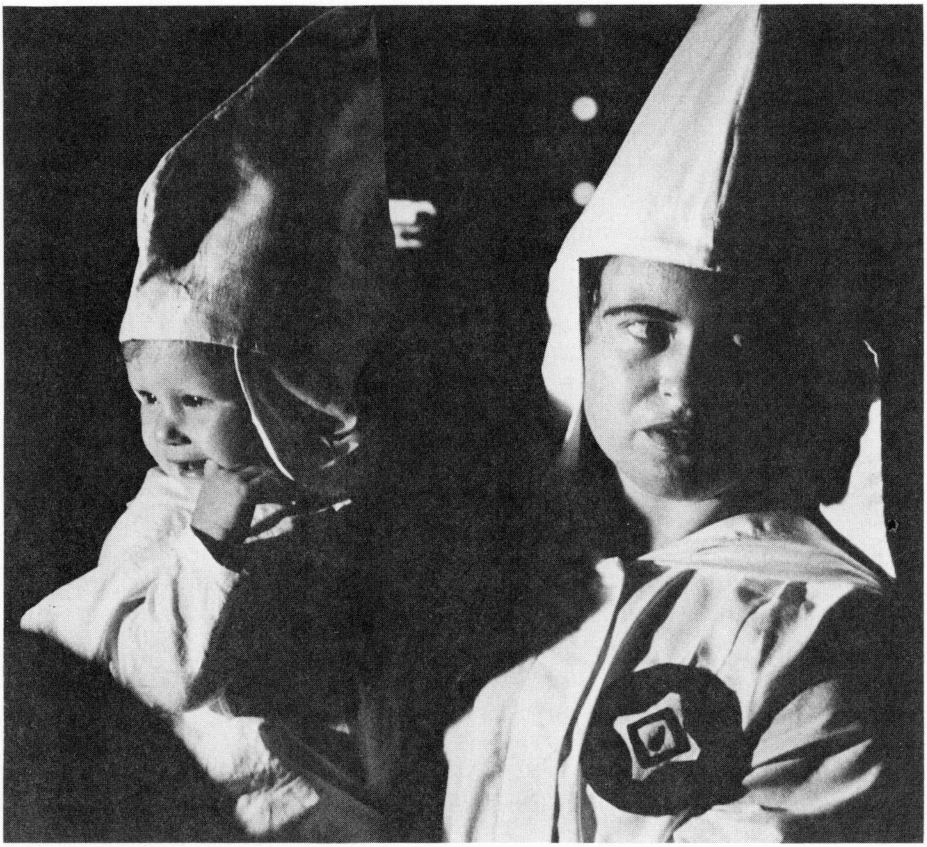

Mother and daughter at a Ku Klux Klan rally.

take it for granted. Thus, we may not be completely aware of why we hold a belief. Many people dislike or fear people of other races, but when challenged to give reasons often find it difficult or impossible to articulate their feelings. Their race attitudes were learned, perhaps informally, uncritically and unconsciously as children, and these early attitudes have often been reinforced, unquestioned, and unchallenged.

Moreover, early learning provides a framework for later learning. Early learning, or its lack, helps set foundations on which later learning may take place or build. Perhaps if we do not learn social cooperation as children, it would be difficult or impossible to learn it as adults. By a process called "psychologic," early learning also helps condition acceptance or rejection of later information and values. Most people systematically, if unconsciously, screen the flow of information and stimuli to themselves. Already accepted attitudes and values help determine whether we will accept or reject new information. If new information agrees with what we already believe, we may pay attention to it. If it disagrees with what we believe, we tend either to ignore it or to make it conform to our beliefs. Thus, our earliest acquired values, images, and attitudes screen out, ignore, or reinterpret values, images, and attitudes that are incompatible with our basic core set of values and attitudes. As we will note later, people do not block out discordant messages forever but may change their beliefs and values when these no longer correspond with reality. Nevertheless, the values and attitudes each of us learned as children help set up a screening framework through which we view institutions, people, and values we meet in later life.

Childhood learning is important, but we must ask, what is its content? Specific content will vary among political systems because political cultures vary. A child born in the People's Republic of China will be socialized to a set of duties and expectations about government different from those of a child in Canada or the United States.

Everywhere, childhood political socialization is a process of *mass socialization*. That is, it involves learning those common political attitudes, values, and behavior that are considered appropriate to the people of a particular political culture. This involves the behavior that "may be performed by the overwhelming majority of people."[20] Appropriate behavior varies among systems but always involves learning what will be expected from "typical" citizens in that system. One country may emphasize a citizen's right, even duty, to participate in selecting leaders or influencing decisions, while another may emphasize the citizen's duty to labor ceaselessly to build a strong nation or reach an ideological goal. Socialization to special roles, such as political behavior appropriate to a certain profession, or to an incumbent role (congressman or school board member) occurs later, usually during adulthood. Such socialization builds on, and often modifies, the mass socialization of childhood.

Political scientists have conducted more socialization studies in the United States than anywhere else. Although patterns of socialization are probably similar, especially in moving from personification of government to acceptance of abstract concepts, we will speak exclusively of the United States in the next few paragraphs.[21]

Initially, children probably conceive of their parents as all powerful. At about two years of age, they begin to become aware of a larger world out-

[20] Jaros, *op. cit.*, p. 27.

[21] This section on the United States is based on Greenstein, *op. cit.;* Jaros, *op. cit.;* and Hess and Torney, *op. cit.* See also, Robert D. Hess and David Easton, "The Role of the Elementary School in Political Socialization," *The School Review,* 70 (1962), pp. 257–65.

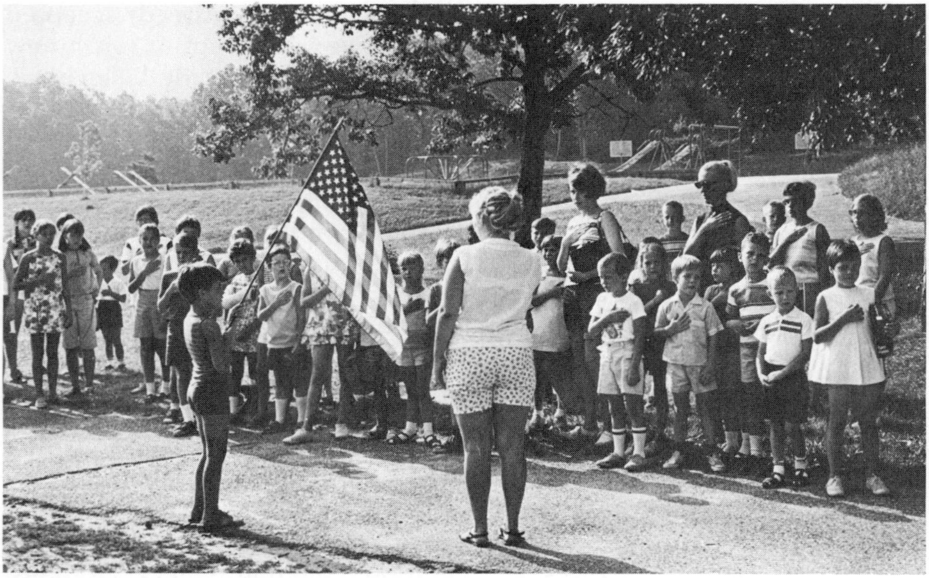

Pledging allegiance to the flag.

side their family and begin to realize this world impinges on their parents and themselves. By age four children are becoming aware of authority, such as traffic lights and perhaps policemen. Children first become aware of larger political institutions by learning the names of a few prominent officials and initially identify government with these officials. Children idealize these officials, thinking they are benevolent and personally helpful. This idealistic assumption about the still distant government encourages children to feel affection for the political system before they acquire information about it. Children also become aware of national symbols, such as the flag or Uncle Sam, before they know what the nation is. These symbols focus their affection on the nation. Cynicism about politics and politicians does not develop until adolescence or adulthood.[22]

In the United States the president is the official children are most familiar with and serves to introduce them to the American political system. Up to grade four, they identify the national government almost exclusively with him. If aware of Congress at all, they tend to assume that congressmen are the president's "helpers," and that it is wrong for them to oppose his

[22] For an argument that children's generally "highly positive views of politics may be a culturally bound phenomenon," see Dean Jaros et al., "The Malevolent Leader: Political Socialization in an American Sub-Culture," *American Political Science Review,* 62 (June, 1968), pp. 564–575.

policies. Though they do not understand who he is or what he does, they feel he is important, powerful, and personally interested in their welfare. They focus on his personal qualities, and only after age ten or so do they begin to distinguish the role of president from the personal qualities of the man. Some political scientists speculate that the young child's high regard for the president is the result of feelings of vulnerability in a world over which children have no control. The president becomes a kind of distant totem who will protect them from harm. In the process they may transfer feelings about authority and helpfulness from the family to this distant

Table I Changes by Grade in Perception of Source of Laws[a]

Grade level	N	Congress makes laws	President makes laws	Supreme Court makes laws	Don't know
2	1627	4.8%	75.6%	11.5%	8.2%
3	1648	11.4	66.1	17.0	5.5
4	1723	27.5	44.1	21.1	7.3
5	1793	57.4	19.4	19.8	3.4
6	1743	65.1	13.2	18.3	3.4
7	1712	72.1	8.9	16.4	2.6
8	1690	85.3	5.4	7.9	1.4
Teachers	384	96.4	.5	3.1	

Changes by Grade in Perception of "Who Runs the Country"[b]

Grade level	N	Congress runs country	President runs country	Supreme Court runs country	Don't know
2	1627	3.9%	86.3%	3.3%	6.5%
3	1662	6.7	85.4	3.1	4.7
4	1725	13.2	77.0	3.4	6.5
5	1796	20.0	71.8	3.8	4.3
6	1744	24.9	66.2	4.5	4.4
7	1711	27.8	64.0	5.3	2.9
8	1683	35.1	58.4	3.6	2.9
Teachers	383	61.4	35.8	3.0	

Source: Adapted from Robert D. Hess and Judith V. Torney, *The Development of Political Attitudes in Children* (Chicago, Aldine, Copyright © 1967, reprinted by permission of the publisher), p. 35. Data for this study were collected December, 1961, through May, 1962.

[a] *Note*—Item: Who makes the laws? Put an X next to the [picture of the] one who does most to make laws.

[b] *Note*—Item: Who does the most to run the country? Put an X in the box next to the [picture of the] one who does most to run the country.

political personage. As seen in Table I, the number of children who think the president makes the laws or runs the country decreases dramatically between the fourth and fifth grades. Children in this age group (9–13) make dramatic and rapid increases in knowledge about the political system's formal and institutional structure.

Acquisition of other attitudes and knowledge occurs at a later age. There may be an actual sequence. Initial development of political awareness is, as we have seen, first "attachment to the nation," followed by development of awareness of government officials and attachment to them. This is followed by a child's awareness of the legal system, his relation to it, and a tendency to equate obeying the law with good citizenship. The child's awareness that citizens may have an impact on political decisions and they, as individuals, may be in a position to influence public policy develops at a later age, generally after fifth or sixth grade.[23] Moreover, the young grade-school child tends to have an image of a conflict-free political world. School emphasizes voting in elections as the paramount citizen activity. Given children's initial expectations about benevolent government, it is often difficult to make them understand political processes or the need for participation. Schools tend to ignore both the conflict attendant upon political decision making and alternative ways through which people make their influence felt, such as political parties, interest groups, and use of personal influence based on wealth or position. Potentially more forceful means of influence, such as organized dissent or resistance, are usually not considered.

ADULT SOCIALIZATION

Political socialization continues throughout our entire lives. The political information and values people learn as children, even if they are the most important political learning, are only part of the adult's necessary intellectual equipment. This is particularly true in modern, dynamic societies where institutions, values, and problems are constantly changing. In relatively stable societies, such as early medieval Europe or some isolated parts of the world today, childhood socialization may be sufficient training for many adult roles and attitudes. Since little in the environment changes, few changes become necessary in people's understanding of, and values about, the political system. Yet even here, the content of socialization changes at different stages of the life-cycle. Even in less complex societies, adulthood may bring changes in status for which childhood socialization cannot prepare people. Even in simple societies, all of the skills necessary for handling adult roles cannot be learned during childhood.

[23] Hess and Torney, *op. cit.*, pp. 24 ff.

Changes in political learning appropriate to different age levels are complicated by other important factors. Modern societies are typified by rapid and frequent socioeconomic change. The values and beliefs people learn in childhood may not refer to any existent reality twenty or thirty years later. In nineteenth-century Europe and North America, people born on farms often had to move into new and frightening urban industries because of changes brought about by the industrial revolution. Here they painfully had to learn new work habits, new patterns of interaction between employer and employee, new family and neighbor relations, and often new political behavior. "Future shock" refers to a phenomenon more than a century old, but sums up the fact that information and values acquired during childhood may be inadequate to the new social, political, and economic realities of an altered world during adulthood.

Many other forces illustrate the need for continued adult socialization. Immigration from one country to another causes obvious environmental changes. Geographical mobility is a fact of life in most nations. Movement from one part of the country to another may place migrants in an entirely new social and political milieu. In the United States movement by a young professional from New York or Chicago to a small town in the Southeast or Midwest often involves movement from a socially permissive, politically liberal climate to one that tends toward political conservatism and conformity to dominant norms. Moreover, typical political participation may shift from interest group activities to personalist politics, emphasizing who you know and manipulation of the political system from within. Simply because different behavior is expected, individuals may feel constrained to modify their behavior in order to function effectively in their new environment. Students entering college also meet a new environment and new stimuli. Typically, these operate to move them in the direction of political liberalism, social permissiveness, acquisition of new political information and ways of viewing the political processes.

Economic and social mobility, either upward or downward, may bring about similar changes in an individual's milieu. These changes may also require readjustment to new values, institutions, and ways of doing things. Quite often a process of "anticipatory socialization" occurs. In anticipatory socialization people consciously try to acquire and emulate the values and attitudes of people who are in the class or occupation into which they are moving. In the United States large increases in salary and movement into the suburbs have often predated a switch from the Democratic Party to either the Republican Party or an independent orientation.

Role

So far we have discussed mass socialization. Acquisition of a specifically political role also entails new political learning. As noted in chapter 2, role refers to a recognized and usually defined social position about which fairly specific performance expectations are made, regardless of who holds that role. Roles can be separated from the person holding a role, and one person may hold many roles. We expect a fireman to perform his primary role—putting out fires—regardless of who he or she is. Often specific rules and a rigid organizational structure define a role, as in a bureaucracy. At other times general expectations, informal folkways, as well as some written rules, define a role, such as in a Legislature. People may acquire a specifically political role when they become involved in politics beyond the activities expected of a "typical" or "average" citizen. Election to office, such as a school board, a local governing body, or Congress; lobbying and other direct involvement in interest group activities; and efforts to affect public policy through personal influence or public protest are all examples of role playing of one sort or another.

Every role, political or nonpolitical, has rules and expectations attached to it. Each role involves learning these basic rules and behavior patterns, which are different from behavior learned through mass socialization. A freshman congressman must learn informal congressional procedures, approaches to other congressmen, times to keep quiet, and how to function in a rather small group of proud individuals if he or she is to have any chance of being effective. It is also possible that learning other nonpolitical adult roles—employer, employee, or parent—may affect political or politically relevant information and values. Such socialization occurs only when the individual is actually in a particular role. It is difficult to learn outside the role, and impossible that such role behavior could be learned during childhood.

AGENTS OF SOCIALIZATION

Numerous agents and events, as well as individual character, contribute to political socialization. There is no agreement about which agent is most important. The impact of different agents varies during an individual's life and also varies according to "the political and cultural milieu in which it operates."[24] In relatively simple, stable systems, the family may be the most important agent of socialization. In societies undergoing rapid change, where traditional or family values conflict with officially approved developmental values, schools may become the major socialization agents. In situations of extreme stress, a political party or religious group may become an important agent of resocialization. Mass media may become increasingly important in homogenizing socialization stimuli. These agents interact, pro-

[24] Kenneth P. Langton and David A. Karns, "Political Socialization and National Development: Some Hypotheses and Data," *Western Political Quarterly,* 27 (June, 1974), pp. 217–238.

ducing a cumulative effect when they agree, producing confusion when they disagree.

Many people expect political socialization to cause political–social–economic–cultural change, as well as stability. This results in conscious efforts to modify socialization agents in a desired direction. Because so many agents are involved and the process of socialization is so complex, it may be difficult to change complicated phenomena such as race and sex attitudes by manipulating only one socialization agent. For example, introducing women's studies in universities will not eradicate sexism since universities are neither dominant nor pervasive agents of socialization; removing violence from Saturday morning TV cartoons may have little influence in socializing children to nonviolence if they are exposed to it in other areas. Modification of all agents, particularly in a reasonably open, pluralistic society, is extremely difficult without either extensive voluntary compliance or force. Therefore, changing any one agent may not produce desired results in the short run. Moveover, any agent's influence may be modified by different generational, class, sex, or subcultural experiences.

The Family

For thousands of years students of politics considered the family the incubator of political man. They assumed that families provided the initial and longest lasting political–social education, and therefore, they must be concerned with family values as the first step toward their preferred political systems. Increasingly in the last two centuries other influences have competed with the family, introducing children to information, values, and ideas different from those inculcated within the family. In many instances this has created painful cross-pressures in which people are torn in different directions. "Generation gap," conflict over values, may result from these cross-pressures. Nevertheless, the family is extremely important.

Our first political and politically relevant learning occurs within the family. Most of this learning is informal, unintentional, and often subconscious. Families initially provide everything necessary for a child to survive and grow—food, shelter, affection, social interaction.[25] Because of this, families influence basic personality development and have great influence on acquisition of nonpolitical but politically relevant values. Thus, children's basic personality orientation, such as capacity for trust and cooperation, receives its initial development within the family. Politically relevant ideas and values, such as proper conduct or orientation to authority, rules, and obedience, also develop within the family. Certain family characteristics, such as a hierarchical, authoritarian family structure,

[25] James C. Davies, "The Family's Role in Political Socialization" *Annals of the American Academy of Political and Social Science,* 361 (September, 1965), pp. 10–19.

may dispose people to obedience of authority figures and a tendency to tyrannize those they consider inferior.

Different family structures may encourage different kinds of expectations about the rest of the world. Thus, families that encourage child participation in family decisions seem to encourage these children to participate in politics when they are adults. Children of politically active parents tend to be more active as adults. This is probably the result of children copying their parents, of transmission of some values to children, and of an enriched environment where awareness of political, social, and economic events is considered normal. Children whose parents deprecate political involvement or rarely discuss political, social, and economic events have few parental examples and less encouragement to participate themselves. Consequently, they tend as adults to be less involved in politics.

Families have a much smaller impact on specifically political values.[26] A child's affection for the nation develops within the family. General attitudes toward other races also develop within the family. However, adult political opinions on specific issues have little measurable correlation with childhood experiences and learning. With the sole exception of party orientation or preference, parental attitudes have little or no direct influence on a child's later adult political opinions. In the United States, Great Britain, and probably in other states with stable party systems, there is a high probability (on the order of 70 percent) that if both parents prefer the same political party, the child will prefer the same party when he or she becomes an adult. Children in second and third grade "know" if they are Democrats or Republicans, Labourites or Conservatives, before they know what these labels refer to. Parents transfer their party preference for a number of reasons. In these countries parties tend to be stable over time and limited in number. As adult voters children face the same party choices as did their parents. Party identification is also simple. In most states it does not require any activity to be a party identifier, and therefore, little conscious choice. Schools do not teach preference for a particular party. In fact, they usually discourage it, so that the parents' preference is dominant during the child's formative years. Moreover, party preference, as with religious preference, is part of the child's accepted milieu. As with so many things we accept uncritically, because learned informally or unconsciously, party preference is acquired before children develop the tools to distinguish different programs or purposes. Many other factors, such as adult experiences, affect party preference, but the family is the most important influence in this area.

None of these reasons operates for specific issue orientations. A child may not be aware of his or her parents' specific preferences on most public

[26] See especially R. W. Connell, "Political Socialization in the American Family: The Evidence Re-Examined," *Public Opinion Quarterly,* 36 (1972), pp. 323–33.

issues. In a dynamic society there are numerous rapidly changing issues and parents and children may not be aware of many of them. Issues may be radically different from those during childhood. One generation's experience with war and inflation may be different from an older generation's experiences with war and economic problems. Unlike choice between two or three parties, there may be an almost infinite range of choices on policy issues. Moreover, many different forces—job, the mass media, friends—influence how we view issues and what information we receive about issues. Therefore, while the family is extremely important in personality development, creation of politically relevant attitudes and, in some countries, party identification, it has much less impact on development of particular issue preferences.

Schools

Though a great deal of informal and unconscious learning occurs in school, the school political socialization process is much more formal, conscious, and intentional than the family process. Schools are conscious societal instruments for transmission of desired values, information, and norms. In terms of helping people acquire necessary political–social tools, in terms of insuring intergenerational continuity, and in terms of providing a forum for value change, schools are among the most important socialization agents. They reinforce other agents while directly contributing to socialization. In adult life, level of education is highly correlated with political participation. In terms of transmitting political information and values, and in developing politically relevant skills, schools have a greater impact than the family. They may serve to overcome some student differences that result from family differences by socializing children to a common citizenship behavior norm. By the time they reach high school, most children in Europe and North America have a fairly clear idea of the formal institutional structure of their political systems and of what citizen roles will be expected of them as adults.

The content of school political socialization is important. Cognitive socialization, toward understanding of the formal structures of society, is very common. This includes how the system operates and who the major figures are. Most schools in the United States ignore the informal aspects of political power. Political parties and interest groups are also usually ignored. Schools in most countries emphasize social interaction, learning, and complying with rules and authority, and do not introduce critical and participatory norms until the upper grades, if at all.

Affective socialization is also an extremely important part of school. "The schools reinforce the early attachment of the child to the nation."[27] Particularly in the first five or six grades, they do this through learning of

[27] Hess and Torney, *op. cit.*, p. 105.

patriotic songs, recitation of pledges of allegiance, emphasis on historical figures, and concentration on historically important buildings, as well as by placing children in an environment that emphasizes their relation to, dependence upon, and duty toward society and the political system. Schools do a much better job of transmitting generalized attitudes such as patriotism and mass citizen duties, for which there is general social support, than of transmitting attitudes about specific issues.

Given their importance, schools have always been major concerns of political systems. Though most western societies are dedicated to depoliticizing their schools, this occurs only when there is widespread agreement over the content of the political values schools are expected to teach. When that agreement breaks down schools have everywhere become involved in political controversy. Schools were a major target for governmental control in Nazi Germany and, after World War II, for efforts to erase Nazism.

In the United States schools have again and again become centers of controversy over whether they were teaching proper American values. In the 1950s schools and teachers were subjected to harassment to "insure" that "communism" and "communists" were not influencing American children. In the 1950s and 1960s many white parents tried to form separate schools, to insure that their ideas about race and racial relations would be passed on to their children. The schools have remained a battleground in the 1970s. Issues such as the busing of children to achieve racial balance illustrate the use to which schools may be put to achieve such social and political goals as equality. Demands for decentralization and for local control over school decision making reveal widespread appreciation of the impact of schools on value transmission. In 1974 and 1975, in Kanawha County, West Virginia, violence broke out over school textbooks. Many parents felt that approved books contained anti-Christian, anti-American, and obscene material. Concerned with maintaining their value system, many were willing to keep their children out of school rather than subject them to what they considered undesirable influences.

In many parts of the world schools have become battlegrounds, as linguistic, cultural, and religious groups seek to control and use them to maintain their special values or separate identities. Everywhere schools transmit information and values. Either to reinforce or change these values, parents and political leaders are concerned with the content of what schools teach, because that content will be an important factor in determining how the next generation will think, feel, and act.

Peer Groups

Peer groups refer to clusters of people with similar status and often similar interests. On an informal basis children and adults learn a great deal from their peers. By frequent interaction they learn other people's values and ideas. If peer contact is homogeneous and stable, people may modify their values and behavior to suit those of the people with whom they interact. If a person interacts with many different groups, he or she may not receive consistent reinforcement and therefore may not conform to the standards of one group. Peer group contact may be very important when there are generational conflicts or very different experiences between groups or generations. Politically, peer group contact is important if peer groups (Boy Scouts, Girl Scouts, etc.) reinforce dominant political–social values. It also becomes important when peer groups take on aspects of a subculture. Then people, especially the young, may develop alternative values, even life-styles. Much of the college-level opposition to American involvement in Southeast Asia in the 1960s and early 1970s grew out of extensive peer group contact in an essentially age-group-isolated environment.

Mass Media

Ever since the invention of printing opened the possibility of communicating a message to large numbers of people, the mass media have had an increasingly important impact on politics and political socialization. In the eighteenth and early nineteenth centuries the spread of cheap periodicals opened increasingly literate middle and working classes to influences from outside their immediate environments, and helped make mass participation, as well as manipulation of the masses, possible. About the turn of this century movies made it possible to present complex visual images, and by the early 1920s radio made it possible to simultaneously convey the same message to millions. Today television makes it possible to present complex messages to tens of millions. In the United States children start to view television at about age two. In the primary grades children watch an average of 15 to 25 hours of television a week, with the number of hours tapering off in high school. By age 18 the average American child will have spent more hours watching television than in the classroom.[28] The important question is, what impact does this have?

We do not yet clearly understand television's impact on political socialization, and there is a great deal of controversy over this question. If television were completely controlled by government and presented a single-minded partisan message, measurement of television's impact would be relatively easy. But in most reasonably democratic states this is not the case. In most Western states television seems to have an impact largely in terms of informal learning, often subconsciously, of politically relevant attitudes, rather than on acquisition of political information and values. This

[28] Robert M. Liebert, et al., *The Early Window: Effects of Television on Children and Youth* (New York: Pergamon Press, 1973), pp. x, xv, 9.

is true despite television's unequalled potential for influencing people through new information or through presentation of different value systems. Nevertheless, television can have a direct impact on mass political socialization if it presents a consistent message, particularly one that is at variance with messages from other agents. Increased cynicism and disillusionment among young Americans may be directly attributable to the impact of seeing and hearing the Vietnam war and the Watergate scandals on television. Vietnam and Watergate have helped to cause a significant decrease in support for the United States because of their revelation of practices so at odds with much of the value system implied in the American socialization process.

Much of television's impact is informal and indirect. This is illustrated by the ongoing argument over the effects of television violence on children. Children learn a great deal by observing adult behavior. Young children may not be able to distinguish fantasy from reality. Also, they are continually bombarded with examples of violence, pain, and injury. It becomes an important part of entertainment, raising the unanswered question of whether constant viewing of violence affects our emotions. More importantly, a constant diet of violence, particularly where it seems to teach that the "good guys" may use violence, deceit, torture, and clandestine activities to obtain their ends, may be breaking down the barriers to social and political violence. If television shows imply that it is legitimate to break laws, intervene in other states, and commit other crimes in order to maintain or get desired results, then they may be teaching a new generation that "might makes right."

Current research indicates that the answer may be yes to these questions. Television "does more than entertain us and our children; it communicates information about ourselves, others, and the world at large."[29] Information and images about social roles are very important, especially if these foster values inimical to political participation. In its early years television tended to perpetuate racial stereotypes, by emphasizing white, middle-class professionals, though this is slowly changing as a result of pressure from civil rights' groups who are concerned with white people's views of racial minorities and also with the self-image of members of minorities themselves. Until quite recently television also perpetuated stereotypes of women and women's roles in society. Under pressure from such groups as NOW (National Organization of Women) stereotypes that portray women as passive and uninvolved are slowly disappearing. Nevertheless, many commercials continue to portray women as happy, but usually simple, even dumb, housewives. Women are also conspicuously absent from roles involving real intelligence. One might also ask if television ads perpetuate acquisitive values. Though not directly political, such values may have an impact on cooperation and willingness to be taxed for common social programs.

[29] *Ibid.*, pp. 18–9 ff.

Television can have a positive and rewarding impact. It can teach cooperation as well as violence. It can open new worlds of information, experiences, and emotion. By bringing inflation, starvation, and war into our homes, it can make us aware of our finite world and increasing interdependence. All of these effects are potential. As with schools, much of the present controversy over television is over whose values it will present. Whose picture of reality will be dominant? As with schools, that question involves more than temporary partisan advantage. It involves rival images of our future world, because it contains disagreement over the values and information we want children to learn.

On a purely political level television's impact is hard to measure. The average voter has more information than at any time in history, but television has not encouraged a larger number of people to vote. Television has, however, changed our image of politics, and by changing our image may be changing what people learn to expect from politics. Television image building and the need to quickly present complex issues encourage simple alternatives. Television usually does not put a premium on careful analysis and explanation of long-standing problems. It may also change what we expect politicians to look like and do. The first Kennedy–Nixon televised debate in 1960 helped Kennedy, because many people concluded that he looked better and fresher.

Television also focuses on the more spectacular aspects of politics, such as national conventions, wars, and summit conferences, and obscures the day-to-day activities of regulatory agencies, local politics, interest group activities, compromise and consensus building that make government possible. This focus may encourage feelings of being a spectator only, while at the same time "teaching" some groups that the way to instant recognition is through an action that will get them national news coverage. Moreover, television may help to create new political demands, by illustrating alternatives, portraying some kinds of political–social behavior, while ignoring others, and by focusing on a few highly visible people, such as presidents and prime ministers, to the exclusion of the majority of people involved in government. Television's exact impact is unknown. It is, however, changing our image of the world, and that makes it important to students of political socialization.

Trauma and Change[30]

Trauma and generalized changes may produce a dichotomy between values and the institutions that embody and support them. Old values seem no longer to fit altered situations. New institutions or new practices seem to undermine or discredit long-established values. War, depression, revolu-

[30] See Jaros, *op. cit.*, pp. 64 ff. See also, Arthur H. Miller, "Political Issues and Trust in Government," *American Political Science Review,* 68 (September, 1974), pp. 951–72.

tion, immigration, and major changes in government are all obvious agents that have an impact on the world and people's image of it. Each of these may force a change in values and institutions. They affect political socialization by forcing changes in established attitudes or by introducing new content into the political socialization process. Other types of change are less obvious. Despite the most elaborate socialization processes, intergenerational change is common in active, vital societies. Each generation, and these may be as short as five years in rapidly changing societies, experiences new events that condition its perception of the validity of older values and institutions, or whether institutions should be changed to conform to dominant values. Experience with economic hardship, especially at a fairly young age, may permanently shift people's loyalty to the party they perceive as eliminating that hardship. Such experience may also lead to emphasis on security from want, perhaps materialism, which a later generation, not knowing hunger, would decry. Experience in war may confirm one generation's belief in its political values, as in World War II. It may shake another generation's beliefs, as in Vietnam, because of the lack of congruence between "defense" of those values and war aims.

In the United States today many people seem to feel that the American system has somehow failed. Systematic government lying about foreign policy; massive resistance to government over civil rights, by both civil rights' supporters and opponents; assassination; and discovery of domestic poverty disillusioned many people in the 1960s. Economic crises in the 1970s are undermining faith in every government and are providing new lessons about government and mutual interdependence. These repeated crises produce fear, disillusionment, and cynicism in people experiencing them. If these feelings or events are intense enough, as in revolution, they may cause a permanent change in political values, institutions, and socialization to these.

THE NONUNIFORMITY OF POLITICAL SOCIALIZATION

In distinguishing types of political socialization—mass socialization from role socialization, child socialization from adult socialization, and the different socialization agents we have indicated that socialization is not an uniform process, even within the same political system. Even if the agents of socialization could operate uniformly on people, individual and environmental variations would produce different results. Despite many shared values, there are significant sources of variation in any political culture which socialize people differently.

Individual Differences

Individual characteristics help determine people's absorption of and response to the socialization process. People are not passive receivers.

Rather, they select, reject, and modify external stimuli. Personality is one such individual difference. We do not fully understand the complex relation between personality and behavior. Nevertheless, people react differently to the same stimuli, and it becomes necessary to explain why in terms of personality. Despite the fact that personality is formed through socialization, once developed, personality has an independent effect on political values, attitudes, and behavior. Different personalities lead people to perceive and respond to the world differently. A confident, open, and cooperative person may view politics as an opportunity and be able to participate easily. A more fearful, closed personality, seeking hierarchy, rigidity, and specific guidelines and rules for interpersonal activities, may feel threatened by an open political process. People who have been taught that they are significant are more likely to participate than are those who have been continually taught they are inferior or should only obey. Different personal needs may also determine people's responses, leading some to demand government protection, others to downgrade it.

Intelligence appears to be a very significant individual difference. Among American children, intelligence, in all social classes, accelerates acquisition of political information and attitudes. More intelligent children find it easier to conceive of politics as a system or set of institutions, rather than as people. This may be the result of a greater facility to abstract. Children with high intelligence appear to have a greater feeling of political efficacy and appear more willing to participate.[31] Greater intelligence may allow a person to see more opportunities for manipulation of politics, or can lead to despair at the complexity of politics. It can encourage people to see their roles clearly, or can encourage antisocial feelings of superiority. Despite our inability to adequately define intelligence, and despite the fact that most intelligence tests measure the ability to take tests, intelligence seems to be a significant variable in determining how people view the world and how they respond to it.

Sex[32]

Intelligence seems to be mainly an individual attribute affecting socialization. Sex and race, while individual, are socially defined. Attitudes toward sex and race are examples of generalized cultural values which, while not usually specifically political in content, affect the content of political socialization and nature and direction of political participation. Everywhere, women participate less in politics than do men, even though this gap is closing in some Western countries under pressure from organized women's groups. Despite similar formal education and despite

[31] Hess and Torney, *op. cit.*, pp. 128 ff.

[32] See Susan C. Bourque and Jean Grossholtz, "Politics an Unnatural Practice: Political Science Looks at Female Participation," *Politics and Society*, 4 (Winter, 1974), pp. 225–66.

similar *formal* political values, women are subject to a variety of informal and often unconscious pressures that push them into politically nonactive roles. These pressures include widespread attitudes that assume women should be passive, occupational roles that are not politically oriented, and attitudes that politics is a male prerogative. This, in turn, has tended to exclude women from politics by blocking their access to political roles.

Thus, the lower rate of participation by women can only be explained in terms of political culture. Men and women are socialized to expect lower participation from women, and act to fulfill these expectations. Changes in attitudes held by men and women, as well as institutional changes to encourage greater participation, can reduce these differences.

Other Factors

Race affects politics and political socialization because of attitudes toward minority participation in dominant racial and ethnic groups. The impact of race is beyond our study. Suffice it to say that in most countries easily identifiable racial and ethnic minorities often develop, or have imposed upon them, different views of the world and their place in it. Attitudes and values about political participation differ, because the real life opportunities of different racial and ethnic groups differ. This in turn is often a reflection of the attitudes and activities of dominant groups. Even if the formal socialization process is the same, children of different races—in the same political system—may learn different values and expectations because of informal learning and attitudes expressed outside the formal socialization process.

Many other factors affect political socialization. Class membership varies in impact among different political cultures, though class differences everywhere affect the rate and direction of political participation, and different family patterns affect acquisition of politically relevant values. Socioeconomic class modifies and structures people's experience with law, police, and the political system; therefore, it affects their political learning. The same thing is true of membership in different subcultures. Many groups develop peculiar cultural patterns that distinguish them from the dominant political culture, while still sharing many common values with it. Racial, cultural, linguistic, religious, and economic groups all may be subcultures. The thing they share in common, as distinct from the rest of society, affects their view of the larger society, and how the larger society views them. This in turn may affect the nature and rate of value, information, and attitude formation/acquisition.

Summary

Political socialization is part of the ongoing political struggle and political processes in every society. Throughout history governments and important groups have considered it too important to leave to chance. Political culture and political socialization help provide a common value system, common assumptions, and common attitudes about proper political behavior within specific political systems. In providing a common framework within which people of a particular political system can function, they make organized political life possible. Nevertheless, political culture and political socialization are not uniform within the political system. While they provide the common framework for political activity, important differences exist. Intergenerational changes, different agents, and different cultural patterns all work to make political socialization an uneven process. Even though political socialization tends toward maintenance of the status quo, enough variation occurs to insure political–social change. Whether this change is conscious or not, in our contemporary world political culture and political socialization are not static. Rather, they are in a state of constant flux, affecting our perceptions of politics and the operations of every political system.

Selected Readings

Students of political culture examine the cultural–political–social–economic environments within which socialization occurs. Donald J. Devine, *The Political Culture of the United States: The Influence of Member Values on Regime Maintenance* (Boston: Little, Brown, 1972) examines the relation between political culture and politics in the United States. The opening chapter is a superb introduction to the study of political culture. For a thorough discussion of political culture, see chapter one of Gabriel A. Almond and Sidney Verba, *The Civic Culture* (Princeton: Princeton University Press, 1963). This book analyzes the interrelation between political culture and participation in the United States, Great Britain, Germany, Italy, and Mexico, and is virtually mandatory reading for more advanced, serious students of politics. Lucian W. Pye and Sidney Verba, eds., *Political Culture and Political Development* (Princeton: Princeton University Press, 1965) is both a summary of the concept of political culture and studies of political culture in eleven nations. Each chapter is a separate study around the common theme of the interrelation of political culture, development of national consciousness, and political development.

Dean Jaros, *Socialization to Politics* (New York: Praeger, 1973) is a basic introduction to political socialization, covering most of the topics in this chapter. A very readable book, this is a good place for students to begin their further study of political socialization. Fred I. Greenstein, *Children and Politics* (New Haven: Yale University Press, 1965) is a basic study of the sources and content of childhood socialization in the United States. Pay particular attention to chapter four, which discusses the development of political information and attitudes. Richard E. Dawson and Kenneth Prewitt, *Political Socialization** (Boston: Little, Brown, 1969) is an analysis of most of the topics discussed in this chapter, including political culture. This book is also a good starting point for further reading. Roberta S. Sigel, *Learning About Politics: A Reader in Political Socialization* (New York: Random House, 1970) is a collection of articles and excerpts dealing with political socialization from a comparative perspective. This is a good basic book for further reading. Charles F. Andrain, *Children and Civic Awareness* (Columbus, Ohio: Charles E. Merrill, 1971) is an empirical study of fifth- through eighth-grade children's political values and information, set within a framework of how children learn about politics. Herbert H. Hyman, *Political Socialization** (New York, Free Press, 1959) is the first modern, full-scale treatment of political learning as a part of political science, summarizing research from other disciplines and concerns as relevant to political analysis. Edward S. Greenberg, ed., *Political Socialization* (New York: Atherton, 1970) is a collection of eight major readings, analyzing socialization in both dominant and subcultural settings in the United States. Greenberg's introduction critically discusses political socialization studies. "Political Socialization: Its Role in the Political Process" is the topic of *Annals of the American Academy of Political and Social Science,* 361 (September, 1965). This important issue includes discussions of the family, education, children's images of government, impact of socialization on personality, and black socialization. One of the most thorough studies into the sources, process, and content of childhood political socialization in the United States is Robert D. Hess and Judith V. Torney, *The Development of Political Attitudes in Children* (Chicago: Aldine, 1967). Based on a study of 12,000 grade school children, this book examines both the development and content of basic political attitudes among American children.

Political socialization is part of the political process, and is analyzed as such by David Easton and Jack Dennis, *Children in the Political System: Origins of Political Legitimacy* (New York: McGraw-Hill, 1969). Jack Dennis, ed., *Socialization to Politics: A Reader* (New York: John Wiley, 1973) is a collection of articles and excerpts covering most of the questions dealt with in this chapter. Kenneth P. Langton, *Political Socialization* (New York: Oxford University Press, 1969) is a cross-cultural analysis of the agents of political socialization. Richard W. Wilson, *Learning to Be Chinese: The Political Socialization of Children in Taiwan* (Cambridge, Mass.: MIT Press, 1970) analyzes the mechanisms of childhood political socialization in Taiwan.

* Available in paperback.

For a brief but insightful discussion of the criticisms and shortcomings of current political socialization research, see Fred I. Greenstein "A Note on the Ambiguity of 'Political Socialization': Definitions, Criticisms, and Strategies of Inquiry," *Journal of Politics,* 32 (1970), pp. 969–78. Susan C. Bourque and Jean Grossholtz, "Politics an Unnatural Practice: Political Science Looks at Female Participation," *Politics and Society,* 4 (1974), pp. 225–66, is a critical analysis of the biases against women that the authors find in political socialization literature. Finding few differences in political attitudes between men and women, the authors call for a reassessment and rejection of assumptions that explain differences in male–female political participation in terms of attitudes.

One of the most controversial political issues in socialization is the impact of television on children. For an excellent summary of research and findings on television's probable effects on American children, see Robert M. Liebert, John M. Neale, and Emily S. Davidson, *The Early Window: Effects of Television on Children and Youths* (New York: Pergamon Press, 1973). For a brief discussion, with specific policy recommendations, see "Violence in Television Entertainment Programs," Chapter 8 in National Commission on the Causes and Prevention of Violence, *To Establish Justice, To Insure Domestic Tranquility, Final Report* (Washington: U.S. Government Printing Office, 1969). *Television and Social Behavior,* 5 vols. of *A Technical Report to the Surgeon General's Scientific Advisory Committee on Television and Social Behavior* (Rockville, Md.: National Institute of Mental Health, 1972) extends beyond our discussion of political socialization, but is a fundamental resource for studying television's impact.

Does the impact of various socialization agents change under different socioeconomic conditions? Kenneth P. Langton and David A. Karns, "Political Socialization and National Development: Some Hypotheses and Data," *Western Political Quarterly,* 27 (1974), pp. 217–38, answer yes. Orville G. Brim, Jr., and Stanton Wheeler, *Socialization after Childhood: Two Essays* (New York: John Wiley, 1966), particularly in Part 1, emphasize that socialization does not end with childhood, but continues throughout each person's life. This is especially true of role socialization in dynamic societies. The following two articles illustrate the need to distinguish between general attitudes and specific political beliefs in discussing political socialization. Many, if not most, students of political socialization assume that the family is the most important socialization agent. R. W. Connell, "Political Socialization in the American Family: the Evidence Re-Examined," *Public Opinion Quarterly,* 36 (1972), pp. 323–33, disputes that belief, claiming that the family, with the exception of political party preference, is "largely irrelevant to the formation of specific opinions" about politics. Both politicians and students of political socialization often assume there is a correlation between childhood values and adult political beliefs. Donald D. Searing, Joel J. Schwartz, and Alden E. Lind, "The Structuring Principle: Political Socialization and Belief Systems," *American Political Science Review,* 67 (1973), pp. 415–32, claim that childhood orientations may not be associated with beliefs on specific political issues.

Throughout history political writers and theorists have discussed the importance of proper education to their ideal societies. Plato, *The Republic** (many editions) is one of the earliest and most influential efforts to create an educational system capable of insuring the proper relation between men and men, and man and the universe. Aristotle, *Ethics,* Books I, II, and III,* and *Politics,* Books VII and VIII* examine the relation of ethnics and education to the good life in the political community. Thomas Jefferson often discussed the need for a widespread system of education to train citizens of a free republic. For analyses of Jefferson's ideas and selections from his writing on education, see Roy J. Honeywell, *The Education Work of Thomas Jefferson* (New York: Russell and Russell, 1964); Gordon C. Lee, *Crusade Against Ignorance: Thomas Jefferson on Education* (New York: Teachers College Press, 1961); Charles Flinn Arrowood, *Thomas Jefferson and Education in a Republic* (New York: McGraw-Hill, 1930). Jean-Jacques Rousseau wrote extensively about the need to properly educate people to freedom and citizenship. See especially his *Emile* (1762),* though large parts of *The Social Contract* (1762)* and his *Considerations Concerning the Government of Poland* (1773, pub. in 1782)* reveal his idea of the relation between education and the political system. John Stuart Mill was shaped by his father's concept of a rigorous education capable of producing a liberal utilitarian. See his *Autobiography* (1873)* and his "Inaugural Address at the University of St. Andrews" (1867),* which set out Mill's general educational philosophy; both are conveniently brought together in Francis W. Garforth, *John Stuart Mill on Education* (New York: Teachers College Press, 1971).

* Available in paperback.

Chapter 5

Political Parties and Interest Groups

Political Parties in the Contemporary World

One of the more succinct definitions of democracy states:

> *Democracy exists where the principal leaders of a political system are selected by competitive elections in which the bulk of the population have the opportunity to participate.*[1]

A democratic political system cannot exist without political parties. The virtues of popular participation have been debated and fought over since at least the fourth century B.C., when Plato and Aristotle were writing as the Greek city-state system collapsed. It is only in the last two hundred years, though, that some variation of democracy has emerged in more than a handful of countries. When the opinions and desires of a substantial number of citizens began to be taken into account by the political elite—either because of philosophical commitment or practical necessity—political parties were organized. Parties brought organization to mass participation, and were originally organized to win popular support. Enfranchisement was a relatively slow process during the nineteenth century, but the pace increased in this century. In the American presidential elections of 1824, for example, when blacks and women were not permitted to vote and tax and property qualifications still existed in many states, 3.8 percent of the

[1] Samuel P. Huntington and Clement H. Moore, "Conclusion: Authoritarianism, Democracy, and One-Party Politics" in Huntington and Moore, eds., *Authoritarian Politics in Modern Society* (New York: Basic Books, 1970), p. 509.

total population voted.[2] A mere 1.1 percent of the Japanese population was eligible to vote in the first national election held in 1890; subsequent lowering of the tax qualification meant that by 1920 the eligible electorate represented 5.49 percent of Japan's population.[3]

Political parties in a pluralistic system are ultimately based on the assumption that over the long run they are the institution most able to provide the maximum opportunity for popular influence on government. This is done by making it possible for the majority of adults to vote in free and competitive elections. The ultimate justification of a competitive party system is that it is the most effective means by which large numbers of people can have a voice in choosing political leaders and in providing some direction to the policies enacted and enforced by the governing authorities.

Many political scientists over the last three decades have averred that the most important institution in a democracy is the political party:

> *Political parties created democracy and . . . modern democracy is unthinkable save in terms of the parties. As a matter of fact, the condition of the parties is the best possible evidence of the nature of any regime.*[4]

Democratic Political Parties Defined

A political party in a democracy is a group of voters organized for the purposes of nominating and electing candidates legally to public office in order to influence and/or control personnel and policy. A party is distinguished from an interest group in that a party nominates candidates for public office. Candidates who win are willing to assume responsibility for the conduct of public affairs generally and do not limit their activities to a few issues such as gun-control legislation, conservation, pollution control, etc.

Even if a party wins few electoral victories, it still may have an impact on the political system and attract loyal supporters and members. In the United States, for example, third parties often act as "issue-finders" for major parties. Norman Thomas, the highly respected and leading American socialist of the century, on numerous occasions wryly observed that though the Socialist Party of America never won an election, many socialist proposals such as minimum wage laws, unemployment compensation, and a separate Department of Labor were enacted by the Democrats and Republicans several decades after they were first proposed by the socialists.

Democratic political parties that enjoy some electoral successes are

[2] Robert Lane, *Political Life* (Glencoe, Ill., Free Press, 1959), p. 19.

[3] Chitoshi Yanaga, *Japanese People and Politics* (New York: John Wiley, 1956), pp. 281–82.

[4] E. E. Schattschneider, *Party Government* (New York: Rinehart & Co., 1942), p. 1.

The 1975 Congress of the Portuguese Central Democratic Socialist Party.

characterized by most of the following features, though no party exhibits every trait or performs each function in a similar way:

Organization

1. Associations of leaders and members seeking to win control of and/or influence government decisions.
2. Local organizations, committees, or branches which maintain some relationship (communication, provide election workers, etc.) with the central headquarters. The organization may be highly centralized or decentralized as in the United States.
3. Institutionalization or permanency of the party organization, which can only occur after there is some means by which party leaders can succeed one another. A new group or generation of leaders replaces the founding members and the party continues to operate under the new leadership.

4. Legal institutions in part constrained by government regulations, in part influenced by the party's own-by-laws and the customs and traditions of the political culture.

Activities

5. Electioneering and mobilizing popular support in order to win elective offices.
6. Combining and balancing the views of receptive interest groups and then articulating policy commitments in order to maintain and expand electoral and financial support for the party, and sometimes manufacturing or blurring issues.
7. Simplifying and structuring the issues so as to obtain the public's attention and support. Some parties even have their own daily newspaper.
8. Establishing itself as a symbol in the minds of people (or a reference group), which provides the typical voter with a means to orient himself to the complex political collage of issues, personalities, and appeals. (Reference groups are groups that are important in a person's thinking. They may evoke positive or negative responses. A person need not be a member of a group even though he positively identifies with it.)
9. Influence the organization of government (personnel) and participate in and influence policy formation.
10. Numerous other functions, some of which are discussed later in the chapter: legitimizing the political system; stabilizing the political system by providing an organization through which the more vocal and compelling claims can influence government (integrating individuals and groups into the political system through participation and avoiding massive alienation, which could lead to sustained violence); acting as a two-way communication process between decision makers and the average citizen outside the more inflexible and impersonal bureaucratic channels; contributing to the orderly succession of political leadership; and recruiting or providing an avenue by which ambitious persons can achieve political elite status.

The ten points listed above describe the democratically oriented party, which competes for popular support against groups holding divergent opinions and which supports constitutional arrangements that guarantee continued political competition. There are, however, organizations—commonly described as political parties—that are dedicated to the overthrow of a political system and will eliminate competitive elections once they have acquired power, either by working through the electoral system (the Nazi party at the end of the German Weimar Republic, 1933) or by working outside the existing system (the Bolsheviks in the 1917 Russian Revolution). If

May Day parade in Prague, Czechoslovakia, 1970.

these parties are tolerated, as the Nazis were in Weimar Germany (1918–1933), they will adopt electoral strategies designed to disorient and cripple the political system. In the declining years of the Weimar Republic, as Depression conditions compounded the ineffectiveness of some of the political leaders, the party system collapsed into street brawls. Uniformed bully boys of the Nazi and Communist parties made it impossible for other political parties to appear in public without the support of a gang of hoodlums. Pitched battles between party militia were difficult to control and systematically weakened party politics.

Frequently, a totalitarian and revolutionary party will reject electoral participation or be prevented from electioneering because the rulers prohibit competitive elections. The party then becomes the "organization weapon" to launch a revolution.[5] Such a party has few of the traits typical of a democratic party. V. I. Lenin (1870–1924), the architect of the October, 1917 Russian Revolution which brought the Communists to power, first described the principles upon which this type of party is founded, and his prescriptions continue to be mainsprings of action for such groups. As Lenin explained to his followers:

And this promise I shall defend no matter how much you instigate the crowd against me for my "anti-democratic" views, etc. . . . 3. that the organization

[5] Phillip Selznick, *The Organizational Weapon: A Study of Bolshevik Strategy and Tactics* (Glencoe, Ill.: Free Press, 1960).

Students of Soviet military academies pass in review on Red Square as part of the parade celebrating the 58th anniversary of the October Revolution.

must consist chiefly of persons engaged in revolution as a profession; 4. that in a country with a despotic government, the more we restrict the membership of this organization to persons who are engaged in revolution as a profession and who have been professionally trained in the art of combatting the political police the more difficult will it be to catch the organization. . . .[6]

If the revolutionary party succeeds, it is the end of competitive politics, and the victorious party becomes an instrument of subjugation. The types of parties that emerge in a country are in large part a result of historical conditions.

ORIGINS

Parties in the organized modern sense first emerged in the United States during the late eighteenth century, almost immediately after the thirteen colonies achieved independence. Not everyone supported these new organizations. George Washington warned in his Farewell Address on September 19, 1796, "against the baneful effects of parties generally, including opening the door to foreign influence and corruption."[7]

From 1797 onward many political leaders throughout the world, often for less charitable and altruistic reasons than President Washington's, have rejected competitive elections. The presence of one and sometimes two or more political parties in a political system has, nevertheless, become a nearly universal phenomenon in this century. The refusal to permit more than one party has been premised on a twofold need: to preserve domestic tranquility and avoid unnecessary quarreling, and to prevent the infiltration of foreign influence.

[6] V. I. Lenin, *What Is To Be Done?* (New York: International Publishers, 1929), p. 116.

[7] U.S. House of Representatives, *Washington's Farewell Address to the People of the United States,* House Document No. 504, 89th Congress, 2nd Session, 1966, pp. 15–16.

The origins of political parties can be traced to five causes, or historical situations, which are discussed below in order of their appearance. Each of the originating conditions occurs in an environment in which traditional institutions and practices are declining and new ideas and techniques are appearing. 1. Political parties first came into being as a consequence of specific constitutional arrangements and laws that provided for or encouraged competitive elections. Political parties in America appeared in the 1790s because state laws encouraged this type of organization by "defining the rules of the game."[8]

Likewise in other countries, parties evolved because the suffrage was expanded and groups of men organized to contest elections. In England, prior to the Reform Act of 1832, members of Parliament were rarely challenged in an election. Many, if not a majority, came from constituencies under the domination of a wealthy landlord (known as pocket boroughs). The MP was not dependent on constituency opinion but on the goodwill of his wealthy sponsor. One of the most infamous examples of a "rotten borough"—a parliamentary district where the population was virtually nil—was Old Sarum. Old Sarum has been described as "a mound of earth, about two miles from the present city of Salisbury, which at the beginning of the nineteenth century had only seven inhabitants and returned two members of Parliament."[9] The seven voters regularly auctioned their votes to the highest bidder. Prior to 1832 the number of voting constituents per MP averaged 330. The Reform Act eliminated some of the worst inequities, such as providing the city of Manchester—population of 180,000—with representation in the House of Commons for the first time. The Reform Act was a modest effort, increasing the eligible electorate by 50 percent, to between 650,000 and 700,000 people, or about 3 percent of the adult population. This numerical increase in the electorate and the enfranchising of the previously disenfranchised sections of the industrializing North led like-minded groups of MPs to initiate electoral organizations, and the development of modern British political parties was set into motion.

Political parties came into being in Japan in about 1881 as mechanisms of protest. The leadership of these groups was composed largely of ex-samurai and former members of the government, who resented the domination of the Choshu and Satsuma clans in the government. A political party opposition (marred by assassination and other political acts of violence) began to evolve. The ensuing kaleidoscope of organizations was partly a result of the

[8] Paul Goodman, "The First American Party System," in William Nisbett Chambers and Walter Dean Burnham, eds., *The American Party Systems: Stages of Political Development* (New York: Oxford University Press, 1967), p. 65.

[9] Sydney Dawson Bailey, *British Parliamentary Democracy* (Boston: Houghton Mifflin, 1962), pp. 110–11.

fact that no constitutional or other legal guide provided an appropriate outlet. With the promulgation of the Emperor Meiji's constitution in February, 1889, party organizations were provided with a logical focus. Chapter III of the new constitution set forth the principles governing the Imperial Diet (the bicameral legislature). Article XXXV described the House of Representatives as "composed of Members elected by the people according to the provisions of the Law of Election." Elections were first held in July, 1890, and within ten years the dominant group in Japanese politics—the Genro, or Elder Statesman—concluded that the most effective way to influence the Diet was to form a political party that could win an electoral majority and organize the House of Representatives. The earlier manipulation and corrupting of individual legislators and party cliques by the executive had brought increasing discredit to the government. The Diet, it was believed, depended on a party system in order to function properly, and the previous techniques could not be relied upon in the future to produce the desired results.

In the fall of 1900 Prince Ito Hirobumi, an Elder Statesman and father of the Meiji Constitution, announced the formation of the Seiyukai party. In a matter of weeks a nonparty man had resigned the premiership, and Ito, president of the Seiyukai, became premier by virtue of the fact that his party had become a majority of the House of Representatives. Japan was moving toward a party government system until the Great Depression and military chauvinists disrupted the trend. Party government ended in the 1930s and did not appear again until the post-World War II American occupation and the "MacArthur constitution."

The announcement of forthcoming elections to be held (1948) by the British colonial authorities in Singapore led to government-sponsored voter registration drives and the formation of the first legal political party, the Progressive Party. As subsequent constitutions expanded the political powers of locally elected officials, more parties registered. Local self-government and compulsory voting came into being between 1957 and 1959. These measures culminated in a flurry of party activity and intense efforts by a wide range of groups to create effective political organizations to contest the upcoming Legislative Assembly elections in which, for the first time, all assemblymen were elected. The People's Action Party, which won the 1959 elections, has governed Singapore since 1959.

In his study of Western party systems, Maurice Duverger refers to those who have a "parliamentary origin" and those "externally created" or "extraparliamentary" in origin.[10] In both instances the party seeks to

[10] See Maurice Duverger, *Political Parties: Their Organization and Activity in the Modern State,* 2nd English ed., trans. Barbara and Robert North (New York: John Wiley, 1959), pp. XIII–XXXVII.

influence or control government because of and through the electoral process. In the former instance groups of men already in parliament who have coalesced on certain questions over time, establish ties with electoral committees as the suffrage is extended. Examples would be the Conservative and Liberal parties in Great Britain and the American Federalists and Jeffersonian Republicans. The external party usually originates among groups who have not participated in an organized manner in the electoral process but now see the time as opportune because many potential supporters have gained the franchise. The activities of the Fabian Society and the Trades Union Congress, which led to the creation of the British Labour Party in 1899, are an example.

While democratic party systems have emerged as a result of constitutional legal prodding, one-party or authoritarian party systems generally have had different beginnings.

2. Nationalist movements against a foreign colonial power have frequently culminated in a single-party system. A successful anticolonial movement was not inclined to tolerate a political opposition within its own ranks. The need for unity in order to confront the manifold economic and political challenges, which threatened to overwhelm a poor, economically underdeveloped system, was the reason commonly advanced to justify a one-party system. A less charitable reason given by an individual who studied the West African party systems is that "single party" states emerged because "it was a goal set by a political elite which then worked self-consciously for its achievement."[11] Political elites, presumably, were first and foremost concerned with remaining in power, and the vehicle to accomplish this was the single-party state. A sure way to stay in power is to prevent effective competition.

Another reason advanced for the creation of one-party states in former colonial territories is that this type of political system is in accord with revered historical–cultural traditions. Rupert Emerson believes that an elite working through a single party is in harmony with traditional practices. He argues that most non-Western traditional societies were generally inclined toward some form of extended deliberation that would result in a consensus, not toward a jarring count of votes with public losers. Majority rule and representative government have no roots in most traditional societies. Tradition reinforced the one-party states of successful nationalist leaders in societies were "the voice of the elders, the wise, and the specially qualified was entitled to extra or even decisive weight".[12]

[11] Aristide R. Zolberg, *Creating Political Order: the Party States of West Africa* (Chicago: Rand McNally and Company, 1966), pp. 35–36.

[12] Rupert Emerson, *From Empire to Nation; the Rise to Self-Assertion of Asian and African Peoples* (Boston: Beacon Press, 1964), p. 284.

3. Beginning with the Russian Communist Party numerous political parties were founded in this century as revolutionary weapons. Some, such as the Nazi Party, adopted a quasi-constitutional strategy. The Nazis pursued their goal within the existing party system, manipulating and disrupting the system in the name of their totalitarian blueprint for the future. Adolf Hitler proclaimed that the Weimar constitution gave the Nazis "the ground on which to wage our battle." Too many ignored Hitler's warning that when the Nazis captured power, "we shall then mould the state into that form which we consider to be the right one."[13] Most revolutionary parties have, however, preferred or been required to adopt a conspiratorial posture. The Communist Party of the Soviet Union (officially founded in 1898 as the Russian Social Democratic Labor Party), for example, seized power through underground conspiracy, revolution, and finally civil war, which did not end until 1920.

Another revolutionary weapon was the Chinese Communist Party (CCP), founded in July, 1921, when the First Party Congress was held in a Roman Catholic girls' school in the French concession at Shanghai—outside the jurisidction of Chinese law. Thirteen Chinese, including Mao Tse-tung, attended this meeting; two Comintern agents, a Soviet citizen and a Dutchman, also attended. The First Congress adopted a hard line and established the party as a revolutionary weapon that refused to cooperate with any existing political group. One document adopted at the Congress urged "aggression" toward existing parties and declared "no relationship with other parties or groups."[14] Today the CCP rules 800 million people, the largest nation in the world.

4. Political parties also were created as a response to the spread of liberal ideas emanating from the West. The nucleus of Japanese parties before the 1890 constitution were partly a consequence of Western ideas and writings, which were widely circulated among the Japanese elites. The overthrowing of the Thai military dictatorship by students in 1973 and the formation of political parties and the January, 1975, elections owed much of their inspiration to liberal political ideas. These ideas came primarily from Western books and journals and from Thais trained abroad, mostly in the United States, who returned to their country with a democratic orientation.

5. A final point of origin for political parties is the need to mobilize and control the growing political consciousness of the masses. Samuel P. Huntington has noted, "Significantly, when authoritarian regimes with weak parties confront crises, the party tends to reemerge as a more important actor."[15]

[13] Frederick Mundell Watkins, *The Failure of Constitutional Powers Under the German Republic*. Cambridge: Harvard University Press, 1939), p. 53.

[14] Stuart Schram, *Mao Tse-tung* (Baltimore: Penguin Books, 1966). p. 66.

[15] Huntington and Moore, eds., *op. cit.* p. 9.

In Egypt, for example, after the late Gamal Abdel Nasser led the Free Officers in the July, 1952, revolution, which overthrew the corrupt monarchy, the new ruler set out to create mass involvement in order to govern Egypt more effectively. Participation by the urban political elite was to be limited by increasing mass involvement. President Nasser perceived the masses as having few immediate demands, the principal one being that "their government be an Islamic-Egyptian one." Three successive "single mobilization parties" were created, the last being the Socialist Union. The Socialist Union coincided with the adoption of a loudly vocal socialist ideology and was designed to organize and mobilize the masses to win their positive cooperation.[16]

Another example is the Burma Socialist Programme Party (BSP), created in July, 1962. It appeared following the seizure of power by General Ne Win and the Burmese army. All other political parties were banned. The BSP was an elitist party, which was to be the nucleus of a future mass party. The BSP constitution declared that the party is a "transitional party" which will lead to a mass party based on democratic centralism and will perform "such basic party functions as recruiting nucleus personnel called cadres, and training and testing them by assigning duties, etc."[17] In Egypt, Burma, and many other areas single parties were created as a means of indoctrinating and controlling the masses, as well as to facilitate rule.

Party origins profoundly influence the objectives and organization of parties. Parties established to seize power by any available means and/or to harness a population are unlikely to assume a democratic character at a very early date.

TYPES OF PARTIES IN COMPETITIVE ELECTORAL SYSTEMS

Political parties have been classified according to a number of criteria. One of the most ambitious efforts to classify political parties is that of Gabriel Almond, who sets forth a tripartite scheme based on party style or behavior in the political arena.[18]

Pragmatic-bargaining or broker-type parties are typical of the Anglo-American system, though this form of party appears to be spreading. This party type is highly voter conscious and attempts to respond to the

[16] Leonard Binder, "Political Recruitment and Participation in Egypt," in Joseph LaPalombara and Myron Weiner, eds., *Political Parties and Political Development* (Princeton: Princeton University Press, 1966), pp. 218–19.

[17] Fred R. von der Mehden, "The Burmese Way to Socialism," in the *Asian Survey*, Institute of International Studies (Berkeley: University of California Press, March, 1963), III, No. 3, p. 133.

[18] Gabriel Almond and James S. Coleman, eds., *The Politics of the Developing Areas* (Princeton: Princeton University Press, 1960), pp. 43–45.

maximum number of interests by policies and campaign statements with the widest appeal. The party appeals to all strata of society and usually attracts support from most identifiable social groupings. Bargaining, compromise, accommodation, responsiveness, and a marketplace atmosphere dominate party strategy. This type of party functions in a system with a broad political consensus, where intense doctrinal issues do not divide society. The bargaining, broker party has been criticized for failing to present the voters with clear-cut alternatives and for failing to lead on the critical issues of the day. One expert on British parties, writing early in this century, criticized British parties for their overriding concern to win "by picking up votes from every quarter. Parties did not lead, but built blocs of votes and were often obliged to conciliate even the representatives of the fanciful movements and the fads."[19]

Absolute value-oriented or ideological parties, such as the Nazi or Communist party, push a rigid, comprehensive program and usually regard compromise and negotiation as weakness. Unflagging commitment to enunciated principles guide party actions and party members are recruited from among the most alienated groups in the population. Appeals for support are limited by the fact that potential members must convert to a highly structured party doctrine. Parties that fit into this category are usually revolutionary or reactionary.

Deviation from the "official" ideology is treason or an act of resignation from the party. Challenging the current leadership and hence party doctrine can produce fatal results. Leon Trotsky, Lenin's most influential comrade, eventually clashed with Stalin and left the Soviet Union in 1929. After living in several countries and maintaining constant public criticism of the Stalin regime, in 1937 Trotsky settled in Coyoacán, Mexico, where he kept up his attacks against Stalin's leadership. Trotsky was assassinated on August 20, 1940, by a trusted supporter, Jacques Mornard, who drove an ice pick into Trotsky's skull. It was soon discovered that the killer was an agent of the Soviet secret police (KGB).

Some parties, of course, are inflexible in only certain policy areas—such as the Prohibition Party in the United States—but would be negotiation-oriented in other matters. Most absolute-value-oriented parties operating in a competitive party system stridently oppose whatever party or parties are in power. Some Communist parties do become more flexible and bargaining-minded as they come closer to power, particularly after they see an opportunity to form a coalition government with non-Communist parties. This is the case in both France and Italy.

Particularistic parties are self-limiting because they combine their appeals

[19] M. Ostrogorski *Democracy and the Organization of Political Parties,* Vol. II (New York: The Macmillan Company, 1902), p. 684.

to specific ethnic, linguistic, or religious groups, such as the Hindu Maha Sabha, a conservative Indian party that restricts its membership to Hindus. These are communal parties dedicated to traditional values or to what Clifford Geertz has described as "primordial sentiments" which are given, "such as being born into a particular language or religious community, ethnic or racial group, kinship, geographic region, etc."[20]

At times these particularistic parties are willing to work within the larger political system and pursue a strategy of negotiation and compromise as the best means of protecting the group's interests. Frequently, though, the party's emphasis on traditional identifications intensifies cleavages in society to the point that political negotiation becomes unlikely. One of the causes of the Nigerian Civil War (1967–1970) was the fact that political parties in independent Nigeria were organized along tribal lines, and old distrusts and misunderstandings were increased after independence. Independence and a new government offer a new prize to be won by ambitious individuals, and it is the primordial sentiments that are often appealed to and politicized by aspiring leaders as they seek to establish a leadership position. For example, one of the best organized Nigerian parties in the pre-Civil War period was the Action Group, whose support was drawn almost entirely from the Yoruba tribe.

Duverger's Typology

The first major effort to deal with specific parties on a comparative basis was published by the French political scientist Maurice Duverger in 1951. Duverger analyzed political parties according to several criteria. One of his hypotheses was that party organization was in part determined by party strategy and objectives; organization in turn influenced a party's political style. Accordingly, he categorized parties according to organizational arrangements at the base of a party pyramid, recognizing that his scheme was "approximate and vague: it describes tendencies rather than any clear-cut distinction."[21]

Indirect membership parties are confined almost entirely to a few Catholic and socialist parties in Western Europe, such as the Social Democratic Party of Germany. This type of party originated in worker-action groups first organized as trade unions and cooperative societies. At a later date socialist-worker parties evolved, and their success depends on the strength of the prior organizations. The British Labour Party is an example

[20] For an analysis of such identifications in contemporary politics, see Clifford Geertz, "Primordial Sentiments and Civil Politics in New States" in *Old Societies and New States; the Quest for Modernity in Asia and Africa* (Glencoe, Ill.: The Free Press, 1963), p. 109.

[21] Duverger, *op. cit.*, p. 3. For a rather rigorous review of Duverger's methodology, see Aaron B. Wildavsky, "A Methodological Critique of Duverger's Political Parties," *Journal of Politics*, XXI, No. 2 (May, 1959), pp. 308–18.

of an indirect membership party. Trade union members vote on whether or not the union should have membership in a political party—in Great Britain's case, the Labour Party. If the vote is affirmative, each union member has another fee added to his regular union dues, which in effect makes him a Labour Party member, the intermediary link being the trade union. The political affiliation can be avoided only if the member "contracts out" by signing a statement declaring that he is unwilling to pay the political fee. Because "contracting out" requires some effort, the pattern is for most union members to pay the additional fee. Individuals may join the Labour Party directly, though with a party membership today of more than 6 million, nearly 80 percent are indirect members.

Direct membership parties are the more common means of affiliation and characterize such diverse parties as the Democrats and Republicans in the United States and the Communist Party of the Soviet Union. Members join parties directly, the requirements and complexity of application procedures depending on the particular party. In the United States, for example, a voter may register as a Democrat or Republican in some states, while in other states he identifies himself as a party member by voting in a party primary election. There is no review of membership declaration and no membership card is issued. The French Socialist Party is another example of a direct membership party. In this case party members complete a membership form, pay local dues, and attend party meetings with some degree of regularity.

Duverger also classifies parties according to whether they are caucus, branch, or totalitarian types.

Caucus parties were the first to emerge. A caucus is a small committee made up of party leaders, a majority sometimes composed of the party's elected office holders. The members of these middle-class parties are predominantly drawn from among the local notables. Party organization is decentralized, activity is largely directed toward electioneering and is, therefore, seasonal. Membership requirements are minimal, and the formal membership is not very large. The greatest influence is held by those who have achieved elective office. The party seeks to win votes, not to build a mass base of ideological members. The Democrats, Republicans, and British Conservatives are examples of this type of party.

Branch parties are typical of European socialist parties, which seek a maximum mass membership. The party depends on membership dues to provide the bulk of its finances. Administration of party fees and membership rolls leads to a growing permanent party bureaucracy. Day-to-day direction of party affairs falls into the hands of party bureaucrats and organization may become oligarchic. These parties have a tendency to be more doctrinaire, and intraparty struggles are often over ideological matters.

Totalitarian (Communist and Fascist) parties are centralized and authoritarian. The vertical chain of command prohibits any type of horizontal links between the cells or other local units. Agitation and propaganda, until recently, take precedence over elections in a competitive party setting. Duverger describes these parties as demanding a total commitment "of the whole human being, which admits of no distinction between public and private life. The faith of a Church is combined with the discipline of an army."[22]

We should note that there are differences between communism and fascism despite many organizational and other similarities. Communists base their organization on workplace cells (15 to 20 members) or on residential cells. The latter came into being because many people, such as writers, doctors, and others, are employed in units that have insufficient party members to justify a workplace cell. The pivot of the Fascist party is the private army of militia, which is steeped in uniforms, ranks, medals, techniques of physical violence, bands, and flags. The Fascists also organized workplace cells and branches based on geographical location, sometimes with hundreds of members.

Based on Karl Marx's utopian philosophy, Communists claim to believe in the innate goodness and rationality of man, which can be nurtured only if he is liberated from the feudal or capitalist institutions that prevent him from achieving his secular salvation. Once existing social institutions are destroyed or reformed, there will be no need for government because rational man does not need to be constrained by instruments of coercion. Fascism is neither as universal in its commitment nor as philosophically optimistic. Man exists to serve the state, which in turn is the embodiment of the chosen race or nation. Government does not wither away because even the elect need the omnipresent inspiration and direction of the Leader and his ideology. When Communists and Fascists have seized power, both have committed monstrous crimes against humanity to achieve their very different self-proclaimed goals.

ONE-PARTY REGIMES

The prototype one-party political regime appeared in the Soviet Union in 1917, in Italy in 1922, and in Germany in 1933, when the Communist, Fascist, and Nazi parties, respectively, came to power. Of these original one-party regimes, only the Soviet system survives today. Over the years as other political systems have become dominated by single parties, the variation among one-party systems has been substantial. We are now at the point where to speak of a single-party regime refers to a wide variety of practices.

[22] *Ibid.*, p. 2.

The common factor that most single-party states share is their authoritarian bias. There are regimes, however, which are in effect single-party states but which are not authoritarian—in Mexico (Institutional Revolutionary Party), for example, and Singapore, where the People's Action Party controls all 65 seats in Parliament.

One-party systems vary in the amount of power the political leadership allows the party as compared with other institutions in society. In some authoritarian systems preponderant influence may remain with the military, civilian administrators, the church, and the economic elite, whether it be big business or the landed gentry. The Communist Party dominates in the Soviet Union but in Spain Franco constrained the National Movement's political influence. The National Movement—Spain's only legal party under Franco—is an outgrowth of Franco's original political organization, the fascist-oriented Falange. National Movement claims are balanced and often disregarded against those of the army, the Church, monarchists, business leaders and, particularly, *Opus Dei,* or "God's Work."

Opus Dei is a rather unique political organization. Founded in 1928 by a Spanish priest, the Sacredotal Society of the Holy Cross and *Opus Dei,* or *Opus Dei* as it is generally described, has a worldwide membership of 50,000, of whom 20,000 are in Spain. Not long ago a Spanish political leader lamented, "It seems incredible that a country should allow itself to be taken over by religious order—*Opus Dei.*"[23]

As Franco prepared to step down as head of state, he appointed more *Opus Dei* members to important government positions, and in turn the appointees have favored fellow-members when choosing associates. *Opus Dei* is not, however, a political organization per se, and its political influence, while pervasive, is more indirect—an outgrowth of the values, beliefs, and actions of laymen who participate in activities analogous to those of a religious order. These include financial obligations, attendance at spiritual retreats, moral discipline, self-study, etc. The dominant political force in one-party Spain for several years was not the National Movement but *Opus Dei.*

Many one-party systems arise out of a social milieu with severe and prolonged cleavages that have led to internal war. The party's initial objective is to restore order and organize the nation as a productive and self-sustaining unit. In a century when mass political consciousness has become a fact of life, the single-party restrains and organizes this consciousness.

[23] *The New York Times,* November 27, 1969, p. 8. The article by Richard Eder is a perceptive overview of *Opus Dei's* evolution. *Opus Dei* is recognized by the Vatican as a secular association which requires Christian discipline and behavior of its members. A principal tenet is sanctification through one's daily work, and members are encouraged to excel in their chosen careers. *Opus Dei* disclaims any interest in politics though its members occupy key positions in government, education, and business.

After the seizure of power the victors carry forward the struggle to purge society of the "enemy." Among totalitarian one-party regimes this is a brutal period in the nation's history, as during the first five years (1949–54) of the People's Republic of China when 10 to 14 million "enemies of the people" were eliminated."

Samuel P. Huntington has analyzed one-party systems in depth and classified them accordingly:[24]

Exclusionary one-party systems maintain divisions in society in order to neutralize politically a major segment of the population. In South Africa blacks and coloreds are excluded; in Ataturk's Turkey of the 1920s and 1930s political participation was restricted to the urban, Westernized population. Political leadership in an exclusionary system does not seek to physically eliminate the subordinate group or groups (as did the Nazis) or resocialize it into a single, acceptable mold. Rather, rulers simply want to assure that the subordinate group will remain apolitical. Once society experiences economic modernization and the subordinated groups begin to participate in the process of social change, it is difficult to maintain the divisions. When the cost of exclusion is acceptable to the ruling group, divisions are maintained through exclusionary practices, as in South Africa today.

A revolutionary one-party system is not interested in maintaining traditional social divisions. It is determined to create a monolithic social and political order. Change, mass mobilization, terror, and absolute loyalty are the hallmarks of a newly established revolutionary one-party system. Those unwilling to convert or those whom the leadership deems unworthy of being converted (for example, Jews or landlords) are destroyed. The revolutionary single party is all-pervasive and its tentacles touch all parts of society and the individual's existence.

Huntington concludes that as exclusionary single-party systems undergo modification, revolutionary one-party systems also change if they survive (as Nazi Germany and Fascist Italy did not). Huntington discusses three stages of development that successful revolutionary one-party systems go through:

Transformation occurs as the old order or aspects of it are destroyed in the name of the law. This is the most brutal if not the most unpredictable period. Purges, executions, summary imprisonments, and confiscation plague the population. The enemy is identified and destroyed or driven out. The systematic snuffing out of human life on unprecedented scales occurred during the early years of the party dictatorship in Nazi Germany, the Soviet Union, the People's Republic of China, and the Democratic Republic of Vietnam.

[24] Samuel P. Huntington, "Social and Institutional Dynamics of One-Party Systems," in Huntington and Moore, eds., *op. cit.*, pp. 3–47. This section is based on Huntington's chapter.

In the *consolidation stage,* the old order has been destroyed and the regime legitimizes itself on the basis of the institutions and performance of the new order. Ideology as it was imposed on the population in the revolutionary stage is eroded. Authoritarian and totalitarian ideology previously emphasized the corrupt and degenerate nature of the present in contrast to the future ideal state to be achieved through the party. In the consolidation stage support or tolerance of the regime rests on the institutions and the performance of the system. Ideology becomes rote chant by the ambitious in order to maintain their credibility and career advancement.

The consolidation stage is the period of institutionalization. The most common result is to limit the power of the leader—as in the Mexican presidency, or to establish an oligarchic system in which power is divided among several individuals. Since the death of Stalin, for example, collective leadership has evolved in the Soviet Union as a means of preventing one individual from acquiring the autocratic power that Stalin held.

Assuming that the party has surmounted the succession crisis, that the founding leader is no longer on the scene, and that the institutions of the new order have taken hold, the party enters the *adaptation stage*. In this stage the party must relate itself to four social developments: (1) the emergence of highly trained technicians and managers who are, (2) responsible for the operation of an economically modernizing society; (3) the reappearance of intellectuals trained under the new order who, nevertheless, frequently criticize the regime; and (4) various groups in society demanding a role in the decision-making process. Technological development and a growing social pluralism suggest a changing role, if not lower status position, for the party bureaucrat or—to use the Soviet term—*apparatchik*.

As in many industrialized systems in the West the intellectual and economic-managerial classes make day-to-day critical decisions that affect the quality and functioning of society. Economic development and specialization encourage the growth of interest groups who begin to make claims on the government. Competitive demands by multitudinous groups and interests may provide the party with its principal role—arbitration of competing demands, whether in a factory, a municipal agency dealing with urban transit or housing, or at the highest government level, deciding between those who seek more emphasis on heavy industry and defense versus those who want more and better quality consumer goods.

Even in the more authoritarian regimes there is evidence of a willingness to become more responsive, if not through an opposition party, at least through the occasional inclusion of more than one officially certified nominee per office. This occurs in Hungary and Poland, for example. Such contests enable the party to acquire a more accurate appraisal of the popular mood, respond to those who maintain the need for popular participation in decision making, and provide a means by which a patently unpopular candidate or issue can be dealt with in a manner that will accrue popular approval and indicate a responsive leadership.

POLITICAL PARTIES IN THE DEVELOPING WORLD

Many political systems in the developing world are dominated by a single party and therefore may be expected to move through the stages outlined above. Countries such as Costa Rica, Malaysia, Thailand, and Venezuela have genuinely competitive elections and cannot be classified as single-party systems. In other political systems, as in Burma, Egypt, Guinea, and North Vietman, the leaders use the party as an instrument to control and mobilize the population. Newly independent countries must face the fact that two or more parties with substantial support could lead to political divisions that would threaten the unity of the country or inhibit a government's developing and implementing programs and policies.

One heritage developing political systems share is *avoidance politics.* In what were subject-oriented political systems the masses did not participate in policy making and implementation. The best that could be hoped for was a condition in which one could avoid government rules or modify government regulations and requirements through an understanding with local officials. Taxes, tranquility, and conscripts were the traditional government requirements. Beyond these, which on occasion were onerous if not unbearable, governments limited their involvement in the local community. Participant systems (for example, the United States, Canada, Japan, and Western Europe), on the other hand, have responsive governments. Governments remain in office because they successfully build coalitions of interests that can command an electoral majority. Participation emphasizes input factors at the electoral and policy making stages.

Transitional policies in the Third World combine the need for nation building (security, stability, economic development, and national integration) with an intellectual movement away from a subject-oriented toward a participatory society. This shift in orientation frequently is more verbal than actual. Leaders whose nations are undergoing internal and external stress may believe that only the discipline and coordination of a subject culture can build a social and economic base necessary for national development. The overlapping challenges to national stability and development are compounded by international opinion, which often judges a regime by its deviation from democratic-participatory norms—norms that few, if any, developing political systems now meet.

Subversive involvement by foreign powers, traditional patterns of internal cleavage, and the limited capacity of the government to solve problems are the ingredients that shape developing party systems. The cumulative impact of these influences pushes a government toward some form of one-party solution. Some developing countries, nevertheless, still seek accommodation with opposition groups, despite the fact that popular participation may appear a luxury the transitional societies cannot afford. In 1945 after the defeat of the Axis powers, Indonesian leaders reacted in this euphoric and democratic atmosphere by adopting the 1945 constitution, which committed them to participatory politics. After a four-year violent struggle against the Dutch, Indonesia became independent in 1949, and the fifth largest country in the world began a democratic experiment. This experiment culminated in the 1955 general elections, in which nearly 38 million Indonesians voted. Four parties—two Muslin, one secular-nationalist, and one Communist—won 78 percent of the vote and captured 198 of the 257 parliamentary seats.[25] The remaining 59 seats were divided among 24 parties and other groupings, such as the two seats held by the Police Employees' Association of the Republic of Indonesia. Coalition governments, preceded by intense bargaining among the parties, continued. Less than fifteen months passed before President Sukarno attacked the 1955 elections. Speaking before a youth conference, Sukarno observed:

> *In November 1945—let us be quite frank—we made a most serious mistake. We suggested the establishment of parties, parties, parties. . . . Just look at the situation. Quite apart from the disease of ethnic and regional loyalties, we are afflicted by the disease of parties which, alas, alas, makes us forever work against one another!*[26]

By 1959 party government had come to an end in Indonesia. Political parties, so runs the argument of numerous Third World leaders, either exacerbate existing tensions and cleavages or create new ones.

SINGLE-PARTY, TWO-PARTY, AND MULTIPARTY SYSTEMS

As the student has seen, political parties can be classified and analyzed according to a number of criteria. One of the most common classifications when considering the political system as a whole is by number of parties: single-party, two-party, and multiparty systems.

Single-Party

An analysis of single-party, or one-party, systems reveals fundamental variations among these systems. There are monolithic, totalitarian parties, such

[25] The Communists won 16.4 percent of the popular vote and elected 39 candiates. For an analysis of the 1955 elections and the future implications of the results see Herbert Feith, *The Decline of Constitutional Democracy in Indonesia* (Ithaca: Cornell University Press, 1962), pp. 424–50.

[26] Sukarno, "Let Us Bury the Parties" in Herbert Feith and Lance Castles, eds., *Indonesian Political Thinking: 1945–1965* (Ithaca: Cornell University Press, 1970), p. 81.

as the Communist Party of the Soviet Union and the Workers' Party of North Vietnam, which are all-pervasive. Parties such as Mexico's Institutional Revolutionary Party and Singapore's People's Action Party (the PAP controls all 65 seats in Parliament) completely overshadow the several legal opposition parties but they do not penetrate society to the degree the ruling parties in the Soviet Union and the Democratic Republic of Vietnam do.

The American South was long described as a single-party system; yet as Hugh Douglas Price has pointed out, this is "a residual category."[27] The term "one-party" in the American context defines a condition where meaningful two-party competition is absent. The South is not a case where a highly organized political machine monopolizes the selection of government officials. One-party in the United States does not imply the existence of a well-oiled monolithic organization, which dominates in an authoritarian manner. The states are constitutionally required to hold elections, and hotly contested electoral battles regularly occur in the primaries if not in the general elections.[28]

This is not to say that political machines or organizations monopolizing local politics do not exist in the United States, such as Mayor Richard Daley's Cook County, Illinois, political organization. The gradual disappearance of long-standing political machines is, however, a phenomenon of contemporary American political life.[29]

Two-Party Systems

Two-party systems are limited to a few countries, principally the United States, Great Britain, New Zealand, Austria, and West Germany. (As we note below, no competitive electoral system has *only* two parties.) A two-party system suggests that decisive encounters occur in elections and in the legislature. The opposition is presumed to be sufficiently united that they can coalesce into a dominant opposition party, which can, if the electoral winds shift, remain united as a governing party. A general mass consensus and homogeneity undergird the system, and both parties concentrate on competing for the dominant bloc of the middle-of-the road electorate. Multiparty systems can tolerate an extremist party, but electioneering cannot continue in a two-party system if one of the two parties is extremist or totalitarian.

The prototype two-party system is generally regarded as the British,

[27] Hugh Douglas Price, "Rise and Decline of Single Party Systems in Anglo-American Experience" in Huntington and Moore, eds., *op. cit.*, p. 77.

[28] A most fascinating, though now somewhat dated, analysis of one-party American states is V. O. Key, *Southern Politics* (New York: Vintage Books, 1949).

[29] A readable though sometimes inaccurate description of the Cook County political organization is Mike Royko, *Boss: Richard J. Daley of Chicago* (New York: Dutton, 1971).

where His/Her Majesty's Opposition is an integral part of the political process. Opposition is regarded as a legitimate public service, and since 1937, the Leader of the Opposition has been paid a special salary by the government. One perceptive analyst of British politics has observed that the two-party system structures and clarifies the issues in a unique manner, and that this need for choice and clarity historically gave rise to two-party systems. "The two-party system is a natural concomitant of a political tradition in which government . . . is the first consideration, and in which the views and preferences of voters and members of Parliament are continuously limited to the single alternative of 'for' or 'against.'"[30]

No functioning two-party system has *only* two parties, but in a two-party system, there are only two major parties. The third party is common to American national politics. In the 1968 presidential election George Wallace's American Independent Party garnered 13.6 percent of the popular vote, but no AIP candidate was elected to office. Between 1946 and 1970 in Great Britain the Liberal Party vote, plus the popular votes of several minor parties, in general elections have ranged between 2.9 percent and 12.5 percent. In the 1972 general election the Liberal Party received 18.9 percent of the popular vote, and the other minor parties received 2.4 percent, yet the Liberals won only 13 of 630 seats in the House of Commons.

In the American two-party system the Democratic and Republican parties are decentralized, with state and even county organizations autonomous of the next higher level in the party hierarchy. The parties compete in elections, but the parties do not remain strictly competitive after the elections. Presidents and governments invariably depend on bipartisan support for many proposals and, almost as inevitably, members of the chief executive's party vote against him on major issues.

Great Britain is often described as having a disciplined two-party system. The average English voter chooses the party and the man he wants to become the next prime minister when he votes in the parliamentary election. The personal magnetism and stature of the individual MP candidate usually neither adds nor detracts more than 500 votes per constituency. The competition of the electoral arena carries over into Parliament, and the term "disciplined parties" means that commonly there are no crossovers when the House of Commons votes. The parties can usually depend on the MPs unanimously registering the party position.

We conclude this section by noting that the term two-party system is never strictly accurate. There are noticeable differences even within the Anglo-American two-party category.

[30] L. S. Avery, *Thoughts on the Constitution* (New York: Oxford University Press, 1947), p. 16.

Multiparty Systems

Multiparty systems describe a situation in which one party is rarely if ever able to win an absolute majority of seats in the legislature. Consequently, in a parliamentary regime a coalition government must be formed. In multiparty systems parties represent fewer, limited-appeal interests and seek to advance these interests by participating in a coalition government. The negotiations in parliament after the elections are decisive. It is at this time that the critical bargains are struck and ministries divided among the parties.

The number of parties, party cohesiveness, and government stability vary among multiparty systems. The Netherlands has a parliamentary system of government in which five or six parties have dominated the political scene in the post-1945 period. These parties generally receive 80 percent or more of the popular vote. The country becomes a single constituency when national elections are held, and a party's representation in the popularly elected Second Chamber of 150 members is determined by its proportion of the national popular vote.[31]

The continuity of popular support for most parties has been a postwar feature of Dutch politics. A poll taken after the 1956 elections revealed that 85 percent of the persons interviewed had voted for the same party they had supported in 1952. Following the elections held in 1971, the six largest parties controlled 124 of 150 seats (39, 35, 16, 13, 11, and 10 seats). The government formed in 1971 was composed of five parties, representing 82 seats in the Second Chamber. Of necessity, any government must be a coalition government, and while it may require several weeks of negotiation to form the coalition, governments normally remain in office for several years. A fragmented, multiparty system has not prevented government stability and the capacity to develop and implement policy in the Netherlands.[32]

The French Fourth Republic (1946–58) stands in sharp contrast to the situation in the Netherlands. The French multiparty system was a contributing factor to the *immobilisme* of French politics before 1958. Cabinets or governments were confirmed and fell with an unhealthy frequency, and between 1946 and 1958 there were twenty different cabinets. Governments ultimately were unable to deal with critical issues, such as Algeria, and important social and economic policies. The Fourth Republic was a parliamentary regime. In 1956, 150 Communist deputies were elected to the 597-member National Assembly. The Communists consistently opposed the

[31] The First Chamber is actually the upper house of the Dutch Parliament. It has 75 members elected by the Provincial Councils for six-year terms. The First Chamber does not propose bills and can only approve or reject proposed bills. It has no right to amend bills it considers.

[32] A brief analysis of the Dutch party system is found in Johan Goudsblom, *Dutch Society* (New York: Random House, 1967), pp. 82–94.

government, and cabinets had to be formed from the remaining groups: the Mouvement Populaire Républician—a social reformist Catholic party with 83 deputies; the Socialists with 95 deputies; and a host of smaller groupings. Some parties other than the Communists, such as the pro-Gaullists and the Poujadists, with approximately 70 seats, also pursued an antigovernment policy. The parties in the middle, which sought to form governments, were limited by the number of parties with which they could realistically negotiate. Throughout most of the Fourth Republic 350 to 400 of the 597 votes in the National Assembly were available to form a government, but all 400 votes were not available at the same time. Another weakening factor was the absence of party cohesion. On 72 crucial votes between 1946 and 1956 in the National Assembly, only the Communists and Socialists maintained party discipline. On numerous votes, from 10 to 40 percent of the parties' deputies voted against the parties' majority. During this same period ten governments were forced to resign because of split voting in parties that originally had voted for installing the cabinet.[33]

In a multiparty system the common denominator is the presence of three or more political parties with substantial and long-term popular support. The ability of the executive branch to govern in a multiparty system varies, depending on the number of parties and party cohesion. There are some political systems, such as Denmark and the Netherlands, where coalition cabinets have a tradition of effective governing.

PARTY ORGANIZATION

One characteristic a group must possess to be considered a political party is some type of formal organization, even if the organization is as restricted as a few legislators consulting one another under a shared party label. Party organization ranges from the decentralized, autonomous, and open-entry arrangements found in many parts of the United States to the hierarchical and centralized pattern common to totalitarian parties.

Party as a Stratarchy[34]

Samuel J. Eldersveld, in an exhaustive survey of political organization in the Detroit metropolitan area, has pinpointed some of the dominant traits of party organizations, not only in the United States but in other democratic and competitive party systems as well. Many democratic parties have a unique form of organizational arrangement called stratarchy.[35] In a stratar-

[33] David S. McLellon, "Ministerial Instability and the Lack of Internal Cohesion in French Parties," *World Affairs Quarterly,* XXVIII (April, 1957), pp. 3–24.

[34] This section is based on Samuel J. Eldersveld, *Political Parties: A Behavioral Analysis* (Chicago: Rand McNally and Company, 1964), especially pp. 1–13.

[35] This concept was first developed by Harold Lasswell and Abraham Kaplan, *Power and Society* (New Haven: Yale University Press, 1950), pp. 219–20.

chical structure there are numerous leaders, and power is dispersed among several levels of the organization. This diffusion of power leads to a reciprocal deference system, whereby the leaders depend on the goodwill of the organization below them. A pattern of accommodation emerges, in which both initiative and indifference at the local and intermediate party level are tolerated by the leadership in order to maintain and expand the membership in the party, which is essentially a voluntary organization.

A democratic party is unlike most organizations because it is "greedy" for supporters. If a party consciously seeks to expand its electoral appeal, it attracts the support of various interests, some of which inevitably have conflicting objectives. The effort to manage intergroup rivalries and maintain the coalition causes a party to mediate the demands made by the groups that support it. No group gets everything it wants; tension arising from conflicting claims is always present, but there should be enough responses on the part of party leaders to retain the support of most, if not all, of the groups. Both the Democratic and Republican parties in the United States receive support from business interests and trade union members. Neither party can afford to ignore either group, but it requires considerable skill on the part of the party leadership to balance the claims of business and labor so as to satisfy some members from each group and maintain maximum electoral coalition.

Tension, conflict, and bargaining are ever present in a democratic, stratarchical party, and most party leaders are unable and unwilling to establish an effective chain of command. This "downward deference" results from the need for votes, the voluntary nature of party support, the few persons interested in working for a party, and the general absence of sanctions that can be applied by party leaders to party workers who are occasionally indifferent or recalcitrant. Obviously, over the long run, the top leadership has some rewards to offer the lower-echelon workers, such as moving up in the party organization or the benefits that can be dispensed by a party that enjoys an electoral success. Both the upper- and lower-echelon party workers mutually depend on one another. This reciprocal dependence, combined with the voluntary character of a democratic party, results in a type of organization called stratarchy.

The Iron Law of Oligarchy

Robert Michels first elaborated on the dangers of the iron law of oligarchy, which is the opposite of a stratarchy, a reciprocal deference system.[36] The German Social Democratic Party, the largest socialist party in the world before World War I, and one presumably committed to democratic principles within its own organization, was the subject of Michels's inquiry.

[36] First published in 1911, Robert Michels, *Political Parties: A Sociological Study of the Oligarchical Tendencies of Modern Democracy* with an introduction by Seymour Martin Lipset (New York: The Free Press, 1966), pp. 15–39.

Michels's research led him to conclude that the weakness of democracy lay in the nature of organizations. He declared that "who says organization says oligarchy," and that oligarchy was control of the organization by a few people at the top. Political parties, the organizations intended to represent the masses, deferred to the elite because of a belief in the superior abilities of the leaders. The complexity of modern society leads to specialization, and the skills and knowledge an organization's leaders acquire extend the power of the leaders. The masses become apathetic, and society is ruled by an entrenched oligarchy.

Michels argued that the leaders of the German Social Democrats did not represent the working class masses. Party leaders eventually became a part of the privileged element in society. Their principal interest became to maintain this privileged status rather than press the interests or claims of their members. Convinced that there was an inherent conflict of interest between leaders and members, Michels explained that the mass membership was unaware of the ever present conflict because of the assets held by the leaders, assets that confirmed the oligarchy's power:

1. Access to vital data and information which is used to win the support of the masses.
2. Domination over the organization's communication flow such as control of all party publications and the ability to send party leaders to the branches to justify the leadership's actions.
3. Political occupational skills that leaders but not members have, for example, speech-making, writing articles, and organizing group activities.[37]

Members have less education and are less sophisticated, and since they attend meetings on a voluntary basis on their own time, mass participation and knowledgeable interest are minimal.

Few parties are purely oligarchical and hierarchical, or decentralized and stratarchical. Two opposite examples of party organization are the Communist Party of the Soviet Union and Japan's ruling Liberal-Democratic Party.

Japan

Japanese political parties, especially the ruling Liberal-Democratic Party, rest on the ties and loyalties of the boss-follower (*oyabun-kobun*) system of traditional Japan. Parties are federations of follower-leader groups—the *ha,* or factions. The electoral strength of the LDP is the association and club affiliated with the *ha* at the constituency level. These groups are loyal to the

[37] A summary of Michels' thesis is found in the "Introduction" by Seymour Martin Lipset to Robert Michels, *Political Parties,* pp. 15–39.

faction, and it is they, rather than the party branch, who provide the decisive electoral and monetary support. Political parties per se are the object of only moderate political loyalty. The Japanese voters' commitment to the faction's secondary associations is the means through which the LDP wins elections. (The Liberal-Democrats, a conservative party compared to the Socialists, have governed Japan since 1949.)

Public opinion polls taken in 1958 revealed that less than 33 percent of the electorate was consciously committed to voting on the basis of party affiliation. The candidate and the faction are the key elements in the LDP's organization: "Leaders extend their benevolence, that is they take care of the group interests, and the members reciprocate by accepting the authority of the leader or 'boss.'"[38]

Traditional affiliations and commitment to group are particularly prevalent in rural areas, where the LDP draws its greatest support. One author reports that in local elections the village community or council usually selects the candidate the village will support, and all villagers are expected to vote for the designated individual. If the campaign heats up, it is not unusual that "in order to block infiltration from the candidates of other villages, watchers are posted on the roads at the entrances to the village."[39]

The prevalence of factions and *oyabun-kobun* relationships in Japanese political parties has continued since World War II. Japan has a parliamentary system with most of the legislature's power residing in the lower house of the Diet, the House of Representatives. The 486-member House of Representatives must be elected every four years, though usually the full term is cut short by dissolution. The lower returns three to five members to the House, but the voter may cast only one vote. Factional rivalry is intensified because the most formidable opponent in the district sometimes is an individual from one's own party.

The organizational and monetary support a candidate can expect is drawn principally from the leader of the *ha*. Each faction leader has his local associations, but more importantly he has built up a network of financial backers, the only source of adequate funding. The candidate or followers, in turn, is to show loyalty to the leader and support him on intraparty and legislative conflicts.

The system holds together at the top because party leaders recognize that the various *ha* forming the party, which in effect is a federation, must receive rewards. In the late 1960s, for example, ten factions were identified in the House of Representatives, each faction identified by the name of the

[38] Robert A. Scalapino and Junnosuke Masumi, *Parties and Politics in Contemporary Japan* (Berkeley: University of California Press, 1962), p. 121–22.

[39] Joji Watanuki, "Patterns of Politics in Present-Day Japan" in Seymour M. Lipset and Stein Rokkan, eds., *Party Systems and Voter Alignments: Cross-National Perspectives* (New York: The Free Press, 1967), p. 463.

leader, or *oyabun*. Among the 289 LDP members in the House, factions ranged in size from 14 to 48.[40] A balance among factions is a prime consideration in allocating ministerial positions and the principal party offices: the president, the secretary-general; the chairman of the Political Research Committee; and the Executive Committee of approximately thirty members who, almost without exception, are members of the Diet.

The Liberal-Democrats have an organization that is distinctly not monolithic, with power more collegial than centralized at the top. Within each faction, however, power is centralized. The viability of the party is apparent, however, from the fact that it has governed Japan since 1949.

The Soviet Union

Lenin, the father of the Communist Party of the Soviet Union, stressed organization as the "kernel" of his doctrine. Lenin and his successors have accepted the dogma first stated by Lenin that "Marxism is fortified by the material unity of organization which welds millions of toilers into an army of the working class."[41] Without organization, ideology would fail, and any army of disciplined communicants was the means to achieve power and then to govern. The term the Communists use to describe their organization is democratic centralism, which in practice means all power is in the hands of a few party leaders, with the democratic component nonexistent. The key features of democratic centralism are:

1. Election of all party executive bodies from bottom to top.
2. Regular accountability of party executive bodies to their party organizations and to higher bodies.
3. Strict party discipline and subordination of the minority to the majority.
4. The absolutely binding character of the decisions of higher bodies upon lower bodies.[42]

Theoretically, the Party Congress, which is supposed to meet every five years, elects the Politburo. At the Twenty-fourth Congress of the CPSU held from March 30 to April 19, 1971, there were 4,949 delegates in attendance. A Central Committee of 241 members and 155 alternates was "elected," and on the last day of the Congress at a plenary meeting, the Central Committee "elected" a Politburo of 15 members and 6 alternates.[43]

[40] Warren M. Tsuneishi, *Japanese Political Style* (New York: Harper and Row, 1966), p. 149.
[41] Selznick, *op. cit.*, p. 8.
[42] Merle Fainsod, *How Russia is Ruled,* rev. ed. (Cambridge: Harvard University Press, 1965), p. 208.
[43] The figures for the size of the various bodies were taken from *Soviet Life,* VI, No. 177 (June, 1971), p. 1.

The Opening of the 25th Congress of the Communist Party of the Soviet Union in the Kremlin Palace of Congresses in Moscow, February 24, 1976.

Members of the 25th Congress of the Communist Party of the Soviet Union in the process of voting.

Elections are not competitive because power is centralized in the Politburo. The Politburo, through the 10-man Secretariat, decides who will have Central Committee membership and who will attend the Congresses. This pattern of selection continues down through the organization. Party leaders are co-opted rather than elected. The Politburo is the decision-making body in the Soviet Union. The Central Committee is too large to act as an executive body except on rare occasions, and it meets, on the average, three to six times a year in plenary session. Party leaders are inviolable insofar as criticism from below is concerned. The CPSU is a military hierarchy, and subordinates must carry out the decisions of the higher authorities. Discussion and some criticism may be allowed about how to best implement policies or why policies are being poorly implemented, but once a decision has been reached by the Politburo or, occasionally, the Central Committee, the decision is binding. Criticism organized to the degree that it might represent the statements of an opposition faction is not tolerated. Communist democratic centralism means a monolithic organization in practice.

PARTY MEMBERSHIP

In the eighteenth century, when political parties were just emerging, the British political writer and statesman Edmund Burke defined a political party as "a body of men united for promoting, by their joint endeavors, the national interest upon some particular principle in which they are all agreed."[44]

Dedication to a particular political philosophy or set of political principles is not an important motivating factor for a majority of party members today. In the United States such an individual would be described as an "ideologue" who "weighs policy alternatives posed in a campaign, making his choice on the basis of agreement or disagreement with the candidate's expressed views on the crucial problems of the day." This person has "a reasonably self-conscious and overarching view of the good life, usually expressed in the form of a liberal or conservative philosophy."[45]

The data available concerning the number of Americans who are predominantly issue-oriented or "ideologues" indicates that they make up a small minority of the voters. The University of Michigan Survey Research Center concluded that in the 1956 presidential election, which pitted President Eisenhower against Adlai Stevenson, only 4.5 percent of the total

[44] Edmund Burke, *Burke's Works,* Vol. I (London: Henry G. Bohn, 1855), p. 375.

[45] Fred Greenstein, *The American Party System and the American People,* 2nd ed. (Englewood Cliffs, N.J.: Prentice-Hall, 1970), pp. 29–30.

sample and slightly under 6 percent of the voters could be classified as "ideologues" or "near-ideology" persons.[46]

The requirements and privileges of party membership are partly determined by the size of the party and the type of party system. The Albanian Communist Party, with a membership of 86,985 represents 3.7 percent of Albania's population of 2,322,600.[47] The opposite extreme is reported for the two African states of Guinea and Mali. In the former, official announcements claimed that the entire adult population—1.6 million—was enrolled in the Parti Democratique de Guinea in 1961. In Mali party saturation of the adult population was purportedly achieved by 1964. Obviously, membership in the elite Albanian Communist Party is more significant than membership in a party that enrolls every adult. In Mali, for instance, one of the principal reasons for expanding the *Union Soudanaise* was to secure additional revenue. One observer reported that "by 1964, party dues seem to be collected as a matter of course from all adults by government as well as party officials along with annual person taxes."[48]

People join political parties for many reasons. The more apparent motives include promotion of selected political policies or doctrines and securing of economic benefits for a particular stratum or category of the population. People also join parties for reasons that are not immediately obvious from looking at the party and its political orientation.

The desire to exercise power, manipulate people, and receive deference motivate some. Harold Lasswell described "political man" as one who accentuates and demands power and orients himself toward experiences that involve power.[49] All behavior allegedly works toward achieving power. The need for power, while not sublimating others, is the dominant need. Both Robert E. Lane and Harold Lasswell noted later, however, that a person with an insatiable desire for power is likely to achieve only a minor political status in democratic political systems. A person dominated by power needs will not have the interpersonal, broker-type skills that are required of successful politicians in democracies. As Lane has noted, "In adult life the search for the jugular of power may very likely lead to the world of finance, journalism, or industry instead of politics."[50]

Without attempting to provide an exhaustive list of conscious and unconscious personal needs that motivate persons to join a political party, we

[46] Angus Campbell et al., *The American Voter* (New York: John Wiley, 1960), pp. 230–31.

[47] Richard F. Staar, ed., *Yearbook on International Communist Affairs, 1975* (Stanford: Hoover Institution Press, 1975), p. 3.

[48] Zolberg, *op. cit.*, p. 105.

[49] Harold Lasswell, *Power and Personality* (New York: W. W. Norton, 1948), p. 57.

[50] Robert E. Lane, *Political Life* (Glencoe, Ill.: The Free Press, 1959), p. 127.

shall discuss selected motivations in order to give an indication of the needs served by political party membership.
People whose curiosity need is highly developed may follow the political

Social adjustment and social interaction are factors that encourage party affiliation. A survey of political leaders in Detroit, beginning at the precinct level, found that precinct leaders were often disillusioned with the political importance of their jobs, but at least 55 percent remained politically active because of "social contacts and association with friends."[51]

Desire for personal economic gain also prompts some to become party members. It is a political truism that it is not only what you know, but who you know. The political arena provides the opportunity to make invaluable contacts with influential persons in the world of business and labor. Most of the "anomalies" that too often make the headlines result from dispensations [or] "inside information" that one may obtain by knowing the right public official at the critical moment. This is not to suggest, of course, that most of the economic gain accruing to an individual with the "right political contacts" is improper or unethical. Eldersveld's Detroit study confirmed the importance of economic motivation.

The career advantages and elite status in a totalitarian political system are even more apparent. Certain jobs are open only to those willing and qualified to join the ruling party. A study of Party membership in the Soviet Union classified selected occupations as "Party restricted," where the number of non-Party members as 1 percent or less: heads of government departments, directorates from the city level up, and the directors of state-owned enterprises. "Virtually Party restricted" occupations included those in which non-CPSU members ranged up to 5 percent: judges, army officers, and probably the police.[52]

Status and ego enhancement are also obviously available to the political activist who has the opportunity to meet various and sundry political personalities of the moment. The "inside information" that swirls throughout any political system enables a party member to stand out among his peers as a person especially knowledgeable and informed and a person to be listened to.

Robert Lane has suggested other needs that are served, including curiosity.[53] Curiosity is a result of the need to come to grips with and understand the environment. For a few, this may include joining a party and comprehending the political world. Lane suggests that the search for meaning may be a "basic" drive to be fulfilled after other basal requirements (temperature, thirst, hunger, sex, security, etc.) have been met.

[51] Samuel J. Eldersveld, *Political Parties* (Chicago: Rand McNally, 1964), p. 290.

[52] T. H. Rigby, *Communist Party Membership in the U.S.S.R.: 1917–1967* (Princeton: Princeton University Press, 1968), p. 449.

[53] Lane, *op. cit.*, pp. 112–20.

world closely and in some instances will become active political party members.

Unconscious, neurotic needs also lead some persons to affiliate with a party. This is not a common phenomenon, but it is a fact that one means of working out inner psychic tensions is to join a political party. Furthermore, it is not only the extremist right-wing and left-wing parties that attract this type of person. Parties in the political center also have members who are too intensely, unreasonably, and rigidly committed to party objectives. Such individuals develop their own rigidly structured value system, and their irrational (often neurotic) dedication prompts them to question the motives and credibility of those who politically disagree with them in the slightest way. The liberal-authoritarian or conservative-authoritarian who takes a middle-of-the-road political philosophy and distorts it to alleviate his inner tensions is found in most democratic parties.

A study in the early 1950s on the nature of Communist Party membership in the United States, Britain, France, and Italy revealed that, particularly in the United States and Britain, Communist membership appealed to those with psychological needs. The militancy of communism in the 1950s stressed the confronting and striking down of civil opponents. In a majority of cases resentment and hostility were induced by the general environment or were a result of party indoctrination. In a substantial number of cases (33 percent in the United States and 34 percent in England), however, the incidence of neurotic hostility in Party members originated as "a pattern of chronic and unconscious hostility resulting from family and childhood experiences."[54]

People join political parties for many reasons. It appears that Edmund Burke's eighteenth-century appraisal of a political party as a group of individuals committed to certain political principles no longer describes the dominant motivation, but is only one among numerous and diverse inducements. Party membership means different things to different people, and any analysis of active political membership must acknowledge this fact. Whatever the various attractions or need satisfactions of party membership, the functions of political parties are of major importance to the political system.

FUNCTIONS

Party Functions in Pluralistic Systems

Political parties in democratic and competitive political systems are first and foremost concerned with controlling or participating in government (the

[54] Gabriel Almond et al., *The Appeals of Communism* (Princeton: Princeton University Press, 1954), p. 261.

executive branch) by electing candidates. Other functions related to this first one include: acting as brokers or mediators/negotiators and balancing competing claims or demands so that conflicting groups resolve their objectives in a peaceful and institutionalized manner; organizing and articulating public opinion for electoral purposes, with the result that it influences government decisions; educating and informing the citizenry on public issues; simplifying and reducing the number of issue alternatives; recruiting and selecting leaders; establishing and confirming procedural standards for the conduct of government, especially the means by which political leaders are chosen; and providing welfare services and social outlets for party members. Parties out of power provide a constant source of criticism, which should illuminate and influence government policy and contribute toward maintaining personal and political liberties. In the American party system and some other party systems such as the French, members of the government party often are as active criticizing the government as members of the opposition parties.

A political scientist and former president of Harvard University, A. Lawrence Lowell, observed that brokerage is the most "universal function" of parties in a democracy and that the broker role is "a new profession whose function consists in bringing buyer and seller together."[55]

> *The process of forming public opinion involves, therefore, bringing men together in masses on some middle ground where they can combine to carry out a common policy. In short, it requires a species of brokerage, and one of the functions of politicians is that of brokers.*[56]

Using a term that has become nearly as familiar as broker, Gabriel Almond describes the distinguishing function of parties as *aggregation,* "the function of converting demands by interest groups into general policy alternatives.[57] Aggregation establishes a few policy alternatives in order to build or maintain an alliance of support groups. It presumes the existence of numerous interest groups (trade unions, business organizations, etc.) whose claims are balanced, mediated, and aggregated by parties. In competitive political systems, it is at the party level that the "inclusive combinatory process" labeled aggregation occurs.

A critical party function is electioneering, although in recent years the ability of parties to sway opinion has been questioned. In the metropolitan Detroit area where party organization is well-developed and active, it is

[55] A. Lawrence Lowell, *Public Opinion and Popular Government,* 2nd ed. (New York: Longmans, Green, and Co., 1930), p. 60.

[56] *Ibid.,* p. 62. Lowell first offered this analysis in 1909 in the James Schouler lectures at Johns Hopkins University.

[57] Gabriel A. Almond and G. Bingham Powell, Jr., *Comparative Politics: A Developmental Approach* (Boston: Little, Brown, 1966), p. 98.

Three 1976 Democratic presidential primary candidates vie for our attention.

reported that approximately 60 percent of the adults in Detroit were "completely unexposed to party structure" and 44 percent had *never* been personally exposed to a party organization.[58] If voters are not contacted face to face or by phone, it suggests that immediate and significant electoral influence may have to come from another source. Frank Sorauf, who has written extensively on American parties, concludes that "the political party no longer monopolizes the important skills or manpower."[59] The trend today is for candidates to rely on public relations specialists, who are experts in appealing to the electorate via mass media exposure. Ad hoc campaign organizations and a phalanx of personal volunteers for a popular candidate are the more common techniques used today. The importance of primary elections in the United States means that most candidates must construct their own organization, at least for purposes of the primary.

[58] Eldersveld, *op. cit.*, pp. 442 and 526.

[59] Frank J. Sorauf, "Political Parties and Political Analysis," in Chambers and Burnham, eds., *op. cit.*, p. 54.

If the electioneering function has been modified in democracies, it has not atrophied. The Cook County "organization," or machine, or Mayor Richard Daley is but one example of an organization with electoral clout. A British example gives further evidence that the electoral role of party should not be disregarded, especially in close elections. Even though most minds may have been made up weeks or months before election day, parties can encourage those who are so busy they might not vote, stimulate the indifferent, and sway a few. The absentee ballot, or postal vote as it is known in Great Britain, indicates how a party with superior organization can be decisive:

> *What is significant is that in nine most marginally won Conservative seats in 1964 the average postal vote was 1772. . . . On the assumption that they split 2:1 in favor of the Conservatives, they would have been decisive in twelve constituencies; at any other election since 1950 they would have been decisive in at least six constituencies.*[60]

Parties perform important though changing functions in democracies. In other political systems party functions are also important.

Party Functions in Authoritarian and Totalitarian Systems

In political systems where there are no competitive elections, the ruling political party performs numerous functions: deciding policies and programs; overseeing the government bureaucracy and the implementation of policy; propagandizing and indoctrinating the masses; supervising the behavior of the population; and selecting and approving party leaders and persons in positions of influence at all levels of society. Joseph Stalin expounded the exclusive position of the Communist Party:

> *The Party must stand at the head of the working class; it must see farther than the working class; it must lead the proletariat, and not follow in the tail of the spontaneous movement.*[61]

A totalitarian party not only attempts to control the most influential stratum of society, but also to colonize it and win its positive support. Academic and professional groups are the most rapidly expanding segment of the Soviet population and the CPSU. The policy-making and supervising functions of the CPSU are the most important, and these functions depend on the allegiance of the academic and professional strata. Table I shows the concern of the leadership in this regard.

[60] Peter G. Pulzer, *Political Representation and Elections: Parties and Voting in Great Britain* (New York: Praeger, 1967), pp. 88–89.

[61] Joseph Stalin, *Foundations of Leninism* (New York: International Publishers, 1934), p. 109, quoted in Merle Fainsod, *How Russia is Ruled,* 2nd ed. (Cambridge: Harvard University Press, 1964), p. 137.

Table I CPSU Membership Among Major Professional Groups

Profession	Number in Party		Approximate Party Saturation in Percent	
	1947	1964	1947	1964
Teachers	80,000	700,000	16.0	25.0
Doctors	40,000	110,000	19.0	22.0
Engineers	148,000	592,000	38.0	42.0
Agriculture specialists	24,000	118,000	19.0	44.0

Source: Adapted from T. H. Rigby, *Communist Party Membership in the U.S.S.R.: 1917–1967.* Copyright © 1968 by Princeton University Press. Adapted by permission of the publisher.

Recruiting and indoctrinating the policy-influential groups is complemented by mobilizing and politicizing the masses. An important means by which the party can accomplish this is through elections, although elections are different from what we regard as normal because generally there is only one candidate per office. Elections are a time for propagandizing and indoctrinating the masses and justifying government policy. Electoral turnout and the percent of valid votes in a district is also an indication of how well the party organization in that district has done its job, and of whether any threatening discontent, as expressed through blank or defaced ballots, is present. Some parties claim to be especially successful. If one is to believe official figures, only *four* persons out of 978,161 registered voters, failed to vote in the 1966 Albanian elections.[62]

Functions in Developing Political Systems

Political parties in the Third World perform many of the same functions as in authoritarian and totalitarian systems, especially if there is only one party or one party overshadows all others. Only a few Third World countries (for example, Costa Rica, Malaysia, Sri Lanka, Venezuela) have competitive elections.

Most developing societies possess only a short political heritage. Traditional institutions, at least at a national political level, are of slight use in the

[62] Julias Birch, "The Albanian Political Experience," *Government and Opposition,* VI, No. 3 (Summer, 1971), p. 63.

contemporary world. If they do exist they are undergoing substantial modification, as in Thailand, where a once powerful king became a figurehead after the 1932 revolution. The inheritances from the European colonial period, while important, were of short duration because of the accelerated and tumultuous events that led to the withdrawal of colonial governments after World War II. Constitutional and government arrangements generally did not have the time to develop.

Samuel P. Huntington has noted that in situations where "political institutions are weak or nonexistent, "stability and the beginning of political integration depend upon a strong party. The party becomes the one institution that can organize and develop the country. It becomes "the distinctive organization of modern politics" whose functions are "to organize participation, to aggregate interests, to serve as the link between social forces and the government."[63]

Political parties, like all organizations, are made up of the interaction patterns of human beings and are subject to local mores, customs, and social institutions. Constitutions and laws provide the formal guidelines within which parties must operate, but the intraparty behavior patterns—including exercise of influence, negotiation, and rewards and patronage for one's supporters—determine the character of the party or party system.

Whether a party can assume important responsibilities can only be answered by looking at specific countries. Aristide Zolberg's analysis of West African states suggests that the demands on party are often too great. The rapid expansion of party organization in order to undertake the governing functions has, on occasion, made the party a point of conflict between traditional and nontraditional interests. Speaking very candidly to this point, President Toure of Guinea admitted:

> *Certain party committees did not represent more than two or three families and the membership was dominated by family discipline or by the family chief who was at the same time the president of the committee.*[64]

Few political parties in the developing world are technologically and ideologically capable of achieving the monolithic character of the totalitarian parties in the West. The largest and most notable effort in this regard was made by the Chinese Communist Party. This attempt began to show public signs of failure with the overt launching of China's Cultural Revolution in 1966. The revolution was launched to rectify the thinking of party cadre who, after nearly two decades in power, were complacent, bureaucratically sluggish, and often more pragmatic, if not opportunistic, than properly revolutionary. The Cultural Revolution was eventually halted in

[63] Huntington, *Political Order in Changing Societies,* p. 91.

[64] *Afrique Nouvelle,* November 20, 1964, quoted in Zolberg, *op. cit., Order* p. 103.

1969 when it became clear that the authority system of the Communist regime was being undermined.[65]

The role of the party in a developing country is potentially unlimited, but the problems associated with institutionalizing the organization and functional responsibilities are of equal magnitude. The struggle to establish authority patterns premised on predictability and stability is the history of the developing world since 1945.

Interest Groups

Most people are gregarious, at least in some of their activities. As society grows and people interact and depend on those beyond their immediate families, they tend to form groups to promote or protect their interests. And as we discussed in the chapter on political theory, a principal reason democratic theorists believed organized government came into being was to protect and facilitate private interests. Much of politics, at least pluralistic politics, is about conflict, negotiation, and government decisions, which often represent a compromise. Many people get involved in politics for reasons of self-interest, or join groups they believe will watch out for their interests. A great deal of political participation is through membership in an organized group.

Robert Dahl lists twenty institutional guarantees that are required if a democratic political system is to exist. The first "requirement" listed is the "freedom to form and join organizations."[66] In a major work published fifteen years earlier, the same author noted that through groups (and other means) a democracy, which Dahl calls a polyarchy, extends "the number, size, and diversity of minorities whose preferences will influence the outcome of governmental decisions."[67]

Defined

An interest group is in most cases an advantage group; it is to an individual's advantage to join. It is an organized body that is supposed to look after the interests of its members. Interest groups are made up of people who share common traits, attitudes, beliefs, and/or objectives, and who organize to promote and protect these interests. Organized groups have

[65] For a succinct overview of the Cultural Revolution, see John Gittings, "The State of the Party," *Far Eastern Economic Review,* LIX, No. 9 (Febrary 29, 1968), pp. 375–380.

[66] Robert A. Dahl, *Polyarchy: Participation and Opposition* (New Haven: Yale University Press, 1971), p. 3.

[67] Robert A. Dahl, *A Preface to Democratic Theory* (Chicago: The University of Chicago Press, 1956), p. 133.

by-laws, formal membership requirements, annual meetings, selected officers, provide information and other services to members, and maintain a communication flow through such things as newsletters, which include explanations of the organization's objectives and the efforts to achieve these objectives.

Although the terms "interest groups" and "pressure groups" are often used interchangeably, some political scientists do distinguish between the two. A pressure group is one that deliberately seeks to influence the public authorities. Some groups are organized specifically for this purpose, such as the Vietnam Veterans Against the War or Concerned Citizens for Initiated Act *X* or for a state constitutional amendment (for example, a state-wide referendum on a state income tax). Others may be interest groups looking after the welfare of their members, which only occasionally attempt to influence a public issue. One example would be the Automobile Association, which provides insurance, tour information, towing, repair, services, and bail bond, etc., but may infrequently engage in political activity, such as opposing an increased gasoline tax or initiating legal action against a well-known and persistent speed trap operation. We use the term interest group in this book because almost all such groups, at one time or another, attempt to influence the public authorities on some issue. Interest groups are distinguished from political parties by the fact that while interest groups attempt to influence government decisions and even support political candidates, they do not nominate candidates for public office. Moreover, most interest groups usually have narrower concerns, such as minimum wages, textile tariffs, gun control, milk supports, etc., while political parties are concerned with all aspects of public policy, both domestic and international.

Evolution of Interest Groups

The twentieth century has witnessed the burgeoning of interest groups. The two principal reasons are functional specialization and social pluralism leading to the evolution of more specialized groups (such as the General Confederation of Beet-Growers in France and the Milk Producers Association in the United States), and the fact that governments through out the world are taking on more and more activities and responsibilities.

Private groups now have much more to gain or lose as a result of government policies. In an effort to influence government decisions, a group is increasingly likely to encounter other organized interests with conflicting objectives, and this leads to greater activity. Government is more persuasive and is more likely to affect the private lives of persons than it was thirty or fifty years ago. In a superior study of the British Medical Association, Harry

Eckstein found the growth of government an important reason for political activity by the BMA:

> *The state of Britain today [1950s and 1960s] disposes directly of 40 percent of the national income; and that fact speaks for itself. We may regard political and actual groups . . . drawn into politics chiefly through the impact of public policies, either policies actually adopted or policies which are "threatened."*[68]

As the population becomes more economically differentiated, groups emerge to organize and represent these specialized interests. When one interest group begins to make claims on government, new groups are organized to counter these claims and increase their bargaining power and protect their clientele.

Self-interest obviously leads to the formation of interest groups. Self-interest as first cause has been described in a general summarized "exchange theory of interest groups," as developed by Robert Salisbury. All groups originally are based on a distinction between the entrepreneur, or organizer, and the individual member, or customer. People belong because they receive some benefits. And the important fact about this explanation is that it provides specific examples of why formal associations are created by the entrepreneur–organizer.[69]

The first broadly successful American farm organization was the Grange, followed by such associations as the Farm Bureau and the Farmers Union. The Grange was originally a lodge, with a secret ritual for both the farmer and his wife. One of its chief objectives was to foster scientific farming at lectures and discussion sessions. Within three years of its founding in 1867, the Grange was spearheading the fight to get state legislatures to regulate railroads, especially setting the maximum shipping rates railroads could charge. The Grange movement also was active in establishing cooperative stores, elevators, creameries, and so on.

Salisbury emphasized the creative and innovative role of the entrepreneur–organizer, who offers future customers (potential members) benefits if they join the organization. When customers "buy" by joining, the group is in business, Organizations are created by leaders who develop a package of advantages that benefit both the leader and the member, and the organization takes shape and grows. This theory emphasizes the roles of specific individuals (entrepreneurs) whose efforts bring about the first

[68] Harry Eckstein, *Pressure Group Politics: The Case of the British Medical Association* (Stanford: Stanford University Press, 1960), p. 27.

[69] The material on the exchange theory is drawn from Robert Salisbury, who explains the origin and continuation of interest groups in terms of benefits and costs. Most of his examples are drawn from the history of farm organizations. See his "An Exchange Theory of Interest Groups," *Midwest Journal of Political Science*, XIII, No. 1 (February, 1969), pp. 1–32.

visible signs of a new interest group. The student should not, of course, overlook the particular environment that allows certain types of organized responses, such as the poor conditions of the farms in nineteenth-century America, nor should the Constitutional freedom to organize be overlooked.

> *The Grange was launched by Oliver Hudson Kelly who, by dint of considerable personal sacrifice and some generous friends, managed to survive until his organizational dream had begun to take hold. Similarly, Newton Gresham, having failed as a newspaper publisher, fed his family on credit and neighbors' largesse for more than a year until his Farmers Union began to attract enough dues-paying members to sustain him.*[70]

Organizations then generally survive if members have the funds to invest, which are compensated by benefits received greater than costs. There emerges a "cyclical pattern of group membership," which is dependent on a member's willingness to commit time, interest, and especially money. In prosperous times organizations grow because members and potential members have dues money to invest. In hard times, despite the fact that the organization may represent fundamental needs under adverse circumstances, membership declines because there is so little money available for dues. During the Depression of the 1930s, farm membership dropped, but during the prosperous decade 1940–1950 "The three main general farm organizations, the Grange, the Farmers Union and the Farm Bureau went from a combined total of 866,224 family memberships to 2,108,849."[71]

Interest groups emerge and grow for a variety of reasons. These are usually a combination of factors including social, economic, and political conditions interacting with the motivations and abilities of individuals who initiate the organizations.

TYPES OF INTEREST GROUPS

We will discuss three interest group typologies so that students can be aware of some of the different ways interest groups are classified and analyzed.

1. One method of classifying groups is according to the type and scope of interests they speak for. The most common is the restrictive interest group, which speaks principally for the specific interests of its members: The National Rifle Association, Real Estate Brokers Association, State Cattlemen's Association are examples of this. Numerous interest groups, among them the AFL-CIO and the National Association of Manufacturers, have come to take public positions on matters of general concern, such as

[70] *Ibid.*, pp. 12–13.
[71] *Ibid.*, p. 9.

foreign aid, the United Nations, and civil rights. These groups can be classified as permanent, multi-issue interest groups, which promote the specific self-interests of members as well as broader interests they believe will benefit not only their members but most of society. Another fairly common phenomenon on the political scene is the temporary, one-issue group that emerges in response to a controversial public question. Often ad hoc groups will organize to support or oppose specific bond issues or urban renewal projects. The Vietnamese war resulted in all varieties of groups supporting and opposing the official American position.

Many interest groups are not, however, organized to represent the specific functional or material interests of the membership. These are promotional or cause groups. In fact, a sizable number of such groups—such as, the American Civil Liberties Union, Common Cause, the League of Women Voters, or the British Royal Society for the Prevention of Cruelty to Children—are continuously supporting positions they feel will improve society in general or in a specific area. These groups are not organized to promote primarily the particular socioeconomic positions of their members.

2. Gabriel Almond's fourfold classification of interest groups is based on the style or method of interest articulation, "the process by which individuals and groups make demands upon the political decision makers."[72] Almond lists four types of interest groups.

Anomic interest groups are spontaneous, immediate-action oriented. Riots, demonstrations, strikes, and the early stages of a revolution are characteristic of their tactics. They are often alienated, and a collectivity spontaneously responds to a precipitant, whether it is a speaker or the arrest of an individual. Many of the student demonstrations in the United States and Europe in the 1960s were anomic, at least in the initial stages.

Nonassociational interest groups are categoric groups, people who share one or more characteristics in common but are not formally organized as such. Examples of these include ethnic or racial, kinship, geographic location, social class (landowners), religion, sex, and age groups. These groups are represented informally and intermittently through village or family heads, individual spokesmen, or cliques. An unofficial spokesman for a group of manufacturers in a developing country, who export a large percentage of their products, may complain to the ministry of foreign trade that the government is not providing enough assistance in finding new markets or is not underwriting the travel expenses required to attend trade fairs. A group of local religious leaders may ask a town official to help build or maintain a mosque, church, or religious school.

[72] For the most elaborate discussion of interest articulation see Almond and Powell, *op. cit.*, especially chapter 7.

Institutional interest groups originally came into being to perform functions other than interest articulation. Presumably these groups are the agents of the policy makers and they are not supposed to spend part of their energy advancing their own interests. Examples include the army, bureaucracy, schools, and church. These groups have certain advantages, among them a professionally staffed organization with a longer history than most other groups in society. Because of the important functions these groups perform (national security, administration, education, etc.), many of them have traditionally been close to the centers of power. These groups are commonly assumed to dominate interest articulation in the developing world. Frequently it is believed that the interests skillfully articulated by institutional interest groups are narrowly self-serving and serve primarily to enhance the position of one segment of an already too-powerful oligarchy. Two qualifications should be made: a) There are innumerable institutional interest groups in developed political systems. The American state university that lobbies for increased appropriations from the state legislature is one example. b) Institutional interest groups may also speak for other groups in society. In developing political systems they may be the only ones with the expertise and access to make claims effectively. Elements of the church, bureaucracy, or the military may speak for social and economic development of certain regions of the country, or for land reform, etc.

Associational interest groups are described by Almond as specialized organizations who have interest articulation as a principal function. They are characteristic of political systems in which some degree of autonomous input is permitted. These groups are well-organized with a full-time professional staff who have regular procedures for influencing public policy. Examples include trade unions, farm organizations, business associations, professional groups such as the American Medical Association, and promotional groups discussed previously, like Common Cause.

3. A third interest group typology categorizes groups according to three principal benefits members perceive themselves receiving from the organization.[73] The first is material benefits, which are tangible—personal rewards such as higher wages, an industrial park that will increase the general business volume in the community, or higher milk prices for the farmer. The second is solidarity values, in which psychological, nonmaterial needs are realized. These would include such needs as affiliation, social interaction, sense of group identification and belonging, status, fun, and congeniality. The third is *purposive* benefits, which are usually suprapersonal and are not confined to the persons promoting these objectives. Examples would be to

[73] This approach to interest groups is rather common and is summarized in Salisbury, *op. cit.*, pp. 16–22.

save the environment, promote freedom of expression, civil rights, opposition to increased defense spending, and patriotism and national loyalty. The expression and support of these values is often personally satisfying. Benefits that result accrue to large numbers of people who have not joined the organization or may not even be aware a group exists promoting an objective.

Individuals may belong to an organization and in the process receive more than one type of benefit. Or one person may perceive one type of benefit while another person perceives a different benefit. The benefits to members may also change over the years. Veterans' organizations are one example of such variations in benefits. The late V. O. Key concluded that "every war has been followed by the establishment of a society of veterans to bring pressure for the creation of conduits from the Federal Treasury to the pockets of the veterans."[74] One of the most successful veterans' organizations in the United States, founded at the end of World War I, is the American Legion, which has nearly 3 million members. The Legion and other veterans' groups have been highly successful in securing material benefits such as bonuses, medical care, educational allowances, and the veterans' 10-point test preference when applying for federal jobs. As these benefits have been secured, solidarity values have become more relevant. For many veterans and their families the American Legion building is a center of social and recreational activities. Purposive benefits are also an aspect of veterans' organizations. Various patriotic contests are held and awards made to high school students and others. In 1921 the Legion was a founding sponsor, with the National Education Association, of American Education Week (now also cosponsored by the U.S. Office of Education and the National Congress of Parents and Teachers). During American Education Week programs are undertaken that alert communities to the achievements and needs of the local schools. A strong America and loyalty to it are important objectives of most veterans' groups. The material benefits were emphasized initially, after major wars when millions of new veterans returned home. The other benefits became more important as material objectives were achieved. Although no survey has been taken, we may assume that veterans belong for different reasons. Some may be most interested in the social benefits, while others may believe membership is the most effective way to identify with and support suprapersonal, educational, and patriotic goals. The delivery of benefits may change over the years as well as the fact that different benefits are seen as important by different individuals at a given moment in time.

[74] V. O. Key, Jr., *Politics, Parties, and Pressure Groups,* 5th ed. (New York: Thomas Y. Crowell, 1974), p. 106.

Functions

The first, if not always obvious, political function of an interest group is to influence public policy. In so doing, it helps to communicate popular feelings and demands to the government. Where a competitive party system exists, part of an interest group's political effort is devoted to influencing one or more of the political parties. A political party in turn attempts to reconcile as many conflicting interests as the party judges ideologically acceptable or practical in order to win electoral support. Interest groups lobby or seek to persuade public officials and they often contribute time, money, and people to support political candidates (electioneering). Many interest groups also function as a source of information to bureaucrats and lawmakers. This information must generally be "straight" and not obviously and systematically manipulated if a group is to build up and retain trust and prestige.

It also has been argued that interest groups function as another "circuit of representation" in pluralistic societies. Interest group membership in a pluralistic society may be relatively low, but the number of individuals

"All I Want Is Just All The Power There Is"

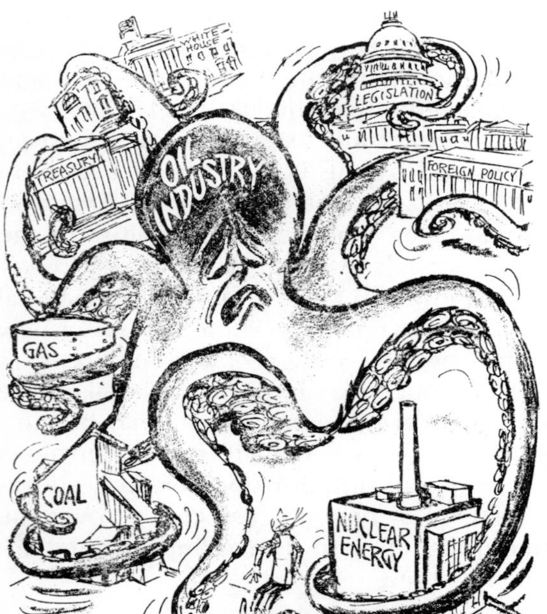

(From *Herblock's State of the Union,* Simon & Schuster, 1972.)

belonging to groups is much larger than the number belonging to political parties. One circuit of representation is elections, but these occur every two years at the most, and generally there are intervals of three to five years between elections. New issues arise and party manifestos are vague. Interests groups, to use Samuel Finer's phrase, supply "emotion."[75] They react, they communicate opinions and provide some measure of public response to officials. And on the complex application of general statutes, groups can represent their interests to bureaucrats as the administrative implementation is worked out.

In a 1959 study, which has become a classic, William Kornhauser warned against the dangers of "mass society."[76] Mass society is a potentially dangerous outcome of the industrial, mobile, technologically sophisticated environment of the Western world. The end result is that "intermediate relations," which are principally interest groups, break down. A mass society is susceptible to being manipulated by the elites with the technology available to them. One example was Nazi Germany where the ministry of propaganda under Joseph Goebbels played a key role in brainwashing the masses.

Based on his concern to avoid the evils of "mass society," Kornhauser lists several positive functions performed by what he terms "intermediate groups," or interest groups.

1. Independent groups assist in dealing with many local problems. For example, in the absence of such associations as the P.T.A., which provide channels of communication between parents and schools, the individual is less likely to develop or maintain interest and participation in aspects of the school program.
2. Most interest group leaders, irrespective of their particular aims (unless they seek to transform radically the political system), help to legitimize the larger system of authority within which their authority system is bound.
3. A large number of stable and independent groups result in diverse and competing interests. The opposition and orderly tension among groups restrains each group's power. This discourages concentrations of power dangerous to both decision makers and the masses.
4. Autonomy also prevents a concentration of power. Groups are more or less autonomous in their own spheres because they are not directly determined in their membership and policies by higher authorities.

[75] An elaboration of this point and a general and recent discussion of interest groups in Great Britain is a cassette, "Parties and Interest Groups," by Samuel Finer (New York: Holt, Rinehart and Wilson, 1972), side 2.

[76] See William Kornhauser, *The Politics of Mass Society* (New York: The Free Press, 1959).

5. There are some overlapping memberships among groups. Because each group is concerned with only limited aspects of its members' lives, groups generally do not seek total domination over their membership.
6. The presence of many groups places an important responsibility on government. The government should have the capacity, and also assume the responsibility, to protect the individual against domination by any group.[77]

Tactics, Strategy, and Effectiveness

The focus and strategy of interest groups vary considerably. Interest groups do not confine their activities to lobbying public officials and electioneering. They engage in strikes and boycotts on occasion. They also seek to build support through education and information campaigns, attempt to influence the civil service, and through court action seek to correct what they consider illegal or inequitable practices. For example, the National Association for the Advancement of Colored People (NAACP) has been especially active in litigation. Much of the civil rights progress in the United States has been achieved by NAACP court-initiated actions, where the organization used the Fourteenth Amendment to argue that many forms of racial discrimination allowed or required by state laws were unconstitutional.

With the federal form of government and separation of powers in the United States there are numerous points of influence for an interest group. A negative response from one agency, one branch, or one level of government will turn the group toward another target. Many interests have found more response from American state legislatures than Congress and vice versa. Interests concentrate their government lobbying at the most responsive points in the decision-making process.

The American Congress has been a special target of interest groups, while in Great Britain greater success has been achieved at the cabinet and bureaucratic levels. There also is increased lobbying of the executive branch and the bureaucracy in the United States. The ever widening scope and technical character of modern economic and social policies have increased the power and responsibilities of the executive–administrative branch. A majority of legislation, even in the United States, is drafted in the executive branch. Bills that become laws tend to be legal frameworks that must be "fleshed out" by administrative interpretation and implemention. Even if an interest group has "lost" and a legislative act has been passed, it may seek to further a relationship with the administering body to secure a congenial interpretation of policy.

Under the British system the cabinet dominates policy making, and the

[77] Adapted and condensed *ibid.*, pp. 76–78.

civil service has much latitude in drafting and implementing laws and regulations. Consequently, most British interest groups focus on the executive branch. Moreover, statutes often require such consultation. In 1972 one political scientist counted more than 600 advisory committees that consulted with the British government in specific areas. The groups were legally built into the system to look after the interests of their own members. In his pioneering study of British interest groups Samuel Finer observed that "on a host of official committees civil servants sit cheek by jowl with representatives of interested associations." For example, The Trades Union Congress is represented on sixty permanent committees, including the Standing Committee on Building Material Prices, the Duty-Free Machinery Imports Committee, and the Joint Advisory Panel for the Decontrol of Fat Stock.[78] It is at these points of contact that much of the influence of interest groups occurs in Great Britain. Not only in Great Britain but in many other countries there are such committees composed of representatives from the government and interest groups.

The French General Confederation of Beet-Growers (GCB) provides an interesting illustration of an interest group that has had to change its tactics. For many years the government-run *Service d'alcools* purchased more alcohol from the farmer than was being used. The alcohol was distilled primarily from beets, apples, molasses, and wine. In more recent years the French government determined to put the *Service d'alcools* on a paying basis. This meant in effect that beet-growers and others were going to have to curtail production. For several years after World War II the GCB had been able to influence many legislators in the French National Assembly, but as its power waned, it began to concentrate on the civil service. Beets are now used increasingly as a source of sugar. The GCB is expanding its laboratories and research. It now works principally with economists and other groups of civil servants. It concentrates its claims on a sugar law that will establish a production target, a favorable price, and a government program that is committed to a five-year plan or longer and that will provide a predictable market for the beet farmers. With the emergence of the Fifth French Republic in 1958, a new group of leaders dominated the government. Shifts in power in Paris, new ideas about balanced budgets, alcohol consumption, and changing technology as beets become a source of sugar, resulted in a change in tactics and strategy on the part of the beet interest group.[79]

Strategy, tactics, and the capability of the group's leadership are not the only factors that contribute to the political effectiveness or ineffectiveness of an interest group. Size can be important, but if the membership is not

[78] Samuel E. Finer, *Anonymous Empire* (London: Pall Mall Press, 1958), pp. 31 and 32.

[79] The discussion of the CGB is taken from Bernard E. Brown, "Pressure Politics in the Fifth Republic," *The Journal of Politics,* XXV, No. 3 (August, 1963), pp. 509–25.

cohesive or does not focus on specific objectives, the group may carry little political influence. The American Medical Association has usually been more politically effective than the much bigger National Congress of Parents and Teachers. The political effectiveness, cohesion, and determination of an interest group are affected by the intensity of concern among the members of the group.

The first objective of a candidate or a party in a competitive political system is to win elections. Ways that an interest group can have a voice in later policy are by contributing money to candidates, giving key campaign organizational support, or having a substantial membership located in electorally close constituencies. The last assumes that group members will vote nearly "en bloc." Through various means interest groups can aspire to participate with success in the electoral process.

The indispensability of a group is also relevant. Milk producers, longshoremen, teamsters, or coal miners are relatively small in number, but their role in the functioning of a modern industrial society makes them very important in many countries. These groups will be successful in achieving many goals, especially those of immediate and personal concern to their members. Finally, we might specify what has been implicit—the composition of the total political system is crucial. In a pluralistic environment autonomous input is allowed and even encouraged. Large numbers of people with various points of view can organize claims and promote their special concerns. In authoritarian systems, this is not the case.

Interest Input in Developing and Authoritarian/Totalitarian Systems

Political systems of the developing world manifest substantial variation in their tolerance of interest groups. States such as Malaysia, Singapore, Mexico, or Venezuela have numerous autonomous interest groups. Other political systems, such as Laos, Burma, Nepal, Saudi Arabia, and many of the African nations, have few if any interest groups with some freedom of input in the political system. In authoritarian political systems, where power is concentrated in the hands of a small group (Soviet Union, North Korea, Algeria, etc.), some interests are represented by individuals or fractions within the leadership. Inevitably, there also are present the institutional interest groups discussed earlier. Too often though, objectives promoted by institutional interest groups are intended primarily to enhance the position of one segment of an already too-powerful oligarchy.

Interest groups in developing nations, where a degree of autonomous group organization is allowed, can play especially crucial roles. Historically, the rulers in these areas have not been expected to consult or respond to the wishes of their subjects. Reliable information about public concerns and attitudes is not available. The newly independent governments, in order to remain in power for very long, must respond to the more urgent claims and demands of a citizenry conscious of the revolution of rising expectations. Persistent failure to initiate responsive programs and policies may lead to some form of internal war in the country, or a coup d'etat, as in the case of the fall from power of Emperor Haile Selassie in Ethiopia in 1974. In the latter instance, young military officers placed the emperor under house arrest. The power of decision making was shifted to a younger generation, but power remained concentrated in the hands of a few. A newly independent, developing society with new responsibilities and problems might find useful some form of interest group development to, if nothing else, apprise the rulers of the more prevalent concerns of the population.

Authoritarian and totalitarian regimes that are publicly committed to a monolithic conformity reject the existence of autonomous groups and the input of the claims into the decision-making process. So-called interest groups, taken over or created by the state, serve principally to mobilize, regulate, and extend the control of government. Any form of independent expression is prohibited.

One function of a group in an authoritarian system is to be a government channel, explaining to members what their true interests are and how government is meeting these interests. Interest groups also regiment and monitor individuals and serve as organizations to implement and reinforce government policy.

An example of totalitarian political system is the People's Republic of China. One method of manipulating the population is to enroll as many persons as possible in one or more state-controlled interest groups. In this case these groups propagandize and control the most populous nation (800 million) in the world. One organization, the All China Democratic Women's Federation, has over 80 million members. Much emphasis is placed on equality, and a major objective is to get women out of the home and into production and defense work. The New Democratic Youth League, with between 12 and 20 million members, is the "reserve force of the party" and is open to all young people between the ages of 14 and 25. All members of the NDYL central committee and most of its higher officers must be members of the Chinese Communist Party. The NDYL sponsors a junior group, the Young Pioneers, for the 9- to 14-year-olds. During the 1950s these two groups were urged to learn and practice the "five loves": love of fatherland, people, labor, science, and public property. Love of parents and family were not mentioned. The NDYL and Young Pioneers mold the minds of the young. They also act as a recruiting device for new leaders by spotting those with leadership abilities and by striving to create in young leaders an enthusiastic devotion to the party and its goals. Interest groups in authoritarian and totalitarian systems are a mechanism for government to dominate the population.[80]

[80] The material on the People's Republic of China is taken from Richard L. Walker, *China Under Communism: The First Five Years,* pp. 36–42. Richard L. Walker, New Haven: Yale University Press, 1955.

Summary

There are obviously many criticisms of interest groups and political parties which we have not dealt with in detail. The quiet negotiations through personal contacts between interest group representatives and political leaders, which take place away from the public limelight, may lead to secret deals. There often is a feeling that a political decision based on the intense pressure of one or two groups means that a "part" benefits to the disadvantage of the general public interest. Producer groups organize more frequently and effectively than consumer groups. Many believe these are narrow, selfish interests intent upon "ripping off" the general public. It is also commonly observed that not all members support the politics of the group with equal zeal. Some members are hardly aware of the group's political positions. Interest group leaders often are not regularly accountable to their members, and some officers may use funds for their personal benefit.

Nevertheless, political parties and autonomous interest groups are probably the best means by which to pluralize a political system and deconcentrate power. They frequently provide the citizen with a means to affiliate in an organized and effective manner and voice demands and opinions independent of the government. Political parties, which of necessity must make appeals broader than any single interest group, moderate group demands as the party draws up general programs to maximize electoral support. The aggregation of interest group claims by political parties means few groups get everything they want.

Political parties and interest groups are objects of much justifiable criticism. Nevertheless, they are the life-blood of politics. They are the most effective means to date to prevent the concentration of power in the hands of a single, ruling oligarchy. A competitive party system strengthens democracy; so also does the autonomous, often competing activity of many interest groups.

Selected Readings

The classic American introduction to political parties and interest groups was written by the late V. O. Key, Jr., *Politics, Parties, and Pressure Groups,* 5th ed. (New York: Thomas Y. Crowell, 1964). In a similar vein, a comparative introduction to parties and interest groups with a European focus is Maurice Duverger, *Party Politics and Pressure Groups,** trans. by David Wagoner (New York: Thomas Y. Crowell, 1972).

* Available in paperback.

There are many studies available on specific party systems. A carefully researched and analytical study of one of the earliest American party systems, first published in 1909, is Carl Lotus Becker, *The History of Political Parties in the Province of New York, 1760–1776* (Madison: University of Wisconsin Press, 1909). Carrying the analysis of American parties into the post-Revolutionary War period is William N. Chambers and Walter Dean Burnham, eds., *The American Party System: Stages of Political Development** (New York: Oxford University Press, 1967). A somewhat dated but excellent analysis of the American party system is Austin Ranney and Willmoore Kendall, *Democracy and the American Party System* (New York: Harcourt, Brace, 1956). A succinct contemporary overview is Fred I. Greenstein, *The American Party System and the American People,** 2nd ed. (Englewood Cliffs, N.J.: Prentice-Hall, 1970).

A selective sample of studies other than American political parties include Samuel H. Beer, *British Politics in the Collectivists Age* (New York: Alfred A. Knopf, 1967); T. McKenzie, *British Political Parties,** 2nd ed. (New York: Frederick A. Praeger, 1964); Thomas J. Bellows, *The People's Action Party of Singapore: Emergence of a Dominant Party System** (New Haven: Yale University Southwest Asia Studies, Monograph Series No. 14, 1970); Leonard Schapiro, *The Communist Party of the Soviet Union* (New York: Vintage Books, 1971); Nathaniel B. Thayer, *How the Conservatives Rule Japan* (Princeton: Princeton University Press, 1970); Paul Harper, "The Party and Union in Communist China," *China Quarterly,* No. 37 (January-March, 1971), pp. 37–56.

Three comparative party studies for the more advanced student are Maurice Duverger, *Political Parties**, 2nd ed., trans. by Barbara and Robert North (New York: John Wiley, Science Editions, 1959); Leon D. Epstein, *Political Parties in Western Democracies** (New York: Frederick A. Praeger, 1967); and Seymour M. Lipset and Stein Rokkan, eds., *Party Systems and Voter Alignments* (New York: The Free Press, 1967). The latter book especially is for the advanced student.

The importance of some form of political opposition either within the ruling party or through the medium of opposition parties is analyzed in three edited volumes: Samuel P. Huntington and Clement H. Moore, eds., *Authoritarian Politics in Modern Society: The Dynamics of Established One-Party System* (New York: Basic Books, 1970); Rodney Barker ed., *Studies in Opposition* (London: The MacMillan Press, 1971); and Robert A. Dahl, ed., *Political Oppositions in Western Democracies** (New Haven: Yale University Press, 1966). Western European Communist parties increasingly appear committed to electoral politics and are inclined to participate in coalition governments if the opportunity arises. A recent study that

* Available in paperback.

describes these 23 Communist parties is Neil McInnes, *The Communist Parties of Western Europe* (Oxford: Oxford University Press, 1975). Two studies that treat the revolutionary and conspiratorial nature of Communist parties are Philip Selznick, *The Organizational Weapon: A Study of Bolshevik Strategy and Tactics* (Glencoe, Ill.: The Free Press, 1960); and Robert Scalapino, ed., *The Communist Revolution in Asia: Tactics, Goals, and Achievements**, 2nd ed. (Englewood Cliffs, N.J.: Prentice-Hall, 1969).

Relatively short but heuristic analyses of the significance of party organization are Samuel J. Eldersveld, *Political Parties: A Behavioral Analysis* (Chicago: Rand McNally, 1964), especially chapter 1 and part III; and Robert T. Golembiewski, William A. Walsh, and William J. Crotty, Chapter XI in *A Methodological Primer for Political Scientists* (Chicago: Rand McNally, 1969). Discussions of political party functions are scattered throughout the literature. Anthony Downs, *An Economic Theory of Democracy,* is especially useful for developing hypotheses. The book analyzes political parties as if they were to follow rationally and consistently a policy of maximizing votes. An introduction to the functional part of the literature through the mid-1960s is Howard A. Scarrow, "The Function of Political Parties," *The Journal of Politics,* XXIX, No. 4 (November, 1967), pp. 770–90.

The standard post-World War II book on interest groups is David Truman, *The Governmental Process: Political Interests and Public Opinion,** 2nd ed. (New York: Alfred A. Knopf, 1971); Harmon Zeigler, *Interest Groups in American Society* (Engelwood Cliffs, N.J.: Prentice-Hall, 1964) is a general treatment. Chapter 1 provides a good introductory summary of the literature and major themes. An appropriate introduction to Robert H. Salisbury's theories is his "An Exchange theory of Interest Groups," *Midwest Journal of Political Science,* XIII, No. 1 (February, 1969), pp. 1–32. His analysis centers on the hypothesis that in order for a group to survive, members must derive benefits and leaders "enough return" or "profit." The standard work on British interest groups is Samuel E. Finer, *Anonymous Empire,* 2nd ed. (New York: Humanities Press, 1966). All of the preceding works can be used to develop hypotheses and principles when studying interest groups in other than the Anglo-American systems.

* Available in paperback.

Chapter 6

Representation and Elections

In political systems where they actually determine who will have the power to make political decisions, elections are one of the most important inputs into the political processes. They provide a link by which the governed can partly control their governors and are a major battleground on which rival interests can fight out their claims. Elections are also the chief institutional mechanism by which representatives are selected. Representation can provide an effective process for making demands and translating them into policy. Though the idea of representation developed independently of democracy, representation and elections are closely identified with modern democratic systems, so closely that many people erroneously think of them as the only means of popular participation and control in large pluralistic states. Nevertheless, elections and representation imply that power and authority come from the people, that they flow from the bottom up. Where this condition is missing, elections and representative type institutions can exist—they are found under almost every form of government—but they do not decide who will govern or how.[1]

THEORIES OF REPRESENTATION

"No taxation without representation" is a well-known battle cry in Western politics. We are all familiar with taxes, but what is representation?

[1] We will use the phrase "representative institutions" rather than legislatures to indicate that many agencies may be involved in speaking or defending popular values and interests. Under some circumstances these may include executives, judicial systems, bureaucracies, even political parties. Legislatures, however, are the major representative bodies.

Representation has many different, even conflicting, meanings. It can mean a typical sample drawn from many similar items; portraying or presenting a likeness of someone or something; a symbol; to act the role of someone or play a part; or to stand in the place of someone and act for them or in their name.[2] Politically, representation means having someone act in your place in governmental decision making. Representatives are people who act for or on behalf of other people in the decision making process. They speak for and commit others to particular courses of action.

There are many different ways in which a person can be understood as representing another politically. Many have nothing to do with either democracy or elections. Throughout history many people have claimed to be representative. Medieval and Renaissance kings claimed to represent or act for their people, regardless of what the masses of people thought. Leninist doctrine creates a role for the disciplined revolutionary party as the representative and embodiment of the proletariat's real interest. According to many Fascists the leader, or *Führer,* somehow incarnates the will and interest of the people. Other theorists, such as Thomas Hobbes (1588–1679) argued that the people give up all their power to a sovereign whose will is then absolute and unchallengeable but is understood as embodying the will of the people.

Such ideas, however, have nothing to do with liberal, Western concepts of representation. These emphasize that representatives are selected by their constituents and are accountable to them, at least through elections. Elections are the key to modern concepts of representation. Linking elections, representation, and responsibility does not, however, tell us what the representative does or what the link or connection is between the representative and represented. Since at least the eighteenth century two persistent, conflicting, though plausible, theories have attempted to explain the relation between representative and represented. Variously called delegate versus trustee, mandate versus independent, or delegate versus independent, the argument centers on how much independence a representative can have from the wishes of his or her constituency. The following answers are typical of a continuing and unresolved debate. This debate is alive today in current controversies over to what extent congressmen should mirror their constituents' demands on issues such as busing, inflation, unemployment, foreign aid, and war.

Independent or Delegate?

Edmund Burke (1729–1797) best stated the argument that elected representatives should be independent of their constituents' wishes when

[2] These and many other meanings are discussed in Hanna Pitkin, *The Concept of Representation* (Berkeley: University of California Press, 1967) pp. 1–13, 241–252 and *passim*; and Hanna Pitkin, ed., *Representation* (New York: Atherton, 1969) pp. 1–23.

those wishes conflict with the representative's best judgment on an issue. Burke argued that we elect representatives for their good judgment, not merely as mirror images of our desires. The exercise of judgment requires independence of thought and action. Burke claimed

> *it ought to be the happiness and glory of a representative to live in the strictest union, the closest correspondence, the most unreserved communication with his constituents. Their wishes ought to have great weight with him. . . . It is his duty to sacrifice his repose, his pleasures, his satisfactions to theirs. . . . But his unbiased opinion, his enlightened conscience, he ought not to sacrifice to you or any set of men living. . . . They are a trust from Providence, for the abuse of which he is deeply answerable. Your representative owes you, not his industry only, but his judgment; and he betrays, instead of serving you, if he sacrifices it to your opinion.*[3]

For Burke the representative's first duty was to look after the national interest. When local interests or opinions clashed with national interest or tradition, representatives should ignore local opinion. To do this the representative must have some independence of action. Moreover, elected representatives are at the center of power and deliberation. They are involved in hearing arguments, presenting ideas, weighing and balancing judgments. This argument is much amplified in our day, by notions of secrecy and exclusive information, with politicians claiming that chief executives should have a larger voice in decision making than legislative bodies. For Burke, representatives could not be bound by local interests or instructions and still perform a deliberative function for the national interest. The representative is, therefore, a trustee, holding the people's power. The people themselves do not hold power. As a trustee it is the representative's duty to work for the constituents' and nation's real interest, not for temporary, often mad, opinions that may seize an unreflective and ill-informed public.

Implicit in Burke's argument is the idea that representatives have superior wisdom, information, and expertise. Many have challenged these assumptions and the idea that representatives can best perform their function if independent of their constituency's wishes. Though no single individual sums up this argument as Burke does for independence, many have argued for and accepted the idea that a representative must reflect the expressed interests and desires of his constituency, that he must be a delegate from the local area to the state or nation.

In its purest form the representative as delegate thesis argues that the representative has no independent function. He or she is merely a proxy, a stand-in, a pipeline for his or her constituency. The representative follows

[3] Edmund Burke, "Speech at the Conclusion of the Poll," Bristol, November 3, 1774, many editions. *Works* (London: 1854, Vol. I), pp. 446–47.

only the instructions from the constituency and has no policy making or deliberative function. His primary duty is to present the constituents' opinions and decisions, defend their interests, and vote according to their instructions. When new situations arise the representative must return to the local constituency and receive new instructions. If he cannot agree with his constituents' wishes, he must either vote against his will or resign.

Although he did not approve of representative government, Jean-Jacques Rousseau (1712–1778) came closest to expressing the delegate view. In the *Social Contract* Rousseau argued that representation was tyranny, control of the sovereign people by their representatives, unless the representatives only conveyed the desires of the people. All they could do was transmit decisions, nothing more.[4]

Without going to this extreme, Thomas Paine, Thomas Jefferson, and John Adams considered that at least one house of the legislature ought to closely reflect the interests and opinions of the people at large. Many European constitutions expressly forbid giving binding instructions to elected representatives, but call for proportional representation to insure that many interests will be heard. Common American attitudes indicate a strong belief that representatives should reflect constituent interests. Yet reflecting constituent interests is far from serving as a pipeline for constituent wishes. To be effective the delegate theory would require small and/or homogeneous electoral districts where people would be very much alike. Probably it would also require simple problems and highly informed voters. As such, we have no national examples of the delegate thesis in practice. The U.S. Congress under the Articles of Confederation, when members were instructed by their state legislatures, and the United Nations General Assembly are the closest examples of the delegate thesis in operation.

Obviously, there is a great deal of tension between these different theories. It is not simply a matter of choosing one or the other. There is no unequivocal answer as to which system would be superior. Your own answer must depend on your values, coupled with your expectations about government and interpretation of political traditions. Politicians are of many minds on this question. In Britain members of Parliament see themselves as being concerned with their constituency but vote according to the determination of their party. In the United States,[5] legislators often say they respond to their constituents' interests, particularly in providing services, but rarely find clear statements of those interests. On many issues the public is uninterested or poorly informed on both basic facts and how

[4] Rousseau's arguments are conveniently collected in Pitkin, *Representation, op. cit.*, pp. 51–72.

[5] John C. Wahlke, *The Legislative System: Explorations in Legislative Behavior* (New York: John Wiley, 1962), chapter 12.

their representatives voted. Many people, as many as 50 per-cent in the United States, do not know who their representatives are. Representatives have a great deal of independence of action on issues that have low visibility to the public. On most questions before a legislature, representatives follow their own minds or respond to interest groups simply because the public at large is not deeply interested in or informed about them. On highly visible, often emotional issues, such as busing, foreign aid, inflation, and unemployment, representatives have less room to follow their own inclinations because their constituents have strong opinions on these issues and long memories at the next election. For example, former Senator J. William Fulbright, Democrat from Arkansas, had independence on most foreign policy issues but little on civil rights.

In fact, these rival theories represent two ends of a continuum. How close to one or the other end a country or even a particular legislator will come depends on many things that may shift over time. These include the strength of the political parties, laws, customs, and traditions; the legislator's view of his duty; the visibility of issues; and the obvious desire for re-election. Weighing these different factors, we can say that one representative or state is closer to being independent, while another is closer to being a delegate. Each, however, will exercise some elements of these rival theories.

WHAT DOES A REPRESENTATIVE REPRESENT?

Theories of representative–represented relations do not tell us exactly what a representative represents. Burke claimed representatives look after the fixed permanent interests of the nation. Delegate theorists claim representatives defend their constituents' expressed interests. Assuming a fair apportionment and the right of everyone to participate, problems remain; it is useful to point out some of the relevant questions even though we can give no concrete answers to them.

The larger states become, the greater the distance and distinction between represented and representative. The more people a representative "represents," the less contact and control each person has over his or her representative. Representatives become more independent as size and pluralism in districts increases simply because there are more people to respond to. Not only are individual voices lost when many people speak, but in large districts representatives depend less on any single group for re-election than they do in small ones.

If increased size makes contact with individuals more difficult, perhaps it can be said that representatives represent a majority of their constituents. Leaving aside what this means for those who are in the minority, we must ask who or what a majority is. This is neither a flippant nor an easy question. Majorities are rarely fixed and permanent. They shift from issue to issue. A person may be in the majority on one issue, in the minority on another, and in different coalitions on each issue. If the representative is to carry out a deliberative function, he or she cannot poll the constituency on every issue, even if the members of the constituency could be expected to have opinions and preferences on all issues.

Perhaps interest groups answer our dilemma. Can we say that representatives respond to and represent the expressed interests of organized groups? They do simply because organized groups are better able to offer programs, rewards, and threats than unorganized masses. But the question then becomes who do the interest groups represent and what do they seek? Moreover, many people are not organized or may never be part of a majority opinion or interest. The theory of representation holds that everyone is represented, but quite often major opinions and wishes are neglected. As noted below proportional representation is one answer to *this* problem.

Finally, despite our political and institutional focus, representation is not confined to formal political institutions. Large private groups, such as professional organizations and labor unions, often maintain representative mechanisms. The American Medical Association has a House of Delegates, and elected representatives from local medical societies meet yearly to decide basic policy. Most large labor unions have similar mechanisms. Moreover, political parties and interest groups are representative of their members in shaping and influencing governmental policy. Often nongovernmental feedback agencies, such as the press or television, are also involved in "representing" opinions. Bureaucracies often "represent" particular clients or interest groups. But are these representative in terms of democratic values? Many argue that these organizations must be made accountable at least to their members. This demand faces all the problems that formal elected representative institutions face, coupled with the fact that the decision-making process of these organizations tends to be hidden from public view.

What a representative does and how he or she responds is therefore not always clear. Despite these problems, representation is still an important key to popular participation in states that are too big for direct decision making by all citizens. Along with interest groups and party activity, representation is one of the most important schemes for including the mass of people in decision making, at least in terms of helping choose who the formal political decision makers will be. Though it does not work perfectly, it provides people with a serious opportunity to influence and set limits to government.

REPRESENTATION IN THE CONTEMPORARY WORLD

The ideas, problems, and tensions discussed above are peculiar to Western liberal-democratic states because the concept of effective representation by elected officials is largely nonexistent elsewhere. Elections occur but they are often more form than substance.

The theory and practice of representation developed in the West before the modern concept of elections. Representation is traceable to the thirteenth century, although only Great Britain has a more or less unbroken record of development. Representative government in secular and church institutions in medieval Europe did not include elections. It was assumed that the nobility, church officials, and burghers spoke for the territories or groups in their realm.[6] It was not until the seventeenth century in England that some theorists began to link representation and responsibility to constituents through elections. Successful institutionalization of this link through widespread adult male participation in moderately honest elections to select representatives did not develop until the late eighteenth and early nineteenth centuries, first in the United States and then in England. Universal adult suffrage was not achieved until the twentieth century, and even then many people could not participate because of prejudice and social pressures. Nevertheless, the struggle to obtain universal suffrage in the selection of representatives was first fought and won in the West.

Efforts to make representative institutions effective and responsive continue today. As recently as 1962 the U.S. Supreme Court in *Baker* v. *Carr* declared that the Constitution requires one person, one vote.[7] The *Baker* v. *Carr* decision helped insure that each urban and suburban resident would have the same representation as a rural voter. The decision required reapportionment of state legislative districts to insure equal population in urban and rural districts. Previously, in most states, rural districts had been smaller, insuring that rural districts elected more representatives per given number of people than urban districts. In effect, rural votes were worth more in terms of elected representatives. Subsequent decisions extended the equal population requirement to such areas as elections within states for the U.S. House of Representatives.[8]

Though decisions such as *Baker* v. *Carr* extend representation, the significance of representation remains a basic question. Today many are dissatis-

[6] See especially R. W. Carlyle, *A History of Medieval Political Theory in the West,* Vol. 5 (Edinburgh: Blackwood, 1971), pp. 128–40; "Medieval Representation in Theory and Practice," special issue of *Speculum,* 29, (April, 1954), pp. 347–476; A. R. Myers, "Parliaments in Europe: The Representative Tradition," *History Today,* 5 (June and July, 1955), pp. 383–390, 446–454.

[7] 369, *United States Reports,* 186.

[8] See especially Gordon E. Baker, *The Reapportionment Revolution* (New York, Random House, 1966).

fied with the apparent inability of representative institutions to solve fundamental problems. Quite often people complain that representative institutions are in decline, unable to cope with an increasingly complex world. This, however, is a problem for all political institutions everywhere, not only representative ones. Yet this is not a comfort to people concerned with the role and place of representation.

Representative type institutions exist in the Communist states of Eastern Europe and the Soviet Union. Their function, however, is different from that in most Western states. Though the Soviet constitution vests all power in an elected "Supreme Soviet," effective power rests with the Communist Party, which controls both the government and nomination to local and Supreme Soviets. The Soviets do not control the government in any meaningful sense. Rather, they serve to ratify decisions taken elsewhere. Instead of reflecting the flow of power and authority from the bottom up, they serve to socialize people and generate support for government policy.[9] Though the situation varies from country to country—in Yugoslavia political institutions have more power—nowhere in Eastern Europe do political representative institutions have the influence over policy that they have in the West.

There is no single way to characterize representative institutions in the developing states. In terms of power and success they range from nonexistent in states such as Saudi Arabia and a few of the one-man-rule states of Africa to almost thriving as in Singapore and, until 1975, India. They have been most influential in former British colonies and in Latin America, but even here representative institutions are weak measured by Western standards. Most developing states have some form of representative institution but almost everywhere they have little power and are dominated by strong executives. In countries such as Chile and India where a tradition of strong representative institutions appeared to be developing, recent coups have virtually eliminated legislatures as effective political voices. As fragile and limited as representative institutions may appear in the West, they have more power and more opportunity to affect policy than anywhere else.

Elections—The Method for Peaceful Change of Leadership

MAJOR ELECTORAL SYSTEMS

Elections in pluralistic societies make it possible for the largest number of persons to participate in politics and permit the largest number of

[9] Frederick C. Barghoorn, "Politics in the USSR," in Gabriel Almond, ed., *Comparative Politics Today* (Boston: Little Brown, 1974), pp. 294–97.

viewpoints to compete for popular support. In authoritarian one-party states elections serve a somewhat different function. They provide legitimacy for the regime, create a sense of mass participation in government, and serve to create a democratic facade for the regime.

Single Member Districts

The simplest type of electoral system is the single-member district with plurality elections. This is used in the United States and Great Britain for choosing members of Congress and the House of Commons. This system exaggerates the legislative representation of the winner and gives the second party a near monopoly of the opposition as will be explained. Minor parties become wasted votes and atrophy. Geographic distribution of electoral support is also crucial.

An American professor, E. E. Schattschneider, was one of the first political scientists to analyze the impact of single-member districts.[10] As Schattschneider noted:

> *If for example, one were told merely that a given party received a total of 10,000,000 votes in all of the 435 [American congressional] districts taken together, out of a vote of 40,000,000 it would be impossible to guess even approximately the number of seats won by the party until something were known of the distribution of the vote.*[11]

In a two party system, votes usually are not evenly distributed geographically. Some districts will be won overwhelmingly, in other districts the popular vote will be extremely close. Each party has its geographical areas of support and is able to survive a major electoral defeat. The second party monopolizes the opposition and accrues support as the inevitable dissatisfaction with the winner occurs. Third and fourth parties enjoy success only when politics is regionalized, and the smaller parties nationally are the first or second party in certain regions. If the third party has no substantial pockets of support it is doomed, as happened in the case of the Liberal Party in Great Britain. During the 1920s and 1930s it became a third party with support distributed throughout the country. Today the Liberal Party holds only a handful of seats in Parliament. In the 1970 parliamentary elections, the Conservatives won 46 percent of the popular vote (as opposed to Labour's 43 percent), and 52 percent of the seats in the House of Commons. The Liberal Party polled 7.4 percent of the vote but won only 6 seats, less than 1 percent. Under single-member districts, voters in a district are effectively limited to two viable alternatives.

The waning of the British Liberal Party in the 1920s illustrates that single-

[10] See E. E. Schattschneider, *Party Government* (New York: Holt, Rinehart and Winston, 1942), pp. 69–84.

[11] *Ibid.*, p. 70.

○ DEMOCRATIC PARTY

FOR UNITED STATES SENATOR:
(Vote for One)

☐ ADLAI E. STEVENSON

FOR STATE TREASURER:
(Vote for One)

☐ ALAN J. DIXON

FOR TRUSTEES OF THE UNIVERSITY OF ILLINOIS:
(Vote for Three)

☐ NINA T. SHEPHERD
☐ ARTHUR R. VELASQUEZ
☐ ROBERT J. LENZ

FOR REPRESENTATIVE IN CONGRESS:
TWENTY-SECOND DISTRICT.
(Vote for One)

☐ GEORGE E. SHIPLEY

FOR REPRESENTATIVE IN THE GENERAL ASSEMBLY:
FIFTY-FIRST DISTRICT.
(Vote for One, Two or Three)

☐ ROLLAND F. TIPSWORD
☐ JOHN F. DUNN

FOR COUNTY CLERK:
(Vote for One)

☐ CHARLES HALL

FOR COUNTY TREASURER:
(Vote for One)

☐ JAMES D. JORDAN

FOR SHERIFF:
(Vote for One)

☐ DARIS L. BOADEN

FOR SUPERINTENDENT OF EDUCATIONAL SERVICE REGION OF CHRISTIAN COUNTY:
(Vote for One)

☐ VANCE A. KAUFFOLD

FOR COUNTY BOARD MEMBER:
(Vote for One)
2 Year Term

☐ ROBERT E. DONOVAN

(Vote for One)
4 Year Term

☐ GEO. HENRY FINCH

FOR JUDGE OF THE APPELLATE COURT:
FIFTH JUDICIAL DISTRICT.
(To fill vacancy of the Hon. Joseph H. Goldenhersh.)
(Vote for One)

☐ JOHN M. KARNS, JR.

FOR JUDGE OF THE APPELLATE COURT:
FIFTH JUDICIAL DISTRICT.
(To fill additional judgeship.)
(Vote for One)

☐ CHARLES E. JONES

○ REPUBLICAN PARTY

FOR UNITED STATES SENATOR:
(Vote for One)

☐ GEORGE M. BURDITT

FOR STATE TREASURER:
(Vote for One)

☐ HARRY PAGE

FOR TRUSTEES OF THE UNIVERSITY OF ILLINOIS:
(Vote for Three)

☐ TIMOTHY W. SWAIN
☐ RUSSELL W. STEGER
☐ GARDNER W. HEIDRICK

FOR REPRESENTATIVE IN CONGRESS:
TWENTY-SECOND DISTRICT.
(Vote for One)

☐ WILLIAM A. YOUNG

FOR REPRESENTATIVE IN THE GENERAL ASSEMBLY:
FIFTY-FIRST DISTRICT.
(Vote for One, Two or Three)

☐ WEBBER BORCHERS
☐ ALLEN F. BENNETT

FOR COUNTY CLERK:
(Vote for One)

☐ JOHN J. AIKEN

FOR COUNTY TREASURER:
(Vote for One)

FOR SHERIFF:
(Vote for One)

FOR SUPERINTENDENT OF EDUCATIONAL SERVICE REGION OF CHRISTIAN COUNTY:
(Vote for One)

FOR COUNTY BOARD MEMBER:
(Vote for One)
2 Year Term

☐ WM. E. NOTHDURFT

(Vote for One)
4 Year Term

☐ RONALD W. NOTHDURFT

FOR JUDGE OF THE APPELLATE COURT:
FIFTH JUDICIAL DISTRICT.
(To fill vacancy of the Hon. Joseph H. Goldenhersh.)
(Vote for One)

FOR JUDGE OF THE APPELLATE COURT:
FIFTH JUDICIAL DISTRICT.
(To fill additional judgeship.)
(Vote for One)

☐ LEHMAN D. KRAUSE

◯ SOCIALIST WORKERS PARTY	◯ COMMUNIST PARTY	INDEPENDENT
FOR UNITED STATES SENATOR: (Vote for One)	FOR UNITED STATES SENATOR: (Vote for One)	
☐ EDWARD THOMAS HEISLER	☐ ISHMAEL FLORY	
FOR STATE TREASURER: (Vote for One)	FOR STATE TREASURER: (Vote for One)	
☐ SUZANNE HAIG	☐ LORRAINE M. ASHBY	
FOR TRUSTEES OF THE UNIVERSITY OF ILLINOIS: (Vote for Three)	FOR TRUSTEES OF THE UNIVERSITY OF ILLINOIS: (Vote for Three)	
☐ ANTONIO DE LEON	☐ JOHN R. LUMPKIN	
☐ MARY R. WISMER	☐ JAY SCHAFFNER	
☐ BRIAN WILLIAMS	☐ VALERIE WITZKOWSKI	
		FOR REPRESENTATIVE IN THE GENERAL ASSEMBLY: FIFTY-FIRST DISTRICT. (Vote for One, Two or Three)
		☐ RUTH A. WILBER

A ballot from Illinois. One point of interest is that a person may vote for one, two, or three candidates for Representative in the Illinois General Assembly.

member districts do not preclude the emergence of new parties. There were several reasons for the Liberal demise. First, as the party to the left of the Conservatives, the Liberals were more susceptible to the competition of the newly organized Labour Party, a party whose extraparliamentary origins and organization were quite different from either the Conservatives or Liberals.

Second, divisions and miscalculations among the leadership damaged the party. Lloyd George and one wing of the party joined a Conservative–Liberal coalition. Fifteen years of intraparty quarreling weakened the party and prevented it from reacting vigorously to the electoral challenges of the Conservatives and Labour.

The record of serious third parties in the United States indicates that the single-member district system has been an important factor in their lack of success. The only third party that replaced one of the major parties was the Republican Party in the 1850s. But it was aided by the fact that the Whig party it replaced was already in a process of dissolution. The Populist party in the 1880s had some electoral success in electing members of both houses of Congress in the West but its weakness was that it was largely a sectional party that could not replace the Democrats as the second party. Its failure was also aided by the fact that the Democrats in 1896 endorsed one of its main planks—the free and unlimited coinage of silver. The two major parties in the United States frequently "steal" proposals from minor parties.

The failure of third parties has been most apparent on the congressional level. Theodore Roosevelt's Progressive Party had little success in electing members to Congress even though Roosevelt was a popular figure who ran second in 1912 in the contest for the presidency. Only for a brief time in the early part of the century were the Socialists able to elect two members, one from a congressional district in Milwaukee, and the other from a district in New York City.

A modification of the single-member district plan is the runoff ballot, which is used in elections to the French National Assembly in the Fifth Republic. In France a second election is held for candidates who fail to receive majorities on the first ballot. In some districts only the two highest plurality candidates participate in the runoff. In others all candidates are on the ballot and occasionally even newcomers may enter the race. In all cases the runoff is decided by a plurality vote. Experience in France to date shows that only a small minority of candidates receive a majority on the first ballot.

The dual-ballot system was adopted in the Fifth Republic principally for two reasons: to encourage the emergence of a majority party in the National Assembly; and to reduce the number of Communist deputies. The law does not work against any particular party, but the final results depend upon the relationships of the parties to one another. The first vote enables each party to secure an accurate reading of its popularity. The week interval between elections enables the parties to consolidate their votes and switch their support to the most likely winners in the second vote. If a party is unable or refuses to enter into electoral alliances or trade-offs, the number of deputies it elects is far below its nationwide popular vote.

In 1958, the year Charles de Gaulle became president of the Fifth Republic, the French Communist Party (PCF) did not enter into alliances with other parties of the left. The alliances could have resulted in left support for Communists in some districts, and in turn the Communists supporting the most popular left candidate in other districts. Thus, while the PCF received 22 percent of the popular vote nationally, it won only 7 percent of the National Assembly seats. By the 1970s the PCF was participating with the Socialists and Radicals in a Union of the Left against the pro-Gaullist Union of Republicans for Progress. In the March, 1973, elections for the 490-member National Assembly, only 12 percent of the candidates won an absolute majority on the first ballot. Therefore, the division of support in the districts among the two "Unions" was crucial. The PCF won 21.4 percent of the popular vote on the initial ballot. At the conclusion of the second ballot, 73 PCF deputies were elected—15 percent of the total seats in the National Assembly—a notable improvement over the earlier "go-it-alone" strategy.

Proportional Representation

Proportional representation is designed to give each political party approximately the same number of legislative seats as the party's voting strength justifies. The two most common forms of proportional representation are the single-transferable vote (Hare) system and the list system. In the former the electoral district is one in which there are a number of seats. The voter indicates his order of preference for candidates by writing in the numbers 1, 2, 3, 4, 5, etc. The numerical preferences equal the number of candidates to be elected. A quota of votes is worked out that will entitle the candidate to a seat.

The list system is the most common type of proportional representation. Prior to an election, the party draws up lists of candidates, equal to the number of seats contested in the multimember district, rank-ordering the names of the candidates. The larger the percentage of the party vote, the more people are elected from the list. The list system was used in Weimar Germany (1919–1933), The French Fourth Republic (1946–58), and is now used in Israel and, in a modified form, in West Germany. List proportional representation reduces popular control—the party, not the voter, selects the names on the list and their rank-order. The lower the position on the list, the less likely it is the candidate will be elected. Power is in the hands of the party hierarchy. Also, the list is a simple device. The voter need only identify with the party or its symbol. The voter, however, may feel isolated from the government because he has no specific representative with whom he can identify and to whom he can turn. The immediate responsibility of the representative is to the party organization, not the voter.

In some countries the voter is allowed some degree of choice in rearranging the list according to his own preferences. Only in Austria is he allowed complete freedom in this respect.

West Germany, which enjoys political stability, has a modified system of proportional representation. To avoid small splinter parties, the country has excluded from representation in the *Bundestag* all parties failing to receive at least 5 percent of the nationwide party vote. West Germany also provides that half of the respresentatives are to be elected by majority vote in one-man districts, while the other half are chosen by party lists in each *Land* which is given a certain number of seats to elect. Under this hybrid system, West Germany has approached a two-party system consisting of Social Democrats and Christian Democrats. A small liberal party comparable to the party of that name in Britain sometimes holds the balance of power.

Advantages and Disadvantages of Proportional Representation

The distinguished nineteenth-century British philosopher John Stuart Mill presented the most important theorectical justification of proportional representation.[12] Supporters of this system contend that it gives a more accurate picture of public opinion than the single-member district plan, because it gives minorities representation proportionate to their voting strength. It is also argued that proportional representation is the best method for independent voters to express their views. Another argument is that it will help eliminate lobbying because of the greater variety of interests represented.

Critics reply that although the majority and minority systems have defects, proportional representation may make it impossible for the majority to govern. Excessive representation for minority parties may divide the legislature into interest groups that prevent the enactment of legislation based on a majority consensus. Perhaps the most effective criticism is that the purpose of elections is to create a broad majority consensus in a parliament that will enable the government to act effectively. This cannot be accomplished, it is said, if every minority group is to have exact mathematical representation.

One of the leading scholars on this subject, Carl J. Friedrich, cites the experience in Weimer Germany as a leading cause of the collapse of the republic in 1933.[13] He feels that the list system stratified party organizations

[12] See his essay, "Representative Government" in *Utilitarianism, Liberty, and Representative Government* (New York: E. P. Dutton, 1947).

[13] See Carl J. Friedrich, *Constitutional Government and Democracy,* 4th ed. (Waltham, Mass.: Blaisdell Publishing Co., 1968), Ch. XV, especially pp. 302–6.

and created new parties because of the ease with which they could be set up. Furthermore, parties were controlled by party bosses who emphasized creed and dogma. At the same time moderate parties came to be identified with some special interest group. This combination of entrenched interests and radical dogmatism made the organization of stable Cabinets very difficult.

On the other hand, Friedrich recognizes the stability of the Scandinavian countries, the Netherlands, and Belgium, under proportional representation but attributes this to the moderating influence of the monarchy in those countries. In these countries the monarch still exerts some political influence and their smallness permits a degree of intimacy between the Court and Parliament.

No conclusive answer is possible on the merits of proportional representation. It cannot be proved that proportional representation causes multiplication of parties in that most states that adopted proportional representation already had multiparty systems. Yet frequently the tendency toward political fragmentation is intensified under proportional representation. In view of the political disintegration of the Weimar Republic and the undermining of popular confidence in the Fourth French Republic, the burden of proof would appear to be on the supporters of proportional representation.

ELECTION OF EXECUTIVES AND MEMBERS OF UPPER HOUSES

There are two types of executive in pluralistic states—the presidential and parliamentary. The former is independent of the legislative branch and is elected directly or indirectly by the people at large, as in the United States and France. The parliamentary executive has the title of prime minister or chancellor and goes before the voters only in his own legislative district. In a two-party system, as in Great Britain, the head of the majority party in the House of Commons is always chosen as prime minister. In some countries as West Germany, the chancellor ordinarily serves for a term of years. In Great Britain the prime minister's tenure depends on his ability to command a majority in the House of Commons. One country, France, has a hybrid system that combines features of the presidential and parliamentary system.

THE EXECUTIVE IN PRESIDENTIAL SYSTEMS

The Constitution of the United States makes no provision for the nomination of candidates for president and vice-president aside from the provision that the presidential electors of each state, who are chosen in such manner as the respective state legislatures may designate, "shall meet in their respective States and vote by Ballot for two Persons of whom one at least shall not be an Inhabitant of the same State with themselves."[14] The intention was that the electors would exercise independent judgment in nominating presidential candidates. As will be explained subsequently, this procedure broke down, and the role of the electoral college is purely formal.

Since the time of Andrew Jackson, candidates for president and vice-president are selected by political conventions called by the respective political parties every four years. The number of delegates from each state are roughly in proportion to the size of their electorates. Delegates are chosen by party conventions or committees and state presidential primaries or a combination of the two methods. In some primaries delegates may be pledged to specific candidates and the primary voter may express a preference for various presidential candidates. The convention meets in the summer preceding the election. Sometimes no candidate has a majority of delegates, in which case a number of ballots may be necessary and party leaders may intervene to break a deadlock. The presidential nomination is followed by the selection of a vice-presidential candidate, which is usually accomplished quickly. The interim between the conventions and the election is devoted to campaigning.

When the voters go to the polls on the first Tuesday after the first Monday in November, they are technically voting for a slate of presidential electors chosen by the respective party organizations. The electoral role of each state is equal to the number of representatives in the House of Representatives plus the two senators. A party may require electors so chosen to cast the state's electoral vote for the presidential and vice-presidential candidate selected by the party's national convention. Only on rare occasions in the absence of a pledge has one or more electors cast a vote for any but the authorized candidates. The electors assemble at their respective state capitals to formally cast the state's electoral vote on the first Monday after the second Wednesday in December.

Thus, the voters do not actually vote for the presidential candidates of their choice, but for presidential electors selected by a political party. To be elected, the winning slate of candidates must receive a majority of the electoral vote. Almost always the candidate with a majority of the popular vote has a majority of the electoral vote. But this is not necessarily so, as the popular vote is distorted in the electoral college. The winning candidate receives the entire bloc of the state's vote even if his winning plurality is very small. Thus in 1888, Benjamin Harrison defeated Grover Cleveland, even though Cleveland had a popular plurality in the nation as a whole. But Harrison received a majority of the electoral vote since he carried New York with its big electoral vote by a small plurality.

The intention of the framers of the Constitution was that electors would

[14] Article II, sec. 1.

exercise independent judgment in performing their task. With the rise of political parties and the selection of electors by popular vote, rather than state legislatures, the original plan broke down. Thus, the form rather than the substance of the electoral procedure is observed.

The greatest weakness of the present system is that if no candidate wins the necessary majority of electoral votes, the president will be picked by the House of Representatives from among the three candidates with the highest number of electoral votes. Each state has one vote and the members vote by states. The vice-president is to be selected by the Senate from between the two highest candidates. These procedures open the door to the selection of a president by a process of crude political bargaining.

Only once, in 1824, was a president—John Quincy Adams—chosen by Congress. In two elections in the present century the shift of a comparatively small number of votes would have thrown the election into the lap of Congress. In 1948, due to the Dixiecrat party of dissident southern states, the loss of a few close states by President Truman to his Republican opponent would have meant the absence of an electoral college majority for any candidate. A similar situation almost occurred in 1968 due to the sizable electoral vote in the South amassed by Governor Wallace of Alabama running as a third-party candidate against Republican Richard Nixon and Democrat Hubert Humphrey.

In the French Fifth Republic the executive branch is a blend of the parliamentary and presidential systems. The president, who is elected by popular vote for a seven-year term, is much more than a titular head of state. He selects the premier and the cabinet and may dissolve the National Assembly but not more than once a year. In a sense he is arbiter between the cabinet, the government, and the parties. The office of president was molded by General de Gaulle, the first president who, despite his death, still casts a shadow over the office.

The premier and cabinet are appointed by the president. Upon taking office, they must resign their seats in parliament if they are members of that body. The premier and cabinet are answerable to both the president and the National Assembly.

The Executive in Parliamentary Systems

In Great Britain the prime minister ordinarily assumes office by virtue of heading the majority party in the House of Commons. He selects his cabinet members from Parliament, primarily from the House of Commons. He is the leader of his party and as head of the cabinet, dominates Parliament. Although he is elected only by the members of his own parliamentary district, his role is in some respects like that of an American president as the voters go to the polls to vote for him and his government.[15]

[15] See Carl V. Friedrich, *op. cit.*, p. 383.

The reigning king or queen is the formal head of the state. As such, the monarch performs the usual ceremonial functions, as does the president of West Germany, and also selects the prime minister. However, the monarch's influence is probably greater than that of a formal head of state in a republic because the monarch is the symbol of the Crown, which is the totality of executive power as well as the office of monarchy.

The chancellor is the moving power in the West German government. Although the office is filled by the president of the republic, the chancellor is selected because he is a party leader who commands a majority in the *Bundestag.* A chancellor cannot be removed unless a majority opposing him adversely changes the political composition of the *Bundestag.* The first chancellor, Konrad Adenauer, served continuously for fourteen years.

The president of the Bonn regime is largely a figurehead chosen by a joint parliamentary body consisting of members of the *Bundestag* and an equal number of members elected by the diets of the *Länder.* He has no power to dismiss the cabinet or the chancellor. All his important acts must be countersigned by the chancellor. His most important function—picking a chancellor—is largely formal, for his choice may be overruled by the *Bundestag.*

Selection of Members of Upper Houses

The manner of selecting members of upper houses is frequently different from that used for lower houses and the units of representation in the two houses usually differ as well. Also, the upper houses frequently possess less power. The United States Senate is a notable exception in this respect. In West Germany and the United States the upper house reflects the federal system. The French Senate is selected by an indirect mode of election and the members of the West German *Bundesrat* are appointed. Membership in the House of Lords is largely hereditary.

The United States Senate is a result of the Connecticut Compromise at the Constitutional Convention, whereby it was agreed that the Senate would represent the states with two senators from each state. The Senate is a continuing body with one-third of the members elected every two years for six-year terms. Since senators are elected from the state at large the state serves as a single member district. The powers of the Senate are substantially the same as those of the House of Representatives.

The House of Lords is an anachronism as a hereditary second chamber in a progressive democracy. The great majority of its membership of over one thousand hold their seats because they are the oldest son of a peer whose ancestor was appointed hundreds of years ago. Its membership also includes princes of the royal blood and 16 peers representing Scotland. There are also members whose seats are not hereditary: the 26 lords spiritual of the Church of England; about a hundred members appointed

A view of the House of Lords at the opening of a parliamentary session. Queen Elizabeth II reads the Opening Speech to the joint meeting of Parliament.

for life under an act of 1958; and the 9 "law lords" who constitute the House of Lords acting as the highest court of the land.

Although once equal to the House of Commons in power, the House of Lords has steadily lost power, especially in this century by custom of legislative act. Its chief functions today are to relieve the House of Commons of the burden of considering private bills and initiating bills of a noncontroversial nature that can pass the House of Commons with dispatch if previously debated in the Upper Chamber.

The Upper Chamber of the Parliament under the Fifth Republic of France has been renamed the Senate[16] and given limited power. Its life-span is nine years with 283 elected indirectly by local electoral colleges consisting largely of local councilors. One-third of the membership is selected every three years. In general, the French Senate may block legislation in which the government is not greatly interested.

The West German *Bundesrat* represents the territorial units of the West German Republic. Unlike the United States Senate, which represents the people of the states, the *Bundesrat* represents the states or *Länder* as such. The membership of the *Bundesrat* is 41 plus 4 nonvoting members from Berlin. All are officials of and appointed by their respective state governments and serve for indeterminate terms. Each state casts a single vote determined by instructions from their governments.

The *Bundesrat* can be overridden by an absolute majority of the *Bundestag* with the exception of legislation affecting state powers. In a legislative emergency proclaimed by the chancellor, and with the consent of the president, bills can become law by action of the government and *Bundesrat* without approval of the *Bundestag*.

VOTING BEHAVIOR

The significance of voting varies with the importance of elections in determining political decision makers. The percent of people voting, however, does not always reflect the actual importance of elections. Thus, some Communist countries such as Albania report voter turnouts of 100 percent, and typical turnouts in Communist states are almost invariably in the 95 percent-plus range. Many Western states report turnouts in excess of 80 percent (see Table I). On the other hand, in the United States congressional elections in non-presidential campaign years typically draw approximately 45 percent of the eligible electorate (see Figure 1). In 1972 55.7 percent of the voting age population voted in the United States, although this figure

[16] The influential second chamber of the Third Republic of France (1871–1940) was called the Senate.

Table I Percentage of Electorate Voting in National Elections (Numbers Are Rounded Off to Nearest Whole Number)

Country	Percentage	Year
Australia	95%	1969
	95	1972
Austria	92	1970
	92	1971
Belgium	90	1968
	92	1971
Canada	76	1968
	77	1972
Denmark	89	1968
	87	1971
Finland	82	1970
	81	1972
France	81	1967
	80	1968
Germany (West)	88	1969
	91	1972
Israel	86	1965
	81	1969
Italy	93	1968
	93	1972
Japan	69	1969
	72	1972
Netherlands	79	1971
	84	1972
New Zealand	89	1969
	90	1972
Norway	85	1965
	84	1969
Sweden	89	1968
	88	1970
Switzerland	64	1967
	57	1971
United Kingdom	76	1966
	72	1970
United States	61	1968
	56	1972

Source: Thomas T. Mackie and Richard Rose, *The International Almanac of Electoral History,* Copyright © 1974 by Free Press. Reprinted by permission of the publisher.

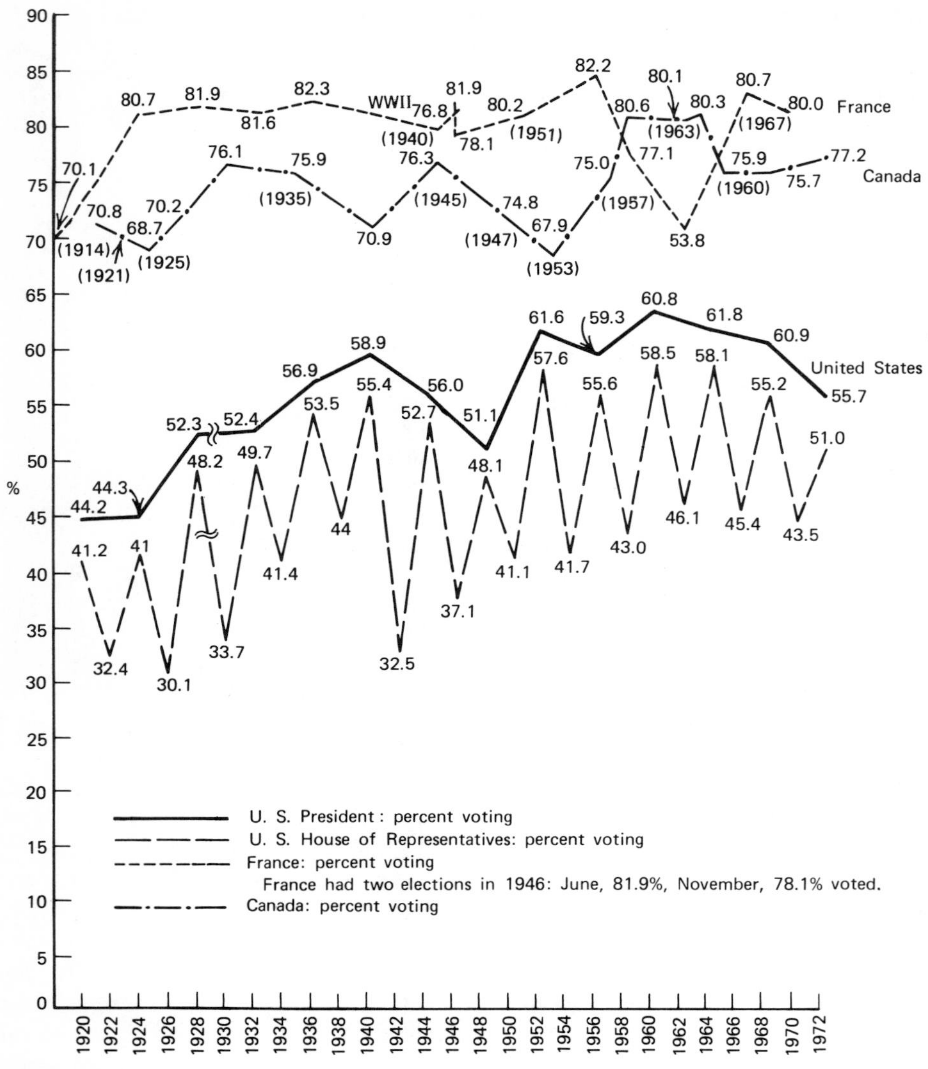

Figure 1. Percentage of eligible voters actually voting in national elections. (Canada has been chosen because it is a North American country, France because it is European with a long history of voting.) Percentages for the United States, 1920 to 1928; are based on population estimates as of July 1. (*Source.* U.S. Bureau of the Census, *Statistical Abstract of the United States: 1962* (Washington, D.C.; 1962), p. 373. Percentages for the United States, 1930 to 1972, are based on population estimates as of November 1. (*Source.* U.S. Bureau of the Census, *Statistical Abstract of the United States: 1974* (Washington, D.C.; 1974), p. 437. Percentages for Canada and France are based on Thomas T. Mackie and Richard Rose, *The International Almanac of Electoral History* (New York, Free Press, 1974, adapted by permission of the publisher), pp. 75, 81, 133, 137.

A scene from the English election riots of 1745, as painted by William Hogarth.

varied from a low of 31.5 percent in the District of Columbia to 69.4 percent in Utah.[17]

These differences force us to ask why there is such profound variation, not only among different countries, but also within the same nation-state. Political participation is a learned activity. The processes of political socialization and rewards and punishments for participation help to account for these differences. Yet what lies behind this political socialization? Who participates? Who does not? Why?

Characteristics such as race, age, sex, class, and education are correlated with voting. In the United States (except where noted our discussion will focus on the United States) black people have traditionally had a much lower turnout than white people. In 1968, 57.6 percent of the black popula-

[17] These figures are adapted from U.S. Bureau of the Census, *Statistical Abstract of the United States: 1974* (Washington, D.C., 1974), pp. 437–38. The 1960 election showed even greater variation from a low of 25.3 percent in Mississippi to 79.7 percent in Idaho. Unless otherwise noted, all U.S. voting statistics are from this source.

tion of voting age *reported* they voted while in 1972 52.1 percent reported they voted.[18] Comparable statistics for the white population were 69.1 percent in 1968 and 64.5 percent in 1972. These figures show a rise from previous years. Moreover, black citizens of voting age tend to have a lower rate of registration than white citizens. This record of lower participation does not, however, reflect any racial characteristics but rather the social and political environment of exclusion and threats and punishments for voting that many black people experienced. Before passage of civil rights legislation in 1964 and 1965, unequal literacy tests, delay tactics, and intimidation prevented large numbers of blacks from registering to vote. In 1960 before massive voter registration drives and federal intervention, 23.1 percent of the black population of the eleven southern states that made up the Old Confederacy[19] were registered to vote as compared to 46.1 percent of the white population. In 1971, 52 percent of the eligible black population was registered as opposed to 59.6 percent of the white population. Moreover, North and South, black people tend to have less education and educational opportunities and a lower socioeconomic status than white people. The less educated and worse off economically tend to participate and vote less than more advantaged groups.[20] This observation holds for minorities in most countries.

As noted in Table II, age and education have a positive correlation with voting. This is true for all races and groups. Here socialization probably accounts for greater participation. As people receive more education, they are exposed to more information about how the system works and their role in it, as well as increased exhortation to participate. People with higher socioeconomic status are more likely to receive more education. Also, as people get older they tend to participate more, probably because they view themselves as having an increased stake in the political system. In the United States in 1972, 48.3 percent of the eligible 18- to 20-year-olds *reported* voting, as opposed to 59.7 percent of people in the 25- to 34-year-old category and 70.8 percent in the 45- to 64-year-old category. If present trends continue and if the trauma of war in Indochina and revelation of governmental corruption do not produce permanent alienation from the political processes, these young voters will probably vote at a higher rate in the future. Lower voter turnout among the young tends to be typical of most Western nations.

[18] The percentage of people who report having voted is always much higher than the number who actually voted.

[19] Alabama, Arkansas, Florida, Georgia, Louisiana, Mississippi, North Carolina, South Carolina, Tennessee, Texas, and Virginia.

[20] In 1973 the median school years completed were 12.3 for the white population and 10.6 for the black population though the median school years completed is tending to even out for whites and blacks in the 25- to 34-year-old category. See *Statistical Abstract,* p. 117.

If this book had been written twenty years ago we would now include a somewhat pious and perhaps tongue-in-cheek discussion of how women vote at a much lower rate than do men. Given socialization patterns all over the world women have traditionally been discouraged from and even punished for participating; "politics is dirty" and "politics is man's work" symbolize this attitude. Moreover, women have been enfranchised only in the twentieth century. Women have had less opportunity to learn participation.[21] This situation is now changing, and as Table II illustrates, the rate of voting for women is rapidly approaching the voting rate of men. New socialization patterns and more out-of-the-home opportunities help account for this convergence. Voting, however, is only one form of political participation, and women still lag far behind men in terms of holding elective offices or participating in political campaigns. Effective resocialization and reform may reduce this difference in the future.

In the United States people with lower socioeconomic status tend to vote less than those with higher status. This is probably the result of less education, less apparent stake in the system, and less reinforcement by other groups that would encourage participation. In European countries with class-based political parties, which actively encourage people to vote, there are smaller differences in participation rates between classes than in the United States. In general, strong identification with a political party or candidate tends to encourage participation.

Many other factors affect participation. For some people political participation may seem threatening to their relation with family and friends. Others may feel it is futile due to a sense of personal inadequacy, a feeling that political forces are unmanageable, or that there is a large gap between democratic ideals and political reality. Many have weak spurs to political involvement, being concerned with their families and friends or seeing few links between political activity and satisfaction of their needs.[22] Some small number of people may simply be satisfied with their political system and see no need to participate. Others, feeling there is no effective choice between candidates or parties, do not vote.

Electoral procedures may also disqualify people from participating. Complex voter registration procedures and residency requirements prevent up to 10 percent of the potential electorate from voting in the United States. Problems with absentee ballots and difficulties in reaching polling stations disenfranchise some people. Even bad weather or a belief that one's candidate or party will win (or lose) may keep some from voting; in these cases

[21] Complete franchise equality on a nationwide level: Belgium, 1948; Canada, 1920; France, 1944; Germany, 1919; Italy, 1946; United Kingdom, 1928; United States, 1920.

[22] Morris Rosenberg, "Some Determinants of Political Apathy," *Public Opinion Quarterly*, 18 (1954), pp. 349–66.

Table II Participation in National Elections, by Population Characteristics, 1968 and 1972[a]

Characteristic	1968				1972			
	Persons of Voting Age	Persons Reporting They Voted		Percent Reporting They Did Not Vote	Persons of Voting Age	Persons Reporting They Voted		Percent Reporting They Did Not Vote
		Total	Percent			Total	Percent	
Total	116,535	78,964	67.8	30.0	136,203	85,766	63.0	37.0
Male	54,464	38,014	69.8	27.6	63,833	40,908	64.1	35.9
Female	62,071	40,951	66.0	32.1	72,370	44,858	62.0	38.0
White	104,521	72,213	69.1	28.9	121,243	78,166	64.5	35.5
Negro	10,935	6,300	57.6	38.5	13,493	7,032	52.1	47.9
18–20 years old	432	144	33.3	64.1	11,022	5,318	48.3	51.7
21–24 years old	11,170	5,707	51.1	45.6	13,590	6,896	50.7	49.3
25–34 years old	23,198	14,501	62.5	35.8	26,933	16,072	59.7	40.3
35–44 years old	22,905	16,223	70.8	27.1	22,240	14,747	66.3	33.7
45–64 years old	40,362	30,238	74.9	22.8	42,344	29.991	70.8	29.2
65 years and over	18,468	12,150	65.8	31.9	20,074	12,741	63.5	36.5
Median age years	45.2	46.7	(X)	(X)	42.4	44.9	(X)	(X)[b]

Metropolitan residence	75,756	51,503	68.0	32.0	99,248	63,799	64.3	35.7
Nonmetropolitan residence	40,778	27,461	67.3	32.7	36,955	21,967	59.4	40.6
North and West residence	81,594	57,970	71.0	29.0	93,653	62,193	66.4	33.6
South residence	34,941	20,994	60.1	39.9	42,550	23,573	55.4	44.6
Years of school completed:								
8 years or less	30,430	16,592	54.5	45.5	28,065	13,311	47.4	52.6
9–11 years	20,429	12,519	61.3	38.7	22,277	11,587	52.0	48.0
12 years	39,704	28,768	72.5	27.5	50,749	33,193	65.4	34.6
More than 12 years	25,971	21,086	81.2	18.8	35,113	27,675	78.8	21.2
Employed	70,002	49,772	71.1	28.9	80,164	52,899	66.0	34.0
Unemployed	1,875	977	52.1	47.9	3,735	1,863	49.9	50.1
Not in labor force	44,657	28,215	63.2	36.8	52,305	31,004	59.3	40.7

Source: U.S. Bureau of the Census, *Statistical Abstract of the United States: 1974* (Washington, D. C. 1974), p. 437.

[a] Persons in thousands. As of November. Covers civilian noninstitutional population. For 1968, persons 18 years old and over in Georgia and Kentucky, 19 and over in Alaska, 20 and over in Hawaii, and 21 and over elsewhere; for 1972, persons 18 years old and over in all States. Includes aliens. Figures are based on a population sample and differ from those based on population estimates and official vote counts. Differences in percentages may also be due to overreporting of voting by persons in the sample. Excludes persons who did not report whether or not they had voted.

[b] X Not applicable.

the nonvoters probably have a low motivation to vote based on some other objection.

One additional factor may discourage people from voting and that is the problem of choosing among candidates or parties. Although it is true that most people do not have well-developed and explicit policy preferences and may have relatively little knowledge about issues, most people do have attitudes about politics. Many express preferred policy outcomes or prefer certain candidate characteristics. The problem is—how should a voter choose when two or more candidates present programs, each program having some policies the voter prefers and some he or she dislikes and rejects? Table III illustrates this dilemma, common especially in countries with weak party systems.

Which candidate should the voter select? Ticket splitting may be one answer, but for some races this is not possible. In such a case powerful cross-pressures are operating because one's vote may be for some issues one favors and others one may oppose. Some voters, unable to choose, may not vote at all.

Voting is a complex act, charged with drama and importance. Whether a person will vote and how he will vote depend on both his political socialization and his environment.

THE SIGNIFICANCE OF ELECTIONS

Western Democracies

Free elections perform a crucial but limited role. They do not mathematically reveal popular sentiment about a long list of controversial public issues. At best, competitive elections are only a rough approximation

Table III Problem of Voter Identification

	Candidate A	Candidate B
Segregation	Yes[a]	No
Religion of candidate	No	Yes
Policy toward Soviet Union	No	Yes
Policy on employment	Yes	Yes
Policy on inflation	No	Yes
Arms spending	No	No
Party identification	Yes	No
Attitude toward women	Yes	No

[b] Yes indicates the voter approves the candidate's position on the issue; no indicates that the voter disapproves.

Bigger Than Either

(Reg Manning/McNaught Syndicate, October 31, 1968.)

Elections can strengthen legitimacy.

of popular feeling. No electoral system goes beyond this indispensable yet restricted function; but in the absence of some type of election and a legislature, free or manipulated, few governments today believe the public will accept them as legitimate.

Even in competitive elections, voters are not knowledgeable about all aspects of a party's program. A vote for a candidate or a party cannot be interpreted as support or even awareness of each item in the electoral program. For example, in the 1962 Wisconsin gubernatorial race, taxes were a major issue. The Democrat supported a higher income tax instead of a sales tax. A voter survey revealed that the percentage of Democratic voters favoring the sales tax was greater than the percentage of people who switched to the Democrat because of his pro-income-tax policy.[23]

Survey research in the United States reveals the impressionistic and unstructured view of politics common to a majority of people. The University of Michigan Survey Research Center concluded that presidential elections in the United States do not decide policy but at most determine "*who shall decide* what government shall do."[24] There is substantial lack of familiarity with even the most important political issues of the time. There is also considerable confusion in the public mind about what effect the election of one party over another would have on specific policies. As a result, according to the study, it may be implied that the electoral outcome is necessarily ambiguous as to what specific policies government should pursue. Also, as a consequence of the public's limited understanding of issues, interpretations as to the meaning of elections are speculative.

As to why the party vote oscillates between the two major parties, political scientists have suggested that a negative public response to the record of the party in power is more likely to influence the electorate than a positive appeal of the party out of power.

> *A majority party, once it is in office, will not continue to accrue electoral strength; it may preserve for a time its electoral majority, but the next marked change in the party vote will issue from a negative response of the electorate to some aspect of the party's conduct in office, a response that tends to return the minority party to power.*[25]

Electoral systems never equitably represent every element in the community. Neither are they as revealing of specific popular feeling as reformers in the nineteenth century had hoped. Despite these qualifications, competitive elections are the best means for the largest number of qualified persons to influence government. Popularly chosen legislatures are the institution that includes the bulk of elected officials, where the widest range of groups have a voice, and where interaction with, and accountability to, the public most frequently occurs.

Communist Societies

Pluralistic societies are not the only political systems that have elections and provide some form of legislative respresentation. Many authoritarian

[23] See Peter G. J. Pulzer who summarizes the paradoxical role of issues in British and American elections in *Political Representation and Elections: Parties and Voting in Great Britain* (New York: Frederick A. Praeger, 1967), pp. 131–137.

[24] Angus Campbell et al., *The American Voter* (New York: John Wiley, 1960), p. 541. This work is an excellent study of voting behavior.

[25] *Ibid.*, p. 288.

political systems also believe elections are important. Elections in the Soviet Union, for example, have several purposes.[26]

1. Elections provide legitimacy. The claim to be "democratic" must be substantiated, at least in part. Electoral support of 98 to 99 percent reassures an elitist ruling party and offers some evidence to the rest of the world.
2. Electioneering imparts a sense of mass participation and involvement and contributes toward building a sense of Communist civic awareness and responsibility. And, in some of the Eastern European countries (for example, Poland), there may be more than one official party candidate for the same seat, thus providing minimal competition and increasing the sense of participation.
3. Limited signs of dissatisfaction are detected. Even a slight percentage of abstentions or *nyets* signals an early warning that there is discontent and trouble in certain districts.
4. Electioneering provides occasions to meet the people, to explain and defend government policies, and to announce new programs. Western observers have noted the "political" personalities of Soviet figures, such as Party Secretaries Khrushchev and Brezhnev. They had or have the ability to communicate and interact with the population and adopt an "on the campaign trail" political style. Campaigns can strengthen bonds of identification between rulers and ruled and bring government to the grass roots, if only sporadically.
5. Elections also are for external consumption. They propagandize the "democratic" character of Soviet institutions, focus attention on the supposed legitimacy and popularity of the regime, and increase the status of the USSR in the international system.

Elections in a one-party state provide minimal popular input. They demonstrate, though, the ambivalent attitude modern authoritarian regimes have toward representative government. Some effort must be made to establish a democratic facade in order to acquire legitimacy. Elections and legislatures are common institutions in modernizing–authoritarian political systems.

Developing Countries

Depending on the nature of the political system, the functions of elections in developing countries range from some of those listed under "Western Democracies" to the manipulated elections of Communist countries.

[26] This section on Soviet elections is drawn from Vernon V. Aspaturian's succinct analysis in Roy C. Macridis and Robert E. Ward, eds., *Modern Political Systems: Europe,* 3rd ed. (Englewood Cliffs, N.J.: Prentice-Hall, 1972).

Some political leaders contend that elections are an integral part of the "democratic" process, even in one-party states. For example, President Julius Nyerere of Tanzania writes and speaks frequently on democracy in Africa.[27] Tanzania has only *one* political party, the Tanzanian African Nation Union, and seats are rarely contested in an election. President Nyerere, nevertheless, claims Tanzania is a democracy. He maintains that a national movement open to every segment of population has nothing to fear from discontented and excluded factions because no such faction exists. If a country has two or more parties, each represents only a segment of the population, but a single party is identified with the nation as a whole. Elections confirm that the one party is a *genuine* national movement, representing the whole nation and excluding none. President Nyerere suggests that frequently there are vigorous debates and the input of grassroots opinion at party meetings. He appears to argue for free debate in private party conferences, but once a policy is decided party discipline prevails. Debate and input occur before elections, but elections are a necessary part of the policy-making cycle and affirm decisions that supposedly have been debated freely within the party.

Elections are also sometimes a means of psychologically reinforcing a leadership, or after a change in government, of ratifying the new leaders. These carefully controlled elections are intended to demonstrate the success of efforts to achieve national harmony and integration. Often elections are an effort to legitimize a political system by demonstrating that a government has popular support, even when some opposition groups are allowed to compete. Beginning in 1967, there were two major elections in South Vietnam before it fell to the Communists in 1975. The Americans pressured the South Vietnamese government to hold both elections so that the Saigon government could demonstrate legitimacy by showing how many Vietnamese were willing to vote despite Communist opposition to voting; and by proving that despite a number of opposition groups, the government could win a majority in relatively free elections. A government that in some way can achieve a popular electoral majority is reinforced in its own sense of legitimacy and by the mandate it can hold before world opinion. In a few developing countries such as Sri Lanka (formerly Ceylon), elections are genuinely competitive, relatively honestly administered, and occasionally result in the incumbent party being turned out of office. Elections can provide voters with the most direct and available means of molding policy, and the Sri Lankans use them accordingly.[28]

[27] A cogent presentation by President Nyerere is "African Democracy," in Frank Tachau, ed., *The Developing Nations: What Path to Modernization?* (New York: Dodd, Mead, 1972), pp. 173–180.

[28] See, for example, the case study by Janice Jiggins, "Dedigama 1973: A Profile of a By-Election in Sri Lanka," *Asian Survey,* XIV, No. 11 (November, 1974), pp. 1000–13.

A particular electoral problem in developing countries is the mobilization of people who have had little or no electoral experience and retain strong traditional ties. Electoral mobilization sometimes inflames existing social cleavages. Clifford Geertz, who has studied this problem, warns of the danger of politicizing "primordial sentiments."[29] Primordial sentiments are the givens of biological and social inheritance, such as family, tribe, caste, language, religion, and ethnic group. Most of the new states of Africa and Asia are multilinguistic, multiethnic, and multireligious. Once a country has achieved independence there is a new and important prize, the new government. If one seeks to mobilize supporters through elections or other means, the most obvious identifications and groups to which to appeal are the primordial groups. Self-rule may actually lead to increased splintering, self-awareness, and suspicion of others, based on traditional ties and obligations. Latent primordial hostilities can be aroused that will lead to bloody and cruel confrontations. Elections may provide a mechanism by which to channel some of these emotions, or they may provide an opportunity to arouse these attachments. Consequently, elections may be rejected or manipulated so as to give the voter no opportunity to identify with and be stimulated by disruptive, centrifugal forces.

There are many reasons for developing countries to reject elections. The wonder is that at this stage of development elections with various degrees of competition are still held in several developing countries.

Summary

Elections, voting, and representation are extremely important political inputs but are not the only means of political participation. As we saw in the last chapter people also participate through interest groups, political parties, and campaigns. In Chapter 11 we will see that political violence may be a form of participation in the political system. Nevertheless, elections and voting provide the most common form of mass participation.

Electoral systems never equitably represent every element in the community. Neither are they as revealing of specific popular feeling as reformers in the nineteenth century had hoped. Despite these qualifications, competitive elections are one means for the largest number of persons to influence government. Popularly chosen legislatures provide a place for the widest range of groups to have a voice and for interaction with, and accountability to, the public. Whether voting, elections, and representation have a major impact on political outcomes varies from

[29] Clifford Geertz, ed., *Old Societies and New States: The Quest for Modernity in Asia and Africa* (Glencoe, Ill.: The Free Press, 1963), pp. 105–57.

country to country. Where they do, they provide one of the most effective means for people to influence decision making.

Selected Readings

For brief selections from various theorists who have dealt with representation see Hanna F. Pitkin, ed., *Representation* (New York, Atherton Press, 1969). See also her *Concept of Representation** (Berkeley: University of California Press, 1967) for an excellent analysis of the conflicting theories of representation. J. Roland Pennock and John W. Chapman, *Representation* (New York, Atherton Press, 1968) provides an excellent introduction to the broad range of issues involved in defining and implementing representation.

There are surprisingly few general histories of the development of representative institutions. See J. A. O. Larsen, *Representative Government in Greek and Roman History* (Berkeley: University of California Press, 1955) for an analysis of the origins of representative institutions, though these were different from the ancestors of modern representative institutions. A. R. Myers "Parliaments in Europe," *History Today,* 5 (1955), pp. 383–390, 446–454, is an accurate and readable account of the development of European representative institutions from Middle Ages to the eighteenth century.

Comparative analysis of voting is important to understand its contemporary significance. Douglas W. Rae *The Political Consequences of Election Laws* (New Haven: Yale University Press, 1971) examines the impact of proportional representation and other electoral arrangements on participation. For an informative analysis of different electoral systems and their impact on political integration within Western, Communist, and developing states, see A. J. Milnor, *Elections and Political Stability* (Boston; Little, Brown, 1969). For a cross-national analysis of participation and voting, see Stein Rokkan et al. *Citizens, Elections, Parties* (New York, David McKay Co., 1970). Though somewhat complex, this book will reward any serious student of politics. Gabriel A. Almond and Sidney Verba, *The Civic Culture* offers many insights into patterns of participation in Germany, Great Britain, Italy, Mexico, and the United States. See especially chapters 5, 6, and 9. Carl J. Friedrich, *Constitutional Government and Democracy* (Waltham, Mass.: Blaisdell Publishing Co., 1968) is a basic, and very important, descriptive analysis of governmental institutions.

There are a number of "classic" studies of political behavior, which while

* Available in paperback.

somewhat dated in terms of data, offer a bonanza of insights into and information about participation. See especially Robert E. Lane, *Political Life** (New York: Free Press, 1959).* Seymour Martin Lipset, *Political Man: The Social Bases of Politics,** (New York, Anchor Books, 1960) examines participation in a very wide perspective. Angus Campbell et al., *The American Voter: An Abridgement** (New York, John Wiley, 1964) is still basic reading for anyone interested in voting in the United States. Paul Lazarsfeld et al. *The People's Choice** (New York: Columbia University Press, 1968), though originally published in 1944, is still enlightening reading. Its successor book, Bernard Berelson, *Voting* (Chicago, University of Chicago Press, 1954) also provides much basic information for understanding American behavior. Angus Campbell, et al., *The Voter Decides* (Evanston, Ill., Row, Peterson, 1954) examines the 1952 election.

Hugh A. Bone and Austin Ranney, *Politics and Voters* (New York: McGraw-Hill, 1971) is a basic introduction to the analysis of why people participate. Angus Campbell et al., *Elections and the Political Order* (New York: John Wiley, 1966) focuses mainly on the United States, with some excellent comparative data from other countries.

William H. Flanigan, *Political Behavior of the American Electorate* (Boston: Allyn and Bacon, 1968) brings together, in a readable form, a large number of findings about how and why Americans act in politics.

Penn Kimball, *The Disconnected* (New York: Columbia University Press, 1972) analyzes the psychological and political factors leading to non-participation in the United States and some of the efforts to increase participation.

For an enlightening discussion of voting and the suffrage within the context of American political parties, see Hugh A. Bone, *American Politics and the Party System* (New York: McGraw Hill, 1971).

Reapportionment is much less of an issue today than after the *Baker* v. *Carr* decision. Nevertheless, it still involves basic questions of representation and government. See Gordon E. Baker, *The Reapportionment Revolution,** (New York: Random House, 1966) and Royce Hanson, *The Political Thickett: Reapportionment and Constitutional Democracy* (Englewood Cliffs, N.J.: Prentice-Hall, 1966).

* Available in paperback.

Part Three

The Output Agencies

Chapter 7

The Legislative Process

INTRODUCTION

Legislatures are popularly regarded as less important today than fifty years ago, but the student should not ignore the special contributions of legislative institutions.

Whenever a society is larger than an extended familial network, many objectives and values can be achieved only through authoritative rules applying to everyone in society. The legislature is the institution that makes rules for the whole society. The numerically and geographically larger a society, the more complex lawmaking and law-enforcing functions become. Legislatures, especially in plural systems, have a key role in the lawmaking process.

During the twentieth century groups and organizations have increasingly turned to government to solve a problem or oppose a proposed solution. Contemporary political systems are more politicized because of a tendency to regard government as having responsibilities in most areas of human concern (ecology, inflation, defense, education, retirement benefits, etc.) In participatory political systems governments devote a majority of their time to negotiating and balancing the claims and counterclaims of diverse ideas and groups demanding an official response or opposing a proposed response. The volume and complexity of political issues and interests continue to expand.

A democratically elected legislature is directly and frequently accountable to the people. Electoral accountability to citizens is the best means to facilitate and organize the flow of claims from the population. Legislatures

Call of the Open Road

(Shanks in the Buffalo Evening News.)

are unique because they are the only political institution providing both broad avenues of access and regular popular accountability. They are also the political body whose members maintain close contact with the general population. Legislature and representation as discussed in the preceding chapter, are inseparable concepts. A legislature, more than any other government institution, includes among its members individuals *representing* the broadest range of interests. Such legislatures provide a breadth of representation and normally include persons articulating a wide range of viewpoints.

THE EVOLUTION OF THE LEGISLATIVE INSTITUTION

Contemporary representative legislatures trace their origins to the American Congress, American state legislatures, and the British House of Commons as they developed in the eighteenth and nineteenth centuries.

The Greek *boule* was the first but only a brief attempt at a popularly chosen, representative legislature. Throughout the Middle Ages the notion of representation and legislative assemblies was nurtured in Europe, but in practice the resemblance to modern legislatures was slight. Nevertheless, a strain of thought persisted among medieval theorists that the king should be limited in his power, though it was usually not clear how this was to be implemented.

Medieval political theorists such as Thomas Aquinas (1227–1274) and William of Occam (1280–1349) sought an ordered society and a government with limited powers. The restraints on government were reason and equity. Rulership was a trust, and ruler(s) were justified because of their contribution to the common good. Justifiable resistance to tyranny was acknowledged as a possibility, but the writers did not lay out a blueprint for popular control of government.[1]

The concept of groups of men consulting and limiting the rulers or monarch never disappeared in Europe, but it was several centuries before effective institutions emerged. Nobility and, later, commoners were first called for consultation to approve new taxes. Subsequently, those called together would submit a list of grievances the monarch often was compelled to acknowledge before taxes were voted. These assemblies did not originate as a method of popular control, but were called into being as a means of strengthening the central government by raising taxes. But the various groups and classes required to attend these meetings gained political information and skills that ultimately undermined the monarchy.[2]

There was ebb and flow in the influence these councils or assemblies had on monarchs. By the fourteenth century the Commons (referring to knights and burgesses from communities rather than commoners) and the Lords were groupings the English monarch felt compelled to deal with, and the maturation of the "Mother of Parliaments" was beginning. The English Parliament was the symbol and visible embodiment of the English people, but it was not an elected or popularly accountable legislature. Nevertheless, toward the end of the centralizing and often authoritarian period of the Tudor dynasty, an English historian could write about Parliament in 1583

[1] A standard discussion of medieval theorists is found in George H. Sabine, *A History of Political Theory,* rev. ed. (New York: Henry Holt, 1950), especially chapters 12–16.

[2] Charles A. Beard and John D. Lewis, "Representative Government in Evolution," *The American Political Science Review,* XXVI, No. 2 (April, 1932), pp. 238–39.

that "every Englishman" was regarded as represented and the consent of Parliament was regarded "to be every man's content."[3]

The turning point came with the expulsion of the Stuart dynasty in the Glorious Revolution of 1688. It affirmed the ascendancy of Parliament over the monarchy, though the monarchy remained an important institution in the decision-making process until the middle of the nineteenth century. The 1689 Bill of Rights required that Parliament meet regularly and parliamentary consent was necessary for all laws involving taxation. Twelve years later the Act of Settlement limited the monarchy to Protestants. It was no longer possible for a strong monarch to reject a law passed by both houses of Parliament. During the next one hundred years constitutional practice (not law) established that the prime minister and cabinet should have the confidence of the House of Commons. The last effort of a king to appoint a prime minister who did not have majority support in Parliament occurred in 1834 when William IV dismissed Melbourne and appointed Peel to form a cabinet. Peel's repeated rebuffs by Commons ultimately forced the king to withdraw the appointment. The "golden age" of parliamentary influence and primacy in the British political system had begun.

Overlapping the assertion of parliamentary supremacy was the movement to democratize Parliament by expanding the suffrage. The great British electoral reform bills were those of 1832, 1867, and 1884. Prior to these the number of voters was small, and sometimes almost nonexistent in a district. Inequitable districts, public voting, and the buying and selling of districts were not uncommon. Occasionally an MP took what we today would regard as a very corrupt view of his legislative role and responsibilities. The following excerpt is from an MP's letter in the first part of the eighteenth century in which he refused a constituent petition:

> *You know, and I know, that I bought this constituency. You know, and I know, that I am now determined to sell it, and you know what you think I don't know, that you are now looking for another buyer, and I know, what you certainly don't know, that I have now found another constituency to buy.*
>
> *About what you said about the excise* [tax]*: may God's curse light upon you all, and may it make your homes as open and free to the excise officers as your wives and daughters have always been to me while I have represented your rascally constituency.*[4]

[3] Sir Thomas Smith quoted *ibid.,* p. 225. Westminster, began as the monastery for the west part of London, became the monarch's palace in the tenth and eleventh centuries, as well as maintaining the monastery. Parliament was called (to Westminster) to consult with the King. By 1550 St. Stephan's Chapel in the Westminster had become the permanent home of the House of Commons.

[4] P. G. Richards, *Honorable Members,* 2nd ed. (New York: Praeger, 1964), p. 157.

A 19th-century election campaign in England.

Parliamentary supremacy preceded democratization of that august institution, but by the end of the nineteenth century universal male suffrage was established in Britain; Commons, the dominant house, was elected and accountable to the popular will. Representative government was secure, and the most corrupt legislative practices were eliminated in the face of competitive elections.

American legislative experience is briefer except to the degree our representative institutions are an offshoot of the British experience. Pre-Revolutionary War events in America had made the colonists distrustful of a strong executive. The Articles of Confederation (1781–89) declared Congress supreme at the national level, though actual power was held by the states, through their legislatures. Each of the thirteen states had one vote in Congress, but a state could have several members in a congressional delegation. States could withdraw delegates from Congress at any time. All important measures required nine votes, and amendments to the Articles required unanimity. In the states, legislatures held power, with governors often elected for only one year at a time with minimal powers. Legislatures were the dominant government institutions in the United States during the nineteenth century and the right of Americans to participate in elections expanded rapidly in that century.[5]

In summary, limitations on the power of the monarchs and the existence of councils and assemblies in some manner representative have a tradition dating back to classical Greece. The prototypes of modern elected legislatures are the English Parliament and American legislative institutions as they have evolved since the eighteenth century. The oft-described Anglo-American political tradition has a representative, democratically elected legislature as one of its principal features.

LEGISLATURES IN PARLIAMENTARY AND PRESIDENTIAL SYSTEMS

Parliamentary Government

Under a parliamentary system, sometimes called cabinet government, a popularly chosen legislature selects the government (prime minister and cabinet) after each election, controls it through debate, discussion, and voting on government proposals, and changes the government if it loses the confidence of the legislature. Generally, parliaments have a maximum life of five years. Usually parliaments are dissolved by the government before the term of office is up, at an auspicious moment when the majority party or parties believe they will enjoy maximum popularity at the forthcoming election. As our discussion of France below indicates, it is unusual, however, for a coalition government to dissolve a legislature simply because it loses a vote of confidence and must resign.

Under a parliamentary system the policy-determining members of the executive—prime minister and cabinet—are, with few exceptions, members of the legislature. In contrast to separation of powers under a presidential system, formal supreme political authority resides with the legislature, and the cabinet depends on continuing legislative support.

Parliament in Great Britain

The prototype of parliamentary systems is the bicameral British Parliament, with power in the popularly elected House of Commons, and the House of Lords exercising minimal influence.

A distinguishing feature of the British Parliament is the highly disciplined two-party system in the House of Commons. Policy innovation, formation, and implementation emanate from the cabinet, not the legislature. The

[5] Suffrage, except for slaves and women, expanded more rapidly even than in England and property tax qualifications were abolished by all but one state (Massachusetts) before the Civil War. See Figure 2.1 in Robert E. Lane, *Political Life* (Glencoe, Ill.: The Free Press, 1959), p. 10.

Table I Party Unity in the House of Commons

	Conservatives	Labour	Liberals
Year	*Coefficient of Cohesion*		
1860	63.0	—	58.9
1871	74.0	—	75.5
1881	87.9	—	83.2
1899	97.9	—	82.5
1906	91.0	88.4	96.8
1914–28	99.2	99.8	88.8
1945–46	99.0	99.9	—

Source: Adapted from Samuel H. Beer and Adam B. Ulam, eds., *Patterns of Government,* 3rd ed. Copyright © 1958, 1962, 1973 by Random House, Inc. Adapted by permission of the publisher. Original data source: Samuel H. Beer, *British Politics in the Collectivist Age,* rev. ed. (New York: Knopf, 1965), pp. 123, 257, 262. Beer states: "Starting from the assumption that a fifty-fifty split in a party signifies zero cohesion, we calculate the coefficient of cohesion by dividing by fifty the difference between fifty and the percentage of party members voting on one side. Thus when 90 percent of the members of a party are on one side, the CoC is 80 percent. . . . Abstainers are not counted."

role of the cabinet has grown considerably in the last century. The phenomenon of disciplined party voting in Commons means that once a government is chosen and is committed to a particular policy, there is little likelihood that the members of Parliament will break ranks and defeat the government.

Parliament rarely makes or breaks governments. The selection of a prime minister is decided at the general elections when the leader of the winning party becomes prime minister. Party discipline and government stability are depicted in Table I, where a unanimous party vote would be a coefficient of cohesion of 100.

Under a disciplined two-party system, party leadership, which is the cabinet, dominates. The cabinet, not the legislature, is the center of power. By and large Parliament today does not possess a choice of governments during a session. Between 1846 and 1860 Commons was supreme and governments suffered eight major defeats. The power to change governments has declined steadily ever since. The last time a government resigned because of a negative vote in Commons was in 1923.[6]

[6] Samuel H. Beer and Adam B. Ulam, eds., *Patterns of Government,* 3rd ed. (New York: Random House, 1973), p. 207.

The House of Commons in session.

Formal voting is not, however, the only way to bring about changes in government personnel or policy, and a ruling party is able to select new leaders in critical political circumstances. Events in 1940 and 1956 demonstrate that a prime minister will resign if a policy erodes the confidence of his party colleagues. In May, 1940, Prime Minister Neville Chamberlain was sharply attacked for his previous diplomatic compromises with Nazi Germany (Munich, 1938) and the deteriorating war situation, signalled by Norway's falling to the Germans. When the division bells rang and the vote of confidence was taken, Chamberlain's normal majority of 200 slipped to 81. Sixty Conservative MPs abstained and 33 supported the opposition. Within the week Chamberlain had resigned, and the House of Commons elected Winston Churchill to lead a national government.

Anthony Eden was prime minister in 1956 during the Suez Crisis. An Israeli attack on Egypt in October/November, 1956, was supported by the British and French, in large part because of Egyptian President Nasser's nationalization of the Suez Canal. Eden subsequently resigned for reasons of health, several weeks after a Middle Eastern ceasefire. There were many pressures on Eden, international pressures from the United States, the Soviet Union, and the United Nations, and also the physical and mental strain in dealing with those dangerous and complicated circumstances. Numerous interpretations of the Suez affair have appeared. One factor leading to Eden's resignation was a revolt in the Conservative Party. There were reports that forty Conservative MPs were prepared to vote against the prime minister, though on a Suez vote following the ceasefire only eight opposed the government.[7] R. T. McKenzie, a leading authority on parties and Parliament in Great Britain, has succinctly described the mix of discipline and deference in the House of Commons: "Once the Conservatives have chosen their Leader he can stay in office . . . until he himself decides to retire or, as has happened on at least three occasions in this century, he is forced from office by a revolt among his followers.[8] The Chamberlain and Eden cases reveal the measure of leadership autonomy and perceived political failure a British parliamentary party will tolerate.

The ultimate constraint of a forced resignation describes unique situations, and must be balanced against the fact the cabinet presides on a day-to-day basis. One indication of the cabinet's dominant position is interest group lobbying. Most British interest groups concentrate their activities on administrative officials and ministries. A case is won if a ministery can be convinced to take or reject a particular action. MPs are approached only as a second or third step in strategy, when the response from the executive has been unsatisfactory.[9]

The size of the executive also has increased, and it has been charged that patronage inherent in this expansion further reduces MP independence and influence.

> *With over a hundred members of the ruling party holding ministerial positions, Mr. Wilson [Labour Prime Minister between 1964 and 1970, and 1974 and 1976] has assuredly dispensed patronage with a liberality which even George III or Lord North might have blushed. Patronage and party discipline have eroded the independence of the members of the legislature . . .*[10]

The House of Commons has 630 members; there are 20 or 21 ministries in the cabinet. If one takes into account noncabinet senior ministers, and junior ministers (usually with the title parliamentary secretary), there are approximately a hundred ministerial appointments to be filled by a government. Thus, 25 to 30 percent of a majority party can anticipate receiving an

[7] R. T. McKenzie, *British Political Parties,* 2nd ed. (New York: Frederick A. Praeger, 1964), pp. 585–56.

[8] *Ibid.,* p. 579.

[9] K. C. Wheare, *Legislatures* (New York: Oxford University Press, 1963), especially chapter 3.

[10] Richard Middleton, "The Problems and Consequences of Parliamentary Government: A Historical Review," *Parliamentary Affairs,* XXIII, No. 1 (Winter 1969–70), p. 57.

executive appointment. Appointments balance and mend differences within the party, but appointments are also reward, control, and "patronage" instruments.

In a constitutional monarchy such as Great Britain, the cabinet does not exercise unlimited power. Not the least of the limitations is the requirement of consultation and negotiation, so party leaders may maintain the confidence of their fellow MPs and present a favorable image to the electorate. British parties are not monoliths, and the spirit of compromise and negotiation permeate the party organizations as well as the entire political system.[11] While formulating policy, British parties are guided by the principle of anticipated response. Policy is drafted and discussed in a manner that takes into account the views of MPs not holding ministerial positions.

Parliament in France

Parliament during the French Fourth Republic (1946–58) had several features missing in Great Britain, but not uncommon in parliamentary systems. The National Assembly, the popularly elected lower house, was a multiparty chamber, with no party ever controlling more than 31 percent of the seats. Except for the Communists, the parties were loosely disciplined, and it was common for a party to have some deputies supporting a bill and others opposing it. The Assembly overshadowed the Cabinet, not the cabinet the Assembly.

The multiparty nature of the Fourth Republic is apparent in Table II.

Certain political parties were unwilling to participate in a government unless the political system was drastically amended. Governing parties in the Fourth Republic did not include the Communists or Gaullists who controlled approximately 33 percent of the Assembly seats. Coalition governments were a necessity, but the range of potential partners was circumscribed. An essential component of government making was *replâtrage* ("replastering"), whereby there was continuity of personalities and parties in the cabinet, with political leaders simply occupying different ministries in successive governments. There was stability of a sort, at least among ministers. One authority has observed that between January, 1946, and December 1952, 16 ministries were held by 66 persons in France (this period includes six cabinets which lasted less than six weeks). During the same period in Great Britain, the 16 counterpart ministeries were occupied by 58 persons.[12]

[11] In his concluding remarks on the British party system, Allen Potter declares: "Great Britain is, socially and politically, a pluralistic society, in which the government no more than any other group or institution is outside the interaction of social forces that constitute the society. British politics is by nature the politics of compromise." "Great Britain: Opposition with a Capital O," in Robert A. Dahl, ed., *Political Oppositions in Western Democracies* (New Haven: Yale University Press, 1966), p. 33.

[12] Philip Williams, *Politics in Post-War France* (London: Longmans, Green and Company, 1954), p. 375.

Table II Representation in the French National Assembly (Fourth Republic)

	1946		1951		1956	
	Deputies	Percent	Deputies	Percent	Deputies	Percent
Communists	182	29.4%	101	16.1%	150	25.2%
Socialists	102	16.5	107	17.1	100	16.8
MRP	166	26.9	97	15.5	83	14.1
Radicals and RGR	71	11.5	91	14.5	94	15.8
Conservatives	67	10.8	98	15.7	121[a]	20.3
RPF (Gaullists)			120	19.1		
Poujadists		4.9			42	7.0
Misc. and unaffiliated	30		13	2.1	6	1.0
	618		627		596[b]	

Source: Walter H. Mallory, ed., *Political Handbook of the World* (New York: Harper & Brothers; for the Council on Foreign Relations), 1947, p. 61; 1952, p. 68; 1957, p. 69.

[a] Troubled conditions in Algeria made it impossible to hold elections for the 30 representatives from that area in 1956.

[b] The Conservatives in 1956 included the remnants of the RPF, the Social Republicans.

Policy innovation and implementation were inhibited, however. Coalition governments were formed on the lowest common denominator of agreement. When a pressing new issue arose, the government would lose a vote of confidence and a new coalition was formed. Governing parties were the reservoirs of the *ministrables*—deputies who had achieved or were eligible for a ministry. On occasion ministers would leave or "abandon" a government at a strategic moment in order to maximize the chances of participating in a subsequent government. A premier always was on the alert to mollify restless coalition partners; moreover, he could not be certain that his own party would continue to support him. Coalition mending and dealing with the smaller, daily questions meant that major problems such as German rearmament and the Algerian revolution did not receive a policy mandate at an election. Governments did not form because of direct electoral choice as in Great Britain, but because of bargains struck among minority parties over matters which, in some instances, were only incidentally relevant at the previous election.

The power to dissolve the legislature and require new elections is a potential weapon in the hands of the executive, but one that may backfire. Dissolution as a means to discipline recalcitrant opponents and increase supporters in the legislature was used only once during the Fourth Republic, and it was unsuccessful. Premier Edgar Faure dissolved the National Assembly in December, 1955. His government was divided over the correctness of a dissolution, and the 1956 election failed to increase the number of pro-Faure deputies. Following the elections, Guy Mollett, a Socialist, formed a government. Faure, a leader of the Radical Party, was expelled from the party in January, 1956, for failing to consult with the party while he was premier.

A principal difference between parliamentarianism in Great Britain and France is that the British system is premised on the need to make and execute policy, while an enduring theme in French political cultures is the politics of defense—parliament restrains government to protect individual or group interests. A French political essayist in the last decade of the Third Republic (1875–1940) expressed an attitude also characteristic of the Fourth Republic when he declared that "the executive is inherently monarchic" and that democracy is "a perpetual struggle by the ruled against the abuses of power."[13] Nevertheless, the constitution of the Fifth Republic (adopted in 1958) includes several changes that increase the executive's authority. The Fifth Republic is a parliamentary–presidential hybrid. The president is popularly elected for a seven-year term; he symbolizes national popular choice and, depending on the election issues, carries some type of policy mandate. The president nominates the premier, who must resign only if he loses a vote of confidence in the Assembly. France has had three strong presidents under the Fifth Republic, Charles de Gaulle (1958–69), Georges Pompidou (1969–74), and Giscard d'Estaing (May, 1974, to date). The Gaullists and their allies have controlled the Assembly and Senate since 1958. The president has exerted great influence on the premier. Resignations were issues between the president and premier, and did not result from a no-confidence vote in the Assembly.

The *ministrable* phenomenon, which previously had led some ambitious deputies to bring about a change in government in the hopes of a ministerial appointment has diminished. A legislator now must resign his seat if he accepts a ministerial appointment. In addition, the government (president, premier, and cabinet) has control of the parliamentary agenda, which was not true in the Fourth Republic. The government decides which bills will be considered and in what order and determines which, if any, committee amendments will be debated and voted on by parliament. A decisive control is the "package requirement," which enables the government to require a vote on the entire bill. Thus, the government need not compromise on technicalities or amendments.

The Fifth Republic provides for executive leadership, and de Gaulle's presidency tipped the balance further in this direction, to the point that even the cabinet had only a minor voice in policy making. Today, however, the politics of negotiation and accommodation are important elements in

[13] Suzanne Berger, "The French Political System," in Beer and Ulam, eds., *op. cit.* p. 361.

parliamentary–executive relations. The president is popularly chosen, and this means he must appeal to many different groups in building a national majority. Parliament does have power, and the president and premier must work with it. The constitution facilitates executive action if there is goodwill between parliament and the executive. Should the two branches find themselves in irresolvable conflict, France could return to the *immobilisme* of the Fourth Republic. The need to avoid this had led the executive to become increasingly receptive to legislative input. A slight majority in the National Assembly (Gaullists and pro-Gaullists had a 58-seat majority in the 490-seat National Assembly following the March, 1973, elections) means the executive must respond to factions and interests within the Assembly majority, as well as acknowledge or pre-empt politically popular opposition arguments.

In summary, we can say that the French and British Parliaments maintain an important role, particularly in facilitating inputs and mediating political conflict through negotiation and bargaining.

The Legislature in a Presidential System

The distinctive feature of a presidential system is separation of powers: the chief executive and the legislature are elected independently of one another; each holds office for a definite period of time which ordinarily cannot be altered by the other; and both the legislature and the executive are not readily controlled by the other.

The American national government is the prototype of presidential government. The president is elected for a four-year term by national popular vote via the electoral college, and can be removed legally by one of two methods, both of which involve Congress: impeachment by majority vote in the House of Representatives, followed by conviction by a two-thirds vote in the Senate. (One president, Andrew Johnson (1865–69) was impeached; he was adjudged not guilty by one vote in the Senate.) The Twenty-Fifth Amendment also provides that if the vice-president and a majority of the cabinet inform Congress that the president cannot discharge his duties, the vice-president will become acting president. If the president subsequently declares no inability exists, Congress must decide the issue within 21 days. Other than these two unique circumstances, the presidential term of office is not controlled by the legislature. Periodically, however, the majority in either the House of Representatives or the Senate does not represent the same party as the president. Between the 80th Congress elected in 1946 and the 94th Congress elected in 1974, the House of Representatives has been controlled by the opposition party 16 of the 28 years, and the opposition has controlled the Senate for 14 years. Even when the opposition party controls one or both houses of the legislature, the president completes his term.

President Ford delivering the 1975 State of the Union address to Congress; behind him are Vice President Rockefeller and Speaker of the House Albert.

Both the legislative and executive branches share broad spheres of power; policy is a compromise between the two branches. The separation of powers associated with presidential government is actually a system of checks and balances. Powers held by one branch are shared in selected but decisive ways with another branch. Congress has the law-enacting responsibility, but the president holds the veto power, which requires a two-thirds majority of those present and voting in both houses to override. Between 1913 and May, 1971, for example, only 37 of 1303 vetoes were overriden by Congress.[14] If Congress is at a disadvantage vis à vis a presidential veto, it possesses considerable control through the authority of the Senate to confirm—"advise and consent to"—major presidential appointments. A majority of appointees serve in the executive branch, but a number also involve the judiciary, the third branch of government. The president nominates, but the Senate confirms. Headlines are made when the Senate rejects a nomination (for example, when the nominations of Carswell and Hainsworth to the Supreme Court by President Nixon were rejected in 1969 and 1970). A continuing dialogue is maintained to avoid an embarrassing rejection. A government acquaintance told one of the authors how the names of "six persons were run by" the Armed Services Committee

[14] Nelson Polsby, *Congress and the Presidency,* 2nd ed., (Englewood Cliffs, N.J.: Prentice-Hall, 1971), p. 81, and *Congressional Quarterly's Guide to Congress* (Washington: Congressional Quarterly Service), 1971, p. 583.

recently before a nomination to the Department of Defense was submitted. One of the important bargaining tools held by Congress, through the Senate, is the power to confirm or reject executive nominations. In a similar vein, the power of the purse, the power to raise taxes and appropriate money, is a restriction the executive branch cannot readily overcome.

A major point at issue, as in parliamentary government, concerns whether or not the legislature is coequal with, or overshadowed by, the executive branch. The president through public messages (State of the Union, Budget Message, etc.) and through bills drafted by the administration has the principal role in recommending and innovating policy. The bulk of the expertise resides in the executive, and in no way is compensated by the nearly 1000 professional staff attached to Senate and House committees.[15]

The Congressional Research Service has been of minor help to Congress in ferreting out new facts. The CRS reports are well-drafted but depend almost entirely on published sources. Unless Congress were to erect a bureaucratic behemoth, it cannot have immediately available to it the necessary technical resources and dispassionate experts responsible only to Congress. Congress is unable, even if it so desired, to monopolize the initiation of programs and legislation; it must share this with the executive, and frequently defer to the president on this first step. As one recent study has shown, however, policy incubation and maturation are fundamental roles enabling Congress to retain important, thought not as apparent, lawmaking duties.

Active politicians are prone to invest solutions to what they perceive to be important issues with popular support or potential support.[16] Much legislation that is subsequently regarded as a "presidential program" actually has its origins in Congress. President Johnson's promotion of consumer protection, pollution control, and auto safety legislation in 1965 and 1966 pre-empted legislative hearings and bills originating at the Congressional level. These happened to be popular issues which lent themselves to pre-emption by the executive. President Nixon, on the other hand, proposed and got a consumer protection agency in the president's Executive Office. The president preferred this to proposals first made in Congress to create a cabinet-level post or establish a new independent regulatory agency.

Executive pre-emption can cause executive–legislative rivalry, even when persons involved are from the same party. The late Senator Kefauver, a

[15] Figure compiled from *Congressional Directory* (Washington: U.S. Govt. Printing Office, 1973), pp. 279–85 and 309–315.

[16] The following two paragraphs draw heavily from the excellent analysis by John R. Johannes, *Policy Innovation in Congress* (Morristown, N.J.: General Learning Press, 1972).

("The Small Society" by Brickman © Washington Star Syndicate, permission granted by King Features Syndicate 1973.)

Government by compromise.

liberal Democrat from Tennessee, initiated a series of committee hearings in December, 1959, on abuses in the drug industry. The hearings gained wide popular attention and roused indignation at apparent abuses. Legislation eventually emerged from the Kefauver Committee in 1962, and the senator requested administration support to push for final passage. The story is complex, but President Kennedy's message and legislative recommendation succeeded in transferring the policy-initiation role to the executive. The law that ultimately came into effect omitted several Kefauver items, but the legislation took its origin and essential framework from Senator Kefauver's hearings and the resulting draft bill. John R. Johannes, who has described this case in detail, concludes that as President Kennedy was signing the bill into law and taking most of the credit, Senator Kefauver remained convinced "that it was Congress, and not the Administration, which had initiated the bill and should receive the plaudits."[17]

The period from proposal to law in a presidential system requires negotiation, trade-offs, and compromising. Congress may occupy the dominant role in lawmaking in the public eye, but its indispensable contribution to policy making is sometimes overlooked. This influence does not always take the form of an amendment or a competing draft bill. Daily contacts between congressmen and congressional staff and administration officials, frequent conferences and briefings, and visits and inspection tours all contribute to an exchange of views. This continual interaction constrains executive actions and reveals on a day-to-day basis legislation that can reasonably be expected to originate in Congress or will be

[17] *Ibid.*, p. 15.

accepted by Congress. Many committee staff and congressmen hold offices much longer than any presidential appointee in the executive (cabinet officers, department heads, undersecretaries, etc.) can hope to, and this longevity and network of contacts is a legislative advantage. This informal and partially concealed network of legislative associations has not received the study it deserves.

Government in a presidential system is essentially compromise government. Many elected officials in Congress, and also the president, must approve if policy is enacted. The American Constitution gave the House of Representatives, the Senate, and the president fixed but different terms of office (two, six, and four years respectively). The heart of the system under these conditions is continuous bargaining, accommodation, and compromise, and despite its label, the role of the legislature remains important in a presidential system.

BICAMERAL AND UNICAMERAL LEGISLATURES

In many countries the division of legislatures into two houses is a historical survival. Bicameral or even tricameral (the three estates under the ancient regime in France) legislatures were first organized by estates or principal classes in the country. As democratic choice and representative government evolved, the lower chamber, for example, the House of Representatives or the British House of Commons, was based on adult suffrage and popular representation, while the "upper" chamber usually was appointed or indirectly elected. The upper chamber was supposed to be a moderating, conservative influence, which would check a potentially tyrannical popular majority. It might also represent certain groups in the community that a government, yielding before the claims of mass participation in the lower chamber, hoped would retain a special voice in the political process.

The British House of Lords in the nineteenth century was nearly coequal with Commons, although the selection of a prime minister rested exclusively with the latter body. Today, the House of Lords has only slight power. The Lords have no budgetary powers. They do have a suspensive veto, rarely implemented, which permits them to reject a bill, which Commons must then repass in a subsequent session.[18] The most important function of the Lords is that of discussion and revision. Technical errors and other flaws, substantive or minor, can be ironed out during the debate in the

[18] The Parliament Act of 1911 prohibited the House of Lords from rejecting any financial bill and reduced the power of delay the Lords could exercise over other bills passed by the House of Commons. The Act of 1949 stated a bill could become law over the House of Lords' opposition if Commons passed the bill in two consecutive sessions and a year had elaspsed between the first reading and final passage.

House of Lords. Broad questions of public policy and new solutions or approaches can be initiated in the Lords, especially since life peers (instituted in 1958) are to be distinguished persons, such as journalists, lawyers, trade unionists, academics, scientists, etc. The Lords is certainly not an historical anarchronism, but its role is diminished. Under a parliamentary government, where the principal executive officers are chosen by the popularly elected lower chamber, it is inevitable that the cabinet and the elective house dominate.

Second chambers also are devised to provide for a different type of representation, even though selection is by popular vote. Japan's House of Councillors exemplifies this principle. The House of Councillors has 250 members who serve six-year terms, half elected every three years. One hundred and fifty are chosen from prefectural districts (Japan has prefectures rather than provinces or states) and 100 are chosen from the nation at large. The voter has two votes, one for the prefectural level and one for the national level. The House of Councillors was to combine territorial representation with the selection of distinguished persons who had achieved eminence in their chosen careers. The latter hope was not realized. Tightly organized interest groups and minority parties are able to elect some candidates at the national level (for example, the Small Business Political League and the Expropriated Farmer's League), and the party organizations of the bigger Japanese political parties play a paramount electoral role. Few independent candidates are elected. Winning candidates often lack the stature envisaged by the drafters of the postwar constitution. In 1962, for example, the largest number of votes was won by a female panelist on the Japanese TV program, "What's My Line?" who ran as a Liberal–Democrat.

The Councillors' power is not coequal to Japan's 492-member House of Representatives. On matters such as the budget and treaty ratifications, the House of Representatives can override Councillors' opposition by a simple majority; in other matters it requires a two-thirds majority. Except for a few special interests and minor political party representation, the partisan composition of the Councillors is similar to the House of Representatives. The wisdom of eminent persons and the calmer and more studied deliberation that were to take place in the House of Councillors has not occurred. The primary difference between the two houses today is the term of office and the size of the electoral district. If, however, a party other than the Liberal Democrats (who have ruled Japan since 1955) should win control of the House of Councillors, the political status of the Japanese upper house would increase perceptibly.

A frequent reason for a bicameral legislature is a federal political system. The upper house, representing territorial units, is organized differently from the lower house. The territorial chamber may represent a different balance of interests, assuming the federal units have special interests or concerns that are a minority at the national level (such as the French-speaking culture of Quebec).

The upper house in West Germany, the Bundesrat, or Federal Council, is made up of delegations from the ten German *Lander,* or states. Each *Land* has three to five representatives, depending on the size of its population, although the two largest *Lander* include 47 percent of the West German population, excluding Berlin. Members of the Bundsrat are selected by the *Land* governments, and most often are *Land* ministers. Each *Land* delegation must vote as a unit. Constitutional amendments must be approved by a two-thirds vote in both the Bundesrat and the lower chamber, the Bundestag (federal parliament). Approximately half of the legislation enacted annually involves what the West German constitution or Basic Law describes as "consent" law, requiring approval by the Bundesrat. The Bundesrat has many political interests: first is to represent the special needs and interests of the state government and maintain the position of the *Lander* under West German federalism. Perhaps because its members are not directly elected, Germans are only slightly aware of the Bundesrat's purpose. The percentage of West Germans who were roughly aware of "what the Bundesrat is here for" rose slowly from 8 percent in 1951 to a mere 14 percent in 1956.[19] The Bundesrat's special concern with sustaining *Land* government interests and its indirect representative character have given it a significant political role, but have failed to attract much public interest.

The upper house under American federalism has, however, achieved a great deal more popular attention than its West German counterpart. The U.S. Senate is organized along state lines, two senators per state elected for six-year terms. Since the Seventeenth Amendment (1913) all senators have been elected by popular vote (before 1913 Senators were chosen for six-year terms by the state legislatures). The Senate shares most powers with the House of Representatives. The Senate alone, however, confirms presidential appointments (majority vote) and ratifies treaties (two-thirds majority). Because the Senate has only 100 members, the individual senator has more visibility than the typical representative. The Senate is generally regarded as the more prestigious and august body. Senators represent their electors and make no claim to watch over state government interests as do Bundesrat delegates.

Countries such as Denmark, Finland, Israel, and Sweden have adopted unicameral legislatures because they believe them to be more efficient due to the concentration of the legislative process into one area or they believe

[19] Karl Deutsch and Eric Nordlinger, "The German Federal Republic," in Roy C. Macridis and Robert E. Ward, eds., *Modern Political Systems: Europe,* 3rd ed. (Englewood Cliffs, N.J.: Prentic-Hall, 1973), p. 402.

bicameralism is less democratic. In some cases there are no compelling reasons for bicameralism: no historical precedents such as the House of Lords need be continued; no special interests require representation; the possibility of calmer and more extended discussion or the presence of eminent but nonpolitical persons is not regarded as mandatory for popular government; or they have a nonfederal system.[20]

FUNCTIONS OF LEGISLATURES

Legislative functions involve interaction between legislators and other political actors, such as constituents, lobbyists, political leaders, presidential spokesmen, and bureaucrats. Legislatures will be regarded as legitimate in a political system because of their representative quality and their willingness to interact with many interests. Figure 1 shows the legislative system, which includes the legislature and the interaction process.

The functions listed are not exhaustive, but they give the student an awareness of the multifunctional character of legislatures:

1. Legislatures share with other institutions and groups the power to initiate, enact, and modify policy through lawmaking and other means. The individual legislator's role in this area is often informal and not open to public view, yet the role is very real. In the British Parliament, for example, disciplined party voting and the cabinet's pre-eminence suggest that the average MP contributes little to policy making. In practice, the MP has considerable leverage with ministers, through the party committee in Commons. Legislative whips in Britain are officially given the duty of "whipping" MPs into line on a vote, but as in many legislatures, spend more of their time apprising the government of MP opinions than "whipping" the legislative party.

The core of the legislature's policy making functions conflict with management. The legislature provides the arena where competing demands can struggle, negotiate, compromise, and hopefully be at least minimally accommodated. Compromise is institutionalized in the legislative process in a democratic system, and legislature negotiation often provides a stability or balance otherwise difficult to achieve. Speaking about the American system, one study recognized that the demands of some interests might not even be partially met, but that legislatures "can grant these interests a hearing—perhaps not obtainable elsewhere—and this hearing can be an important factor in the management of conflict."[21]

[20] J. Blondel reports that in 1971 there were 52 bicameral legislatures out of 108 countries having legislatures. *Comparative Legislatures* (Englewood Cliffs, N.J.: Prentice-Hall, 1973), p. 32.

[21] Malcolm E. Jewell and Samuel C. Patterson, *The Legislative Process in the United States,* 2nd ed., (New York: Random House, 1971), p. 12.

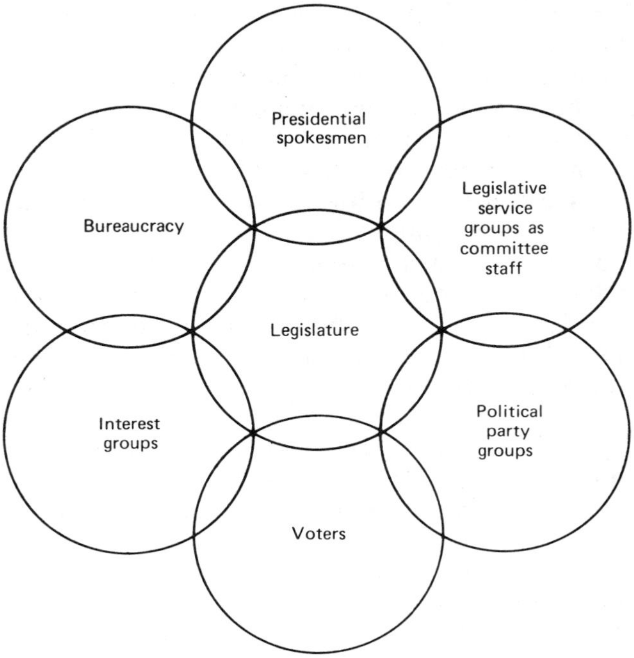

Figure 1. A legislative system. Adapted from Malcolm E. Jewell and Samuel C. Patterson, *The Legislative Process in the United States*. **Copyright © 1966 by Random House. Adapted by permission of the publisher.**

A legislature generally will not have among its members individuals with the depth of technical expertise that serve in the executive or interest groups, but it possesses a perspective that the experts will not have. En masse, legislators have a range of knowledge and experience in terms of class, ethnic, religious, and geographic origin and an awareness of constituent views, which makes them exceptionally sensitive to public opinion and demands and most able to judge the acceptability and feasibility of policy. Legislatures' size may inhibit efficient procedure, but size also has its attributes.

2. Legislatures usually influence the composition of the chief executive officers. Under a parliamentary system the prime minister and the cabinet are legally responsible to the legislature. British practice provides that the prime minister invariably is the leader of the party that won the election. Even in Great Britain, though, the composition of the cabinet is decided by negotiation and bargaining with various elements of the majority party. The

House of Commons no longer makes and unmakes governments during a parliamentary term, but it can make or cripple reputations. A minister must be a "good House of Commons man" and be able to hold his own in parliamentary debate, else he falter and feel compelled to resign. One Conservative minister, in describing his first months in office, observed "the remorseless interest of the House of Commons in seeing a man brought down."[22] Commons provides a setting in which ministers must regularly justify their actions and show competence.

When choosing his cabinet and making appointments, an American president must give consideration to the temper and anticipated reaction of the Senate. The Senate does not make a habit of rejecting presidential nominees, but the occasional refusal to confirm an appointment makes it clear the president should consult with senators prior to announcing a key appointment.

3. While performing a lawmaking function, committee hearings may perform a valuable role in discovering and/or making public new information. The United States has the most developed legislative committee system.

A case study of the Kefauver hearing on prices and practices in the drug industry (conducted by the Antitrust and Monopoly Subcommittee of the Senate Judiciary Committee) shows that they began in a situation where "practically no data on the subject were available in usable form, and the staff commenced a laborious research job."[23] Not only did the hearings make nationwide headlines, they also publicized facts that only a few insiders had been aware of up to that time. Similarly, the Watergate hearings conducted by the Senate Select Committee on Presidential Campaign Activities brought together and organized information in a situation when most if not all participants themselves had knowledge that was restricted to only small segments of the affair. Committee hearings serve many purposes, including preparation of legislation and supervision of other branches of government. In doing so, they make public and organize information that might not be revealed under any other circumstances.

4. Legislatures legitimize government actions and in turn serve to legitimize the political system. In following procedural norms, legislatures reassure the public of the rightness and propriety of the policy process. The legitimizing functions include outputs as well as procedural standards. Ultimately, legitimacy is determined by the output and the success in responding to the most pressing demands and accommodating a diverse range of interests.

Transitional political systems that are moving from authoritarianism to a

[22] *Economist,* February 27, 1971, p. 17, quoted in Beer and Ulam, eds., *op. cit.,* p. 238.
[23] John R. Johannes, *op. cit.,* p. 14.

limited pluralism focus on procedures. At the beginning of the transitional stage, the legislature is barely involved in formulating laws and policy. The Supreme Soviet, which is the bicameral Soviet legislature, illustrates this first step in the legitimating function. One of the Supreme Soviet's functions is to enact laws and thereby bestow a certain legality and acceptability on them. This adherence to proper procedure is a significant first step. Important policy is no longer simply party or administrative directive. The rule of law, legitimacy, and authority are at a very early though developing stage in the Soviet Union. The Supreme Soviet is one institution through which procedural norms will evolve if this transition continues.

5. Democratic legislatures should oversee other branches of government and thereby uphold freedom to critizice and evaluate programs and officials. In the United States a majority of the supervisory functions occur in committee hearings. It would be hard to find an American high school or college student who is unaware of at least one congressional investigation that has turned the glare of publicity on some government agency or official. In Great Britain the most telling public overview takes place during the Question Hour, which occurs the first four days each week when the House of Commons convenes at 2:30. Ministers must respond to questions (written and then followed up orally) submitted by an MP. Individual responsibility and explanation are rigorously and regularly enforced during the Question Hour. Many ambitions have been lofted or deflated during this grilling period.

6. Educating and informing the public are functions best performed by democratic legislatures. This is a corollary to the above functions, but is of sufficient importance to be included in a separate category. The educative–informational function occurs in legislative debates, committee hearings, in elections, and during the period between elections when legislators attempt to maintain ties with constituents by interpreting major issues in newsletters, in TV and radio talks, and through back-home visits.

7. Legislatures can be a bulwark of democracy. Some also function as a transitional institution to a more open society. Legislatures are one focus for promoting diverse viewpoints not always in harmony with the government of the moment. In political systems that are making an effort to be more tolerant of differing political viewpoints, legislatures will play an essential role in the movement toward liberalization. Throughout the world a majority of political systems constrain political competition. Where there is an effort to expand the boundaries of political expression, the legislatures will be among the first arenas in which political discussion and criticism are allowed, first during the elections and then in the legislative sessions.

8. Legislatures function as electioneering forums, particularly during the period between elections. The publicity and controversies generated are relevant to the winning and losing of popular support. This is true of both

John Dean arrives to testify at the Senate Watergate hearings.

developed and developing political systems. In one sense governing is a protracted election campaign. At a news conference on the day following the 1972 parliamentary elections, Singapore's prime minister was asked when the next election would take place. He replied that the next election began the day after election day. The British Parliament has been described as "the agreed arena in which most of the campaign is fought." The parliamentary sessions are the place where the political parties "obtain something like equal access to the ear of the electorate in the long formative period between official campaigns."[24]

In developing countries, where parties are relatively new and party organization at an embryonic state, action in the legislature can be the most important way to win attention and build electoral support. In Singapore, for example, the period between 1955 and 1959, when the country was moving toward self-government, was critical. The People's Action Party, which has governed Singapore since June, 1959, had only four members in the 1955–59 Assembly. Several factors accounted for the PAP's electoral victory in the May, 1959, elections. One was the ability of the future prime minister, Lee Kuan Yew, through his incisive rhetoric, to dominate a good

[24] Bernard Crick, *The Reform of Parliament* (Garden City, N.Y.: Anchor Books, 1965), pp. 25–26.

Representatives at the opening meeting of the USSR Supreme Soviet.

portion of the legislative debate. His statements and proposals also won support from some of the English-educated in Singapore and convinced most of the English-educated community that PAP leaders, as distinct from the PAP grassroots organization, were not pro-Communist.[25] The legislative forum was critical for building up mass support and wooing key segments of society.

9. The eight functions discussed thus far characterize democratic legislatures or those where the political system is transiting toward a more open and competitive situation. Legislatures in authoritarian systems fulfill functions much the same way as one-party elections (discussed earlier in the chapter on representation and elections). Authoritarian legislatures function as a recruiting device, to reward the upwardly mobile regime-faithful or, in some cases, to take a closer look at an ambitious individual. The Supreme Soviet is careful to represent major vocational and national groups. The legislative overseeing function is minimal, if not nil. The Supreme Soviet is sometimes a device permitting the government to educate the members on objectives and policies, who in turn will represent

[25] Thomas J. Bellows, *The People's Action Party of Singapore: Emergence of a Dominant Party System* (New Haven: Yale University Southeast Asia Studies, Monograph Series No. 14, 1970).

The Soviet of the Union (lower house of the USSR Supreme Soviet) in session.

these views to the masses. The Soviet legislature functions as an educative-control instrument of an authoritarian government and provides one method to reach the masses.

LEGISLATIVE DYNAMICS

Legislative dynamics and policy making are important subjects, but space limitations prevent a detailed discussion. Therefore, only two aspects are discussed in order to provide the student with some appreciation of influences that affect the workings and output of a legislature.

The American Congress and Legislative Committees

The American system disperses power. Congress has been described as a conglomerate of little legislatures—the congressional committees (twenty in the House, sixteen in the Senate). Once a bill is introduced into either the House of Representatives or the Senate, it is referred to a committee. Which committee can sometimes be extremely important. Civil rights bills in the Senate have been sent to either the Judiciary Committee or the Commerce Committee. The membership of the latter is more liberal and more likely to result in a favorable vote for the bill. The most common way to kill a bill is to table it or simply not bring it up for consideration, the agenda determined by the committee chairman. If a bill is reported out (positive vote) in the House of Representatives, it must then go to the Rules Committee, which decides when or if it shall appear on the House agenda, the nature and extent of debate that will be allowed, and whether or not amendments can be offered.

More than 10,000 bills are introduced in Congress annually. (See Figure 2.) Without a division of labor, these bills would never be even superficially reviewed. The political system would be buried under a landslide of legislation if the reviewing, sifting, and culling process did not, as it does now, eliminate 90 percent of the bills introduced. After a bill has cleared subcommittees, and each chamber, there inevitably are discrepancies. This requires a Conference Committee composed of members from both houses. The Conference Committee can usually work out a compromise bill, but in the event that the committee cannot or Congress adjourns, the bill is dead and must be reintroduced and go through the entire procedure again. Congress has been called an obstacle course: "For sheer difficulty the way of a serious legislative proposal through Congress is equalled only by that of a camel through the eye of a needle or a rich man into the Kingdom of God."[26]

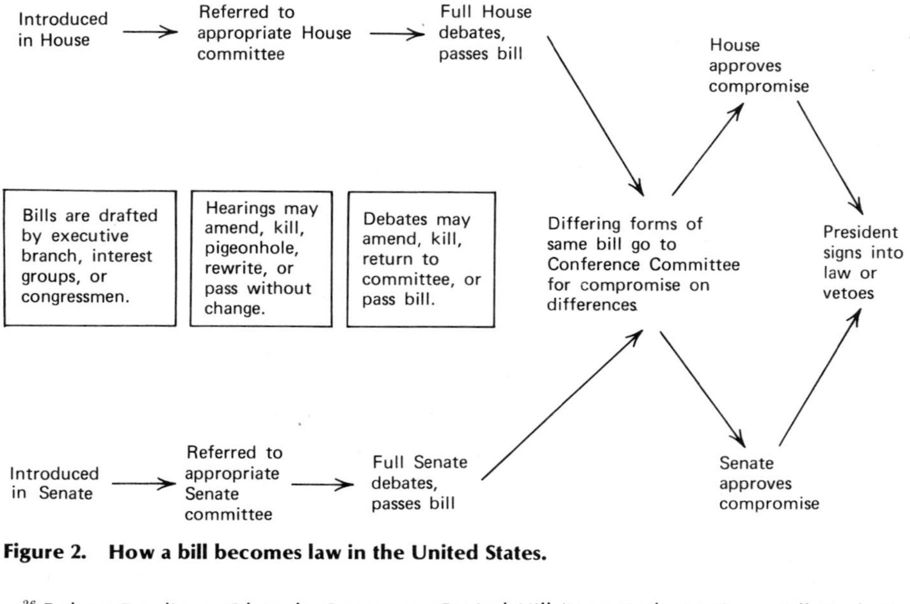

Figure 2. How a bill becomes law in the United States.

[26] Robert Bendiner, *Obstacle Course on Capitol Hill* (New York: McGraw-Hill Book Company, 1964), p. 15.

"Next I want to sing a song about the House Rules Committee and how the legislative functions of Congress are tyrannized over by its procedural calendar, dominated in turn by an all-powerful chairman hamstringing the processes of democracy."

(Drawing by Koren; © 1964 The New Yorker Magazine, Inc.)

Legislatures have their critics.

Three facts stand out: First, the committee system is a key to the American congressional process. Legislative committees are the only way a large and great nation can handle the many issues and proposals that must be considered. The need for specialization is juxtaposed by the fact that pockets of power are controlled by a few persons—committee members and, notably, committee chairmen—and the range of representative input is necessarily reduced.

Second, guiding a bill to law requires procedural expertise. Wooing majority support occurs at several points and involves different persons. Not one vote but many are involved. Actors and conditions change during the legislative gamut; negotiation and adjustment are a continual process for the bill's sponsors up to the point the bill reaches the president's desk, to be signed or vetoed.

Third, the legislative road is complex, and there are many points where the bill can be amended or defeated. Supporters of the bill must win each vote; those who wish to amend or kill the legislation can focus on one or two votes. Few bills arrive on the president's desk in their original form or one nearly identical to it.

Great Britain

While a thousand bills may become law during a congressional session, the British Parliament enacts only about two hundred. (See Figure 3.) Bills originate in the ministries in discussions involving ministers and the civil service and, oftentimes, interest groups. The Future Legislation Committee of the cabinet reduces the proposals to a manageable number, and these become the basis for the government's program. Individual MPs cannot introduce bills involving taxation or expenditure. A "private" bill involves primarily minor subjects with a narrow focus, and if it is to be enacted the government must be sympathetic or at least neutral. (Private bills are included in the two hundred figure.) Backbenchers have some influence, as do the arguments of the opposition, but a legislative proposal is highly developed before the government introduces it. Further, since a government regards each bill as a vote of confidence, a test-of-strength showdown will fall to the government.

There are only six standing committees in the House of Commons. A, B, C, D, E, and the Scottish Committee. All except the last consider bills without regard to subject. Committees have from twenty to fifty members, they do not call in outside experts, and as soon as they have reported on one bill they receive another, in order of consideration, not according to subject matter. Following a Second Reading, committee A, B, C, etc., considers the bill. The bill cannot be tabled, because the cabinet ultimately determines the order of business before the House. The standing committee goes through the bill line by line, noting any discrepancies or ambiguities. The government usually accepts only technical amendments at this stage. It is at this stage that MPs, speaking for various points of view or interests, can seek modifications, though the policy guidelines are definitely settled at the Second Reading.[27]

Congressional committees in the United States and some legislative committees in Continental Europe have much broader policy authority than do committees of the House of Commons, which do not have the power to table a proposal or substantially amend bills. Nevertheless, as we have seen, there can be some policy input at this stage, though under a disciplined

[27] The First Reading is a formality; only the title is read. The bill is subsequently printed and within three weeks, at the Second Reading, general policy is affirmed by a vote after the bill is debated by the government party and opposition.

Before a public bill is presented, the ministry concerned reviews its terms and makes suggestions, recommendations, and amendments. After receiving cabinet approval, the bill goes to the parliamentary counsel for drafting. Here, civil servants with legal training check on the bill's wording and its relation to other legislation. This process can be repeated as many as 25 times.

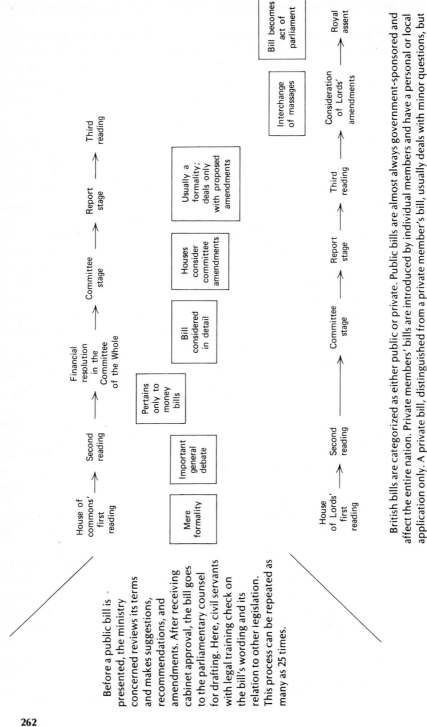

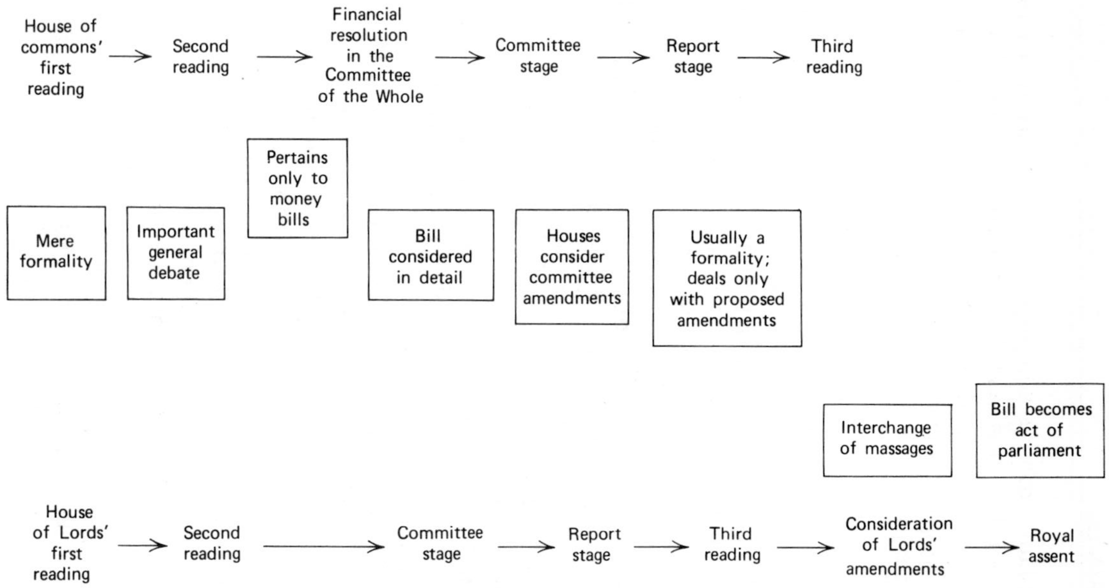

British bills are categorized as either public or private. Public bills are almost always government-sponsored and affect the entire nation. Private members' bills are introduced by individual members and have a personal or local application only. A private bill, distinguished from a private member's bill, usually deals with minor questions, but on rare occasions involves controversial issues that a party does not wish to sponsor.

Figure 3. How a public government-sponsored bill becomes law in the British parliament.

parliamentary system the willingness to accept amendments rests with the executive or cabinet. The principles of accommodation and negotiation that undergird British politics make the process more democratic than it might otherwise be. In authoritarian systems with a weak or nonexistent committee system, legislators find that they have negligible influence on policy formation.

Institutional Behavior and Rules of the Game

The formal structure of a legislature—the committee system—can be critical in the policy process. The rules of behavior discussed in this section are not formally written down, but they are generally understood within the institution itself and exemplify another key aspect of legislative policy making.

Legislative role requirements shape a legislator's actions by virtue of membership in a specific institutional context. When many persons or groups share roughly similar expectations about how to behave or how others should behave in a given situation, the result is referred to as a role. A role involves interactions with other persons, in this case fellow legislators. People develop expectations about how they and others will behave in specific situations. Role is a concept that assumes regularized interaction patterns, guides the actor's behavior, and inclines the individual to be conscious of, and responsive to, the reactions of significant others—in this case, legislative colleagues.

Role defines what should be done and what cannot be tolerated. Depending on the length of time the role has existed, the specific behavior patterns that have evolved, and the flexibility and adaptability that have developed during the evolution, a role can be specific down to the most minute behavioral and ceremonial detail, or it can simply define behavior limits in broad and general terms. Role requirements in modern legislatures tend toward broad guidelines, rather than specific details. In a modernizing, democratic context roles adapt and change and allow more variation in behavior patterns as compared to a traditional, status quo, or authoritarian system, which stresses rigid, highly structured behavior patterns covering nearly all aspects of behavior.

A legislator must relate to his colleagues in an acceptable way or he will not achieve maximum influence. Unwritten rules, custom, rules of the game, or folkways may tolerate several behavior patterns, but the institutional setting determines the limits of appropriate behavior. What we have said thus far assumes, of course, that the institution (in this case, the legislature) is viable, performs relevant functions in the political system, and does not include a substantial number of persons determined to destroy or radically transform the institution.

A perceptive analysis of legislative role behavior was done by Donald R.

Matthews in his study of American senators.[28] Senatorial folkways facilitate the operational efficiency and effectiveness of the American Senate. These norms discourage verbosity in an institution that seldom formally limits debate. Specialization and expertise are encouraged and a senator is discouraged from publicly debating each issue of the moment. Toleration, mutual respect, and friendship guide personal relations. Senators are encouraged to be "compromisers and bargainers" and to use their powers in a restrained and careful manner.

The most generally accepted rule is apprenticeship. Freshmen senators receive the less attractive committee assignments. For two years, and even more, freshmen are discouraged from speaking frequently, if at all, on the Senate floor. Respect for senior members, bordering on deference, makes a senator acceptable to many of his colleagues. As one new senator explained: "Keep on asking for advice, boy, the committee chairman told me. That's the way to get ahead around here."[29]

A senator must specialize if he wants to influence his colleagues. If most senators spoke on each issue, Senate work would move considerably slower. Specialization provides a necessary division of labor, encourages more action and less talk, and builds a senator's reputation and effectiveness among his colleagues. "The really effective senators are those who speak only on the subjects they have been dealing with at close quarters, not those who are on their feet on almost every subject all the time."[30]

Courtesy fosters the civility that one hundred important men must have if they are daily expected to function as a decision-making body on controversial issues—issues that often are the center of intense popular feelings. Conflicts inevitably exist, but debate is usually restrained by the underlying courtesy rule. A colleague's motives are never questioned, nor are other states criticized. Less personal address formalizes debate and reduces personal incentive; for example, Senator *X* is not referred to by name on the Senate floor, but as the "Senator from State *Y*." Courtesy allows strong personalities and potential competitors to achieve a necessary degree of cooperation. Courtesy is absolutely necessary to muffle the rivalries and potential personal conflicts in a problem-solving institution like the Senate.

Institutions cannot expect 100 percent commitment to the unwritten rules of conduct by members, and the American Congress is no exception. The political novice may not immediately understand that he has the time to accept a deferential apprenticeship of several years. The Appropria-

[28] Donald R. Matthews, *U.S. Senators and Their World* (Chapel Hill: The University of North Carolina Press, 1960), see especially chapter 5. The information on senatorial rules of the game is drawn from this book.

[29] *Ibid.*, p. 93.

[30] *Providence Evening Bulletin,* February 8, 1956.

tions Committee is a highly valued assignment in the House of Representatives. Members of the committee consider themselves among the hardest working group in the House. There is also consensus in the large committee (40 to 50 members) that it is the guardian of the federal budget and there is an obligation to hold spending down to the minimum. New committee members go through an acute socialization experience in which they learn the norms and learn to compromise. Speaking too often, or even speaking much at all during the first couple of years on the committee, or being abrasive and contentious can lead to punishments—"raised eyebrows, not being sent on a trip to Europe, a change in subcommittee assignment, or not being given anything to do."[31] Most members who wish to continue on the Appropriations Committee and be effective absorb the committee's folkways. One example of the reverse side of the coin is the case of the senator who has loftier political ambitions, especially the presidency. This individual speaks on many issues, appeals to many national groups and potential constituencies, and of necessity disregards the axiom of specialization and limiting public exposure to specific issues. Presidential ambitions are nurtured by groups outside the Senate, and Senate norms become secondary. One example was the late Senator Kefauver from Tennessee. Once a vice-presidential nominee of the Democratic Party, and nearly a presidential nominee, he had, however, limited influence in the Senate, partly the result of his disregard for some Senate norms.

Unwritten rules by their very nature do not specify penalties; but diminished status in the institution is the obvious result, and penalties are tangible. Rules of the game socialize new members into the institution, influence the decision-making process within the institution, and affect the legislative output. These rules are an integral component of the legislative process of most legislatures.

Summary

The diminished role or status of legislatures remains a debated question. Clearly, during the last few decades in even pluralist systems, the executive and the courts have initiated policy and engaged in rule making to the point that they frequently overshadow legislatures.

Complex crises also seem to work against the importance of the legislative process. Extended consideration, negotiation, and compromise, which characterize democratic legislatures, seem to impede public opinion and encourage a sluggish response to issues that require quick decisions. Those who stress the necessity of clear-cut and speedy decisions, because they

[31] *Idem.*

honor rationality, efficiency, and an immediate response as supreme virtues or who identify themselves as strict majoritarians, find the legislative process cumbersome and in violation of the public will.

Nevertheless, legislatures are the single institution that can give public voice to the widest range of claims and groups in the rule-making process. Democratic legislatures provide the continuous maximum breadth of representation in society and are also regularly accountable through elections. No other institution has this type of representativeness or accountability. In authoritarian systems that are becoming more pluralistic, it is often in the legislature that the pluralism is mostly effectively manifested and nurtured. Participation in the rule-making process is only one of several valuable functions performed by legislatures.

As we have seen, legislatures perform many other functions. A principal function of viable legislatures is rule making. Rule executing, discussed in the next chapter, is an executive administrative function, but the executive branch also performs more than the single function of rule executing.

Selected Readings

A classic and not difficult introduction to the role and importance of democratic legislatures is K. C. Wheare, *Legislatures,* 2nd ed. (New York: Oxford University Press, 1967). An equally readable and helpful overview but one focusing on rule making as a function rather than legislatures as institutions, is Gabriel A. Almond and G. Bingham Powell, Jr., *Comparative Politics: A Developmental Approach* (Boston: Little, Brown, 1966), pp. 128–42.

One of the first efforts to systematically collect similar data on the 108 existing legislatures throughout the world today is J. Blondel, *Comparative Legislatures* (Englewood Cliffs, N.J.: Prentice-Hall, 1973). An earlier work, heavily institutional and legalistic, is Michael Ameller, ed., *Parliaments: A Comparative Study on the Structure and Functioning of Representative Institutions in Fifty-Five Countries,* 2nd ed. (London: Published for the Inter-Parliamentary Union by Cassell & Company, 1966). For an early effort that has continuing theoretical implications, and that studied characteristics and behavior of legislators mostly at the state level, see John C. Wahlke et al., *The Legislative System* (New York: John Wiley, 1962). Still valuable today because of the theoretical and methodological issues raised is John C. Wahlke and Heinze Eulau, eds., *Legislative Behavior: A Reader in Theory and Research* (Glencoe, Ill.; Free Press, 1959).

The idea of rule making by legislatures is more than 2500 years old. The sometimes successful efforts to establish representative institutions in the classical world are described by J. A. O. Larsen, *Representative Government in Greek and Roman History* (Berkeley: University of California Press, 1966). A good overview of what representation and assemblies meant in the Middle Ages is found in the symposium sponsored by the International Commission for the History of Representative and Parliamentary Institutions, "Medieval Representation in Theory and Practice," *Speculum,* Vol. XXIX, No. 2 (April, 1954), pp. 347–476. Covering some of the same period is an historical description of representation until the seventeenth century by A. R. Myers, "Parliaments in Europe: The Representative Tradition, I and II," *History Today,* Vol. V, Nos. 6 and 7 (June and July, 1955), pp. 383–90 and 446–54.

The functions of legislatures and individual members are widely discussed. Two collections that provide various viewpoints on the importance or decline of legislative functions are Elke Frank, ed., *Lawmakers in a Changing World* (Englewood Cliffs, N.J.: Prentice-Hall, 1966); and Gerhard Loewenberg, ed., *Modern Parliaments: Change or Decline?* (Chicago: Aldine-Atherton, 1971).

There are a number of good studies of specific legislatures or legislative systems. The most extensive writing has been done on American legislatures. Malcom E. Jewell and Samuel C. Patterson, *The Legislative Process in the United States,* 2nd ed. (New York: Random House, 1972) is a basic introduction to American legislative systems. Robert Bendiner, a journalist, describes the difficulties, equal to passing "a camel through the eye of a needle," of getting a proposal through the congressional committee system in *Obstacle Course on Capital Hill* (New York: McGraw-Hill Book Company, 1964). Randall B. Ripley, *Congress: Process and Policy* (New York: W. W. Norton, 1975) presents a wide-ranging analysis of Congress in the belief that Congress plays an important policy-making role. The book includes an extensive and helpful bibliography on the American Congress. Following a similar though briefer format and also including a good bibliography, Lawrence C. Dodd, *Congress and Public Policy* (Morristown, N.J.: General Learning Press, 1972), shows through a series of case examples that despite arguments to the contrary, Congress retains considerable policy initiative. A critical study of Congress written for the popular market emerged from the Ralph Nader Congress Project: Mark J. Green, James M. Fallows, and David R. Zwick, *Who Runs Congress?* (New York: Bantam Books, Grossman Publishers, 1972).

A brief introduction to American state legislatures is Wilder Crane, Jr., and Meredith W. Watts, Jr., *State Legislative Systems* (Englewood Cliffs, N.J.: Prentice-Hall, 1968). The Eagleton Institute of Politics, Rutgers University, has done considerable research on state legislatures. A recent Eagleton-sponsored study by Alan Rosenthal urges an expanded role for state legislative committees to upgrade the performance of state legislatures: *Legislative Performance in the States: Exploration of Committee Behavior* (New York: The Free Press, 1974). The Citizens Conference on State Legislatures has undertaken a massive study of America's fifty state legislatures and has recommended many improvements. One spinoff of this study is John Burns, *The Sometimes Governments** (New York: Bantam Books, 1971). This book, written in layman's language and intended for popular consumption, makes 1300 recommendations.

Much also has been written on the British legislative process. The history of parliamentary reform in Great Britain is traced by Bernard Crick, *Reform of Parliament** (Garden City, N.Y.: Anchor Books, 1965). Ronald Butt argues that critics have overestimated the extent to which the role of Parliament is being undermined in his *Power of Parliament: An Evolutionary Study of the Functions of the House of Commons in British Politics* (New York: Walker, 1968). As the qualifications of members of Parliament appear to have increased, it is paradoxical that the status of the average MP seems to have decreased. A recent volume of readings, almost half of which were contributed by MPs, indicates that the backbencher has more influence than commonly assumed: Dick Leonard and Herman Valentine, eds., *The Backbencher and Parliament* (London: Macmillan Press, 1972).

Two highly regarded studies of European parliaments are Gerhard Loewenberg, *Parliament in the German Political System* (Ithaca, N.Y.: Cornell University Press, 1967); and Philip M. Williams, *The French Parliament: Politics in the Fifth Republic* (New York: Praeger, 1968). One early contribution of elected legislators in a developing country is that they can help to link the government with the prople. David Morrell analyzes such a situation in "Legislative Intervention in Thailand's Development Process: A Case Study," *Asian Survey,* Vol. XII, No. 8 (August, 1972), pp. 627–46.

Three major efforts to carry forward legislative research on a comparative basis are Herbert Hirsch and M. Donald Hancock, eds., *Comparative Legislative System* (New York: The Free Press, 1971); Allan Kornberg and Lloyd Musolf, eds., *Legislatures in Developmental Perspective* (Durham, N.C.: Duke University Press, 1970); and Samuel C. Patterson and John C. Wahlke, eds., *Comparative Legislative Behavior: Frontiers of Research* (New York: John Wiley, 1972). A new journal, *Legislative Studies Quarterly,* published by the University of Iowa's Comparative Legislative Research Center, intends to include theoretical and conceptual articles as well as studies of specific representative assemblies.

* Available in paperback.

Chapter 8

Executive Leadership and Public Administration

The executive branch is the second of the "output" agencies. It includes the executive government and the bureaucracy. Both agencies are charged with implementing policies made by the legislative branch but partake, as we shall see, in the policy-making process too. We would like to begin our discussion of the executive branch by recalling a major event that occurred not too long ago.

On August 9, 1974, newspapers in many countries of the world featured on their front pages an unprecedented happening—the resignation of Richard M. Nixon from the presidency of the United States. For two years Mr. Nixon had tried to stymie an increasing number of charges made against him, such as his knowledge and coverup of the Watergate burglary, his misuse of governmental agencies, his alleged acceptance of illegal campaign contributions, and his illegal income tax deduction. Faced with the certainty of impeachment, Mr. Nixon resigned the evening of August 8. Because part of this chapter will deal with the presidential and the parliamentary executive, the following statement by Louis W. Koenig is of some relevance:

> *In a parliamentary system, Nixon, after only a few of his infractions, would have been swiftly ousted from office. But the cumbersome impeachment machinery and a fixed term of office enabled Nixon to dodge and parry for more than two years while the nation suffered and drifted.*[1]

[1] Louis W. Koenig, *The Chief Executive,* 3rd ed. (New York: Harcourt Brace Jovanovich, 1975), p. 73.

Though the orderly succession of Mr. Ford gave proof "that the American system works," the Watergate crisis left a deep scar in American society.

Was "Watergate" just an historical accident or does it include other ramifications, such as a decline of executive leadership? Some analysts point out that the contemporary world does not have any of the "great leaders" of the caliber of a Churchill, Roosevelt, or de Gaulle. While this may be true, one needs to add that there has been a steady growth in the complexities of government and the issues that leaders need to deal with. At no time have the strains and stresses on executive leadership been greater than they are now. With the above in mind, let us examine the evolution of the executive and its role in various contemporary political systems. Our emphasis will be primarily on the national executive.

THE EVOLUTION OF THE MODERN EXECUTIVE

All political units (villages, towns, cities, states, and countries) have had and have now some form of central leadership in the form of one person or a small group of people. This central leadership has become known as the executive. Prior to the establishment of viable legislative and judicial institutions, the executive virtually constituted the government, and even in recent decades its role has often gone substantially beyond that of simply executing policy. Throughout most of history executive leadership has been in the form of hereditary kingship, with brief exceptions such as

Athenian democracy in ancient Greece and the republican governments of the Roman Republic. Feudal kinds ruled in Europe from the Dark Ages until the Reformation. Modern nation-states developed in Western Europe during the sixteenth and seventeenth centuries, and these were ruled by absolute monarchs. The last ruler of this type was perhaps Haile Selassie of Ethiopia, who was overthrown only a few years ago.

England was the first country to move toward a constitutional monarchy, when Parliament in 1689 placed specific constitutional limitations on the crown, a step that became known as the "Glorious Revolution." The next important development occurred again in England when in the early eighteenth century Sir Robert Walpole established himself as the first prime minister, thereby giving rise to the dual executive consisting of a chief of state and a chief executive. Finally, the Founding Fathers of the United States provided for a president, that is, a nonhereditary "king" as chief executive, thus establishing the system of a single nonhereditary executive.

In the nineteenth century the role of the strong king was, in some countries, taken over by strong prime ministers such as Metternich in Austria and Bismarck in Prussia and, after 1871, in the German Empire.

During the first few decades of the twentieth century some Western legislatures gained enough power to challenge effectively their executive counterparts. In the United States, for example, Congress in early 1920 defeated President Wilson's quest for American membership in the League of Nations. In 1937 Congress defeated President Roosevelt's "Court-packing" proposal, a plan designed to shift the Supreme Court's viewpoint. More specifically, President Roosevelt had introduced legislation that would permit him to appoint additional Supreme Court justices equal in number to those incumbents who had reached the age of seventy. The president hoped that this new Court would rule more favorably on the items of his New Deal legislation. A short-lived ascendancy of parliamentary power can be noticed in continental Western Europe during the 1920s too.

A number of strong leaders came to office during World War II and during the subsequent decade to cope with the complex issues at hand. Is it an historical accident that Churchill became British prime minister after Dunkirk? That de Gaulle took over the leadership of the Free French forces after Petain's surrender in 1940? That Tito emerged as the leader of the Yugoslav partisans during that country's occupation? And that after World War II De Gasperi became prime minister of Italy and Adenauer chancellor of the new West Germany? Did Ghandhi and Mao Tse-tung rise to leadership by sheer accident? According to Max Lerner:

> *Often the great leaders have arisen after great catastrophes, to meet the crisis of spirit that follows. . . . The qualities of greatness must be there in the man*

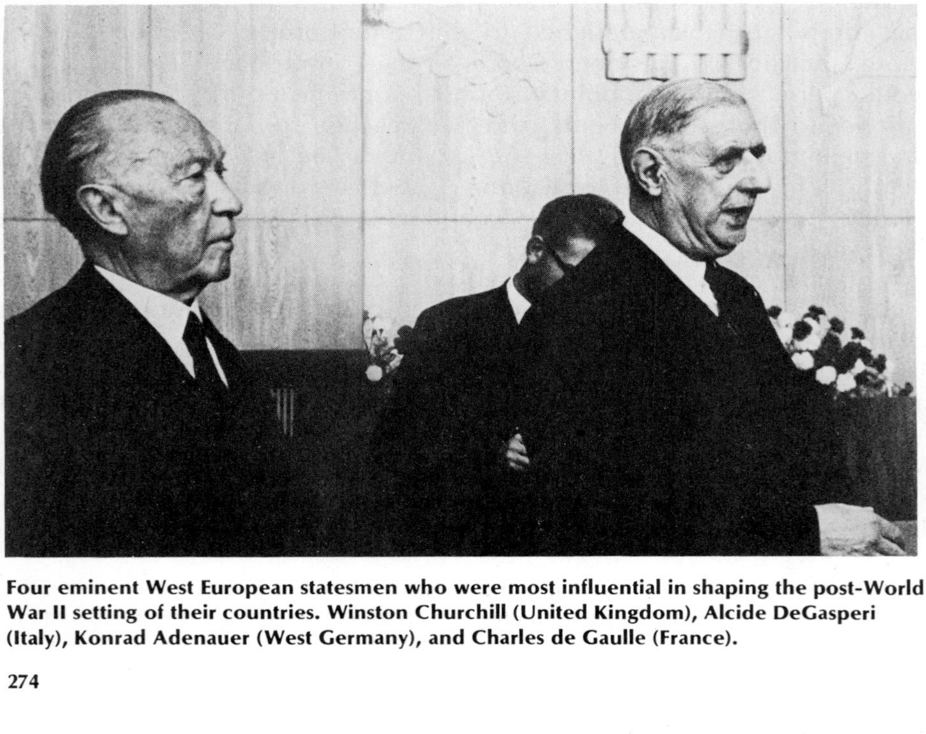

Four eminent West European statesmen who were most influential in shaping the post-World War II setting of their countries. Winston Churchill (United Kingdom), Alcide DeGasperi (Italy), Konrad Adenauer (West Germany), and Charles de Gaulle (France).

> *before he can rise to his stature. But the demands of the occasion and the need and receptiveness of the people are what bring the qualities out.*[2]

In the meantime most of the great and strong leaders of the post-World War II era have died. From this earlier group, only the octogenarians Tito and Mao Tse-tung remain in office at the time of this writing.

The steady growth in the real role and power of the chief executive, however, has continued worldwide. Reasons for this development can be found in the growing complexity of economic issues and the many political and military crises throughout the world. The tremendous technological advances of recent decades, especially in the areas of armaments, communications, and transportation have produced a setting that often requires quick and knowledgeable governmental decisions. Much of this needs to come from the executive because it is the central collection and evaluation source of important information and it can act much more speedily than legislative bodies, which are by nature deliberative.

However, the Watergate incident clearly illustrates the growth of distrust of executive leaders. While this noticeable lack of trust may have arisen first in the United States in conjunction with our military involvement in Southeast Asia and with Watergate, it has spread to other Western countries too. It seems that the people of these countries are rather ambivalent toward their executive leadership. On the one hand, they distrust strong leadership. On the other hand, however, they do look to the president (or prime minister, premier, or chancellor) to come forth with speedy answers to the monumental economic and other problems that confront Western societies. This ambivalence is found in its strongest form in the United States because of the Watergate trauma.

Looking at the Communist countries, we see a growing desire among the intelligentsia for their leaders to rule in a more restrained, humane fashion and for a greater degree of civil liberties. The writings of such eminent Russian spokesmen as Andrei Sakharov and Alexander Solzhenitsyn give ample proof of the presence of this quest.

Frequent coups d'état provide short executive tenure in many of the developing countries. One aspect of interest in regard to executive leadership in developing countries is that during the initial years following independence some indigenous people rose meteorlike to power. A good illustration is Joseph Mobutu. He had been a sergeant in the Belgian forces in the Congo, the highest rank a Congolese could obtain. Following the Belgian withdrawal in 1960 Mobutu advanced within a few months to the rank of general and commander-in-chief of the Congolese forces. He became president of the Congo (now Zaire) in 1965. The point is that as

[2] Max Lerner, "Where Is Strong Leadership in the World Now That We Need It Most?" *The Providence Journal,* January 1, 1975.

more young people from developing countries are being trained for professional positions, their rise to power will be substantially slower and more tedious than that of present incumbents.

The political executives of today have many different titles, and their range of duties differs from country to country. A number of countries, such as the United States, have a presidential type of executive, with the president serving as chief of state and chief executive. Others, such as Britain, have a parliamentary system of government, which provides for a dual executive. Here the chief of state may be a hereditary ruler (the British Queen) or an elected president (as in France or West Germany). In most parliamentary systems the chief of state serves as a symbolic ruler, having very little political power. Exceptions to this are the Shah of Iran, the presidents of France and Zaire, and a few other chiefs of state who wield considerable power. But in many societies the actual decision-making process is directed by the chief executive, who may carry the title prime minister (in English-speaking countries), premier (in French-speaking countries), or chancellor (in German-speaking countries).

An important point to note is that the degree of industrialization and the political culture of a given society have considerable bearing on the scope of power a chief executive may wield in his society. For example, presidents and prime ministers in the countries of the postindustrialized Atlantic community are subject to substantially more restrictions than many of the leaders in developing countries and the Communist nation-states.

A PROFILE OF EXECUTIVE LEADERS

The people holding the top political job in their countries come from different levels of society and different types of training. Very few executives remain who have inherited their position. The Shah of Iran is one of the last in this category. A large number of leaders, especially in the developing countries, come from the military. This group includes President Mobutu of Zaire, Colonel Qaddafi of Libya, and a number of others. In the United States, we may recall, some military men ascended to the presidency—Washington, Grant, and Eisenhower, for example. Many of the top leaders in the advanced countries are professional politicians. British prime ministers, for example, have usually spent between fifteen and twenty-five years in the House of Commons before gaining the office of chief executive. All chancellors of the Federal Republic of Germany (Adenauer, Erhard, Kiesinger, Brandt, and Schmidt) have been fulltime politicians before becoming chief executive. All the top political leaders in the Communist countries were fulltime party officials and/or administrators in their earlier career years. A number of presidents in the United States have served in

Congress or as governors prior to being elected to the highest office. A few top political leaders in the advanced countries have had extensive training in business before moving into politics and ultimately gaining the top office. One example in this category would be Georges Pompidou, second president of the Fifth French Republic.

Additional common features, but also differences between generations of executive leaders, can be found within political regions, that is, the Western democracies, the Communist countries, or the developing nation-states. Victor T. Le Vine, in his discussion of political leadership in Africa, states that:

> *Political leadership in most independent African states is still in the hands of a generation of "elder statesmen"—men who carried the fight against colonialism, who founded the principal political parties, and who developed nationalist ideologies and doctrines. These are men whose backgrounds, political styles, and ideological commitments often seem more appropriate to the winning of independence than to its consolidation or to the establishment of a legitimized political order.*[3]

Turning to the second generation of African leaders, Le Vine remarks:

> *At the same time a new generation of leaders—usually a group of men who have become politically important since independence—is concerned with the attainment of political goals much different from those that constituted the horizons of the older generation: instead of independence, the elimination of the foreign presence, and greater measures of political freedom and participation, the newer goals are more directly relevant to the post-independence situation—various kinds of economic development, the establishment of effective central government, and the satisfaction of specific political, economic, and social demands.*[4]

Le Vine's observations regarding first- and second-generation leaders in Africa could be applied, at least in part, to first- and second-generation leaders in Communist regimes. For example, Stalin was much more set on building "communism in one country" than Lenin, and there are also considerable differences in leadership between Khrushchev and Stalin. Other similarities are found as we look at other Communist countries, such as Hungary, Poland, and Romania.

Having briefly examined the backgrounds of contemporary top political executives, we may wish to look at some psychological aspects and traits connected with the incumbents. These are men and women who are in the

[3] Victor T. Le Vine, *Political Leadership in Africa* (Stanford, Cal.: Stanford University Press, 1967), p. 1.

[4] *Idem.*

category of the powerful.[5] According to Dahl, they possess substantial resources (wealth, influence, skill, and motivation) and use their resources efficiently and skillfully. We may add that these people have considerably charisma, a strong desire for power,[6] are highly motivated, employ considerable tenacity, and have a superior instinct for political survival.

A number of psychologists have researched the phenomenon of "leadership traits." One of the more comprehensive surveys, undertaken by R. M. Stogdill, identifies the following as "leadership traits": physical and constitutional factors and appearance (height, weight, physique, energy, health); intelligence; self-confidence; sociability; will (initiative, persistence, ambition); dominance; and surgency (talkativeness, cheerfulness, geniality, enthusiasm, expressiveness, alertness, and originality).[7] While the above list of "leadership traits" is not complete, it does give some idea of the ingredients that may help a person to obtain the top political position in a society.

In terms of their effectiveness, rulers have differed widely. Some political historians in this country have ranked American presidents, according to their performance, as "great presidents" (George Washington, Thomas Jefferson, Andrew Jackson, Abraham Lincoln, Theodore Roosevelt, Woodrow Wilson, and Franklin D. Roosevelt); near-great presidents (Harry Truman, for example); average presidents (such as Dwight D. Eisenhower); and weak presidents (as typified by James Polk and Warren G. Harding). A good comparison of leadership stature among British prime ministers would be the contrast between the soft-spoken Neville Chamberlain, who let himself be "hoodwinked" by Hitler at the Munich Conference (1938) and his successor, Winston Churchill, who led Britain successfully through World War II. Churchill undoubtedly would be ranked as one of Britain's great prime ministers. In recent French political history, the charismatic and strong performance of President Charles de Gaulle differs starkly from the weak leadership rendered by his predecessors of the Fourth Republic.

In a broader sense history depicts many different kinds of rulers. Some have exercised strong leadership, others have been weak, and many others have been moderate in their role as leaders. The reigns of some rulers have been more beneficial to the masses than the reigns of others. Some rulers have been outright cruel to their subjects, indicating clear mental deficiencies. Among twentieth-century rulers Hitler and Stalin would fall into

[5] See our discussion of Dahl's categorization of man's political role in Chapter 1.

[6] Some theorists consider the "drive to power" as perhaps the major trait among many of those who reach the top political office. For an eloquent exposition of this theory, see Harold D. Laswell, *Power and Personality* (New York: W. W. Norton, 1948).

[7] See Murray G. Ross and Charles E. Hendry, *New Understandings of Leadership,* (New York: Association Press, 1957), p. 18. The book is an excellent survey of research on the topic of "leadership."

the category of "sick personalities." Certainly, the world would have been better off without them. Fortunately, the cases of Caesar and Ghengis Khan, as well as Hitler and Stalin, constitute the exception to the rule. In most instances rulers have been and are substantially more sane and responsible than these four men. In addition, modern rulers have advisers who can exercise a moderating influence if needed. Nevertheless, it is imperative in our times that "sick personalities" be kept from obtaining high political and military office. In the age of nuclear weaponry there exists the danger that a number of countries will obtain atomic warheads. Accordingly, the number of political leaders who, potentially, could cause substantial harm will increase correspondingly.[8]

What are the socioeconomic backgrounds of chief executives? Many of the political leaders of Western countries, including Latin America, have come from middle- or upper-class family backgrounds. The "log cabin" heritage has been the exception to the rule. British prime ministers have usually been graduates of Cambridge or Oxford University. The above thesis also holds true for most leaders in the continental European democracies and for Japan. The case of Willy Brandt, who came from a rather poor background, is one of the few exceptions. We do find a difference, however, when we look at the Communist countries. Lenin and Stalin came from middle-class families. They were seminary students before becoming professional revolutionaries. Khrushchev, in contrast, was an illiterate coal miner during his late teens. He received all his formal education under party auspices. Several other Communist leaders have made their way from blue-collar ranks to the top executive office in their respective countries.

What are the socioeconomic backgrounds of the leaders in the developing countries of Africa and Asia? The large majority came from fairly well-to-do family backgrounds. This obviously holds true for the Shah of Iran and the kings of Saudi Arabia, Jordan, and Morocco. But it applies also—perhaps to a lesser degree—to many of the nonhereditary rulers in Africa and Asia.

In summary, we find that the top political executives throughout the world have certain attributes and traits in common, and it is on the basis of these attributes and traits that these leaders have arrived at top positions. The large number of people who do not become chief of state or chief executive may also have some of the attributes and traits, but they will have

[8] Two superb anthologies on the role of leadership in political systems are Lewis J. Edinger, ed., *Political Leadership in Industrialized Societies* (New York: John Wiley, 1967); and James D. Barber ed., *Political Leadership in American Government* (Boston: Little, Brown, 1964). A less scholarly but rather interesting book on the subject is Viscount Montgomery, *The Path to Leadership* (New York: G. P. Putnam's, 1961).

them to a lesser extent and/or will maximize them less than those who become chief executives.

The study of leadership phenomena is one of the more recent areas of academic inquiry. Much still needs to be learned about the factors and variables that are responsible for elevating a person to a leadership position.

Major Varieties of Executive Government

The two major kinds of the executive are the presidential and the parliamentary forms. The only exception to these two major forms are the transitional military regimes, presently found in Chile, Ethiopia, and Portugal, for example. As we shall see below, the parliamentary and presidential executives exist in many different varieties, leading some writers to use other classification schemes, such as democratic executives, restrictive executives, and totalitarian executives.[9] We believe, however, this approach involves a fallacy, since the categories are variations or perversions of either the genuine presidential or parliamentary executive. Any executive branch, as well as the other parts of the government, will reflect the political culture and heritage of a society, including its democratic, authoritarian, or totalitarian tradition. Let us examine the presidential and parliamentary types of the executive and the functions each performs.

THE PRESIDENTIAL EXECUTIVE

Some fifty countries have presidential executives. Among them are the United States, most Latin American countries, and some in Africa and Asia. A basic characteristic of the presidential type of executive is that the offices of chief of state and chief executive are held by the same person. A president serves as the ceremonial and symbolic leader of his nation-state, but he also has to attend to the day-by-day issues of governmental business. Thus, he often will become involved in party politics, unlike the chief of state in a parliamentary system.

In some ways the president is the modern counterpart to the king of ancient days. He is the central point of power in a society. How does he arrive at this highest political poisition a country has to offer? Some presidents are popularly elected for a specific term of office. For example, the president of the United States is elected for a four-year term and, since

[9] See D. George Kousoulas, *On Government and Politics,* 2nd ed. (Belmont, Cal.: Duxbury Press, 1971), pp. 228–233.

the passage of the Twenty-Second Amendment to the Constitution, may not be elected to this office more than twice. In countries where democratic elections are less established or less meaningful, presidential hopefuls often obtain the presidency through a coup d'état and stay in the office until they are overthrown. The latter practice is still widespread in Latin America and the developing countries of Africa and Asia.

Presidents in democratic societies are subject to greater limitations and restraints than their counterparts in more authoritarian countries in Latin America, Africa, and Asia. The president of the United States, for example, may make treaties only with the advice and consent of the U.S. Senate, and while he may nominate candidates for high federal positions in the executive and judiciary, the final appointment of these persons, again, requires Senate approval. Moreover, the Vietnam and Watergate affairs have shown that public opinion and the mass media have become important watchdogs on the actions of U.S. executives. The strong presidents of authoritarian Latin American or African societies, as typified by General Stroessner of Paraguay or Mobutu of Zaire, face substantially less internal restraint.

Presidential Functions

The constitutional functions and powers of a president can perhaps be best explained by examining the responsibilities of the president in the United States. The presidential system in this country has served as a model for many other nation-states.

1. The president serves as *chief of state,* a symbolic and ceremonial function. In this capacity he is expected to exhibit and symbolize the glory, greatness, and values of the United States. He will receive and entertain leading officials from other countries and award medals and other tokens of recognition. The citizenry expects him to be above reproach in his manners and personal life. It is this expectation that, among other things, Mr. Nixon grossly violated during the episode that became known as the "Watergate crisis." Some presidents in developing countries serve an additional function in this category in that they try to develop an ideology suitable to their society. A good example could be found in the efforts of President Nyerere of Tanzania to build African socialism.[10]

2. The president is the *chief executive* of his country. He carries final decision-making power and ultimate responsibility. President Truman had the famous "THE BUCK STOPS HERE" sign on his desk. President Kennedy went on nation-wide television to take full responsibility for the abortive Bay of Pigs invasion in 1961. The president provides leadership for his cabinet and attempts to direct the bureaucracy. Finally, he needs to main-

[10] His ideological thoughts are cogently expressed in Julius K. Nyerere, *Freedom and Unity* (London: Oxford University Press, 1966).

tain open channels of communication with the people and inform them of major steps taken by the government. Franklin D. Roosevelt used his "fireside chats" for this purpose; more recent presidents have addressed the people via television during prime-time hours.

3. The president serves as the *chief legislator* of his country. He will keep pressure on Congress to have it perform according to the charge contained in his State of the Union address. He must cajole and persuade congressional leaders and other influentials to do the things he believes need to be done in the interest of the country. As President Truman put it at one time:

> *I sit here all day trying to persuade people to do the things they ought to have sense enough to do without my persuading them. . . . That's all the powers of the President amount to.*[11]

The point is that the assertion of presidential leadership in legislative matters is very important. He must, however, lead in a positive and constructive fashion, so as not to annoy those whose action and support he seeks. Since legislative assemblies are still in a formative stage in many of the developing countries, their presidents have considerably more leeway in dictating terms than does a president of the United States.

4. The president is the *commander-in-chief* of the armed forces in his country. The philosophy underlying this role is that of civilian control of the military. Presidential command of the armed forces, coupled with congressional fiscal control of military expenses, was intended by the Founding Fathers to forestall military *coups d'état*. However, not all countries that have a presidential executive also provide for civilian control of the military. In Latin America, for example, presidents often have been brought to power by the military and they may wish or are forced to retain the military as their main arm of support thereby creating "a state within the state."

5. The president serves as the *chief diplomat* of his country. The U.S. Constitution stipulates presidential leadership in foreign relations by stating that the president "shall have the power, by and with the Advice and Consent of the Senate, to make Treaties, provided two-thirds of the Senators present concur," and "he shall nominate, and by and with the Advice and Consent of the Senate, shall appoint Ambassadors." The president can bypass the consent of the Senate provision by concluding an executive agreement, instead of a treaty, with the leader of another country. A famous example of the above is the agreement concluded between

[11] Quoted in Richard E. Neustadt, *Presidential Power: The Politics of Leadership* (New York: John Wiley, 1960), pp. 9–10.

President Ford conferring with Canadian Premier Trudeau. The meeting is attended by Canadian Foreign Secretary MacEachen and Secretary of State Kissinger, his American counterpart.

President Roosevelt and Prime Minister Churchill in 1940, whereby the British received fifty overage American destroyers in return for United States' leases on British territories along the east coast of the American continent for the purpose of constructing air bases on some of these islands. An increasing number of executive agreements have been concluded since World War II. Some U.S. presidents have been more active in the making and execution of foreign policy than others. Some have delegated most of the duties in this area to the secretary of state, as, for example, President Eisenhower did with John Foster Dulles. The increasing use of summit meetings since World War II has, generally speaking, further enhanced the role of the U.S. president and other chief executives in foreign relations.

6. A final role of the U.S. president, which should be mentioned, is that he is the *leader of his political party.* In this capacity he is expected to play an active role in directing the overall affairs of the party and to speak at party gatherings. The president's role as party leader is a difficult one. As president of the United States he is the spokesman of all people in this country. But on partisan issues his role as leader of his party may limit his

The President is the leader of his party. President Ford waves to the crowd as he campaigns in Rock Hill, South Carolina, in support of 5th Congressional District candidate Len Phillip (1974).

capacity to perform his spokesman role in full. According to Louis W. Koenig:

> *The President's uneasy party role is aggravated by the continual tension between his responsibilities to his office and the claims of his party. His office, and therefore its duties and problems, presumably exceed any obligation the party can impose upon him. He is a politician who must also be a statesman. Yet the party often insistently violates this assumption.*[12]

The above six roles are, by and large, the major constitutional roles

[12] Louis W. Koenig, *op. cit.*, p. 116.

performed by all chief executives in countries with presidential systems. There exist, of course, a number of variations. In some of the developing countries, for example, the single dominant political party has been created by the imcumbent president and his role as party leader is still more closely integrated with his larger role as chief executive than would be the case in the United States. An example of this is the relationship between President Nyerere and the TANU movement in Tanzania. The more autocratic a society, the more all-embracing the real powers of a president will be. Recent examples of extreme dictatorial presidential rule are the cases of François ("Doc") Duvalier of Haiti and Idi Amin of Uganda.[13]

THE PARLIAMENTARY EXECUTIVE

The parliamentary system, characterized by its fusion of power of the executive and legislative branches, has a dual executive, consisting of a chief of state and a chief executive. The former may be a hereditary ruler (as for example, in Belgium, Morocco, Thailand, or the United Kingdom) or an elected president (such as in Austria, France, Italy, or Israel). The latter is usually the leader of the country's majority party or of a coalition government and may carry the title prime minister, premier, or chancellor. The power of the chief of state has declined considerably in most countries during the past century. Leading exceptions are France and Iran. In France the writers of the Constitution of the Fifth Republic (adopted in 1958) shifted sizable powers from the office of the premier to that of the president. In Iran the shah exercises nearly exclusive power, with the prime minister relegated to an office of relatively little significance.

With the few exceptions, the chief of state performs primarily symbolic and ceremonial functions. He personifies his nation-state and, by taking care of the official ceremonial functions, relieves the chief executive of many time-consuming duties. The political influence wielded by the British queen or the president of the Federal Republic of Germany, to cite two examples, depends to a large extent on the political circumstances as well as the ability, intelligence, personality, and wisdom of the incumbent. But the presence of the office adds stability to the parliamentary system. Many of the chiefs of state in advanced Western countries have made it a point to stand above domestic politics. Queen Elizabeth has no clear association

[13] For a detailed discussion of the functions of the U.S. president, see Koenig, *op. cit.* and Neustadt, *op. cit.* Shorter discussions of the subject are found in Fred R. Mabbutt and Gerald J. Ghelfi, *The Troubled Republic: American Government, Its Principles and Problems* (New York: John Wiley, 1974), and Peter Woll and Robert H. Binstock, *America's Political System,* 2nd ed. (New York: Random House, 1975). For an examination of the Latin American presidency, see Alexander T. Edelmann, *Latin American Government and Politics* (Homewood, Ill.: The Dorsey Press, 1965), pp. 393–427.

with any of the political parties in Britain. Neither do the monarchs of the Benelux or Scandinavian countries. President Heuss, the first president of the Federal Republic of Germany, resigned his membership in the Free Democratic Party when he was elected to his office in 1949. He thought that party membership was incompatible with holding the office of president. Even Charles de Gaulle, after becoming president in 1958, declined to partake in the party work and leadership of the "Gaullists," a political movement he had helped to establish in 1947. He felt that his office required him to stand "above" the squabbles of French party politics.

The typical prime minister (premier or chancellor) is the chief executive, the chief legislator, the chief diplomat, and leader of the majority party. By "typical," we mean the prime minister in a parliamentary system as it exists in the United Kingdom. He is usually a person of considerable political experience, having served for a number of years as party official, legislator, and usually as a minister in a previous administration of his party. The functions of the prime minister as chief executive, chief legislator, and chief diplomat differ from those of a president, who makes ultimate decisions and carries final responsibility. The prime minister, in contrast, shares his decision-making power in all three areas with his cabinet. The prime minister of yesteryear used to be labeled a *primus inter pares* ("first among equals") within the cabinet. Major decisions were made collectively by that body, with the prime minister serving as the chairman of the meetings. However, most students of British politics maintain that the contemporary prime minister is substantially more powerful than the Latin phrase indicates. According to Humphry Berkeley:

> *The Prime Minister is not, and has not been for a long time, primus inter pares. . . . If the Cabinet discusses anything it is the Prime Minister who decides what the collective view of the Cabinet is. A Minister's job is to save the Prime Minister all the work he can. But no Minister could make a really important move without consulting the Prime Minister, and if the Prime Minister wants to take a certain step the Cabinet Minister would either have to agree, to argue it out in Cabinet, or resign.*[14]

Despite the growth of the prime minister's power, the ultimate responsibility for major governmental decisions rests with the whole cabinet, rather than with the prime minister alone.

A brief comparison of the real powers of the U.S. president and the British prime minister shows a mixed bag of similarities and dissimilarities. Both have extensive powers of patronage, although major appointments in the United States are subject to Senate confirmation. Both are leaders of their party, but the British prime minister is in a stronger position than his

[14] Humphry Berkeley, *The Power of the Prime Minister* (London: George Allen and Unwin, 1968), pp. 23–24.

James Callaghan, British Prime Minister.

counterpart in the United States. The president serves a fixed term of office, while the prime minister's tenure is not constitutionally set but rather, depends on retention of majority support in the House of Commons. More generally speaking, the president of the United States has substantially broader constitutional powers than does the British prime minister. Lastly, because the president is chief of state as well as chief executive, his office portrays the incumbent as a person of greater prestige than the British prime minister.[15]

[15] See Berkeley, *op. cit.* and, for a discussion of the cabinet system, John P. Mackintosh, *The British Cabinet*, 2nd ed. (London: Stevens & Sons, 1968).

The power relationship between the president and the chancellor in the Federal Republic of Germany is in many ways similar to that of the British monarch and prime minister. The president performs largely ceremonial functions and the chancellor serves as the political leader of the nation-state. Similar statements can be made about the relationship between the chief of state and the chief executive in most other postindustrial societies having a parliamentary system, with the exception of France because of its strong president and appointed (rather than elected) prime minister in the Fifth Republic.

What types of countries have a parliamentary, rather than a presidential, system of executive leadership? As indicated above, the United Kingdom can be considered the prototype of the parliamentary system. Many countries in the British Commonwealth have followed its example. They have been joined by all the democratic states of Europe, as well as Israel and Japan.

Most Communist countries, according to their constitutions, have some kind of parliamentary system too. The Soviet Union, for example, has a prime minister (the chairman of the Council of Ministers) and a chief of state (the chairman of the Presidium of the Supreme Soviet). The latter performs a number of the ceremonial duties exercised by chiefs of state in other societies. However, there is a substantial difference between the functions performed by the executive in the Communist countries and those of the executive in Western parliamentary systems. The highest decision-making body in the Soviet Union (and other Communist countries) is not the prime minister's cabinet but the Politburo of the Communist Party. Furthermore, the secretary-general of the Communist Party often performs duties rendered by either the chief of state or the chief executive in Western countries. The Soviet prime minister executes the policies passed down from the Politburo. Thus, while the Soviet constitution provides for a parliamentary system with a dual executive, its functions differ from those performed by parliamentary executives in Western countries.

ADVANTAGES AND DISADVANTAGES OF THE PARLIAMENTARY AND THE PRESIDENTIAL EXECUTIVES

The parliamentary executive (resembling the British type) is found in most of the postindustrialized societies. In order to function satisfactorily, the parliamentary system requires a well-developed and well-functioning political party system—a level of political sophistication found presently only in the more advanced countries. The presidential executive, in turn, is found in the United States and in many of the developing countries.

The fusion of executive and legislative powers under the parliamentary system provides for a much closer and smoother working relationship between these two branches of government than does the prevailing practice under the presidential system. In turn, one of the advantages of the presidential form lies in the fixed term of office of the incumbent (assuming that he does a satisfactory job). The prime minister, in order to stay in office, must maintain majority support in the lower chamber of the legislature. Does either system provide for better executive leadership? The answer, we think, depends very much on the circumstances. One could argue that the presidential stature and prestige of Lincoln, Wilson, and Roosevelt increased their eminence as wartime leaders. To achieve a similar effect, Churchill, when appointed prime minister in the early days of World War II, established a coalition government, which included all parties represented in the British Parliament. This move created a base of united support for him at home, made him a kind of "super-prime-minister," and put him on a more equal footing with the president of the United States.

In turn, however, the Watergate dilemma shows that the president and the office of the presidency can suffer inordinate loss of popular respect if the incumbent involves himself—or gets drawn into—the kind of nefarious activities that Mr. Nixon did. The parliamentary system offers a better setting for handling crises of this nature. If a prime minister loses his credibility, he can resign or be forced to resign. When a prime minister resigns, the presence of the chief of state may lend continuing stability to the system, a kind of stability that was not present in the United States during the later phases of the Watergate crisis.

Let us cite an example to illustrate the above theory. The Federal Republic of Germany experienced a type of "Watergate crisis" in May of 1974, which involved the rather popular Chancellor Willy Brandt. Intelligence sources had discovered that a member of the chancellor's immediate staff, Gunter Guillaume, was a spy in the pay of the Communist German Democratic Republic. Mr. Brandt reacted quickly and resigned from his office. A new chancellor was elected within ten days, and the transition was very smooth. The office of chancellor suffered little loss of prestige on account of the crisis. The important point is that the presence of a chief of state, separate from the chancellor (as the chief executive), provided some stability to the West German government during the crucial days because the executive was not completely void of leadership. It must be added, however, that Mr. Brandt's quick resignation—in contrast to the drawn-out struggle fought by Mr. Nixon—helped to keep the problem within manageable limits. In terms of seriousness, however, the Guillaume case, though quite different from Watergate, was probably as dangerous a matter as the wrongdoings that occurred in Washington during the Watergate crisis.

Both systems, the presidential and the parliamentary executive, lend themselves to perversion and dictatorship. Hitler and Mussolini rose from parliamentary settings, while many of today's semideveloped and developing countries are ruled by autocratic or dictatorial presidents.

A last item that deserves mention has to do with the workload of the incumbents. Observers of the presidency of the United States have found that, especially in more recent years, the president's obligation to perform both ceremonial and executive functions places an ever increasing burden on the shoulders of the incumbent. In this setting political analysts have raised the question of whether the duties of the presidency have become too large to be performed by one person.

PUBLIC ADMINISTRATION AND NATIONAL BUREAUCRACIES

Presidents and prime ministers direct the national bureaucracies, the administrative arms of their governments. We use the term bureaucracy (or administration) in a broad sense, encompassing the whole hierarchy of employees in the executive branch, from the ministers (or secretaries) at the top down to the lowest-ranking civil servant. The national bureaucracy administers and implements the central government's policies throughout the country. It carries on the process known as public administration, which can be defined as consisting of "all those operations having for their purpose the fulfillment or enforcement of public policy."[16] Public administration covers an enormously wide scope of activities, ranging from the negotiation of a treaty to the delivery of mail. It includes the multitudinous governmental administrative activities in such areas as education, health, welfare, public works, conservation, and many others. Public administration takes place at all levels of government—national, state, and local. Our following discussion will focus largely on the national aspects of public administration.

Bureaucracies, we have said, administer and implement policies. At times they also participate in the policy-making process. Members of the bureaucracy, usually those at a higher level, become involved in policy making because most legislative statutes are general prescriptions and often need to be interpreted by members of the executive branch before they can be applied to specific situations. This interpretation may add new substance to a law, and thus constitute a kind of policy making. In turn, members of the bureaucracy may initiate new legislation by reporting difficulties they have experienced in the process of implementing existing

[16] Leonard D. White, *Introduction to the Study of Public Administration,* 4th ed. (New York: Macmillan, 1955), p. 1.

rules. A multitude of complaints regarding a particular law may lead legislators to enact improved legislation.

National bureaucracies in all countries have a tendency to grow in size and complexity. They range in size from a few hundred national employees in the smallest countries to a number of millions in the largest countries. The People's Republic of China and the Soviet Union have, by far, the largest and most complex national bureaucracies.

In terms of classification, members of the bureaucracies fall into one of the following categories; political appointees; non-civil service career officials; and civil servants. Members of the first group are appointed to office for one of many reasons, ranging all the way from particular qualifications to nepotism. The second category encompasses professional governmental officials in countries that do not have a standardized civil service system. The third group consists of career governmental employees recruited and employed under a (civil service) merit system. The basic concept underlying the civil service system is that people employed under its auspices are politically neutral and will faithfully carry out the policy instructions of their superiors. Their jobs are tenured in contrast to those of political appointees, who come and go with individual administrations.

In order to discuss national bureaucracies in more detail, we would like to examine and compare the administrations of the United States, the United Kingdom, the Federal Republic of Germany, the Soviet Union, and complete our discussion with a more generalized discussion of the bureaucracies in the developing countries.

THE BUREAUCRACY IN THE UNITED STATES

The federal administration in this country consists of approximately 3 million civilian employees. It is divided into eleven departments[17] and some thirty independent agencies, such as the Civil Service Commission and the Postal Service. The personnel at the top of the federal bureaucracy consists of nearly 3000 political appointees, such as the secretaries of the eleven departments and, within each department, undersecretaries, assistant secretaries, as well as the deputies and assistants of those listed above. All these political appointees are nominated by the president, and their appointment requires the consent of the Senate. They serve at the pleasure of the president. Each incoming administration will ultimately select its own people for the appointive positions, even if the same party stays in power with a new president. For example, when Mr. Johnson took office, he kept the Kennedy appointees in office during the transition period, but then

[17] Departments of State; Treasury; Defense; Justice; Interior; Agriculture; Commerce; Labor; Health, Education, and Welfare; Housing and Urban Development; and Transportation.

replaced many of them with his own people. Secretary of State Dean Rusk was one of the few who served in his position from the start of the Kennedy administration through the end of the Johnson administration.

Customarily, an incoming president will select the nominees to head departments and they, in turn, will propose to the president candidates for the subordinate political positions in their departments. The candidates are usually members of the president's party. Mr. Kennedy's nomination of Robert McNamara, a Republican, for secretary of defense, and Mr. Nixon's nomination of a democrat, John Connally, for secretary of the treasury, are exceptions to the rule.

What is the professional background of these political appointees?[18] Some have served in the executive branch during a previous administration of their party. Others are recruited from business, as in the case of Mr. McNamara. In more recent years some candidates for high executive office have come from among academicians, as for example Secretary of State Henry Kissinger. Defeated candidates for gubernatorial office, if they belong to the president's party, may be offered an appointive position in the federal executive. John Chafee, after having been defeated in the 1968 gubernatorial election in Rhode Island, was appointed secretary of the navy by Richard Nixon.

The Civil Service in the United States

Most federal employees below the rank of the political appointees in the cabinet departments and independent agencies are under the merit system. They have been recruited and employed under the auspices of the United States Civil Service Commission or the Civil Service programs of particular agencies, such as the State Department's Foreign Service or the postal service. The system of a civil service was established in the United States with the passage of the Pendleton Act in 1883.[19] Today more than 90 percent of all federal employees hold civil service status.

The United States Civil Service Commission uses two types of classifica-

[18] An excellent profile study of federal executives is W. Lloyd Warner, et al., *The American Federal Executive* (New Haven: Yale University Press, 1963). The study examines the profiles of nearly 13,000 civilian and military executives, ranking from GS 14 (or equivalent) through cabinet secretary.

[19] A classic source on the development of the civil service in the United States is Paul P. Van Riper, *History of the United States Civil Service* (Evanston, Ill.: Row, Peterson, 1958). See also Herbert Kaufman's chapter "The Growth of the Federal Personnel System" in the American Assembly, *The Federal Government Service,* 2nd ed. (Englewood Cliffs, N.J.: Prentice-Hall, 1965). His table on pp. 41–43 lists the number of federal employees under the merit system from 1884 to 1963. For an analysis of the competitive position of the federal government as an employer see the excellent but dated study by Franklin P. Kilpatrick, Milton C. Cummings, Jr., and M. Kent Jennings, *The Image of the Federal Service* (Washington, D.C.: The Brookings Institution, 1964).

tion systems for its employees: the CPC (Crafts, Protective, and Custodial) grouping encompasses all the blue-collar jobs—about one-fifth of all the positions; the large majority of all federal employees under the merit system, those holding white-collar jobs, are under the GS (General Schedule) system, which ranges from grade GS 1 to grade GS 18. College graduates are recruited at the GS 5 or GS 7 level, depending on their previous experience and performance in the PACE (Professional and Administrative Career Examination). Information about the test and employment matters can be obtained from the nearest federal civil service office. The United States government is the largest employer in the United States. Its range of employment involves thousands of job categories. Its pay scale, as well as conditions of employment, have been steadily improved and are presently competitive with comparable private occupations.

THE BRITISH BUREAUCRACY

The British have perhaps the most professional administration in the Western world. Professional in the sense that there are few (substantially fewer than in the United States) political appointees, and nearly all of these have been members of Parliament for years and, quite often, have had previous administrative experience in the executive branch. The number of ministers customarily ranges between forty and fifty, with approximately twenty of them being members of the prime minister's cabinet. A ministry may have from three to six political appointees at the top of its hierarchy. They are ranked in the following order: minister (or secretary), minister of state, under-secretary, parliamentary secretary, and parliamentary private secretary. These officials are appointed by the prime minister and serve at his pleasure. Most ministers are long-term members of the House of Commons. A few department heads customarily are members of the House of Lords. In these instances the second-ranking political appointee must be a member of the House of Commons in order that he can represent the ministry in the lower house. Most ministers of state, under-secretaries and parliamentary secretaries are members of the House of Commons. They, too, are career politicians and many of them aspire to become ministers at a later date. The parliamentary private secretary is a junior official, usually serving his first or second term in the House of Commons. All in all, there are some two hundred political appointees at the helm of the British bureaucracy. Their small number, as well as the presence of civil servants at the highest level of government, has led one British scholar to comment:

The great advantage of having permanent officials at the highest levels is that they make available to new Ministers an unrivalled fund of experience. The American practice whereby the equivalents of our Permanent Secretaries,

Deputy Secretaries and Under-Secretaries, are political appointments have corresponding disadvantages.[20]

As suggested by Stacey, the obvious advantage of this particular British system is far more continuity at the highest levels of the ministries.

The British Civil Service

As implied above, the British civil service reaches higher into the top-level administration than its counterpart in the United States. The highest-ranking British civil servant, the permanent secretary, would about equal a GS 21 or, in other words, an assistant secretary in the United States.

The British civil service is the oldest in the Western world. It was started in the 1780s, and its merit system now covers nearly all the civilian employees of the British national government. Until the early 1970s the British civil service consisted of four distinct parts: the administrative class (the top echelon administrators); the executive class (the middle-level administrators); the professional, scientific, and technical class (this category was added during the 1950s and encompassed professional specialists such as engineers, physicians, and scientists); and a two-tier clerical class. Each category had its own entrance route.

Britain's civil service has been subject to periodic reviews, the most important and most recent being the inquiry by the Fulton Committee (1966–1968). Its proposals included a strong recommendation to abolish the strict quadripartite division with the separate entrance routes, replacing it with a single hierarchical structure similar to the system in the United States, which would cover all civil servants in one system. This proposal was accepted by the government and the changeover to the new system began in 1971. According to the Fulton Committee, a single-structure civil service would do away with the "caste system" and could considerably increase the mobility within the ranks. In the past, promotions from the executive class to the administrative class took place in very exceptional cases only and each class had become "a small world of its own." Members of one group had little contact with members of the other. One of the particular features of the administrative class has been its exclusive educational background. Approximately two-thirds of its members have been graduates of Oxford or Cambridge University.[21]

The British bureaucracy is broader in scope than its counterpart in the United States because of its administration of the nationalized industries and public corporations. Government intervention in the economy has taken place on a much larger scale in Britain than in the United States.

[20] Frank Stacey, *The Government of Modern Britain* (Oxford: Clarendon Press, 1968), p. 343.

[21] An excellent study of the social structure of the former administrative class is R. K. Kelsall, *Higher Civil Servants in Britain* (London: Routledge & Regan Paul, 1966).

Presently, the British government controls in full or in major part the following industries: electricity, gas, radio and television, civil aviation, coal, and steel, among others. Some of the nationalized industries are under the direct control of a minister while others are governed by government-appointed boards, similar to the independent agencies in the United States.

PUBLIC ADMINISTRATION IN THE FEDERAL REPUBLIC OF GERMANY

The number of federal ministers in West Germany is considerably smaller than in Britain, having ranged between fourteen and nineteen. They are appointed by the chancellor and, as in Britain, serve completely at his pleasure. In contrast to Britain, all West German ministers are members of the chancellor's cabinet. They do not have quite an equal footing in the cabinet, however. Some play a more important role than others. The minister's importance in the government depends on the particular department he heads, his standing as a party leader, and his personal relations with the chancellor. In regard to the first point, the ministers of foreign affairs, defense, interior, and finance enjoy an elevated position in the cabinet because of the great importance of their departments. The ministers are usually members of the *Bundestag,* the lower house of the West German legislature. Their length of parliamentary experience, however, is often less than that of their counterparts in Britain.

Most West German administrations have been coalition governments consisting of two parties. One of the coalition arrangements has been the practice, since 1966, that the position of minister of foreign affairs be held by the parliamentary leader of the junior party in the coalition. Thus, Willy Brandt of the Social Democratic Party served as foreign minister from 1966 to 1969, Walter Scheel from 1969 to 1974, and since 1974 Hans-Dietrich Genscher, both of the Free Democratic Party.

Formerly, all administrative positions below the rank of minister were staffed with civil servants. More recently, however, one or two positions in each ministry analogous to that of an undersecretary in the United States or parliamentary secretary in Britain have been made appointive. The appointees are members of the *Bundestag* and carry the title parliamentary state secretary. They are primarily responsible for maintaining liaison between their ministry and the legislature.

The West German Civil Service

The roots and traditions of the German civil service system were formed in early nineteenth-century Prussia and perpetuated in the German Empire and the Weimar Republic. During those years the civil service developed into a kind of caste or "state within the state," known for its efficiency and loyalty to the government. During the Third Reich efforts were made to politicize it in the sense that those who joined the Nazi Party were promoted over those who did not. Little modernization of the civil service has occurred in the post-World War II era. Efforts to democratize it—in the sense of making it more similar to the American civil service—have largely failed. According to a leading West German political scientist:

> *The main problem of the German administration is its lack of open personnel policy and the fact—seen from the point of view of the citizen—that the federally organized administration is too complex to understand. The tendency of the administration to be autonomous towards the political decision-makers by referring to a pressure exerted by the logic of facts has made the problem of the technocracy acute in the Federal Republic too. The civil service as the supposed neutral authority of the state interest tends to be a power factor with a strong dynamic of its own that is politically difficult to keep under control, a bureaucracy in the strictest meaning of the word.*[22]

Many reform proposals, such as the establishment of a specific college for the training of higher civil servants, similar to the *Ecole Nationale d'Administration* in France, have been examined and temporarily shelved. A strong hindrance to any large-scale reform is the provision in Paragraph 5, Article 33 of the West German constitution stating that "law regarding the public service shall be regulated with due regard to the traditional principles concerning the status of professional civil servants."

In terms of structure, the West German civil service is divided into three major categories, which are similar to the former British system: On top of the hierarchy is the higher service, the most important and influential category. Its members are customarily graduates of law schools. They receive their initial appointment after passing a competitive examination. After a three-year training period a second examination must be passed before the candidate receives life-term tenure in the higher civil service. *Beamte* (the general label for tenured civil servants) have enjoyed an extraordinarily high social status in German society, but that seems to be declining today. Personal connections have had some bearing on promotions within the ranks. Graduates of the "right" university and the "right" fraternity of that university have been looked after favorably by their older fraternity brothers in the upper ranks.

The second category of the West German civil service is the salaried service, consisting of the clerical employees. Most of them, too, enjoy a high degree of job security but less prestige than the members of the higher service. The third category is that of wage earners, essentially blue-

[22] Kurt Sontheimer, *The Government and Politics of West Germany,* translated from the German by Fleur Donecker (New York: Praeger, 1972), pp. 145–146.

collar workers whose jobs may be of either a temporary or permanent nature.

One substantial difference between the West German civil service and those of the United States and Britain is that while West Germany has a unified civil service structure (encompassing federal, state, and local employees in the executive and judicial branches of government), the number of civil servants in the employment of the federal government (approximately 15 percent of the total) is substantially smaller than in Britain or the United States. About 53 percent of the West German civil servants serve at the state level, and the remaining 32 percent with local governments. These figures reflect a main feature of West German federalism: no ministries, with the exception of defense and finance, have field offices at the state or local level. Consequently, the federal ministries depend on state and local agencies for the implementation of federal policies at these levels, which explains the large number of civil servants at the state and local levels.

In terms of scope the West German bureaucracy is broader than its counterpart in the United States but not as broad as the British. In addition to the comparable areas under public control in the United States, the West German government administers—under the Ministry or Transport, Posts and Telecommunications—radio, television, telegraph, and telephone service as well as civil aviation and railroads—areas that are basically in private hands in the United States.[23]

ADMINISTRATION IN THE UNION OF SOVIET SOCIALIST REPUBLICS

The Soviet bureaucracy differs substantially from its counterparts in the United States, Britain, and West Germany. The scope of Soviet administration is vast because it directs and supervises nearly all areas of societal endeavors: the traditional areas of public responsibility, such as foreign affairs, defense, finance, justice, as well as agriculture, civil aviation, communication, culture, education, all industries, public health, and transportation. The Communist Party is dominant over governmental agencies. Decisions on all major issues are made by the highest council of the party, the

[23] There are relatively few primary English-language sources dealing at length with the bureaucracy of the Federal German Republic. Two early studies are John H. Herz, "Political Views of the West German Civil Service" in Hans Speier and W. Phillips Davison, *West German Leadership and Foreign Policy* (Evanston, Ill.: Row, Peterson, 1957); and Karlheinz Neunreither, "Federalism and the West German Bureaucracy," *Political Studies* (October, 1959), pp. 233–245. A recent publication of interest is Renate Mayntz and Fritz W. Scharpf, *Policy-Making in the German Federal Bureaucracy* (New York: Elsvier Scientific Publishing Co., 1975).

Politburo. The executive branch, therefore, becomes largely a tool for implementing policy, being less involved in the policy-making process than its counterparts in non-Communist countries. There is no Western-type civil service in the Soviet Union; however, most of the bureaucratic officials are career people. The above are some, but by no means all, of the differences between Western bureaucracies and those of the Soviet Union (which has served as a model for the bureaucracies of other Communist countries).

At the top of the Soviet administrative structure is the Council of Ministers, directed by the prime minister who, in turn, is a member of the Politburo of the Communist Party. The members of the council are "elected" by the Supreme Soviet, an automatic procedure after their names have been proposed to the legislature by the party leadership. According to the present constitution of the Soviet Union the Council of Ministers is "the highest executive and administrative organ of state authority. . . . "It is responsible to the Supreme Soviet (the legislature of the Soviet Union) and accountable to it. . . . [It] "issues decisions and orders on the basis and in pursuance of the laws in operation of the USSR. . . ." The primary function of the Council of Ministers is to supervise the huge administrative apparatus and to implement all the basic party decisions that pertain to the vast area of executive–administrative jurisdiction in the Soviet Union, including the allocation of resources in the economic realm, the overall direction of economic and social affairs, and the execution of defense and foreign policies. The Council of Ministers is very large. In its present composition it consists, in addition to the prime minister (known as chairman of presidium of the Council of Ministers) of two first deputy chairmen, nine deputy chairmen (the above twelve form the presidium and serve as a cabinet), and approximately one hundred other members, including some thirty ministers in charge of functional departments, chairmen of nationwide committees, and the fifteen chairmen of the presidia of the Republic Councils of Ministers. The components of the Council of Ministers have been subject to constant change.[24]

The national ministries in the Soviet Union are of two kinds: all-union and union-republic. All-union ministries are in complete charge of their sphere of administration throughout the Soviet Union. For example, civil aviation is administered by an all-union ministry, which has its main office in Moscow and field offices in the fifteen republics and their local districts.

[24] A detailed chart depicting all the components of the Council of Ministers as of 1971 can be found in Frederick C. Barghoorn, *Politics in the USSR,* 2nd ed. (Boston: Little, Brown, 1972), pp. 340–41. See also the slightly less detailed diagram in Robert J. Osborn, *The Evolution of Soviet Politics* (Homewood, Ill.: The Dorsey Press, 1974), pp. 268–69, depicting the composition of the council as of July, 1973.

Union-republic ministries, in contrast, have a central ministry in Moscow and corresponding ministries in the fifteen republics. Agriculture is such a ministry. Its national programs are administered at the republic and local level through the officials of the republic ministry rather than those of the national office.

The vast Soviet bureaucracy employs a large number of officials at the national, state, and local levels. Estimates of their number range from ten to fifteen million. These employees can be loosely classified into three categories: party officials whose job it is to see that party policies are properly implemented in the administrative realm; administrators who put into practice the governmental programs (as distinguished from party policies) and managers who direct the work in agriculture and industry; and specialists such as architects, artists, biologists, chemists, dentists, educators, physicians, physicists, and so forth. Recruitment to positions in the bureaucracy and promotions within the ranks is supervised by the party and based on capability, performance, and political loyalty. The last criterion is often the most important consideration. According to Barghoorn:

> *The tightly centralized Soviet recruitment system tends to protect the mediocre and exclude much talent from participation in public life. Nevertheless, from the Kremlin's point of view it has compensatory advantages. Perhaps the most important is that it tends to assure the filling of all strategic posts in party, state, and other areas by politically reliable personnel.*[25]

In addition to political loyalty, membership in the Communist Party is practically a must for those who wish to advance in the administration.[26]

One of the astonishing features of the Soviet higher administrative elite has been the extraordinary longevity of people in office, despite the severe purges that occurred under Stalin and, to a lesser degree, under Khrushchev. Mr. Kosygin is only the eighth prime minister in the history of the Soviet Union. Still more remarkable is the longevity at the ministerial and subministerial levels. Some ministers have been in charge of their departments for twenty and more years. Andrei Gromyko is perhaps the world's most senior foreign minister, having been promoted to that position in 1957.

Perhaps the greatest shortcoming in the Soviet bureaucracy is that its complexity—resulting from size and duplications caused by the existence of concurrent party and governmental agencies in nearly all areas of administrative endeavors—has given rise to an inordinate amount of red

[25] Barghoorn, *op. cit.*, p. 174.

[26] An interesting in-depth study of the bureaucratic elite in the Ukraine is John A. Armstrong, *The Soviet Bureaucratic Elite: A Case Study of the Ukranian Apparatus* (New York: Frederick A. Praeger, 1959).

tape. Reports from visitors to the Soviet Union and accounts in major Soviet newspapers abound with complaints about the prevalent administrative inefficiency, apathy, and nepotism. While the Soviet leadership has tried to remedy the more flagrant abuses and shortcomings, it has made little headway in its attempts to make the bureaucracy more efficient. The larger a bureaucracy, the more difficult it is to reform it. The monstrous size of the Soviet bureaucracy makes any kind of reform difficult. Moreover, some possible reforms, such as eliminating the duplication caused by overlapping party and administrative agencies would run counter to basic principles of the Soviet system and are, obviously, not desired by the ruling elite.

BUREAUCRACIES IN THE DEVELOPING COUNTRIES

Since the late 1940s a large number of countries in Africa, Asia, and Latin America have achieved independence. Prior to independence, these countries were ruled by an administrative structure centered in the mother country and the governor of the colony. The administration under the governor was customarily patterned and structured along the lines of the mother country's bureaucracy. The colonial administrative personnel consisted of a small number of Europeans (such as Britishers in British colonies) in the higher positions and indigenous officials in the middle and lower ranks. In the British colonies, for example, Britishers filled about 4 or 5 percent of the administrative positions. But since these were the higher positions, the European administrators in fact controlled the bureaucracy.

When the colonies became independent, most of them had fairly well-established administrative systems with built-in civil services, but little in terms of other political institutions. A resulting problem has been described by Fred Riggs:

> *A phenomenon of the utmost significance in transitional societies is the lack of balance between political policy-making institutions and bureaucratic policy-implementing structures. The relative weakness of political organs means that the political function tends to be appropriated, in considerable measure, by bureaucrats. Intra-bureaucratic struggles become a primary form of politics. But when the political arena is shifted to bureaucracies—a shift marked by the growing power of military officers in conflict with civilian officials—the consequences are usually ominous for political stability, economic growth, administrative effectiveness, and democratic values.*[27]

The point made by Riggs is that in many new countries the administrations are far more developed than the fledgling legislatures and therefore play an inordinately large role in the policy-making process.

[27] Fred W. Riggs, "Bureaucracy," in Frank Tachau, ed., *The Developing Nations: What Path to Modernization?* (New York: Dodd, Mead, 1972), p. 115.

Let us now examine some of the features of the transition period.

The first generation of chief executives in the new countries has usually been people who either moved up from an administrative position held under the old order or who came from the military. They appointed some of their own people as ministers and other immediate subordinates, but also retained the services of a number of European administrative experts who had been present under the colonial order. The speed with which the foreigners have been replaced by indigenous experts has varied from country to country and, obviously, depended on the availability of trained natives; there were more, for example, in India, Pakistan, and the West Indies than in Africa. As Henry L. Bretton points out:

> *Few of the first-generation African leaders possessed the skills, though many possessed the intelligence, to understand let alone manage and direct complex ministries in the crucial sectors of finance, foreign and domestic trade, industry, the central banks, and the sensitive areas of telecommunications. The potential of high-level civil servants increased in direct proportion to the lack of experience, know-how, and expertise of the African heads of ministries.*[28]

In the former British colonies of Africa, the degree of Africanization of the civil service at the time of independence differed considerably from country to country and in the case of Nigeria from region to region. Moreover, there were interesting differences in the subsequent further Africanization. According to J. F. Maitland-Jones:

> *The degree to which the public services in ex-British Africa have been Africanized/localized, and the speed with which it had taken place, clearly varied very greatly. . . . Ghana and Uganda, which were relatively speaking always the most advanced countries, kept British permanent secretaries for longer than the other countries—because . . . an Africanization policy had been seen by the public to be in operation for so long they could believe in it, and they did not therefore need to exert pressures experienced elsewhere to Africanize speedily at the expense of efficiency.*[29]

The new leaders of the developing countries have changed little in their countries' administrative systems. By and large these bureaucracies today have the structure they had during colonial time.[30] The replacement of foreigners with indigenous administrators went ahead more rapidly in ex-British colonies than in ex-French colonies, because Francophone Africa had, relatively speaking, substantially fewer indigenous administrators at

[28] Henry L. Bretton, *Power and Politics in Africa* (Chicago: Aldine Publishing, 1973), p. 177.

[29] J. F. Maitland-Jones, *Politics in Africa: The Former British Territories* (New York: W. W. Norton, 1973), p. 99.

[30] For a detailed discussion of the civil service in Anglophone Africa, presented by an eminent African administrator, see A. L. Adu, *The Civil Service in Commonwealth Africa: Development and Transition* (London: George Allen & Unwin, 1969).

independence than Anglophone Africa, and the Francophone countries have generally maintained closer ties with France than the Anglophone countries with Britain. Most Britishers were phased out of the bureaucracies of African countries within the first ten years of independence, although a number of British advisers have been retained in such countries as Kenya, Malawi, Nigeria, Sierra Leone, and Zambia. In contrast, the reduction of French personnel has been rather slow in ex-French Africa with the exception of Algeria and Tunisia. During the 1960s the number of French civil servants leaving Africa was easily matched by the arrival of French technicians and agricultural experts. Rubin and Weinstein report that:

> *Even though French civil servants in the states of West Africa, Equatorial Africa, and Madagascar decreased from 10,278 in 1960 to 8,423 in 1966, 1,500 more military men arrived to work as technicians, and 3,800 agricultural specialists were sent. Those Frenchmen still in administrative post rose in rank, to have control over a greater number of African civil servants than in the past.*[31]

Several Francophone African governments have maintained themselves in office with the help of French troops. As late as 1971 a regiment-sized French unit put down a rebellion in Chad.

The above discussion indicates that the bureaucracies of many developing countries are still in a transitional phase, in the sense that the transfer of administrative responsibilities to a completely indigenous staff has not yet been completed. Some of these countries will depend on the help of foreign administrative experts for some years still.

Summary

The above has been a survey discussion of the executive branch of government. We described the parliamentary and presidential forms with their similarities and differences. It is important to be aware that there exist many varieties of the single and the dual executive. Some of them may differ considerably from our two models, the British parliamentary executive and the presidency in the United States.

The primary constitutional function of the executive is to implement policy, but we have noted that chief executives also participate in the policy-making process. The degree of involvement will vary from country to country, depending on the viability of legislative bodies (especially in the developing countries) and the role of party leadership, especially in the

[31] Leslie Rubin and Brian Weinstein, *Introduction to African Politics: A Continental Approach* (New York: Praeger, 1974), p. 201.

Communist countries. Generally speaking, the increasing complexities of societal and worldwide problems have contributed to the growth of the *informal* powers (as distinguished from the constitutional powers) of chief executives in recent years.

Presidents and prime ministers preside over vast bureaucracies. We compared briefly the administrations of the United States, the United Kingdom, the Federal Republic of Germany, the Union of Soviet Socialist Republics, and concluded the section with a more general discussion of the bureaucracies in developing countries. The number of political apointees at the top of the administrative hierarchy differs from country to country. Likewise, the features of the civil service may vary. One common characteristic of nearly all bureaucracies is their continual growth. Since people look increasingly to their national governments for help of one kind or another, there are no easy ways to arrest the trend of bureaucratic growth.

Selected Readings

Four insight discussions of political leadership are James D. Barber, ed., *Political Leadership in American Government** (Boston: Little, Brown, 1964); Lewis J. Edinger, ed., *Political Leadership in Industrialized Societies: Studies in Comparative Analysis** (New York: John Wiley, 1967); R. Barry Farrell, ed., *Political Leadership in Eastern Europe and the Soviet Union** (Chicago: Aldine, 1969); and Victor T. Le Vine, *Political Leadership in Africa* (Stanford, Cal.: Stanford University Press, 1967).

A number of biographies provide valuable information on an individual's rise to power and political leadership. Some of the better biographies of recent political leaders are Lewis Broad, *Winston Churchill,* 2 vols. (New York: Hawthorn, 1958); Alexander Werth, *De Gaulle: A Political Biography* (New York: Simon and Schuster, 1966); Terence Prittie, *Adenauer* (London: Stacy, 1971); and by the same author, *Willy Brandt: Portrait of a Statesman* (New York: Schocken, 1974). The best book on Stalin is Issac Deutscher, *Stalin: A Political Biography,** 2nd ed. (New York: Oxford University Press, 1967). A well-written biography of his successor is Edward Crankshaw, *Khrushchev: A Career** (New York: Viking, 1966).

Among the more useful discussions of the U.S. presidency are Louis W. Koenig, *The Chief Executive,** 3rd ed. (New York: Harcourt Brace Jovanovich, 1975); Richard E. Neustadt, *Presidential Power: The Politics of Leadership** (New York: John Wiley, 1960); and James D. Barber, *The Presidential Character: Predicting Performance in the White House**

* Available in paperback.

(Englewood Cliffs, N.J.: Prentice-Hall, 1972). Two helpful sources on the office of the British chief executive are Humphry Berkeley, *The Power of the Prime Minister* (London: George Allen and Unwin, 1968); and Andrew Alexander and Alan Watkins, *The Making of the Prime Minister* (London: Macdonald, 1970).

A detailed study of federal executive officials in the United States is W. Lloyd Warner et al., *The American Federal Executive* (New Haven: Yale University Press, 1963). The standard work on the U.S. Civil Service is Paul P. Van Riper, *History of the United States Civil Service* (Evanston, Ill.: Row, Peterson, 1958). For a more recent survey, see Herbert Kaufman, "The Growth of the Federal Personnel System," in the American Assembly, *The Federal Government Service,* 2nd ed. (Englewood Cliffs, N.J.: Prentice-Hall, 1965).

The classic work on the British cabinet is John P. Mackintosh, *The British Cabinet,* 2nd ed. (London: Stevens, 1968). There are no books on the recent reform of the British civil service. The best sources for the pre-1970 civil service in the United Kingdom are R. K. Kelsall, *Higher Civil Servants in Britain* (London: Rutledge & Kegan Paul, 1966); and Edgar N. Gladden, *Civil Services in the United Kingdom,* 1853–1970, 3rd rev. ed. (London: Frank Cass, 1967).

There are no English language books dealing exclusively with the West German executive. The Adenauer and Brandt biographies cited above provide some insight. For an up-to-date but brief discussion of the subject, see Arnold J. Heidenheimer and Donald P. Kommers, *The Governments of Germany,** 4th ed. (New York: Thomas Y. Crowell, 1975). Various aspects of the bureaucracy are discussed in John H. Herz, "Political Views of the West German Civil Service," in Hans Speier and W. Phillips Davison, *West German Leadership and Foreign Policy* (Evanston, Ill.: Row, Peterson 1957); and Renate Mayntz and Fritz W. Scharpf, *Policy-Making in the German Bureaucracy* (New York: Elsevier, 1975).

Some information on the national administration in the USSR is to be found in Frederick C. Barghoorn, *Politics in the U.S.S.R.,** 2nd ed. (Boston: Little, Brown, 1972). Post-Khrushchev reforms are analyzed by Jerry F. Hough in "Reforms in Government and Administration" in Alexander Dallin and Thomas B. Larson, eds., *Soviet Politics Since Khrushchev** (Englewood Cliffs, N.J.: Prentice-Hall, 1968). An informative study of state and local administration is John A. Armstrong, *The Soviet Bureaucratic Elite: A Case Study of the Ukranian Apparatus* (New York: Frederick A. Praeger, 1959).

* Available in paperback.

The best source on political leadership in Africa is Le Vine's book cited above. Another useful publication is Henry L. Bretton, *Power and Politics in Africa** (Chicago: Aldine, 1973). The most authoritative study of the civil service in Africa is A. L. Adu, *The Civil Service in Commonwealth Africa: Development and Transition* (London: George Allen and Unwin, 1969). His discussion focuses on Anglophone Africa. For an Asian comparison, see C. P. Bhambhri, *Bureaucracy and Politics in India* (Dehli, India: Vikas, 1971).

* Available in paperback.

Chapter 9

The Judicial Process: Law and the Courts

Law and Justice

The judicial branch constitutes the third governmental output agency. It entails law, judges, and courts. These forces play a role in all political systems. It is difficult to think of the state without law because when people live in great proximity they require rules and regulations to define their respective rights and obligations as members of society.

Law is generally regarded as one of the greatest achievements of civilization. It is concerned with basic rules of conduct that reflect to some degree the concept of justice. These rules concern the relationships of the individual with his government and with other men.

An ideal of justice frequently expressed is that government should be a government of laws and not of men. Whether this goal can be achieved is questionable, as laws are made and administered by men. But in practice this ideal is generally interpreted to mean a legal system that treats everyone equally and is not subject to change through the arbitrary acts of a dictator, or even the whim of transient majorities.

There are many kinds of law and no single definition of the term is possible, as scholars are not in agreement on the nature of law. The rules of law are based on custom or legislation and court decisions. But the language of the law is technical and not easily understood, and the proceedings through which the courts function are frequently complex.

Positive Law and Natural Law

Positive law is associated with the nineteenth-century English utilitarian philosopher, John Austin, who defined law as consisting of well-defined rules of human conduct, enforceable by appropriate sanctions of government.[1] Law, in this sense, is man-made and is essentially a relationship between ruler and ruled. This conception of law does not exhaust the meaning of that term, but it does describe the aspect of law with which political scientists are most concerned.

To many there is another type of law, one traditionally called natural—a law more basic than man-made law and one that is based on fundamental principles of justice. A human law that conflicts with natural law is void. The idea of natural law was first developed by the Greek and Roman Stoic philosophers. The Roman jurist Cicero (106–43 B.C.) defined the law of nature as "right reason" implanted in nature, which is the basis of measuring justice and injustice. This concept was adopted by the Christian church and incorporated into the philosophy of the great medieval thinker Thomas Aquinas. In more modern times it became part of the philosophy of John Locke, the seventeenth-century English philosopher who derived the idea of natural rights from the concept of natural law. When Thomas Jefferson spoke of "life, liberty, and the pursuit of happiness" in the Declaration of Independence, he was stating in new language Locke's ideas of natural rights.[2]

Civil and Criminal Law

Civil law, in its most widely used sense, is concerned with the relations between individuals and their legal rights. A typical civil suit would be for breach of contract, a divorce action, or tort action (an injury to one's person or property), such as a suit growing out of an automobile accident. Usually civil actions are between private individuals, but it is possible for the government to be party to a civil suit. For example, the United States government might sue a corporation for breach of contract.

All crimes are against society and the state as the representative of society charges the individual or corporation with a violation of law. A penalty for such violation is usually provided by statute. Crimes may be serious, such as murder or arson, or petty, such as violation of a traffic law. Punishment ranges from death or imprisonment to a fine.

International Law

International law consists of a body of rules and principles regulating the behavior of nations, international organizations like the United Nations, and

[1] See John Austin, *Lectures on Jurisprudence,* Vol. 1, 3rd ed. (London: J. Murray, 1869), pp. 182–183.

[2] See George H. Sabine and Thomas L. Thorson, *A History of Political Theory,* 4th ed. (New York: Dryden Press, 1973), Chapters 9, 14, and 27.

individuals of other countries with different legal systems. International law lacks the effective sanctions of the governments of national states, as there are no effective international organizations with enforcement power.[3]

Constitutional, Administrative, and Statutory Law

A constitution may be unwritten in the sense that it is not limited to a single document. The British constitution, for example, consists of historic documents such as the Great Charter of 1215, which the English barons forced King John to sign at Runnymede; acts of Parliament of extraordinary importance such as the Great Reform Act of 1833, which enfranchised much of the middle class; important judicial decisions; and custom and tradition. Even the United States, with its written Constitution, has a supplementary "unwritten Constitution" growing out of judicial decisions, important acts of Congress and the president, and custom and tradition. American political parties, for example, had their origin in custom and tradition and are not part of the written Constitution.

Constitutional law consists of interpretations of a nation's constitution by the courts. In the United States, for example, the Supreme Court may decide the meaning of congressional power over interstate commerce.

A relatively new kind of law is administrative law, which is concerned with the legal accountability of government officials in carrying out government policy as expressed in statutes. In the United States, for example, Congress has delegated to administrators extensive rule-making authority. The federal courts may review the rules and regulations of the Federal Trade Commission concerning "unfair and deceptive" trade practices to determine whether the administrators have acted within the scope of the law.

In many instances the courts interpret the meaning of statutes. Legislatures must inevitably state the rules embodied in statutes in general terms, for they cannot anticipate all the problems that will arise over specific provisions. The final decision about the meaning of a statute is made by the courts. One important standard the courts employ is to determine the "legislative intent."

Anglo-American Law

The Common Law

The basis for the legal system of Great Britain, the United States, and most of the English-speaking countries is the common law. The common law is

[3] See J. L. Brierly, *The Law of Nations,* 6th ed., rev. by Sir Humphrey Waldock, (New York: Oxford University Press, 1963) for a good brief introduction to international law. The subject is discussed in more detail in Chapter 13.

judge-made law. Its roots go back to the twelfth century in England when the king sent itinerant justices throughout the realm to settle local disputes on the basis of general customs. Gradually a body of legal precedents was developed from the various decisions of the royal judges.

In hearing disputes, the judges would consider previously decided cases. The judge, in determining the relevance of a previous decision, reasons by analogy to reach a decision. He determines whether an earlier case of a similar nature is sufficiently comparable to the case at hand to constitute a binding precedent. If so, it becomes the basis for deciding the case. This process of following earlier precedents is known as *stare decisis.* On the other hand, the judge may distinguish the controversy before him from an earlier precedent. But this is no simple, mechanical process, as no two cases are exactly alike, and the judge ordinarily has considerable latitude in reaching his decision. *Stare decisis* leads to both stability and flexibility in the law. It also permits the judge to modify old law to meet new social conditions. Regulations of public utilities, for example, grew out of old common law doctrines regulating innkeepers.

The common law was carried to English colonies in various parts of the world. When many of these countries became independent, they continued to apply the common law. In the United States the states generally apply the common law to varying degrees but, as in Great Britain, it has been modified considerably by statute. Common law marriages, for example, are not usually recognized by statute.

Equity

Another source of Angle-American law is equity, which developed out of the feeling that the early common law courts did not always insure justice. These courts, for example, usually allowed only monetary damages as a remedy in most civil cases. Litigants who could not get justice in the regular courts appealed to the chancellor, the king's legal adviser, who frequently provided relief on the basis of general principles of justice. Eventually, a complementary system of law was developed by a new court known as a Court of Chancery. The primary difference between the justice administered by the two systems of law was in the remedy. A Court of Equity or Chancery would issue, for example, an injunction to prevent irreparable harm to property. Under the common law a person whose property rights were threatened could take no action until the injury occurred, in which case he could sue for damages. An injunction, on the other hand, prohibits a person or persons in general from committing acts that would result in injury to the property. For violations of an injunction, the judge may summarily punish by fine or even imprisonment in some instances. Injunctions have frequently been used in labor disputes. Another difference between common law and equity is that juries are not used in equity cases.

Equity, like the common law, was carried overseas into new English-speaking settlements. But in England and most of the American states today the same courts administer both law and equity. The American federal courts have jurisdiction in all cases in law and equity involving the Constitution, laws, and treaties.

The Judicial System in Great Britain

The British court system is headed by a lord chancellor who is a member of the cabinet. He presides over the House of Lords and advises on all judicial appointments. The highest court is the House of Lords, but only a small group of appointed law lords, headed by the lord chancellor, act as a court in the name of the House of Lords. At the very bottom of the judicial hierarchy are justices of the peace who try petty criminal cases. The British courts are known for the outstanding legal qualifications of their judges.

The legal profession in Great Britain is divided into two categories—solicitors and barristers. The former are office lawyers who handle legal problems before the trial stage. Unlike barristers, solicitors are not required to have university training. They become members of the Law Society by passing special examinations. The barristers, who have greater prestige, are exclusively trial lawyers who are trained in one of the four famous Inns of Court, which are both law schools and guild associations and which enforce very high standards on their members. Judges are chosen from the more outstanding barristers.[4]

The American Judicial System

Because the American governmental system is federal in nature, this country possesses a dual court system of federal and state courts. Although there are variations among the state court systems, typically the lowest courts are police magistrates or justices of the peace. Usually there are general trial courts based on a county or combination of counties, which are courts of general jurisdiction. These courts also hear appeals from police magistrates and justices of the peace. Above the general trial courts appellate courts are common. Usually each appellate court hears appeals from general trial courts within its district. At the top every state has a court of appeals with statewide jurisdiction, usually called the supreme court.

States judges are usually elected for a term of years, commonly on a party basis. In a few states the governor appoints judges. Two states, California

[4] See William Martin Geldart et al., *Elements of English Law,* (London: Oxford University Press, 1959) for an excellent introduction to English law.

and Missouri, have developed a mixed elective–appointive system divorced from parties or politics. A judge goes before the voters at the end of his term or after a fixed number of years to determine whether or not he should be retained in office for another term. The essence of this plan is that judicial vacancies are filled by the governor from a list of nominees submitted by a nonpartisan commission.[5]

Election of state judges has been subject to considerable criticism on the ground that the quality of the state judiciary has suffered. The most frequent criticism is directed at police magistrates and justices of the peace, who frequently are laymen with little knowledge of the law. Municipal court judges or other local judges are frequently indebted to a local political machine. State supreme court judges are rarely appointed to the United States Supreme Court. Notable exceptions were Oliver Wendell Holmes and Benjamin N. Cardozo, both of whom were not only distinguished jurists but also well-known as philosophers of the law.

The only court required by the Constitution is the Supreme Court. Since 1789, however, Congress has provided for a system of lower federal courts. Today, there are 87 district courts within the fifty states and territories. While each state has at least one district court with at least one judge, some districts have more than twenty judges and many states have more than one district court. These are courts of general jurisdiction where most law suits originate.

Above the district courts are the 11 judicial circuits, each one of which has a court of appeals. Most cases never get beyond the court of appeals. The minority of cases that reach the Supreme Court usually do so through the writ of *certiorari,* which may be granted at the discretion of a least four judges of the Supreme from the highest state court if a federal question is raised.

All federal judges are appointed by the president, subject to confirmation by the Senate. Most judicial appointments are of the same political party as the president. Supreme Court appointees are usually men who reflect the same philosophy of government as the president, even when they are chosen from the opposite party. Other judicial appointments, especially district court judges, are subject to "senatorial courtesy." This means that the president, in filling appointments for judicial vacancies, must consult with the state's senator or senators if they are of his own party. "Senatorial courtesy" is a custom that permits a senator of the president's party to block the confirmation of an objectionable appointee from his own state. In effect, the president does not have a free hand. Where there

[5] See Charles Aiken, "A New Method of Selecting Judges in California," *American Political Science Review,* XXIX, (June, 1935), pp. 412–14; and Thomas E. McDonald, "Missouri's Ideal Judicial Selection Law," *Journal of American Judicial Society,* XXIV, (April, 1941), pp. 194–99.

"I WANNA SEE AGNEW'S LAWYERS!"

(Editorial Cartoon by Paul Conrad © Los Angeles Times, Reprinted with permission.)

Equal justice?

is no senator from the president's party in a given state, his range of choice is greater.

Anglo-American Civil and Criminal Procedure

Courts generally will take jurisdiction over a question only if there is a real controversy between two or more parties and not simply an abstract question of law to be decided. Thus, in a civil case a typical justiciable issue would be a suit by *A* against *B* alleging that *A* was injured by *B* who, while negligently driving his automobile, ran into *A* who was crossing the street. *A*'s attorney would file a complaint alleging the above facts. *B* would respond with an answer. If *B* denied any negligence in his answer, the issue before the court would be whether *A*'s injury was due to *B*'s negligence.

Criminal procedure begins with the law enforcement process. Six steps are involved in this process: arrest of law violators; preliminary hearing; preferring of charges; arraignment; trial; and punishment of convicted persons.

On the local level law enforcement is primarily the function of the police or, in rural areas, the sheriff. Persons arrested for violating the law are brought before a minor magistrate for a preliminary hearing, the purpose of which is to decide whether the evidence against the accused is sufficient to hold him for action by the prosecutor or grand jury. If he is held for further action, the magistrate would set bail unless the offense is a nonbailable capital crime. Traditionally, the next step is action by the grand jury, a body of five to twenty-three persons. The latter is summoned by the prosecutor to determine whether the evidence against the accused justifies returning an indictment, a simple statement describing the essential ingredients of the crime. The local prosecutor is usually an elected county official, whereas in the federal courts there is a district attorney for each district court appointed by the president with the consent of the Senate.

In Great Britain there is no official comparable to either the United States federal or state district attorney. There is a director of public prosecutions, who may direct the prosecution in serious criminal cases, such as murder. In England and Wales the police initiate and conduct most prosecutions. This arrangement is possible only because of the lower crime rate in Great Britain.

Great Britain has also abolished use of the grand jury. Some American states have virtually discontinued use of the grand jury. A majority of our states permit some use of an alternative procedure known as prosecution by information for lesser crimes. This differs from the traditional indictment only in that it is filed by the prosecutor without a grand jury. After the charges are filed, the accused is arraigned before the trial court where a plea of "guilty" or "not guilty" is entered.

The Anglo-American court system is based on the adversary principle. Each side in a law suit, whether civil or criminal, presents evidence to support its case. The jury, if one is used, is traditionally a body of twelve competent men and women who render a unanimous verdict on the basis of the facts and the law. Today, some states in civil cases and trials for lesser crimes have relaxed the unanimity rule and provided for juries of less than twelve members. It is assumed that the jury can arrive at the truth from the testimony presented by each side. The role of the judge is essentially that of an impartial referee, who is responsible for observance of the rules of evidence and procedural safeguards. If there is no jury, the judge performs the function of the jury. In a criminal action the state must prove its case beyond a reasonable doubt, whereas in a civil case the plaintiff, the party who institutes the suit, need only present a preponderance of the evidence in his behalf.

If a verdict of guilty has been returned by the trial jury in a criminal case, the court pronounces the sentence.

THE CIVIL LAW OF EUROPE

In countries of Western Europe the law is based on Roman law and generally tends to be codified in contrast to common law. Its origins go back to the code prepared for the Roman Emperor Justinian in A.D. 533. During the Middle Ages the Roman Catholic church based its canon law on Roman law. In the French and Italian universities of the twelfth and thirteenth centuries, Roman law was rediscovered. It had great appeal to the educated and rising mercantile classes and to many European monarchs who in particular liked its authoritarian features. In more modern times the law codes of Napoleon I have been of great importance. They have influenced not only the legal systems of European countries and Latin America, but the Canadian province of Quebec and the state of Louisiana as well.

The codes assume that the fundamentals of the nation's law can be stated in comprehensive statutes. The codes, of course, require interpretation and elaboration. This task is more the responsibility of law teachers than of the judges. Typical subjects of a code are civil and criminal procedures, property, commercial law, etc.

The differences between code and common law should not be overstated. Although the code law is more the work of the legislature than the courts and the judges tend to see the law as written reason, the common law systems also rely on statutes and have legal commentaries and some codification, but to a lesser degree. Even in interpreting a statute, Anglo-American judges refer to prior relevant decisions. Under the code law judges are supposed to follow the code alone.

Another difference between the two systems of law is found in criminal procedure.[6] In a typical code-law country such as France the first step in a criminal case is a preliminary examination of the accused and chief witnesses by an investigating judge who determines whether the accused should be formally tried. The trial itself repeats this "inquisitorial" procedure to get at the truth. The role of the judge is that of an active participant in the procedure and there is little emphasis on procedural safe-

[6] See Henry J. Abraham, *The Judicial Process,* 2nd ed. (New York: Oxford University Press, 1968), pp. 98–103, for a comparison of the Anglo-American adversary system with the accusatorial practice of code countries.

guards for the defendant. But the French system gives the judge complete control of the trial and permits him and the prosecutor to develop the case against the accused on the basis of the *dossier* resulting from the preliminary examination.

By the time a suspect has undergone this thorough preliminary examination and is standing trial, the general assumption is that he is probably guilty. This is unlike the Anglo-American law which, through its many safeguards for the defendant, seeks to minimize the possibility of an innocent person being found guilty. French code law lays more stress on preventing a guilty person from escaping punishment.

The French legal system seeks to provide justice economically and to make it readily available to the French people. The system as streamlined under President de Gaulle in 1958 rests upon 172 courts of grand instance distributed throughout the country. These courts, which have three judges each, have unlimited civil jurisdiction. The criminal court on this level is the correctional court. Below the courts of grand instance are special labor and commercial courts and courts of instance, which have jurisdiction over less serious crimes and minor civil cases. The courts of grand instance have appellate jurisdiction over those minor courts.

An important feature of the French judicial system, as well as those of most continental European democracies, is that judges and prosecutors are part of the same public service. Prosecutors are under the Ministry of Justice, but judges have seniority of tenure and are not subject to government discipline. Another difference is that in France an individual decides at the beginning of his career whether he will become a lawyer or a member of the judiciary.

Another important feature of French law is the separate system of administrative law, which utilizes special administrative courts. There are no comparable courts in England and the United States. These tribunals hear complaints and law suits against the state itself and afford the citizen protection against arbitrary decisions of government officials. The function of the administrative courts is the annulment of rulings where officials have exceeded their power. The highest administrative court is the Council of State which has an excellent reputation both in France and abroad. The Council has frequently awarded generous damages to individuals injured by the government. It has also protected civil servants wrongfully dismissed by the government.

In Anglo-American countries the state may not be sued without its consent for the actions of government employees committed in the discharge of their duties. In the United States and Great Britain the public official himself who is charged with dereliction, and not the state, is sued in the regular courts. Other code-law countries follow the French practice in having a separate system of administrative law.

COMMUNIST LAW AND LEGAL SYSTEMS

The Marxian Conception of Law

The Communist conception of law is fundamentally different from that of Western democratic states. The latter assume that law is binding upon governors and governed alike and that the individual should be guaranteed certain rights that protect him against state action.

Marx and Engels assumed that law is a tool of the state and that the state in turn is the instrument of the ruling class. Judges in capitalistic states, according to Marx, because of their training and background would favor the interests of property in their decisions. He felt that even guarantees of equality before the law were of little value to the poor because they could not afford the best lawyers and the high cost of legal proceedings.

In his views of a Communist state, Marx was a utopian. He believed that coercion would ultimately become unnecessary and the power of public opinion would be sufficient to maintain an orderly and peaceful society. Marx, however, recognized that there would be a short period of transition between the Communist revolution and the attainment of this ideal state. During this interim period it would be necessary to revise bourgeois law so that it would no longer protect property rights against justice for the masses. The selection of judges sympathetic to communism would also be necessary.

The Soviet Conception of Law

Needless to say, the Soviet Union, although it came into existence in 1917, has not attained the condition of pure communism where law is unnecessary. In fact, law is very much a part of the Soviet system. But Soviet law assumes that, as the Soviet state is the product of the type of revolution Marx and Lenin predicted, it embraces all the interests of its citizens. Thus, according to this assumption, there can be no conflict between the interests of the state and the rights of the individual. Because the Soviet Union is a state presumably based on the welfare of the proletariat, or working class, its law and court decisions always reflect the interests of the working class in theory.

In practice, law plays a greater role in the Soviet system than in Western democratic states because all spheres of life are subject to government control. For example, there are commercial courts that have jurisdiction over state enterprises and organizations that buy or sell from each other.

Whenever the interests of the regime are affected, law is simply an instrument of state policy. This explains the lack of procedural safeguards in criminal procedure and the fact that the bill of rights in the Soviet constitution of 1936 is a mere declaration of intention, of no legal significance and not enforceable in the courts. The law codes aver that the state is supreme

"Guilty Of Revolutionary Activities! Take Him Away"

(From *The Herblock Gallery,* Simon & Schuster, 1968.)

over the individual and the conduct of a criminal trial reflects this fact. The defense attorney, who is a state employee, is chosen from a lawyers' collegium which is subsidized by the state. Neither the defense attorney nor the defendant is shown the state evidence until the day before the trial. The judge, as in countries with code law, questions the defendant and witnesses. Furthermore, the defendant must prove his innocence. And cases may be reopened by a higher court after acquittal in a trial court.

The structure of the Soviet courts is in many respects like that of Western European countries. At the bottom of the regular court system are regional courts with a supreme court in each of the union republics. At the top of the pyramid is a supreme court of the union, which is primarily an appellate court. There are also people's, or comrades courts which are quite informal. These were organized during the Krushchev era in neighborhoods and places of work and are administered by laymen. Minor cases such as drunkenness and petty theft are tried in these courts, which consist of one lay judge and two lay assessors. Their jurisdiction is limited to the simplest of disputes. Judges are elected but candidates are always politically reliable.

During the Khrushchev era the government issued new and less harsh rules of both civil and criminal law. For example, in criminal law punishment by analogy is abolished. Under this doctrine, in force since the revolution, an act that was not a crime but similar to a criminal act, could be made punishable as a crime by a judge. Nevertheless, Soviet criminal law is still harsher than that of Western democratic states. Political crimes are still usually tried in military courts, which exist in every military district. These courts are conducted in secret. Civilians convicted for treason, espionage, and assassination of a public official abroad, to name some of the more serious crimes, can be sentenced to death.

An important post in the Soviet legal system is that of the Procurator General of the Soviet Union. There are also procurators in each of the republics and districts as well. The procurator's duties extend to the organization of the courts and execution of the rules of law in use, as well as the traditional duties as prosecutor for the state. The Procurator General of the Soviet Union is one of the most important officials in the country and is always a high-ranking member of the Communist Party.[7]

LAW IN DEVELOPING NATIONS

Influence of Western Legal Systems

The term "developing states" is used to refer to those nations that differ from modern Western societies in a number of ways, including a low rate of literacy, low per capita income, a basically rural economy, and little

[7] For excellent studies of Soviet law see the following:
George Fiefer, *Justice in Moscow* (New York: Dell Publishing, 1964); Eugene Karneuba, "The Soviet View of Law," *Problems of Communism,* (March–April 1965), pp. 8–16; John A. Hazard, "Soviet Law and Justice," in John W. Strong, ed., *The Soviet Union under Brezhnev and Kosygin* (New York: Van Nostrand, 1971); Alfred C. Meyer, *The Soviet Political System: An Interpretation,* (New York: Random House, 1965), pp. 300–55.

technological development. Some of these countries have primitive economies with no food reserves, a limited cultural and artistic life, and limited political development. The newly independent nations of Africa and Asia are typical of this Third World, but the older political societies of Latin America also share many of the characteristics of developing nations.

Western legal systems generally were introduced in the developing states of Africa and Asia prior to independence. But the impact of Western law was negligible, since colonial rulers generally permitted much of customary law and practice to remain in force on the village level. One of the important problems facing the newly independent governments has been to reconcile Western legal standards with existing customary practices.

The new governments of the developing nations frequently have looked upon Western law as an obstacle to desirable new programs. This has often resulted in disregarding established legal procedures. In some instances ruling ethnic or racial groups have used established law to dominate minorities. The result has been that the role of law continues to be in a state of flux.

African Law

A brief survey of the judiciary in a few of the new African states will illustrate some of the problems of these countries. Many changes have been made in the legal systems imposed by former colonial rulers because the African leaders believed the inherited system did not reflect contemporary needs and aspirations. Customary law has also been modified in many ways. For example, in some African states the giving of gifts at a time of marriage or a feast at baptism is limited to minimize the impoverishment of African families. Marriage has been secularized and arranged marriage forbidden.

As to the new legal codes, Marxian influence appears to be minimal. The French governmental structure is retained in the former French colonies. Although the old courts administering customary laws are abolished, specialists in the old law are advisers in the new courts.[8]

Latin American Law

The civil law of Spain and Portugal was carried over to the New World and became firmly established. Since countries achieved independence the civil law of other European countries has had considerable influence. But the influence of the United States has not been absent. The writ of habeas corpus, for example, has had widespread adoption in Latin America. But Latin American countries have adopted many laws that are responses to

[8] See John H. Hazard, "Law and Social Change in Marxist Africa," in *American Behaviorial Scientist* Columbia University, Vol. XIII, No. 4 (March-April, 1970), pp. 575–84.

their own local problems. Examples are the mining codes of Peru and Mexico's agrarian reform laws.[9]

Judicial procedure in Latin America is quite unlike that of the United States and Great Britain. In Argentina procedures are fairly typical of Latin America. A trial of a civil action is usually a private hearing in which a secretary presides over the proceedings and keeps a detailed record of everything that takes place. The judge usually does not bother to attend the hearing. Instead, he bases his decision on the written record.

Criminal procedures offers the defendant fewer safeguards than Anglo-American practices. A person arrested and charged with a criminal offense is brought before an instruction judge who combines the functions of a committee magistrate and grand jury. He decides whether the accused will be held for trial and under what circumstances, if any, he will be released on bail. Pending trial, the accused may be held incommunicado for a number of days. During this time the police attempt to obtain criminal evidence. When the trial takes place, it is held without a jury and usually behind closed doors. The trial judge is frequently absent during part of the proceedings. Sometimes he bases his judgment to a large extent on written evidence prepared by a secretary. It is said that justice often depends on the accuracy of a secretary's notes. Another variation from Anglo-American practices is that the public prosecutor, as well as the accused, may appeal the verdict. This makes it possible for a person found innocent in a lower court to be adjudged guilty in a court of appeals.[10]

Judicial Independence

In the newly independent African states judges generally are appointed by the executive, often without requiring approval by the legislature. Judges usually serve for life, subject to removal from office for high crimes and misdemeanors.

Sometimes removal power is vested in the president, as in Ghana where, under former President Nkrumah, the constitution provided that the president could remove the chief justice at will and judges of the lower courts if two-thirds of the assembly concurred. Since a one-party system prevailed in Ghana, Nkrumah was able to get the necessary legislative majority to remove three supreme court justices after the court failed to convict three persons of plotting to overthrow the president. A special court was then selected to retry the case. The defendants were convicted and sentenced to death. This action of Nkrumah's led the International Jurists Commission to condemn him for violating the independence of the

[9] Alexander T. Edelmann, *Latin American Government and Politics,* rev. ed. (Homewood, Ill.; The Dorsey Press, 1969), pp. 465 ff.

[10] Alexander T. Edelmann, *op. cit.,* pp. 480–82.

judiciary. Other African states have created special courts to try cases involving threats against the government.

Since most African states do not have judicial review, parliament can override court decisions under the doctrine of legislative supremacy. Such action has occurred on several occasions and usually does not involve any great difficulties, for government majorities are typically large. Even where judicial review formally exists, as in Tanzania and Nigeria, judicial decisions have been overruled.[11]

It would be incorrect to assume from the preceding illustrations that the judiciary always lacks independence in developing states. The courts of many states of Southeast Asia have frequently shown a high degree of independence. In Burma, for example, the government, believing the existence of the state was threatened, invoked a preventive detention act in the 1960s. The higher courts, however, frequently released detained persons because of insufficient grounds for holding them. And the Philippine supreme court, during the presidential campaign of 1965, unanimously upheld an injunction preventing the national board of censors from banning a movie that portrayed the opposition candidate for president, Ferdinand Marcos, as a man of destiny. The judges, several of whom had been appointed by the incumbent president, Macopagal, resisted strong pressures to support the government, which wished to prevent showing of the movie.[12]

Clearly, relatively independent courts can and do exist in developing states. The commonly accepted view that internal political pressures undermine judicial independence, as exemplified in Ghana, Mexico, and other states, requires reservations.

JUDICIAL REVIEW

Judicial review is the process by which courts determine whether the legislative and executive branches, especially the former, have exceeded their power. Judicial review is most likely to exist in a federal system such as the United States and in countries with written constitutions. In a federal system, with power divided between the central government and the member states, the courts are the logical branch of government to determine the power boundaries between the two levels of government.

Although judicial review exists in a number of countries, its scope is broadest in the United States. In nations where judicial review exists the

[11] Dorothy Dodge, *African Politics in Perspective* (Toronto: D. Van Nostrand, 1968), pp. 136–38.

[12] See Theodore L. Becker, *Comparative Judicial Politics: The Political Functioning of Courts* (Chicago: Rand McNally, 1970), pp. 159–60.

judiciary usually plays a more significant role in the governmental process than in countries where the courts do not exercise this power. In the United States both federal and state courts have held federal and state laws invalid under the federal Constitution. The United States Supreme Court has the last word on the constitutionality of a federal or state law. Judicial review is important not only because of its use, but also because of the threat of the judicial veto. Congress and the president, in making policy, must always consider the possible unconstitutionality of their acts.[13]

Judicial review is not specifically granted in the Constitution, but it has been exercised since 1803 with respect to acts of Congress.[14] Many more state laws have been held unconstitutional, however, than acts of Congress or the president. Since 1789 about eighty congressional laws have been held unconstitutional. The instances where executive acts have been held beyond the power of the president are relatively few. One of the more recent examples occurred in 1952 during the Korean War when the Supreme Court held that President Truman did not have authority to seize the steel industry to avert a strike.[15] Although originally the subject of controversy, judicial review is generally accepted today.

After *Marbury* versus *Madison* no act of Congress was held unconstitutional until 1857, more than fifty years later. It was in the period from about 1890 to 1937 that the Supreme Court acquired the reputation of being a "super legislature" by striking down many federal and state laws. Since the Court during this period generally reflected conservative economic and political values, many of the laws held unconstitutional were regulations of property rights. Following the "constitutional crisis" of 1937, provoked by President Franklin D. Roosevelt's unsuccessful attempt to enlarge the Supreme Court's membership to make the liberal minority of judges a majority, the Supreme Court has generally deferred to the judgment of Congress and the states with reference to laws regulating property rights. This shift in the Court's position is explainable by the fact that two of the "middle of the road" judges joined the liberal minority after 1937 to constitute a new majority and the replacement of the conservative members of the Court following their retirement or death. Since the mid 1950s the Court has actively used judicial review to promote civil rights. This trend is discussed in the sections "Civil Liberty" and "The Judicial Process."

[13] See Loren P. Beth, *Politics, the Constitution, and the Supreme Court* (Evanston, Ill., Row Peterson, 1962), pp. 58–61 for a succinct discussion of judicial review.

[14] *Marbury* versus *Madison,* 1 Cranch 137 (1803). The opinions of the Supreme Court are now published by the U.S. government. Until 1875 the reports were cited according to the name of the reporter, in this instance Cranch. The first number refers to the volume and the second to the page.

[15] *Youngstown Sheet and Tube Co.* versus *Sawyer,* 343 U.S. 579 (1952).

Judicial review exists in some European countries but in no country has it existed as long as in the United States. Nor does the judiciary in these countries play a role comparable to the United States Court.

In France under the Fifth Republic the constitutional council is a body consisting of all ex-presidents of France and nine other appointed individuals. The council, which is not part of the regular judicial system, may hold unconstitutional certain laws of Parliament if referred to it by the president of the republic, the premier, or the presidents of both Houses of Parliament. This is very limited judicial review, for no individual can challenge the constitutionality of a law. The weakness of the council is illustrated by its refusal to rule on President de Gaulle's referendum on direct election of the president of France in 1962, despite the fact that the French constitution did not authorize such action.[16]

West Germany has a special constitutional court, which may decide the validity of any federal or state (*Land*) law and which protects the fundamental rights of citizens. This court has assumed a role of importance in the West German governmental system. Among its important decisions were two that declared both the Communist Party and a neo-Nazi party to be unconstitutional as organizations detrimental to a democratic state.[17]

The postwar Japanese constitution, as a result of the American occupation and influence, allows the review of all laws, ordinances, administrative regulations, and official acts of government. The final authority rests with the Japanese supreme court. In practice, however, the Japanese court has not exercised this power to any great extent.[18]

Judicial review is also common in Latin America, due to the influence of Anglo-American law. Mexico has a unique form of judicial review in the form of the writ of *amparo*, which permits a citizen to apply to a federal court for redress if a law or act of a governmental official impairs any right guaranteed by the constitution of Mexico. But this writ is less than real judicial review since the judges do not grant relief to each petitioner who files a complaint. There may be thousands of cases resulting from a single law.[19]

JUDICIAL INTERPRETATION OF STATUTES

Interpretation of statutes by the courts, as well as judicial review, is important in analyzing the role of the courts in making national policy. In the United States, the country where judicial review is most important,

[16] Henry V. Abraham, *op. cit.*, pp. 296–99.

[17] *Ibid.*, pp. 311–12.

[18] See Warren M. Tsuneishi, *Japanese Political Style* (New York: Harper and Row, 1966), chapter 10. See also *Law in Japan: The Legal Order in a Changing Society,* ed. by A. T. Van Hehren (Cambridge: Harvard University Press, 1963).

[19] See Alexander T. Edelmann, *op. cit.*, pp. 483–84.

statutory interpretation and development of doctrines growing out of the common law substantially enhance the power of the courts. Many acts of Congress are complex and their meaning is not always clear. Ultimately, a statute means what the Supreme Court says it means.

For example, Congress in 1940 enacted the Smith Act, which made teaching and advocacy of the overthrow of the government by force a criminal offense. What is the meaning of this provision? It presumably would not prevent the teaching of the revolutionary doctrines of Marx and Lenin in a college class. But on the other hand, is there a distinction between abstract advocacy of violent overthrow of the government and incitement to violence now or as soon as practical? In *Yates* v. *U.S.* (1957) Justice Harlan, speaking for the Supreme Court, gave the Smith Act a narrow interpretation by holding that to convict under the act, the government would have to prove advocacy of violent action now or in the future. Mere belief in the desirability of violent overthrow of the government as an abstract doctrine is not enough to convict.[20]

What is true of the United States would also be true in other countries where the courts play an important role in judicial interpretation.

CIVIL LIBERTIES

The courts frequently play a leading role in the preservation of civil liberties. The United States Supreme Court under Chief Justice Warren (1953–1969) lent support to the "civil rights revolution" through its interpretation of the "equal protection" clause of the Fourteenth Amendment as a prohibition of segregation laws.

In general the Supreme Court has furthered the cause of civil liberties by "nationalizing civil rights." Since the 1920s the Court has held that the First Amendment freedoms (speech, press, assembly, and religion) are incorporated into the "due process clause" of the Fourteenth Amendment, which restricts the states from abridging the rights of citizens. In recent years more and more of the Bill of Rights have been incorporated into the Fourteenth Amendment. Since the Bill of Rights restricts Congress, the result of the "nationalizing of civil rights" has been to make much of the Bill of Rights indirectly binding on the states through the Fourteenth Amendment. Today the result is that the Supreme Court not only protects the First Amendment freedoms from violation at the state level, but also extends the application of procedural rights, such as the right to counsel and protection against self-incrimination, to the state level. In *Escobedo* versus *Illinois,* the court held in a five to four vote that in criminal prosecutions the right to representation by counsel extended back to the time a

[20] 355 U.S. 66 (1957).

suspect is subjected to questioning.[21] Two years later the Court, in another five to four decision (*Miranda* v. *Arizona*) ruled that in order for a conviction to stand—if obtained by evidence introduced at the trial as a result of "custodial interrogation"—it would be necessary to show that the suspect had been told he could remain silent, informed that any information volunteered could be used against him, told that he may have an attorney present during interrogation, informed that an attorney would be furnished if he could not afford one, and lastly, allowed to end police interrogation at any time.[22]

The purpose of these rules is to protect the prisoner against self-incrimination and preserve his right to counsel. Not only is the Supreme Court divided on the wisdom of extending procedural safeguards this far, but so is public opinion. Critics claim that the Court is discouraging the use of voluntary confessions and making the conviction of criminals difficult. Defenders of the Court point to the unquestioned fact that in the past the procedural rights of suspects have frequently been violated, especially on the state level. Probably an important factor in polarizing opinion of this issue is that the Court has acted at a time when the public is understandably concerned about the rising tide of crime in our cities.

In Great Britain the primary responsibility for the preservation of civil liberties rests upon alert public opinion. It is part of the "unwritten constitution" of that country that Parliament pass no law infringing upon the traditional civil liberties of the realm. Nevertheless, as we have seen, while the courts cannot hold an act of Parliament unconstitutional, judges in Great Britain do have the authority to restrain executive officials from depriving people of their rights. Any invasion of civil rights is usually raised in Parliament. Any British citizen who believes his rights have been violated can usually find a member of Parliament to cross-examine an appropriate member of the ministry to get all the facts. Evidence of a violation of basic rights may lead to extended debate in Parliament. Even without the power of judicial review, the courts are effective in protecting civil rights. They make certain that the executive branch adheres to the rules of procedure laid down by law in carrying out their functions. And through judicial interpretation the courts have construed seditious conspiracy narrowly. Although violence may not be used to change the constitution or the laws, any type of agitation that does not include violence may be used.[23]

The preservation of civil liberties is of particular importance in West

[21] 378 U.S. 478 (1964).

[22] 384 U.S. 436 (1966).

[23] See Sydney D. Bailey, *British Parliamentary Democracy,* 2nd ed. (Cambridge, Mass.: Houghton-Mifflin, The Riverside Press, 1966), pp. 97–100; and Gwendolyn M. Carter and John H. Herz, *Major Foreign Powers,* 5th ed. (New York: Harcourt, Brace & World, 1967), pp. 52–53.

Germany today. The Nazi regime (1933–1945) not only destroyed the independence of the judiciary but also established special courts not bound by any law. Fortunately, the West German regime has shown an awareness of the importance of civil liberty. The Bonn constitution restored the principle that punishment must be inflicted only according to law after a fair trial. Furthermore, the establishment of extraordinary courts is forbidden and double jeopardy (more than one prosecution for the same offense) prohibited. The constitutional court of West Germany is authorized to hear all complaints by individuals against any violation of their constitutional rights. The court's record is generally considered to be progressive.[24]

In Japan the concept of basic civil rights has not become firmly rooted in Japanese constitutionalism. The pre-World War II Japanese constitution authorized basic civil rights "subject to the limits of the law." In practice this meant little, as few rights were allowed. The postwar constitution grants a wide range of specific rights, including freedom of the press, assembly, speech, and academic freedom. In addition, a variety of procedural safeguards are included—such as protection against self-incrimination, the right to speedy trial, and the writ of habeas corpus. The last is a court order to any official holding a person in custody, directing him to bring the prisoner before the court to explain why he is confined. If the court finds the person unlawfully detained, he is released. In Japan the only restriction is that these rights may not be used so as to jeopardize the public welfare. The Japanese supreme court has interpreted the scope of civil rights narrowly. The constitutionality of every law challenged as a limitation of freedom of expression has been upheld as necessary to preserve the public welfare.[25]

There are no civil liberties in the Western sense in the Soviet Union. Although the constitution of 1936 contains a bill of rights, the emphasis is on social and economic rights, such as the right to work and the right to a free education rather than freedom from interference by the government. The social and economic rights are merely declarations of intention not enforceable by the courts. Even such political guarantees as freedom of association and the press are only for those who support the regime.

Neither procedural rights such as habeas corpus nor bail are allowed. A Soviet citizen who is arrested can be detained in jail for nine months while the charges against him are investigated. Nor can he have an attorney until the day before his trial.[26]

Many African constitutions provide for substantive civil liberties, such as

[24] See Arnold V. Heidenheimer, *The Governments of Germany,* 3rd ed. (New York: Thomas Y. Crowell, 1971), chapter 7, for a discussion of the constitutional court,

[25] Tsuneishi, *op. cit.,* pp. 185–87.

[26] Ellsworth Raymond, *The Soviet State* (New York: Macmillan, 1968), pp. 211–12 and 240.

freedom of the press, speech, and religion. In these countries, however, there is less emphasis on procedural rights, such as right to counsel and jury trial. In Nigeria during what was known as the Action Group crisis of 1962, which grew out of a split in the leadership in the western region of that country, the governor removed the prime minister and a struggle developed over control of the office. The leader of the opposition party and others were charged with treason, felony, and conspiracy against the government. The defendants were not allowed to use counsel brought from England in their defense. When the late Tom Mboya was minister of justice in Kenya, he indicated jury trial was foreign to Africans. On issues of evidence, some African courts have ruled that they would make a presumption in favor of the government.[27]

Ghana's postindependence republican constitution had no bill of rights. In its place the president, upon assuming office, was required to declare his adherence to certain fundamental principles. But the Ghana supreme court held that this was of moral significance only and did not restrict either the president's or the legislature's legal powers.[28]

What are the future trends likely to be? Professor L. C. B. Gower of Lagos University believes that it is likely that if African courts apply provisions of bills of rights frequently, civil rights will either be abolished completely, whittled away, or the bench will be packed with judges who will do the government's bidding.[29]

In the United States considerable progress has been made in advancing civil rights, especially through court decisions outlawing segregation and imposing the procedural guarantees of the Bill of Rights on state courts as well as national. In Great Britain civil rights continue to be protected despite the absence of judicial review. Communist nations reject the Western conception of civil rights. On the other hand, progress has occurred at least in a formal sense in Japan and many of the developing states, which have included bills of rights in their new constitutions.

THE AMERICAN JUDICIAL PROCESS

When an attorney is appointed to the judiciary, he carries with him his social and political philosophy. Most judges seek to be objective in deciding a case and to avoid prejudices. But all judges possess basic attitudes that are outgrowths of social background, legal training, professional experience as a lawyer, and political affiliation. Attitudes toward what are

[27] Dorothy Dodge, *op. cit.*, pp. 138–40.

[28] L. C. B. Gower, *Independent Africa: The Challenge to the Legal Profession* (Cambridge: Harvard University Press, 1967), p. 79.

[29] *Ibid.*, pp. 82–83.

commonly called "liberalism" or "conservatism" will frequently be reflected in judicial opinions, especially where questions of social policy are involved. As we have seen, American presidents, when they appoint judges, usually are influenced by what they consider to be a judge's social philosophy. President Nixon, in appointing Chief Justice Burger, sought a man who would be a "strict constructionist" and less "activist" than his predecessor, Chief Justice Warren.

In deciding cases, judges make law. Obviously, they do not do so in the sense that a member of the legislature does. But they do make policy. Today the traditional idea that judges "discover" the law has generally been discarded. This "slot machine" idea of the law assumed that a judge arrived at his decision by applying the correct rule or principle to the case at hand. If the case involved the constitutionality of an act of Congress, the Supreme Court merely laid the law alongside the Constitution to see if there was a conflict. If Congress, for example, passed a law making income tax rates higher in Illinois than elsewhere, its invalidity would be obvious, for the Constitution provides that national taxes shall be uniform throughout the United States. The type of controversy that comes before the Supreme Court is far more complex, and cannot be resolved by such a simple test.

To state that American courts do not decide cases by a process of logical deduction is not to suggest that they act in an arbitrary manner. Courts generally take precedents seriously, but frequently there are competing judicial doctrines available with respect to open-ended clauses of the Constitution, such as interstate commerce. Precedents are not always consistent and can be interpreted narrowly or broadly, as the decision demands. At times the Court will specifically overrule an earlier precedent. But most judges usually try to decide cases on the basis of sound legal reasoning and to provide some continuity to the law.

The recent decision of the Supreme Court in *Oregon* versus *Mitchell* illustrates the operation of the judicial process.[30] In this case the Court, by a five to four opinion, held that Congress could by statute reduce the voting age to eighteen in federal elections but that Congress lacked the power to reduce the voting age to eighteen in state and local elections.

Contrary to popular belief of recent years, there is no specific provision of the Constitution granting Congress the power to fix voting qualifications. In fact, the determination of who shall vote has been considered a state function. Article I, section 2 of the Constitution states that the electors for the House of Representatives "shall have the qualifications requisite for electors of the most numerous branch of the state legislature." The Seventeenth Amendment providing for direct elections of senators has identical qualifications for voters. Article II provides that presidential elec-

[30] 400 U.S. 112 (1970).

tors shall be chosen in the manner the state legislature directs. The two suffrage amendments, however, require that in fixing qualifications the states cannot discriminate on account of race or sex. (The Fifteenth and Nineteenth amendments are worded in the negative.) And Article I, section 4 grants to state legislatures the power to determine the "times, places and manner of holding elections" for Congress, subject to such alterations as Congress may make. Lastly, the "equal protection" clause of the Fourteenth Amendment also has a bearing on the problem in the opinion of four of the Supreme Court justices.[31] This clause states that no state may deny to anyone within its jurisdiction the equal protection of the laws. The Fourteenth Amendment grants Congress the power to enforce its provisions by appropriate legislation.

The act of Congress authorizing eighteen-year-olds to vote in federal, state, and local elections was an amendment to the Voting Rights Act of 1965. The primary constitution argument advanced on behalf of the law was that Congress, in exercising its enforcement powers under the Fourteenth Amendment, could determine that the denial of suffrage to eighteen-year-olds was a denial of "equal protection."

What is novel about the constitutional argument is the broad interpretation of congressional power to enforce the equal protection clause. Generally, the equal protection clause has been used to hold invalid state legislation that was alleged to be unconstitutional because of its discriminatory nature. An example would be *Brown* versus *Board of Education,* which held that segregation in education was a denial of equal protection.[32]

Actually, the court in *Oregon* versus *Mitchell* was even more deeply divided than the five to four decision might indicate. Justice Black who wrote the official opinion held that Congress on the basis of Article I, sections 2 and 4, had general supervisory power over congressional and presidential elections but not state or local elections. But no other member of the court agreed with his reasoning or conclusions. Four of his colleagues—Douglas, Brennan, Marshall, and White—believed the equal protection clause gave Congress power to determine age limits for voting in all elections in the interests of equal protection. On the other hand, Justices Stewart, Blackmun, Harlan, and Chief Justice Burger held that the states had exclusive authority over age limits for voting. Justice Stewart contended that the "manner" of holding elections does not include the qualifications of voters, as section 2 of Article I spells out what these qualifi-

[31] The relevant portion of the Fourteenth Amendment states: No state shall make or enforce any law which shall abridge the privileges or immunities of citizens of the United States; nor shall any state deprive any person of life, liberty or property, without due process of law; nor deny to any person within its jurisdiction the equal protection of the laws. . . . The Congress shall have power to enforce, by appropriate legislation, the provisions of this article. . . .

[32] 347 U.S. 483 (1954)

cations are. As to state and local elections, Stewart held that the power to decide on qualifications for voting, if it means anything, must include the power to select twenty-one as a reasonable voting age.

The dissenting judges' views reflected a conservatism that laid greater stress on earlier precedents and the importance of preserving a constitutional balance between the nation and the states. The issue, according to Justice Stewart, was not whether it was good policy for eighteen-year-olds to vote, but whether Congress had the power to decide the issue in this way, rather than through the slower and more complex process of a constitutional amendment.[33]

In *Oregon* versus *Mitchell,* the Supreme Court made important public policy by upholding part of a controversial act of Congress. Sometimes the court breaks new ground by dealing with a problem that Congress refuses to act on for political reasons. For many years segregated public schools were common in the South and parts of the north. In 1896 the court in the case of *Plessy* versus *Ferguson* had set forth the "separate but equal" doctrine, which allowed segregation in public facilities as long as facilities were "equal."[34] By holding that southern segregation laws did not violate the equal protection clause of the Fourteenth Amendment, the justices encouraged segregation as a policy.

By the 1930s and 1940s there was growing criticism of this policy by Negroes and many whites. At first the Supreme Court responded by "tightening up" the requirement of equal facilities for Negroes. The best solution would have been for Congress to outlaw state segregation by passing a law under its enforcement powers under the Fourteenth Amendment. This was politically impossible due to southern opposition and the possibility of a filibuster in the Senate. Finally in 1954, as we have seen, the Court repudiated segregated education in *Brown* versus *Board of Education* by holding it a form of "invidious discrimination."[35] This was followed by cases holding other forms of segregation unconstitutional. This policy gave a boost to the "Negro Revolution" and ultimately (despite southern opposition) contributed to the creation of a climate of opinion that forced Congress to act by passing the various civil rights laws between 1957 and 1968.

A danger in judicial activism, of course, is that of getting ahead of public opinion and making judicial pronouncements that are not enforceable. Court decisions always require the cooperation of the executive branch and sometimes the legislative branch to be effective. For a while there seemed to be a danger that the desegregation decisions might be ineffec-

[33] Since this decision, the Twenty-Sixth Amendment has been added to the Constitution. This grants suffrage to eighteen-year-olds and over in both federal and state elections.

[34] 163 U.S. 537 (1896).

[35] 347 U.S. 483 (1954).

tive because of southern opposition and less than enthusiastic executive cooperation and enforcement by President Eisenhower. There is also the risk of too broad judicial intervention. And some problems are incapable of judicial solution. Possibly *de facto* segregation in schools in northern cities, due to the concentration of blacks in certain neighborhoods, as opposed to legal segregation, falls into this category.

Summary

There are a variety of legal systems in the world. The two systems generally associated with democratic regimes, the Anglo-American common law system and the code law of Western Europe, differ in numerous ways. The former is to a greater degree based on judge-made law and stresses procedural safeguards for defendants in criminal cases, limiting the role of the judge to that of an impartial referee in the conduct of a trial. Judicial review, so important in the American legal system, is not found in the British system, but is provided for in some code-law countries.

The Communist legal system reflects to varying degrees the authoritarian nature of the Communist governmental systems. Japan and the developing states are influenced by both the Western legal systems and indigenous factors.

It is clear that courts make policy. In a sense in the United States, the Constitution is what the judges say it means. In the short run there may be a conflict between the ways in which a majority of the Supreme Court justices interpret the Constitution and the manner in which the majority of the people desire the Constitution to be interpreted. But in the long run, the Supreme Court is likely to interpret the Constitution in the way the majority desire. This is because presidents are likely to appoint judges who reflect dominant policy values. Also, failure on the part of the Court to reflect such values over a period of time is likely to undermine its prestige.

Except in Communist countries, courts generally try to exercise independence from political pressures and to maintain objectivity. That this is not always possible in developing states is illustrated by Ghana, to name only one example. It is likely that there is some relationship between the relative independence of the courts and the countries whose judicial system is based on the common law. Perhaps, as Theodore L. Becker has suggested, "Where judges can rely, in a common law system, on norms *they* produce, they need rely less on other norm-producing structures, that is, the legislature, the administrative agencies, etc."[36]

[36] Becker, *op. cit.*, p. 161.

Selected Readings

Henry J. Abraham, *The Judicial Process,** 3rd ed. (New York: Oxford University Press, 1975) is an excellent comparative introduction to the judicial process and administration of justice of leading Western states, with emphasis on the United States, England, and France. A study that emphasizes judicial politics and the role and function of the courts of various judicial systems is Theodore L. Becker, *Comparative Judicial Politics* (Chicago: Rand McNally, 1970).

There are a number of good studies of the judicial systems of particular foreign countries. For a study of Soviet law, see Harold J. Berman, *Justice in the U.S.S.R.: An Interpretation of Soviet Law** (New York: Vintage Press, 1963). A. T. Van Meren, *Law in Japan: The Legal Order in a Changing Society* (Cambridge: Harvard University Press, 1963) is a study of Japanese law. An introduction to African law is found in L. C. B. Gower, *Independent Africa: The Challenge to the Legal Profession** (Cambridge: Harvard University Press, 1967). Delmar Karlen, et al., *Anglo-American Criminal Justice* (New York: Oxford University Press, 1967) is a study of criminal justice in the United States and Great Britain from the role of the police to post-sentence remedies.

There are several specialized works dealing with various aspects of the American judicial system. Charles Warren, *The Supreme Court in United States History,* rev. ed., 2 vols. (Boston: Little, Brown, 1935) is still a valuable study, although outdated in some respects. Oliver Wendell Holmes, Jr., *The Common Law* (Boston: Little, Brown, 1948) has become a classic study of the common law. This work was first published in 1881 by one of the most distinguished justices of the United States Supreme Court. An early study of the judicial process by a distinguished legal scholar and Supreme Court justice is Benjamin N. Cardozo, *The Judicial Process* (New Haven: Yale University Press, 1921).

Edward H. Levi, *An Introduction to Legal Reasoning** (Chicago: University of Chicago Press, 1948) is an excellent introduction to legal reasoning in the field of constitutional law. Professor Levi, the present attorney general of the United States, was formerly president of the University of Chicago and dean of the University of Chicago Law School. For an excellent beginners' book on American law for college students whose interests center in the social sciences, see C. Gordon Post, *An Introduction to the Law** (Englewood Cliffs, N.J.: Prentice-Hall, 1963).

* Available in paperback.

C. Herman Pritchett, *The American Constitution,* 2nd ed. (New York: McGraw-Hill, 1968) is an analytical summary of what the American Constitution means. Professor Pritchett begins with the Constitutional Convention and its background and presents analytical summaries of leading Supreme Court decisions under topical headings, such as the executive, interstate commerce, and the various amendments.

A good introduction to the behavioral approach to American constitutional law is found in Glendon Schubert, *Judicial Policy Making** (Glenview, Ill.: Scott Foresman, 1965). Professor Schubert approaches constitutional law through the analytical framework known in social science as "systems analysis."

Alexander M. Bickel,* *The Supreme Court and the Idea of Progress** (New York: Harper and Row, 1970) is a friendly criticism of the Supreme Court under Chief Justice Warren. The late Professor Bickel of Yale believes that the Warren Court was inclined to read its liberal philosophy into the Constitution, just as conservative courts of an earlier day "found" the economic philosophy of laissez-faire in the Constitution. Another commentary on the Warren Court is Philip B. Kurland,* *Politics, the Constitution, and the Warren Court** (Chicago: University of Chicago Press, 1970). Professor Kurland of the University of Chicago Law School has published a series of lectures examining the significance of the Warren Court, both historically and in its relationship to other branches of government. Like Professor Bickel, he is a friendly critic.

A commentary on the American judicial system that is challenging but not in the mainstream of thinking is Macklin Fleming, *The Price of Perfect Justice* (New York: Basic Books, 1974). A California judge argues that the current quest for "perfect justice" has resulted in an overemphasis on procedural rights, which has frequently led to needless and costly litigation.

* Available in paperback.

Part Four

Dynamics of Political Change

Chapter 10

Political Change and the Developing World

The developing world, or Third World, includes Africa, Asia, Latin America, and the Middle East. This is in contrast to the free world of Western Europe, the United States, Canada, Australia, New Zealand and Japan; and the Communist states of Europe. Depending on the speaker and the context, the People's Republic of China (PRC), with a population of 800 million, is sometimes included in the Communist world, but more often in the Third World. We include the PRC in the developing country category. Altogether, the developing world accounted for 70 percent of the world's population in 1970 and at current growth rates will contain 80 percent of the world's population in 2020. It is a majority of the world we *cannot* ignore. (See Figure 1.)

The Third World often includes Latin America. In several ways, however, Latin America is unique and is not always identified as a Third World region. Almost all of the Latin American countries achieved their independence by 1824. For the rest of the developing world, independence came generally after World War II. Latin America also has a shared inheritance, which many developing countries, even those that border one another, do not have. Most of Latin America was a Spanish colony. Its social, political, and economic conditioners were similar. These countries shared common religious, political, and economic structures for many years before independence. When one looks at other developing countries, one sees contiguous countries where in one case a colony was ruled by Great Britain, and neighboring colonies by France, Belgium, Portugal, or the Netherlands. The colonial heritages and traditions are much more diverse in Asia, Africa, and the Middle East than in Latin America.

THE GROWTH OF THE MODERN NATION–STATE SYSTEM

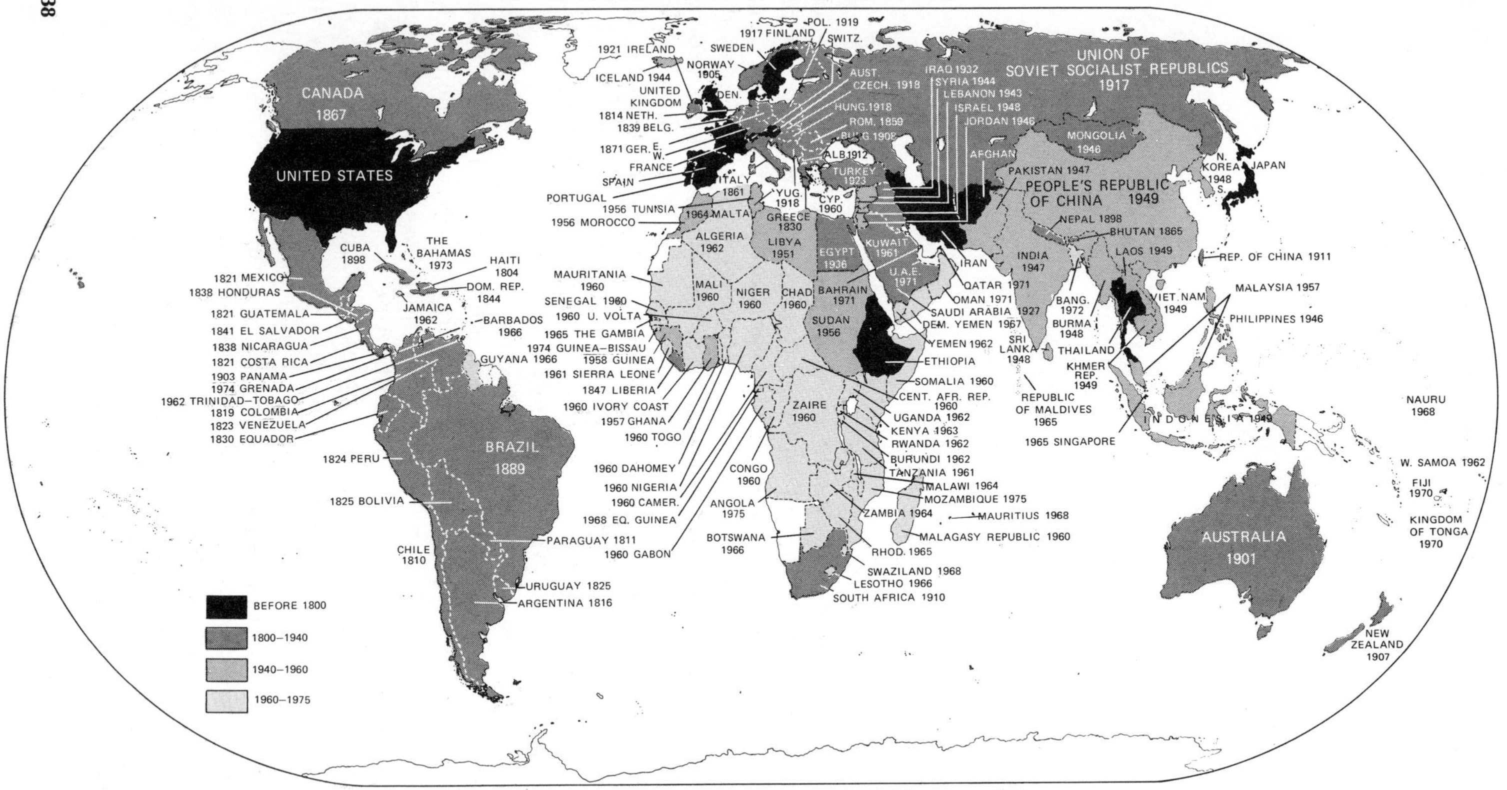

For most countries we give the most recent dates of independence, even though some countries, such as China and Poland, have existed as nation–states for centuries. No dates are given for independence before 1800.

Korea was divided in 1948. Germany was divided in 1949. Vietnam was unified in 1976.

The People's Republic of China claims all territory known as the Republic of China (Taiwan).

The Growth of the Modern Nation-State System

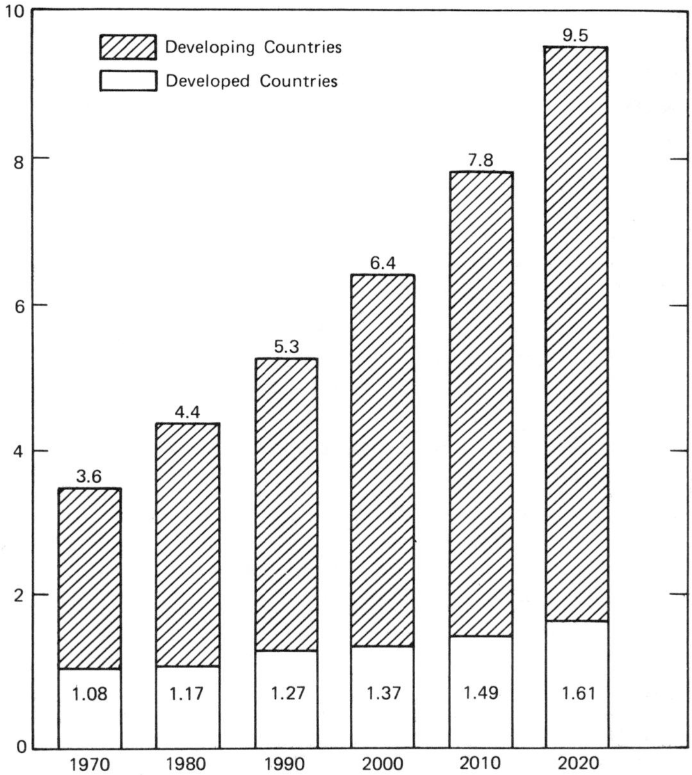

Figure 1. The growing population crisis, 1970–2020 (populations in billions), based on projected current annual growth rates of 2.3 percent (developing countries) and 0.8 percent (developed countries). *Source.* **War on Hunger: A Report from the Agency for International Development, Vol. IX, No. 9 (September, 1975), p. 1.**

There are about 150 sovereign nation-states in the world today. More than half of these have come into existence since World War II. These new states that emerged from colonial rule after 1945 are commonly referred to as developing countries or developing political systems. United States government publications refer to these countries as LDC's, or Less Developed Countries. We do not use that term in this book because it suggests that countries labeled LDC have an inferior status.

These new developing political systems share certain characteristics:

1. Their formal independence is relatively recent. Most are less than thirty years old.
2. The government and constitutional structures are new and still evolv-

ing, as are the organization and responsibilities of the executive branch; the organization, training, and functioning of the administrative service; and the organization and functioning of legislative and judicial institutions. These structures are just beginning to institutionalize, and their organization and duties are often subjects of intense political disputes.

3. Many political organizations, such as political parties, are unsure of their objectives (whether to participate in government or overturn the political system), have weak organizations, and are searching for an effective style of participation (electioneer, demonstrate, or be bought off by the ruling elites).
4. There are few interest groups, such as trade unions and business organizations, which have a history of making claims on government or have an input in policy making.
5. There has been a tradition of avoidance politics, where the village headman, village council, or religious or clan leaders seek to minimize the impact of government. The masses had no opportunity to influence policy making, but they were concerned with avoiding or mitigating more arbitrary or demanding government requirements.
6. Government usually limited itself to providing security, transportational facilities, and occasionally irrigation and flood control projects. It required taxes, military conscripts, and the corvée (unpaid contributed labor for public works projects). Governments could be and often were oppressive, but their functions were limited.
7. A number of easily quantifiable characteristics are present, such as low per capita income; limited distribution of technology; a predominantly rural society, with often as high as 80 to 85 percent of the population living in rural areas; small percentage of the population working in manufacturing; lower levels of caloric consumption; limited medical and health facilities, with fewer doctors or nurses per 1000 population; limited educational opportunities and high unemployment for those who do earn a college degree; relatively low literacy, often below 50 percent; high birth rate; limited social mobility, and so on.
8. Exports are largely primary products, such as bauxite, copper, oil, rubber, wood, rice, copra, spices, coffee, tea, and other agricultural products. It has been estimated that 80 percent of the developing world's foreign earnings come from such sales. There is little local processing of these goods, and it is the processing and manufacturing that provides more jobs, profits, and tax revenue. The processing and distribution of the final product usually occur in the developed, industrialized countries.

Each of the more than eighty developing countries do not have all of the traits listed. This is simply a summary of some characteristics common to most of them.

MAJOR PROBLEMS

Problems facing the developing countries are numerous, sometimes overwhelming. In many ways they seem even greater when compared to the situations new countries were facing fifty or a hundred years ago. A simple listing gives one some indication of the unprecedented demands that are being made on these countries and particularly on the governments, which are regarded as responsible for responding to most of the challenges:

1. Rapid urbanization since there are no jobs in the countryside or there is rural violence, but with only limited increase in employment in the urban centers.
2. The challenge of communism either as an insurgency movement or through organized and sustained demands for revolutionary change and reform.
3. A popular revolution of rising expectations with regard to the material standard of living.
4. Encouraging economic development, with an effort to improve productivity in the rural areas and industrialization to provide jobs and offset dependence on the often impoverished agricultural sector.
5. Population growth, which can reach over 3.5 percent annually.
6. Social mobilization (discussed later).
7. The communications revolution, which brings to many an awareness of the fruits of modern society, stimulating consumer appetites. It also provides an entrée for revolutionary ideologies.

An example of the communications revolution is seen in the following experience of an acquaintance of one author. While he was doing geographical fieldwork in Laos in the 1960s, the only radio station he could get regularly on his transistor was Radio Peking. He remembers one day when the pleasant-voiced female speaker requested all listeners to join in and sing the following song: "Somebody Throw a Stone at Eisenhower because He Is Nothing Better than a Rat," sung by the People's Liberation Band to Free Taiwan. Even the most isolated villages can be reached through the transmitter radio, and it is very rare for a village not to have at least one such link with the "modern" world.

Population growth, hunger, and oil prices are interlocking problems that seem to grow in intensity. One-half of all the deaths in the developing world are of children under age five. Most of these deaths are caused by a combination of infection and malnutrition. Each year there are 200 million cases of malaria, a similar number of snail fever cases, and 40 million cases of river blindness.[1] More than half a billion people are permanently malnourished, and starvation or inadequate diet is probably responsible for more than 100,000 deaths a year.

Despite the absence of adequate medical and health care, conditions are better than they were at the beginning of this century. The number of people killed in local wars in the developing world is much reduced as compared to the eighteenth century. The result, despite the earlier depressing statistics, is that the birth rate, survival rate and life expectancy have increased to the point that today the population growth rate (birth minus death rate) for the developing world is more than three times that of the developed world. For example, at present high growth rates South Asia (Bangladesh, India, Nepal, Pakistan, and Sri Lanka) will double its population in 29 years. It will take the United States and Canada 110 years to double their populations and Europe 147 years![2]

The number of people increases, but there is not a corresponding growth in food production. There are real possibilities that the food shortfall may increase since even some "developed" countries, such as the Soviet Union, import large quantities of foodstuffs because their grain production is below consumption needs. South Asia's 1975 foodgrain production was 150 million tons or 192 kilograms per person, about 45 percent of the world average. Grain consumption in this region is 202 kilograms per person, or approximately 5 percent more than the production.[3]

South Asia presents the most serious crisis, but other regions of the Third World face similar problems. Food production has not shown any noticeable increases in most of the developing world since 1970, and the Third World does not have the money to import more fertilizer and equipment to accelerate production.

During the 1960s there occurred what is popularly known as the Green Revolution, making available "miracle rice" and "miracle wheat" hybrid strains. Production jumped in the late 1960s (for example, from 105 million tons of food grain in South Asia in 1966 to 148 million tons in 1970), but this increase leveled off in the 1970s. There were many problems. The wealthier, middle and large farmers had the money and the larger-size farms to buy and effectively use fertilizer and farm equipment. The wealthier farmers could build and maintain the necessary irrigation and

[1] A basic summary of the dramatic statistics is "The Growing Crisis," *War on Hunger: A Report from the Agency on International Development,* No. 2 (September, 1975), pp. 1–9.

[2] *Ibid.,* p. 5.

[3] Data from Shahid Javed Burki and Shahid Yusuf, "Population: Exploring the Food-Fertility Link," *Finance and Development,* Vol. XII, No. 4 (December, 1975), p. 32.

'TELL ME MORE ABOUT THIS ENERGY CRISIS OF WHICH YOU SPEAK . . .
(Editorial Cartoon by Pat Oliphant (c) Washington Star, reprinted with permission Los Angeles Times Syndicate.)

drainage systems. The small farmer did not have the surplus to invest, and in too many cases lost his land as his production and profits fell behind. In some ways, what was to be a humanitarian breakthrough created more inequality. Now, even the wealthier farmers are finding it more difficult to purchase fertilizer and other needs from abroad to maintain production levels.

Acting as a unit, the Organization of Petroleum Exporting Countries quadrupled the price of oil during the last three months of 1973.[4] The cost of this price increase to the developing world was approximately $10 billion in 1974, an amount equal to almost all forms of development assistance the developing countries receive from industrialized, donor nations. The non-oil-producing Third World needs oil not only as a fuel but for many other products as well, such as commercial fertilizer, most of which is petrochemical in origin. Well over half of the developing countries have annual per capita incomes of under $200. These countries with the least money are hurt most by quadrupling oil prices, which then leads to price increases on almost all other imported items.

As discussed earlier, the exports of most developing countries are primary products. Paradoxically, as oil prices and the prices of manufac-

[4] A readable analysis of petroflation and its consequences is the Committee for Economic Development, *International Economic Consequences of High-Priced Energy* (New York: CED, 1975).

Famine in the Sahel: People collect and eat animal fodder dropped by French military planes for livestock.

tured goods inflate, the prices received by developing countries for other primary products drops (copper, for example, sold at $3,000 a ton in early 1974, at $1,000 a ton in December, 1975). It is estimated that the combined trade deficit for the developing world, excluding oil-exporting countries, was $35 billion in 1975.[5] The peoples of the developing world are caught in a vicious cycle just to survive physically until the year 2000. Medical and health improvements, though limited, have contributed to high population growth. Increasing food availability, which now is perilously close to a mass-starvation level, requires extensive imports. Most of these countries do not have the hard cash earned through exports to purchase the necessary items to increase agricultural and industrial production. A difficult situation is tragically complicated by increased oil prices, which penalize the developing world most. The problems confronting the political leaders of the Third World are as great in the 1970s as they have ever been. As you read this book, you are aware that no one has an answer to the population–food production–petroflation crisis.

Even under the best of conditions, where the government is making a reasonable effort to solve major problems and is not being subjected to a local or externally supported insurgency, it is obvious that government

[5] *New York Times,* December 18, 1975, p. 1.

resources are overtaxed. Governments are confronted with responsibilities that most governments in these areas have not been required to respond to in the past. The new governments have limited resources in terms both of finances and of a trained public service that can analyze problems, draw up a policy response, and then have access to the necessary materials and skills to implement the policy.

Some of these problems, for analytical purposes, can be broken into two general categories: control of the environment; and political integration.

Control of the Environment

The maximum control over and efficient use of the environment refers to the physical, economic, and social aspects of the environment. This has been one approach used to summarize the principal tasks of governments in the developing countries. Often the emphasis is on the technological, but of course technology has important implications for social and political control of the human resources. A historian, Karl Wittfogel, has shown that in China the development of complex hydraulic (irrigation and flood control) systems along the Yellow River and other major Chinese rivers resulted in a highly organized, hierarchical, and authoritarian society. In order to maintain the hydraulic infrastructure for hundreds of miles, it was necessary to mobilize and regulate the populations and to create a complex bureaucratic system to supervise and administer the geographic and human environment. Traditional Oriental government was semimanagerial. It possessed total political power, but it exerted only limited social and intellectual control over its subjects. The result was, in Wittfogel's terminology, "Oriental despotism."[6]

Claude Welch, who uses the term modernization rather than development, describes the process as one that utilizes natural and human resources in the most rational way aiming at the "establishment of a modern society." He defines a modern society as one that applies technology to achieve the optimum control and development of the environment.[7]

The development of a public policy to meet the essential economic and political needs of a state may result in a population so organized and regimented that it will lose all essential political liberties. Society may be harnessed to achieve what government officials believe should be the maximum use of the environment, but the consequence can be a hierarchical and authoritarian political system. The latest in technological

[6] See Karl J. Wittfogel, *Oriental Despotism* (New Haven: Yale University Press, 1957); and "The Historical Position of Communist China: Doctrine and Reality," *The Review of Politics,* XVI (1954), pp. 463–74.

[7] Claude E. Welch, Jr., *Political Modernization: A Reader in Comparative Social Change,* 2nd ed. (Belmont, Cal.: Wadsworth Publishing Company, 1971), p. 2.

development, as Karl Wittfogel warned us, does not necessarily increase personal freedom.

Samuel P. Huntington points out that the one common denominator of political development (or political modernization) is the weakening of what we call a traditional political system. Subsequent events are not always a coordinated series of changes moving toward modernization in the social, economic, and political systems. What is common is the initial weakening of traditional practices or patterns. Urbanization and industrialization may occur, industrialization may lead to a larger Gross National Product, and the Green Revolution in agriculture may increase total agricultural output. Literacy and the exposure to newspapers and radio may spread. Social and political inequalities can, however, be intensified. The measurable assets of the state may climb as the result of industrialization policy and new technology in the rural areas, but the urban worker may suffer for many years while new industries are established. The small farmer may find that he is unable to take advantage of the latest technology and expensive fertilizers, with the result that he loses his land to the more affluent landowner who has access to credit and can adopt the new agricultural technology. Even though some progress may be occurring in the economic system and pockets of economic and social change taking place, positive political and social changes may be restricted to a small middle class. Change can be compartmentalized. Advances in one aspect of society may actually lead to disintegration or disequilibrium in other parts of the social system. Control of the environment can place unusual if not impossible strains on the political system to the point that there occurs regression, or as Huntington describes it, "decay."[8]

It is obvious that one aspect of development or modernization is more rational and effective exploitation of the natural resources these new countries possess. Will the development of these resources lead to further social and economic inequity in society? How much investment of resources and management skills is required and who will bear the burden of this investment? Only a relatively small percentage of the population—10 to 20 percent—may benefit for the first few years, while the majority may find that conditions are worse for several decades. European experiences are not encouraging. The British industrial revolution began in 1760 and continued for over a century. The average Englishman was actually worse off as industrial development took place than he had been in the preindustrial period. Charles Booth's 17-volume *Life and Labor of the People of London* shows that 30 percent of London was at or beneath the level of base subsistence in 1900. Joseph Chamberlain, a Conservative Party leader, quoted scholarly sources to the effect that the English working class was

[8] Samuel P. Huntington, "Political Development and Political Decay," in *World Politics,* Vol. XVII, No. 3, (April, 1965), pp. 386–430.

worse off in the nineteenth century than it was at the close of the fifteenth century.

Substantial changes in the economic and social systems can place policy responsibilities on governments in the developing countries that sometimes appear insurmountable. Development or control of the environment may require sacrifices that only regimentation can enforce. Coordination of resources can quickly lead to authoritarian and arbitrary government policies by a government beset with innumerable claims and pressures.

Political Integration

Some form of political integration is necessary if a country is to survive. This is true if only to prevent the twin problems of *separatism,* where a segment of the community, usually geographically concentrated, wishes to break away as an independent nation (Bangladesh from Pakistan), and of *irredentism,* where a segment of the community, again usually geographically concentrated, wishes to become part of a neighboring political system and separate from the nation they are currently a part of, such as some Irish Catholics in Northern Ireland.

Political integration implies a relationship and a feeling of community among people within the same geographic–political boundary. There are social, economic, psychological, and political ties existing which give the population a feeling of identity, self-awareness, and exclusiveness, a sense of belonging to a common nation or political system. Political integration is both a goal and a process. It occurs when government contributes to the material and psychological cohesion of the political system. A sense of interdependence and cooperation exists. Citizens recognize that in some cases community cooperation is best achieved through the government. There is a belief that personal well-being depends in part on membership in the national unit and, at least in some ways, personal well-being can be advanced by government policies. A minimum requirement is that government provide the individual with an acceptable degree of security while political integration is occurring. If political integration is taking place, the bulk of the population will not be inclined to respond to irredentist or separatist appeals. There also will be little popular support for rapid, drastic, and violent changes in the political system.

The colonial experience often complicates political integration. The political boundaries of many of the new nations were decided by an outside colonial power in response to the creation of colonies by other expanding colonial powers in the same general area. The African state of Gambia, a former British colony which became independent in 1965, is a rather extreme example of a geopolitical boundary that has scant relationship to previous identities. Gambia "defies all principles of boundary making. There are no geographical features or other lines of demarcation, whether economic, cultural, or racial, separating it from the country surrounding it."[9] Newly independent government must then promote policies that will foster social, economic, and psychological interdependence and will begin the process of political integration. Political integration does not assume that tensions, conflicts, and policy disagreements will cease. It does, however, suggest that most of the public issues can be handled within a broad framework of rules of the game so that the fundamental existence of a particular political system is not challenged. Otherwise, simple survival instead of problem solving becomes the paramount concern of government officials.

TRADITIONAL AND TRANSITIONAL SOCIETIES: SOME MISPERCEPTIONS

The study of developing political systems is frequently complicated by incorrect assumptions. Four examples are discussed so that students will be aware of some of the pitfalls to avoid.

The Static-Stability Error

Traditional societies are often described as stable and experiencing slight or no change in social and political patterns. Traditional societies are usually farming, hunting, fishing, gathering, and sometimes nomadic. There is no regular flow and acquisition of inventions, technology, or innovation, and trade is minimal and often by barter. There is little economic specialization and most of the labor force is in primary (agricultural, fishing, etc.) production. Loyalty is to the family, clan, tribe, or village. Rule is usually by one man or a few (oligarchy). The masses do not participate and their freedom of action is usually limited because society is hierarchical with a ruling and a subject class, the latter far more numerous. Landowning is often the single source of wealth and power. Custom dominates much of existence with limited need to respond to new circumstances. An article written by the sociologist F. X. Sutton in the 1950s contrasted "intensive agricultural" (traditional) and "industrial" (modern) societies.[10] A distinguishing feature of traditional society is stability, both with regard to work patterns within the village and spatial mobility or migration away from the village. The status of groups is constant, determined by such things as birth, age, sex, etc. "Access to facilities and rewards" is continuous and unchanging. People are familiar with and committed to the locality and the social status quo. Change is minimal.

[9] E. W. Evans, *Britannia Overseas* (London: Thomas Nelson, 1946), pp. 55–56.

[10] "Representation and the Nature of Political Systems," *Comparative Studies in Society and History,* Vol. II (October, 1959), pp. 1–10.

Traditional, non-Western, or historically older societies do, though, undergo fundamental changes. Non-Western societies should not be treated as inevitably rigid and static. When British colonial officials began to assert control over northern Burma, they encountered a group of hill peoples known as the Kachin, who lived adjacent to the Chinese border and near the Assam area in India. E. R. Leach, a British anthropologist who has studied the Kachin in detail (300,000 people in an area of 50,000 square miles), describes a revolutionary political transformation occurring as late as 1870, shortly before the British arrived.[11]

Typically, Kachin villages had been ruled by an hereditary leader called a *sawbwa*. Villagers had to cultivate the *sawbwa's* land without compensation and were required to pay various taxes to him. During the latter part of the nineteenth century a series of village "revolutions" occurred. Many *sawbwas* were killed and were replaced by popularly responsible headmen.

The revolutionary villages, those without *sawbwas,* were called *gumlao,* or "rebel villages." At one point Leach speaks of the "spontaneous" emergence of the revolutionary or *gumlao* villages. It is clear that among the Kachin, at that time little affected by Western, British contacts, fundamental changes occurred in the political system. The spread of *gumlao* villages either was the result of new settlements (three or more "original" houses of equal status which intermarry) or of political revolt.

> *There is a tradition of revolution in which the former gumsa chiefs were either driven out or reduced to the status of lineage headman having no special rights.*[12]

Interestingly, British officials, who might be said to represent modernization, opposed the republicanism of the gumlao villages. It was much easier to deal with a *gumsa* or *sawbwa*-owned village where the *swabwa* was friendly and could control his subjects. The newly emergent "representative" form of *gumlao* government developed by the Kachin was inconvenient in the eyes of British officials and they opposed it. Revolution, not stability, took place in this "traditional" society, and not as a consequence of Western colonial contacts. British colonial officials eventually succeeded in reversing the trend toward indigenous "representative" village government among the Kachins and actually discouraged change.

Adaptability of Traditional Institutions

Sometimes traditional institutions are analyzed as an impediment to political change. They either attract a loyalty that contradicts efforts to

[11] E. R. Leach, *Political Systems of Highland Burma* (Boston: Beacon Press, 1965; first published in London, 1954). Material for this section was taken principally from pp. 197–207.

[12] *Ibid.,* pp. 206–07.

establish a national identity and loyalty, or they impede the growth of more open, participatory political processes. This is not always so.

One example of a traditional institution that assumed a new democratic function is the Indian caste association. This is a rather paradoxical and unusual example. Over the centuries the Indian caste system was an indispensable feature of India's repressive and stratified social system.

> *Membership in a caste is completely ascriptive: once born into a caste, a man has no way to change social identity insofar as the social structure and cultural norms recognize caste. Caste norms prescribe the ritual, occupational, commensal, marital and social relationships of members, and caste organization and authority enforce these norms. . . . The unit of action and location of caste has been, until recently, the sub-caste in the village or group of villages.*[13]

The caste association in postindependence India (1948) has been described as "one of the chief means by which the Indian mass electorate has been attached to the processes of democratic politics."[14]

Today, caste associations are most influential at the state level in the Indian federal system, rather than at the national level. Caste organizations with specific objectives emerged in the nineteenth century with the spread of communications, transportation, and a market economy during the British colonial period. At first the lower caste associations concentrated on upgrading their position in the social hierarchy by encouraging members to adopt the behavior of the higher castes: for example, vegetarianism, abstention from liquor, and preventing widows from remarrying. The associations also began to turn to the state to correct grievances, such as allowing more administrative positions and greater access to university education. After independence the local associations supported members for elective office either through existing parties or by forming new parties. The intention of the caste associations is to maximize caste influence and representation in governing bodies at the state and local level. The adaptability and performance of new functions by the caste associations have been rather successful. The associations have been praised for their capacity "to organize the politically illiterate mass electorate, thus making possible in some measure the realization of its aspirations and educating large sections of it in the methods and values of political democracy."[15] Castes, then, have participated in and even facilitated India's "modernizing" or developmental process.

Modernization and Political Development

Modernization and political development are terms that have been used interchangeably. Both terms are used widely in the literature. We have dis-

[13] Lloyd I. Rudolph and Susanne Hoeber Rudolph, "The Political Role of India's Caste Association," *Pacific Affairs,* Vol. XXXIII, No. 1 (March, 1960), p. 6.

[14] *Ibid.,* p. 5.

[15] *Ibid.,* p. 8.

cussed political development. This section questions the assumption that modernization is usually an integrated process moving all elements of a society in a single direction, reducing differences in society through an homogenizing process. Daniel Lerner, in his study of Middle Eastern societies, concludes that "urbanization, industrialization, secularization, democratization, education, media participation do not occur in a haphazard and unrelated fashion." They seem to be "highly associated" and "went together so regularly because, in some historical sense, they *had* to go together."[16]

We have discovered, however, that components of "modernization" (or of political development) do not interact in the same way or move uniformly in the same direction. Some parts of society may change while others remain isolated and unaffected by the changes. Interaction between "modernizing and traditional" segments of society may be delayed, the cause of interaction uncertain, the stimulus and reasons for interaction unclear and the results unpredictable. Compartmentalized changes occur in societies. Some segments of society may remain relatively unaffected for a long time. A perceptive study of Sicily, one of the more traditional regions in Europe, illustrates these observations.[17]

The Sicilian case shows that modernization and development are not identical concepts and that change can affect some groups in the population, but not others. The case study of Sicily defined modernization as imported change: ideologies, behavior patterns, institutions, commodities, expectations, etc., that are stimulated by contact with established industrial-developed centers. The example of Sicily suggests that as a modernizing region becomes dependent on urban-industrial centers, it imports nonselectively those items that are easier to acquire and that have more appeal. Development is defined as being more difficult—a region's efforts "to acquire an autonomous and diversified industrial economy on its own."[18] Some incomes may rise, fewer people are employed in agriculture, and urbanization and mass communications expand, but general productive output fails to increase, and the changes occur primarily in a few urban areas that have economic linkages with distant industrial-urban centers. Some changes take place because of foreign investment, although these often are isolated pockets of economic change that do not have a

[16] Daniel Lerner, *The Passing of Traditional Society: Modernizing the Middle East* (Glencoe: The Free Press, 1958), p. 438. Samuel Huntington has listed nine characteristics that various writers on modernization assign to this concept. See "The Change to Change," *Comparative Politics,* Vol. 3, No. 3 (April, 1971) pp. 288–90.

[17] The Sicilian data is taken from Peter Schneider, Jane Schneider, and Edward Hansen, "Modernization and Development: The Role of Regional Elites and Noncorporate Groups in the European Mediterranean," *Comparative Studies in Society and History,* Vol. XIV (June, 1972), pp. 328–29.

[18] *Ibid.,* p. 341.

spillover on the rest of society. Frequently, workers leave the region for employment in distant, prosperous areas and remit portions of their salaries to their home, increasing purchasing power and consumption. Between 1950 and 1961, for example, more than 400,000 men left Sicily for employment in Western Europe. A third source of funds that changes life-styles is tourism. One town near the Sicilian coast is a case in point. The local youth equate the behavior and possessions of the American, British, French, and Scandinavian youth with the "desirable and modern."

> *Coca-Cola and Scotch became prestigious drinks, juke boxes in glossy new bars blared hard rock music, and sexual standards of local maidens were threatened by comparison with the reported conduct of foreign girls on the coast. This too is modernization.*[19]

Regions exposed to modernization through tourism or limited economic ties with affluent industrial centers—and there are hundrends of such regions with tens of millions of people in the Third World—are in a dependent position. The prosperity they enjoy is tied closely to the economic well-being of the metropolitan industrial centers. Modernization also brings changes that are not necessarily cumulative, nor do they set into motion a series of further changes. In some cases, of course, modernization has set into motion fundamental, interrelated, and far-reaching changes as Karl Deutsch suggested would happen in his theory of social mobilization. Sicily is an example of instances where modernization has not brought about such changes. A middle class emerges, but it invests for short-range profit. It does not invest in industrial or agrarian enterprises which require a slower profit return. The principal investments of the Sicilian middle class

> *include real estate speculation, commerce appropriate to the new consumer markets which modernization engenders, and perhaps agricultural or light industrial production, cautiously capitalized because of its vulnerability to fluctuations on world markets. . . . If anything, modernization implies either the fragmentation and dispersal of money, or its waste.*[20]

Modernization and development are not two different words to describe the same phenomena. One interpretation of modernization, which has some basis in fact, is that it is contemporary, often superficial, and does not automatically lead to progressive changes throughout most of society. One means of distinguishing between development and modernization is to regard the former as an evolutionary process in which indigenous institutions adapt and control change and are not simply caught up in imitating and reacting to outside forces. Modernization often is contemporary, imported, and creates a dependency on the technologically advanced

[19] *Ibid.*, p. 343.
[20] *Ibid.*, p. 344.

urban–industrial centers without helping local political and social institutions to grow and adapt. Development means that a system has some ability to be selective in the type and pace of changes, often imported, that occur in a country.

Second, modernization is not, as Daniel Lerner described it, a "consistent whole," a unifying set of changes and responses. Modernization is not always associated with social mobilization. Social mobilization, to use Karl Deutsch's term, is a set of changing components, "correlated" and moving in the same direction, preparing people for change, and uplifting their intellectual curiosity, imagination, and outlook with an homogenized "world culture" as the usual outcome.

Modernization may sometimes be only the most current in personal lifestyles. Often its impact on society is haphazard. The modernization process can lead to the introduction of serious discontinuities rather than laying the groundwork for a series of interrelated changes moving toward the objective of a transformed society.

Western-Style Democracy

A fourth misconception assumes that unless a political system has freewheeling, competitive, national elections, with one or more major opposition parties, it is not "politically developed."

The movement toward individual freedom need not necessarily be led, symbolized, or guaranteed by a competitive party system at the national level. This was often the case in Anglo-American experience, but there are other potential patterns of change. An anthropologist, Clifford Geertz, has persuasively argued that competitive electioneering in some of the newly independent societies may have negative consequences. Part of the reason for this is that many peoples in these new, heterogeneous nations believe that their individual identities and inalienable values are tied to primordial attachments, such as kinship, race, ethnic group, religion, language, region of birth, etc. These attachments are combined with a growing awareness in this century that the state and its governing institutions can, depending on which group is in control, protect and enhance these values. Competitive politics may arouse and organize these primordial attachments as the surest and easiest way to attract popular support. Universal suffrage and competitive elections can temporarily place intolerable strains on governments with limited resources and a host of other problems.[21]

A rule of law, with protection of civil liberties and the increasing

[21] For an overview of primordial attachments and some political implications, see Clifford Geertz, "The Integration Revolution: Primordial Sentiments and Civic Politics in the New States" in Clifford Geertz, eds., *Old Societies and New States: The Quest for Modernity in Asia and Africa* (Glencoe: The Free Press, 1963).

autonomy of individuals and groups in society, may be another approach to nurturing political pluralism in a developing country. The opportunity for individuals to involve themselves in those choices that most directly affect them might provide a better strategy than instant national elections, which are soon abolished or become transformed into plebiscites to ratify government leaders. Two examples that appear to be working are Yugoslavia and the Republic of China (Taiwan). There are 571 communes or county councils in Yugoslavia. Their job is to plan and carry out functions similar to local governments in the United States. These activities include such things as provision of roads, education, city planning, building codes, local social services, etc. The local communes have some taxation powers and they also receive funds directly from the national government. The commune councils have the power to make decisions within a general framework of national policies established by the central government in Belgrade.

Council members are elected and they hire their own administrative staffs. At one time the councils had authority over industrial development within their commune, but this responsibility has been transferred to the workers' councils. One student of the Yugoslav political system has spoken of local self-management and direct democracy in the sense that "wide participation among the populace" is encouraged. As a result an "impressive variety of committees, commissions, citizens' councils, public boards, and other bodies now exist." There are also "voters' meetings" which allow the individual citizen to express himself on local government issues. There is widespread participation as long as there is no direct challenge "to central authority and socialist foundations." Decentralization in this Marxist, socialist state has led to substantial and increasing participation by individual citizens in matters that directly affect their livelihoods, their environment, and their living conditions.[22]

In the case of Taiwan, there are 22 county farmers' associations and 324 township farmers' associations.[23] The effective level of operation of the farmers' association is at the township. Each association has an elected board, which is the policy-making instrument of the local organization. This board selects the administrative staff, somewhat analogous to our county agents, as well as budget officers, managers of the cooperative store, etc. Approximately 6 percent of the regular members of the farmers' association hold elected positions in the association. Another 3 percent are members of village extension committees, while other villagers hold office in the local government, irrigation associations, farmer tenancy committees, credit unions, etc. The elections and decision making by local farmers at this level are not controlled by the central government except in terms of

[22] M. George Zaniovich, *The Development of Socialist Yugoslavia* (Baltimore: Johns Hopkins Press, 1968), pp. 119–21.

[23] For an historical analysis of Taiwan's changing rural society, see Martin C. Yang, *Socio-Economic Results of Land Reform in Taiwan* (Honolulu: East-West Center Press, 1970).

general policies such as encouraging greater use of fertilizer, encouraging sugar cane production, and so on.

The farmers' associations were developed in conjunction with a far-reaching land reform campaign in Taiwan in the 1950s. The associations have been effective in increasing production and making available marketing arrangements for the rural economy. The various office-holding opportunities opened up by the development of the associations have created a large number of new leadership positions in society, beyond the number of traditional, or village lineage, leadership positions that existed in pre-World War II, Japanese-occupied Taiwan. Two foreign aid specialists who have studied Taiwan and a number of other developing countries concluded that new leadership positions

> *are a way of subjecting traditional leaders to competition. But most important of all, the application of this principle confronts the traditional leaders with a choice. Either they must become leaders of development or run the risk of losing their positions.*[24]

The new local institutions have not been taken over by the traditional elites or officials from Taipei, the capital. The central government insists that farmers' associations prepare annual work programs and budgets, assisting them and making sure that these programs are carried out. They also assist the associations in obtaining financial aid, budgeting information, and general information about production and marketing. In such a way the potential abuse and power at the local by traditional elites or the more wealthy farmers is controlled. Individual villagers are not only concerned with carrying out decisions affecting their personal livelihood, but they also have the opportunity to have a voice in making these decisions. One sees a form of representative pluralism emerging at the grassroots level in Taiwan. The local cooperatives involve the farmers in participating in rural change and using the most efficient agricultural techniques. They also provide an opportunity for autonomous decision making that has been carried forward to local township government councils, where there is growing freedom of political choice in electing members.

The importance of self-conscious participation and a growing sense of efficacy and identification are affirmed by Gabriel Almond and Sidney Verba in *The Civic Culture,* a book that studies the political cultures of five countries—West Germany, Great Britain, Italy, Mexico, and the United States:

> *Organizations in which there is some opportunity for the individual to take an active part may be as significant for the development of democratic citizenship as are voluntary organizations in general . . . Democracy depends upon citizen*

[24] Edgar Owens and Robert Shaw, *Development Reconsidered* (Lexington, Mass.: D.C. Heath, 1972), pp. 27–28.

participation, and it is clear that organizational membership is directly related to such participation. . . . Membership in a politically oriented organization appears to lead to greater political competence than does membership in a nonpolitical organization, and active membership in an organization has a greater impact on political competence than does passive membership.[25]

Participation is an integral aspect of political development. Participation may be initiated more effectively at the local level, evolving upward, than at the top in national elections. Habits and skills of participation often do not percolate downward very rapidly, if at all, but participation can contribute to nation building.

THEORIES OF POLITICAL DEVELOPMENT

There is no universally accepted theory of political development. Many of the definitions various authors have drawn up overlap and share several features. There are also differing emphases, and some characteristics are unique to a definition. Four representative theories discussed are those of the Committee on Comparative Politics, C. E. Black (a Sovietologist); and Karl Deutsch and Samuel P. Huntington (political scientists).

Committee on Comparative Politics

One of the early and still widely used definitions that represented the thinking of the Committee on Comparative Politics of the Social Science Research Council was set forth by Lucian W. Pye. Pye's "development syndrome" suggested a linear movement whose ultimate objective seemed to be a pattern similar to what had been achieved in the Western world. He saw the emergence of a "world culture":

But at an ever-accelerating rate the direction and volume of cross-cultural influences has become nearly a uniform pattern of the Western industrial world imposing its practices, standards, techniques, and values upon the Non-Western World.[26]

The development syndrome (a syndrome is a pattern of interrelated traits) included three general characteristics. The first was *equality,* which as an ultimate political goal anticipated universal adult participation, with popular interest and involvement. Interestingly, Pye included totalitarian mobilization as one possible type of participation that supposedly would provide a "pretense" of popular rule. Equality also meant a general system of laws that would apply to all citizens equally. Social mobility was an aspect of equality, particularly as related to political office or the public service. Achievement standards were introduced, rather than a spoils

[25] Gabriel A. Almond and Sidney Verba, *The Civic Culture: Political Attitudes and Democracy in Five Nations* (Boston: Little, Brown, 1965), pp. 262–63.

[26] Lucian W. Pye, *Aspects of Political Development* (Boston: Little, Brown, 1966), p. 9.

system or a system that emphasizes ascriptive or inherited status qualities, such as ethnic group, religion, kinship, nobility over commoner, region of the country. Demonstrated merit was the principle for hiring and advancement.

A second feature of the development syndrome referred to the *capacity* of a political system in terms of the types and range of activities government was undertaking and its effectiveness and efficiency in making and implementing public policy. Professional standards in the public service, and government decision-making in general, would include such things as professional training, technical skills, and rational, empirical and analytical approaches to policy.

The third characteristic, *differentiation* and *specialization,* drew heavily on anthropology and sociology. We assume that as society and government become more complex, specialized, and interdependent, political pluralism will emerge. Specialization or expertise was considered important. Each agency would perform specialized and limited functions and therefore could be more responsive and capable in its activities. Unfortunately, there was little thought given to the coordination of the various specialized, functionally specific government departments. A hundred subdepartments approaching a problem from multiple angles can, as we have learned, be a major impediment to effective and responsive public policy.

The development syndrome recognized that there would be inherent tensions between various groups, some making demands for quality, others emphasizing capacity, and still others stressing technological innovation as social pluralism evolved. The particular mix of these demands and the way the political system reacted would result in patterns of development. There was no common progression described through which each country would go. The three characteristics listed above would enable a student to compare any number of political systems at a point in time (spatial comparison), but would not enable one to measure political development through time (longitudinal comparison). As outlined by Pye, the Committee on Comparative Politics of the Social Science Research Council drew up a list of six crises, later reduced to five,[27] which they believed every political system must confront and deal with if it is to evolve as a "modern state." The crises listed below will not necessarily be followed in sequence by each country, though it was obvious that the order in which they were discussed was based on British experience:

1. The *identity crisis* is identification by a people within a given territory, recognizing that this is their national territory. It can be described as a sense of togetherness and the absence of significant

[27] The seventh volume of the Committee on Comparative Politics, which discusses these issues, is Leonard Binder et al., *Crises and Sequences in Political Development* (Princeton: Princeton University Press, 1971), *passim.*

separatist or irredentist pressures. It is similar in many respects to the political integration problem discussed earlier.

2. The *legitimacy crisis* refers to the constitutional nature of the political system or the commonly accepted rules of the game. Legitimacy is also related to the responsibilities or function of a government and the popular feeling toward the scope and general effectiveness of government responsibilities.
3. The *penetration crisis* concerns the ability of government to influence basic policies and decisions in areas where it desires or is obligated to perform certain functions. A government that is restricted to the major towns and a few of the main roads during the daylight hours will not be able to penetrate society effectively, carry out its work, and develop feelings of confidence and rapport between government officials and citizens.
4. The *participation crisis* is concerned with the number of people participating in the political system and the range of alternatives the individuals may consider when making political input. The participation crisis is worked out principally through the evolution of interest groups and a political party system. Participation requires choice in terms of numbers of alternatives that can be popularly discussed and the availability of selecting between competing candidates at an election. In most developing countries if universal suffrage is bestowed almost immediately after independence, there is no question of formal participation. We might question, however, if this participation is really effective or whether voting is simply a controlled election with no choice mobilized by the political leadership.
5. The *distribution crisis* occurs as government attempts to encourage the distribution of goods and services throughout society, eliminating the more flagrant inequities and equalizing the benefits received by the population. Such undertakings as unemployment legislation, social welfare, public parks, etc., tend to reduce gaps between the wealthy and the poor. Government may be active in providing opportunities for groups that had previously been at a disadvantage, such as through job quotas or scholarships. An industrialization program that provides help, even modestly, for the under- and unemployed is a form of distribution response.

These five crises were based on the British experience. In the British case each crisis took decades, if not centuries, to solve. The appearance of these "crises" occurred in the order they have been discussed. Frequently, generations of people were involved in the emergence and facing of a particular "crisis."

Many of the developing countries face a situation where several crises are occurring simultaneously. An unbearable strain may be placed on government. An insurgency, which generally is a legitimacy crisis, can make it impossible for a government to deal with other "crises," such as penetration, participation, and distribution. The inability of the government to deal with other pressing issues makes its legitimacy even more suspect and unstable. As a result, the government is in the untenable situation of not being able to respond to some of the problems that might strengthen its legitimacy. An administrative apparatus, systematically subjected to a war of attrition, cannot perform even the minimal output functions that are necessary to build legitimacy in a new political system. A tragic example is South Vietnam where figures reveal that there were 6700 deliberate political assassinations between 1957 and 1963.[28]

> *The common characteristic of this activity against individuals is that it was directed at the village leader, usually the natural leader—that individual who, because of his age, sagacity, or strength of character, is the one to whom people turn for advice and leadership. Many were religious figures, schoolteachers, or simply people of integrity and honor. Since they were superior individuals these persons were more likely to stand up to the insurgents when they came to the village and thus most likely to be the first victims. The assassination rate declined steadily from 1960 to 1965 for the simple reason that there was only a finite number of persons to be assassinated. Many villages by 1966 were virtually depopulated of their natural leaders, who are the single most important element in society.*[29]

Political systems cannot survive this systematic terrorism against a government infrastructure over a period of many years. Legitimacy in the developing countries requires young governments to win popular support by delivering outputs. Without an administrative service, no government can do more than survive for a few years. Public policies cannot be developed and implemented because of the day-to-day need for physical survival. Political development becomes impossible under such circumstances. Too many developing countries face a brutal and extended internal war which is an intolerable drain on already limited resources.

The Longitudinal Perspective

C. E. Black, a historian, has looked at development from an historical or longitudinal perspective, as well as compared spatially the experiences of many political systems. He concludes that development or, as he describes it, the shift from tradition to modernity, is a revolutionary change comparable to the fundamental adjustments and changes that were required as man shifted from prehuman to human existence and from primitive to civilized

[28] Douglas Pike, *Viet Cong* (Cambridge: The M.I.T. Press, 1966), p. 102.
[29] *Ibid.*, p. 248.

societies. Black emphasizes institutions, their responses to challenges, and their ability to assume innovative functions in the face of various challenges or changes in society. The essence of modernization is new knowledge, its application in terms of technology and social organization and its transmission through education. The political system in any given state is a major influence in setting the pace and determining the scope and nature of change.

Having reviewed the role of change in the European Renaissance, Black sees modernization in the contemporary world occurring when traditional societies are confronted by modernity and the resulting response. Most developing countries must confront change and respond to it in a relatively short time as compared to the history of the Western world. Black outlines seven "patterns of modernization": 1. France and Great Britain, which emerged early in modern history as organized states within a well defined territory; 2. the United States, Canada, Australia, and New Zealand which were offshoots of the British pattern; 3. other European countries where administrative institutions were weakened by excessive colonial undertakings (Spain and Portugal), by fragmentation of territory (Germany and Italy) or by separatist and irredentist movements of subject nationalities against ruling dynasties (Eastern and southeastern Europe); 4. Latin America offshoots of the third pattern; 5. China, Japan, Russia, Thailand, Turkey, and a few other countries which, by defensive borrowing, withstood or reduced Western expansionist policies; 6. in some recent colonies (southern Asia and the Middle East) traditional cultures and institutions were developed enough to interact and adapt from the tutelary colonial experience (usually British); 7. the remaining societies (sub-Saharan Africa and parts of Asia) which had no cultural or institutional basis for interaction as in category 6.

Several of the countries in these seven patterns have experienced the four phases Black sees: 1. challenge of modernity; 2. consolidation of modernizing committed leadership; 3. economic and social transformation; and 4. integration of society. Political events such as revolutions and political institutions such as new constitutions are critical for the movement from one phase to the next. Some countries have transited all four phases; most in categories 6 and 7 have not.[30] Black enables us to see the patterns of development from an historical perspective. He does not provide a solution.

Social Mobilization

Patterns of political development have also been studied as a set of dependent variables, as political responses to changes that occur in the

[30] See C. E. Black, *The Dynamics of Modernization: A Study in Comparative History* (New York: Harper and Row, 1966), *passim*.

general social structure and that in turn require reactions by government if the political system, those particular political leaders, and the existing rules of the game are to survive. Implicit in this interpretation is the notion that many of the general social changes that occur are not directed or inspired by government policies, but evolve as the society responds and adapts to complex environmental pressures. Karl Deutsch, who was one of the first to interpret political development in this way, developed a widely quoted approach known as social mobilization.[31]

Deutsch maintained that social mobilization increases the probability of political tensions and demands in society and brings about fundamental changes in the nature of the political system because of the "changing range of human needs that impinge upon politics." People expect their government to do more. Social mobilization occurs as more people move to the cities and as more people are exposed to political events through newspapers and radios, both in the cities and in the rural areas. People come to believe there are needs the villages no longer meet, either because they have new concerns for better schools, better water supplies, the introduction of a partial cash economy, etc., or because they have left the village and moved to a new location. The result is that more people take part in political discussions, possibly in riots and demonstrations, in strikes, in insurgencies, and in various organizations that speak to government officials in the name of the membership.

The variables that Deutsch identifies as part of social mobilization are empirically measurable and most are available in various statistical data books, such as *The United Nations Statistical Yearbook* or the *World Handbook of Political and Social Indicators.*[32] The traits are considered to go together in terms of recurrent association, but no single trait is related to a specific effect on the political system. It is assumed that all of these characteristics interact and complement one another. Social mobilization politicizes individuals who previously did not play an active role in the political process. The number of claims on government increase in scope and intensity. Government is held responsible for the changes and their effects on society or it is regarded as the only institution capable of responding to the new and diverse challenges. Some of the social mobilization variables are:

1. Increase in gross national product and per capita gross national product.
2. Percentage of labor force in agriculture and in manufacturing.

[31] Karl Deutsch, "Social Mobilization and Political Development," *American Political Science Review* LV (September, 1961), p. 495.

[32] The latter is edited by C. L. Taylor and M. C. Hudson, *World Handbook of Political and Social Indicators,* 2nd ed. (New Haven: Yale University Press, 1972), *passim.*

Thousands of Portuguese demonstrate against communism and in support of the church.

3. Percentage of population in cities with 100,000 or more inhabitants.
4. Percentage of population over age 15 that is literate.
5. Number of radios, television sets, and newspaper circulation per 1000.
6. Population growth (the lower the rate the better).
7. Voting participation as percent of adult population.
8. Persons who have changed residence locality since birth.

Social mobilization exposes people to "modernity" and makes them susceptible to change. It encourages or makes it possible for them to change their residences, their occupations, their communication patterns, their reading habits, their peer groups, their aspirations, their political outlooks, levels of political information, their general attitudes toward the political system, and expectations about what the political system should do. These various traits increase or decrease at different speeds, but they all supposedly move in the direction of "modernity."

It is implicit that the final outcome in terms of literacy, birth rate, life expectancy, exposure to mass communication, and so forth will approach contemporary Western standards. A "world culture" bias is apparent in social mobilization analysis. Also apparent is the belief of a general "forward" movement in society, which affects most groups more or less equally. Government becomes more a dependent variable than a cause in the social mobilization process. We believe there is a certain weakness in an approach that overlooks the fact that political actors and institutions influence the social system more significantly than most social changes.[33]

Institutionalization and Political Change

Samuel P. Huntington has written on political development and political change for many years.[34] He is a political scientist who has changed his perspectives over the years and has acknowledged this change in his own writings. He was one of the first to point out that we cannot assume that all political systems will be moving together in a progressive, linear development pattern. There is also a possibility that some political systems will regress or "decay."

Huntington believes that one should distinguish between political development and political modernization. Political development is one aspect of modernization, but to use the terms interchangeably artificially

[33] For an elaboration on this point, see Giovanni Sartori, "From the Sociology of Politics to Political Sociology," *Government and Opposition,* Vol. IV, No. 2 (Spring, 1969), pp. 195–214.

[34] A superior overview of the political development literature, including summaries of his own works, is found in Samuel P. Huntington, "The Change to Change: Modernization, Development, and Politics," *op. cit.,* pp. 283–322. Most of the references to Huntington are taken from this article. Huntington documents all of his previous political development writings in this essay.

restricts one's focus. It would be very difficult to analyze political development in the time of the Roman Empire or the Middle Ages because *ipso facto* these periods are not modern by our standards. Political development has occurred over the centuries and is not a term that should only be applied to recent events.

In *Political Order in Changing Society,* Huntington presents his institutionalization thesis. Here he is concerned with interaction between the demands of political participation and the necessity of political institutionalization. The pressure for political participation is nearly universal in the contemporary world and can be set into motion by a multitude of historical experiences, or catalysts. Political institutionalization is regarded as a means by which societies respond to this single most important demand—the striving for some form of political participation. It is assumed that traditional or colonial political systems that have experienced a high level of institutionalism (for example, a bureaucracy, a governing council, or a partly elected legislature) would be more capable of responding to pressures for political participation and input claims. He also suggests that certain leadership groups drawn from the traditional aristocracy, the military, or a revolutionary leadership, might be able either to adapt or create new institutions that would allow a political system to respond to pressures in an orderly fashion. Stability and the ability to survive by ordered responses (incrementalism) would be achieved through functioning political institutions in the society rather than the wholesale creation of new ones in a revolutionary atmosphere. One difficulty is that a highly institutionalized political system, such as the Soviet Union, could be classified as politically developed. This would be true in terms of institutionalization but not true in terms of civil rights, personal and group autonomy, and some freedom of choice in articulating political inputs. The participation "crisis" can be averted by constraining, if not prohibiting it. A second difficulty is that by stressing political participation as a catalyst, the focus remained on the modern or contemporary. This was an orientation Huntington had previously criticized.

Huntington subsequently expanded his thesis and argued that two modifications should be made: there were factors other than political participation that should be taken into consideration; and political development more properly should be called political change.[35] There should be an effort to relate changes in one part of the system to changes in another part, to begin to establish some cause and effect relationships. Political scientists should concentrate on the most important institutions and processes in the political system, those that seem to have the predominant impact at the moment. There should be some effect to measure the rate,

[35] This proposed analytical approach is discussed *ibid.,* pp. 315–19.

direction, and scope of change and recognize that one part of the political system has an effect on other parts. Huntington saw five components as particularly useful for persons interested in political change in any given political system:

1. Culture—the values, attitudes, orientation, myths, and beliefs relevent to politics and dominant in the society.
2. Structure—the formal organizations through which the society makes authoritative decisions, such as political parties, legislatures, executives, and bureaucracies.
3. Groups—the social and economic formations, formal and informal, that participate in politics and make demands on the political structure.
4. Leadership—the individuals in political institutions and groups who exercise more influence than others on the allocation of values.
5. Policies—patterns of governmental activity that are consciously designed to affect the distributions of benefits and penalties within the society.

Summary

The advantage of stressing change is that it has universal application since every political system is experiencing change. Analysis is not restricted to a particular time period. A single political system can be studied over a period of time (longitudinal comparison) or one can study one or more political systems during a given period of history, limited, of course, by the availability of data. Our concern is back to the political, where it should be for political scientists. Political institutions and political leaders are independent factors that shape the natural and social environment. Segments of the political system also have a direct bearing on other segments or "components." Intervening social and economic factors often are more a result of political decisions than many writers have acknowledged. Industrial zones, the commitment of resources to hydroelectric or nuclear power plants, defense expenditures, increasing literacy, the availability of basic medical facilities, birth control programs, government assisted foreign trade programs—all influence the intensity and scope of demands made on governments. But these factors are often the result of decisions made in the first instance by political leaders. A focus on change recognizes the determinant role of political decisions and their consequences for the country.

POLITICAL DEVELOPMENT: AN OUTMODED TERM?

Recent years have witnessed a shift in emphasis away from the term political development, which many believe implies that the ultimate objective is some type of Anglo-American democracy based on a two-party system, underpinned by a popular political consensus. Early writings on political development went so far as to dichotomize the world's political systems into Western and non-Western and to speak of a unique non-Western political process. Lucian Pye drew up a "generalized model" of 17 traits that were "dominant and distinctive characteristics of a non-Western political process."[36] Non-Western countries were fundamentally different. These differences would affect the way these societies transited on the path to a more rational, prosperous, and Western-style political system. Almost immediately a lucid rejoinder by Alfred Diamant appeared in the same journal in which Pye had published. Diamant believed it was dangerous to see a "new world" of political systems where the concepts, trends, and social-political relationships observed by social scientists studying Western nations had little relevance to the study of developing countries. Diamant warned against the "drifting apart of Western and non-Western comparative politics" and instead stressed "the continuities and similarities between the two political processes."

> *The problem of rapid change in non-Western societies attempting to Westernize and industrialize is neither new nor unprecedented. . . . I refer here chiefly to the writings of laymen, as well as clerics, both Catholic and Protestant, who dealt with the political, social and economic impact of the French Revolution, the industrial revolution and capitalism on the traditional societies of Europe [in the nineteenth century.]*[37]

A seminal work, *The Politics of Developing Areas*, published in 1960, argued convincingly that all political systems were "mixed." For analytical purposes one might draw a continuum with traditional at one pole and modern at the other: Traditional ⊢——⊣ Modern. Almond insisted that the "dualism" of political structure was "characteristic of modern Western political systems [and] non-Western and primitive" political systems.[38] Every political system is in some degree of transition and each has a mixture of modern and traditional elements. Almond illustrated this "mixed" character of modern political systems with an American example.

During and immediately after World War II, several analyses of the impact of mass communications (radio, newspapers, and movies) in the United States suggested a situation where there was an electorate of "atomized individuals" linked "to a system of mass media which were

[36] "The Non-Western Political Process," *The Journal of Politics*, Vol. 20 (August, 1958), pp. 468–86.

[37] Alfred Diamant, "Is there a Non-Western Political Process?" *The Journal of Politics*, Vol. 21 (February, 1959), pp. 123–24.

[38] Gabriel A. Almond and James S. Coleman, eds., *The Politics of the Developing Areas* (Princeton: Princeton University Press, 1960), p. 23.

assumed to monopolize the communication process." Further research revealed that this model of modern political communications was inaccurate. Important political communication and political cues occurred below the mass media level beamed directly at the individual. Mixed with the modern communications process were "particularistic" (emphasis on personal ties and relationships), "diffuse" (spread out, not highly structured), and "ascriptive" (traits ascribed to, often born with, rather than achieved) features. The opinion leader was commonly "a trusted individual whose political influence was often a diffuse consequence of other roles." He might be listened to and respected because he was the landlord, a well-liked and respected friend in the peer group, a religious leader in the village or parish, or a vigorous and extroverted personality. There was a "mixed" (modern/traditional) two-step communication process. The opinion leader was often the intermediary who made his/her group of associates aware of significant political information and interpreted this information. Awareness, cues, and interpretation were mediated through the traditional, informal opinion leader. The opinion leader in turn was influenced more by other people than the mass media. The opinion leader was considered traditional when compared with "modern" political parties:

> *The modern, mass, bureaucratically organized, political party has not supplanted the informal coteries of notables which preceded it, but combines with this "more primitive" type of structure [local organization leaders] in what amounts to a mixed system.*[39]

This recognition that political systems in all parts of the world share fundamental features led some to reject the notion of political development as artificially separating and compartmentalizing Western and non-Western systems. Nevertheless, the concept of political development still carries the connotation of being concerned with non-Western countries, which are or should be purposively acquiring the chief features of their older, more mature, and successful Western counterparts. This underlying theme, often present in political development literature, also presumes a movement toward a "Western" objective and does not consider seriously the possibility of regression or decay. If a military junta or a Communist-led insurgent group takes over a country, it is frequently seen as an unpleasant necessity on the road to rationality, functional specialization, efficiency, and maximum use of national resources.

Reacting to the political scientists' concern with modernization, transition, and non-Western versus Western societies, Samuel Huntington, as we have seen, foresees a more general interest in political change emerging,

[39] *Ibid.*, pp. 20–21.

not limited to particular parts of the world or to specific periods in history. In earlier major writing, there was a bias toward the contemporary and the nondemocratic aspects of a political system.[40] He believed the principal challenge to institutionalization, or a regularized and stable functioning of the political system, was the pressure of political participation, which on a worldwide scale is essentially a movement of this century. In later writings he emphasized that change occurs in all political systems and that understanding political change should be a principal objective of political scientists.

Nevertheless, this recognition of change and transition as the essential focus for political science should not discourage us from studying something called political development with all the inherent problems the term suggests. Political change with special reference to the problems of the developing or emerging countries is an appropriate focus.

We listed at the beginning of the chapter certain characteristics shared by most Third World countries that set them apart from Western countries. Most were under colonial rule until well into this century. Third World countries are geographically separate from the Western world, do not share the Judeo-Christian heritage, and are technologically less advanced. Their political institutions are newer and more inclined to be unstable, and these countries are usually behind the West in terms of per capita GNP, persons employed in manufacturing, literacy, health care, etc. The study of developing countries does not rule out study and appreciation of the Western experience. The recognition that political change is universal, that there are discernible stages of development or regression in political systems, an historical perspective, and recognition of the "mixed" nature of political systems allow for comparisons that draw on Western examples to comprehend better underlying changes, "crises" or major problems, and contemporary government responses in developing countries. The universal presence of political change in all political systems is generally recognized. A political scientist may be especially concerned with political change and response in non-Western countries without being oblivious to meaningful comparisons of similarities and differences in Western experience. Many of the same problems or stages occurred in the West decades or even centuries ago.

It is clear that political development as a subfield in the discipline has shed its non-Western exclusiveness. In the future, political development will refer to challenge, response, and change, with a bias toward stable, nonrevolutionary, and nonviolent adjustments. Political development does not have an Anglo-American democratic model as its objective. Its essence

[40] Samuel P. Huntington, *Political Order in Changing Society* (New Haven: Yale University Press, 1968).

is innovative, non-self-serving responses by political leaders which make possible orderly adjustments. It is committed to the optimum degree of social, economic, and political freedoms, recognizing that each country has unique qualities. Therefore, no single pattern will emerge. Political development also presumes that new political institutions will emerge or there will be substantial modifications in existing institutions. The burden of performance is on the leadership of these new countries. They must live within political boundaries that often were drawn by colonial powers more concerned with avoiding disputes among competing metropolitan nations than with drawing boundaries in accord with the ethnic and geographic realities of the local situation. Problems of village parochialism, primordial sentiments, such as first loyalty to religion, language group, region, and so on, and the need to create employment and reduce the population growth rate are juxtaposed against government leadership with only limited resources. This makes it difficult to implement public policies that will solve these problems. There is an inadequate tax base, a shortage of motivated and skilled manpower and, all too frequently, an externally supported insurgency, which may force a government to concentrate on military and physical survival, passing over important social and economic problems. At this moment in time the burdens and capacities of the developing countries differ in important ways from those of the Western nations. The developing countries are a separate category of countries. We believe it is appropriate to concentrate on them in terms of their political development.

AUTHORITARIANISM AND SYMBIOSIS

This section is concerned with two divergent approaches to political change in developing countries: the authoritarian, whose naive faith in the unique integrity and capacity of governments in developing nations places an inordinate responsibility on these signal institutions; and the symbiotic, which recognizes aggregation and accommodation as critical in effective nation building, which assumes that policy is not simply administration but includes a broad range of inputs, and favors "organic" rather than a monolithic, imposed solidarity.

The attraction of government intervention is not limited to those who perceive government as an authoritarian and pervasive institution. Whenever a society is composed of more than an extended familial network, most members believe that certain objectives and values can be achieved only by authoritative rules applicable to everyone in society. As society becomes numerically and geographically larger and more complex and impersonal, citizens regard government as the most promising way of promulgating and enforcing laws binding on everyone in the social system.

Disagreement over who will make the laws, what the laws should be, and how they shall be applied is political conflict. The amount of participation and discussion allowed and the administration of enforcement procedures locate a political system on the continuum between authoritarian and pluralistic.

There are several reasons to assume that a strong, authoritarian, flexible government is the "action and responsive" institution to confront the challenges of the 1970s. This is especially true in the Third World where the demands made on new governments are cumulatively greater than demands made at similar points in Western political development, when problems such as national identity, industrialization, population growth, social mobilization, Communist subversion, universal suffrage, and the revolution of rising expectations were sequential rather than concurrent.

Renewed interest in the achievements of the People's Republic of China (PRC), reported throughout the world press but instantly observable via satellite television, has strengthened the association of such terms as development, order, and authority. Rosy and myopic analyses of mainland China's accomplishments and weaknesses result.[41] Some China visitors apparently are overwhelmed by a political system that can create order, cleanliness, discipline, smiling faces, overt consensus, and a sufficient, albeit plain, food supply for 800 million people who had experienced increasing degrees of political chaos and anarchy since the Taiping Rebellion (1850–1864). If a harsh, even totalitarian system is necessary for the PRC, the lessons drawn from this case are appropriate for other developing nations.

We often ignore the psychological and human suffering that have occurred on the Chinese mainland since 1949. Some overlook the fact that thousands of Chinese continue to flee the mainland. Hong Kong has absorbed more than 1.5 million refugees since 1950, and illegal immigrants from the mainland continue to arrive regularly. Some 20,000 people entered the British colony in 1971 (though less than 25 percent were detected and temporarily detained by the authorities); and 70 percent of those interviewed by the police were between 17 and 25.[42] Recent modifications in PRC policy responded to serious mistakes made by overly ambitious, authoritarian policies. The late Premier Chou En-lai had several times rebuffed foreign visitors whose sycophantic plaudits overlooked the stresses still present in the system. The appeals of authoritarian, reformist, modernizing governments have not had their source in the PRC experience, but renewed interest in, and awareness of, the PRC's political system has lent support to

[41] See, for example, Harrison E. Salisbury, *To Peking—And Beyond: A Report on the New Asia* (Chicago: Quadrangle Books, 1973).

[42] See the *Far Eastern Economic Review* Vol. 76, No. 18, (April 29, 1972) pp. 18–20; and Vol. 76, No. 20 (May 13, 1972), p. 23.

those who maintain that a firm hand is the means to political, economic, and social progress.

The number of authoritarian governments in the Third World, the successes of disciplined Communist insurgents, and the imposition of martial law in countries such as the Philippines may suggest that the practical turn of events is a reasonable justification for authoritarian political systems. This is reinforced by academics who analyze and evaluate political development in the Third World. Since man first made tools, weapons, and laws, a principal theme in Western tradition is man's struggle to master nature and history. Behind the Enlightenment of the eighteenth century and subsequent events is the belief that reason, progress, and modernization are measured by the degree that man controls his natural and social environment. Absolute commitment to reason and change can soon lead to a doctrinaire rationalism which judges human progress by the amount of institutionalized control in a system. Even those with a personal liberal philosophy sometimes urge developing nations to adopt authoritarian solutions. A sympathetic overview of the emancipation of African and Asian peoples written a decade ago by Rupert Emerson of Harvard University declared:

> *For a backward people precariously moving out from under colonialism with all the problems of economic development still ahead of them, it is highly doubtful that the sovereign remedy is a full-scale installment of democracy. . . . [T]he prime requirement is not more freedoms but for discipline and hard work, not for opposition but for a national consolidation of all forces and talents.*[43]

A few weeks after the end of World War II, the New York-based Social Science Research Council undertook to sponsor a Committee on Comparative Politics. This committee was discharged in 1972 by the SSRC. One of its main tasks was to publish a series entitled *Studies in Political Development,* which we have referred to earlier. The seventh volume in this excellent collection appeared in 1971. One of its functions was to summarize and reconsider conclusions in the previous volumes. Progressively, the series and published spinoffs by persons associated with the committee emphasized the crucial role of a strong (if necessary, authoritarian) government for developing nations. In writing on the need for governmental capacity, the authors discussed "penetration" as an indispensable variable:

> *Penetration means conformance to public policy enunciated by central government authority. The degree of penetration may be viewed as the probability that governmental policies regarding the polity as a whole, or any of its subdivisions will be carried out. . . .*
>
> *Penetration refers to whether they, the governing authorities, can get what they want from people over whom they seek to exercise power. Such power clearly*

[43] Rupert Emerson, *From Empire to Nation* (Boston: Beacon Press, 1962), pp. 289–90.

refers to areas of governmental policy that go considerably beyond taxation, conscription, and control of deviant behavior.[44]

We would like to suggest that the values of national political integration and respect for the autonomy of the individual spirit can usually be better achieved through less authoritarian political arrangements. In part, this is because of our bias against authoritarian regimes, practically, because we believe that better results can be achieved via a more democratic form of politics. Developing nations are usually heterogeneous—multiethnic, multitribal, multilinguistic, multireligious, having valley and hill peoples, etc. Authoritarian, or "strong," governments have a disturbing tendency to represent only one community in the country. Consequently, other groups become increasingly alienated and cumulative grievances beget various degrees of insurrection, leading to more authoritarian government responses before legitimate claims are recognized.

Nonauthoritarian solutions are not without their advocates. Emile Durkheim (1858–1917), one of the first modern social scientists, investigated conditions in the Third French Republic similar to those facing much of the developing world today. During the latter part of the nineteenth century France was experiencing a multitude of social and economic changes; the empire had just been replaced by a republic, but in the transition France had narrowly escaped a return to strongman rule. Durkheim's discussion of mechanical and organic solidarity was both a description of, and prescription for, the Third Republic. It remains equally incisive today as we evaluate political policy in the developing nations.

Symbiosis is a related though not identical term describing the organic solidarity Durkheim advocated. Symbiosis describes the interdependence of dissimilar components. Mutual benefits encourage cooperation, although factors inducing cooperation may be dissimilar for each actor. For example, Singapore became a part of Malaysia because it perceived economic, common market benefits, while the central government in Kuala Lumpur saw the union as a means to constrain Communist elements on the island and prevent Singapore from becoming Malaya's Cuba. The eventual separation in 1965, with Singapore achieving independence, occurred because the symbiotic relationship had not evolved. Singapore's Communists were in disarray, but the economic benefits were slow in coming. Except for conflicting political ambitions, the symbiosis could have been achieved as it has for the former territories of Malaya, Sabah, and Sarawak, which now make up Malaysia.

Emile Durkheim was one of the first to recognize that there was such a problem as nation building. He theorized that orderly change and a

[44] Leonard Binder et al., *Crises and Sequences in Political Development* (Princeton: Princeton University Press, 1971), pp. 208–209.

minimal national consensus built on a monolithic and all-embracing set of shared values was less satisfactory than a society based on the accommodation and aggregation of diverse and legitimate interests. Successful modern societies are based on a broad range of mutually beneficial symbiotic relationships.

Influenced by Auguste Comte and Charles Darwin, Durkheim sought to discover laws that would explain social development. Development meant individual differences, autonomous groups, economic complexity, and specialization rather than standardization of thought and behavior.

National integration or "solidarity" could be achieved "mechanically" or "organically." Mechanical solidarity occurs, not because it is produced by artificial means, but because it is analogous "to the cohesion through which living organisms are united." Under mechanical solidarity, beliefs and values are to be common to all members and "solidarity increases with the extent of the preponderance of the common ideas and tendencies over the personal ones." Mechanical solidarity and individualism are inversely related. Mechanical solidarity typifies traditional societies or contemporary authoritarian and totalitarian systems.

Organic solidarity describes a more open, pluralistic society, one that has achieved functional specialization and a division of labor, or is moving in that direction. It assumes that political, social, and economic development interact and that changes in one system affect the other systems. Durkheim stated that individualism, innovation, and independence increased in society as organic solidarity evolved. Further, he argued that the human potential could only be realized in a society based on organic rather than mechanical solidarity. An individual's specialized and creative functions are possible only "if each one has an individual sphere of action, consequently a personality." Each unit "has its special physiognomy, its autonomy. Yet as the unity of the organism increases the more marked is the individuality of its parts."[45] Political integration and development require autonomy and creativity, both of which ultimately depend on the contributions of symbiotic relations.

We do not advocate a return to the night watchman state, which confined itself to external and internal security and maintaining a communications and transportation infrastructure. The numerous crises telescoped into a narrow time span in the developing nations require active, efficient, rational, and honest governments to deal with problems ranging from external subversion to rice shortages caused by drought or flood. Simultaneously, we must realize that the capacity of governments in the

[45] These quotes are taken from Book 1, chapter 3 of Emile Durkheim's *Division of Labor,* first published in 1893. For a succint interpretation of Durkheim's writings, see George Simpson, *Emile Durkheim: Selections from his Work, with Introduction and Commentaries* (New York: Thomas Y. Crowell, 1963).

developing world is limited. One of the dilemmas of the Third World is that as more demands are made on governments, the demands must be balanced against a rather narrow resource base upon which these governments can draw for taxes, technicians, etc. In addition to all their internal problems, there are external forces that impinge on the functioning of developing political systems.

INTERNATIONAL FACTORS

Political development cannot be studied simply as a result of forces and decisions operating *within* the boundaries of a particular nation. The majority of the developing countries have a history of being significantly influenced by pressures outside the nation over which they have little or no control. Students should also note, however, that the Western or developed nations are also influenced by groups not readily subject to national control. The international environment as a source of factors influencing internal stability, development, and decay has generally been neglected. While there are many examples we could discuss, such as the need for foreign markets and foreign investment, we offer two examples of international influence to illustrate the types of problems facing the Third World.

Insurgency and International Intervention

The case of the Tho, concentrated in the mountainous Vietnam–China border area, illustrates the problems of nation building from both an historical and international perspective.[46]

When the French took control of various parts of what is now Vietnam in the nineteenth century, it was a time of vigorous territorial expansion. This territorial spreading out of Vietnamese threatened the non-Vietnamese hill tribes who had been the only inhabitants of the sparsely populated highlands. The French separated uplanders, or *Montagnards,* from Vietnamese administration and ruled these peoples directly or through local tribal officials whom they appointed. There was general acceptance of this policy by the Montagnards, except in the case of the 400,000 Tho. The Tho had supported an unsuccessful Vietnamese usurper in the sixteenth century. Determined to avoid this in the future, the victorious Vietnamese emperor had sent Vietnamese officials to intermarry with the Tho and to administer them. The descendants of the resulting intermarriages—the Tho-ti—became the ruling elite, were accepted as rulers, and became the political link with the lowland Vietnamese. The Tho-ti were alienated because they

[46] See John T. McAlister, Jr. "Mountain Minorities and the Viet Minh: A Key to the Indochina War," in Peter Kunstadter, ed., *Southeast Asian Tribes, Minorities, and Nations,* Vol. 2 (Princeton: Princeton University Press, 1967), pp. 780–88.

were passed over by the French, as the new French rulers appointed local officials. Unhappiness with the new political arrangement festered and intensified because of this political slight. A major Tho tribal rebellion against the French occurred in 1940. The scattered remnants of the Indochinese Communist Party, which had been weakened by an unsuccessful revolt against the French in 1930–31, now fled from the lowlands and delta to the Tho area. They promised equality and autonomy to the Tho. The Tho mountain area became the first major Communist base, as both groups joined against the common French enemy. When the first Vietnam war, against the French, ended in 1954, 20 percent of the anti-French insurgents (Vietminh) were composed of Tho tribesmen. The international aspects of this Tho–Vietminh alliance is summarized by a political scientist who has studied this situation in detail:

> *But possession of a base area in the Tho homeland was more important to the Viet Minh for another reason. The Tho homeland provided the all-important supply route to China through which the Viet Minh obtained external assistance—thereby internationalizing the Viet Minh war.*[47]

Before the Communists seized all of China in 1949, the Vietminh and Tho had traded opium for guns. After 1949 political motives were the source of Chinese support for the insurgents. One writer has said that if it were not for the weapons from China, the Vietminh insurgency would have failed.[48]

The results of the protracted Vietnamese Communist insurgency are self-evident. In April–May, 1975, South Vietnam fell to the insurgents, and Saigon became Ho Chi Minh City. One factor that influenced the continuation of the Vietnam wars for twenty-nine years (1946–1974) was the outside assistance contributed by the Chinese, the Russians, the French, and the Americans. The United States alone spent more than $150 billion between 1960 and 1975. This "international aid" was a crucial factor influencing political development and political decay in Vietnam.

After Vietnam fell to the Communists, the next area of big-power involvement became the Angolan Civil War. Angola was given independence by Portugal in 1975. The victorious Peoples Liberation Movement of Angola was supported by the Russians, Cubans, and Nigerians. Two other political–military movements received support from the United States, the People's Republic of China, South Africa, and Zaire, among others.

The relatively weak internal condition of many developing countries makes them susceptible to outside political forces that wish to influence specific policies or the type of political system that will endure. If one

[47] Gary D. Wekkin, "Tribal Politics in Indochina: The Role of Highland Tribes in the Internationalization of Internal Wars," in Mark W. Zacher and Stephen Milne, eds. *Conflict and Stability in Southeast Asia* (Garden City, N.Y.: Anchor Press, 1974), pp. 129–30.

[48] David Feingold, "Opium and Politics in Laos," in Nina S. Adams and Alfred W. McCow, eds., *Laos: War and Revolution* (New York: Harper & Row 1970), pp. 335–36.

This picture depicts the Soviet freighter *Olga Varentsova* as it ties up in the port of the Angolan capital, Luanda, in 1975. The Soviet Union supported the MPLA during the civil war with both military and civilian equipment.

considers foreign economic influences on the developing world, it is also apparent that the impact of multinational corporations is increasing.

Multinational Corporations

The nation-state and the multinational corporation (MNC) have been described as the "two dominant institutions in the world in the late twentieth century."[49] One way to show the impact of MNCs is to draw up two lists, a list of countries according to their gross national product and a list of corporations according to their gross annual sales. The lists should be rank-ordered, with the countries having the highest GNP at the top of the list. Similarly, the companies should be rank-ordered, with those having the highest gross annual sales at the top of the list. If these lists are then merged and the 100 names at the top are separated, 59 names on the list are nation-states and 41 are multinational corporations. General Motors' gross annual sales are higher than the GNPs of Switzerland, Pakistan, and South Africa. Or Ford Motor Company's sales are higher than Austria's GNP.[50]

[49] Lester R. Brown, "The Multinationals and the Nation-State," *Vista: The Magazine of the United Nations Association,* Vol. VIII, No. 6 (June, 1973), p. 15.

[50] U.S. Senate, Committee on Finance, *Multinational Corporations, Hearings,* before a Subcommittee on International Trade and Finance, 93rd Congress, 1st Session (February 26, 27, 28, and March 1 and 6), p. 404.

An MNC is a corporation that has parallel or complementary operations in several countries. Firms are duplicating their activities or dispersing essential parts of their operation among several different states.[51] One of the first MNCs was Bata, which was founded in Czechoslovakia and later transferred to Canada in World War II. In 1968 Bata was manufacturing shoes in 79 countries and selling them in 89 countries.

An IBM Corporation executive has summarized IBM's overseas operations:

1. We operate in 126 countries overseas with some 125,000 employees.
2. We do business in 30 languages, in more than 100 currencies.
3. We have 23 plants in 13 countries.
4. We have 8 development laboratories in as many countries.
5. And we have a very healthy offshore growth rate, going from $51 million in gross income in 1950 to $5.14 billion in 1973. In fact, since 1970 our overseas business has accounted for more than half the corporation's net income.[52]

Developing countries seek outside investment to provide jobs, to introduce technology, as a source of investment dollars, and to be affiliated with a worldwide marketing network. Most of this investment in the developing countries comes through multinational corporations. If one looks at the total world product (WP), that portion dominated by the multinational corporations accounts for 14 percent of WP, and the percentage increase in MNC sales has steadily grown faster than WP. Jobs, economic development, urbanization, unemployment, and equitable or unreasonable distribution of profits and wages are often important factors contributing to the stability of a political system. Not only will the local economic condition help to prevent widespread discontent, it also may provide important taxation resources for a new government faced with numerous demands. Many of the economic decisions that then have political implications are not solely or even principally within the jurisdiction of the political system, as the following hypothetical case shows:

Many decisions once considered the province of the nation-states are now being made by externally based MNCs, particularly in such matters as the nature, timing, and location of investment. These decisions may affect the employment level, the rate of economic growth, the balance of payments, or whether a given natural resource is developed. A planning commission sitting

[51] For a review tracing the development of the term multinational corporation, see Howe Martyn, "Development of the Multinational Corporation," in Abdul A. Said and Luiz R. Simmons, eds., *The New Sovereigns: Multinational Corporations as World Powers* (Englewood Cliffs, N.J.: Prentice-Hall, 1975), pp. 30–43.

[52] Jacques Maisenrouge, "How a Multinational Corporation Appears to Its Managers," in George W. Ball, ed., *Global Companies: The Political Economy of World Business* (Englewood Cliffs, N.J.: Prentice-Hall, 1975), p. 15.

in Accra, the capital of Ghana, may make certain decisions concerning, say, the creation of additional employment, but critical decisions influencing the number of new jobs to be created in Ghana may be made in the executive offices of the MNCs headquartered in New York, Amsterdam, or Osaka.[53]

Important economic and social decisions to which older governments and nation-states were previously able to respond without considering external forces now must carefully operate within the parameters of outside interests. The political system is concerned, among other things, with poverty, overpopulation, possible rising unemployment, and the taxation base, but these factors do not occupy a prominent position in terms of the corporate strategies of MNCs. Each MNC's global strategy is concerned with such decisions as where to secure raw materials, which components will be manufactured in what factory in which particular country, where the assembling of various components will occur, in which countries or with which banks one should seek capital for financing, and where assembly plants, manufacturing plants, employee training, research plants, management offices, and research laboratories should be located. These types of problems continue to impinge upon the public policy decisions of many of the developing countries, particularly because of the size and range of activity of many of the MNCs active in the developing world.

One indicator of sovereignty or national independence is the number and scope of decisions influenced by forces outside the country. In important ways many economic decisions are by MNCs in circumstances under which the local government has little control. On occasion, however, the MNC may become directly involved politically in order to continue operating in a country.

A recent disclosure by Gulf Oil Corporation that it "donated" $4 million over a five-year period to South Korea's Democratic-Republic Party is an unpleasant reminder of the political role a wealthy MNC can play in a developing country. Gulf Oil has a $350 million investment in South Korea in oil, fertilizer, petrochemical, and shipbuilding facilities. The Democrat-Republicans won only 51 percent of the vote in the 1971 Korean general elections. The party's finance chief, who was described by a Gulf executive as being "as tough a man as I ever encountered," explained his request in 1971 to Gulf as follows: "Here we are, a struggling young democracy, and as you know it takes money to run an election. We therefore are appealing to business people to accomplish this."[54] In the Korean case, Gulf apparently was a reluctant political contributor. The company official testifying before the Senate Foreign Relations Committee did, however, admit that the $3 million contribution to the 1971 election campaign was "an

[53] Lester R. Brown *op. cit.*, p. 50.
[54] *New York Times*, May 17, 1975, p. 37.

unwarranted interference" in Korean internal politics. The Gulf–Korean episode is one example of how MNC policy and the local government's actions may influence one another in important political ways that most of us do not consider proper or legal.

Summary

Unity, national integration, political development, political modernization, or political change—whatever one chooses to call it—is better achieved by maximum accommodation of diverse claims, recognizing that much of the impetus to change and evolution must be extragovernmental. An evolving political integration is superior to an imposed political uniformity. History shows that authoritarian regimes seldom maintain a spirit of reason, efficiency, and charity. In general, an optimal level of political and social freedom is the surest way to proceed toward political, economic, and social development. The problems that confront developing systems oftentimes seem insurmountable. Authoritarian solutions are too frequently adopted for purposes of short-run survival. Unfortunately, political change in the developing and developed world sometimes assumes the form of political violence. This is the subject of the next chapter.

Selected Readings

The literature abounds and there are many ways for the student to introduce himself or herself effectively to the major issues that confront a large majority of the world's population. Sometimes rather detailed, but among the most stimulating books written, is Samuel P. Huntington, *Political Order in Changing Society** (New Haven: Yale University Press, 1968). Huntington's book should be read in conjunction with Gabriel A. Almond and G. Bingham Powell, Jr., who use a functional approach: *Comparative Politics: A Developmental Approach** (Boston: Little, Brown, 1966). A work that emphasizes becoming modern and political leadership is Dankwart A. Rustow, *A World of Nations* (Washington, D.C.: The Brookings Institution, 1967). Well-organized overviews of many of the characteristics associated with the developing world are: John H. Kautsky, *The Political Consequences of Modernization** (New York: John Wiley, 1972); and Fred R. von der Mehden, *Politics of the Developing Nations** 2nd ed. (Englewood Cliffs, N.J.: Prentice-Hall, 1969). A not difficult conceptual

* Available in paperback.

introduction is Lucian Pye, *Aspects of Political Development** (Boston: Little, Brown, 1966).

Most of the writing on political development has been by American writers. A good collection of British authors is Colin Leys, ed., *Politics and Change in Developing Countries* (Cambridge, Eng.: At the University Press, 1969). For recent trends in the developmental literature as it applies to Latin America, see Ronald H. Chilcote and Joel C. Edelston, eds., *Latin America: The Struggle With Dependency and Beyond** (New York: John Wiley, A Halstead Press Book, 1974). Finally, for a superior review of the literature and the various approaches that have emerged, see Samuel P. Huntington, "The Change to Change: Modernization, Development and Politics," *Comparative Politics,* Vol. III, No. 3 (April, 1971), pp. 283–322.

There are numerous introductory readers on political development available. Three of the better ones are Jason L. Finkle and Richard W. Gable, eds., *Political Development and Social Change,** 2nd ed. (New York: John Wiley, 1971); John H. Kautsky, ed., *Political Change in Underdeveloped Countries* (New York: John Wiley, 1962); and Claude E. Welch, Jr., *Political Modernization: A Reader in Comparative Political Change,** 2nd ed. (Belmont, Calif.: Wadsworth Publishing, 1971).

The Committee on Comparative Politics of the Social Science Research Council has sponsored an excellent *Studies in Political Development* series, which includes conceptual chapters as well as individual country chapters. The case studies are drawn from both Western and non-Western countries. The following books in the series are all published by Princeton University *Press: Joseph LaPalombara, ed., Bureaucracy and Political Development,** rev. ed., 1967; Robert E. Ward and Dankwart A. Rustow, eds., *Political Modernization in Japan and Turkey,** 1964; James S. Coleman, ed., *Education and Political Development,** 1965; Lucian W. Pye and Sidney Verba, eds., *Political Culture and Political Development,** 1965; Joseph LaPalombara and Myron Weiner, eds., *Political Parties and Political Development,** 1966. The seventh published volume in the series, Leonard Binder et al., *Crises and Sequences in Political Development,** 1971, does not include any case studies and is rather esoteric in places.

Political pluralism is not easily achieved in the developing countries, but we should not discount it as an objective. Robert Dahl, *Polyarchy: Participation and Opposition,** (New Haven: Yale University Press, 1971) considers on a worldwide basis the possibility and problems of authoritarian political systems becoming more pluralistic. One of the few works that argues that there are sound, practical reasons for a developing country to become

* Available in paperback.

more pluralistic is William A. Douglas, *Developing Democracy* (Washington, D.C.: Heldref Publications, 1972). Competitive elections are relatively rare in the Third World. Internal war and insurgency make it even more difficult to hold elections that provide some choice. Surprisingly, major elections held in South Vietnam in 1967 and 1971 provided more choice and were fairer than is popularly assumed. A thoughtful analysis is Howard R. Penniman, *Elections in South Vietnam** (Washington D.C.: American Enterprise Institute for Public Policy Research, 1972).

Two publications that argue for autonomy and innovation at the local level as a basis for effective socioeconomic development and as an impetus to a widening political pluralism are Thomas J. Bellows, "Political Development, Authoritarianism and Symbiosis," *Journal of Thought,* Vol. VIII, No. 2 (April, 1973), pp. 123–30; and Edgar Owens and Robert Shaw, *Development Reconsidered* (Lexington, Mass.: D. C. Heath, Lexington Books, 1972).

An effort to explain why bureaucratic elites dominate in so many developing countries is Gerald A. Heeger, "Bureaucracy, Political Parties, and Political Development," *World Politics,* Vol. XXV, No. 4 (July, 1973), pp. 600–07. A thorough case study of a bureaucracy's role and importance in a developing political system is Robert O. Tilman, *Bureaucratic Transition in Malaya* (Durham: Duke University Press, 1964).

Big-power involvement in the destinies of the developing world is a matter of continuing discussion. Alvin Z. Rubinstein has edited a volume which suggests that in many instances the two Communist big powers have not achieved their objectives: *Soviet and Chinese Influence in the Third World* (New York: Praeger, 1975).

Political development and political change are not confined to non-Western countries. The processes also occur in the West. Two works that include numerous case studies from Western Europe are the eighth volume in the SSRC Studies in the Political Development Series, Charles Tilly, ed., *The Formation of National States in Western Europe** (Princeton: Princeton University Press, 1975); and Gabriel Almond, Scott C. Flanagan, and Robert J. Mundt, eds., *Crisis, Choice, and Change: Historical Studies of Political Development* (Boston: Little, Brown, 1973).

* Available in paperback.

Chapter 11

Political Violence

Images of violence, assassination, war, terrorism, revolution, and death fill our newspapers, magazines, and television news shows. We have all directly or vicariously experienced the trauma of a seemingly violent nation and world. Almost against our wills, we are forced to ask whether man is normally a violent creature. Is our society violent or not? What causes violence? How can we separate pathology from the coercion and force that seem intrinsic to many political activities? What are the costs of allowing groups to engage in violent activities? What are the equally important costs of creating a society where there will be no dissent? Is all violence bad? What is violence?

The potential questions are endless. We will not find completely acceptable answers to many. Nevertheless, most problems center on the place or role of violent activity in politics. Though politics and violence are distinct, politics and a threat of violence are not separable. Political activity, particularly that centered on making basic decisions for society, implies a struggle for authority, which in many countries involves bullets instead of ballots. Even in democratic states there is a real possibility that excluded groups will dissent or even resort to nonrevolutionary violence. Moreover, violence is much more than a political issue. It involves our most fundamental ethical, religious, and moral convictions. Philosophy, sociology, psychology, and economics offer insights into violent behavior. No one view is adequate alone. In this chapter we will examine violence that seeks a fundamental political, social, or economic change. Criminal violence, strikes, riots, and demonstrations—while important—will form only a small part of our discussion.[1]

ON DEFINING VIOLENCE

If violence and politics often mix, what is violence? Immediately we run into many conflicting answers, some based on scholarly disagreement, others on ideological differences. Perhaps the most common meaning emphasizes physical force and aggression that produces personal or property loss, pain, or injury. This is particularly true when there is an intention to injure someone, such as in robbery, rape, murder, assassination, or war. Thus, we rarely talk about an accident as violence even if accompanied by injury. The object of violence is either to control a person, take something from him, punish him, gain power, or otherwise incapacitate the individual. Except in cases of sadism and nonrational behavior, such violence has some purpose whether we agree with it or not.

But violence may involve more than physical assault and punishment. It includes nonphysical assault and psychological manipulation that may leave people more incapacitated than physical assault. In other words, violence is much more than holding a gun to a person's head or threatening his life. Force of this kind is relatively easy to recognize, but it is an incomplete description of violence. Common language, which identifies threats, intimidations, terror, climates of uncertainty, and denial of human dignity as violence, indicates that more than force is involved. Chalmers Johnson has written a commonly accepted definition. Violence is "action that deliberately or unintentionally disorients the behavior of others."[2] It may involve direct physical coercion or it may involve manipulation of the psychological climate in which we exist. Such action prevents people from developing stable expectations about other people. While this definition is somewhat broad, it indicates that more is involved than force. It indicates that social-political stability is dependent on people expecting that others will act in certain, predictable patterns—police, teachers, strangers on the street will not be a threat, but rather will govern their actions by widely accepted rules of conduct. Violence, by instituting force and making

[1] There is a vast literature on the subject of strikes, riots, demonstrations, etc. Some useful sources include *Report of the National Advisory Commission on Civil Disorders* (Washington: U.S. Govt. Printing Office, 1968); *To Establish Justice, to Insure Domestic Tranquility,* Final Report of the National Commission on the Causes and Prevention of Violence (Washington: U.S. Govt. Printing Office, 1969); Louis H. Masotti and Don R. Bower, eds., *Riots and Rebellion: Civil Violence in the Urban Community* (Beverly Hills: Sage, 1968); Thomas Rose, ed., *Violence in America* (New York: Random House, 1969); James A. Geschwender, *The Black Revolt* (Englewood Cliffs, N.J.: Prentice-Hall, 1971).

[2] Chalmers Johnson, *Revolutionary Change* (Boston: Little, Brown, 1966), p. 8.

changes in these patterns of normal activity, makes it difficult, if not impossible, for people to know what to expect (unless they are perpetrating the violence or have come to accept uncertainty as "normal"). This definition also indicates that violence may have a purpose—to change people's values, actions, and habits. Thus; violence, in Johnson's definition, is an important indicator of change.

A third definition of violence is one increasingly connected with the question of poverty and racism. Are political, social, economic deprivations, poverty, and the institutional constraints and structures that support them forms of violence directed against the poor? Have slavery, misery, poor education, discrimination, bad health, and unequal opportunities combined to produce violence against the poor today?[3] This argument has become increasingly popular and would seem to follow from the distinction between purely physical violence and violence as a social and psychological reality.

Political violence is a special, often purposeful, form of violent activity. By political violence we mean the use of force and coercion—restraint, threats, and actual infliction of pain, injury, or deprivation of a desired object—to influence other people, to impose one group's will on another, to influence or take over the decision making structure of society, particularly the government. This influence or takeover may be conducted to benefit the first group politically, socially, or economically. Political violence may be used to punish opponents or simply to express displeasure with current policies without making an effort to alter them in a specific way. Or political violence may involve some higher social purpose, such as reform. In some countries political violence may be an important or major route for achieving political office. Though political violence is usually directed at the government or armed forces, it may have lesser targets, such as businesses, schools, churches, and private associations. Political violence is, therefore, essentially purposeful, even if it contains irrational or pathological elements, great cruelty, and other elements of which we disapprove. Generally pain and injury are the means, not a goal in themselves, although Nazi death camps were an end—destruction of the Jewish people. Political violence is, however, only one way of influencing people. Persuasion, inducement, bribery, appeals to common interests, and simple log-rolling are other means. Political violence is different from these because it embraces any activity that is designed to use force or coercion as the means of enforcing wants, policies, and programs. Political violence

[3] For a negative view of these questions, see Ernest van den Haag, *Political Violence and Civil Disobedience* (New York: Harper and Row, 1972). For a good, brief discussion of different forms of violence, see Newton Garver, "What Violence is," in Thomas Rose, *op. cit.*, pp. 5–13.

ranges from picketing to demonstrations to riots to threats to terrorism to direct revolutionary activities designed to replace one set of decision makers by another. War is a special form of political violence, which must be examined as part of international politics.

A Definitional Caution

All definitions of violence involve some value judgment. In describing violence, language is not neutral. "Violence" is an emotion-charged word, and what we consider as violence will depend partly on our ideology. Labeling an activity violent will depend on how we perceive the purpose of the action, what our moral values are, and what our perception of a need for the action is.[4] Many examples are available. In describing urban violence, commentators often reveal as much about their own values as about the violence they are describing. The term "civil disorder" used by the National Advisory Commission on Civil Disorder in 1968 implies value neutrality. To call the same events a battle, such as the "Battle of Detroit" or the "Battle of Chicago," or to call it a revolution confers on the event a dignity and sense of legitimacy that such terms as riots, mobs, murder, and looters do not convey. To pin one or another label on the same event goes very far in condemning or supporting the event in public opinion.

Every political and social system may be viewed as discriminatory from someone else's point of view. There may be severe disagreement over each other's rights and activities, and people may be willing to use coercion to uphold what they consider to be their rights. Many civil rights' advocates have felt compelled to break the written law in the name of higher values. Some consider these activities as violent attacks on the established order, yet many Americans agree that discrimination is a form of violence against black people. Many revolutionaries, including Thomas Jefferson and George Washington, as well as Fidel Castro and Mao Tse-tung, have been willing to employ force and coercion and have considered their activities legitimate because they felt they were fighting grave injustices. Few Americans consider Jefferson and Washington traitors; we approve of the political system they helped to create. Yet if their revolution had failed they would surely have suffered execution as rebels because the British government and one-third of the colonial population did consider them dangerous revolutionaries.

How we interpret actions will largely determine whether we accept or reject them. This observation, however, does not reduce us to complete relativism about what is or is not legitimate violence. Violent activity, whether mugging, war, or psychological torture, injures people. Pain and

[4] The best single discussion of ideology and violence is Charner Perry, "Violence—Visible and Invisible," *Ethics,* 81 (October, 1970), pp. 1–21.

injury are the irreducible core of violence, regardless of its purposes. We may inquire whether or not that injury was deserved or undeserved, and why we believe as we do. We may ask whether or not the injury was avoidable; whether a particular example of governmental use of force upholds our values or undermines them; whether the group turning to violence has exhausted all of its alternatives in defending its position, or whether it turns to violence as a shortcut to achieving power, and many other questions. We cannot escape the fact that force, coercion, and violence cause pain and injury, regardless of the cause in whose name they are inflicted.

ON THE HISTORY AND FREQUENCY OF POLITICAL VIOLENCE

Political violence is as old as organized society. Aristotle (384–322 B.C.) wrote extensively about revolutions, making the study of political violence one of the oldest aspects of political analysis.[5] Greece partly destroyed itself with communal violence. Assassination and civil war kept Rome in constant flux. Medieval and Renaissance Europe suffered from unremitting conflict, murders, and violence. Modern man has increased the destructiveness of political violence and has transformed it into a mass activity instead of a sport of aristocrats, but we have little to teach our ancestors about political violence.

And yet we are rightly troubled by political violence. There have been hundreds of coups, revolutions, and attempted coups and revolutions and other major examples of widespread violence since World War II.[6] Robert S. McNamara has noted that between 1958 and 1966

> *there were no less than 166 internationally significant outbreaks of violence, each of them specifically designed as a serious challenge to the authority or the very existence of the governments in question. Eighty-two different governments were directly involved . . . only 15 of these 164 significant resorts to violence were military conflicts between two states. . . . At the beginning of 1958 there were 23 prolonged insurgencies going on around the world. As of February, 1966, there were 40.*

[5] Aristotle, *The Politics of Aristotle,* translated by Ernest Barker (New York: Oxford University Press, 1958), Book V, passim.

[6] Isaac Kramnick, "Reflections on Revolution: Definitions and Explanations in Recent Scholarship," *History and Therory,* 11, 1972, pp. 26–63. On p. 29 he notes that you will get widely different figures, depending on what you seek to measure. If you look only at violent changes in government, there were 135 between 1946 and 1965. If you look at major violence, there were more than 1600 examples between 1946 and 1958. See especially Peter Calvert, *A Study of Revolution* (Oxford: Clarendon Press, 1970), pp. 189–194. Here Calvert lists 179 governmental transitions involving assassinations or violence between 1946 and 1969. He did not list attempts that failed or any other widespread violence that failed to remove figures in power.

Delacroix's painting, *Liberty leading the people,* **of the uprising in Paris, July 28, 1830.**

McNamara went on to note that the incidence of violence was increasing all over the world.[7] Since 1966 there have been violent demonstrations, insurrections, terrorist activities, coups or attempted coups, guerrilla wars, and revolutions involving the loss of life in dozens of countries. Among these are Angola, Argentina, Bolivia, Brazil, Cambodia, Canada, Ceylon, Colombia, Ecuador, Egypt, France, Ghana, Greece, Guinea, India, Iraq, Israel, Italy, Japan, Jordan, Laos, Lebanon, Libya, Mexico, Mozambique, Mali, Malaysia, Nigeria, Northern Ireland, Peru, the Philippines, Pakistan, the People's Republic of China, Poland, Portugal, Rhodesia, Spain, the Sudan, Syria, Turkey, Uganda, the Union of South Africa, the United Kingdom, the United States, Uruguay, Vietnam, Venezuela, West Germany, and Yemen.[8]

[7] Robert S. McNamara, *The Essence of Security: Reflections in Office* (New York: Harper and Row, 1968), p. 145.

[8] It is quite popular to call the United States a violent society, and it does experience frequent personal violence. But there has been relatively little direct political violence, although terrorist activities, such as the Ku Klux Klan, aimed at political and economic domination as well as social control. For a discussion of early political violence, see David Grimsted,

CAUSES OF POLITICAL VIOLENCE

As soon as we ask what causes political violence, we are confronted with a vast and contradictory body of ideas that dates back to the ancient Greeks. Some have sought the cause of revolution in economic changes, political motivation, and psychological disturbances. Others, following Crane Brinton, have looked for features common to different revolutions.[9] There are many taxonomies, or classification schemes, of revolutions (such as this chapter), which study political violence by examining the purposes of the actors, the means they employ, and the part of the government or society that they seek to change. Still others, such as Mao Tse-tung, Che Guevara, and Regis Debray, have concentrated on the mechanics of how to bring about a revolution. Some theorists have emphasized broad social, political, and economic movements as the cause of revolution, while others have emphasized micro-theory, looking at individual feelings of frustration and psychological abnormalities. To the basic question of what opens the floodgates of political violence, we have a vast number of different answers, some contradictory.[10]

We may distinguish political, economic, psychological, and sociological explanations.[11] Political causes offer perhaps the oldest explanations. Aristotle maintained that men struggling for equality, for justice, and for property caused revolutions. John Locke (1632–1704) argued that revolutions are caused by the tyrannical behavior of government which, in effect, breaks the social contract and rebels against the people by oppressing them.[12]

Factors such as nationalism, indignation, a sense of oppression, thirst for power, loss or efforts to gain or regain political liberties—while they may have an economic or a psychological component—motivate people's lives and must be considered in any examination of causes. They are not merely manifestations of economics, nor can they be explained solely in psychological terms. Rather, they illustrate that we must pay some attention to the reasons people give for their actions. We must remember that much

[9] Crane Brinton, *The Anatomy of Revolution* (New York: Vintage Books, 1965).

[10] For a fairly complete list of different hypotheses about the causes of domestic political violence, see Harry Eckstein, "On the Etiology of Internal Wars," *History and Theory,* 4 (1964), pp. 133–63.

[11] This distinction is adopted from Kramnick, *op. cit.,* pp. 26–63.

[12] Aristotle, *The Politics,* Book V. Aristotle also looks at states of mind and elite splits. John Locke, *Second Treatise of Government,* edited by Peter Laslett (London: Cambridge University Press, 1967), Chapters 17–19.

"Rioting in its Jacksonian Setting," *American Historical Review,* 77 (April, 1972), pp. 361–97. For a good discussion of the perennial and unanswerable question of whether man is violent, see James C. Davies, "Violence and Aggression: Innate or Not?" *Western Political Quarterly,* 23 (September, 1970), pp. 611–23.

political violence and revolution is purposeful. People often want specific gains and decisions, such as to share power or have exclusive control over the basic decision-making apparatus of their community. Because most political violence is directed toward change in the decision-making structure of society and/or changes in the kind and nature of decisions made, economic and psychological reductionism may miss the fact that the heart of political activity and contests for political control is the right and ability to make basic decisions for society.

Nevertheless, much political violence has an economic component and even an economic cause. While Karl Marx is most commonly associated with the argument that economic conditions and economic change are the root of political violence and revolution, both conservative and liberal theorists have pointed to economic causes of violence. Marx argued that economics is the propelling force and foundation of history, bringing about changes in the political and social superstructure. For Marx, revolution occurred when one type of political system was being replaced by another political system as a result of inevitable economic change. Moreover, capitalism produced intolerable conditions for workers, making their conditions worse or at least increasing the gap between proletariat and bourgeoisie. This gap, coupled with capitalism's dynamic to aggregate thousands of workers together, led to the development of class consciousness which would eventually propel workers to overthrow the capitalist system by violent revolution, substituting the exploited for the exploiters. Political revolution was, therefore, rooted in economic exploitation and misery.

Some commentators have argued, however, that improving, rather than deteriorating, conditions are associated with the commencement of a revolution. Alexis de Tocqueville (1805–1859) noted that the French Revolution occurred during a period of increasing economic prosperity, which triggered hope for more and more rapid improvement. Support for the revolution was greatest in the most prosperous parts of France, indicating that when conditions were improving and people could hope for still better conditions, then revolution occurred.[13] This explanation is particularly popular among theorists examining unrest among black Americans.

James C. Davies has offered a theory that reconciles improving and deteriorating economic conditions.[14] Davies combines the concepts of economic advancement and regression. Political violence and revolution are most likely to occur when a period of real economic advancement is followed by a short but rapid economic reversal or downturn. According to

[13] Melvin Richter, "Tocqueville's Contributions to the Theory of Revolution," in Carl J. Friedrich, ed., *Revolution, Nomos VIII* (New York: Atherton Press, 1967), p. 119.

[14] James C. Davies, "Toward a Theory of Revolution," *American Sociological Review*, 27 (February, 1962), pp. 5–19.

Davies, there is usually a gap between people's expectations and their actual achievements, but as long as this gap is small there will be little or no revolutionary violence. As conditions improve, people's expectations increase. With a sudden downturn in economic advancement, actual conditions deteriorate, creating an "intolerable gap" between what people have come to expect and what they are actually getting. This gap leads to frustration and anxiety because expectations are thwarted and people feel anxious that they may lose the gains they have already made. This anxiety, particularly when the threat of economic loss can be blamed on the government, may lead to violence and/or revolution. The type of violence will be determined by which groups are dissatisfied and what means they have available for expressing their dissatisfaction.

Davies's critics argue that he is too monocausal and deterministic. There are many other causes of frustration besides economic dissatisfaction. These include relative deprivation and downward mobility. Moreover, feelings of affection and legitimacy toward the government and political system, or even bread and circuses, may moderate or rechannel frustration that could lead to aggression. As Davies admits, the paramount example of the nonoccurrence of a violent revolution, as opposed to political violence, during conditions of advance and regression, was the Great Depression of 1929 to the mid-1930s in the United States. Millions were economically ruined, extremist programs gained currency; yet shared values and feelings that the American government was legitimate and was attempting to meet unemployment prevented a violent revolution. This indicates that economic conditions alone are not sufficient to explain the prevalence or absence of political violence or revolution, although in many cases they may provide important clues as to why a particular violent activity occurred.

The inadequacy of political and economic explanations alone has led many scholars to turn to psychological explanations of violence and revolution. This is implicit in Davies' work for he admits that frustration and anxiety are produced by economic changes. What people feel and think about their actual condition is extremely important in determining whether they will engage in violent activities or not. Psychological, or more generally behavioral, analysis is concerned with who engages in violence and why.[15] It is particularly concerned with personality development among leaders, the dynamics of group leadership and membership, and the nature of people who engage in political violence. Perhaps the most popular explanation, particularly for urban riots, is the frustration-

[15] See Erich Fromm, *Escape from Freedom* (New York: Holt Rinehart and Winston, 1941) and Erik Erikson, *Young Man Luther* (New York: Norton, 1958); Ted Gurr, "Psychological Factors in Civil Violence," *World Politics,* 20, (January, 1968), pp. 245–78; Kramnick, *op. cit.* pp. 53–62, and Johnson, *op. cit. passim.*

aggression thesis. This holds that frustration, or the subjective feeling of being deprived of your rightful place in society or of your fair share of its goods, or a growing gap between yourself and others, or the feeling that you are lost and aimless, without guidance or goals, leads to antisocial behavior we term aggression. In other words, because people's values and expectations are unfulfilled, they turn to violence either as a way of fulfilling their wants or at least as a release for their tensions. While this may explain many violent outbursts, it does not explain all of them. It does not tell us why or how conditions were generated that have produced frustration. Moreover, many if not most frustrated people do not engage in violence. They may sublimate or transfer their frustrations to other objects, as in much personal violence in ghettos. Or they may be so repressed that frustration will turn into apathy and dejection. Clearly, the environment in which frustration develops helps to determine the way in which that frustration will express itself. It may result in political action, but whether it will or not depends on social conditions and opportunities, such as leaders willing to aggregate and articulate discontent, opportunities to express it politically, and the feeling that government is the enemy. Frustration, discontent, and even psychological pathology are not enough to produce political violence and revolution, though they may fuel it when other conditions are present.

Sociological analysis has concentrated on viewing society as a system of mutually interacting parts, roles, organizations, institutions, and relations, rather than looking at individuals, economics, or politics as such. It seeks the explanation of political violence in terms of social structure: creation of new classes; elite decay or intransigence; alterations in family structure; or brutalizing conditions of particular political–social systems, such as those found in the urban ghetto. One of the primary examples of this kind of analysis is found in Chalmers Johnson, *Revolutionary Change*. Johnson argues that society is characterized by "homeostatic equilibrium"—the different parts of society are in an interdependent balance with each other. When one part changes, the other parts must change in synchronization with each other. Stability depends on the basic values and institutions of society being in agreement with each other. Viewing society as a system, he assumes that it exists in an environment made up of the economy, moral-religious values, and other systems, which influences and is influenced by the social system. Change can be introduced from one of four sources: value changes occurring spontaneously within the system; value changes being introduced from the environment through propaganda, a new ideology, or missionaries; institutional changes within the system produced by technological innovations; and institutional changes coming from outside the system through trade or conquest. Changes in any one of these areas can produce changes in all the others, as they adapt themselves to each other. Thus, a new philosophy or political ideology may demand institutional changes, such as a new distribution of income or even new governmental structures. If these are forthcoming, society will remain in balance, and there will be no political violence or revolution. If values and institutions do not change in congruence with each other, an increasingly large gap will develop, people will feel frustrated, and violence, even destruction of the system, may result.

Johnson's scheme is quite sophisticated, but it requires a great deal of effort to translate its abstractions into an explanation of a particular revolution or act of political violence. Moreover, it assumes that the normal state of society is one of balance, characterized by gradual and evolutionary change that gives all parts of society time to adjust. We must ask if society is like this. Despite the difficulty of turning Johnson's analysis into concrete description and explanation, it does emphasize one important factor—change. Social, political, and economic change produces dislocations in people's perceptions of the world, as well as in the actual functioning of institutions. This change in turn sets the stage for further change which, if there are weak institutions, excessive demands and value conflicts, may lead to political violence and revolution.

One final type of analysis is worth noting—the attempt to find and explain uniformities in seemingly diverse revolutionary activities. Perhaps the best example is Crane Brinton's *Anatomy of Revolution.*[16] Brinton was concerned with the "great" revolutions: England in the 1640s and 1650s, America in the 1770s and 1780s, France from 1789 to 1815, and Russia from 1917 to the mid 1920s. In studying these events, he and other analysts after him discovered a number of common points. In each of these revolutions there were important structural, economic, and political weaknesses, and economic problems coupled with economic advance for some people who felt cramped and restrained by inefficient governmental machinery. In other words, each of the societies experienced economic advance, but many people felt that governmental neglect, excessive taxation, even stupidity, prevented the advance from moving as rapidly as they felt it should.

In each revolution an important group or groups felt constrained by the system. There were also bitter and complex class antagonisms. It was not simply nobility versus bourgeoisie or bourgeoisie versus proletariat, but complex emotions generated by deep gaps between what groups were getting and what they thought they should be getting (see our discussion of James Davies).

In each revolution studied there was both widespread dissatisfaction and

[16] Brinton, *op. cit.*, pp. 27–66, 250–58 and *passim.*

what Brinton calls "transfer of allegiance" of many of the intellectuals from the government and the dominant political–social values that supported it to other principles and values. This process undermined governmental stability by denying the government legitimacy and chipping away at values that supported it (see our discussion of Chalmers Johnson). Intellectuals teach the young, provide intellectual justification for concrete actions, dream dreams, and may even act as policy advisers. Widespread intellectual alienation from government, particularly when accompanied by adoption of alternative political, social, and economic values, signals the breakdown of the myths and ideologies upon which every society is based and may be an important clue to potential revolutionary occurrences.

In each case the government was too inefficient to handle all the problems it faced. The ruling class became increasingly inept, unwilling or unable to govern, and split within itself. This, coupled with inefficient governmental machinery, has been one of the most frequently commented upon conditions of a prerevolutionary situation. Some observers have gone so far as to argue that elite disintegration is either one of the most important causes of extensive political violence or a precondition for successful revolution. Either someone who can rule will push the old elite out of the way or elite inabilities will make suppression of dissent and violence difficult; this, in turn, encourages more dissent and violence. The success of the February and October revolutions in Russia and Castro's revolution in Cuba were the result more of the incredible stupidity and inefficiency of the regimes they overthrew than of the force and support the revolutionaries commanded.

In each case studied there was growth in agitation before the revolution. Each government suffered a dramatic reversal such as financial breakdown or loss of a war. The actual outbreak of revolutionary violence was triggered by a dramatic outburst of violence, which the government, because of its ineptness, elite splits, and loss of control over the coercive machinery of society, was unable to respond to with sufficient force. Variously called an "accelerator," a "catalytic event," or simply a "trigger," such events simultaneously show the weakness and odium of the regime and act as a catalyst for would-be revolutionaries. This type of event is not the cause of a revolution or of extensive political violence. Rather, it is merely the final point from which pressure that has been building up over a long period of time finally explodes, producing widespread political violence and/or revolution. At this point, the revolutionaries are often uncertain of what their action should be.

In each revolution moderates and the middle class played an important role. As the revolution proceeded, moderates tended to be pushed out of power as the revolution gathered momentum and made wider and wider appeals. Events after the revolution all showed some uniformity. Each revolution experienced a reaction to extremists and terrorist activities. (In the

American Revolution moderates never lost control.) Each revolution achieved greater governmental efficiency. Despite a more efficient government and the eventual return of moderates to power, a revolutionary tradition had a continuing effect on each of the societies, providing a set of values and an ideology that could be appealed to in order to attack or defend current governments.

Brinton noted a number of other uniformities, but these illustrate his main points. They serve to demonstrate that political violence and revolution are not spontaneous, totally unpredictable events. Rather, they rise out of specific cultures, political, social, economic, and psychological phenomena or conditions. Nevertheless, they do reveal some uniformities. Brinton, however, correctly noted that the uniformities are not necessary predictors for political violence today. They were "discovered" only in retrospective analysis. Though they speak to current problems, we must remember that we still do not have any accurate way of measuring how much elite cohesion is necessary to stability as opposed to stifling dissent or even participation. We have not yet developed completely accurate measures of governmental efficiency though we can generally tell when a government is not performing basic functions. Nor have we yet developed accurate measures of support for a government or for general political beliefs and values. We must admit that we do not know all the causes of political violence, nor are we able to spell out all the causes of a particular example of political violence. No single factor, whether political, economic, psychological, or sociological, is enough to explain political violence. Poverty alone is not a cause. Agitation and ideology can only operate if there are grievances that can be manipulated. Relative deprivation and feelings of oppression are factors, but they do not always lead to political violence. Political, economic, and social change set the stage for more change, and if this change is too rapid or destabilizing, it may encourage political violence. Rapid change often portends political violence, but is not an inevitable cause of such violence. Various social and political conditions, such as lack of mobility or too much mobility, a small, closed elite or a large, fragmented elite, class conflict, or inefficient government certainly are associated with revolutionary causation but not in every case. Feelings about the government's legitimacy, the legitimacy of violence, even the honesty or criminality of political leaders are all factors in revolutionary causation but again not in every case. Many causes contribute to political violence, requiring multidisciplinary, cross-national analysis to understand it.

TYPES OF POLITICAL VIOLENCE

In the following discussion we will briefly mention crime and anomie, and then focus on political violence, particularly revolution. We will look at governmental use of force; low levels of political violence in the form of strikes, demonstrations and riots; representational violence; terrorism; and revolutionary violence, distinguishing such violence by technique and purpose. In slighting criminal violence at one end and ignoring international war at the other (though a revolution may in fact be a disguised international war), we are not saying that these do not affect politics. That they do is attested by the "law and order" issue in American, Canadian, and European politics and by the impact of a lost (or won) war in reshaping or expanding political institutions. In the interest of brevity and coherence, we will discuss only domestic political violence.

The following discussion consists of ideal types, not mutually exclusive categories. In the real world distinctions between kinds of violence are more difficult to make. There is often a great deal of overlap, and any particular episode may involve several different kinds of political violence. The Russian Revolution included defeat in a war, a reform coup d'état, a civil war that took on the character of a mass-based revolution, guerrilla war, and international intervention as well as strikes, riots, demonstrations and outright anomic and criminal behavior. While in many cases it may be difficult to distinguish crime from pathology from political violence, we will destroy any chance of understanding political violence if we do not attempt to separate them.

Nonpolitical Violence

Crime and anomie may have an impact on the political system but are not specifically political.

Crime: Definitions of crime have varied widely among different ages, countries, and ideologies. Typical definitions state that it is an act that is morally blameworthy, harmful to individuals and society, and is prohibited by law. To have a crime we must have a prohibition, enforced by the coercive authority and power of the state, against a specific act.[17] However, prohibitions are not constant. At one time witchcraft was a crime. Current controversy in the United States centers on whether homosexual behavior between consenting adults, possession and use of marijuana, or publication of literature describing sexual acts should be considered crimes.

Moreover, most revolutionary activity is considered criminal by the people against whom it is directed. Governments constantly try to label "criminal" those who challenge their authority outside accepted electoral activities, and occasionally will call any dissent, disagreement, or challenge a crime or, as is increasingly evident in the Soviet Union, a mental abnormality. Conversely, people using violence to challenge or defend a govern-

[17] See the brief definition by J. E. Hall Williams in Julius Gould and William L. Kolb, ed. *Dictionary of the Social Sciences* (New York: Free Press of Glencoe, 1964), pp. 147–48.

ment, no matter how base the activity may be—airline hijackings, Nazi death camps, My Lai, Viet Cong extermination of village chieftains, Stalin's youthful bank robberies—will defend their activities as politically necessary. In normal circumstances, however, crime is not a political issue except as to which party or politician is more opposed to it. Crime may, however, be an indicator of the breakdown of social cohesion, which can be a step in the development of revolutionary conditions.[18]

Anomie and Anomic Violence. Anomie is not a political question. But like crime, it may overlap with political violence or indicate that social cohesion and integrative values are disintegrating. Anomie refers to a situation of personal or individual disorientation, when norms or guides to action are either missing or in conflict with each other. In such a situation the individual may have nothing to guide his behavior. When people in such a situation engage in violent activities they rarely have political purposes in mind. Rather, violence may serve to release personal tension, reduce personal disorientation, meet personal problems, and express dissatisfaction with their lives; but it is not directed at specific changes in the political, social, or economic systems. Revolutions and economic change, which often attack established values and norms, may increase anomic behavior.

Governmental Use of Force

All governments attempt to monopolize the use of force. Ideally, governmental use of force would be conceived as a purely nonpolitical and dispassionate dispensation of justice and protection of the innocent.[19] In fact, it is often politically oriented. Certainly the fact that it often protects society and the political system colors it politically. More importantly, many black critics of American society, in addition to neo-Marxists and Marxists, have argued that governmental force is actually violence against the black community and/or the proletariat, designed to keep them in a state of permanent subjugation. The fact that governmental use of force can generate intense controversy illustrates that many people want to limit this power to carefully defined areas. Charges of police brutality indicate that while most people acknowledge the necessity of having police forces, they feel some police either exceed their authority or use more force than most people consider necessary to maintain social stability. The killing of four students by Ohio National Guardsmen at Kent State University on May 4, 1970, illustrates the continuing controversy in American society about the

[18] *The Final Report of the National Commission on the Causes and Prevention of Violence* (Washington: U.S. Government Printing Office, 1969) looks primarily at crime and civil disobedience, not revolutionary violence.

[19] Even here critics have questioned the legitimacy of the manner in which this function is often carried out. See Karl Menninger, *The Crime of Punishment* (New York: Viking Press, 1968).

legitimate and illegitimate uses of force by governmental agencies. Whether you view their deaths as murder or an unpleasant concomitant of maintaining "law and order," they raise the uncomfortable and unanswered question of the role of governmental force in a democratic society.

Whether or not a government's use of force will be considered legitimate by the citizens of that society depends on their perception of threats to their values, ideology, and the government's conformity with established rules and norms. It is a commonplace of politics that most people will allow governments a wider scope of activity in a genuine crisis, war, or national emergency than they will sanction in normal times or periods of tranquility. Moreover, values and ideology determine acquiescence or opposition to governmental use of coercion. While most Americans are agreed on basic political and social values, they often disagree about their implementation. Thus, diagreement over capital punishment (clothed in constitutional terms of whether or not it is a "cruel and unusual punishment"), riot control methods (what is a riot?), and the limits and nature of "legitimate" dissent reveal disagreements over rights, values, and legitimate means of governmental control, *not* whether government should be able to suppress violence or punish criminals. Finally, we measure the legitimacy of government's use of force and coercion by the values of that government. Does it allow dissent or suppress it, even if it calls itself free and democratic? What rights do the accused have? Unfortunately, in most political systems governmental use of coercion, spies, and even terror does not conform to expressed values of freedom and dignity. In many instances similar to those in France during the Algerian revolution, 1954 to 1962, governmental use of violence and revolutionaries' use of violence fed on each other. Inept, clumsy, and unsuccessful employment of force may also make a government illegitimate.

Society is held together by more than force and coercion. Nevertheless, security depends on a governmental monopoly or near monopoly of force. The paramount question is how that force is used, and to what extent governments need means of coercion, not whether that force needs to exist or not.

Political Violence

Demonstrations and Riots

Political violence involves the use of force and coercion to achieve a desired end. There are, however, many gradations of political violence, ranging from strikes, which are widely accepted, mild forms of coercion, to mass-based revolutionary activity that has all the attributes of civil war.

Radical Japanese students, wearing helmets and armed with long bamboo poles, scuffle with riot police near Tokyo International Airport. The occasion was President Ford's visit to Japan in November, 1974.

Peter Calvert distinguishes among public demonstrations, riots, and terrorist activities,[20] which we will treat as an entirely separate category. While public demonstrations and riots may be the beginning of a revolution or used as a revolutionary tactic, they are not necessarily revolutionary acts. Public demonstrations may or may not be violent, but they always carry the implication that they may turn to violence, particularly if their demands are not met or if there is a brutal effort to repress them.

It is difficult to establish when a demonstration turns into a riot, but the dividing line seems to be widespread, unsystematic, and uncontrolled violence. In weak political systems riots carry with them the possibility of overthrowing the government. This has happened on a number of occasions in Latin America and almost took place in France in May, 1968, when student demonstrations in Paris touched off demonstrations, strikes, and riots by students and workers throughout the country. France was probably

[20] Peter Calvert, "Revolution: The Politics of Violence," *Political Studies,* 15 (February, 1967), p. 4 and Calvert, *op. cit.,* pp. 21–4.

spared a revolution because the students and workers did not systematically make common cause; there was no obvious leadership to assume command; and the police and army remained neutral or loyal to the government. In the United States demonstrations and riots by students have tended to be nonrevolutionary, although political.[21]

Demonstrations and riots are complicated by the fact that governments may encourage them for their own purposes or tolerate them as an efficient means of controlling political opponents or of letting unrepresented people vent their anger. "Church and king" mobs in England at the beginning of the French Revolution coerced English liberals and radicals while at the same time they organized mass support for the prosecution of war against revolutionary France. In France during the May, 1968, violence pro-government demonstrations revealed a widespread desire to maintain the de Gaulle regime in power or at least to avoid a civil war.

Representational Violence[22]

Representational violence refers to the conscious use of force or coercion as a way of presenting a group's problems and demands. This occurs when normal channels to bring grievances or demands to the attention of relevant elites are blocked or do not exist. Lacking direct elite access, often the disenfranchised can only present their demands through public demonstrations. They use direct action to articulate what they consider legitimate demands. To be effective, however, such actions usually carry with them the veiled threat of further and more intensive violence if the original request is not met. Representational violence does not attack the state. It demands that elites or the state include groups or issues previously excluded from participation or consideration. It may also demand that government actually implement its values or perform its duties. Representational violence aims at meeting demands, at gaining meaningful access to the system, or at actual inclusion of unrepresented groups within the political, social, and economic systems. Such demands may look revolutionary to people within the system. If they are met, they may change or enlarge the system in some fundamental way. Nevertheless, revolution is not the purpose of representational violence.

Unlike the violence we have discussed previously, the term "representational" refers to the purposes or ends of the violence. Unlike mobs and

[21] For an excellent analysis of the demonstration of power capabilities that could lead to extensive political violence, see Charles W. Anderson, *Politics and Economic Change in Latin America* (Princeton, N.J.: van Nostrand, 1967), pp. 97–101. He distinguishes demonstrations, general strikes, and symbolic terror, as well as various levels of military force and democratic electoral processes.

[22] Martin C. Needler, *Political Development in Latin America: Instability, Violence and Evolutionary Change* (New York: Random House, 1968), pp. 47–9.

demonstrations it is an end, not purely a means to an end. Though representational violence may contain anomic elements or lead to revolutionary violence, it is a distinct and useful way of looking at some political violence.

Moreover, mob action may be an effective control on elites that is at least tolerated by the government. This was true for eighteenth-century America and England. There was endemic nonrevolutionary violence in eighteenth and early nineteenth-century England. It cropped up everywhere, in cities and countryside. Violence was virtually a traditional control over elite activities. "Collective bargaining by riot" frequently released pent-up social pressures among the poor. It was common, even accepted, and was often the only method the poor had to voice their grievances. This violence took many forms, ranging from hunger riots to organized machine breaking. Often violence was well organized, with the poor setting or enforcing customary prices on food, forcing wage increases, and even collecting and paying out money for products. Riots and other forms of violence were, in fact, the most effective way for the socially, politically, and economically disenfranchised to articulate demands.[23]

In nineteenth-century England the great Chartist movement which, between 1838 and 1848, organized hundreds of thousands of English workers into massive demonstrations and gathered several million signatures for petitions, was designed to achieve universal adult male suffrage and a reorientation of parliamentary concerns toward problems of the poor. In the United States Shays' Rebellion in 1786 and the militant section of the women's suffrage movement employed varying degrees of violence to represent their cause before the public, change hated laws, and achieve actual inclusion within the American political system. While much student unrest during the 1960s and 1970s had anomic overtones, it can only be understood as representational violence since students considered that they were protesting injustices that could not be removed by other means.

Although the United States has a long and often brutal history of racial violence, much of the black response has been representational in nature. The National Association for the Advancement of Colored People (NAACP) has employed almost exclusively legal and constitutional protest through the courts and in lobbying legislators. Crossing the threshold toward the hint of political violence, the Southern Christian Leadership Conference (SCLC) has employed mass demonstrations and organized sit-ins and civil disobedience to protest treatment of black people. (It has also organized

[23] For America see Grimsted, *op. cit.*, p. 362; for England see E. J. Hobsbawm and George Rudé, *Captain Swing* (New York: Random House, 1968), pp. 16–18; and R. B. Rose, "Eighteenth Century Price Riots and Public Policy in England," *International Review of Social History*, 5 (1961), pp. 275–92.

self-help programs and engaged in legal cases.) When we talk of black violence, however, we often talk of ghetto violence: Watts in 1965; Detroit, Washington, D.C., and Newark in 1966; Chicago, Washington, and Baltimore in 1968; and Hartford, Connecticut, in 1969. Here the situation is much more complex. It is true that frustration, looting, desire to get back at "whitey," easing of personal tension, and simply letting off steam were important elements in these instances of violence. A vast number of causal factors can be and have been offered to explain and analyze this violence, no one of which is a complete answer. Representational violence is also a partial explanation. To the extent that many participants in the disorders felt they were forcing the rest of America to take notice of their problems, that this violence was one way to insure that government would focus its attention on ghetto problems, even on such mundane matters as garbage collection and street lighting, and to the extent that the violence has helped to remove obstacles to black people entering into all parts of the economy and politics, the ghetto disorders may be partially viewed as a form of representational violence. There is a noticeable shift toward electoral politics within the system even if the purpose is to change the system; we need only look at the recent election of a small number of black mayors and legislators, Bobby Seale's efforts to run for mayor in Oakland, California, and the Black Panthers' breakfast program for ghetto children. This shift also indicates that most of the violence was not revolutionary.

Terrorism

In the last several years we have experienced many examples of terrorist activities: terror and counterterror in Indochina; the IRA in Northern Ireland; the Lod Airport massacre in May, 1972, when 26 people were killed

The scene on August 11, 1976, after pro-Palestinian guerillas exploded bombs at the Yesilkov Airport, Istanbul, Turkey, killing four persons.

and 76 wounded; the murder of Israeli athletes at the Munich Olympic games in September, 1972; the killing of 16 Israeli hostages at a school in 1974; a continual parade of skyjackings, kidnapings, and assassinations of foreign representatives. Terrorism involves destruction of property and/or the elimination of people in what appears to be a random manner. It can be employed as a tool of opposition or a tool of oppression. In Hitler's Germany and Stalin's Soviet Union the government deliberately fostered fear to fragment the population, making it easier to control people. Terror creates feelings of fear and anxiety that divide the individual from people around him so that he feels there is no one he can trust. In terrorist activities there is no effort to distinguish the "guilty" from the "innocent," civilians from soldiers. All who are not open supporters of the terrorists are potential targets. As Hitler and Stalin proved, even fanatical followers were not safe from elimination, show trials, and execution. Controlling the state's repressive machinery, they could prevent the ensuing anxiety from developing into open opposition or revolution.

Terrorism, whether it is a prerevolutionary act, part of government policy, or part of a revolutionary strategy, generally has a political purpose. It is more than pathology even if it is sometimes pathological. Thomas Perry Thornton has defined terrorism as *"a symbolic act designed to influence political behavior by extranormal means, entailing the use or threat of violence."*[24] Thornton explained these terms, and a little elaboration here will illustrate the political nature of terrorist activities.

1. "A symbolic act." Terrorism is designed to show the relative impotence of the government and to demonstrate the ability of terrorist groups to disrupt normal activities and kill opponents at will.[25] It can be a token or symbolic act to convey a broader meaning than the act itself. Thus, the destruction of mailboxes or public monuments and selective assassination may damage or inconvenience society, but generally terrorists see such action more as an effective way of protesting society and bringing public attention to their cause than as a direct means to gain power.

2. Terrorists generally try to influence political behavior. All terrorists have some purpose, and generally this purpose is at least remotely political—to influence political behavior in a way beneficial to the terrorist cause. All terrorist activity is not directly political however. Particularly when the cause is as remote or vague as "world revolution," terrorist activities may be designed to salve the impatience of terrorist groups or to give them the feeling or myth that they are actually pursuing a worthwhile

[24] Thomas Perry Thornton, "Terror as a Weapon of Political Agitation," in Harry Eckstein, ed., *Internal War: Problems and Approaches* (Glencoe: Free Press of Glencoe, 1964), p. 73.

[25] See Anderson, *op. cit.*, p. 99 where he notes that occasionally violence is used in Latin America to damage or destroy symbols of governmental authority without any effort to injure anyone or to destroy major property holdings.

aim. Moreover, terrorists' political aims may be considered criminal by society at large or at least by those against whom the violence is directed. In the Arab-Israeli struggle each side considers the others' terror and retaliation criminal, just as the North Vietnamese labeled American bombings criminal and their own guerrilla activities patriotic.

All analysts agree that one of the primary aims of terrorist activity is to disorient people's behavior (see Johnson's definition of violence above). For those challenging an incumbent regime the purpose of this disorientation is to create a feeling of exposure to danger and normlessness, which undermines the values, symbols, and institutions that tie people to the regime. Terrorism may frighten people away from supporting an incumbent government and demonstrate that safety and a set of values that will reintegrate the individual into a recognizable community can be found only through support of the terrorist organization. The primary political purpose of terrorism is, therefore, to strip people of their loyalties to existing governments, values, and institutions in preparation for undermining the government toward the final step of creating new men and structures fashioned after the terrorists' ideals.

This creation of new men is one of the reasons for terrorism by totalitarian governments. Random violence, knocks in the night, torture, prison and labor camps, job insecurity, and secret police all fragment the population, cutting people off from friends and institutions, making them distrustful. This makes opposition or any non-regime-sanctioned organization difficult if not impossible. The regime then offers rewards to people who support it. Through ideology, mass parades and rallies, sports events, and the promise of a better future it tries to offer people something in which they can find a home, friends, values, purpose, and trust; in turn the people will support the government. Disorientation is also the goal of governmental terror in nontotalitarian regimes, but here the terror is aimed at supporters and potential supporters of revolutionary organizations. During the Algerian war Algerian revolutionaries and the French government each employed terrorist tactics against the other. The same was true of the conflict in Southeast Asia. Terror became a weapon on both sides designed to deprive the opposition of potential support while frightening people into neutrality or active support for those employing terror. Terrorism may also be a tool by which a dominant minority, such as whites in South Africa, or representatives of a dominant majority, such as the Ku Klux Klan, attempt to maintain their social, economic, and political position. In such cases terror may be enforced by law through unequal treatment and discriminatory legislation or it may be informally condoned by those charged with implementing the law. The purpose of such "private" terrorism, whether it is lynching, beatings, or deprivation of jobs and education, is the same as "public" terrorism—to keep a group in a state of fear and anxiety which will prevent its members from organizing or rebelling.

Terrorism may, therefore, be understood as an aimless response to confusion and disorientation, as the beginnings of a revolutionary movement, particularly to advertise the movement and generate enthusiasm for it among would-be supporters, as a revolutionary tactic, and as a counter-revolutionary tactic. It may also be an effective instrument for physically eliminating opposition elements and prominent personalities—doctors, village leaders, businessmen. This action physically weakens the opposition and symbolically demonstrates the opposition's weakness and inability to protect its supporters. Bombed and twisted aircraft and mutilated bodies on prominent display serve this purpose. Terrorists, however, must be careful to avoid alienating the broad population, for then people may turn on them. Too much terror, particularly against potential supporters, may be counterproductive. Perhaps this is one reason for the almost universal observation that terrorism is a weapon of the weak. When insurgents or the government gain support, the stronger opponent decreases its terrorist activities. Conversely, when one side sees its support slipping it is often tempted to increase its terrorist activities.

Electoral participation and peaceful demonstration are not terrorist tools. Rather, the terrorist's purpose is to disrupt society deliberately. Force and coercion—creating a climate of uncertainty and fear—are the means. Assassination, particularly in a flamboyant manner; indiscriminate bomb throwing; seemingly random killing; physical mutilation and torture; kidnaping; destruction of highly visible property; and extreme statements that evidence no regard for life, either for that of the terrorist or his targets, are the most common tools of terrorism. Quite often terrorism becomes rational use of the irrational. It may benefit terrorists to appear irrational in their dedication to destruction. If your opponent appears to place no regard on the consequences of his act to himself, you may be tempted to meet his demands out of fear that he will destroy both you and himself. Seemingly irrational threats may lead rational men to pay close attention to terrorists or extortionists, to give them what they want, although this may backfire if people decide to relieve their tension by eliminating the terrorist. The seemingly cruel and senseless murder of tourists at Lod airport in Israel in 1972 may actually have been planned to appear irrational in order to strike fear among Israel's supporters. In this case the terrorists may have wanted to focus world attention on their cause, frighten tourists from visiting Israel, provoke Israel into a counterattack that would condemn its leaders in world eyes, and to shake its confidence and pride.[26]

[26] Edmond Taylor, "The Terrorists," *Horizon,* 15 (Summer, 1973), p. 59.

Terrorism is a two-edged sword that can destroy both terrorists and their victims. Moreover, it can leave a feeling of bitterness and alienation in a community for generations. As a political weapon it is not sufficient in itself to achieve the terrorists' aims, nor is it sufficient to overthrow a government. For that we must turn to revolution.

Revolutionary Violence

> Ye sons of France, awake to glory . . .
> Shall hateful tyrants mischief breeding,
> With hireling hosts, a ruffian band,
> Afright and desolate the land,
> While peace and liberty lie bleeding.
> To arms, to arms, ye brave
> The avenging sword unsheath.
> March on! march on!
> All hearts resolved on liberty or death.

Nearly two centuries after it was written, *La Marseillaise* still stirs our emotions with its call to revolutionary fervor. In a few lines it captures the romantic revolutionary ethos in an appeal to patriotism, denigration of the tyrants, hirelings, ruffians, and probably foreigners who are different from true patriots, therefore dangerous, perhaps criminal. It claims that the patriots are only defending the country, not causing violence; it promises a better world through cathartic but legitimate violence; and it is a stirring tune that arouses the emotions.

La Marseillaise, images of liberty storming the barricades, the notion that evil can be liquidated and the good society created at one stroke have dominated popular tradition concerning revolution. At the other extreme people have condemned revolution as unnecessary, waged only by selfish and bloodthirsty men. The truth lies somewhere in between. Revolution can be a messy, dirty affair. Evil does not necessarily disappear with one swipe at reaction's head. Change is often slow. We are not playing games but are dealing with people's lives, the structure and fate of societies, states, and perhaps of international society itself. On the other hand, much good has come from revolutions. We like to think that the American Revolution was legitimate, justifying itself through the creation of a free and democratic society. People in China, the Soviet Union, Mexico, Turkey, Algeria, and France think the same about *their* revolutions. The notion of written constitutions and widespread suffrage were invented during the English Revolution of the 1640s. Clearly, we are dealing with a complex phenomenon that defies any single-minded approach.

When discussing revolution, we immediately run into the problem that there are no exact and unequivocal definitions. We do not even have

North Vietnamese tank, flying Vietcong flag, enters Saigon on April 30, 1975.

agreement about what constitutes a revolution. To Hannah Arendt there were no real revolutions before the eighteenth century because revolution to her implies a search for freedom and an attempt to create a new society, a new order of things. To Manfred Halpern a revolution "is any action, which transforms the political order to transform society." For Isaac Kramnick, revolution involves change from one great set of organizing social principles to another set. For Chalmers Johnson, revolution is a conscious, structural change employing violence to bring about that change.[27] For some it is any illegal effort to change government; for others revolution must bring about widespread social changes. Many theorists make a distinction between rebellions, which do not attempt to change the class that rules or the basic values of society, and revolutions. Many distinguish coups d'état from revolutions. The list is almost endless, but these few definitions illustrate some areas of disagreement.

Revolution covers many different actions, from peasant uprisings to civil wars. To account for this we will call a revolution any action, using or threatening violence, that attempts to or succeeds in removing the present

[27] Hannah Arendt, *On Revolution* (New York: Viking Press, 1965), pp. 2, 21ff.; Manfred Halpern, "The Revolution of Modernization in National and International Society," in Friedrich, *op. cit.*, p. 187; Kramnick, *op. cit.*, p. 34; Johnson, *op. cit.* p. 57; Lawrence Stone, "Theories of Revolution," *World Politics*, 18 (January, 1966), pp. 160–64.

holders of political authority and replacing them with new persons or programs more to the liking of those using or threatening to use violence. This definition focuses on the political nature of revolution as an attempt to replace one set of incumbents with another set through the use of violence. Every political revolution includes or threatens violence, but all violence is not revolutionary. For the moment we are ignoring different kinds of revolutions, different purposes, and different methods of eliminating those who already hold positions of power in order to focus on the point that lies at the heart of our concept of revolution: overthrow of a government. The purpose of all revolution is some variety of governmental change. We may distinguish between revolutions by the means they employ to replace the government and the goals they seek. Thus we will link both coups d'état and guerrilla movements because both direct a violent blow against government. As with all political violence we must avoid a completely inflexible distinction between types of coups and revolutions because quite often a particular event will manifest elements of several types of political violence or there may be alternation between one and another type.

The coup d'état.[28] The coup d'état is a technique for taking over a government, for seizing power from above instead of involving the masses. In itself it tells us nothing about the purposes of those who employ coups. The coup d'état is a sudden, forceful change or alternation of one ruling group by another. Usually, the coup is carried out by those who are already in a position of power and trust, and who have access to the means of coercion and levers of power in a society. The higher their power the greater the chance of success. The coup tends to be sudden and unpredictable, based on small numbers of armed men at the center of power. Because it is secret and involves small numbers, it can be very dangerous for the participants.

A successful coup requires a number of things:

1. The first requirement is secret, careful planning. It must be secret because any hint of preparation would lead to the conspirators' fall from power and possibly the loss of their lives. Further, because small numbers are involved, they must be carefully placed and ready to move at the correct moment. Many coups have failed because of poor timing. Leaks and poor timing, which give incumbents time to prepare, will prevent most coups from succeeding.
2. Coups work best against highly centralized governments, with a single seat of power that can, in fact, be seized. Federal systems,

[28] For an interesting "how to do it" study, see Edward Luttwak, *Coup d'Etat: A Practical Handbook* (Greenwich, Conn.: Fawcett, 1969). See also David C. Rapaport, "Coup d'Etat: the View of the Men Firing Pistols," in Friedrich, *op. cit.*, pp. 53–74.

particularly as in the United States, where fifty state governors control sizable military forces in the form of the National Guard and where Congress has much independent power, make poor candidates for coups. If all power and authority radiate from one center, and people are accustomed to looking to that center for authority and leadership, it will be easier to seize that center than if real power were divided among competing branches or centers of government.

3. The conspirators must know what the sympathies of the armed forces are. In the typical coup the vast bulk of armed forces do not become involved. Both civilian and military conspirators must know if other military commanders will act against them, acquiesce in the coup, or be unable to act even if they wished. Again, secrecy and proper timing are of the utmost importance for success. Moreover, it is generally more important to control or neutralize the army than naval or air force units which, by their nature, find it difficult to use force to intervene in politics.
4. The conspirators must be fairly certain that there will be no foreign intervention. In the 1960s in a number of African states former colonial rulers were invited to put down military mutinies. The fate of the Dominican Republic in 1965 illustrates the danger of foreign intervention against would-be revolutionaries. Generally speaking, the larger a country is, the less likely it is that intervention will occur.
5. A passive population is probably necessary. Mass opposition can destroy most coups, particularly if it becomes a prod for the bulk of the uncommitted armed forces to intervene against the conspirators.
6. There should be a low level of political legitimacy in the country. If people are hostile, indifferent, and apathetic to the government, there is more likelihood that a coup will succeed. Coups are almost impossible when directed against a highly popular government, but we have no measure of the degree of support necessary to forestall a coup. Moreover, in countries that do not have a long tradition of electoral rotation in office, large numbers of people may see nothing illegitimate in shooting their way into office. The best guarantee against coups seems to be a long tradition of electoral rotation in office, plus a high degree of public support for the form of government. Unfortunately, this is not the case in most countries. Since World War II more than half the countries of the world have experienced coups. Syria holds the current record for successful coups—nine.

In some countries electoral legitimacy is very low. Either elections take place very infrequently or they are only tentative demonstrations of support, not binding decisions. Because of this some writers have argued that coups may be a functional equivalent of elections in that they insure rotation in office. While there is an element of truth in this, coups are extraordinary, illegal in every country, dangerous for both plotters and those in power, and offer fewer guarantees than elections (where possible and meaningful) that they will be concerned with the wants and needs of the population. Coups have no mass support even if widespread discontent encourages the conspirators to act. They depend on secrecy and force. By their nature they raise the question of political legitimacy. They can undermine political legitimacy, agreement on basic issues, and even simple administration of government.

But coups do occur. The coup itself is merely a means or a particular style of overthrowing governments. As with all violence that overthrows government, the actual seizure of power may not be the really important event, despite its profound political, legal, and moral implications. Seizure of power merely releases other forces. The really important question is what do successful conspirators do with their new position. What do they do with power once they have it? One answer to this question is to distinguish palace coups, reform coups, and revolutionary coups.[29] While "coup" refers to the means by which power is seized, "palace," "reform," and "revolutionary" refer to the goals or purposes of the seizure of power—they answer what the successful conspirators do with power once they have it.

Palace coups. Palace coups refer to conspiratorial and potentially violent changes of leaders, not policies. They generally occur in countries with a small, powerful elite, where the bulk of the population is excluded from or apathetic about politics. Incumbents change; policies generally do not. Though there may be a rather thorough redistribution of governmental rewards, few if anyone outside the circle of conspirators and their supporters benefit from the change. Often the successful conspirators will argue that their purpose was to "protect the constitution" or "guarantee good government," but often their major ambition is personal motivation, minor changes, and the more successful implementation of agreed-on policies, not any fundamental change in policies, beneficiaries of governmental programs, nor ideology. Usually such palace coups are carried out with a minimum of violence. Incumbent legitimacy is often low, requiring little violence to topple those in office, and the conspirators must expect that they too may one day be the target of a coup. It is palace coups, with their generally low level of violence and reshuffling of personnel without

[29] This distinction is based on Samuel P. Huntington, *Changing Patterns of Military Politics* (New York: Free Press of Glencoe, 1962), pp. 32–40; Raymond Tanter and Manus Midlarsky, "A Theory of Revolution," *Journal of Conflict Resolution,* 11 (September, 1967), p. 265.

fundamental policy changes, that encourage some analysts to conceptualize coups as the equivalent of elections.

In the nineteenth and twentieth centuries palace coups by those already near the center of power became a popular means of changing governments. Examples include most Latin American countries in the nineteenth century, as various factions often labeled "liberal" or "conservative" battled for control of government; France under Louis Napoleon; and many Asian and African states today. In the last 25 years it has become increasingly difficult to label a particular coup a palace coup because successful conspirators have felt forced by increasing mass expectations to broaden benefits to a wider group than the conspirators themselves. Nevertheless, many coups have occurred which, in fact, have produced few widespread changes. Ghana, Vietnam, Cambodia, Syria, and Argentina have all experienced such coups. Perhaps even the ouster of Premier Khrushchev of the Soviet Union in October, 1964, may be considered such a coup. With increases in at least the myth of popular participation and the growing feeling that coups or revolutions can be justified only if the mass of the people eventually benefit, purely palace coups are becoming increasingly rare.

Reform coups. With an increasing emphasis on economic development and ideological purity, more and more successful conspirators feel compelled to justify their coup in terms of mass benefits and/or increasing national pride and integration. Many conspirators genuinely hope to improve the lot of their countrymen, and some have succeeded in actually helping to create an environment and programs beneficial to the masses. Reform coups are often program or action oriented. The successful conspirators have a set of ideas and perhaps policies they will attempt to implement, though often without mass support or mass organizations. Such coups bring reform from above where policy decisions are imposed on the nation by self-appointed leaders who "understand" the real needs of their country. They will often attempt to meet these needs through technocratic leadership. Thus, they may condemn politics, arguing it is slow and cumbersome, that politics condemn the nation to inept leadership and compromise while the real problems go unmet. They often emphasize economic growth, limited economic gains to keep the population contented, and nationalism. Generally, reform coups promise improvement but do not attempt widespread social, economic, or political change, though they may help set the stage for these. Samuel Huntington has noted that reform coups are often followed by conservative coups, which moderate reform programs.[30]

A good example of a modern reform coup oriented toward economic

[30] Huntington, *op. cit.*, pp. 33–6.

development and nationalism occurred in Peru in October, 1968, when a military junta overthrew the government of President Fernando Belaunde Terry, which had been elected in 1963 after a coup in 1962.[31] The new government called itself revolutionary, and many of its policies aimed at basic changes, but they were largely economic changes, imposed from the top down that did not attempt basic political and social transformation. Peruvian military leaders see themselves as having a mission to develop Peru. Political dissent, political parties, mass organization, and popular participation are not part of the program. Though this economic modernization is firmly based in capitalism, the government is attempting to "guide" private investment into desired areas such as mining and manufacturing, reduce dependence on imports and foreign investment, reform the fiscal system, and encourage agrarian reform. Accompanying this effort to increase production and expand industrialization, the new government engaged in a form of selective nationalization of foreign owned assets, which is extremely popular with many Peruvians, while avoiding total nationalization. Another coup took place in 1975. The new rulers promised to continue reform.

An extremely important variant of the reform coup, one that borders on the revolutionary coup, is the overthrow of a government to install wider participation and reform, or a coup to create a workable government. Venezuela and France provide examples of both. In January, 1958, political violence and military opposition in Venezuela ousted Perez Jimenez who had himself come to power through a coup. The resulting election in December, 1958, which was one of the few honest elections in Venezuela's history, brought Romulo Betancourt to the presidency. This was followed by elections in 1963, 1968, and 1973, the first time in Venezuelan history that there had been successive honest elections. Although Venezuela still has numerous economic and political problems, and the military is extremely important in domestic politics, the country is on its way to establishing a system that has widespread economic and political participation.

Nineteen-fifty-eight was also a fateful year for France. The Fourth French Republic, which had been established after World War II, was increasingly incapable of governing. War in Algeria was tearing apart the French people. There was widespread apathy and fear that France was headed for disaster. In May, 1958, Charles de Gaulle came to power in what amounted to a virtual coup. He had widespread support from the army, parts of the left and right, and from many French citizens, though all for different

[31] James F. Petras and Robert La Porte, Jr., *Cultivating Revolution: the United States and Agrarian Reform in Latin America* (New York: Random House, 1971), pp. 253–330; Jane S. Jaquette, "Revolution by Fiat: The Context of Policy-Making in Peru," *Western Political Quarterly*, 25 (1972), pp. 648–66.

reasons. Under de Gaulle a new constitution was written, a new republic created, and the bloody Algerian war ended with complete independence for Algeria. Under de Gaulle's constitution more power was concentrated in the president, and it became more difficult to overthrow the prime minister in the Parlement. De Gaulle survived an attempted coup led by four French army generals in Algeria in April, 1961, and extensive riots in May, 1968, only to retire in 1969 after losing a national referendum. De Gaulle's assumption of power in 1958 and his subsequent election to the presidency ended a disastrous war and helped set France back onto the road of national integration, renewed pride in the country and government which, in fact, could govern.

Revolutionary coups. Revolutionary coups aim at the seizure of power in order to achieve a widespread or total reorganization of the political, social, and economic systems of a society. They are not always easily separated from reform coups. Perhaps the main distinction lies in the means of enforcing social-political reorganization and, to a lesser extent, in ideology. The major examples of revolutionary coups have often generated violence, opposition, and even civil war after the initial seizure of power. The successful conspirators have sought such major changes that other groups saw more value in resistance than in acquiescence to change. In the case of Communist and Fascist revolutionary coups, ideology has been very important in providing justification for the coup and both justification and subsequent models for societal reorganization. In England, Turkey, and Egypt, however, ideology developed during and after the efforts to achieve societal reorganization. In addition reform coups may grow revolutionary; sometimes moderate reformers are pushed into revolutionary policies by the need to appeal for popular support to maintain their position or by the logic and momentum of events pushing them into more extreme positions. This occurred to the English Parliament during the English Revolution of the 1640s, to the Egyptian army officers who removed King Farouk in 1952, and to the young Turkish reformers at the beginning of the twentieth century. Moreover, revolutionary coups are relatively rare probably because most people who want fundamental changes in society and politics are outside the main center of power and cannot easily make use of the coup d'état. Lenin's seizure of power in Petrograd in 1917 and the Communist seizure of power in Prague, Czechoslovakia, in 1948 have many of the characteristics of the coup that aimed at total revolution.[32] The Japanese military's acquisition of power in the 1930s and Hitler's rise to power in 1933, while fulfilling many of the outward signs of legality, amounted to coups that aimed at widespread political, military, and social reorganization. Finally, coups can occur within revolutions. This happened with

[32] Rapaport in Friedrich, *op. cit.*, p. 56.

Pride's Purge during the English Civil War, in the French Revolution, in Algeria in 1965, and in Portugal in 1974.

The coup, therefore, is a very popular technique for seizing power. What successful conspirators do with their power depends on their ideology and the opportunities and difficulties they face. Further, many coups do not fit the distinction among palace, reform, and revolutionary. Some have elements of two or even all three, as events propel the conspirators to alter their plans. Some aim only at ending impasses in government, removing obstacles to change, or ending growing corruption in government, as the Turkish army coup of May, 1960, attempted. Finally, coups may overturn reasonably popular or radical governments, which may or may not be economically efficient, in the hope of returning to more conservative principles such as happened in Brazil in 1964, in Ghana in 1966, and in Chile in 1973, when President Allende, the first freely elected Marxist was murdered.

Whether or not conspirators turn to a coup instead of mass-based revolution will depend on a number of questions. How close are the conspirators to the center of power? If they are close, they may choose a coup or the seizure of power from above. If they are far from the center of power or face an united elite, they may turn to mass-based revolution and guerrilla war, gradually chipping away at governmental support and building their own support. Such tactics, however, take considerably longer than coups and generally involve more violence.

Mass-based Revolution

In the study of political violence the most common question is, what is a revolution? How can we distinguish it from other types of widespread political violence? Most contemporary commentators emphasize that revolution involves widespread political violence aimed at removing the government. It aims at fundamental transformation of the government, political and economic systems, and social structure. To avoid the question of how widespread violence and subsequent changes must be to qualify calling a particular event a revolution, we will examine mass-based revolution in a way similar to our discussion of the coup d'état, emphasizing mass-based revolution as a technique, not merely a result of violence. As with coups, such revolutions may have different purposes, ranging from economic development to democratization to creation of a socialist commonwealth. The most important distinguishing characteristic is mass participation in the effort to overthrow a government. Unlike the coup d'état, large numbers of people who are effectively outside the basic decision-making process engage in violence to remove a government and replace it with another. Although they are usually led by a dedicated elite who may on occasion manipulate the mass of people for their ends, the mass revolution is characterized by its being made by the relatively powerless. It is revolution from the bottom up. Mass participation, as a key to revolution, goes back to the American Revolution of the 1770s.

Since mass-based revolutions involve an assault on the political system from the outside by large numbers, they must be organized for greatest effect. This goes beyond the creation of an effective fighting force to creation of values and ideals that will justify suffering and deprivation in the name of a cause. In short, mass-based revolutions require an ideology. There must be some set of ideas and ideals that can explain to people why they should participate in the dangerous business of revolution and that can promise them a better future. In seventeenth-century England the ideals fashioned modern liberalism: constitutionalism; individual rights, particularly religious freedom; greater economic liberty; and limited government. In the American and French Revolutions liberalism coupled with increasingly vocal demands for wider political participation. Throughout the nineteenth century in France, Germany, Italy, Austria, Poland, and Russia demands for greater political participation merged with increasing demands for a better economic–social distribution, and eventually the end of capitalism either through cooperative and socialist evolution or Communist revolution. In the twentieth century some variant of Marxism, often coupled with nationalism or the desire to set up strong, independent states, has proved to be one of the most potent sources of revolutionary ideology. In Russia from 1917 to 1921 and in China from 1927 to 1949 they combined to produce two of the greatest and most far-reaching revolutions in history. In Turkey starting in 1908 and in Mexico from 1910 to 1920 nationalism combined with demands for wider participation and limited social–economic redistribution to create massive revolutionary potential that helped force these countries into the twentieth century. Particularly in Mexico the revolution has provided an ideology of development, a potent image of what Mexico can become, and a rallying standard for national integration. In many of the developing states nationalism, occasionally combined with varying degrees of socialism, helped undermine the status, if not the actual power, of colonial powers such as England, France, and Belgium. In most newly independent states the transfer of power from colonial rulers occurred peacefully. In Vietnam and Algeria it occurred only after long and bloody wars. In Angola and Mozambique Portugal's effort to retain possession of what it considered to be integral parts of Portugal helped lead to revolution at home.

Ideology is, therefore, an important part of any revolution because it provides justification for destroying the old order and models for creating a new order. As models for future revolutions, the French and Russian Revolutions produced vast amounts of revolutionary ideology.[33] In a very real

[33] Carl Leiden and Karl M. Schmitt, *The Politics of Violence: Revolution in the Modern World* (Englewood Cliffs, N.J.: Prentice-Hall, 1968), pp. 97–100.

sense Karl Marx (1818–1883) helped to bridge the ideological gap between these two revolutions. Deeply influenced by the revolutions of 1789, 1848, and 1871, Marx attempted to synthesize a theory of history which, though based on economic determinism, saw political revolution as essential to real progress. Marx argued that industrialization had created a new, urbanized, industrial proletariat, which was destined to destroy capitalism through violent revolution. Revolution would overthrow the old social–political order, which was based on private ownership of the means of production, and create a totally new order based on collective ownership. Thus, revolution ended one political–economic system and helped to create another. Ironically, Marxist justification for revolution has had the greatest impact in countries with relatively small pockets of industrialization. Whether his theories of history and inevitable revolution are accurate or not, they have provided inspiration for revolutionary agitation for countless men and women.

One of the most important of these men was Vladimir Ilich Lenin (1870–1924). Lenin accepted most of Marx's analyses of capitalist society but made a few additions. In *Imperialism* he explained why proletarian revolution had not yet occurred in the most industrially advanced states as Marx had predicted. In effect, the capitalists had bought off their proletariat with superprofits earned through imperialism—the systematic plunder of the underdeveloped parts of the world. The proletariat, satisfied with higher than starvation wages, allowed the industrialists their superprofits and their constant attempts to divide up the world, which inevitably led to war (an inevitability that Premier Khrushchev said had disappeared by 1956). In order to overcome this lack of revolutionary zeal, the suppressive apparatus of the state, and the low level of proletarian development in such states as Russia, Lenin argued that a small revolutionary and conspiratorial cadre was required to help create the conditions for revolution. Thus, Lenin added one of the most essential ingredients of modern mass revolution: creation of a disciplined revolutionary party which can educate and organize the masses to carry out revolution. After the success of the Russian Revolution, which was really a coup followed by a vicious civil war, and after Lenin's death, his followers split. Leon Trotsky (1879–1940) supported permanent revolution, proclaiming that socialism could never be completed in Russia unless it was also achieved in the industrialized West. Joseph Stalin (1879–1953), on the other hand, emphasized "socialism in one country," which in practical terms meant only limited support for foreign revolution, industrialization of the Soviet Union, and ruthless consolidation of Stalin's personal power.

Mao Tse-tung has modified these elements, particularly in terms of emphasizing agriculture and peasants as the raw material and basis of revolution. Instead of urban-industrial insurrection, he emphasizes guerrilla warfare, wars of "national liberation," gradual creation of popular support, creation of secure bases, and political indoctrination of the army. This, in turn, has led to increasing emphasis on guerrilla war as the basis of mass revolution.

Guerrilla war. The chances of a classic mass-based revolution of the American, French, or Russian type occurring today are remote. This is due partly to the special circumstances of those revolutions and partly to the increasingly sophisticated suppressive techniques available to governments that still command support from their police and military. For would-be revolutionaries who lack direct access to power centers and thus cannot mount a coup d'état, guerrilla war has become an increasingly attractive alternative for capitalizing on discontent to overthrow a hated regime. It promises to wear down opposition forces through terrorism, small defeats, propaganda, and gradual undermining of the government's position. To be successful, guerrilla war must precipitate a breakdown in government, the military, and popular support. At the very least, it must neutralize government support by getting large sectors of the military and the population to withdraw their allegiance from the government, even if they do not transfer their allegiance to the guerrillas.

Mao, Che Guevara, and Regis Debray have written classic works on guerrilla war. For Mao the goal of revolution is political even if military force is used to reach that goal. The primary purpose is to destroy the opposition army, but this is only a means to political control and reconstruction. Military victory is not an end in itself. To achieve victory, it is necessary first to mobilize the population by appeals to patriotism, nationalism, a better way of life, etc., then to organize the population for the ensuing revolutionary struggle. Third, it is necessary to begin to build a large, dedicated revolutionary army with a significant number of party members. This force can be built up gradually. Its primary aim is political. In selecting tactics the army is to avoid contact with the enemy if the enemy is superior, attack and destroy isolated units, and gradually build up strength while undermining the opposition until it is able to defeat the opposition in open battle. Thus, the revolutionary's commitment is to a long, drawn-out war of attrition where political goals cannot be subordinated to military means.[34] For Guevara and Debray it was possible to go out and create the conditions for revolution even if the population was not yet ready for revolt. They felt that it was possible for small, dedicated, armed bands to enter the countryside and create widespread discontent against the government, encourage governmental attempts at suppression (which would bring new recruits to

[34] For a brief summary, see Chalmers Johnson, *Revolution and the Social System* (Stanford: Hoover Institute on War, Revolution and Peace, 1964), pp. 58–61; Henry Bienen, *Violence and Social Change: A Review of Current Literature* (Chicago: University of Chicago Press, 1968), pp. 42–45ff.

the revolutionaries), undermine governmental support, and gradually build up an efficient revolutionary force. In the last several years increasing attention has focused on urban guerrillas, who have foresworn the countryside in order to create revolution within the increasingly brutal conditions of city life in many developing countries.

With the success of guerrilla war in China, in Indochina against the French, in Algeria, and Cuba, it began to appear to many that guerrilla war was an almost unbeatable way of overthrowing a government. Especially to many revolutionary romantics, it appeared to be a cheap but inevitable method of eliminating entrenched elites and creating total social, political, and economic transformation in the name of the oppressed proletariat. Yet there are some special conditions that have enabled guerrilla war to succeed in some areas.[35] In China, Algeria, and Vietnam the guerrillas, at least initially, could appeal to feelings of nationalism in ousting a foreign invader (Japan) or a colonial master (France). In noncolonial situations, guerrilla war has succeeded only in China and Cuba, and the Cuban Revolution has taught elites to pay close attention to the early signs of insurgency and to their own means of counterinsurgency. Che Guevara was killed in Bolivia in 1967 (where *he* was the foreigner) before he had the opportunity to organize a real guerrilla force. Without a foreign enemy whom everyone can see, moderate elements will rarely support guerrilla forces. And guerrillas cannot succeed without substantial moderate and middle class support. In the absence of a direct foreign enemy, guerrilla war immediately takes on the color of civil war.

Although guerrilla wars are still being waged and undoubtedly more will break out in the future, other factors work against successful outcomes. International support for such wars, whether in terms of U.N. resolutions against colonial governments, worldwide sympathy, or even the practical issue of foreign arms and support, have decreased. Cuba and the Soviet Union are offering less support for guerrilla war at precisely the same time that governments faced with a guerrilla conflict are finding more and more international sympathy and support for their antiguerrilla activities. Moreover, guerrilla groups in Latin America and Africa are often splintered into several small and sometimes warring factions. Disagreement and confusion over goals, strategy, and tactics make it very difficult for revolutionary groups to succeed. This is particularly true because many have not been successful in building up popular support. In addition, the techniques of suppression have become more sophisticated. Counterinsurgency training, improved communications, middle class fear of revolution, counterter-

[35] Joseph S. Kraemer, "Revolutionary Guerrilla Warfare and the Decolonization Movement," *Polity,* 4 (Winter, 1971), pp. 148–51; Brian Crozier, *Masters of Power* (Boston: Little Brown, 1969), pp. 259–62; Alan Riding, "The Death of the Latin American Guerrilla Movement," *World,* August 3, 1973, pp. 29–32.

rorism, torture, and even the growth of nationalism among nonrevolutionary elites have undermined, but not eliminated, revolutionary possibilities via guerrilla war. A successful guerrilla war takes a long time. Increasingly, modernization, elite repression, and the difficulties of organization rob potential guerrillas of that time.

REVOLUTION TODAY AND YESTERDAY[36]

Revolutions are not new, but there are numerous differences between those of today and previous centuries. Even if we include coups, perhaps the greatest distinction in past and present political violence aimed at overthrowing the government is mass participation. Even if the bulk of the population does not directly participate in violence, today most revolutions are made in their name.

A second and equally important distinction is ideological. Most modern revolutionary violence justifies itself with an appeal to dogma and values to justify violence and provide models of a better system. Ideology became important with the French Revolution and is basic to current revolutionary efforts.

Thirdly, organization has changed. There are very few spontaneous revolts today. More often than not they are planned and organized by a small group. While they rarely create widespread discontent, they may take advantage of discontent. Lenin's revolutionary cadre and Guevara's efforts to create revolutionary movements illustrate this phenomenon.

Fourth, the scale or extent of upheaval is greater than in previous centuries. Previously, small numbers were involved. Today whole societies are involved, and revolution may have profound effects on international politics. Many revolutionaries aim at fundamental and total change, whereas before 1789 revolution largely involved only a change in governors.

Finally, modern revolutions have sought to extend themselves over time and space. Perhaps this is a function of ideology and their aim of total change. Mao seeks to bring a new generation to direct experience with China's revolution. In the United States, the Soviet Union, France, and Mexico there are constant appeals to the values and policies of their respective revolutions. Revolution provided both the basis for these governments and a large part of their political language. In addition, the great revolutions have tried to export themselves to nonrevolutionary countries. This is not a new phenomenon even if Communists today appear to have made it a fine art. Both Athenians and Spartans systematically aided their internal allies in other city-states during the Peloponnesian War. In

[36] This section is based in part on Johnson, *Revolutionary Change, op. cit.*, pp. vii–viii.

the late 1640s and early 1650s some English revolutionaries confidently expected much of Europe to follow England's lead and create republics. Americans invaded Canada in the 1770s and during the War of 1812, aided the Latin American revolutions of the 1820s, and the U.S. Congress debated whether we should send aid to Greece during its revolution in the 1820s. (Congress decided not to do so.) French revolutionary armies threatened to forcefully export the French Revolution. The Soviet Union and Cuba thus stand in the long tradition of revolutionary exportation, even if at times their revolutions have seemed more permanent and dangerous than previous upheavals.

POLITICAL VIOLENCE AND POLITICAL, ECONOMIC, AND SOCIAL CHANGE

Political violence is generally purposeful. People employ violence to achieve some end they feel would otherwise be unattainable. Despite its destructive aspects, political violence may have some positive aspects.[37] One of the most common justifications for political violence is to achieve social justice by eliminating oppression, redressing grievances, improving the lot of the masses. Whether we look at the American, French, or Russian Revolutions or at representational violence, civil disobedience, or guerrilla war, most political violence has as primary goals elimination of abuses in a particular society and improvement of the conditions of the masses. Whether they achieve this or not will depend on the real motivations of people employing violence, as well as the actual conditions they meet before, during, and after their action. Elimination of social–political–economic abuse is extremely difficult and is usually a long-term project. The initial violent act often only symbolically improves conditions while helping to create conditions for long-term reform efforts.

This is not a warning against violence as much as a caution that something more than violence is necessary to end injustice ultimately. It seems clear that land seizures have helped Latin American peasants, and that ghetto violence has removed many obstacles to black Americans, but these are not ends in themselves, merely the beginning of unfolding possibilities.

Political violence and revolution may also put modernizers into power. By weakening or eliminating existing institutions and the people who currently hold power, violence may eliminate obstacles to change and allow groups eager for change to assume power. Historically, political violence

[37] Among important sources, see Anderson, *op. cit.;* Martin Needler, *op cit.;* Hedley Bull, "Violence and Development," in Robert E. Hunter and John E. Rielly, eds., *Development Today: A New Look at U.S. Relations with the Poor Countries* (New York: Praeger, 1972), pp. 99–115; Bienen, *op. cit.*, pp. 78, 102–03.

and revolution have helped to place classes into power who wanted extensive economic, social, or political change. The English, American, French, Russian, and Chinese Revolutions helped lead directly to economic modernization. In cases such as the Meiji Restoration in nineteenth-century Japan and the Young Turk movement in the 1900s, judicious use of violence placed in power people who wanted to improve their nation's power and standing vis à vis other nations.

Moreover, violence may help to create national unity, particularly if it is directed against a foreign opponent. Nation building is a severe problem for most developing states today. Creation of common loyalties, values, and affections—a sense of belonging together as a nation—may be partially created by actual conflict or the image of danger, hostility, and encirclement by enemies. History is filled with examples of conflict helping to cement national unity: the United States in the Revolution and the War of 1812; the French Revolution and the development of French nationalism; Germany in the Franco-Prussian War of 1870; Stalin's appeal to Russian nationalism in the early years of World War II; the Arab-Israeli conflicts of 1948, 1956, 1967 and 1973; and colonial struggles in general. Unity forged through war has a price, however. That price may involve international bitterness and further war. In the case of a civil war, bitterness and resentment may unite members of each contending faction but divide them as groups for generations. Once the conflict has ceased, feelings of common loyalty may end if they have nothing beyond the conflict to sustain them.

Many other advantages have come from conflict. Most revolutionary wars have led to the development of stronger, more efficient governments. Even if violence does not cause great changes, it may act as a safety valve. By releasing pressure or demonstrating the need to release growing pressure, low levels of political violence may actually prevent development of situations that could cause widespread violence. Thus, some low levels of violence may actually be conducive to stability. Further, according to Franz Fanon (1925–1961) and Georges Sorel (1847–1922) violence may be a constructive, liberating act for the individual or class committing it (though certainly not for the victims). Finally, violence may be a means of defense for a legitimate and popular political order against an armed minority.

Violence, however, can be both constructive and destructive. Most theorists who have spoken of the need for violence, whether Niccolò Machiavelli, V. I. Lenin, or Mao Tse-tung, have argued that it is an instrument to achieve political ends such as unification and order, and that indiscriminate use of violence defeats those ends.

We are not completely certain about the long-term effects of violence. There has been very little empirical analysis of actual changes that have occurred in societies that have experienced extensive political violence. Moreover, massive violence may bring about no major changes at all; this was typical of the violence in and between the Greek city-states and the violence of feudal societies.

Every revolution carries with it both constructive and destructive elements.[38] There is no guarantee that one will dominate the other. Even the most successful political violence will carry costs that detract from its benefits. Political violence and revolution are costly in terms of arms spending, resources destroyed, and lives lost. Less obviously, the resort to violence may weaken or destroy political legitimacy, trust, and national unity. Since 1789 France has suffered fourteen constitutional changes. Political violence may encourage frequent coups as conspirators feel they cannot trust each other, or see the rewards of seizing power for themselves. Violence may encourage constant recourse to violence as an attempted means of overcoming opposition or lack of legitimacy and cooperation. Violence may not only weaken political values; it may also weaken or destroy law and political institutions that provide the framework for social interaction. A social situation lacking values and institutions will probably lead to chaos; therefore, we can be certain that someone will attempt to impose some values, order, and institutions, and this may lead to renewed conflict and destruction. Decades, even generations, may elapse before elimination of widespread social conflict.

Political violence is always directed at someone. Some people or groups are injured, and this injury may engender deep opposition and hate if the group is not completely eliminated (as happened with much of the landlord class in the People's Republic of China) or bought off (as is true of many landowners in Latin America). Even groups employing violence may be brutalized by it or fall out among themselves out of fear and suspicion. Many people will be cut off from solid foundations and group interaction by violence. Uncertainty and confusion are concomitants of all political violence, atomizing society. Cleavages may become so great that actual economic or social progress will be retarded as people lose confidence in each other, resources are destroyed, institutions break down, and as values no longer explain reality.

Finally, one of the costs of political violence may be elimination of opposition, silencing of dissent, destruction of other opinions that could point out or develop alternative programs and policies. Society is extremely complex. No single road or ideology has all the answers. As John Stuart Mill noted more than a century ago, we choke off opposing opinions at peril of losing or ignoring part of the truth. Nevertheless, political violence is often employed to protect dissent and opposing opinions.

[38] Leiden and Schmitt, *op. cit.*, p. 62.

A Few Concluding Notes

Given widespread poverty, discontent, injustice, rapid change, and ideological conflict in our contemporary world, political violence will not disappear in the near future. Political violence, despite its shortcomings and problems, has helped to create better, more responsive political, economic, and social systems. To disavow it completely would mean disavowing our own revolutionary heritage and the institutions and liberties forged out of that heritage. To embrace violence overeagerly would destroy many of those same values and institutions. Every part of the world, however, faces political violence. While it may be more frequent in the developing states, none of the developed states is free of the conditions that encourage violence. Political conflict and violence are common in every society.

Problems remain, and questions remain unanswered and perhaps unanswerable. What about civil disobedience? How can we justify it? How can we justify suppressing it? What is its relation to democracy? A second series of questions involves man's use of violence. Why is violence so prevalent? Where does it come from? Can we distinguish criminal from noncriminal violence? What are the safeguards against violence? Can we eliminate violence? Where can we eliminate violence? Thirdly, we must ask ourselves what the role of political violence is. Is it always an oppressive instrument? When do groups or individuals have a right to resort to violence? Can we create any a priori standards for use of violence? Finally, we must end with the question of whether this will be the complacent 1970s as opposed to the radical 1960s. Was the violence at home and abroad during the 1960s simply an interlude that we can forget or the opening volley of a new Thirty Years' War? Have we learned anything from the civil wars, guerrilla wars, riots, assassinations, confrontations, and killings of the last thirty years?

Selected Readings

Carl Leiden and Karl M. Schmitt, *The Politics of Violence: Revolution in the Modern World** (Englewood Cliffs, N.J.: Prentice Hall, 1968) is a general discussion of most of the topics covered in this chapter, as well as four contemporary revolutions: Mexico, Turkey, Egypt, and Cuba. It is one of the best brief introductions to the study of political violence. David V. J. Bell, *Resistance and Revolution** (Boston: Houghton Mifflin, 1973) is a general

* Available in paperback.

introduction to both the philosophical and empirical aspects of political violence, including analysis of causes, types, and structure of resistance behavior. Carl J. Friedrich, ed., *Revolution* (New York: Atherton, 1967) is a collection of eleven studies concerned with the nature, typology, philosophy, and ideology of revolution within its international setting. Any serious student of revolution should read Crane Brinton, *The Anatomy of Revolution,* Rev. ed. (New York: Vintage Books, 1965). In studying the English, American, French, and Russian revolutions, Brinton examines their common features in terms of causes, events that signal revolution, triggers, stages, and outcomes.

For a thorough introduction to contemporary theories of violence, see Henry Bienen, *Violence and Social Change, a Review of Current Literature* (Chicago: University of Chicago Press, 1968). Chalmers Johnson, *Revolutionary Change** (Boston: Little Brown, 1966) is a theoretical examination of the social system out of, and within which, revolution occurs. Based on systems analysis of the interrelation of values and institutions, this is one of the most important social analyses of revolution. Peter Calvert, *A Study of Revolution* (Oxford: Clarendon Press, 1970) is a general study of the characteristics of twentieth-century political violence and revolution. Two important appendices list governmental power transitions that have occurred through violence, 1901–1969. For a brief but incisive discussion of the problems of studying political violence, and of the types and levels of political violence, see Peter A. R. Calvert, "Revolution: The Politics of Violence," *Political Studies,* 15 (Feb., 1967), pp. 1–11. Lawrence Stone provides an excellent, brief, critical discussion of major contemporary analytic theorists of revolution—Crane Brinton, Chalmers Johnson, Harry Eckstein—and such trends as the application of behavioralism to revolution studies. See *World Politics,* 18 (1966), pp. 159–176. Isaac Kramnick, "Reflections on Revolution: Definitions and Explanation in Recent Scholarship," *History and Theory,* 11 (1972) pp. 26–63, discusses the basic problem of defining what scholars mean by revolution, and then critically examines the political, economic, sociological, and psychological theories of the origin of political violence and revolution. Harry Eckstein "On the Etiology of Internal Wars," *History and Theory,* 4 (1964–65) pp. 133–163, examines the various theories of the origins and causes of domestic political violence, cautioning against too much reliance on any single theory. Eckstein also briefly discusses obstacles to internal war.

Harry Eckstein, ed., *Internal War, Problems and Approaches* (New York: Free Press, 1964) is a collection of twelve major studies examining the causes and varieties of domestic political violence. James C. Davies, "Toward

* Available in paperback.

a Theory of Revolution," *American Sociological Review,* 27 (1962) pp. 5–19, is one of the most reprinted and discussed "economic" theories of the origin of revolution. Davies claims that revolution is most likely to occur when a period of economic and social advance is interrupted by a sharp reversal, creating a gap between wants and the expectation of fulfilling those wants. U.S. National Commission on the Causes and Prevention of Violence, *To Establish Justice, To Insure Domestic Tranquility, Final Report* (Washington: U.S. Gov. Printing Office, 1969) is basic reading. Though dealing with violence in general, several chapters are very relevant to the topic of political violence: group violence, civil disobedience, assassination, and campus violence. Hugh Davis Graham and Ted Robert Gurr produced a staff report for the National Commission, which is a balanced and thorough analysis of political and nonpolitical violence in the United States: *Violence in America: Historical and Comparative Perspectives* (Washington: U.S. Gov. Printing Office, 1969). Though the title may seem flippant, Edward Luttwak, *Coup d'Etat, A Practical Handbook** (Greenwich, Conn.: Fawcett, 1969) is a serious study of the causes of the coup d'etat, carefully explaining why it succeeds or fails.

Numerous studies of specific revolutions or revolutionary theories are available. Three of the best are: Michael Walzer, *Revolution of the Saints** (New York: Atheneum, 1969). This is one of the most readable political studies of the causes of the Puritan Revolution in England. Pauline Maier, *From Resistance to Revolution: Colonial Radicals and the Development of Opposition to Britain, 1765–1776* (New York: Alfred A. Knopf, 1972) is a superb analysis of the popular and theoretical roots of both the American Revolution and, more generally, American revolutionary thinking. Michael Walzer, ed., also has a book dealing with the French Revolution, *Regicide and Revolution: Speeches at the Trial of Louis XVI* (Cambridge: Cambridge University Press, 1974). Walzer's introduction examines the development of a justification to execute a monarch, and justifies Louis' death. The book also contains selected speeches dealing with Louis' trial, including one by Thomas Paine.

There are many discussions of political violence and revolution in classical political philosophy. Two of the most important are Aristotle, *Politics,** Book V and John Locke, *Second Treatise of Government,** chapter 18 and 19. For a timeless defense of the use of power in politics, see the fifteenth-century theorist Niccolò Machiavelli, *The Prince.** Each of these is available in many inexpensive editions. See also Machiavelli's *Discourses on the First Ten Books of Titus Livius* (many editions) for a classical study of politics, violence, state building, and loyalty. Edmund Burke, *Reflections on*

* Available in paperback.

*the Revolution in France** (1790, many editions) is the classical conservative critique of rapid change and revolution, defending tradition, order, and an organic society, while still admitting the necessity for change. See also Burke's *An Appeal from the New to the Old Whigs* (1791, many editions) for his defense of the Glorious Revolution of 1688 and basic Whig principles. Robert C. Tucker, *The Marxian Revolutionary Idea* (New York: W. W. Norton, 1969) examines Marx's and Marxist ideas of revolution over time. For a "conservative," normatively oriented analysis that admits the occasional need of civil disobedience and even violence, but places most emphasis on order, law, authority, and obedience within a formal, political, democratic context, see Ernest van den Haag, *Political Violence and Civil Disobedience** (New York: Harper and Row, 1972). For an intelligent discussion of the interrelation of rights, interpretations of rights, violence, and differing meanings of political violence within different value contexts, see Charner Perry, "Violence—Visible and Invisible", *Ethics,* 81 (1970), pp. 1–21.

Civil disobedience in a democracy is popularly treated by two former Supreme Court justices. Abe Fortas, *Concerning Dissent and Civil Disobedience** (New York: Signet, 1968) attempts to define the right to dissent and the permissible methods of dissent within the American framework. William O. Douglas, *Points of Rebellion** (New York: Vintage Books, 1970) extends the permissible methods of dissent to argue that violence has often been "the only effective response" to governmental and establishment oppression, even though it can never have a constitutional sanction.

* Available in paperback.

Part Five

The International System

Chapter 12

Components of International Politics

We believe that it is highly appropriate to conclude our survey of politics with a discussion of politics on the international scene. As discussed in the first chapter, the phenomenon of politics extends from the smallest group of people to the international community.

The need to know more about the larger world around us has steadily grown, because of rapidly increasing international interaction. Figuratively speaking, the world has shrunk considerably in recent decades. Today a person can travel around the globe by jet plane in a matter of some twenty hours, in contrast to the three years needed by the adventurer sailors of the sixteenth century. Via telephone one can contact people in Africa, Asia, and Europe in a matter of minutes. Formerly mountains and oceans helped to protect nation-states. Today, airplanes and missiles defy these barriers. Technological revolutions have been accompanied by a substantial expansion in trade. Our supermarkets and department stores feature goods from many different countries, while some of our goods are sold around the world.[1]

The growing interchange on the international scene has not been accompanied by a commensurate educational growth. How much do we know about the people in other parts of the world? How much do they know

[1] The present energy crisis clearly illustrates the crucial nature of economic interdependence and what happens when major oil-producing countries reduce their sales to postindustrial societies. For a lucid discussion of the growing economic interdependence of nation-states, see Lester R. Brown, *World Without Borders* (New York: Random House, 1972), pp. 183–208.

about us? Experiences derived from the United States' military involvement in Southeast Asia and the Soviet intervention in Czechoslovakia verify this lack of commensurate knowledge. How much did our policy makers know in 1964 about the aspirations, desires, and hopes of the masses in Vietnam? How much did our G.I.'s sent to Southeast Asia know about the indigenous people? Though Czechoslovakia is geographically much closer to the Soviet Union than Vietnam is to the United States, we know that the Soviet soldiers sent into Czechoslovakia in 1968 were greatly misinformed about the hopes and wishes of the large majority of the Czech people.

PROGRESS OF MAN

(Parrish, reprinted courtesy of The Chicago Tribune.)

The need to have as much information as possible about the people abroad is especially crucial for the power elites, the policy makers of the leading powers. In order to make wise decisions regarding another country, a government needs to have a high degree of accurate information and knowledge about that society.

The technological discoveries of recent decades have not been unilateral blessings. In addition to their merits, they have encouraged the production of weapons capable of destroying mankind. Scientific discoveries *appear* to have outstripped man's capability to control them permanently. Today the United States and the Soviet Union possess enough nuclear weapons to kill each other's populations many times over. Will the world community succeed in establishing sufficient social and political counterbalancing forces to nuclear weaponry? We believe that man has the ability to control and correct the ecological, economic, military, and social problems of our time.

SIMILARITIES AND DIFFERENCES BETWEEN DOMESTIC AND INTERNATIONAL POLITICS

In some points international politics is similar to domestic politics. Political actors in both settings try to achieve their desires, and some succeed more than others. The actors on the domestic scene are individuals or groups of people in private or public organizations. In international politics the actors are the spokesmen of nation-states (that is, the leaders of the United States, the Soviet Union, France, Japan, Nigeria, and so on). Moreover, in both spheres the more powerful will customarily wield more influence on economic, military, and political processes than those with less power.

The main point of difference between domestic and international politics has to do with the degree of authority and order, in the sense of law, that prevails in each sphere. Domestic governments, by and large, have a preponderance of authority and power in their societies. This means that these governments will have enough military and police support to make their decisions stick and to squash internal unrest. In addition, a national government is the source of final sanction in the judicial sphere. Should a government lose its preponderance of power, it will be overthrown by coup d'état or revolution–civil war. The Russian Revolution (1917), the Spanish Civil War (1936–39), the Cuban Revolution (1958–59), and the multitude of coups d'état in the developing countries serve as examples. By and large, however, the domestic scene has been substantially more peaceful than the international scene. According to Quincy Wright, only 70 out of 244 wars in which European countries participated between 1480 and 1941 were civil wars.[2] Since 1945, however, the number of civil wars has

[2] Quincy Wright, *A Study of War,* 2nd ed. (Chicago: The University of Chicago Press, 1965), p. 651.

increased to equal the figure of wars among countries. One major reason for the change is found in the fact that, because of the immense arsenals of nuclear weapons, war between the global powers and their respective European allies has become prohibitive. The above figures indicate that there has been more anarchy on the international than on the domestic scene. The reason is that internationally there is no institution having a preponderance of power. The Security Council and the General Assembly of the United Nations are at best weak facsimiles of their domestic counterparts. War is still the ultimate method of sanction on the international scene, and conflicts among nation-states are often settled on a "might makes right" principle, rather than on the basis of what is right according to international law. History abounds with examples of an action successfully executed by the stronger party becoming "the just decision" in the minds of the victors and their supporters.

THE ACTORS IN INTERNATIONAL POLITICS

We have said that the spokesman of nation-states or countries are the political actors on the international scene. Nation-states have certain common characteristics. They are political entities separated from other states by boundaries that are usually officially recognized. In some instances, however, boundaries of a country, or even the existence of a country, may be disputed by some other countries. The Indian-Pakistani conflict is an example of the former, while the Chinese claim to Taiwan exemplifies the latter.

Nation-states have central governments and maintain diplomatic relations with other countries depending upon their standing in the world community. For instance, the United States, Canada, and Sweden maintain diplomatic relations with many other nation-states, while Taiwan, Albania, and Rhodesia have diplomatic relations with relatively few countries. Nation-states are said to be sovereign according to international law. Sovereignty implies equality with other nation-states and independence from outside interference in the pursuit of domestic and international affairs. In reality, however, no country enjoys absolute sovereignty. The policies and pursuits of one country will frequently have bearing on the actions of others. Powerful countries will often limit the foreign policy range of weaker nation-states or even interfere directly with their domestic affairs. An example of the first type can be seen in the relationship between the Soviet Union and its European allies and has been spelled out in the Brehznev doctrine.[3] The United States committed actions of direct interference in Guatemala in 1954, in Laos in 1962, in the Dominican

[3] This doctrine was promulgated by the Kremlin after the 1968 occupation of Czechoslovakia and, in essence, holds that the Soviet Union has the right to intervene in a Warsaw Pact country if the Communist system there is in danger of being overthrown or radically changed.

("The Wizard of Id" by permission of Johnny Hart and Field Enterprises, Inc.)

Republic in 1965; the Soviet Union in East Germany in 1953, in Hungary in 1956, and in Czechoslovakia in 1948 and 1968.

The present world community consists of some one hundred and fifty nation-states. They range in size from the Soviet Union, with 8,650,000 square miles and Canada, with 3,851,809 square miles, to such minute entities as the Vatican (109 acres) and Monaco (433 acres). In terms of population, the nation-states vary from the People's Republic of China (some 800 million) and India (more than 550 million) down to the Vatican with a population of about 1000 and Nauru with about 7000 people.[4]

Obviously, these nation-states differ greatly in terms of power. By power we mean the capability to make one's influence or will prevail over others. Some are labeled superpowers, with others are ranked in a second, third, or fourth category. What are the ingredients that help to make one country more powerful than another?

The following are some of the major elements that contribute to power:

1. *The Geographic Element* (size, climate, natural resources, location, and terrain). Most of human history has been made between 25° and 60° North Latitude, in the temperate zone. Natural resources are important for agricultural and industrial production. The more self-sufficient a country, the better off it is. Size lends itself to power in that it provides flexibility for retreat and relocation of manpower and industry. The vast size of the Russian state presented an insurmountable problem to Napoleon and Hitler. In turn, countries like Andorra or Liechtenstein have not become great powers. Certain locations and terrains have constituted advantages in the premissile age. For example, the British Isles have not been invaded by a conquering force since the eleventh century, while the mountains have protected Switzerland. In World War II Hitler's High Command refrained from invading either of the two, primarily because of logistical considerations.

[4] The above figures and estimates are from *The 1973 World Almanac and Book of Facts* (New York: Doubleday, 1973).

2. *The Demographic Element* (population). A large population will lend power to the country, provided that the people are adequately nourished, well trained in industrial and professional skills, and highly motivated in supporting the aims of the incumbent power elite. Without the above ingredients a large population may be a deterrent to power. For example, the Soviet government found itself greatly weakened during the early 1930s because of the widespread famine leading to substantial starvation in many areas of the country, including the Ukraine—the primary breadbasket of the USSR. Likewise, the government of the People's Republic of China was largely occupied during the 1950s with raising enough food for its many millions of people. The Chinese intervened militarily in Korea only after United Nations Forces came close to the Yalu River, and even then the Chinese limited their involvement. India, with the second largest population of any country in the world, still struggles to meet the basic necessities of its people.

3. *Natural Resources, Technology and Transportation.* Extensive natural resources readily accessible for exploitation and an adequate plant system to transform the natural resources into commercial and military goods add considerably to the power of a country. Essential to the production process and the maintenance of domestic unity are up to date and well-functioning systems of communication and transportation. Keeping in mind the confusion and chaos an occasional brown-out, black-out or strike by airline employees causes, the results of a complete breakdown of communication and/or transportation facilities would be infinitely more chaotic and confusing and could render a postindustrial society completely helpless. Technological superiority will customarily give a nation-state an advantage over those who are less developed. The perpetuation of the power-potential depends on the continuous allocation of resources (manpower and money) for further research. A society that calls a halt to scientific and technological developments will soon come to a technological standstill. The vicious arms race between the United States and the Soviet Union since World War II is, among other factors, a sign of the perpetual technological-military competition between the two superpowers. Present efforts aim at a curtailment of this race, though both societies will continue their technological–militiary research in order to protect their national interests,[5] that is, the minimum requirements, as conceived by the power elite, for protecting and sustaining the continuation of societal development.

4. *Military Power and Preparedness.* The presence of a strong and well-

[5] The term "national interest" is rather elusive and difficult to define precisely. One thoughtful definition is that of Frederick Hartmann, who states that "national interests may be defined in terms of what states seek to protect or achieve vis-à-vis other states." Frederick H. Hartmann, *The Relations of Nations,* 4th ed. (New York: The Macmillan Company, 1973), p. 6.

trained military establishment equipped with up to date weaponry is perhaps the most obvious element of national power. There is some difficulty in calculating actual military power. How many infantry battalions, how many tanks, how many pieces of artillery equal a 5-megaton nuclear bomb? To what extent does the tremendous manpower potential in the People's Republic of China equal Soviet nuclear stength? Another question pertains to the speed with which the resources in manpower and weaponry can be mobilized.

Whatever system of calculation is used, the United States and the Soviet Union are substantially ahead of all other states in military power. Both have vast quantities of nuclear weapons and the delivery systems for short-, medium-, and long-range missiles. The other members of the nuclear club are France, the People's Republic of China, and the United Kingdom. A number of other countries have the capability to produce nuclear weapons, but have refrained from producing them. An expansion of the "nuclear club" would make international relations more complex and more dangerous. At this time the governments of the United States and the Soviet Union are vitally interested in preventing an expansion of the "nuclear club," in order to forestall international complications.

5. *Governmental Leadership.* Last but not least, the quality of governmental leadership has considerable bearing on the power of a nation-state. The leaders in the national government set the priorities and determine the allocation of resources for the armed forces, foreign aid, and domestic purposes. It is of paramount importance for society that the top leaders in the national government keep fully informed about the happenings at home and abroad. Furthermore, it is extremely important that these leaders make wise decisions, wise in terms of short-term and long-term implications. History abounds with examples of statesmen who have fumbled and have led their societies into catastrophes, such as those committed by Napoleon, Mussolini, the Japanese military oligarchy of World War II, and Hitler.

Strength and wisdom in leadership help to produce a stronger country, and it is a rare quality of a society to develop the kind of political system that brings the most able men into the top national positions and supports and sustains their decisions.

The above elements are some of the main criteria of national power. Obviously, they are not all-inclusive, and exceptions to the rule as well as special circumstances need to be taken into consideration when examining a particular case.[6]

[6] The main points of the above discussion are drawn from Vernon Van Dyke, *International Politics,* 3rd ed. (New York: Appleton-Century-Croft, 1972), pp. 223–242. Related discussions of the elements of national power are found in Hans Morgenthau, *Politics Among Nations,* 5th ed. (New York: Alfred A. Knopf, 1973), pp. 112–149; and Hartmann, *op. cit.,* pp. 41–66. Hartmann's discussion includes some very useful tables comparing the manpower, production of vital materials, and armed forces of selected countries.

THE NATURE OF INTERNATIONAL POLITICS

The origin of the modern nation-state system dates back to the sixteenth century. The Italian writer and diplomat Niccolò Machiavelli (1469–1527) provided an early analysis of and justification for statesmanship and centralized power at the national level in *The Prince*. Since those days the number of existing nation-states has increased considerably. Many of the 90-plus countries customarily classified as "developing nation-states" have become independent only in recent years, since World War II. A large number of nation-sates have been born in a revolutionary or semirevolutionary setting. The people in the United States declared their independence from Britain during the Revolutionary War. Other colonies were granted independence from their mother countries under more peaceful settings. A recent example would be that of Britain granting independence to the Bahamas in 1973.

The community of nation-states exists in a setting of constant change. While some new countries are being born, others are being swallowed up by more powerful ones. For example, the former Baltic countries of Estonia, Latvia, and Lithuania were annexed by the Soviet Union during World War II. Still other countries have been divided and temporarily swallowed up by adjacent nation-states. A good example of this would be Poland, which was divided three times during the eighteenth century and again during World War II. Germany and Korea were divided at the end of World War II, and in both instances two quite different political units have developed. A temporary division of Vietnam was decreed by the Geneva Conference of 1954, and much of the turmoil in Vietnam in recent years has been over dissatisfaction with the Geneva arrangement and its unfulfilled promises. Because of perpetual shifts in the power relationship among countries, the process of change in the nation-state community will exist as long as the nation-state remains the primary unit of the international community.

The Viability of a Nation-State

Which nation-states are likely to remain in their present geographical form, which will experience losses of territory, divisions, or will disappear completely? The perpetuation of a nation-state in its present geographical make-up is based on external and internal considerations. External factors include the nation-states's power position vis à vis its neighboring countries and other potential adversaries, the presence of natural frontiers, and the presence of enlightened leadership on both sides of the frontiers. The power of a country (as defined in our earlier discussion) will exercise restraints upon the ambitions of other governments. Natural frontiers, such as the Pyrenees between France and Spain, are unlikely to lead to boundary disputes. Finally, enlightened statesmen will try to resolve their disputes with other leaders in amicable rather than belligerent ways, thereby refraining from endangering the existence of their state.[7]

The opposite example would be the story of the Third Reich, where the policies of the super-belligerent and paranoid Hitler regime led to the destruction of Germany and the death of many millions of people. One could conjecture that if German leaders had continued the enlightened Stresemann spirit as exhibited in the Locarno Treaties (1925) during the 1930s and 1940s, there still would be a Germany today with the boundaries of 1937. The above presupposes, of course, that the leaders of the surrounding countries would have continued their enlightened spirit of 1925 too.

Internal factors are very important to the viability of a state. For a country to remain viable, there must exist a high degree of national integration, including a certain degree of nationalism, sufficient ethnic homogeneity, a uniting language, and wise leadership. Nationalism, as related to the viability of a nation-state, refers to the public loyalty put forth by the citizenry. The large majority of citizens must extend their public loyalty in the first instance toward their nation-state, rather than a subunit thereof or a foreign country. Ethnic homogeneity and a unifying language serve as helpful ingredients. Countries such as Iceland, Norway, and Sweden are leading examples of the above requirements, and the homogeneity of their societies has reinforced considerably their viability as nation-states. In contrast, the Austro-Hungarian Empire, which was a conglomerate of national groups and languages, fell apart in 1918 because the individual national groups desired to achieve independence. The people in former East Pakistan, having little in common with the people and government in West Pakistan, fought successfully for independence and established their own state, Bangladesh, in 1971.

In contrast, some years earlier, the Ibos fought for independence from Nigeria and lost. But despite the Ibos' defeat, boundary changes and efforts toward tribal independence can be expected in Africa in years and decades to come. The present boundaries, drawn arbitrarily by the colonial powers in the nineteenth century, frequently fail to reflect tribal locations and language considerations. A case in point would be Nigeria, where the population consists of a number of tribes—the largest ones being the Hausa, the Ibo, and the Yoruba. The Hausa are the most populous tribe in Nigeria, but they also overlap into neighboring Niger. The Yoruba, in turn, overlap into Dahomey. Most likely, some of the tribal aspirations will be contained through domestic power struggles (such as the violent conflicts between the Hutu and Tutsi in Burundi and Rwanda), others through civil wars as

[7] For an extensive treatment of the issues of national integration, see Karl Deutsch, *Nationalism and its Alternatives* (New York: Alfred A. Knopf, 1969), pp. 3–91.

the Ibo case illustrates. Some other ethnic conflicts will undoubtedly lead to boundary changes in the years to come.[8]

An Asian example of geopolitical complexity is India. The country features about a dozen major languages and several hundred dialects. Various efforts to make Hindi, the most widely spoken language, the official language of the country, have been opposed by measures that at times included demonstrations, violence, and bloodshed. As a consequence, the Indian government has seen no choice but to retain English as the official language of the country. Only about 30 percent of the Indian people speak Hindi.[9] Would a future imposition of Hindi as the national language lead to separatist movements by the non-Hindi-speaking groups?

Foreign Policy and International Politics

The term international politics embraces the sum total of the nation-states' foreign policies. A nation-state's foreign policy consists of its government's relations with other countries. More specifically, these relations are based on considerations of national interest and may involve political, economic, cultural, and military measures. Fundamental elements of foreign policy are such desires as safeguarding the country from foreign invasions and maintaining an adequate foreign trade balance. Foreign policy involves sets of objectives and strategies often conceived over a period of time, involving three ingredients—conception, content, and implementation. In the words of Frederick Hartmann:

> *Since a foreign policy consists of selected national interests presumably formulated into a logically consistent whole that is then implemented, any foreign policy can be viewed analytically in three phases: conception, content, and implementation. Conception involves the strategic appraisal of what goals are desirable and feasible. Content is the result and reflection of that appraisal. Implementation looks to both the coordinating mechanisms within a state and the means by which it conveys its views and wishes to other states. Although inefficiencies and failures can be very costly in any of these three phases, it is apparent that the most critical phase is conception.*[10]

Hartmann's three-step formula can be applied to the foreign policy making process of all countries. What differs, however, are the goals pursued by the individual countries. These differences have to do with the power capabilities of a country, its needs, location, and so forth. The Soviet Union and the United States, our present-day superpowers, pursue worldwide

[8] A good source for ethnic information and country profiles of Sub-Saharan Africa is Donald G. Morrison, ed., *Black Africa: A Comparative Handbook* (New York: The Free Press, 1972).

[9] See A. H. Hanson and Janet Douglas, *India's Democracy* (New York: W. W. Norton, 1972), p. 2.

[10] Hartmann, *op. cit.*, p. 67.

interests and have these reflected in their foreign policies. Botswana or Paraguay, in contrast, are underdeveloped and land-locked countries with rather limited foreign policy aims and pursuits.

THE CONDUCT OF INTERNATIONAL POLITICS

Once foreign policy has been formulated, by what means is it put into effect? How do nation-states deal with each other? The range of possible relations is wide, stretching from friendly diplomatic acts on the one hand to warfare on the other. Diplomacy, according to Nicolson, quoting from the *Oxford English Dictionary,* is

> *the management of international relations by means of negotiation; the method by which these relations are adjusted and managed by ambassadors and envoys: the business or art of the diplomatist.*[11]

Diplomacy is the means by which governments conduct business with each other. In order to facilitate the conduct of diplomacy, nation-states customarily establish some degree of diplomatic relations with each other. For example, country *A* may have a trade mission in country *B* and use this trade mission for conducting trade and diplomatic matters. A case in point would be the East German trade mission in Bonn. Or a country may maintain a special office or legation in another country, headed by a charge d'affaires or minister. For example, the United States was represented in some of the Arab countries by charges d'affaires after the 1967 war. Some countries maintain only consular relations with each other. The Republic of South Africa, for example, has only consular relations with Denmark, Iran, and Japan. While the South African government would like to maintain full diplomatic relations, the three countries mentioned above prefer for political reasons to keep relations at a less conspicuous level. In the three cases the representatives of both sides have consular rather than diplomatic titles, but perform all or most of the functions normally handled by accredited diplomats. The highest diplomatic rank is that of an ambassador. He is in charge of an embassy abroad. All of the above officials are considered diplomats and are under the jurisdiction of the state department or foreign ministry of their home countries. Diplomats enjoy certain privileges such as diplomatic immunity. Should a diplomat violate laws of the host country, he may not be tried there. Rather, he would be declared persona non grata and asked to return to his home country.

How are diplomatic relations established? As a new country comes into being, the governments of the other countries will decide whether to establish diplomatic relations with it or not. Various political considerations

[11] Harold Nicolson, *Diplomacy* (New York: Oxford University Press, 1963), p. 15.

are involved in this decision-making process. For example, will our establishment of diplomatic relations with country *X* offend country *Y*, a friend of ours? What will be our economic and political gains in establishing these relations? For instance, when Bangladesh became independent in December of 1971, the United States government temporarily held back extending diplomatic recognition to that new nation-state in order not to offend our CENTO and SEATO ally, Pakistan. However, after a number of other states had recognized Bangladesh, the United States followed suit. The United States government did not recognize the Communist regime in Russia until 1933,[12] and some degree of diplomatic relations with the People's Republic of China has been established only since President Nixon's 1972 visit to that country. At the time of this writing, the United States' government maintains some diplomtic relations with every country but Albania, Cuba, North Korea, and Vietnam. Since the break of diplomatic relations between Cuba and the United States, Swiss diplomats have represented our interests in that country.

Disputes between countries will at times lead to a reduction in diplomatic relations or a complete severance. Such steps may be initiated unilaterally or be based on reciprocity. For instance, the United States government severed diplomatic relations with some of the Eastern European countries after they had been taken over by Communist regimes at the end of World War II. Following the abortive Hungarian Revolution of 1956, our government reduced its diplomatic representation in Hungary by recalling the ambassador and leaving a chargé d'affaires in control of our embassy. Full restoration of diplomatic relations occurred some years later after a considerable improvement in United States–Hungarian relations had taken place. Most Latin American countries broke diplomatic relations with Cuba after the Castro takeover, but in recent months some have begun to move toward reconciliation. The point is that diplomatic recognition is often used as an instrument of political expediency and a means of reward or punishment. Generally speaking, however, governments will find it more convenient to maintain diplomatic relations with other countries than not to do so. In the absence of diplomatic relations, other sources have to be found to negotiate existing issues. For example, during the late 1950s and most of the 1960s our ambassador in Warsaw met on a fairly regular basis with his Communist Chinese counterpart to negotiate matters of interest to both countries.

Before a government appoints a person as ambassador inquiries will be made whether he or she is acceptable (*persona grata*) to the host country.

[12] The issues surrounding the late U.S. recognition of the USSR are discussed in detail in Edward M. Bennett, *Recognition of Russia: An American Foreign Policy Dilemma* (Waltham, Mass.: Blaisdell Publishing Company, 1970).

If not, a more suitable person will be selected. Diplomats serve two primary functions: they represent the home government in the host country; and they keep the home government adequately informed about the cultural, economic, military, and political happenings in the host country in order that the state department or foreign ministry at home can formulate intelligent policies toward the other country. The diplomats stationed abroad attend to the day-to-day items of business. Issues of great concern are more likely to be dealt with by special negotiators appointed to conduct a particular conference, by secretaries of state or foreign ministers, or by the heads of states themselves.

The "Big Three" at the Potsdam Conference. From left to right: Prime Minister Winston Churchill, President Harry S. Truman, and Generalissimo Josef Stalin.

In addition to the embassay, a country may maintain one or more consulates in the host country. The consular staff attends to matters such as issuing visas, assisting citizens traveling abroad, trade promotion, and public information activities.

Since World War II a number of *Summit Meetings* have been held between the leaders of the major countries, as well as those who are still in a developing stage. For such meetings to be successful, a great deal of preliminary work needs to be done at the professional diplomatic level. Three important summit meetings took place during and at the end of World War II: Teheran, 1943 (Churchill, Roosevelt, Stalin); Yalta, 1945 (Churchill, Roosevelt, Stalin); and Potsdam, 1945 (Churchill, Attlee, Truman, Stalin). At these three meetings the Allies' war aims, the fate of the vanquished countries, and the creation of the United Nations were discussed, and important final decisions were made on these subjects. In 1955 Bulganin, Eden, Eisenhower, and Faure met in Geneva to consider the future of Germany and European security. The meeting between Kennedy and Khrushchev in Vienna in 1961 served as an exchange of United States' and Soviet views on confrontation issues in Europe and Southeast Asia. Finally, Nixon's 1972 visit to the People's Republic of China, leading to the

A history-making foursome. From left to right: Premier Nikolai Bulganin, President Dwight D. Eisenhower, Premier Edgar Faure, and Prime Minister Anthony Eden at the Geneva Conference, 1955.

Contemporary summitry: President Ford meets with the three important West European leaders during the 1975 Helsinki Conference. From left to right: British Prime Minister Harold Wilson, President Gerald Ford, French President Giscard d'Estaing, and West German Chancellor Helmut Schmidt.

establishment of partial diplomatic relations between the United States and China, his subsequent visit to the Soviet Union, and Brezhnev's 1973 visit to the United States are recent examples of big-power summit meetings.

Methods for Conducting International Relations

The above focus has centered on the channels used by nation-states to conduct their official affairs with each other. The following discussion deals with the *methods* used by governments in the pursuit of their foreign relations. International problems can be solved through amicable political or judicial methods, or through nonamicable means, including retortion, reprisal, or even war. The main amicable political instrument is that of *negotiation*. Representatives of two or more countries will meet with the purported purpose to achieve agreement on a given issue. The process of negotiation is based on the assumption that the parties involved have some interest in solving the problem at hand. Fred Charles Iklé classifies the objectives of governments in international negotiations into the following four types: extension or renewal of an existing agreement with perhaps slight changes of the former; the normalization of relations, such as the negotiations that led to United States' recognition of the Soviet Union in 1933; a redistribution of territory and/or political power. This type of negotiation is conducted between an offensive and a defensive party, with the offensive side trying to acquire something from the other. For example, the Icelandic government claimed in 1958 a 12-mile offshore zone for native fishery exclusively. The British, having fished previously in that area, began to comply with the Icelandic demand in order to forestall future difficulties which, however, developed anyway. Of greater politico-military importance were Khrushchev's repeated demands during the late 1950s for a change in the status of West Berlin. In this instance, the West did not acquiesce. The fourth type of negotiation includes innovation agreements that serve to establish a new relationship between the parties involved. The Treaties of Rome (1957), which set up the European Economic Community and Euratom, serve as a good example.[13]

Do statesmen always negotiate to achieve agreement on an issue of concern? According to Iklé:

> *Side-effects—that is, effects not concerning agreement—may be an important part of the outcome, even if all parties negotiate primarily for the purpose of reaching agreement. They may arise either by accident or by design of one party or all parties involved. When diplomacy produces agreements only rarely—as between East and West—the objective of producing side-effects, in fact, often dominates.*[14]

[13] Fred Charles Iklé, *How Nations Negotiate* (New York: Frederick A. Praeger, 1967), pp. 26–42.

[14] Iklé, *op. cit.*, p. 43.

Iklé lists six major points of negotiating for side effects:

1. The purpose of one or both negotiators may be plainly that of maintaining contact with each other, to keep open the channels of communication. An example of this would be the negotiation between the Soviet Union and the United States regarding the German question and, more specifically, the status of West Berlin during the 1950s and early 1960s. Though the parties had arrived at a stalemate on these issues, the leaders in Moscow and Washington decided that the negotiations should be continued to prevent a worsening of the situation, which could have dire consequences for both.

2. Negotiations can serve as a substitute for violent actions. The argument made in support of this thesis is that the process of negotiations can be so pleasing to one's adversary or catalyze in him the feeling of obligation to see the negotiations through that he will refrain from taking the violent action he would have otherwise. Iklé goes on to say that the thesis holds true in some instances, while it does not apply to others. For example, contrary to Neville Chamberlain's hopes, the Munich Conference did not keep Hitler from starting World War II; neither did the United States-Japanese negotiations in 1941 forestall Japan's attack on Pearl Harbor.

3. Negotiations may be used to gather intelligence information about the adversary. During the process of negotiation the opponent may reveal some of his intentions, his long-term aims, or his range of negotiability—that is, the minimum and maximum desires. There is some evidence that President Nixon's talks with the Chinese and Russian leaders served in part to get a reading of their views regarding Southeast Asia, and that the president developed his subsequent policies accordingly.

4. The major purpose of a particular negotiation may be deception—to deceive the opponent about one's aims. An example of deception took place during the Hungarian Revolution in 1956. During the first four days of the uprising the Soviet ambassador in Budapest negotiated with the leaders of the new Hungarian government about their political aims and the withdrawal of the Russian troops. This period gave the Soviet Politburo enought time to plan its counterattack to overthrow the Nagy government.

5. Negotiations are sometimes used for propaganda purposes. In this setting one or both sides will set forth proposals, knowing that they are unacceptable to the other side. The prime aim is to gain favorable publicity. Important forums, such as summit meetings, and the rostrums of the Security Council and the General Assembly of the United Nations lend themselves well to gaining publicity and prestige. Presidential speeches, here and abroad, are filled with statements favoring peace and the well-being of mankind. While there may be some true intention in these comments, the point is that often one side tries to outdo the other in order to score points with the rest of the world by making the other side look hypocritical. One case in point is the publicity during the disarmament

conferences of the past eight decades and, in particular, the Russian proposals, commencing with Lenin, for complete disarmament. In addition, it appears that past Soviet and United States' proposals concerning the unification of Germany contained a good deal of farce too.

6. Negotiations for the purpose of influencing third parties. In this instance the real purpose of the negotiation may be to intimidate a third country. During the 1960s some governments of developing countries have tried to play Washington against Moscow and vice versa in order to obtain favorable economic deals. One can also conjecture that President Nixon's visit to the People's Republic of China had a wholesome effect on Soviet–United States relations.[15]

In summary, negotiations have often been used for purposes other than those purported. Nevertheless, negotiations are far preferable to less amicable alternatives. But in order for negotiations to make sense, there must be a negotiable issue, the parties involved must have some desire for agreement, and furthermore must show some flexibility—because the outcome of successful negotiations is usually a compromise solution.

Sometimes the process of mediation is employed. Here a third party is called upon to disentangle the problem between two parties and to help to bring about an agreement. Most likely, this third party will be an outside government or an international forum such as the Security Council of the United Nations. In 1966 Premier Kosygin invited the leaders of India and Pakistan to Tashkent in order to help them delineate a ceasefire line and to improve relations between the two countries. Kosygin's efforts were of some success and contributed to a temporary easing of tensions between India and Pakistan.

While a number of international problems have been settled through negotiations in a fairly amicable fashion, other conflicts have led to nonamicable measures, customarily involving a good deal of coercion. Vernon Van Dyke identifies four types of nonamicable methods: retortion, reprisal, intervention, and war.

Retortion is a deliberately unfriendly but legal act, which has a coercive or retaliatory purpose. For instance, government *A* may be displeased by an action taken by government *B* and, to show its indignation, will reduce or sever diplomatic relations with the latter. A less severe step would be a temporary curtailment of trade or trade privileges.

The term *reprisal* refers to a deliberately unfriendly act, the purpose of which is coercive or retaliatory. One case in point has to do with the Gulf of Tonkin incident of 1964. While even today very few facts about this affair are known to the public, the point is that as a consequence the president of the United States ordered an all-out air attack on North Vietnamese oil

[15] For a more detailed discussion of the above see Iklé, *op. cit.*, pp. 43–58.

storage facilities and PT boat bases, thereby substantially escalating our military involvement in Southeast Asia.

Intervention means interference by one state in the affairs of another. This is an illegal act committed by governments for one of several purposes. Intervention may involve meddling in the electoral process of another country, to insure the election of a candidate favorable to the intervening country. Or it may lead to pressure on the other government to pursue or not to pursue a certain foreign policy. Intervention may involve the sending of troops into another country to force that government "to fall into line." In the early decades of this century the United States government sent marines into several Latin American republics. It may involve the blockade of another country's coast or ports. In more recent years the United States' intervention in 1965 in the Dominican Republic, the Soviet reoccupation of Hungary in 1956 and its occupation of Czechoslovakia in 1968 were obvious examples of intervention.

In the absence of an international authority that has a preponderance of power, *war* remains the ultimate means for settling a conflict on the international scene. History abounds with examples of countries having gone to war against each other after they had unsuccessfully exhausted the existing political and judicial means for settlement, or even before they had tried some or all of them. Thus, war still plays an important function in international politics. It remains the ultimate method for settling a problem. This fact makes it more difficult to successfully reduce or to outlaw war on the international scene.[16]

The above discussion of methods used in international relations does not include judicial means such as arbitration and adjudication. They will be explained in the next chapter having to do with international law. The choice of method used by governments to solve a given problem will very much depend on the circumstances at hand, the objectives pursued, the attitude of the statesmen (reasonable and rational or belligerent and revengeful), the power ratio between the nation-states involved, the willingness of both sides to compromise, and other factors. Suffice it to say that it is better to talk with each other than to shoot at each other. Hopefully, in the years to come more and more statesmen will be able to solve their disputes by amicable means rather than through warfare.

INTERNATIONAL POLITICS IN THE POST-WORLD WAR II ERA

Having examined the elements of international politics and the methods employed by nation-states in their relations with each other, it may be

[16] Van Dyke, *op. cit.*, pp. 294–96.

worthwhile to scrutinize briefly the major international developments since World War II.

The Bipolar Development

The United States and the Soviet Union emerged from the war as the two global powers. Clearly, in 1945 the United States was substantially stronger than the Soviet Union, which had suffered considerably from the effects of the war. But the immense size of the Soviet army, its presence in most of the Balkan states, in Poland, in the heart of Germany, in Manchuria, and in the northern part of Korea, plus the strength derived from the dictatorial government of the country, compensated for some of the points of Russian weakness and gave the Soviet Union a power position nearly on a par with that of the United States.

In comparison to the two giants, other major World War II allies had become, at best, secondary powers. The United Kingdom emerged economically weakened from the war. Its hold over the vast colonial empire began to crumble, and with the independence of the Indian subcontinent in 1947 a movement was set into motion that in the next fifteen years led to the independence of most of the British colonies. France after World War II was economically weak and politically divided. A major general strike in 1948 led the country to near chaos. In addition, domestic political instability and the Indochina crisis, as well as the problem in Algeria, kept France from playing any influential role in foreign affairs until the return to office of de Gaulle in 1958. In the Far East, the end of World War II signaled the resumption of the civil war between the Communists led by Mao Tse-tung and the government forces under Chiang Kai-shek. In 1949 the Communists won the war and Chiang Kai-shek fled with the remnants of his forces to Taiwan. These developments and others left the Soviet Union and the United States temporarily the uncontested global rulers.

The governments of both powers set out to consolidate their areas of influence and, by doing so, established a bipolar order. The major line between these two spheres cut through the center of Europe. As Sir Winston Churchill stated so appropriately in his famous May 5, 1946, speech at Westminster College, Missouri:

> *From Stettin in the Baltic to Trieste in the Adriatic, an iron curtain has descended across the Continent. Behind that line lie all the capitals of the ancient states of Central and Eastern Europe. Warsaw, Berlin, Prague, Vienna, Budapest, Belgrade, Bucharest and Sofia, all these famous cities and populations around them lie in what I must call the Soviet sphere, and all are subject in one form or another not only to Soviet influence but to a very high and, in many cases, increasing measures of control from Moscow.*[17]

[17] Randolph S. Churchill, ed., *The Sinews of Peace: Post-War Speeches by Winston S. Churchill* (London: Cassell and Company, 1948), p. 100.

Churchill's classic statement points at the iron curtain as the man-made division between the two spheres of interest and alludes to the commencement of the Cold War era, an epoch that continued, with a varying degree of severity, until after the Cuban missile crisis.

The only Western enclave behind the iron curtain has been West Berlin, the part of the city occupied by British, French, and United States' troops since the summer of 1945 and governed by the Western Allies. During the late 1940s and 1950s the Soviet government made several attempts to eliminate Western presence in Berlin, the more serious ones being the 1948–49 blockade and Khrushchev's demands in 1958 and 1959 to turn West Berlin into a "free city" after the withdrawal of the Western troops. All these attempts failed, and the status of West Berlin has not been changed.

The two superpowers differed in the kind of hegemonic control they exercised. The United States' approach was Western-democratic oriented, providing substantial economic aid (the Marshall Plan), and intervening in a subtle fashion only when such intervention was deemed necessary. The Soviet approach, in contrast, was dictatorial, brought economic hardship on the subjected countries, and involved open and direct military intervention on several occasions. One consequence of the different approaches can be seen in the fact that substantially more people fled, or tried to flee, from East to West than vice versa. There is also clear evidence that in the early 1950s, in the absence of foreign military attacks, the Adenauer government in West Germany and its Western type of democratic order could have sustained itself quite readily without the presence of British, French, and United States' troops in the country. In contrast, evidence shows, that during the same time period the incumbent regimes in Czechoslovakia, East Germany, Hungary, and Poland were kept in power only with the help and as a result of the presence of Soviet troops.

Over the years, however, both major powers have faced difficulties in maintaining hegemony in their respective area. A general assessment of the developments in Europe and Asia shows that the Soviet Union clearly faced the greater difficulties. Let us examine these developments in some detail.

CHALLENGES TO SOVIET AND UNITED STATES' HEGEMONY

The first open conflict in the Soviet empire occurred in 1948, when Marshal Tito of Yugoslavia asked Russian advisers to leave his country and commenced a course of policies independent of Moscow. In 1953 widespread demonstrations against the Ulbricht regime occurred in East Germany. This uprising threatened to overthrow the incumbent Moscow-loyal power elite and was suppressed only by large-scale intervention of Soviet troops. Further unrest in the German Democratic Republic led to the building of the infamous Berlin Wall in 1961. A revolutionary type of uprising occurred in Hungary in 1956 and led temporarily to the withdrawal of Russian troops from that country and the installation of a popular government under Imre Nagy. A few days later, however, Russian troops reinvaded Hungary and forcefully replaced the Nagy government with Hungarian Communists loyal to Moscow. During the same year demonstrations in Poland led to a change in leadership and brought Wladyslaw Gomulka into office. On the basis of subsequent negotiations between Gomulka and Khrushchev the Soviet power elite decided against a military intervention in Poland. A similar situation occurred in Poland in late 1970, when fairly widespread demonstrations forced Gomulka out of office and brought the rather popular Edward Gierek to power.

In the Balkans Albania shifted its alliance from Moscow to Peking in the early 1960s. The government of Romania began in 1963 to pursue a foreign policy semi-independent of that of Moscow and the Warsaw bloc. The Soviet government refrained from intervening directly into the separate pursuits of the governments of Yugoslavia, Albania, and Romania.

The development in Czechoslovakia in 1968 was a different story. The liberal Communist government that had come to power under the leadership of Alexander Dubcek constituted, according to the majority of the members of the Soviet Politburo, a threat to the Russian national interest. As in the Hungarian episode of 1956, Soviet leaders feared in 1968 that Dubcek's experiments with a high degree of freedom of speech and of the press would become contagious—they might affect the thinking of people in Poland and, especially, East Germany. Moreover, there was fear in Moscow that Dubcek, in his foreign policy, might align himself with the West, thereby exposing a stretch of the Russian border to the West. The same would have occurred, according to Soviet reasoning, if Nagy would have remained in government in Hungary. The Hungarian as well as the Czech case threatened to blow a hole into the *cordon sanitaire* (buffer zone) that the Russians had established so carefully since World War II between their western boundary and the United States' sphere of influence.

The ultimate Soviet reaction to Dubcek's policies was a logistically smooth, large-scale military intervention by Warsaw Pact troops, the occupation of the country, a forced change in the Czech leadership, and the declaration of the Brezhnev Doctrine, which in fact states that the Soviet Union has the right to intervene in any Warsaw Pact country where the Communist system is in danger of being overthrown.

Finally, in our discussion of difficulties the Soviet power elite has experienced in maintaining control of its "bloc," some mention needs to be made of the Sino–Soviet dispute. When Mao initially came to power, he accepted quite readily Moscow's leadership in the bloc and, in turn, received extensive economic and technical aid from the Soviet Union. The deterioration of relations began in about 1960 and gained momentum during and after the Chinese–Indian border war (1962). The 1960s abounded with serious verbal clashes between the Chinese and the Soviet leaders, growing to such momentum that the Chinese seriously challenged Moscow's leadership of the Communist bloc. But the conflict did not stay in the realm of rhetoric. In March of 1969, Chinese and Russian troops engaged in two military clashes on the Ussuri River, resulting in hundreds of casualties on each side.[18] The Sino–Soviet dispute is intense and complex. It will be with these two countries in one form or another for some years to come. The dispute is not only over doctrine, but more basically has to do with the substantial differences in the national interests as conceived by the power elites of both countries.

While the Soviet Union has had its share of problems, the United States did not remain unscathed either. The post-World War II United States' sphere of influence—the Americas and Europe west of the iron curtain—has been subject to a number of economic and political developments that have catalyzed changes in the relations between these countries and the United States. In comparison with the Soviet Union, however, the United States has experienced substantially fewer traumatic experiences.

Generically speaking, the nation-states of the American continent have become more independent of the United States. Castro established a Communist-type government in Cuba in 1959 and associated that country with Moscow. In Chile a socialist-type of system gained control in legitimate elections in 1970, but was overthrown three years later. The relations of other American states with the United States differ from country to country. Some relations are closer, others are less so. The main point is that the era in which the United States dominated these states politically and U.S. business and industry exploited these states (more or less) is over, and a new relationship is in the making. This relationship is, in the case of some American states, a new partnership, in the cases of others a somewhat strained relationship.

Turning to Western Europe, the countries there have changed colossally since 1945. At the end of the war, they were war-torn, devastated, and prostrate. Their relationship with the United States at that time could be compared to the relationship between very small children and an all-powerful parent. In the meantime, however, these European states have grown to adulthood; they have become mature economically and politically and require a much more equal relationship with the United

[18] A perceptive English-language analysis of the March, 1969, clashes is found in Thomas W. Robinson, "The Sino-Soviet Border Dispute: Background, Development, and the March 1969 Clashes," *The American Political Science Review*, LXVI (December, 1972), pp. 1175–1201.

States than years ago. The required change in relations has been an agonizing experience for the policy makers in Washington. Their reaction has been slow. Confessedly, it is much easier to leave a policy as it is than to change it, but history does not stand still.

The primary West European challenge to U.S. foreign policy came from France during the 1960s. President de Gaulle pursued for some years the plan to weld Western Europe, under French leadership, into a third superpower that would serve as a balancing force between the Soviet Union and the United States. Former Chancellor Brandt in West Germany, with the blessings of Washington, undertook an important initiative with his *Ostpolitik,* aimed at puncturing the iron curtain by improving relations with the East European countries.

The termination of United States' military involvement in Southeast Asia has provided an opportunity for this country to re-examine relations with Western Europe, and it is no coincidence that Secretary of State Kissinger sometime ago called 1973 "the year of Europe" and recommended the negotiation of a new Atlantic Charter. The growing economic strength of the countries of the European Economic Community, especially West Germany, has had some dire consequences for United States' foreign trade and the stability of the dollar and has increased the need for our government to establish, jointly with our Canadian and West European allies, a new framework to meet more adequately the needs of the Atlantic community in the 1970s. Similar considerations apply to the relations between the United States and Japan.

In sum, a thorough re-examination of the relations between the United States and its West European allies is overdue. It is not true, however, that Western Europe has become anti-American. As former Chancellor Brandt and other West European statesmen have pointed out repeatedly, the shouts of "Ami, go home" are the rhetoric and thinking of a small minority of people in Western Europe. The countries of Western Europe need the alliance with the United States, and in turn the United States needs the alliance with Western Europe.

The above discussion has alluded from time to time to the critical international issues of the 1970s. However, before we can examine these, a discussion of the rise of the Third World is in order.

THE GROWTH OF THE THIRD WORLD

Following World War II the remaining colonial empires controlled by the British, Dutch, and French disintegrated rapidly. After the British had granted independence to the Indian subcontinent, some sixty countries in Africa, Asia, and Latin America achieved independence within the next two decades. The new countries and others who have been independent for some time but are still in the developmental state, such as Ethiopia and Liberia, are customarily referred to as the Third World, to distinguish them from the postindustrial societies of the West and the Communist countries. This division, however, is more academic than real. For example, the leaders of Yugoslavia and of the People's Republic of China have played important roles at Third World meetings.

The countries of the Third World have several important features in common. They are still in an early stage of industrial development and are trying to industrialize their societies as quickly as possible. Their governments are putting forth considerable efforts to build cohesive nation-states. This applies especially to sub-Saharan Africa, where substantial tribal differences still need to be overcome. Common to almost all these countries is a strong spirit of nationalism and the desire not to be dominated or manipulated by either of the two superpowers. As a consequence, most of the developing countries try to remain as nonaligned and uncommitted as possible. The initial tenets of the doctrine of nonalignment were first stated in form of the doctrine of *Panch Sheel* (Five Principles of Peaceful Coexistence) in the Sino-Indian Agreement on Tibet of 1954 and reiterated by President Nehru at the Bandung Conference in 1955.[19] While the members of the conference ascribed to the five principles, the members of the Third World have not always adhered to the doctrine in later years. The border clash between India and the People's Republic of China, the repeated military conflicts between India and Pakistan, Nasser's intervention in Yemen, and a number of conflicts between African countries are obviously in violation of the spirit of Bandung.[20]

The developing countries have become an important element for the superpowers. The Third World makes up about two-thirds of the membership of the United Nations. In addition, some of these countries contain large resources of oil, minerals, and other materials of importance to the advanced industrial societies. The governments of the People's Republic of China, the Soviet Union, the United States, and some European powers have put forth considerable efforts to gain and increase their influence in the Third World countries via foreign aid, peace corps, information offices, and other methods. Neither of the great powers or other developed countries has gained—or will gain—a monopoly of

[19] The five principles of *Panch Sheel* are: (1) mutual respect for each other's territorial integrity; (2) mutual nonaggression; (3) peaceful coexistence; (4) mutual noninterference in each other's internal affairs; and (5) equality and mutual benefit. A detailed discussion of the significance of the Bandung Conference is found in Michael Brecher, *The New States of Asia* (New York: Oxford University Press, 1966), pp. 153–215.

[20] The most exhaustive though not up to date discussion of intervention among the nation-states of Africa is found in I. William Zartman, *International Relations in the New Africa* (Englewood Cliffs, N.J.: Prentice-Hall, 1966).

influence in the Third World. Rather, the competition for influence will continue in the future.[21]

In recent years the phrase "the north–south split" has become popular among many students of international relations. The term refers to great cleavages in living standards of the postindustrial societies on the one hand and many of the developing countries on the other. The point is that now and in the years to come the developing countries need various kinds of help from the postindustrial societies, but they want it on their own terms, with no strings attached. The desire to remain independent of outside influence is a natural desire but does not always jibe with the pursuits of the great and near-great powers in their dealings with the developing countries. While the latter need the help of the former in some areas, the same holds true in reverse. However, as the developing countries become more viable, their leaders will insist still more strongly on receiving equal treatment in the family of nations. The governments of the People's Republic of China, the Soviet Union, and the United States, as well as others, will have to adjust their foreign policy dealings with the developing countries accordingly and at times will have to learn to cope with temporary behavior pattern that are enigmatic at best.[22]

THE CRUCIAL INTERNATIONAL ISSUES OF THE 1970s

Having surveyed the major international developments since the end of World War II, let us examine now the present-day relations and major policy schemes of the global powers, as well as the primary international issues of the 1970s as we see them at this time. While there have been considerable changes in world politics since 1945, the Soviet Union and the United States have retained their position as global powers primarily because of their immense military power. However, the governments of both countries have realized over the years that their countries cannot play the role of world policemen in perpetuity. In the case of the United States, our large-scale military involvement in Southeast Asia in the recent past has raised a number of questions and has led ultimately to a large-scale reappraisal of United States' foreign policy on a global scale. The beginning of a

[21] For a detailed discussion of the interrelationship between foreign aid and foreign policy, see Robert E. Asher, *Development Assistance in the Seventies* (Washington, D.C.: The Brookings Institution, 1970); David A. Baldwin, *Foreign Aid and American Foreign Policy* (New York: Frederick A. Praeger, 1966); Marshall I. Goldman, *Soviet Foreign Aid* (New York: Frederick A. Praeger, 1967); and Jacob J. Kaplan, *The Challenge of Foreign Aid* (New York: Frederick A. Praeger, 1967).

[22] The above discussion of "International Relations in the post-World War II era" is an expansion of a brief part of a former publication of mine in Bellows, Erikson, and Winter, eds., *Political Science: Introductory Essays and Readings* (Belmont, Cal.: Duxbury Press, 1971), pp. 456–458.

new approach was enunciated by President Nixon in his Guam speech of July, 1969. As stated in a Department of State publication, the new policy—known as the Nixon Doctrine—calls for a more restrained style of conducting foreign affairs:

> *We will attempt, consistent with protection of our own interests, to reduce our official presence and visibility abroad. We will emphasize mutuality and multilateralism. We will encourage others to assume a greater share of the responsibilities for the security and economic development of the area.*[23]

Soviet foreign policy appears to be undergoing a similar transformation and, at least presently, features restraints in Russian dealings with the People's Republic of China, caution in the Middle East, and a friendlier attitude toward the West, especially as shown in recent negotiations with West Germany and the United States.

The two superpowers are basically in agreement on several crucial issues of world politics. The most important of these is an understanding that the governments of both countries must do their utmost to prevent a war between themselves. Such a war, and both sides are fully aware of the consequences, would be mutual suicide and would mean the annihilation of the Northern Hemisphere. Both superpowers are also in agreement that the United Nations (which will be discussed in the next chapter) serves a worthwhile purpose and deserves continuing support. This is not to say that the governments of the Soviet Union and the United States always see eye to eye in the United Nations and on matters pertaining to it, but both countries will refrain from wrecking that foremost international organization. There is also some tacit agreement between the superpowers to follow a cautious line of pursuit in the Middle East and to prevent the outbreak of a major military conflict in that crucial area. Finally, the Soviet Union and the United States would like to keep the "nuclear club" limited to its present five members. A proliferation in the number of nuclear powers would increase the chance of nuclear war, be it by accident or by intent. Whether the superpowers can prevent secondary powers (other than China, France, and the United Kingdom) from developing such weapons is one of the crucial questions of our decade.[24]

It is difficult to categorize the major current international issues in terms

[23] From *United States Foreign Policy 1969–1970: A Report of the Secretary of State.* (Washington: U.S. Govt. Printing Office, Department of State Publication #8575), p. 36. The implications of the Nixon Doctrine are discussed in some detail in subsequent pages of this publication.

[24] For a more detailed discussion of the proliferation issue, see William C. Davidon et al., *The Nth Country Problem and Arms Control* (Washington: National Planning Association, 1960); R. N. Rosecrance, ed., *The Dispersion of Nuclear Weapons* (New York: Columbia University Press, 1964); and Alastair Buchan, ed., *A World of Nuclear Powers?* (Englewood Cliffs, N. J.: Prentice-Hall, 1966).

of priority. Some of them are equally important, and most of them are interrelated. Major efforts should be directed in the 1970s toward reducing the arms race between the Soviet Union and the United States; preventing the spread of nuclear weapons to countries outside the "nuclear club"; reducing the military confrontation between East and West in Central Europe; diminishing the tensions in the Middle East; and helping to improve the standard of living in the developing countries.

The arms race between the superpowers has been going on since 1945, and thousands of billions of dollars have been spent in military pursuits. Over the years the United States has maintained a two- to four-year advantage over the Soviet Union. For example, the United States had its first operational atomic bomb in 1945 and the hydrogen bomb in 1949. The respective years for the Soviet Union are 1949 and 1953. This trend continued in about the same pace with the development of missiles and the sophistication of warheads. The most recent development in the arms race has been the production and employment of MIRVs (Multiple Independently Targeted Warheads). The United States has several hundred operational MIRVs on land—as well as submarine-based missiles. In July of 1973 United States intelligence sources found out that the Russians had just successfully flight-tested their first MIRVs. What will be the Pentagon's counteraction?

The governments of both superpowers have in recent years come under increasing pressure at home to allocate more resources for domestic improvements and less for military efforts. The disarmament conference of the 1960s produced the 1963 Nuclear Test Ban Treaty (banning nuclear tests in the atmosphere) and the Nuclear Nonproliferation Treaty of 1968. The Strategic Arms Limitation Talks (SALT) between the Soviet Union and the United States commenced in 1969. Meeting alternately in Helsinki and Vienna, the two negotiation teams worked out the details of the Anti-Ballistic Missile Treaty, which was signed by President Nixon and General Secretary Brezhnev in May of 1972 during the president's visit in Moscow. The results of SALT I, the ABM Treaty, deals with the *defensive* part of the two country's nuclear weapon systems. In essence, the treaty limits the Soviet Union and the United States to the construction of two ABM (Anti-Ballistic Missile) sites only, thus preventing both from building nationwide ABM systems.[25] In the meantime, SALT II negotiations have been held between representatives of the Soviet Union and the United States for the purpose of limiting the production and employment of *offensive* nuclear weapons and some agreement has been achieved in this area.

The main hindrance in disarmament and arms control discussions in

[25] The text of the Anti-Ballistic Missile Treaty is published in *The Department of State Bulletin,* 66, June 26, 1972.

"Basically, of course, we've got to pull together."
(Le Pelley in The Christian Science Monitor (c) 1966 TCSPS.)

(From *The Herblock Gallery*, Simon & Schuster, 1968.)

general, and in the negotiations between the United States and the Soviet Union in particular, has been the psychological element of suspicion. Each side fears that the other side may not comply in full with the provisions of the agreement. In the case of the nuclear treaties between the two superpowers, the Russians' constant refusal to permit on-site inspection and verification in their country used to be a hindrance to the negotiations. In recent years, however, the development of satellite surveillance has decreased significantly the importance of on-site inspection. Nevertheless, the growth of reciprocal good will—that is, an improvement in political relations—remains very important for success in arms control and disarmament negotiations.

ARMS WRESTLING

(Jim Dobbins, The Boston Post.)

Regarding the nonproliferation of nuclear weapons, mention should be made of the fact that perhaps a dozen countries in addition to those in the nuclear club have the know-how to produce such weaponry. Others will gain the capability in years to come. The Nuclear Nonproliferation Treaty of 1968 forbids signatories in the nuclear club to supply nonnuclear countries with nuclear weapons or weapons technology. In addition, the treaty prohibits nonnuclear signatories to use their nuclear facilities for military purposes. A majority of the members of the United Nations have signed the Nuclear Nonproliferation Treaty. The nonsignatories include France and the People's Republic of China, two members of the nuclear club.[26]

The issue of bringing about a partial military disengagement in Central Europe has received considerable attention in recent years. Since 1945 the Soviet Union and the United States, supported by their respective allies, have maintained vast military establishments along the iron curtain. The Cold War of yesteryear has given way to a new set of relationships between East and West, which foreshadow the possibility of some degree of disengagement. Recent statements from both sides have indicated some interest in discussing the possibility of balanced force reductions. At the Moscow summit of 1972 the governments of the Soviet Union and the United States agreed that

> *the goal of ensuring stability and security in Europe would be served by a reciprocal reduction of armed forces and armaments, first of all in Central Europe. . . . Agreement on the procedures for negotiations on this subject should be reached as soon as practicable between the states concerned.*[27]

The military balance of power in Europe has been very delicate since the start of the Cold War—delicate in the sense that potentially a small incident along the iron curtain could trigger a nuclear holocaust. The time is ripe for taking a fresh look at this potential Pandora's box. Hopefully, forthcoming negotiations can lead toward force reductions. These reductions, however, must be reciprocal and balanced in order to continue to insure the security interests of the Soviet Union and the United States, as well as their respective allies. As former Chancellor Brandt mentioned on various occasions, a unilateral force reduction by the West would not serve the purpose of peace in Europe, rather it could bring forth dire consequences. President Nixon and General Secretary Brezhnev, during the latter's visit to the United States, decided that negotiations on the mutual reduction of military forces in weapons in Europe should begin in Vienna on October 30, 1973. The subject of the discussions is complex, the road ahead is tough,

[26] For an extensive treatment of the Nuclear Nonproliferation Treaty, see Mason Willrich, *Non-Proliferation Treaty: Framework for Nuclear Arms Control* (Charlottesville, Va.: Michie, 1969).

[27] Department of State, "Foreign Policy Outlines," June, 1973, 24–31, p. 1.

but with some good will on both sides success can be achieved on this crucial issue.

The Middle East has been a powder keg for some time and presumably will constitute the major regional area of conflict in the next few years. We all are acquainted with the generalities of the Arab–Israeli struggle between 1948 and the present time. Suffice it to say that the conflict is still going on. Both superpowers have wisely kept their role in this quagmire limited, in order to forestall a direct confrontation in that area. Somehow an agreement has to be arrived at by the Arabs and Israel in which the Arabs would give legal recognition to the existence of the nation-state Israel and all privileges connected with it. In this accord, the boundaries between Israel and the adjacent Arab states need to be freshly delineated in a fashion acceptable to both sides. Finally, the problem of the Palestinian refugees has to receive more proper international attention than in the past. A better way of living and a future have to be provided for these people in order to curtail their hatred and acts of terrorism. Israel has the potential to contribute considerable know-how to the development of its Arab neighbors, and both sides would benefit from better relations.

The final issue mentioned has to do with the developing countries, populated by about two-thirds of the world's people. Most of these people are poor and illiterate. A "revolution of rising expectations" is sweeping the Third World. Generally speaking, the leaders of the developing countries would like to move their societies into the twentieth century as quickly as possible—to industrialize and increase the general welfare. These societies need aid and advice in many areas. The postindustrial societies have the means to render help. We believe that this aid ought to be channeled more through international sources, rather than bilaterally. Ways should be found to reduce the cleavage between the rich and the poor nation-states more successfully than in the past.

Many other current problems—and problems in the making—are not only of national but of international scope. Pollution, disease, and food scarcity transcend national boundaries. These problems lend themselves more readily than politico-military issues to international collaboration. Some degree of international cooperation has already been established to examine these problems. Hopefully, in years to come more and more statesmen and their citizens will realize that there exist problems that threaten the survival of mankind, and that out of this realization stronger international ties of brotherhood will grow to serve the well-being of all of mankind.

In this chapter we have examined the nature of international politics, its actors, the characteristics of the nation-state system, the methods used for interaction on the international scene, the major developments in international politics since World War II, and the major issues of our time. Collective efforts toward peace through balance of power, collective security, international and regional organizations, as well as the role of international law, will be the subject of the following chapter.

Selected Readings

Good general treatments of the subject of international politics are, among others, Frederick H. Hartmann, *The Relations of Nations,* 4th ed. (New York: Macmillan, 1973); K. J. Holsti, *International Politics: A Framework for Analysis,* 2nd ed. (Englewood Cliffs, N.J.: Prentice-Hall, 1972); Hans J. Morgenthau, *Politics Among Nations: The Struggle for Power and Peace,* 5th ed. (New York: Alfred A. Knopf, 1973); Steven J. Rosen and Walter S. Jones, *The Logic of International Relations** (Cambridge, Mass.: Winthrop Publishers, 1974); John G. Stoessinger, *The Might of Nations: World Politics in Our Time,** 5th ed. (New York: Random House, 1975); Richard W. Sterling, *Macropolitics: International Relations in a Global Society* (New York: Alfred A. Knopf, 1974); and Vernon Van Dyke, *International Politics,* 3rd ed. (New York: Appleton-Century-Crofts, 1972).

A highly readable examination of contemporary worldwide issues and problems is Lester R. Brown, *World Without Borders** (New York: Vintage Books, 1972). For a contrasting study that explores the force of nationalism and the potential for developing international loyalties, see Karl W. Deutsch, *Nationalism and Its Alternatives* (New York: Alfred A. Knopf, 1969). An interesting psychological discussion of international problems is Otto Klineberg, *The Human Dimension in International Relations** (New York: Holt, Rinehart and Winston, 1964).

The foreign policies of ten leading countries are examined in F. S. Northedge, ed., *The Foreign Policies of the Powers,** 2nd ed. (New York: The Free Press, 1974). Two excellent analyses of the relations between the major powers are Adam B. Ulam, *The Rivals: America and Russia Since World War II** (New York: Viking Press, 1971); and John G. Stoessinger, *Nations in Darkness: China, Russia, and America,** 2nd ed. (New York: Random House, 1975). For an examination of the development of foreign relations among the new states of Africa, see I. William Zartman, *International Relations in the New Africa** (Englewood Cliffs, N.J.: Prentice-Hall, 1966).

An excellent treatment of United States' foreign policy is Frederick H. Hartmann, *The New Age of American Foreign Policy* (New York:

* Available in paperback.

Macmillan, 1970). Of special interest should be the writings of Henry A. Kissinger, which include *Nuclear Weapons and Foreign Policy** (New York: Doubleday, 1957); *The Necessity for Choice: Prospects of American Foreign Policy** (New York: Doubleday, 1962); and *American Foreign Policy** (New York: W. W. Norton, 1974). Useful discussions of the process of foreign policy making are John Spanier and Eric M. Uslaner, *How American Foreign Policy is Made** (New York: Praeger, 1974); and Marian Irish and Else Frank, *U.S. Foreign Policy: Context, Conduct, Content** (New York: Harcourt Brace Jovanovich, 1975). The public influence on foreign policy making is analyzed in Bernard C. Cohen, *The Public's Impact on Foreign Policy** (Boston: Little, Brown, 1973).

A standard work on the development of organized diplomacy and recent changes in diplomatic practice is Harold Nicolson, *Diplomacy,** 3rd ed. (New York: Oxford University Press, 1963). Two informative treatments of the activities of diplomats are Humphrey Trevelyan, *Diplomatic Channels* (Boston: Gambit, 1973); and Eric Clark, *Diplomat: The World of International Diplomacy* (New York: Taplinger, 1973). The practice of international negotiations is superbly analyzed in Fred C. Iklé, *How Nations Negotiate** (New York: Frederick A. Praeger, 1967); and Arthur Lall, *Modern International Negotiations: Principles and Practice* (New York: Columbia University Press, 1966).

For a skillful discussion of the role of multinational corporations in international politics, see the anthology by Abdul A. Said and Luiz R. Simmons, eds., *The New Sovereigns: Multinational Corporations as World Powers** (Englewood Cliffs, N.J.: Prentice-Hall, 1975).

Three good treatments of foreign aid and its role in U.S. foreign policy are David A. Baldwin, *Foreign Aid and American Foreign Policy** (New York: Frederick A. Praeger, 1966); Jacob A. Kaplan, *The Challenge of Foreign Aid: Policies, Problems, and Possibilities* (New York: Frederick A. Praeger, 1967); and John D. Montgomery, *Foreign Aid in International Politics** (Englewood-Cliffs, N.J.: Prentice-Hall, 1967). For information on Soviet foreign aid, see Marshall I. Goldman, *Soviet Foreign Aid* (New York: Frederick A. Praeger, 1967); and James Richard Carter, *The Net Cost of Soviet Foreign Aid* (New York: Frederick A. Praeger, 1971).

The classic study on warfare is Quincy Wright, *A Study of War,** 2nd ed. (Chicago: University of Chicago Press, 1965). For a comprehensive treatment of the potential implications of the nuclear arms race, see Herman Kahn, *On Escalation: Metaphors and Scenarios* (New York: Frederick A.

* Available in paperback.

Praeger, 1965). A highly readable case study of war is John G. Stoessinger, *Why Nations Go to War** (New York: St. Martin's Press, 1974). Recent data on worldwide military expenditures and on arms trade are compiled in *World Military Expenditures and Arms Trade—1963–1973** (Washington, D.C.: U.S. Arms Control and Disarmament Agency, 1975). A good comparative analysis of defense costs is Bruce M. Russett, *What Price Vigilance?** (New Haven: Yale University Press, 1970).

The following recent publications are informative treatments of arms control and disarmament: Georges Fischer, *The Non-Proliferation of Nuclear Weapons,* trans. by David Willey (New York: St. Martin's Press, 1971); Morton A. Kaplan, ed., *SALT: Problems and Prospects** (Morristown, N.J.: General Learning Press, 1973); and Trevor N. Dupuy and Gay M. Hammerman, eds., *A Documentary History of Arms Control and Disarmament* (Dunn Loring, Va.: T. N. Dupuy Associates, 1973). The texts and histories of the arms control and disarmament agreements concluded in the twentieth century are published in *Arms Control and Disarmament Agreements** (Washington, D.C.: U.S. Arms Control and Disarmament Agency, 1975).

* Available in paperback.

Chapter 13

Collective Means for Cooperation and Integration in the International Community

AT the time this chapter was drafted, two members of the United Nations and of the North Atlantic Treaty Organization—Greece and Turkey—came close to going to war because of the coup d'état on Cyprus. The Security Council of the United Nations, Secretary-General Waldheim, and the United Nations Emergency Forces stationed on Cyprus tried to curtail bloodshed on the island and endeavored to prevent the outbreak of war between Greece and Turkey.

The above illustrates a major facet of the history of mankind, namely the presence of violence on the one hand and attempts toward peaceful settlement on the other. International lawlessness has existed since antiquity, but so have efforts toward establishing a greater degree of order by formulating international rules applicable to all of mankind, and by establishing international organizations to maintain peace and order. We have pointed out in the previous chapter that the international community has faced a greater degree of anarchy than domestic society because there is no single international government having a preponderance of power.

This chapter attempts to examine briefly the nature of international law and international and regional organizations and the role these play in international politics today.

International law and organizations are collective in the sense that they are supposed to apply to and serve all countries and all of mankind, rather than one group of people or one country. These forces are means that can and do place limitations on the behavior of states in their relations with each other. Let us first look at international law.

THE NATURE OF INTERNATIONAL LAW

Queries about the existence of international law are of a rhetorical nature, because the body known as international law is of a somewhat different nature than domestic law. The governments of nation-states, usually having a preponderance of power in their respective societies, enforce domestic law. On the international scene, however, there is no world government and therefore no agency that can enforce international law. Definitions of international law usually recognize this important difference between the roles of domestic and international law. According to J. L. Brierly, "The Law of Nations, or International Law, may be defined as the body of rules and principles of action which are binding upon civilized states in their relations with one another."[1] A still more pointed definition comes from Charles Hyde, who states:

> *The term international law may fairly be employed to designate the principles and rules of conduct declaratory thereof which states feel themselves bound to observe and, therefore, commonly observe in their relations with each other.*[2]

Hyde's definition points at the aspect of voluntarism in international law, the fact that nation-states "feel themselves bound to observe" this rule or that, for common sense reasons.

Governments of nation-states will adhere to certain aspects of international law for one of several reasons: many rules are followed customarily. This would apply, for example, to most of the practices in the field of diplomacy. The reasons of expediency and/or morality may be relevant in some other situations. Governments will refrain from violating international principles out of the consideration that otherwise other countries would do likewise. An example of this category would be the general adherence of Western states to the Prisoner of War rules as stated in the Geneva convention of 1929 and revised in 1949. In World War II, for example, the authorities of the United States, Britain, and Germany treated their respective prisoners more humanely, as compared with the treatment of German POWs in the Soviet Union or Russian POWs in Germany. The final category would be that of sanctions, which may take the form of condemnation by other governments and outside public opinion or the threat of or initiation of retaliatory actions, such as severing diplomatic relations, economic sanctions, or military actions. These economic or military actions may be pursued against the perpetrator by one or several countries, a regional organization, or the United Nations. Examples of the last would be the eco-

[1] J. L. Brierly, *The Law of Nations,* 6th ed., rev. by Sir Humphrey Waldock (New York: Oxford University Press, 1963), p. 1.

[2] Charles Cheney Hyde, *International Law Chiefly As Interpreted and Applied by the United States,* Vol. 1 (Boston: Little, Brown, 1945), p. 1.

nomic sanctions imposed by the United Nations against Rhodesia and the application of military sanction to combat aggression in Korea.

What, specifically, does international law consist of? This question may be answered best by citing a classification scheme developed by Vernon Van Dyke. He divides the scope of international law into four major categories.[3]

The Law of Peace. This category includes principles and rules having to do with the establishment of nation-states, their recognition by other countries, and the obligations of new nation-states. It also contains the rules relating to the extent of the national domain (that is, questions about boundaries and coastal jurisdiction), the rights of governments, the concept of domestic jurisdiction, the determination of nationality, and the rights of aliens.

The Law of War. Van Dyke's second category deals with rules that have been developed for regulating the conduct of military hostilities. This rubric includes procedures for the declaration and termination of war, as well as the treatment of enemy civilians and soldiers and their property. An examination of warfare in past decades and centuries shows that some countries have adhered more closely to rules in this category than others. In recent years the development of nuclear weaponry has rendered some of the rules of the law of war obsolete.

The Law of Neutrality. Rules in this category define the obligations and rights of the belligerent vis a vis neutral countries and vice versa.

The Law Concerning Resort to War. These rules have their origin in the twentieth century. The earliest restriction of the freedom of nation-states to go to war is found in the Covenant of the League of Nations and was buttressed by the Kellogg-Briand Pact (1928). In this treaty, which was signed by most countries, the governments pledged themselves "to condemn recourse to war for the solution of international controversies, and to renounce it as an instrument of national policy" and to seek peaceful settlement of their disputes. The United Nations Charter constitutes the most recent source of limitation. The signatories have promised under Article 2 that they "shall settle their international disputes by peaceful means in such a manner that international peace and security, and justice, are not endangered." Further that they "shall refrain in their international relations from the threat or use of force against the territorial integrity or political independence of any state. . . ." Recent history has shown, however, that these provisions have not prevented some countries from going to war against each other. The attacker usually has claimed to fight in "self-defense."

[3] Vernon Van Dyke, *International Politics,* 3rd ed. (New York: Appleton-Century-Crofts, 1972), pp. 304–310.

THE DEVELOPMENT OF INTERNATIONAL LAW

When the Dutch scholar Hugo Grotius, commonly known as "the father of international law" published his famous work *De jure belli ac pacis* ("On the Law of War and Peace") in 1625, he categorized and codified in his book all aspects of international law that had been developed in the previous centuries of Western civilization. He placed into a modern setting the interstate rules and principles that had been developed by the Greeks, the Romans, and subsequent Western cultures. His book was the first comprehensive treatment of the subject, and it has served as the basis for further study and growth.[4]

In the modern nation-states era, which began roughly with the Treaty of Westphalia (1648), international law has grown in a fashion similar to the growth of common law, and this process of growth is steadily continuing. New features were added in recent decades in the form of international forums and agencies rendering decisions on disputes between two or more nation-states.

The first permanent international court of Arbitration was established by the First Hague Conference (1899). This body is still in existence and, over the years, has decided some twenty issues between nation-states. A second international judicial body was established in 1920 as part of the League of Nations. It became known as the Permanent Court of International Justice. In 1945 the founders of the United Nations established the International Court of Justice as successor to the Permanent Court of International Justice. The International Court of Justice is one of the six principal organs of the United Nations. Located, like its predecessors, in The Hague, it consists of fifteen judges who are elected by the General Assembly and the Security Council of the United Nations. The members of the court are elected for nine-year terms on a staggered basis (five every three years) and may be reelected.[5] The court deals with legal cases (that is, questions having to do with what the law is in a particular case) rather than political cases (questions about what the law should be). Issues of the latter category cannot be adjudicated by the court. They have to be dealt with by methods producing peaceful change (diplomacy) or, if these fail, by means of violence (such as war or threat of war).

Only nation-states may be parties in cases before the International Court

[4] For an English-language translation of Grotius' writings, see A. C. Campbell, *The Rights of War and Peace including the Law of Nature and the Law of Nations Translated from the Original Latin of Grotius* (Washington and London: M. Walter Dunne, Publisher, 1901). A useful biographical discussion of Grotius is Hamilton Vreeland, *Hugo Grotius* (New York: Oxford University Press, 1917).

[5] The United Nations has published an informative handbook on the court. See United Nations Office of Publications *The International Court of Justice* (New York: United Nations).

of Justice. The court can try only those cases that parties in dispute submit voluntarily. It does not have any enforcement powers enjoyed by domestic courts. Even if two states agree to submit their dispute to the International Court, they do not have to adhere to its judgment. An exception to the foregoing statement is that in conjunction with Paragraph 2 of Article 36 of the Statute of the International Court of Justice a number of countries have pledged themselves to accept compulsory jurisdiction of the court.[6] By 1971 forty-seven states had pledged themselves to this "optional clause," some however with various kinds of reservations that limit their cooperation with the International Court of Justice.

All in all, the role of the International Court of Justice is different from and weaker than that of domestic courts.

THE SOURCES OF INTERNATIONAL LAW

As domestic law has grown from the needs of people living within societies, international law has grown out of the needs of nation-states. The major sources of international law are listed in Paragraph I of Article 38 of the Statute of the International Court of Justice:

1. *The Court, whose function is to decide in accordance with international law such disputes as are submitted to it, shall apply:*
   a. *international conventions, whether general or particular, establishing rules expressly recognized by the contesting states;*
   b. *international custom, as evidence of a general practice accepted as law;*
   c. *the general principles of law recognized by civilized nations;*
   d. *subject to the provisions of Article 59 [stating that the decision of the Court has no binding force except between the parties and in respect of that particular case], judicial decisions and the teachings of the most highly qualified publicists of the various nations, as subsidiary means for the determination of rules of law.*[7]

Let us briefly examine the sources stated above:

International Conventions. The term refers to treaties and related agreements concluded on a multilateral basis. Bilateral treaties rarely create

[6] The states parties to the present statute may at any time declare that they recognize as compulsory ipso facto and without special agreement in relation to any other state accepting the same obligation, the juristiction of the court in all legal disputes concerning:

1. The interpretation of a treaty.
2. Any question of international law.
3. The existence of any fact which, if established, would constitute a breach of an international obligation.
4. The nature or extent of the reparation to be made for the breach of an international obligation.

[7] See United Nations, *Yearbook of the United Nations 1971* (New York: United Nations Publications, 1974), p. 779.

a new rule of international law. They are usually built upon and declaratory of existing rules. Treaties constitute an important part of international law. As an international practice, they date back as far as written records have been found. In our century a number of multilateral treaties and agreements have come into existence. While none of them have obtained universal ratification, they have achieved the support of enough nation-states to be considered part of international law. The Covenant of the League of Nations of 1919, the Kellogg-Briand Pact of 1928, the Charter of the United Nations of 1945, the Nuclear Test Ban Treaty of 1963, and the Non-Proliferation Treaty of 1968 are examples of multilateral treaties. Under the auspices of the United Nations, three Law of the Sea conferences have been held, the latest in 1976 at the United Nations in New York. This meeting achieved nearly universal representation. The most important issue of that conference and its predecessors concerns the zone of sovereignty over coastal waters. Under existing international law territorial waters extend to 3 miles from the coast. During the past two decades some nation-states have unilaterally declared larger zones of sovereignty, amounting to 12 miles and in a few instances even 200 miles. The representatives at these meetings have made some progress toward a new agreement. Hope exists that a compromise solution will be arrived at, producing a new international agreement on coastal sovereignty, which will revise existing international law.

While bilateral and multilateral treaties are considered binding on the signatories, history shows a number of examples of the governments of some participant states having broken their promises and having either partially or fully terminated their respective international obligations. This, obviously, decreases the force of international law. The Nazi German government, for example, unilaterally terminated several treaties with the questionable assertion that the other party had violated them.

In recent years copies of some multilateral treaties have been deposited with the United Nations, in order to give them a greater degree of international legal standing. This practice was followed by the United States and the Soviet Union after their ratification of the Nuclear Test Ban Treaty and the Nuclear Non-Proliferation Treaty. We may assume that this practice will be followed by these countries and others in the future.

International Customs. Established customs among the nation-states constitute an important part of international law. These are rules of behavior that were introduced decades or even centuries ago by one or some countries in dealing with each other and slowly were adopted by others because they found them useful. Once an adoption of this kind has become nearly universal, a new international law has been established. A great number of customs that are now universally accepted have developed over the centuries in the area of displomacy and the rights and privileges of diplomats. A good example is the principle of diplomatic immunity enjoyed by accredited diplomats throughout the world.

General Principles of Law. A third source of international law is made up by generic principles of law, which are recognized by "the civilized nation-states" of this world. What are these general principles? While there is some disagreement among students of international law on the nature of these principles, a number of them point out that Article 38 of the Statute of the International Court of Justice refers to the general principles of justice and reason as found in natural law as rationally understood and applied to modern society. How are these principles applied to present-day cases? According to Frederick H. Hartmann:

> *The "general principles" of law, to be applied at all, must be applied in a particular case to specific facts that are the corollaries of those principles. The question asked is: what does the principle mean in this case? The answer is the result of the use of reason and, where necessary, analogies from principles pervading the municipal law of nations in general.*[8]

It appears from the above that the "general principles" stated in Article 38 constitute an element of international law that is less defined and more difficult to apply than the principles originating from treaties and customs.

Judicial Decisions and Writings of Scholars. Both are indirect and subsidiary sources of international law. Decisions rendered in domestic courts may here and there help international jurists in forming their opinions. More important are the decisions rendered by international tribunals. The growing body of these decisions will serve as precedents for international jurists in years and decades to come.

The writings of experts were very important during the formative stage of modern international law. However, with the formation of a body of modern international law and the establishment of international tribunals, the publicist has become a commentator and interpreter, rather than a maker of international law.[9]

THE ROLE OF INTERNATIONAL LAW IN CONTEMPORARY TIMES

Because of the lack of universal executive enforcement powers, international law has not taken on the effectiveness of domestic law, nor has the

[8] Frederick H. Hartmann, *The Relations of Nations*, 4th ed. (New York: Macmillan, 1973), p. 113.

[9] For more extensive discussions of the sources of international law see Gerhard von Glahn, *Law Among Nations: An Introduction to Public International Law*, 2nd ed. (London: The Macmillan Company, 1970), pp. 10–22; Charles A. Fenwick, *International Law*, 4th ed. (New York: Appleton-Century-Crofts, 1965), pp. 84–97; Brierly, *op. cit.*, pp. 56–68; and Ahmed Sheikh, *International Law and National Behavior* (New York: John Wiley, 1974), pp. 62–69.

International Court of Justice achieved the important role of national supreme courts. According to Stanley Hoffmann:

> *The nature of the international system condemns international law to all the weaknesses and perversions that it is so easy to deride. International law is merely a magnifying mirror that reflects faithfully and cruelly the essence and the logic of international politics. In a fragmented world, there is no "global perspective" from which anyone can authoritatively assess, endorse, or reject the separate national efforts at making international law serve national interests above all.*[10]

Modern international law has developed essentially within the framework of the Western states. The rise of the Communist countries and the Third World of the developing nation-states has brought about a high degree of pluralism on the international scene which, in turn, calls for the revision of formerly accepted international principles in order to make them universally applicable. The discussions at the Law of the Sea conference serve as an illustrative example of this process of revision to produce principles of international law acceptable to the West, the Communist world, and the developing countries. One may assume that this adjustment will continue for years to come. All countries, whether postindustrial Western, Communist, or developing, engage in similar basic activities. They all have certain interests in common. It is in the area of commonality that universal principles can be achieved first. As stated by Oliver J. Lissitzyn:

> *The conflicts of interest do not prevent mutually acceptable regulation of transnational activities in the areas of international relations where there is some community of interest, however limited. Since all states engage in such activities, there is a basis for the existence of "universal" international law in the sense of a number of concepts and norms understood, invoked, and honored by all states, as well as of "particular" international law-norms that apply to some but not all states. Both universal and particular international law may be expected to grow in scope and complexity as the volume and variety of transnational activities increase.*[11]

The governments of all nation-states have common interests (though there may be a difference in degree) in internationally accepted rules pertaining to the exercise of diplomacy, the issue of maritime jurisdiction, traffic on the high seas, regulation of outer space, treatment of enemy nationals and their property during wartime, as well as the rights and obli-

[10] Stanley Hoffmann, in Lawrence Scheinman and David Wilkinson, eds., *International Law and Political Crisis: An Analytic Casebook* (Boston: Little, Brown, 1968), p. xvii.

[11] Oliver J. Lissitzyn, "International Law in a Divided World," *International Conciliation* (March, 1963), pp. 3–69. The author examines very incisively the impact the rise of the Communist bloc of countries and the developing nation-states have had on existing international law.

gations of neutrals. In this context, it is of some interest that two adversary states, Cuba and the United States, were able to conclude a reciprocally beneficial agreement against skyjacking.

The presence of international law exercises a moderating influence on the foreign policy activities of governments. It provides basic norms of conduct governments can use for their communication with each other. It furnishes means for channeling conflict so that issues can be decided by peaceful means instead of force. It serves as a moral force in that international condemnation can be directed against the violator of universally established norms.

The problematic nature of international law will continue for some time. Its plight, in the words of Stanley Hoffmann,

> *is that, now as before, it shows on its body of rules all the scars inflicted by the international state of war. The tragedy of contemporary international law is that of a double divorce: first, between the old liberal dream of a world rule of law, and the realities of an international system of multiple minidramas that always threaten to become major catastrophes; second, between the old dream and the new requirements of moderation, which in the circumstances of the present system suggest a down-playing of formal law in the realm of peace-and-war issues, and an upgrading of more flexible techniques, until the system has become less fierce.*[12]

In the complete absence of international law, the world of ours would be much worse off than it is now. One can only hope that the world community will make speedy headway in transforming traditional international law into the norms and principles that can be accepted universally by the multiple world we live in. Moreover, it is hoped that governments will increasingly use the existing body of international law to settle disputes by peaceful means, so that the world can become a more lawful community.

INTERNATIONAL ORGANIZATION

The Historical Perspective

International organization is a response to insecurity in the multination system. The League of Nations was established after World War I to prevent another worldwide war. In 1945 the United Nations was created "to save succeeding generations from the scourge of war.[13]" The underlying aim of international organization is to increase cooperation among the nation-states and to decrease friction and violence on the international scene.

Attempts at international organization date back as far as the League of Greek City-States at the time of Plato and Aristotle. The modern era of

[12] Stanley Hoffmann, *op. cit.*, pp. xvii and xix.

[13] From the Preamble to the Charter of the United Nations.

international conferences commenced with the Treaty of Westphalia (1648), when hundreds of envoys, representing nearly every European state, met and catalyzed a new era of European relations. A number of interesting plans toward international federation and organization were proposed during the seventeenth and eighteenth centuries. For example, the Frenchman Emeric Cruce advocated a world union of independent states; the "Grand Design" of Henry IV of France called for converting Europe into a Christian Republic to be composed of fifteen equal units; William Penn and Abbe de Saint-Pierre proposed related plans for a "Parliament of Europe."

The Congress of Vienna (1815) set the stage for the Quadruple Alliance and its periodic congresses—a system that became known as the "Concert of Europe," which in essence was a system of balance of power maintained by the four great continental powers of that time.

In 1899 and 1907 two international conferences were held in The Hague, Holland. The professed aim of these meetings was to bring about general disarmament and to develop means for the peaceful settlement of disputes. While these conferences were far from being successful, they had some importance for the development of international organization because representatives of a number of non-European states joined their European colleagues at these gatherings, and the principle of one country–one vote (as found in voting procedure of the General Assembly of the United Nations) was put into operation.

The prevalent political climate at the end of World War I led to the establishment of the first nearly universal organization, the League of Nations. Its permanent headquarters were located in Geneva, Switzerland. The major bodies of the League were the Assembly, in which all member countries were represented, and the Council, which was made up of the great powers. The day-to-day staff work was handled by a permanent Secretariat under the direction and supervision of the Assembly and Council. The organizational structure of the League as well as its practices and experiences had, as we shall see later on, a considerable influence on the shaping of the United Nations in the 1940s.

While the existence of the League of Nations lent itself to improved international relations during the 1920s, it did not fulfill the Wilsonian hopes of preventing another world war. By the late 1930s the League, for all practical purposes, had become a defunct organization. While a number of reasons could be cited for this, the two most important ones are that the major powers never showed a concurrent full commitment to support the League and its principles. The United States, whose president had been the prime mover in establishing the League, did not even become a member of the organization. Related to the above, the principle of collective security, written in rather loose language into Articles 10 and 11 of the League Covenant, never became operative. The concept of collective security denotes a security arrangement wherein all members pledge themselves to common retaliatory action in the case of an attack against a member country. The League failed to stem the tide of aggression that commenced when Japan invaded Manchuria in 1931.

One of the greatest long-range values of the League of Nations, perhaps, lies in the fact that the founding fathers of the United Nations were able to learn from the League experience and, accordingly, write a United Nations Charter—a document substantially superior to the League Covenant.[14]

THE UNITED NATIONS

Representatives of fifty-one states met in San Francisco in the spring and early summer of 1945 to draft and discuss the charter for a new international organization—the United Nations. The final document was signed on June 26, 1945. The name "United Nations" was coined by President Roosevelt and Prime Minister Churchill during their Arcadia Conference (1941). During the early 1940s the governments of the United Kingdom and the United States spearheaded the drive toward establishing this new international organization. The Soviet Union, having become a wartime partner of the Western allies, was kept informed about the initial developments. In September, 1944, a meeting of representatives of the three Allies was held in Dumbarton Oaks, an estate in Washington, D.C., and dealt exclusively with United Nations matters, centering around the issues of membership, security provisions, and the veto (explained in our discussion of the Security Council). Different views regarding the veto between East and West continued to exist until an agreement was arrived at in Yalta (February, 1945).

In contrast to 1919, public opinion in the West (especially in the United States) was rather favorably disposed toward a United Nations, and it was a forgone conclusion that the United States would play a leading role in creating the organization and would be one of the major members of it.

The other original charter members, including France and China who were to become permanent members of the Security Council, played peripheral roles in shaping the United Nations prior to the San Francisco conference. By the end of June, 1945, the participants of the conference had completed the United Nations Charter, and the document came into force on October 24, 1945, after the necessary number of nation-states had ratified it. Since 1945 the charter has been amended twice. Amendments

[14] For readings on the League of Nations, we suggest M. E. Burton, *The Assembly of the League of Nations* (Chicago: University of Chicago Press, 1941); D. F. Fleming, *The United States and the League of Nations* (New York: Putnam, 1932); Francis P. Walters, *A History of the League of Nations* (New York: Oxford University Press, 1952); and Alfred Zimmern, *The League of Nations and the Rule of Law* (New York: Macmillan, 1939).

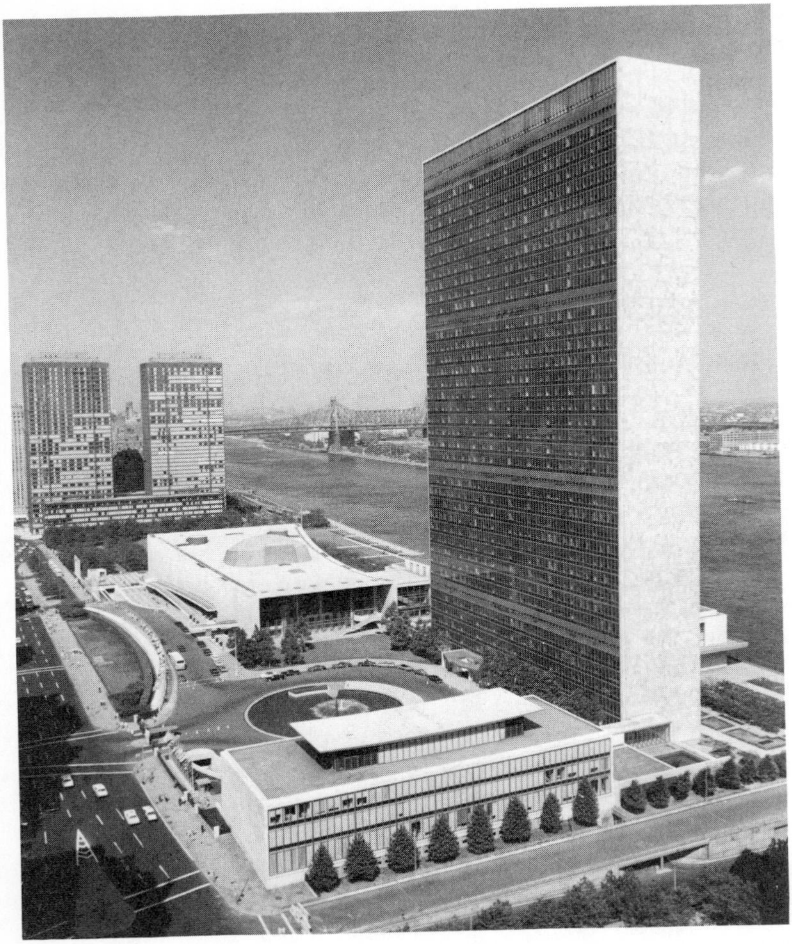

A general view of the permanent headquarters of the United Nations in New York. The 39-story Secretariat is flanked by the General Assembly building and the Library (foreground).

adopted in 1963 enlarged the membership of the Security Council and of the Economic and Social Council and adjusted the voting procedures of these two organs to reflect the larger membership. The second adoption of an amendment occurred in 1965 and relates to provisions having to do with the review of the charter.

The first meeting of the United Nations was held in London in January, 1946. In the next few years a permanent headquarters was built along the East River in New York City and became operative in early 1950.

THE FUNCTIONS OF THE UNITED NATIONS

The functions and purposes of the United Nations are clearly stated in Article I of the charter:

1. To maintain international peace and security, and to that end: to take effective collective measures for the prevention and removal of threats to the peace, and for the suppression of acts of aggression or other breaches of the peace, and to bring about by peaceful means, and in conformity with the principles of justice and international law, adjustment or settlement of international disputes or situations which might lead to a breach of peace.
2. To develop friendly relations among nations based on respect for the principle of equal rights and self-determination of peoples, and to take other appropriate measures to strengthen universal peace.
3. To achieve international cooperation in solving international problems of an economic, social, cultural, or humanitarian character, and in promoting and encouraging respect for human rights and for fundamental freedoms for all without distinction as to race, sex, language, or religion.
4. To be a center for harmonizing the actions of nations in the attainment of these common ends.[15]

THE STRUCTURE OF THE UNITED NATIONS

Article 7 of the United Nations Charter delineates six principal organs of the organization: 1. the General Assembly, 2. the Security Council, 3. the Economic and Social Council, 4. the Trusteeship Council, 5. the International Court of Justice (located in The Hague and discussed in the earlier part of the chapter) and 6. the Secretariat.

A number of specialized agencies are directly affiliated with the United Nations. The following listing gives the date of their establishment and their place of headquarters in parentheses: Universal Postal Union (1875, Berne); International Telecommunications Union (1865, Geneva); International Labor Organization (1919, Geneva); Food and Agriculture Organization (1944, Rome); International Monetary Fund (1944, Washington); International Bank for Reconstruction and Development (1944, Washington); United Nations Educational, Scientific, and Cultural Organization (1945, Paris); World Health Organization (1946, Geneva); International Civil Avia-

[15] The full text of the charter is published in, among other sources, the *Yearbook of the United Nations* (New York: United Nations Office of Public information, published annually). A helpful and popular source of information about the United Nations and its affiliated agencies is *Everyman's United Nations* (New York: United Nations Office of Publications).

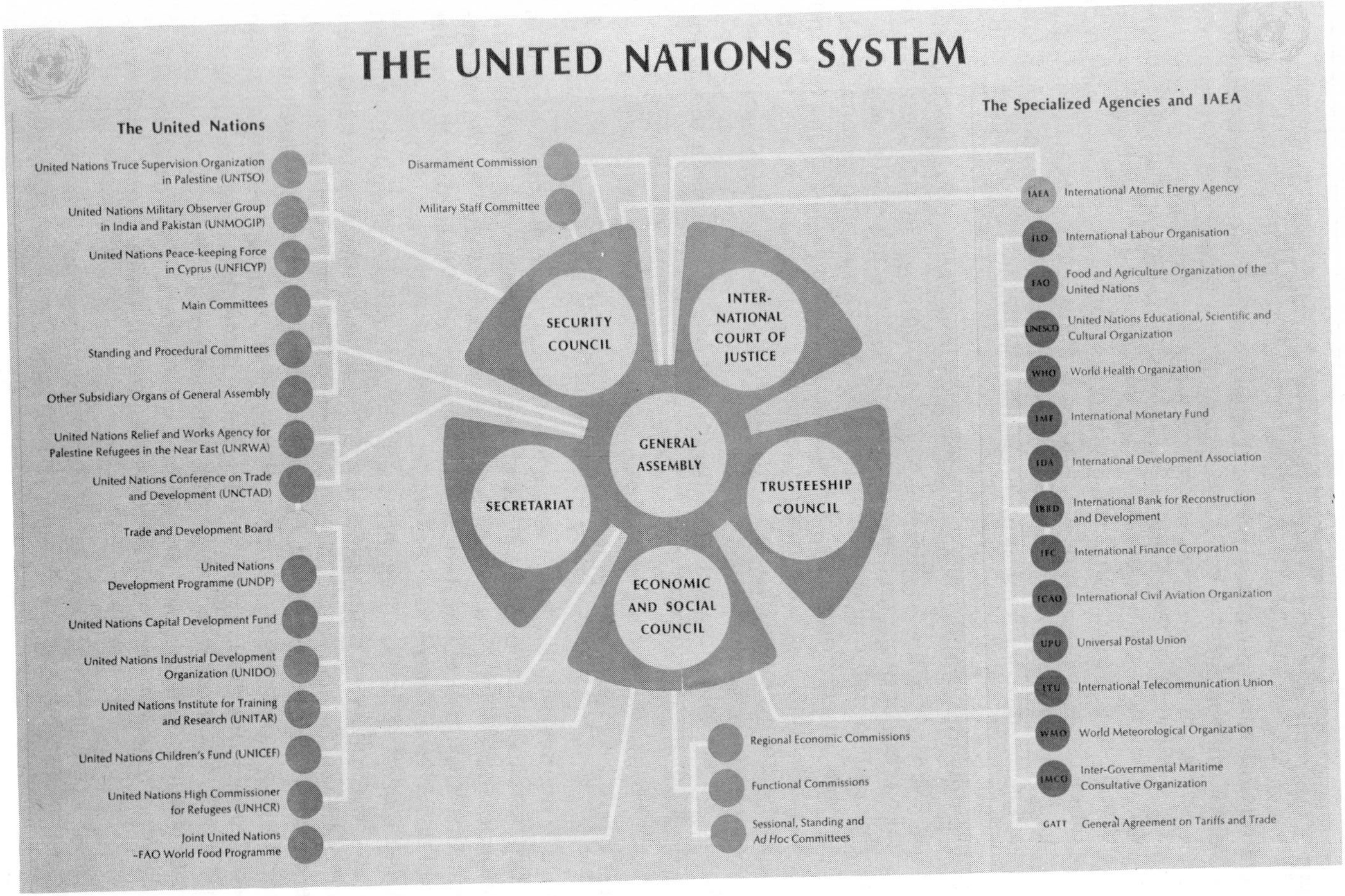
THE UNITED NATIONS SYSTEM
The United Nations
United Nations Truce Supervision Organization in Palestine (UNTSO)
United Nations Military Observer Group in India and Pakistan (UNMOGIP)
United Nations Peace-keeping Force in Cyprus (UNFICYP)
Main Committees
Standing and Procedural Committees
Other Subsidiary Organs of General Assembly
United Nations Relief and Works Agency for Palestine Refugees in the Near East (UNRWA)
United Nations Conference on Trade and Development (UNCTAD)
Trade and Development Board
United Nations Development Programme (UNDP)
United Nations Capital Development Fund
United Nations Industrial Development Organization (UNIDO)
United Nations Institute for Training and Research (UNITAR)
United Nations Children's Fund (UNICEF)
United Nations High Commissioner for Refugees (UNHCR)
Joint United Nations -FAO World Food Programme
Disarmament Commission
Military Staff Committee
SECURITY COUNCIL
INTER-NATIONAL COURT OF JUSTICE
GENERAL ASSEMBLY
SECRETARIAT
TRUSTEESHIP COUNCIL
ECONOMIC AND SOCIAL COUNCIL
Regional Economic Commissions
Functional Commissions
Sessional, Standing and Ad Hoc Committees
The Specialized Agencies and IAEA
IAEA International Atomic Energy Agency
ILO International Labour Organisation
FAO Food and Agriculture Organization of the United Nations
UNESCO United Nations Educational, Scientific and Cultural Organization
WHO World Health Organization
IMF International Monetary Fund
IDA International Development Association
IBRD International Bank for Reconstruction and Development
IFC International Finance Corporation
ICAO International Civil Aviation Organization
UPU Universal Postal Union
ITU International Telecommunication Union
WMO World Meteorological Organization
IMCO Inter-Governmental Maritime Consultative Organization
GATT General Agreement on Tariffs and Trade

The structure of the United Nations.

tion Organization (1947, Montreal); World Meteorological Organization (1950, Geneva); International Finance Corporation (1956, Washington); Intergovernmental Maritime Consultative Organization (1958, London); and International Development Association (1960, Washington).

THE GENERAL ASSEMBLY

The General Assembly is the basic forum of the United Nations in that all member nation-states are represented in it. Voting in the Assembly emphasizes the principle of equality, with each member country having one vote in its decisions. The only exception is the Soviet Union, which has three (one for the Soviet Union at large, one for the Ukraine, and one for Belorussia—a compromise forced by Stalin at Yalta). The General Assembly holds annual sessions that start in September and may continue until the early spring of the following year.

The functions and powers of the General Assembly are very broad. According to the charter:

> *The General Assembly may discuss any questions or any matters within the scope of the present Charter or relating to the powers and functions of any organs provided for in the present Charter, and, except as provided in Article 12 [which states that the General Assembly shall not make any recommendation on a dispute while it is being discussed by the Security Council], may make recommendations to the Members of the United Nations or to the Security Council or to both on any such questions or matters.*

In size, the General Assembly has grown from its original 51 members to 144 in 1975. It has served as a valuable forum for debate and exchange of views. In the decision-making area, it has left by and large specific actions on security matters and peace-keeping functions to the Security Council. It should be pointed out, however, that in this area the General Assembly has

("The Small Society" by Brickman (c) Washington Star Syndicate, permission granted by King Features Syndicate, 1973.)

(OFF THE RECORD by Ed Reed, reprinted courtesy The Register and Tribune Syndicate.)

become a backstop of the Security Council with the passage of the Uniting for Peace Resolution in 1950. This resolution grew out of the experience derived from the early part of the Korean conflict—the recognition that a permanent member of the Security Council could easily block a majority-approved U.N. peacekeeping action. To circumvent this, Article I of the Uniting for Peace Resolution provides that in emergencies, when the Security Council is prevented from acting (on account of a veto or the threat of a veto), the General Assembly is authorized to meet on short notice and to recommend any appropriate collective measures, including the use of armed force. The resolution enabled the General Assembly to deal with several important security problems during times of a deadlock in the Security Council, such as periods of the Korean conflict and the Congo crisis.

The rapid increase in membership has given the General Assembly a near universal flavor and representation. Over the years its function as a forum for discussion and debate of regional and worldwide economic, military, political, and social issues has been of considerable value to the world community.

THE SECURITY COUNCIL

Underlying the composition and the voting procedure in the Security Council is the concept of big-power control or "world sheriff" as embodied in the Concert of Europe. The Council, as created in 1945, consisted of eleven members. Five of these were permanent members: China, France, the Soviet Union, the United Kingdom, and the United States. The remaining and nonpermanent six members were to be elected for two-year terms by the General Assembly. In 1963 the number of non-permanent members was increased to ten, in recognition of the growing membership of the United Nations.

Some mention needs to be made of the voting procedure in the Security Council. Each member has one vote. Decisions on procedural matters (recommendations that do not include sanctions) require the affirmative vote of any nine of the fifteen members. Substantive decisions, however, require the affirmative votes of nine members including those of all five permanent members. It is here that the veto may occur. The negative vote of a permanent member on a substantive issue constitutes a veto and will block Security Council action.[16]

According to Article 24 of the United Nations Charter the member-states "confer on the Security Council primary responsibility for the maintenance of international peace and security, and agree that in carrying out its duties under this responsibility the Security Council acts on their behalf." The particular powers granted by the charter to the Security Council to discharge its duties are laid down in Chapters VI (Pacific Settlement of Disputes), VII (Action with Respect to Threats to Peace, Breaches of the Peace, and Acts of Aggression), VIII (Regional Arrangements), and XII (International Trusteeship System). In essence, the actions of the Security Council will involve one or several of the following: it may suggest methods of reconciliation; it may offer specific resolutions (this was done, for example, in the Congo crisis); it may order a provisional truce (as on Cyprus in 1964 and 1974); it may invoke nonmilitary sanctions (in 1965 the Security Council invoked economic sanctions against Rhodesia); and finally it may resort to military sanctions, as it did in Korea and in the Congo.

Over the years the Security Council has often been handicapped by the quarrels among its permanent members and has not been fully able to mobilize the United Nations as intended by the founding fathers. Its best area of success has been—and is—in disputes where the aggressor is not a permanent member of the Security Council and is not being directly supported by a permanent member. The presence of the veto usually prevents the Security Council from taking action against a permanent member or another state actively supported by a permanent member.

The peacekeeping capability of the United Nations was enhanced in 1956 when the General Assembly passed a resolution creating the United

[16] Both the governments of the Soviet Union and the United States insisted during the preparatory stage that the veto principle be built into the United Nations Charter. For an excellent discussion on the use of the veto, see Sidney D. Bailey, "Veto in the Security Council," *International Conciliation* (January 1968), pp. 5–66.

Nations Emergency Force (UNEF), an international military force with the task of supervising armistice arrangements decreed by the United Nations. The members of this military force were to be drawn from member-states, with the exception of the permanent members. Since 1956 UNEF has served in the above capacity in the Middle East and in the Congo (where it was known as ONUC). A number of countries have contributed troops to UNEF; for example, Finland, Sweden, Canada, Austria, Ireland, India, and several African countries sent troops during the Congo operation. In the fall of 1974 UNEF troops were stationed on Cyprus, along the Suez Canal, and in the Golan Heights area. The United Nations Emergency Force is the first step in modern history toward establishing an international military force.

By and large the actions taken by the Security Council mirror the particular state of international relations. Any change in its composition, functions, and powers will continue to require the consent of its permanent members. Of these the United States and the Soviet Union have remained superpowers. The United Kingdom and France have lost some of their former influence in world affairs and are second-rate powers, at best. The fifth permanent seat, for a long time held by the Chiang Kai-shek government, was turned over to the People's Republic of China in 1971.

Could the Security Council be made more viable by further additions and/or changes in membership? The 1963 amendment, enlarging the number of nonpermanent members from six to ten, was designed to give more voice in the Security Council to the rapidly growing membership of the United Nations. But as of 1975 no nation-state from Latin America, Africa, or the Middle East held a permanent seat.

THE SECRETARIAT

The Secretariat performs the day-to-day administrative tasks of the United Nations. It is directed by the secretary-general, who is appointed by the General Assembly upon recommendation by the Security Council. The functions of the secretary-general are spelled out in Chapter XV of the United Nations Charter:

> *He shall be the chief administrative officer of the Organization.*
>
> *The Secretary-General shall act in that capacity in all meetings of the General Assembly, of the Security Council, of the Economic and Social Council, and of the Trusteeship Council. . . . The Secretary-General shall make an annual report to the General Assembly on the work of the Organization.*
>
> *The Secretary-General may bring to the attention of the Security Council any matter which in his opinion may threaten the maintenance of international peace and security.*

As the highest administrative officer, he oversees the work of thousands of international civil servants, recruited from many of the member-states. Most of the Secretariat's employees work at the headquarters in New York, but others are in Geneva or at one of the several field offices the United Nations maintains throughout the world.[17]

The present secretary-general, Dr. Kurt Waldheim (Austria), is the fourth person to hold this position. He was preceeded by Trygve Lie (Norway), 1945–1952; Dag Hammarskjöld (Sweden), 1952–1961; and U Thant (Burma) 1961–1971).[18] All four have been persons of high ability and have contributed considerably to the viability of the United Nations. Their major problem has been that the concept underlying their position, namely to act as the leading international spokes nan, is still relatively new. The job of the Secretary-general has an unavoidable problem–for most of the time he has "to walk a tightrope." If in fulfillment of his duties, he speaks out too loudly and forcefully, he may incur the wrath of one or several of the permanent members of the Security Council. Yet if he does not speak out at all, he would doom his office to sterility. It takes a most talented person to play, under the strains of this dilemma, a forceful and productive part in the work of the United Nations.

THE ECONOMIC AND SOCIAL COUNCIL

One of the main purposes of the United Nations, as stated in the charter, is "to achieve international cooperation in solving problems of an economic, social, cultural, or humanitarian character." The Economic and Social Council was established to serve as the key agency for coordinating the United Nation's activities in the economic and social realms. The functions of the council are spelled out in Chapter X of the charter and include the initiation of studies and reports on international economic, social, cultural, and educational matters, preparing recommendations for the General Assembly and assisting the Security Council on economic and social matters when so requested. The Economic and Social Council consists of twenty-seven members, of whom nine are elected each year for three-year terms.

The founding fathers of the United Nations had hoped that the organization's activities in the economic and social realms could be kept out of the arena of political conflict which, as they correctly envisaged, might trouble

[17] For an examination of some of the complexities of international administration, see Robert S. Jordan, ed., *International Administration: Its Evolution and Contemporary Applications* (New York: Oxford University Press, 1971).

[18] For a useful discussion of the office of secretary-general and the experiences of the first two incumbents, see Trygve Lie, *In the Cause of Peace* (New York: Macmillan, 1954); and Brian Urquart, *Hammarskjöld* (New York: Alfred A. Knopf, 1972).

the General Assembly and the Security Council from time to time. Moreover, they hoped that the habit of peaceful collaboration in the economic and social realms could later be extended to the organization's political and military activities. However, international struggles have been reflected from time to time in the activities of the Economic and Social Council, and the hopes of the founding fathers have not fully materialized. In the composite perspective, however, we find that it has become a very important organ of the United Nations and a stimulant of international cooperation. Over the years there has been a steady growth of the activities supervised by the Economic and Social Council.

THE TRUSTEESHIP COUNCIL

This is the successor to the League of Nations Mandate System, which was established after World War I to render some degree of international control over former German colonies and over territories once held by the defunct Ottoman Empire. With the establishment of the United Nations those former League mandates that had not yet achieved independence were turned into trusteeships of the United Nations.

The Trusteeship Council consists of the permanent members of the Security Council, other countries administering trust territories, and enough additional member-states (elected by the General Assembly) to insure an equal balance on the council between countries administering trust territories and those that do not.

Chapter XII of the charter declares that the basic objectives of the Trusteeship Council are "to promote the political, economic, social, and educational advancement of the inhabitants of the trust territories, and their progressive development toward self-government or independence." Since 1945 most of the former trust territories have become independent. As of 1976, only the Carolines, Marianas, and Marshall Islands in the Pacific (administered as a strategic trust territory by the United States) remain under the jurisdiction of the Trusteeship Council.

A perpetual bone of contention between the United Nations and the Republic of South Africa has been the status of Namibia (South-West Africa). This territory was a mandate under the League of Nations and the United Nations has claimed jurisdiction over the area. The government of South Africa, in turn, has maintained that South-West Africa has become an integral part of the Republic of South Africa.[19]

[19] For a concise analysis of the United Nations dispute with the Republic of South Africa in the historical context, see Ronald B. Ballinger "United Nations Action on Human Rights in South Africa," in Evan Luard, ed., *International Protection of Human Rights* (London: Thames & Hudson, 1967). See also Amry Vandenbosch, *South Africa and the World* (Lexington: The University of Kentucky Press, 1970, pp. 203–227); and Rosalyn Higgins, "The International Court and South West Africa: The Implications of the Judgment," *International Affairs* (October, 1966), pp. 573–599.

A BRIEF EVALUATION OF THE UNITED NATIONS

The shortcomings of the United Nations mirror the problems of today's world. Its strength and productivity rest, in essence, on the support given by the member-nations, especially by the great powers. The major problem of the United Nations was candidly stated by Secretary-General Waldheim in 1973:

> *At the present there does not appear to be a clear agreement between member-countries on the way the organization should proceed, and there are times when it is hard not to feel that not all governments fully accept the consequences that arise from their membership of [sic] the United Nations. . . .*[20]

The major powers, especially the United States and the Soviet Union, have found it expedient to bypass the United Nations on many occasions and have negotiated most of their bilateral issues outside the international organization. But this should not be interpreted to mean that the two

(Justus, The Minneapolis Star.)

[20] *Frankfurter Allgemeine Zeitung,* September 17, 1973, as translated and reprinted in *The German Tribune,* October 4, 1973.

global powers have forsaken the United Nations and that they do not care about it at all. The viability of the United Nations was threatened on several occasions, especially during the Congo crisis in the early 1960s and the fiscal impasse during the Nineteenth General Assembly (1964), which was created by the refusal of the Communist countries, France, and some other non-Communist members to pay their part of the expenses of United Nations peacekeeping operations in the Congo and the Middle East. At these two instances—and at many other times—the governments of the United States and the Soviet Union have exercised enough flexibility to insure the continuation of the United Nations. While the two global powers may not agree about the kind of United Nations they like to see in operation, they are in fundamental agreement that the United Nations serves a useful purpose and must continue to exist.

Over the years the United Nations has undergone a great deal of change. Its membership has nearly tripled. Its discussion has shifted to many new issues. After rapid growth in membership during the 1950s and 1960s the United Nations has arrived at a consolidation stage, which may provide the basis for striking out toward new horizons in the future. According to John G. Stoessinger:

> *Political institutions pass through periods of growth and periods of consolidation. The United Nations is no exception, and, in the overall assessment, it is vital to bear in mind this time dimension. In this fundamental sense, it is not true that the United Nations has fallen so low as many fear; it has merely not yet been permitted to rise as high as many had hoped.*[21]

To cope with the changing fortunes of international politics, the United Nations has exercised flexibility in various ways. First, it has amended the charter to enlarge the membership of the Security Council and the Economic and Social Council in recognition of the organization's growing membership. Second, it has reinterpreted the charter on several occasions. For example, it has established the United Nations Emergency Forces in such a way that the global powers are excluded from partaking in the actual peacekeeping operations. Third, it has shifted, depending upon the need, the initiation of action between the Security Council, the General Assembly, and the Secretariat. This has been made possible through the passage of the Uniting for Peace Resolution and initiatives taken by the secretary-general, such as the actions taken by Dag Hammarskjöld during the Congo crisis. Finally, the secretary-generals have succeeded in maintaining, at all times, enough political consensus within the United Nations to insure the internal stability of the organization.

Any evaluation of the United Nations will leave the observer with mixed reactions. It has not met the founding fathers' hopes in some areas, while

[21] John G. Stoessinger, *The United Nations and the Superpowers: China, Russia, and America,* 3rd ed. (New York: Random House, 1973), p. 209.

meeting or surpassing them in others. The plain fact is that the United Nations can not be much stronger than it is because of the limitations imposed by our present-day nation-state system and its ramifications.

The United Nations has helped to bring spokesmen of the various people of the world closer together. The General Assembly constitutes the only permanent worldwide forum where the representatives of the many member-countries can meet, exchange opinions, and publicly voice their views on regional and worldwide problems. The importance of this forum should not be underestimated. In the area of economic and social development the United Nations renders important help to many of the developing countries and has contributed, beyond original expectations, to the improvement of the general welfare. Finally, the United Nations helps to maintain peace throughout the world. While its intended role as mediator and conciliator has not borne fruit at every occasion, its partial results have been of help to the world community. Any composite and realistic evaluation of the United Nations must lead to the conclusions that the international institution has made a positive contribution to international order and well-being. The global community has been in need of a United Nations and will need its services in the future.

REGIONAL INTEGRATION

Since World War II a number of regional organizations have been created. These systems may be defined as groupings of three or more nation-states which have formed distinct arrangements for the purposes of economic, military and/or political integration. Regionalism, according to some theorists, can serve as "a steppingstone toward universalism." Advocates of this theory emphasize that the present world is too diverse culturally, economically, ideologically, and psychologically to develop global common loyalties. Integrating commonalities could be more readily established within regions. The building blocks created by regional integration can serve in the future for the creation of a greater degree of worldwide order. Some supporters of regionalism support the "federal approach" and others the "functional approach." The first calls for the establishment of supranational agencies within regional organizations. The members would surrender part of their sovereignty to the supranational bodies. The "functionalists," in contrast, have encouraged the development of broad-scale intergovernmental collaboration in lieu of supranational agencies. According to their view, economic, social, and cultural cooperation is a paramount prerequisite to political integration. The regionalism that has developed in recent decades appears to contain aspects of both theories.[22]

[22] For a theoretical discussion of regional integration, see Ernst B. Haas "International Integration, the European and the Universal Process," and Amitai Etzioni, "The Dialectics of Supranational Unification," in *International Political Communities, An Anthology* (Garden City, N.Y.: Doubleday, 1966), pp. 93–147.

Articles 52 through 54 of the Charter of the United Nations give international recognition to regional arrangements and define the relationship between such bodies and the United Nations. According to Article 52:

> *Nothing in the present Charter precludes the existence of regional arrangements or agencies for dealing with such matters relating to the maintenance of international peace and security as are appropriate for regional action, provided that such arrangements or agencies and their activities are consistent with the Purposes and Principles of the United Nations.*
>
> *The Members of the United Nations entering such arrangements . . . shall make every effort to achieve pacific settlement of local disputes through such regional arrangements before referring them to the Security Council.*
>
> *The Security Council shall encourage the development of pacific settlement of local disputes through such regional arrangements . . . either on the initiative of the states concerned or by reference from the Security Council.*

In addition, Article 51 provides legitimacy for the collective security provisions found in the treaties establishing military regional alliances. This states:

> *Nothing in the present Charter shall impair the inherent right of individual or collective self-defense if an armed attack occurs against a Member of the United Nations, until the Security Council has taken the measures necessary to maintain international peace and security.*

The important point is that according to the United Nations' Charter regionalism is compatible with the United Nations and should be utilized to help the Security Council in its peacekeeping function. Have regional organizations developed along these guidelines?

Some degree of "regionalism," in the sense of grouping a number of nation-states together for the pursuit of a common policy, existed prior to the United Nations. The defense alliances formed before and after World War I and the British Commonwealth serve as examples. Regional organization gained considerable momentum in the late 1940s and during the 1950s, leading to the establishment of a large number of military, economic, and political arrangements, which will be discussed below. The move toward regional association was spearheaded by arrangements in the Atlantic community area and in the Americas. They were countered in the 1950s by regional arrangements among the Communist countries. Other regional organizations were established in the Middle East, Africa, and Southeast Asia.

Generally speaking, the multitude of regional organizations developed after World War II can be divided into three categories: military associations; political and security associations; and economic associations. Some of the regional organizations are more clearly within one category than others, which may perform overlapping functions. These may include security, political, and economic matters.

MILITARY REGIONAL ORGANIZATIONS

Regional arrangements whose primary function is that of security include the North Atlantic Treaty Organization (established in 1949), the Warsaw Treaty Organization (1955), the Rio Pact (1947), which became one of the three basic documents of the Organization of American-States established one year later, the Central Treaty Organization (1955), and the Southeast Asia Treaty Organization (1954).

Underlying all of the above security-oriented regional arrangements is the principle of collective security—that is, the concept that an attack upon one member of an association should be considered as an attack on all members, and all shall rally to the defense of the attacked nation-state. For example, Article 3 of the Rio Pact states:

> *The High Contracting Parties agree that an armed attack by any State against an American State shall be considered as an attack against all American States, and, consequently, each one of the said Contracting Parties undertakes to assist in meeting the attack in the exercise of the inherent right of individual or collective self-defense recognized by Article 51 of the Charter of the United Nations.*[23]

Similar provisions are found in the treaties that serve as the constitutional foundation for the North Atlantic Treaty Organization (NATO), the Warsaw Treaty Organization (WTO), the Central Treaty Organization (CENTO), and, in a watered-down version, the Southeast Asia Treaty Organization (SEATO).

Let us briefly look at the specific purposes of the above military arrangements. The Rio Pact was designed to provide an inter-American treaty of military assistance and to establish a system of collective security in the Americas. The North Atlantic Treaty Organization was created to contain the Communist threat to Western Europe. Further Western attempts to restrain communism led to the treaties establishing the Central Treaty Organization and the Southeast Asia Treaty Organization, thereby completing the encirclement of the Communist bloc of nation-states. To counter the Western military alliance system, the Soviet government converted in 1955 its bilateral military treaties with other East European countries into a multilateral agreement, the Warsaw Treaty Organization, commonly referred to as the Warsaw Pact.

The North Atlantic Treaty Organization and the Warsaw Pact are more structurally developed than the other military alliances. NATO and WTO each consist of semi-integrated military systems that have been perpetually

[23] The text of the Rio Pact is reprinted in M. Margaret Ball, *The OAS in Transition* (Durham: Duke University Press, 1969). For the text of the Atlantic Treaty see, among others, A. H. Robertson, *European Institutions* (New York: Frederick A. Praeger, 1958). The English-language text of the Warsaw Treaty is published in Robin A. Remington. *The Warsaw Pact* (Cambridge: the MIT Press, 1971).

commanded by United States and Russian officers respectively. The large-scale development of nuclear weaponry in recent years has rendered questionable some of the basic premises upon which the two military alliances (and the others, too) were built. In essence, how much credibility does the assumption of collective security carry in a time when warfare in the Northern Hemisphere could lead to nuclear annihilation? This credibility gap was, allegedly, one of the primary reasons for de Gaulle to take France out of NATO.

The move toward reform has been stronger in NATO than the other military regional organizations. A number of conferences have been held in recent years on how to reinvigorate NATO and to make it more relevant to present-day issues. Its endeavors have been broadened to include political, economic, and environmental issues. In the composite, however, the reform of NATO is still far from a satisfactory completion.[24]

SEATO appears to be the least viable among the five military regional arrangements under discussion. It had little cooperative strength from the beginning, and the military struggles in Southeast Asia as well as the growing new political order in that area have rendered that organization obsolete.

NATO, CENTO, SEATO, Rio Pact, and Warsaw Pact are basically defensive military alliances established to protect the hegemonical interests of the United States and the Soviet Union respectively. Depending upon the circumstances, these interests may be potentially opposed to those held by a majority of the members of the United Nations. This being the case, the pursuits of military regional organizations do not necessarily jibe with the expectations as set forth in Article 52 of the United Nations Charter.

POLITICAL AND SECURITY REGIONAL ORGANIZATIONS

Major regional organizations that are commonly labeled political organizations are the Council of Europe (formed in 1949); the Organization of American States (OAS, 1948); the Arab League (1945); and the Organization of African Unity (OAU, 1963).

Of these four the Council of Europe has maintained perhaps the lowest and most limited political profile. Over the years its activities have been overshadowed by questions and issues relating to NATO and European economic integration. The Organization of American States was established as a follow-up to the Rio Pact. Under the active leadership of the United States OAS has been used to coordinate hemispheric American politics. In contrast to the Council of Europe, OAS has occupied itself with a number

[24] One of the more recent evaluations of NATO is Edwin H. Fedder, *NATO: The Dynamics of Alliance in the Postwar World* (New York: Dodd, Mead, 1973).

of broad issues, involving political, economic, and military matters. For example, the Alliance for Progress program was carried on, at least technically, under the auspices of OAS. Generally speaking, the Alliance for Progress was based on the United States commitment to Latin American countries to help them to raise their standard of living. The most notable military action of the OAS occurred in 1965 in conjunction with a governmental crisis in the Dominican Republic. Civil war and the threat of an apparent Communist takeover in late April and early May of that year led the United States government to send troops to the Dominican Republic. After a ceasefire had been achieved between the warring factions, an Inter-American Peace Force was established under OAS auspices, consisting of United States troops plus contingents from Brazil, Costa Rica, El Salvador, and Nicaragua. The force was directed by a Brazilian general and it remained at the scene until the fighting was stopped and a new, viable government was established.

The Arab League is the oldest of the four political regional organizations. Its espoused purpose has been to foster and increase cooperation among the Arab states. While its first aim was essentially to seek the liberation of all Arab countries from colonial rule, it soon became involved in military actions when it sought to prevent the establishment of the nation-state of Israel. Integrated economic pursuits were added to the Arab League's responsibilities in later years. Perennial divisions of interest among some of the Arab states have limited the effectiveness of the Arab League over the years.

The Organization of African Unity is the newest of the political regional organizations. It is the only regional organization combining the black and Arab African countries, most of which have become independent only recently. Established in 1963, it has sought to unite under its framework the divergent groupings of African nation-states. The charter of the Organization of African Unity calls for achieving the aspirations of the African people through economic and political development. The members of OAU have pledged themselves to coordinate their policies, to defend their sovereignty, and to eradicate colonialism in Africa. Some of OAU's major accomplishments have been related to the prevention or settlement of disputes between members. The most successful achievements occurred in 1963, when OAU officials achieved a ceasefire in the border dispute between Algeria and Morocco. Subsequent OAU meetings helped in bringing about a settlement.

Unlike some of the other regional organizations, OAU has been subject to various internal strains. However, the organization has endured all crises during the past and has succeeded in achieving growing international importance. Perhaps one of its greatest problems in recent years has been the growing division between the Arab member countries on the one hand

and the black countries on the other. Requests for economic aid made by the drought-stricken countries of the Sahel region have not yet been met with an adequate response by the newly rich oil-producing countries of the north. It appears that this problem and the rivalry over black or Arab leadership in OAU will continue for some time to come. Thus, while OAU has had some success as a regional arbitrator, it has done little to further "pan-African Unity."

ECONOMIC REGIONAL ORGANIZATIONS

The largest number of regional organizations have developed in the economic realm. Some of them have achieved substantially more structure and organizational viability than others. They differ also in size, ranging from the macrosized Organization of Economic Cooperation and Development (OECD), which includes twenty-three developed countries, to such microsized organization as the Nordic Council (which consists of the five Scandinavian countries) or the East African Community (EAC), consisting of Kenya, Uganda, and Tanzania. The basic effort underlying the economic regional groupings has been to decrease trade barriers between the member countries and to increase commerce between them. This pursuit has led to substantially increased economic cooperation in some parts of the world. The most important strides toward economic integration have taken place in Europe: In Western Europe under the auspices of the European Economic Community (the Common Market) and in Eastern Europe under the Council for Mutual Economic Assistance (COMECON or CEMA).

The European Economic Community was established in 1957 for the purpose of integrating the economic policies of the Benelux countries, France, the Federal Republic of Germany, and Italy. These were joined in 1973 by the United Kingdom, Denmark, and Ireland. In 1951 the original six countries mentioned above, also known as the "Inner Six," had established the European Coal and Steel Community to provide a common market in coal and steel and its byproducts among the six members. The European Economic Community provided a still broader scope and aimed to integrate the entire economies of the member countries. A European Atomic Energy Community (Euratom), with the purpose of establishing a basis for the joint exploitation of atomic energy, was created simultaneously with the Common Market.

The ostensible purpose of the moves toward West European economic integration was to achieve functional integration and to increase the economic well-being of all the member countries. In actuality, however, the major impetus came from French statesmen, especially Robert Schuman, and sought integration as a means of eliminating the danger of armed conflict between France and Germany. It is in this aspect that one of the major rationales underlying West European integration differs considerably from those of economic integration in other parts of the world.

While there has been considerable economic integration among the Common Market countries, progress has been faster in some specific areas than in others. Accomplishments include the creation of a Customs Union which became operative in 1968; the establishment of a common agricultural policy, which by 1974 encompassed most of the community's agricultural production; the creation of a community-wide Monetary Cooperation Fund, and endeavors toward common policies in environmental, scientific, and technological affairs.

West European economic integration showed its greatest momentum during the early and mid-1960s and has leveled off in more recent years. Among other problems, the oil crisis of late 1973 led to divisive tendencies among the Common Market countries, and policies that were based on an "each for his own" attitude rather than constructive, joint endeavors. In a larger sense, current inflation and questions of how to cope with it present a formidable challenge today to economic unity within the Common Market. But despite all these problems, the European Economic Community has achieved more economic integration among its members than any other regional economic organization in the non-Communist part of the world.

The Council of Mutual Economic Assistance (COMECON or CEMA) is the regional economic organization of Communist countries. In 1974 the members were the Soviet Union, Poland, the German Democratic Republic, Czechoslovakia, Hungary, Bulgaria, Romania, the Mongolian Republic, and Cuba. Albania, one of its original members, left COMECON in 1961. Its creation came as a reaction to the Marshall Plan and subsequent West European economic integration. Over the years a close system of economic interdependence has been developed under the auspices of COMECON between the Soviet Union and the other members. During the 1950s and 1960s COMECON members conducted most of their foreign trade within the organization and a considerable portion thereof with the Soviet Union. However, a leveling-off tendency in this trade pattern has occurred in recent years, with Romania, for example, increasing its trade with the West. Other countries pursuing a similar pattern, though at a smaller level, are Poland and Hungary.

Two unique COMECON projects are the construction of an oil pipeline linking the Soviet Union with Poland, Hungary, Czechoslovakia, and the German Democratic Republic and an electric power grid system connecting the Soviet Union with the above countries plus Bulgaria and Romania. One may deduce from these examples that integration within COMECON, at least in some areas, has gone still farther than among the Common Market countries.

One of the basic differences between the Common Market and COMECON is that in the latter the Soviet Union, because of its power and influence, has played a dominant role in COMECON. No such great predominance has been exercised by any country within the Common Market. The Soviet leadership has been able to utilize COMECON to increase, at least temporarily, its control over the member countries, despite occasional setbacks such as the departure of Albania and the defeat in 1963 of Khrushchev's plan to introduce a still greater degree of specialization among the industries of the COMECON countries.

AN EVALUATION OF REGIONAL ORGANIZATIONS

What has been the success of regional organizations in the post-World War II era? What has been their contribution to peace? Have they performed in the expectation of the founding fathers of the United Nations as stipulated by Article 52 of the charter? The composite picture of regional organizations shows a "mixed bag" situation, in that some regional organizations have been much more successful than others. Regional organizations dominated by one or the other superpower, such as NATO, OAS, the Warsaw Pact, or COMECON, have been used extensively and perhaps understandably to protect and perpetuate their spheres of influence.

According to Nye:

> *Regional organizations are not a major cause of spheres of influence, but to some extent they help to perpetuate them. One can argue that these spheres of influence have been useful no-trespassing signs that help to prevent miscalculation by the superpowers and thus help to avoid nuclear holocaust.*[25]

An alternate argument, however, is that regional spheres are "likely in the long run only to provoke rather than prevent further conflict both within and without.[26]"

In any case, regional organizations have made some constructive contribution to world peace. They have helped in varying degrees to create a greater sense of commonality among the populations of the member countries. Good examples are the Council of Europe and the Common Market. Both organizations have contributed much toward overcoming the historic national rivalries between France and Germany. The regional consciousness in Western Europe—the feeling of belonging together—is greater today than ever before. Regional organizations have helped in curtailing conflict among member countries. Admittedly, the disputes set-

[25] J. S. Nye, *Peace In Parts: Integration and Conflict in Regional Organization* (Boston: Little, Brown, 1971), pp. 179–80.

[26] Evan Luard, *Conflict and Peace in the Modern International System* (Boston: Little, Brown, 1969), p. 167.

tled by regional organizations were cases of low intensity in terms of their seriousness for the global community.[27]

The composite evaluation of the roles played by regional organizations shows that while they do not constitute a panacea for world order, they have made a definite contribution to peace and have complemented the work of the United Nations in a number of instances.

Selected Readings

The classic introduction to international law is J. L. Brierly, *The Law of Nations,* 6th ed., rev. by Sir Humphrey Waldock (New York: Oxford University Press, 1963). For a more recent and broader study, see Gerhard von Glahn, *Law Among Nations: An Introduction to Public Law,* 2nd ed. (New York: Macmillan, 1970). An excellent behavioral interpretation of contemporary international law is Ahmed Sheikh, *International Law and National Behavior** (New York: John Wiley, 1974). Several good case studies are featured in Lawrence Scheinman and David Wilkinson, eds., *International Law and Political Crisis** (Boston: Little, Brown, 1968).

A very informative discussion of the creation of the League of Nations, its years of growth, stability, and demise, written by a former deputy-general of the League, is Francis P. Walters, *A History of the League of Nations* (New York: Oxford University Press, 1952). The best source on the structure, functions, and activities of the United Nations and its related agencies is *Everyman's United Nations** (New York: UN Office of Public Information). For a good text on international organization, see Inis L. Claude, Jr., *Swords into Plowshares: The Problems and Progress of International Organization,* 4th ed., (New York: Random House, 1971). The primary scholarly journal in this area is *International Organization* (published quarterly by the University of Wisconsin Press). Two books that provide considerable insight into the early years of the United Nations are the autobiography of the first secretary-general, Trygve Lie, *In the Cause of Peace* (New York: Macmillan, 1954), and the extensive discussion of Hammarskjöld's years as secretary-general by a close associate in Brian Urquart, *Hammarskjöld* (New York: Alfred A. Knopf, 1972). Two good treatments of U.S. foreign policy and the United Nations are Lincoln P. Bloomfield, *The United Nations and U.S. Foreign Policy,** rev. ed. (Boston: Little, Brown, 1967); and Robert E. Riggs, *U.S./U.N., Foreign Policy and International Organization** (New York: Appleton-Century-Crofts, 1971). A superb comparative analysis of the

[27] See Nye, *op. cit.*, pp. 129–172 for his penetrating analysis of the OAS, OAU, and Arab League and their performance in controlling conflicts.

* Available in paperback.

roles of the United States, the Soviet Union, and the People's Republic of China in the United Nations is John G. Stoessinger, *The United Nations and the Superpowers: China, Russia, and America,** 3rd ed. (New York: Random House, 1973).

For a good comprehensive treatment of regional organization, see J. S. Nye, ed., *Peace in Parts: Integration and Conflict in Regional Organization** (Boston: Little, Brown, 1971). A standard work on European integration is A. H. Robertson, *European Institutions* (New York: Frederick A. Praeger, 1958). A more recent publication of similar style is Michael Palmer, John Lambert et al., *A Handbook of European Organizations* (New York: Frederick A. Praeger, 1968). For a good analysis of the North Atlantic Treaty Organization, see Edwin H. Fedder, *NATO: The Dynamics of Alliance in the Postwar World** (New York: Dodd, Mead, 1973). The best comprehensive discussion of its Communist counterpart is Robin A. Remington, *The Warsaw Pact* (Cambridge, Mass.: The MIT Press, 1971). The evolution, principles, structure, and activities of the Organization of American States are treated extensively and competently in M. Margaret Ball, *The OAS in Transition* (Durham: Duke University Press, 1969). For an informative and detailed analysis of political integration in Africa, see Zdenek Cervenka, *The Organization of African Unity and Its Charter* (New York: Frederick A. Praeger, 1969).

* Available in paperback.

Epilogue

In this book we set out to analyze, discuss, and describe the major aspects and processes of political systems in the contemporary world. Three major themes underlie our discussion: (1) that the various political processes are interrelated; (2) that all countries share some similar political characteristics, and (3) that all political systems are subject to change. Emphasizing systems analysis and pluralism, we have explained the political processes in terms of interacting groups and forces, none of which are autonomous.

Since the days of Plato the number of political societies has multiplied, and they have developed into very complicated systems. Much of this change has occurred in the present century. This growing complexity is found in politics, both domestic and international. Political science, as we said in Chapter 1, involves the systematic analysis and study of politics in the public realm, the sum total of all activities of public authorities, and those seeking to influence public decision making.

Politics has been an integral part of man's behavior for centuries, and we may assume that it will be with man as long as humanity exists. Man has the intellectual ability to improve politics and to improve his life. The political scientist, especially, can suggest ways for refining the methods of politics in the public realm.

We have shown that the political world of today is one of great diversity. Although all countries share some similar political characteristics, the specific political features of each country are different. The more than 150 nation-states of our time are in various stages of development and exhibit diverse degrees of pluralism. *No one* single system of political parties, interest groups, executive, legislature, or judiciary can be advocated as the best for all countries. Many of us living in the West concur with Winston Churchill's aphorism that "democracy is possibly the worst form of government—except for any other." But Western type democracy is, at least for the time-being, not a suitable system of government for many of the other countries.

Even without advocating one particular type of government as a panecea for the world, political scientists can make worthwhile contributions to society. Many contribute by researching the multitudinous facets of political systems to learn the detailed facts and establish similarities and dissimilarities. By bringing their knowledge to bear in the classroom and in their publications, political scientists help to inform and to educate the citizenry. Perhaps this, more than anything else, is their most important function. To deal adequately with different kinds of political systems requires an open mind—an analytical capability that restricts personal biases in the analysis of a problem.

Political scientists can help to improve their own political systems by bringing shortcomings in the public realm along with constructive suggestions for improvement to the attention of public officials. For the person who would like to keep the political system exactly as it has been, the political scientist will appear as a semi-revolutionary—the advocate of constructive change. But the basic criterion for suggesting change must be the betterment of man's life. All of us can participate in this process, but effective participation requires some understanding and knowledge of political systems and processes, their relations to other aspects of societies and their place in the larger world. We hope that students, after having read this book, will be more knowledgeable about political affairs and will become more constructive participants in the political arena.

Credit List

Chapter 2
Page 31 U.P.I.
Page 34 Wide World Photos
Page 42 Wide World Photos
Page 52 Henri Bureau/Sygma

Chapter 3
Page 67 Ny Carlsberg Glyptotek/Art Reference Bureau
Page 74 New York Public Library Picture Collection
Page 83 Brown Brothers

Chapter 4
Page 108 Wide World Photos
Page 106 Tass from Sovfoto
Page 118 Ray Ellis from Rapho/Photo Researchers
Page 116 Bob Combs from Rapho/Photo Researchers

Chapter 5
Page 141 Gamma/Liaison
Page 167 (top) Tass from Sovfoto
Page 167 (bottom) Tass from Sovfoto
Page 173 Martin Adler Levick/Black Star
Page 143 Eastfoto
Page 144 Tass from Sovfoto

Chapter 6
Page 204 & 205 Courtesy State Board of Elections, State of Illinois
Page 213 Wide World Photos
Page 217 Courtesy Trustees of Sir John Soane's Museum, London, England

Chapter 7
Page 237 New York Public Library Picture Collection
Page 240 Wide World Photos
Page 246 J. Tiziou/Sygma
Page 256 Marc Godfrey/Magnum
Page 257 Tass from Sovfoto
Page 258 Tass from Sovfoto

Chapter 8
Page 272 Sylvia Johnson/Woodfin Camp
Page 274 (top) Eric Lessing/Magnum
Page 274 (bottom) Wide World Photos
Page 283 J. Tiziou/Sygma
Page 287 Henri Bureau/Sygma

Chapter 10
Page 344 Alain Nogues/Sygma
Page 362 S. Julienne/Sygma
Page 376 Wide World Photos

Chapter 11
Page 388 Alinari/Art Reference Bureau
Page 399 Wide World Photos
Page 402 Wide World Photos
Page 407 Sygma

Chapter 12
Page 441 Wide World Photos
Page 442 Wide World Photos
Page 443 Phillipe Ledru and Alain Nogues/Sygma

Chapter 13
Page 478 United Nations
Page 480 United Nations

Index